EDITION

6

CRIMINALISTICS

An Introduction to Forensic Science

RICHARD SAFERSTEIN, Ph.D.

Forensic Science Consultant, Mt. Laurel, N.J.
Lecturer, Widener University School of Law

Prentice Hall
Upper Saddle River, NJ 07458

Library of Congress Cataloging-in-Publication Data

Saferstein, Richard, (date)
    Criminalistics: an introduction to forensic science/Richard
Saferstein.—6th ed.
      p.   cm.
    Includes bibliographical references and index.
    ISBN 0-13-592940-7
    1. Criminal investigation. 2. Forensic ballistics. 3. Chemistry,
Forensic. 4. Medical jurisprudence.
    HV8073.S2 1998
    363.25—dc21   97-6295
                                        CIP

Acquisition Editor: Neil Marquardt
Editorial Assistant: Rose Mary Florio
Managing Editor: Mary Carnis
Project Manager: Linda B. Pawelchak
Production Coordinator: Ed O'Dougherty
Design Director: Marianne Frasco
Cover Director: Jayne Conte
Cover Design: Bruce Kenselaar
Cover Illustration: Richard Tuschman
Electronic Page Layout: Clarinda Company
Electronic Art Creation: Asterisk Group
Marketing Manager: Frank Mortimer Jr.
Copy Editing: Susan Korb
Proofreading: Maria McColligan
Printing/Binding: RR Donnelley & Sons, Harrisonburg, VA.

© 1998, 1995, 1990, 1987, 1981, 1977 by Prentice Hall, Inc.
Upper Saddle River, NJ 07458

Printed in the United States of America
10 9 8 7 6 5

ISBN 0-13-592940-7

Prentice-Hall International (UK) Limited, *London*
Prentice-Hall of Australia Pty. Limited, *Sydney*
Prentice-Hall of Canada, Inc., *Toronto*
Prentice-Hall Hispanoamericana, S. A., *Mexico*
Prentice-Hall of India Private Limited, *New Delhi*
Prentice-Hall of Japan, Inc., *Tokyo*
Pearson Education Asia Pte. Ltd., *Singapore*
Editora Prentice-Hall do Brasil, Ltda., *Rio de Janeiro*

To the Memory of Fran and Michael

Contents

CHAPTER
3 PHYSICAL EVIDENCE   66

CHAPTER
4 PHYSICAL PROPERTIES: GLASS AND SOIL   97

CHAPTER
5 ORGANIC ANALYSIS   129

PREFACE

The criminal trial is over. The verdict finds millions of Americans in vehement disagreement with the jury's assessment of the evidence. Even though one may tend to characterize the Simpson verdict as a failure of the judicial system, in a sense, it was a triumph for forensic science. An overwhelming number of Americans are convinced of Simpson's guilt. Undoubtedly, this attitude stems from the quantity and quality of scientifically evaluated physical evidence linking O. J. Simpson to the murder site. During the trial, forensic scientists systematically placed Simpson at the crime scene through DNA analyses, hair and fiber comparisons, and footwear impressions. In this case, the quantity of forensic evidence simply overwhelms and submerges defense contentions that the evidence was planted and/or contaminated. In the court of public opinion, science, logic, and common sense prevail.

As millions of Americans watched the O. J. Simpson case unfold, they, in a sense, became students of forensic science. Intense media coverage of the crime-scene search and investigation, as well as the ramifications of findings of physical evidence at the crime scene, all became the subject of study, commentary, and conjecture. For those of us who have taught forensic science in the classroom, it comes as no surprise that forensic science can grip and hold the attention of those who otherwise would have no interest in any science subject. The O. J.

Simpson case amply demonstrates how intertwined criminal investigation has become with forensic science. Through six editions, *Criminalistics* has striven to depict the role of the forensic scientist in the criminal justice system. The current edition builds on the contents of its predecessors and seeks to update the reader with the latest technologies available to crime laboratory personnel. Like all facets of modern life, forensic science has been touched by the Internet. This new edition introduces the reader to basic concepts of Internet use and encourages exploration of Web sites particularly relevant to forensic science and criminal investigation.

Making science relevant and pertinent to the interests and goals of the student is a desirable but often elusive goal pursued by educators. *Criminalistics* is written with such lofty objectives in mind. The sixth edition of *Criminalistics* retains the purpose and intent of the previous editions. First and foremost is a presentation of the techniques, skills, and limitations of the modern crime laboratory for a reader who has no background in the forensic sciences. The nature of physical evidence is emphasized along with the limitations that technology and knowledge impose on its individualization and characterization.

A major portion of the text centers on discussions of the common items of physical evidence encountered at crime scenes. These chapters include updated techniques describing forensic analysis as well as procedures and practices relating to the proper collection and preservation of evidence at crime scenes. Particular attention is paid to the meaning and role of probability in interpreting the evidential significance of scientifically evaluated evidence.

The implications of DNA typing are important enough to warrant their inclusion in a chapter in *Criminalistics*. In keeping with the style and content of the book's previous editions, the DNA subject is described in a manner that will make it comprehensible and relevant to readers who lack a scientific background. The discussion focuses on giving the reader insight into what DNA is and explains its central role in controlling the body's chemistry. Finally, the chapter describes the process of DNA typing and illustrates its application to criminal investigations through examples of actual case histories.

In selecting the subject matter for the book, I have drawn upon my experience both as an active forensic scientist and as an instructor of forensic science at the college level. No prior knowledge about scientific principles or techniques is assumed of the reader. He or she is introduced to those areas of chemistry and biology relating to the analysis of physical evidence with a minimum of scientific terminology and equations. It is not the intent of this book to make scientists or forensic experts of the reader. For this reason, the chemistry and biology discussed are limited to a minimum core of facts and principles that will make the subject matter comprehensible and meaningful to the nonscientists. Nevertheless, it will certainly be gratifying if this effort motivates some students to seek further scientific knowledge and perhaps direct their education toward a career in forensic science.

Although *Criminalistics* is an outgrowth of a one-semester course offered as part of a criminal justice program at many New Jersey colleges, its subject matter is not limited to the college student. Optimum utilization of crime laboratory services requires that criminal investigators have a knowledge of the techniques and capabilities of the laboratory that extends beyond any summary that may be gleaned from departmental brochures dealing with the collection and packaging of physical evidence. Only by combining a knowledge of the principles and techniques of forensic science with logic and common sense will the investigator gain a comprehensive insight into the meaning and significance of physical evidence and its role in criminal investigations. Forensic science begins at the crime scene. If the investigator cannot recognize, collect, and package evidence properly, no amount of equipment or expertise will salvage the situation.

Likewise, there is a dire need to bridge the "communication gap" that presently exists between lawyers, judges, and the forensic scientist. An intelligent evaluation of the scientist's data and any subsequent testimony that may follow will again depend on the familiarity of the underlying principles of forensic science. Too many practitioners of the law profess ignorance of the subject or at best attempt to gain a superficial understanding of its meaning and significance only minutes before meeting the expert witness. To this end, it is hoped that the book will provide a painless route to comprehending the nature of the science.

In order to merge theory with practice, a number of actual forensic case histories are included in the text. It is intended that these illustrations will remove forensic science from the domain of the abstract and make its applications relevant to the real world of criminal investigation.

I am indebted to many people for their assistance and advice in the preparation of this book. Many faculty members, colleagues, and friends have read and commented on various portions of the text. Particular thanks go to the following people for their critical reading and discussions of the manuscript: Norman Demeter, John Lintott, Charles Midkiff, Raymond Murray, Jay Siegel, and Richard Tidey, as well as the reviewers of this edition: Richard James, Kansas State University; and John Swan, Harrisburg Area Community College.

In addition, I would like to acknowledge the contributions of Jeffrey C. Kercheval, Robert Thompson, Roger Ely, Jose R. Almirall, Darlene Brezinski, and Michael Malone.

I want to credit the assistances of Pamela Cook whose research efforts and editorial skills are an integral part of this revision. I am also appreciative of the time and talent given by Peggy Cole and my production editor, Linda Pawelchak.

I would like to give credit to those law enforcement agencies, governmental agencies, private individuals, and equipment manufacturers cited in the text for contributing their photographs and illustrations. Finally, I particularly wish to express my appreciation to Major E. R. Leibe (retired) and Major V. P. O'Donoghue (retired) for their encouragement and support.

Anyone who expects to write a textbook must be prepared to contribute countless hours to the task, often at the expense of family obligations. This effort was no exception. My efforts would have fallen well short of completion without the patience and encouragement of my wife Gail. Her typing and critical readings of the manuscript, as well as her strength of character under circumstances that were less than ideal, will always be remembered.

Richard Saferstein, Ph.D.

ABOUT THE AUTHOR

Richard Saferstein, Ph.D., retired in 1991 after serving 21 years as the Chief Forensic Scientist of the New Jersey State Police Laboratory, one of the largest crime laboratories in the United States. He currently acts as a consultant for attorneys and the media in the area of forensic science. During the O. J. Simpson criminal trial, Dr. Saferstein provided extensive commentary on forensic aspects of the case for the *Rivera Live* show, the E! television network, ABC radio, and various radio talk shows. Dr. Saferstein holds degrees from the City College of New York and earned his doctorate degree in chemistry in 1970 from the City University of New York. From 1972 to 1991, he taught an introductory forensic science course in the criminal justice programs at the College of New Jersey and Ocean County College. These teaching experiences played an influential role in Dr. Saferstein's authorship in 1977 of the widely used introductory textbook *Criminalistics: An Introduction to Forensic Science,* currently in this sixth edition. Saferstein's basic philosophy in writing *Criminalistics* is to make forensic science understandable and meaningful to the non-science reader, while giving the reader an appreciation for the scientific principles that underlie the subject.

Dr. Saferstein presently teaches a course on the role of the expert witness in the courtroom at the law school of Widener University in Wilmington, Delaware. He has authored or co-authored more than 30 technical papers covering a variety of forensic topics. He has also edited the widely used professional reference books *Forensic Science Handbook, Volumes I–III* (Prentice Hall, 1982, 1988, 1993) dealing with important forensic science topics. Dr. Saferstein is a member of the American Chemical Society, the American Academy of Forensic Sciences, the Forensic Science Society of England, the Canadian Society of Forensic Scientists, the International Association for Identification, the Mid-Atlantic Association of Forensic Scientists, the Northeastern Association of Forensic Scientists, the Northwestern Association of Forensic Scientists, and the Society of Forensic Toxicologists.

INTRODUCTION

DEFINITION AND SCOPE
OF FORENSIC SCIENCE

Forensic science in its broadest definition is the application of science to law. As our society has grown more complex, it has become more dependent on rules of law to regulate the activities of its members. Forensic science offers the knowledge and technology of science for the definition and enforcement of such laws.

Each year, as government finds it increasingly necessary to regulate those activities that most intimately influence our daily lives, science merges more closely with civil and criminal law. Consider, for example, the laws and agencies that regulate the quality of our food, the nature and potency of drugs, the extent of automobile emissions, the kind of fuel oil we burn, the purity of our drinking water, and the pesticides we use on our crops and plants. It would be difficult to conceive of any food and drug regulation or any environmental protection act that could be effectively monitored and enforced without the assistance of scientific technology and the skill of the scientific community.

In the arena of criminal justice, laws are continually being broadened and revised to counter the alarming increase in crime rates. In response to public concern, law enforcement agencies have expanded their patrol and investigative functions, hoping to stem the rising tide of crime. At the same time they are looking more and more to the scientific community for advice and technical support of their efforts. Can the technology that put astronauts on the moon, split the atom, and eradicated our most dreaded diseases be enlisted in this critical battle? Unfortunately, science cannot offer final and authoritative solutions to problems that stem from a maze of social and psychological factors. However, as the contents of this book will attest, science does occupy an important and unique role in the criminal justice system—a role that relates to the scientist's ability to supply accurate and objective information that reflects the events that have occurred at a crime. It will also become apparent to the reader that a good deal of work remains to be done if the full potential of science as it is applied to criminal investigations is to be realized.

Considering the vast array of civil and criminal laws that regulate society, forensic science, in its broadest sense, has become so comprehensive a subject as to make a meaningful introductory textbook treatment of its role and techniques most difficult, if not overwhelming. For this reason, we must find practical limits that narrow the scope of the subject. Fortunately, common usage provides us with such a limited definition: **Forensic science is the application of science to those criminal and civil laws that are enforced by police agencies in a criminal justice system.**

Even within this limited definition, we will restrict our discussion in this book to only those areas of chemistry, biology, physics, and geology that are useful for determining the evidential value of crime-scene and related evidence, omitting any references to the subject of medicine and the law. Forensic pathology, psychology, and odontology certainly encompass important and relevant areas of knowledge and practice in law enforcement, each being an integral part of the total forensic science service that is provided to any up-to-date criminal justice system. However, except for a brief discussion at the end of this chapter, these subjects go beyond the intended range of the book, and the reader is referred elsewhere for discussions of their applications and techniques.[1] Instead, we will attempt to focus on the services of what has popularly become known as the *crime laboratory*. It is here that the principles and techniques of the physical and natural sciences are practiced and applied to the analysis of crime-scene evidence.

For many, the term *criminalistics* seems more descriptive for describing the services of a crime laboratory. However, it will serve no

---

[1]Two excellent references are André A. Moenssens, Fred E. Inbau, James Starrs, and Carol E. Henderson, *Scientific Evidence in Civil and Criminal Cases,* 4th ed. (Mineola, N.Y.: The Foundation Press, Inc., 1995); and Werner U. Spitz, ed., *Medicolegal Investigation of Death,* 3rd ed. (Springfield, Ill.: Charles C Thomas, Publisher, 1993).

useful purpose to rationalize whether the subject matter included in this book can best be classified as criminalistics or forensic science, if indeed this distinction can be made at all. For all intents and purposes, the two terms are taken to be one and the same and will be used interchangeably in the text. Regardless of title, criminalist or forensic scientist, the trend of events has made the scientist in the crime laboratory an active participant in the criminal justice system.

HISTORY AND DEVELOPMENT OF FORENSIC SCIENCE

Forensic science owes its origins first to those individuals who developed the principles and techniques needed to identify or compare physical evidence, and second to those who recognized the necessity of merging these principles into a coherent discipline that could be practically applied to a criminal justice system.

Today, many believe that Sir Arthur Conan Doyle had a considerable influence on popularizing scientific crime-detection methods through his fictional character Sherlock Holmes. It was Holmes who first applied the newly developing principles of serology, fingerprinting, firearm identification, and questioned-document examination long before their value was first recognized and accepted by real-life criminal investigators. Holmes's feats excited the imagination of an emerging generation of forensic scientists and criminal investigators. Even in the first Sherlock Holmes novel, *A Study in Scarlet,* published in 1887, we find examples of Doyle's uncanny ability to describe scientific methods of detection years before they were actually discovered and implemented. For instance, here Holmes is probing and recognizing the potential usefulness of forensic serology to criminal investigation:

> "I've found it. I've found it," he shouted to my companion, running towards us with a test tube in his hand. "I have found a reagent which is precipitated by hemoglobin and by nothing else. . . . Why, man, it is the most practical medico-legal discovery for years. Don't you see that it gives us an infallible test for blood stains? . . . The old guaiacum test was very clumsy and uncertain. So is the microscopic examination for blood corpuscles. The latter is valueless if the stains are a few hours old. Now, this appears to act as well whether the blood is old or new. Had this test been invented, there are hundreds of men now walking the earth who would long ago have paid the penalty of their crimes. . . . Criminal cases are continually hinging upon that one point. A man is suspected of a crime months perhaps after it has been committed. His linen or clothes are examined and brownish stains discovered upon

them. Are they blood stains, or rust stains, or fruit stains, or what are they? That is a question which has puzzled many an expert, and why? Because there was no reliable test. Now we have the Sherlock Holmes test, and there will no longer be any difficulty."

There are many who can be cited for their specific contributions to the field of forensic science. The following is just a brief list of those who made the earliest contributions to formulating the disciplines that now constitute forensic science.

Mathieu Orfila (1787–1853).   Orfila is considered the father of forensic toxicology. A native of Spain, he ultimately became a renowned teacher of medicine in France. In 1814, Orfila published the first scientific treatise on the detection of poisons and their effects on animals. This treatise established forensic toxicology as a legitimate scientific endeavor.

Alphonse Bertillon (1853–1914).   The first scientific system of personal identification was devised by Alphonse Bertillon. In 1879, Bertillon began to develop the science of anthropometry, a systematic procedure of taking a series of body measurements as a means of distinguishing one individual from another. For nearly two decades, this system was considered the most accurate method of personal identification. Although anthropometry was eventually replaced by fingerprinting in the early 1900s, Bertillon's early efforts have earned him the distinction of being known as the father of criminal identification.

Francis Galton (1822–1911).   Galton undertook the first definitive study of fingerprints and developed a methodology of classifying them for filing. In 1892, he published a book entitled *Finger Prints,* which contained the first statistical proof supporting the uniqueness of his method of personal identification. His work went on to describe the basic principles that form the present system of identification by fingerprints.

Leone Lattes (1887–1954).   In 1901, Dr. Karl Landsteiner discovered that blood can be grouped into different categories. These blood groups or types are now recognized as A, B, AB, and O. The possibility that blood grouping could be a useful characteristic for the identification of an individual intrigued Dr. Leone Lattes, a professor at the Institute of Forensic Medicine at the University of Turin in Italy. In 1915, he devised a relatively simple procedure for determining the blood group of a dried bloodstain, a technique that he immediately applied to criminal investigations. Even to this day Dr. Lattes's procedure is often utilized by forensic scientists.

Calvin Goddard (1891–1955). To determine whether or not a particular gun has fired a bullet requires a comparison of the bullet with one that has been test-fired from the suspect's weapon. Calvin Goddard, a U.S. Army colonel, refined the techniques of such an examination by utilizing the comparison microscope. Goddard's expertise established the comparison microscope as the indispensable tool of the modern firearms examiner.

Albert S. Osborn (1858–1946). Osborn's development of the fundamental principles of document examination was responsible for the acceptance of documents as scientific evidence by the courts. In 1910, Osborn authored the first significant text in this field, *Questioned Documents.* This book is still considered a primary reference for document examiners.

Hans Gross (1847–1915). The first treatise describing the application of scientific disciplines to the field of criminal investigation was written by Hans Gross in 1893. Gross, a public prosecutor and judge in Graz, Austria, spent many years studying and developing principles of criminal investigation. In his classic book, *Handbuch für Untersuchungsrichter* (later published in English under the title *Criminal Investigation*), he detailed the assistance that investigators could expect from the fields of microscopy, chemistry, physics, mineralogy, zoology, botany, anthropometry, and fingerprinting. He later introduced the forensic journal *Kriminologie,* which still serves as a medium for reporting improved methods of scientific crime detection.

Edmond Locard (1877–1966). Although Gross was a strong advocate of the use of the scientific method in criminal investigation, he did not make any specific technical contributions to this philosophy. It was left instead to a Frenchman, Edmond Locard, to demonstrate how the principles enunciated by Gross could be incorporated within a workable crime laboratory. Locard's formal education was in both medicine and law. In 1910, he persuaded the police department in Lyons to give him two attic rooms and two assistants to start a police laboratory.

During his first years of work, the only instruments available to Locard were a microscope and a rudimentary spectrometer. However, his enthusiasm quickly overcame the technical and monetary deficiencies he encountered. From these modest beginnings, Locard's research and accomplishments became known throughout the world by forensic scientists and criminal investigators. Eventually he became the founder and director of the Institute of Criminalistics at the University of Lyons; this quickly developed into a leading international center for study and research in forensic science.

It was Locard's belief that when a criminal came in contact with an object or person, a cross-transfer of evidence occurred (Locard's Exchange Principle). Locard strongly believed that every criminal can be connected to a crime by dust particles carried from the crime scene. This concept was reinforced by a series of successful and well-publicized investigations. In one case, confronted with counterfeit coins and the names of three suspects, Locard urged the police to bring the suspects' clothing to his laboratory. Upon careful examination, he located small metallic particles in all the garments. Chemical analysis revealed that the particles and coins were composed of exactly the same metallic elements. Confronted with this evidence, the suspects were arrested and soon confessed to the crime. During the post–World War I period, Locard's successes served as an impetus for the formation of police laboratories in Vienna, Berlin, Sweden, Finland, and Holland.

It was in the United States that the most ambitious commitment to forensic science was undertaken. In 1932, the Federal Bureau of Investigation, under the directorship of J. Edgar Hoover, organized a national laboratory that aimed to offer forensic services to all law enforcement agencies in the country. During its formative stages, extensive consultations were made with business executives, manufacturers, and scientists whose knowledge and experience were useful in guiding the new facility through its infancy. The FBI Laboratory is now the world's largest forensic laboratory, performing over one million examinations every year. Its accomplishments have earned it worldwide recognition, and its structure and organization have served as a model for forensic laboratories formed at the state and local levels in the United States as well as in other countries. Furthermore, the opening of the FBI's Forensic Science Research and Training Center in 1981 gave the United States, for the first time, a facility dedicated to conducting research to develop new and reliable scientific methods that can be applied to forensic science. This facility is also used to train crime laboratory personnel in the latest forensic science techniques and methods.

The oldest forensic laboratory in the United States is that of the Los Angeles Police Department, created in 1923 by August Vollmer, a police chief from Berkeley, California. In the 1930s, Vollmer headed the first U.S. university institute for criminology and criminalistics at the University of California at Berkeley. However, this institute lacked any official status in the university until 1948, when a school of criminology was formed. The famous criminalist Paul Kirk (see Figure 1–1) was selected to head its criminalistics department. Many of the graduates of this school have gone on to become actively engaged in the development of forensic laboratories in other parts of the state and country.

Figure 1–1.
Paul Leland Kirk, 1902–1970.
Courtesy Blackstone-Shelburne, N.Y.

Presently, California has numerous federal, state, county, and city crime laboratories located within its boundaries. Many of these facilities operate independently of one another. However, in 1972 the California Department of Justice embarked on an ambitious plan to create a network of state-operated crime laboratories. As a result, California has created a model system of integrated forensic laboratories consisting of regional and satellite facilities. An informal exchange of information and expertise is facilitated among California's criminalist community through a regional professional society, the California Association of Criminalists. This organization was the forerunner of a number of regional organizations that have developed throughout the United States to foster cooperation among the nation's growing community of criminalists.

In contrast to the American system of independent local laboratories, Britain has developed a national system of regional laboratories under the direction of the government's Home Office. England and Wales are serviced by six regional laboratories, including the Metropolitan Police Laboratory that services London. In the early 1990s, the British Home Office reorganized the country's forensic laboratories and instituted a system whereby police agencies were charged a fee for services rendered by the laboratory. It is anticipated that this approach will make the regional laboratory system more efficient and improve accountability for services rendered to police agencies.

THE ORGANIZATION OF A CRIME LABORATORY

The development of crime laboratories in the United States has been characterized by rapid growth accompanied by a lack of national and regional planning and coordination. At present, there are approximately 320 public crime laboratories operating at various levels of government—federal, state, county, and municipal. This represents more than a threefold increase over the number of crime laboratories operating in 1966.

The size and diversity of crime laboratories make it impossible to select any one model that can best describe a typical crime laboratory. Although the majority of these facilities function as elements of police departments, others have been placed under the direction of the prosecutor's or district attorney's office; and some have had their functions combined with laboratories of the medical examiner or coroner. Far fewer are affiliated with universities or exist as independent agencies in government. Laboratory staff sizes may range from one person to over a hundred, and their services may be diverse or specialized, depending on the responsibilities of the agency that houses the laboratory.

For the most part, crime laboratories have been organized by those agencies that either foresaw their potential application to criminal investigation or were pressed by the increasing demands of casework. A number of reasons can rightfully be cited for explaining the unparalleled growth of crime laboratories during the past 25 years. There is little doubt that Supreme Court decisions in the 1960s were responsible for the police placing greater emphasis on securing scientifically evaluated evidence. The requirement to advise criminal suspects of their constitutional rights and their right of immediate access to counsel has all but eliminated confessions as a routine investigative tool. Today, successful prosecution of criminal cases requires a thorough and professional police investigation, frequently incorporating the skills of forensic science experts. Fortuitously, modern technology has provided forensic scientists with many new skills and techniques to meet the challenges accompanying their increased participation in the criminal justice system.

Coinciding with changing judicial requirements has been the staggering increase in crime rates in the United States. This factor alone would probably have sufficed to account for the increased utilization of crime laboratory services by police agencies were it not for the fact that only a small percentage of police investigations generate evidence requiring scientific examination. There is, however, one important exception to this observation, and that is drug-related arrests. All illicit drug seizures must be sent to a forensic laboratory for confirmatory chemical analysis before the case can be adjudicated in court. Since the mid-1960s, drug abuse has accelerated to nearly uncontrollable levels and has resulted in crime laboratories being inundated with drug specimens.

The impact of this trend can be gauged by the experiences of the New Jersey State Police Laboratory. Since 1968, this organization has seen a significant rise in drug cases. For 1996, approximately 29,000 drug-related cases were analyzed, compared to 21,000 cases in 1987 and 9000 cases in 1968. To cope with this increase, and to adequately perform other casework as well, it has been necessary to add some 70 chemists to the laboratory's staff and to expand its facilities to include three new regional laboratories. The demand for laboratories to perform drug analyses has probably been the single most important factor in the recent expansion of forensic services in New Jersey and elsewhere in the United States.

Historically, a federal system of government, combined with a desire to retain local control, has produced a variety of independent laboratories in the United States, precluding the creation of a national system. Crime laboratories to a large extent mirror the fragmented law enforcement structure that exists on the national, state, and local levels. The federal government has no single law enforcement or investigative agency that has unlimited jurisdiction. Four major federal crime laboratories have been created for the purpose of assisting in the investigation and enforcement of criminal laws that extend beyond the jurisdictional boundaries of state and local forces. The FBI (Department of Justice) maintains the largest crime laboratory in the world. Its expertise and technology support its broad investigative powers. The Drug Enforcement Administration Laboratories (Department of Justice) are responsible for the analysis of drugs seized in violation of federal laws regulating the production, sale, and transportation of drugs. The laboratories of the Bureau of Alcohol, Tobacco, and Firearms (Department of Treasury) have responsibility for analyzing alcoholic beverages and documents relating to tax law enforcement, as well as for examining weapons, explosive devices, and related evidence received in conjunction with enforcement of the Gun Control Act of 1968 and the Organized Crime Control Act of 1970. The U.S. Postal Inspection Service maintains laboratories concerned with criminal investigations relating to the postal service. Each of these federal facilities will offer its expertise to any local agency that requests assistance in relevant investigative matters.

Most state governments maintain a crime laboratory to service state and local law enforcement agencies that do not have ready access to a laboratory. Some states, such as Alabama, California, Illinois, Michigan, New Jersey, Texas, Washington, Oregon, Virginia, and Florida, have developed a comprehensive statewide system of regional or satellite laboratories. These operate under the direction of a central facility and provide forensic services to most areas of the state. The concept of a regional laboratory operating as part of a statewide system has successfully increased the accessibility of many local law enforcement agencies to a crime laboratory, while at the same time minimizing the duplication of services and assuring maximum interlaboratory cooperation through the sharing of expertise and equipment.

Local laboratories provide services to county and municipal agencies. Generally, these facilities operate independently of the state crime laboratory and are financed directly by local government. However, as costs have risen, some counties have found it desirable to combine resources and create multicounty laboratories to service their jurisdictions. At this time, many of the larger cities in the United States maintain their own crime laboratories, usually under the direction of the local police department. Frequently, high population and high crime rates combine to make a municipal facility, such as New York City's or Chicago's, the largest crime laboratory in the state.

Like the United States, most countries in the world have created and now maintain forensic facilities. Reference has already been made to the British regional laboratory system. In Canada, forensic services are provided by three government-funded institutes: (1) six Royal Canadian Mounted Police regional laboratories, (2) the Centre of Forensic Sciences in Toronto, and (3) the Institute of Legal Medicine and Police Science in Montreal. Altogether, over 100 countries throughout the world are known to have at least one laboratory facility offering services in the field of forensic science.

SERVICES OF THE CRIME LABORATORY

Bearing in mind the independent development of crime laboratories in the United States, the wide variation in total services offered in different communities is not surprising. There are many reasons for this, including (1) variations in local laws, (2) the different capabilities and functions of the organization to which a laboratory is attached, and (3) budgetary and staffing limitations.

In recent years, many local crime laboratories have been created solely for the purpose of processing drug specimens. Often these facilities were staffed with few personnel and operated under limited budgets. Although many have gone on to expand their forensic services, some are still engaged primarily in performing drug analyses. However, even among crime laboratories providing services beyond drug identification, the diversity and quality of services rendered will vary significantly. For the purposes of this text, I have taken the liberty of arbitrarily designating the following units as those that should constitute a "full-service" crime laboratory.

BASIC SERVICES PROVIDED BY FULL-SERVICE CRIME LABORATORIES

Physical Science Unit.   The physical science unit applies principles and techniques of chemistry, physics, and geology to the identification and comparison of crime-scene evidence. It is staffed by criminalists who have the expertise to utilize chemical tests and modern analytical instrumentation for the examination of items as diverse as drugs, glass, paint, explosives, and soil. In a laboratory that has a staff large enough to permit specialization, the responsibilities of this unit may be further subdivided into sections devoted to drug identification, soil and mineral analyses, and the examination of a variety of trace physical evidence (see Figure 1–2).

Biology Unit.   The biology unit is staffed with biologists and serologists who apply their knowledge to the identification and typing of dried bloodstains and other body fluids, the comparison of hairs and fibers, and the identification and comparison of botanical materials such as wood and plants.

Firearms Unit.   The examination of firearms, discharged bullets, cartridge cases, shotgun shells, and ammunition of all types is conducted by the firearms unit. Garments and other objects are also examined in order to detect firearm discharge residues and to approximate the distance from a target at which a weapon was fired. The basic principles of firearm examination are also applied here to the comparison of marks made by tools.

Document Examination Unit.   The handwriting and typewriting on questioned documents are studied by the documentation unit to ascertain authenticity and/or source. Related responsibilities include analysis of paper and ink, as well as examination of indented writings (the term usually applied to the partially visible depressions appearing on a sheet of paper underneath the one on which the visible

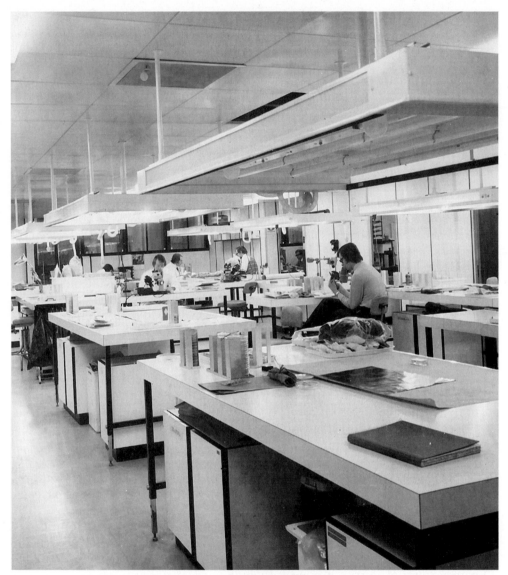

Figure 1–2.   Work area of the chemistry section of the Metropolitan Police Laboratory. *Courtesy* Metropolitan Police Laboratory, London, England.

writing appears), obliterations, erasures, and burned or charred documents.

Photography Unit.   A complete photographic laboratory is maintained to examine and record physical evidence. Its procedures may require the use of highly specialized photographic techniques, such as

infrared, ultraviolet, and X-ray photography, to make invisible information visible to the naked eye. This unit also aids in the preparation
of photographic exhibits for courtroom presentation.

OPTIONAL SERVICES PROVIDED BY FULL-SERVICE CRIME LABORATORIES

Toxicology Unit. Body fluids and organs are examined by the
toxicology group to determine the presence or absence of drugs and
poisons. Frequently, such functions are shared with or may be the sole
responsibility of a separate laboratory facility placed under the direction of the medical examiner's or coroner's office.

In most jurisdictions, field instruments such as the Intoxilyzer
are used to determine the alcoholic consumption of individuals. Often
the toxicology section has the responsibility of training operators as
well as maintaining and servicing these instruments.

Latent Fingerprint Unit. The responsibility for processing and
examining evidence for latent fingerprints when they are submitted in
conjunction with other laboratory examinations belongs to the latent
fingerprint unit.

Polygraph Unit. The polygraph, or lie detector, has come to be
recognized as an essential tool of the criminal investigator rather than
the forensic scientist. However, during the formative years of polygraph technology, many police agencies incorporated this unit into the
laboratory's administrative structure, where it sometimes remains
today. In any case, its functions are handled by people trained in the
techniques of criminal investigation and interrogation.

Voiceprint Analysis Unit. In cases involving telephoned threats
or tape-recorded messages, investigators may require the skills of the
voiceprint analysis unit to tie the voice to a particular suspect. To this
end, a good deal of casework has been performed by the sound spectrograph, an instrument that transforms speech into a visual graphic
display called a *voiceprint.* The validity of this technique as a means of
personal identification rests on the premise that the sound patterns
produced in speech are unique to the individual and that the voiceprint displays this uniqueness.

Evidence-Collection Unit. The concept of incorporating crime-
scene evidence collection into the total forensic science service is
slowly gaining recognition in the United States. This unit dispatches
specially trained personnel (civilian and/or police) to the crime scene to

collect and preserve physical evidence that will later be processed at the crime laboratory.

THE FUNCTIONS OF THE FORENSIC SCIENTIST

ANALYSIS OF PHYSICAL EVIDENCE

First and foremost the forensic scientist must be skilled in applying the principles and techniques of the physical and natural sciences to the analysis of the many types of evidence that may be recovered during crime investigation. However, in doing this the scientist must also be aware of the demands and constraints that are imposed by the judicial system. The procedures and techniques that are utilized in the laboratory must not only rest on a firm scientific foundation but also satisfy the criteria of admissibility that have been established by the courts.

In rejecting the scientific validity of the lie detector (polygraph), the District of Columbia Circuit Court in 1923 set forth what has since become a standard guideline for determining the judicial admissibility of scientific examinations. In *Frye* v. *United States*,[2] the court stated the following:

> Just when a scientific principle or discovery crosses the line between the experimental and demonstrable stages is difficult to define. Somewhere in this twilight zone the evidential force of the principle must be recognized, and while the courts will go a long way in admitting expert testimony deduced from a well-recognized scientific principle or discovery, the thing from which the deduction is made must be sufficiently established to have gained general acceptance in the particular field in which it belongs.

To meet the *Frye* standard, the court must decide if the questioned procedure, technique, and principles are "generally accepted" by a meaningful segment of the relevant scientific community. In practice, this approach required the proponent of a scientific test to present to the court a collection of experts who could testify that the scientific issue before the court is one that is generally accepted by the relevant members of the scientific community. In recent years, this standard engendered a great deal of debate as to whether or not it is sufficiently flexible to deal with some new and novel scientific issues that for some

---

[2]293 Fed. 1013 (1923).

reason may not have gained widespread support within the scientific community.

As an alternative to the *Frye* standard, some courts came to believe that the Federal Rules of Evidence espoused a more flexible standard that did not rely on "general acceptance" as an absolute prerequisite for admitting scientific evidence. Part of the Federal Rules of Evidence governs the admissibility of all evidence, including expert testimony, in federal courts, and many states have adopted codes similar to those of the Federal Rules. Specifically, Rule 702 of the Federal Rules of Evidence deals with the admissibility of expert testimony:

> If scientific, technical, or other specialized knowledge will assist the trier of fact to understand the evidence or to determine a fact in issue, a witness qualified as an expert by knowledge, skill, experience, training, or education, may testify thereto in the form of an opinion or otherwise.

In a landmark ruling in the 1993 case of *Daubert* v. *Merrell Dow Pharmaceutical, Inc.,*[3] the U.S. Supreme Court asserted that "general acceptance" or the *Frye* standard is not an absolute prerequisite to the admissibility of scientific evidence under the Federal Rules of Evidence. According to the Court, the Rules of Evidence—especially Rule 702—assigns to the trial judge the task of ensuring that an expert's testimony rests on a reliable foundation and is relevant to the task at hand. Although this ruling applies only to federal courts, many state courts are expected to use this decision as a guideline in setting standards for the admissibility of scientific evidence.

What the Court advocates in *Daubert* is that trial judges must assume the ultimate responsibility for the admissibility and validity of scientific evidence presented in their courts. The Court offered some guidelines as to how a judge can gauge the veracity of scientific evidence, emphasizing that the inquiry should be flexible:

1. Whether the scientific technique or theory can be (and has been) tested;
2. Whether the technique or theory has been subject to peer review and publication;
3. The technique's potential rate of error;
4. Existence and maintenance of standards controlling the technique's operation; and
5. Whether the scientific theory or method has attracted widespread acceptance within a relevant scientific community.

Some legal practitioners have expressed the concern that abandoning *Frye's* general acceptance test will result in the introduction of absurd

---

[3] 113 S. Ct. 2786 (1993).

and irrational pseudoscientific claims in the courtroom. The Supreme Court rejected these concerns:

> In this regard the respondent seems to us to be overly pessimistic about the capabilities of the jury and of the adversary system generally. Vigorous cross-examination presentation of contrary evidence, and careful instruction on the burden of proof are the traditional and appropriate means of attacking shaky but admissible evidence.

A leading case that exemplifies the type of flexibility and wide discretion that the *Daubert* ruling apparently gives to trial judges in matters of scientific inquiry is *Coppolino* v. *State*.[4] Here a medical examiner testified to his finding that the victim had died of an overdose of a drug known as succinylcholine chloride. This drug had never before been detected in the human body. The medical examiner's findings were dependent on a toxicological report that identified an abnormally high concentration of succinic acid, a breakdown product of the drug, in the victim's body. The defense argued that this test for the presence of succinylcholine chloride was new and the absence of corroborative experimental data by other scientists meant that it had not yet gained general acceptance in the toxicology profession. The court, in rejecting this argument, recognized the necessity that exists for devising new scientific tests to solve the special problems that are continually arising in the forensic laboratory. It emphasized, however, that although these tests may be new and unique, they are admissible only if they are based on scientifically valid principles and techniques:

> The tests by which the medical examiner sought to determine whether death was caused by succinylcholine chloride were novel and devised specifically for this case. This does not render the evidence inadmissible. Society need not tolerate homicide until there develops a body of medical literature about some particular lethal agent.

PROVISION OF EXPERT TESTIMONY

Because their work product may ultimately be a factor in determining a person's guilt or innocence, forensic scientists may be required to testify with respect to their methods and conclusions at a trial or hearing. Trial courts have broad discretion in accepting an individual as an *expert witness* on any particular subject. Generally, if a witness can

---

[4]223 So. 2d 68 (Fla. App. 1968), app. dismissed 234 So. 2d (Fla. 1969), cert. denied 399 U.S. 927.

establish to the satisfaction of a trial judge that he or she possesses a particular skill, or has knowledge in a trade or profession that will aid the court in determining the truth of the matter at issue, that individual will be accepted as an expert witness. Depending on the subject area in question, the court will usually consider that knowledge acquired through experience, training, or education or a combination is sufficient grounds for qualification as an expert witness.

In court, the qualifying questions that are asked of the expert by counsel are often directed toward demonstrating the witness's ability and competence pertaining to the matter at hand. Competency may be established by having him or her cite educational degrees, participation in special courses, membership in professional societies, and any professional articles or books published. Also important to the issue is the number of years of occupational experience in which the witness has engaged in areas related to the matter before the court.

Unfortunately, there are few schools that confer degrees in forensic science. Most chemists, biologists, geologists, or physicists prepare themselves for careers in forensic science by combining training under an experienced examiner with independent study. Of course, formal education provides the scientist with a firm foundation for learning and understanding the principles and techniques of forensic science. Nevertheless, for the most part, courts must rely on training and years of experience as a measurement of the knowledge and ability of the expert.

Before the judge rules on the witness's qualifications, the opposing attorney will be given the opportunity to cross-examine the witness and to point out weaknesses in background and knowledge. Most courts are very reluctant to disqualify an individual as an expert even when presented with someone whose background is only remotely associated with the issue at hand. The question of what credentials are suitable for qualification as an expert is one that is obviously ambiguous and highly subjective and one that the courts wisely try to avoid. However, the weight that a judge or jury will assign to "expert" testimony in subsequent deliberations is quite another matter. Undoubtedly, education and experience are factors that have considerable bearing on the value assigned to the expert's opinions. Just as important may be the witness's demeanor and ability to explain scientific data and conclusions clearly, concisely, and logically to a judge and jury composed of nonscientists. The problem of sorting out the strengths and weaknesses of expert testimony falls to prosecution and defense counsels, who must endeavor to prepare themselves adequately for this undertaking.

The ordinary or lay witness must give testimony on events or observations that arise from personal knowledge. This testimony must be factual and, with few exceptions, cannot contain the personal opinions of the witness. On the other hand, the expert witness is called upon to evaluate evidence that the court lacks the expertise to do. This expert will then express an opinion as to the significance of the findings. The views expressed are accepted only as representing the expert's opinion and may later be accepted or ignored in jury deliberations.

It must be recognized that it is not possible for the expert to render any view with absolute certainty. At best, one may only be able to offer an opinion that is based on a reasonable scientific certainty derived from training and experience. Obviously, the expert is expected to defend vigorously the techniques and conclusions of the analysis, but at the same time there must be no reluctance to discuss impartially those findings that could minimize the significance of the analysis. The forensic scientist should not be an advocate of one party's cause, but only an advocate of truth. An adversary system of justice must give the prosecutor and defense ample opportunity to offer expert opinions and to argue the merits of such testimony. Ultimately, it will be the duty of the judge or jury to weigh the pros and cons of all the information presented in deciding guilt or innocence.

FURNISHING TRAINING IN THE PROPER RECOGNITION, COLLECTION, AND PRESERVATION OF PHYSICAL EVIDENCE

The competence of a laboratory staff and the sophistication of its analytical equipment have little or no value if relevant evidence cannot be properly recognized, collected, and preserved at the site of a crime. For this reason, it is important that the forensic staff have responsibilities that will influence the conduct of the crime-scene investigation.

The most direct and effective response to this problem has been to dispatch specially trained evidence-collection technicians to the crime scene. A growing number of crime laboratories and the police agencies they service have recognized the necessity of having trained "evidence technicians" on 24-hour call to aid criminal investigators in retrieving evidence. These technicians are trained by the laboratory staff to recognize and gather pertinent physical evidence at the crime scene. They are administratively assigned to the laboratory to facilitate their continued exposure to forensic techniques and procedures. They have at their disposal all the proper tools and supplies that will make possible the proper collection and packaging of evidence for future scientific examination.

Unfortunately, many police forces have still not adopted this approach. Often a patrol officer or detective is charged with the responsibility of collecting the evidence. His or her effectiveness in this role will be dependent on the extent of his or her training and working relationship with the laboratory. If maximum utilization is to be made of the skills of the crime laboratory, training of the crime-scene investigator must go beyond superficial classroom lectures to involve extensive personal contact with the forensic scientist. Each must become aware of the other's problems, techniques, and limitations.

The training of police officers in evidence collection and their familiarization with the capabilities of a crime laboratory should not be restricted to a select group of personnel on the force. Every officer engaged in fieldwork, whether it be traffic, patrol, investigation, or juvenile control, will often have to process evidence for laboratory examination. Obviously, it would be a difficult and time-consuming operation to give everyone the in-depth training and attention that a qualified criminal investigator requires. However, a familiarity with crime laboratory services and capabilities can be facilitated through periodic lectures, laboratory tours, and the dissemination of manuals prepared by the laboratory staff that outline the proper methods for collecting and submitting physical evidence to the laboratory. Examples of such manuals are shown in Figure 1–3.

Figure 1–3. Representative evidence-collection guides prepared by various police agencies. *Courtesy* New Jersey State Police.

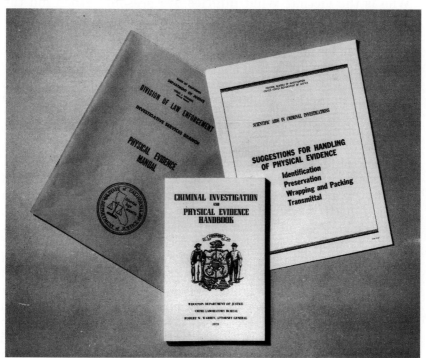

A brief outline describing the proper collection and packaging of common types of physical evidence is found in Appendix I. The procedures and information summarized in this guide will be discussed in greater detail in forthcoming chapters.

OTHER FORENSIC SCIENCE SERVICES

Even though this textbook is devoted to describing the services normally provided by a crime laboratory, it must be emphasized that the field of forensic science is by no means limited to those areas covered in this book. The fact is that there are a number of specialized forensic science services outside the crime laboratory that are routinely available to law enforcement personnel. These services are important aids to a criminal investigation and require the involvement of individuals who have highly specialized skills.

Forensic Pathology.   This field involves the investigation of sudden, unnatural, unexplained, or violent deaths. Typically, forensic pathologists, in their role as medical examiners or coroners, are charged with the responsibility of answering several basic questions: Who is the victim? What injuries are present? When did the injuries occur? Why and how were the injuries produced? The primary role of the medical examiner is to determine the cause of death. If a cause cannot be found through observation, an autopsy is normally performed to establish the cause of death. The manner in which death occurred is classified into five categories: natural, homicide, suicide, accident, or undetermined, based on the circumstances surrounding the incident.

After a human body expires, it goes through several stages of decomposition. A medical examiner participating in the criminal investigation can often estimate the time of death by evaluating the stage of decomposition in which the victim was found. Immediately following death, the muscles relax and then become rigid without the shortening of the muscle. This condition, *rigor mortis,* manifests itself within the first 24 hours and disappears within 36 hours. Another condition occurring in the early stages of decomposition is *livor mortis.* When the human heart stops pumping, the blood begins to settle in the parts of the body closest to the ground. The skin will appear as a dark blue or purple color in these areas. The onset of this condition begins immediately and continues for up to 12 hours after death. The skin will not appear discolored in areas where the body is restricted by either clothing or an object. Obtaining this information can be useful in determining if the victim's position was changed after death occurred.

Other physical and chemical changes within the body are also helpful in approximating the time of death. A condition referred to as *algor mortis* is the process in which the body temperature continually cools after death until it reaches the ambient or room temperature. The rate of heat loss is influenced by factors such as the location of the body, victim size, clothing, and weather conditions. Because of such factors, this method can only estimate the approximate time period since death.

Another approach helpful for estimating the time of death is determining potassium levels in ocular fluid (vitreous humor). After death, cells within the inner surface of the eyeball release potassium into the ocular fluid. By analyzing the amount of potassium present at various intervals after death, the forensic pathologist can determine the rate at which potassium is released into the vitreous humor. This rate then allows for approximating the time of death. During the autopsy, other factors can be observed that may indicate the time period in which death occurred. For example, the amount of food in the stomach can help to estimate when a person's last meal was eaten. This information can be valuable when investigating a death.

Frequently, medical examiners must perform autopsies if a death is deemed suspicious or unexplained. The cause of death may not always be what meets the eye. For example, a decedent with a gunshot wound and a gun in his hand may appear to have committed suicide. However, an autopsy may reveal that the victim actually died of suffocation and the gunshot wound occurred after death to cover up the circumstances surrounding the commission of a crime.

Forensic Anthropology.   Forensic anthropology is a specialty that is concerned primarily with the identification and examination of human skeletal remains. Skeletal bones are remarkably durable and undergo an extremely slow breakdown process that will last decades or centuries. Because of their resistance to rapid decomposition, skeletal remains can provide a multitude of individual characteristics. An examination of bones reveals their origin, which sex they belong to, approximate age, race, and skeletal injury. For example, a female's bone structure will differ from a male's, especially within the pelvic area because of a woman's childbearing capabilities. This area of expertise is not limited just to identification, however. A forensic anthropologist may also be of assistance in creating facial reconstructions to aid in the identification of skeletal remains. With the help of this technique, a composite of the victim can be drawn and advertised in an attempt to identify the victim. Forensic anthropologists are also helpful during the identification of victims of a mass disaster, such as a plane crash. When such a tragedy occurs, forensic anthropologists can help identify victims through the collection of bone fragments.

Forensic Entomology. The study of insects and their relation to a criminal investigation is known as forensic entomology. Such a practice is commonly used to estimate the time of death when the circumstances surrounding the crime are unknown. After decomposition begins, insects such as carrion flies are the first to infest the body. Their eggs are laid within the human remains and ultimately hatch into maggots or fly larvae. The maggots are responsible for the consumption of human organs and tissues. The forensic entomologist can identify the specific insects present in the body and approximate how long a body has been left exposed by examining the stage of development of the fly larvae. These determinations are not always straightforward, however. The time required for stage development is affected by environmental influences such as climate and weather conditions. For example, cold temperatures will hinder the progress of fly eggs into adult flies. The forensic entomologist must take these conditions under consideration when estimating the postmortem interval. The knowledge of insects, their life cycles, and their habits make entomological evidence an invaluable tool for an investigation.

Forensic Psychiatry. Forensic psychiatry is a specialized area in which the relationship between human behavior and legal proceedings is examined. Forensic psychiatrists are retained for both civil and criminal litigations. For civil cases, forensic psychiatrists normally determine whether people are competent to make decisions about preparing wills, settling property, or refusing medical treatment. For criminal cases, they evaluate behavioral disorders and determine whether people are competent to stand trial. Forensic psychiatrists also examine behavioral patterns of criminals as an aid in developing a suspect's behavioral profile.

Forensic Odontology. Practitioners of forensic odontology provide information for the identification of victims when the body is left in an unrecognizable state. Teeth are composed of enamel, the hardest substance within the body. Because of its resilience, the teeth will outlast tissues and organs as decomposition begins. The characteristics of teeth, their alignment, and the overall structure of the mouth provide individual evidence for identifying a specific person. With the use of dental records such as X-rays and dental casts or even a photograph of the person's smile, a comparison can be made between a set of dental remains and a suspected victim. Another application of forensic odontology to criminal investigations is bite mark analysis. At times in assault cases, bite marks are left on the victim. A forensic odontologist can analyze the marks left on a victim and the teeth structure of the suspect in order to make a comparison. See Figure 1–4.

Forensic Engineering. Forensic engineers are concerned with failure analysis, accident reconstruction, and causes and origins of fires or explosions. Forensic engineers answer questions such as, How

Figure 1–4. (a) Bite marks on victim's body: (b) and (c) Dental impressions showing characteristics of suspect's teeth. *Courtesy* The Forensic Science Laboratory, Dublin, Ireland.

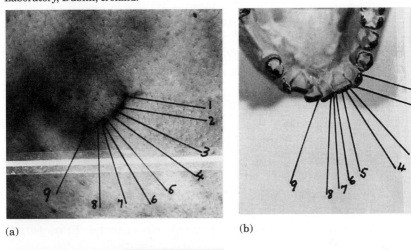

(a)

(b)

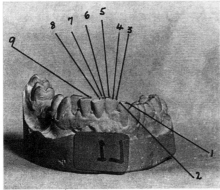

(c)

did an accident or structural failure occur? Were the parties involved responsible? If so, how were they responsible? Accident scenes are examined, photographs are reviewed, and any mechanical objects involved are inspected.

REVIEW QUESTIONS

1. The application of science to law describes _____.
2. The fictional exploits of _____ excited the imagination of an emerging generation of forensic scientists and criminal investigators.
3. A system of personal identification using a series of body measurements was first devised by _____.
4. _____ is responsible for developing the first statistical study proving the uniqueness of fingerprints.
5. The Italian scientist _____ devised the first workable procedure for typing dried bloodstains.
6. The comparison microscope became an indispensable tool of firearm examination through the efforts of _____.
7. Early efforts at applying scientific principles to document examination are associated with _____.
8. The application of science to criminal investigation was advocated by the Austrian magistrate _____.
9. One of the first functional crime laboratories to be formed existed in Lyons, France, under the direction of _____.
10. The first forensic laboratory in the United States was created in 1923 by the _____ Police Department.
11. The state of _____ is an excellent example of a geographical area in the United States that has created a system of integrated regional and satellite laboratories.
12. In contrast to the United States, Britain's crime laboratory system is characterized by a national system of _____ laboratories.
13. The increasing demand for _____ analyses has been the single most important factor in the recent expansion of crime laboratory services in the United States.
14. Four important agencies offering forensic service at the federal level are _____, _____, _____, and _____.
15. A decentralized system of crime laboratories presently exists in the United States under the auspices of various governmental

agencies at the _____, _____, _____, and _____ levels of government.

16. The application of chemistry, physics, and geology to the identification and comparison of crime-scene evidence is the function of the _____ unit of a crime laboratory.

17. The examination of blood, hairs, fibers, and vegetative materials is conducted in the _____ unit of a crime laboratory.

18. The examination of bullets, cartridge cases, shotgun shells, and ammunition of all types is the responsibility of the _____ unit.

19. The examination of body fluids and organs for drugs and poisons is a function belonging to the _____ unit.

20. The _____ unit dispatches trained personnel to the scene of a crime to retrieve evidence for laboratory examination.

21. The "general acceptance" principle, which serves as a criterion for the judicial admissibility of scientific evidence, was set forth in the case of _____.

22. In the case of _____, the Supreme Court ruled that in assessing the admissibility of new and unique scientific tests the trial judge did not have to rely solely on the concept of "general acceptance."

23. A Florida case that exemplifies the flexibility and wide discretion that the trial judge has in matters of scientific inquiry is _____.

24. An _____ is one who can demonstrate a particular skill or has knowledge in a trade or profession that will assist the court in determining the truth of the matter at issue.

25. The expert witness's courtroom demeanor may play an important role in deciding what weight the court will assign to his or her testimony. (True, False)

26. The testimony of an expert witness incorporates his or her personal opinion relating to a matter he or she has either studied or examined. (True, False)

27. The ability of the investigator to recognize and collect crime-scene evidence properly is dependent on the amount of _____ received from the crime laboratory.

28. When _____ sets in after death, the skin will appear as a dark blue or purple color in those areas closest to the ground.

29. One method for approximating the time of death is determining body temperature. (True, False)

FURHER REFERENCES

Berg, Stanton O., "Sherlock Holmes: Father of Scientific Crime Detection," *Journal of Criminal Law, Criminology and Police Science,* 61, no. 3 (1970), 446–52.

Cohen, Stanley A., "The Role of the Forensic Expert in a Criminal Trial," *The Canadian Society of Forensic Science Journal,* 12 (1979), 75.

Doyle, Sir Arthur Conan, *The Complete Sherlock Holmes,* Vol. 1. New York: Doubleday, 1956.

Farley, Mark A., "Legal Standards for the Admissibility of Novel Scientific Evidence," in *Forensic Science Handbook,* Vol. 3, R. Saferstein, ed. Englewood Cliffs, N.J.: Prentice Hall, 1993.

Kagan, J. D., "On Being a Good Expert Witness in a Criminal Case," *Journal of Forensic Sciences,* 23 (1978), 190.

Kuzmack, Nicholas T., "Legal Aspects of Forensic Science," in *Forensic Science Handbook,* Vol. 1, R. Saferstein, ed. Englewood Cliffs, N.J.: Prentice Hall, 1982.

Lucas, D. M., "North of 49—The Development of Forensic Science in Canada," *Science & Justice,* 37 (1997), 47.

Peterson, J. L., S. Mihajlovic, and J. L. Bedrosian, "The Capabilities, Uses, and Effects of the Nation's Criminalistics Laboratories," *Journal of Forensic Sciences,* 30 (1985), 10.

Starrs, James E., "Montebanks Among Forensic Scientists," in *Forensic Science Handbook,* Vol. 2, R. Saferstein, ed. Englewood Cliffs, N.J.: Prentice Hall, 1988.

Thorwald, Jürgen, *Crime and Science.* New York: Harcourt, Brace & World, 1967.

———, *The Century of the Detective.* New York: Harcourt, Brace & World, 1964.

Walls, H. J., "The Forensic Science Service in Great Britain: A Short History," *Journal of the Forensic Science Society,* 16 (1976), 273.

CASE READING

The case of *State* v. *Jascalevich* offers an excellent example of the legal and scientific issues involved in assessing the admissibility and value of scientific evidence in the courtroom. Dr. Jascalevich was accused of murdering a number of his patients by administering lethal doses of the drug curare. The issue of whether the curare was detected and identified in the exhumed bodies of the alleged murder victims was central to proving the state's case against the defendant. What ensued at the trial was a classic illustration of conflicting expert testimony on both sides of a scientific issue. Ultimately, it was the jury's task to weigh the data and arguments presented by both sides and to reach a verdict.

DETECTION OF CURARE
IN THE JASCALEVICH MURDER TRIAL

Lawrence H. Hall

The Star-Ledger, Newark, New Jersey

Roland H. Hirsch

Chemistry Department, Seton Hall University, South Orange, New Jersey

The murder trial of Dr. Mario E. Jascalevich was one of the most complicated criminal proceedings ever tried in an American courtroom. The 34-week trial before a Superior Court judge in New Jersey resulted in a not-guilty verdict for the Englewood Cliffs, N.J., surgeon. The questions concerning analytical chemistry raised in the trial will continue to be discussed in years to come.

Not since the controversial trial of Dr. Carl Coppolino—convicted in a Florida courtroom in 1967 of murdering his wife with succinylcholine chloride—have so many forensic experts of national and international stature labored so long over the scientific questions at issue in the case:

What happens to human tissue, embalmed and interred for a decade?

Assuming lethal doses of a drug such as curare were given to hospital patients, would the drug have changed chemically or have been destroyed entirely over a 10-year period?

Assuming again that the drug had been injected, what analytical techniques could be employed to trace submicrogram amounts of it?

Could components of embalming fluids or bacteria in the earth react chemically, forming substances giving a false positive reading in the analytical procedures used?

Forensic scientists first grappled with these questions during the latter part of 1966. Two of Jascalevich's colleagues at Riverdell

---

Hospital in Oradell, N.J.—Dr. Stanley Harris, a surgeon, and Dr. Allan Lans, an osteopathic physician—suspected him of murdering their patients with curare. There were no eyewitnesses to the alleged murders, but Drs. Harris and Lans discovered 18 vials of curare in Jascalevich's surgical locker after breaking into it.

They took their suspicions to the Bergen County Prosecutor's office in November 1966, and a brief but unpublicized investigation was launched. Items taken from the surgeon's locker, including the vials of curare and syringes, were sent for analysis at the New York City Medical Examiner's office.

In the interim, Jascalevich told authorities he used the muscle-relaxant drug in animal experiments at the Seton Hall Medical College. The surgeon presented the prosecutor his medical research papers and other documentation to support his contention. In addition, he reviewed the medical charts of the alleged murder victims and told the prosecutor there was no need for the operations the patients received. Malpractice and misdiagnosis were the causes of the deaths, Jascalevich stated at that time.

Dr. Milton Helpern, chief of the New York City Medical Examiner's office, and his staff in early 1967 concluded their testing on the items taken from Jascalevich's locker. Dog hair and animal blood were detected on the vials of curare and syringes.

The prosecutor's office terminated its investigation and stated there were more reasons to look into allegations of malpractice than murder at the small osteopathic hospital.

In January 1976 a series of articles about a "Doctor X" suspected of murdering patients at Riverdell Hospital appeared in the *New York Times,* and the Bergen County Prosecutor's office reopened its case.

A month prior to the case being officially reopened, however, New York Deputy Medical Examiner Dr. Michael Baden supplied an affidavit to the Superior Court in Bergen County stating that at least a score of patients who died at Riverdell in 1966 succumbed from other reasons than those stated on death certificates.

In his affidavit in support of exhumation of the patients' remains, Dr. Baden stated,

> It is my professional opinion that the majority of these cases reviewed are not explainable on the basis of natural causes and are consistent with having been caused by a respiratory depressant.
>
> [The deputy medical examiner continued] I am aware that because unexplainable respiratory arrests have been involved in many of these deaths, the possibility of poisoning by a curare-like substance (specifically d-tubocurarine) was considered and investigated at the time of the initial inquiry in 1966.

The ability to identify *d*-tubocurarine, often referred to as curare, in human tissue was limited at the time of the initial investigation.

It is my professional opinion that recent technological advances now permit the detection of very minute amounts of *d*-tubocurarine in tissues removed from dead bodies. This is because *d*-tubocurarine is a chemically stable compound that can exist unaltered for many years.

Therefore, the aforementioned new techniques to detect curare-like compounds can be applied to tissues removed from bodies that have been interred for long periods of time.

A Superior Court judge signed the order in January 1976, granting the prosecutor's office the right to exhume the bodies of Nancy Savino, 4; Emma Arzt, 70; Frank Biggs, 59; Margaret Henderson, 27; and Carl Rohrbeck, 73.

All these patients entered Riverdell Hospital between December 1965 and September 1966 for routine surgical procedures and succumbed days afterward.

In mid-January 1976 the body of the Savino child was exhumed from a gravesite in Bergen County and taken to the medical examiner's office in New York City.

There, Dr. Baden, in the presence of New Jersey State Medical Examiner Dr. Edwin Albano and others, began performing the almost 4-hour examination of the child's body, which was said to be well preserved.

Assisting Dr. Baden in the analytical studies carried out on the tissues were Dr. Leo Dal Cortivo, chief toxicologist for Suffolk County, N.Y., and Dr. Richard J. Coumbis, chief toxicologist for the New Jersey Medical Examiner's office. The defense experts, headed by former Westchester County (N.Y.) Medical Examiner Dr. Henry Siegel, were not permitted to be present at the reautopsies.

The state began its work. In March, a week before the grand jury met, a newspaper article declared that curare had been detected in the Savino child. However, in his grand jury testimony weeks later, Dr. Baden stated his experts could not be certain if curare could be detected: "We have to look and see whether or not we can develop adequate procedures."

On May 18, 1976, Dr. Jascalevich was indicted for five murders.

A little more than a year later, the state's forensic experts began using radioimmunoassay (RIA) and high-performance liquid chromatography (HPLC) on the tissue specimens. In the fall of 1977, the defense received from Drs. Baden and Dal Cortivo samples of tissues and embalming fluids of the alleged murder victims.

For the remainder of the year, both the defense and the state experts worked to develop analytical procedures to settle the question of detection of curare in human tissue.

In addition, there were numerous pretrial hearings at which time the defense, headed by Jersey City attorney Raymond Brown, requested medical slides, reports, and patient charts relating to the alleged murder victims, as well as the methodologies used in treating the specimens.

On February 28, 1978, a panel of 18 jurors was chosen for what was to become the second longest criminal trial in the nation's history. At the outset, the defense wanted a hearing to ascertain the validity of the scientific procedures employed by the state to reportedly detect curare.

The defense contended that RIA and HPLC were relatively new procedures and could not be used to detect curare in human tissue. RIA, for example, could only be used to detect drugs in blood and body fluids, according to defense experts.

The defense motion for a hearing outside of the presence of the jury was denied by Superior Court Judge William J. Arnold, who maintained the motion could be made later in the trial when the evidence obtained by the analytical techniques would actually be scheduled for presentation to the jury.

The trial got underway with testimony by osteopathic physicians, nurses, and other hospital personnel employed by Riverdell during the time the alleged murders were committed. The physicians told Assistant Prosecutor Sybil Moses that in each instance the patient had been recovering from surgery when he succumbed.

However, on cross-examination, the physicians admitted they had misdiagnosed their patients' conditions and that there was inferior postoperative care. For example, in the case of the Savino child, the defense experts held that the little girl died of acute diffuse peritonitis—the source of her abdominal pain when she was brought into Riverdell after having been diagnosed as having acute appendicitis.

After the prosecution completed presentation of the medical aspects of its case, the defense renewed its request for a special hearing on the admissibility of the evidence obtained by radioimmunoassay, liquid chromatography, and other analytical techniques. This request came as Dr. Baden took the witness stand to explain why he had recommended reautopsy of the bodies. The prosecution was opposed to a hearing:

> The techniques used by the State are not new toxicological methodologies, but are standard methods, used widely throughout the field. These methodologies include radioimmunoassay and high-pressure liquid chromatography. . . .
>
> Since the methodologies used to detect the curare are widely accepted in the scientific community, there is no necessity for the Court to conduct a hearing as to their reliability.

Nevertheless, Judge Arnold ruled that a hearing should be held. Arguments began, in the absence of the jury, on June 10. Both sides presented statements by their technical experts and affidavits from other scientists regarding the validity of the analytical methods. The prosecution cited various cases in support of its position:

> Practically every new scientific discovery had its detractors and unbelievers, but neither unanimity of opinion nor universal infallibility is required for judicial acceptance of generally recognized matters [*State* v. *Johnson,* 42 N.J. 146, 171 (1964)].
>
> The law, in its efforts to enforce justice by demonstrating a fact in issue, will allow evidence of those scientific processes, which are the work of educated and skillful men in their various departments and apply them to the demonstration of a fact, leaving the weight and effect to be given to the effort and its results entirely to the consideration of the jury [*State* v. *Cerciello,* 86 N.J.L. 309, 314 (E&A 1914)].

The prosecution stated, "Federal courts have held that newness or lack of absolute certainty in a test does not require its inadmissibility." In one case involving neutron-activation analysis, a federal appellate court held in part:

> Every useful new development must have its first day in court. And court records are full of the conflicting opinions of doctors, engineers, and accountants to name just a few of the legions of expert witnesses [*United States* v. *Stifel,* 433 F. 2d. 431, 437, 438 (6th Cir. 1970)].

The prosecution noted,

> The Florida Appellate Court in *Coppolino* v. *State.* . . held that not only established techniques but methods developed specifically for that case could be used to detect a previously undetectable drug in the body of the decedent. . . .
>
> The tests by which the medical examiner sought to determine whether death was caused by succinylcholine chloride were novel and devised specifically for this case. This does not render the evidence inadmissible. Society need not tolerate homicide until there develops a body of medical knowledge about some particular lethal agent. The expert witnesses were examined and cross-examined at great length and the jury could either believe or doubt the prosecution's testimony as it chose [*Coppolino* v. *State,* 223 So. 2d. 75 (Fla. App. 1968)].

Finally, the prosecution noted the following holding of the New Jersey Superior Court Appellate Division:

The general rule in New Jersey regarding the admissibility of scientific test results is that, if the equipment or the methodology used is proven to have a high degree of scientific reliability, and if the test is performed or administered by qualified persons, the results will be admissible at trial [*State* v. *Chatman,* 101 N.J.L.S. index 307, 308 (App. Div. 1973)].

The defense contended that

The methodologies of thin layer chromatography (TLC), high pressure liquid chromatography, ultraviolet spectrophotometry, and radioimmunoassay which have been utilized by the State do not meet the required level of acceptance under the circumstances of the tissues in this case. . . . Since there have never been any attempts to demonstrate the presence of *d*-tubocurarine in embalmed, buried tissue . . . the State cannot even assert that the techniques it wishes to utilize to demonstrate this have been generally accepted.

The defense presented affidavits from a variety of forensic scientists, from which we present one example:

It should be noted that even though the newer analytical methods and some of the sophisticated equipment are extremely sensitive for drug detection, the sensitivity of some method is not a criterion of its specificity. Sensitivity is the minimum amount of an unknown substance below which a test gives a negative result. Specificity is the ability of a test to establish the individual characteristics and/or configuration of a particular substance by differentiating it from all other substances, especially in a biologic mixture.

Currently, the reported analytical methods, which include ultraviolet absorption spectrophotometry, thin layer chromatography and radioimmunoassay, alone or in conjunction, lack such a degree of specificity with any degree of scientific certainty required to support the opinion that they identified the isolated material as *d*-tubocurarine in embalmed, decomposed and skeletonizing tissues that have been in the ground for ten years under varying climatic conditions [Abraham Stolman, Chief Toxicologist, State of Connecticut Department of Health].

On June 20 the judge ruled that the analytical evidence was admissible. He stated,

All I'm saying is under the law the evidence is admissible. I'm not going to comment on the value or trustworthiness of the witnesses [who testified]. The ultimate decision must be made by the jury.

Following this decision, the jury began listening to the scientific evidence, with the State's and the defense's witnesses in the process explaining such points as: What is curare, and specifically *d*-tubocurarine? What is radioimmunoassay? What is an antibody, and how is the antibody for *d*-tubocurarine created? What is high-pressure liquid chromatography?

Dr. Richard Coumbis testified about his finding tubocurarine in tissues from four of the five patients: ". . . can only state there is presumptive evidence" that curare was discovered in the fifth patient. Under cross-examination by defense attorney Raymond Brown, Coumbis maintained that the RIA and HPLC procedures were valid methods of detecting curare because "on the basis of my personal experience, I did not find any other substance interfering with curare."

The toxicologist admitted that the counting efficiencies of the instruments he used to get the RIA displacement values varied from day to day and were subject to error. Brown disagreed with the displacement figures Coumbis arrived at, and wanted to know whether there was a "cut-off point" whereby he arrived at the conclusion that curare was or was not present in tissues. The RIA results ranged from as low as 77 counts all the way up to 700. Somewhere within that range, Brown argued, was a point at which Coumbis arrived at the decision that the drug was detected or not. Where, he asked, was that point? The toxicologist responded by saying that the higher the figure, the more likely curare was present. He said in many instances, however, he had to use his discretion to determine the cut-off point.

Dr. David Beggs of Hewlett-Packard then testified that he found curare in the Savino lung and liver samples using mass spectrometry. He said the Biggs and Arzt samples contained possible traces of curare; however, he could not be scientifically certain of this. He stated that mass spectrometry "is not an absolute test" for curare, but "just indicated that it is probably there." He did carry out a solvent blank as a means of eliminating false positives. He held under cross-examination that the electron impact technique used by him resulted in a spectrum with 12 major peaks and that 10 were sufficient for "fingerprint" identification of curare.

Dr. Sidney Spector of the Roche Institute testified about how he had developed the antibody for *d*-tubocurarine and applied it in RIA analysis of body fluids such as urine and blood. He had not himself run any tests for curare in human tissue samples and stated, "If there were curare in tissues, there is the possibility it could be detected." He said that the State's RIA experiments were "inadequate" in relying on aqueous solutions of curare to develop a standard curve. He held that the RIA procedure could give an indication that curare was present, but that the finding would only be presumptive evidence and not sufficient to say that the muscle-relaxant drug was positively present. He made the same point about HPLC and said that even if the two techniques were used together, there still would only be presumptive proof that the drug was present.

Dr. Leo Dal Cortivo then took the witness stand and testified that he had found curare in tissue remains of three of the patients using HPLC. He also had measured curare in vials found in the defendant's locker at Riverdell Hospital in 1966, which the defense contended had been used in animal experiments conducted by Jascalevich at the College of Medicine in Jersey City. It was necessary to use RIA for the detection of curare in the HPLC eluates. The samples were prepared for LC analysis by an extraction procedure which Dal Cortivo stated gave a 75% recovery. He rejected the contention that the extraction and LC method might have allowed positive results because of an interfering substance.

The prosecution then completed its case. At this point Judge Arnold dismissed two counts of murder and stated that the prosecution had not presented scientific evidence for the presence of curare in the bodies of Emma Arzt and Margaret Henderson. The defense then began presentation of its case with testimony about the medical aspects.

In September, attention returned to the analytical data. Drs. Frederick Rieders and Bo Holmstedt testified about the experiments they carried out on the samples provided by the prosecution. The major question they addressed was that of the long-term stability of curare under the conditions to which the bodies were subjected between 1966 and 1976.

Dr. Rieders maintained that, in his opinion, the RIA was not specific enough and "could only raise suspicions that something is there but it might not be there." The only procedure he found specific enough to be confident of identification of curare is mass spectrometry, using the entire spectrum, not just selected ion monitoring. In critical analyses, a four-step extraction procedure was used to isolate d-tubocurarine from the samples. . . .

Rieders tested for the stability of curare and found that both embalming fluids and tissue juices (from the patients) had destructive effects on this compound. He added curare to these liquids and could detect it by TLC initially, but after a few days could find no trace of it or other nitrogenous bases. These liquids altered curare chemically to the point where it was no longer recognizable as such. He concluded that the rapid rate of decomposition meant that to detect curare in the specimens in 1976 would have required huge, medically impossible amounts to have been present in 1966.

Rieders tested the samples for curare and found it only in the liver specimen of Nancy Savino. He stated that mass spectrometry indicated that the curare in this sample was highly pure and could not have been present in the ground for 10 years. Furthermore, if curare was present in the liver, it should also have been found in the child's muscle tissue. That it was not detected in the latter specimen was a "tremendous inconsistency."

Dr. Bo Holmstedt then stated that curare could not survive in embalmed bodies for 10 years, especially because of the effects of bacteria and repeated fluctuations in temperature of the bodies. He reviewed experiments which showed that curare, upon injection, shows levels of the same order of magnitude in liver and muscle tissues. After 10 minutes, "40% of the drug is to be found in the muscle and 3% in the liver."

On October 14 the defense rested its case. On October 23, after both sides had presented summations of their cases, Judge Arnold gave his charge to the jury. The next day, October 24, 1978—seven and a half months after the trial had begun—the jury received the case. After just over 2 hours of deliberations, the jury returned a unanimous verdict of not guilty on all three remaining counts of murder. Two years and five months after the indictments against him had been returned, Dr. Mario Jascalevich was free.

CHAPTER

2 THE CRIME SCENE

PROCESSING THE CRIME SCENE

As automobiles run on gasoline, crime laboratories "run" on physical evidence. **Physical evidence encompasses any and all objects that can establish that a crime has been committed or can provide a link between a crime and its victim or a crime and its perpetrator.** But if physical evidence is to be effectively used for aiding the investigator, its presence first must be recognized at the crime scene. If *all* the natural and commercial objects within a reasonable distance of a crime were gathered so that the scientist could uncover significant clues from them, the deluge of material would quickly immobilize the laboratory facility. Physical evidence can only achieve its optimum value in criminal investigations when its collection is performed with a selectivity governed by the collector's thorough knowledge of the crime laboratory's techniques, capabilities, and limitations.

Forthcoming chapters will be devoted to discussions of methods and techniques available to forensic scientists for the evaluation of physical evidence. Although it is true that present-day technology has given the crime laboratory capabilities far exceeding those of past decades, these advances are no excuse for complacency on the part of criminal investigators. Crime laboratories do not solve crimes; only a thorough and competent investigation conducted by professional police officers will enhance the chances for the successful outcome of a criminal investigation. To be sure, forensic science is, and will continue to be, an important element of the total investigative process; but it is only one aspect of an endeavor that must be a team effort. The investigator who believes the crime laboratory to be a panacea for laxity or ineptness is in for a rude awakening.

Forensic science begins at the crime scene. If the investigator cannot recognize physical evidence or cannot properly preserve it for laboratory examination, no amount of sophisticated laboratory instrumentation or technical expertise can salvage the situation. The know-how for conducting a proper crime-scene search for physical evidence is not beyond the grasp of any police department, regardless of its size. With proper training, police agencies can assure themselves of competent performance at crime scenes. In many jurisdictions, police agencies have delegated this task to a specialized team of technicians. However, whether this task is carried out by a specialist or by a patrol officer, it must be emphasized that the techniques of crime-scene investigation are not difficult to master and certainly lie within the bounds of comprehension of the average police officer.

Not all crime scenes require retrieval of physical evidence, and in reality, limited resources and personnel have forced many police agencies to restrict their efforts in this area to crimes of a more serious nature. Once the commitment is made to completely process a crime site for physical evidence, however, it is imperative that certain fundamental practices be adhered to.

SECURE AND ISOLATE THE CRIME SCENE

It is the responsibility of the first officer arriving on the scene of a crime to take steps to preserve and protect the area to the greatest extent possible. Of course, first priority should be given to obtaining medical assistance for individuals in need of it and to arresting the perpetrator. However, as soon as it is possible, extensive efforts must be taken to exclude all unauthorized personnel from the scene. As additional officers arrive, measures are immediately initiated to isolate the area. Ropes or barricades along with the strategic positioning of guards will prevent unauthorized access to the area.

Sometimes the exclusion of unauthorized personnel proves to be a more difficult task than expected. Crimes of violence are especially susceptible to attention by higher level police officials and members of the press, as well as by emotionally charged neighbors and curiosity seekers. Every individual who enters the scene is a potential destroyer of physical evidence, even if it is by unintentional carelessness. If proper control is to be exercised over the crime scene, the officer charged with the responsibility for protecting it must have the authority to exclude everyone, including fellow police officers not directly involved in processing the site or in conducting the investigation. Seasoned criminal investigators are always prepared to relate horror stories about crime scenes made totally valueless for physical evidence by hordes of people who, for one reason or another, trampled through them. Securing and isolating the crime scene are critical steps in an investigation, the accomplishment of which is the mark of a trained and professional crime-scene investigative team.

RECORD THE SCENE

Investigators will have only a limited amount of time to work a crime site in its untouched state. The opportunity to permanently record the scene in its original state must not be lost. Such records will not only prove useful during the subsequent investigation but are also required for presentation at a trial in order to document the condition of the crime site and to delineate the location of physical evidence. Photography, sketches, and notes are the three methods for crime-scene recording (see Figure 2–1). Ideally all three should be employed; however, as is often the case, personnel and monetary limitations may prohibit the utilization of photography at every crime site. Under these circumstances, departmental guidelines will establish priorities for deploying photographic resources. However, no reason exists for failing to utilize sketches and notes at the crime scene.

Photography.   The most important prerequisite for photographing a crime scene is to have it in an unaltered condition. Unless there are injured parties involved, objects must not be moved until they have been photographed from all necessary angles. If objects are removed, positions changed, or items added, the photographs may not be admissible as evidence at a trial, and their intended value will be lost.

Each crime scene should be photographed as completely as possible. This means that the crime scene should include the area in which the crime actually took place and all adjacent areas where important acts occurred immediately before or after the commission of the crime. Overview photographs of the entire scene and surrounding area, including points of exit and entry, must be taken from various angles. If the crime has taken place indoors, the entire room should be photographed to show each wall area. Rooms adjacent to the actual crime site must be similarly photographed. If the crime scene includes a body, photographs must be taken to show the body's position and location

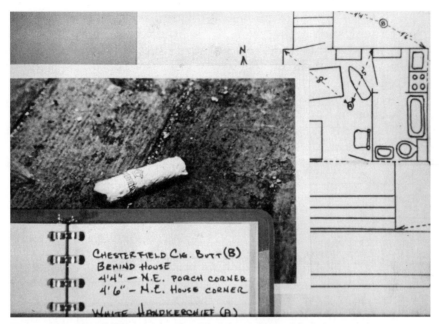

Figure 2-1. The finding of an evidential cigarette butt at the crime scene requires photographing it, making a sketch showing its relation to the crime scene, and recording the find in field notes. *Courtesy* Police Science Services, Niles, Ill.

relative to the entire scene. Close-up photos depicting injuries and weapons lying near the body are also necessary.

As items of physical evidence are discovered, they are photographed to show their position and location relative to the entire scene. After these overviews are taken, there should be close-ups to record the details of the object itself. When the size of an item is of significance, a ruler or other measuring scale may be inserted near the object and included in the photograph as a point of reference.

The use of videotape at crime scenes is becoming increasingly popular as the cost of this equipment is decreasing. The same principles used in crime-scene photographs apply to videotaping. As with conventional photography, videotaping should include the entire scene and the immediate surrounding area. Long shots as well as close-ups should be taken in a slow and systematic manner. Furthermore, it is desirable to have one crime-scene investigator narrate the events and scenes being taped while another does the actual shooting.

While videotaping can capture the sounds and scenes of the crime site with relative ease, the technique cannot at this time be used in place of still photography. The still photograph remains unsurpassed in the definition of detail it provides to the human eye.

Sketches.   Once photographs are taken, the crime-scene investi-gator will sketch the scene. The investigator may have neither the skill nor the time to make a polished sketch of the scene. However, this is not required during the early phase of the investigation. What is necessary is a "rough" sketch containing an accurate depiction of the dimensions of the scene and showing the location of all objects having a bearing on the case.

A rough sketch is illustrated in Figure 2–2. It shows all recov-ered items of physical evidence, as well as other important features

Figure 2–2.   Diagram of a crime scene.

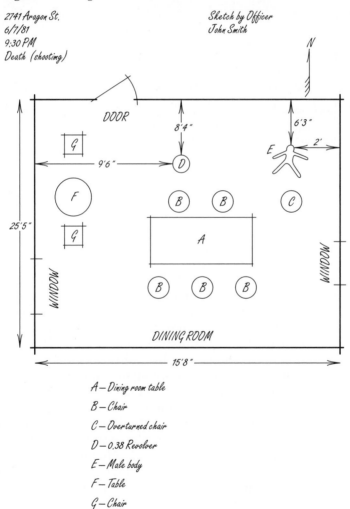

2741 Aragon St.
6/7/81
9:30 PM
Death (shooting)

Sketch by Officer
John Smith

N

DOOR

8'4"

6'3"

9'6"

E

2'

F

B

B

C

25'5"

A

WINDOW

G

WINDOW

MAGNUM

B

B

B

DINING ROOM

15'8"

A — Dining room table
B — Chair
C — Overturned chair
D — 0.38 Revolver
E — Male body
F — Table
G — Chair

of the crime scene. Objects are located in the sketch by distance measurements from two fixed points, such as the walls of a room. It is important that distances shown on the sketch be accurate and not the result of a guess or estimate. For this reason, all measurements are made with a tape measure. The simplest way to designate an item in a sketch is to assign it a number or letter. A legend or list placed below the sketch will then correlate the letter to the item's description. The sketch should also show a compass heading designating *north*.

Unlike the rough sketch, the finished sketch is drawn with care and concern for aesthetic appearance. It is usually prepared with the aid of templates and drafting tools by a skilled individual and is frequently drawn to scale. When the finished sketch is completed, it must reflect information contained within the rough sketch in order to be admissible evidence in a courtroom. Computer programs are becoming available to law enforcement agencies to reconstruct crime scenes with computer-aided drafting (CAD). The software, ranging from simple, low-cost programs to complex, expensive programs, contains predrawn intersections and roadways or buildings and rooms onto which information can be entered. A generous symbol library provides the operator with a variety of images that can be used to add intricate details such as blood spatters to a crime-scene sketch. Equipped with a zoom function, computerized sketching can focus on a specific area for a more detailed picture. The CAD programs allow you to select scale size so that the ultimate product can be produced in a size suitable for courtroom presentation.

Notes.   Note taking must be a constant activity throughout the processing of the crime scene. These notes must include a detailed written description of the scene with the location of items of physical evidence recovered. They must also identify the time an item of physical evidence was discovered, by whom, how and by whom it was packaged and marked, and the disposition of the item after it was collected. The note taker has to keep in mind that this written record may be the only source of information for refreshing one's memory months, perhaps years, after a crime has been processed. The notes must be sufficiently detailed to anticipate this need.

Tape-recording notes at a scene can be advantageous—detailed notes can be taped much faster than they can be written. Another method of recording notes is by narrating a videotape of the crime scene. This has the advantage of combining note taking with photography. However, at some point the tape must be transcribed into a written document.

CONDUCT A SYSTEMATIC SEARCH
FOR EVIDENCE

The search for physical evidence at a crime scene must be thorough and systematic. For a factual, unbiased reconstruction of the crime, the investigator, through his or her training and experience, must not overlook any pertinent evidence. Even in those cases in which suspects are immediately seized and the motives and circumstances of the crime are readily apparent, it is imperative that a thorough search for physical evidence be conducted at once. Failure in this, even though it may seem at the time to be unnecessary, can lead to accusations of negligence or charges that the investigative agency knowingly "covered up" evidence that would be detrimental to its case.

Assigning those responsible for searching a crime scene is a function of the investigator in charge. Except in major crimes, or where the evidence is very complex, it is usually not necessary to have the assistance of a forensic scientist at the crime scene; his or her role appropriately begins with the submission of evidence to the crime laboratory. As has already been observed, some police agencies do have trained field evidence technicians to conduct the search for physical evidence at the crime scene. They have the equipment and skill to photograph the scene and examine it for the presence of fingerprints, footprints, tool marks, or any other type of evidence that may be relevant to the crime.

How one proceeds to carry out a crime-scene search will depend on the locale and size of the area, as well as on the actions of the suspect(s) and victim(s) at the scene. When possible, it is advisable to have one person supervising and coordinating the collection of evidence. Without proper control, the search may be conducted in an atmosphere of confusion with needless duplication of effort. Evidence collectors may choose to subdivide the scene into segments and search each segment individually, or the search may start at some outer point and gradually move toward the center of the scene in a circular fashion (see Figure 2–3). The areas searched must include all probable points of entry and exit used by the criminals.

What to search for will be determined by the particular circumstances of the crime. Obviously, the skill of crime-scene investigators at recognizing evidence and searching relevant locations is paramount to the successful processing of the crime scene. While training will impart general knowledge for conducting a proper crime-scene investigation, ultimately the investigator must rely on the experience gained from numerous investigations to formulate a successful strategy for recovering relevant physical evidence at crime scenes. For example, in the case of homicide, the search will be centered on the weapon and any type of evidence left as a result of contact between the victim and

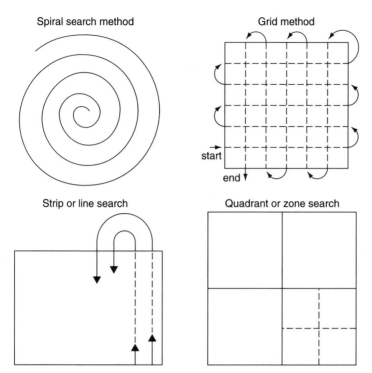

Figure 2–3. Several typical examples of crime-scene search patterns. The pattern selected will normally depend on the size and locale of the scene and the number of collectors participating in the search.

the assailant. The cross-transfer of evidence, such as hairs, fibers, and blood, between individuals involved in the crime is particularly useful for linking suspects to the crime site and for corroborating events transpiring during the commission of the crime. During the investigation of a burglary, efforts will be made to locate tool marks at the point of entry. In most crimes, a thorough and systematic search for latent fingerprints is required.

Vehicle searches must be carefully planned and systematically carried out. The nature of the case determines how detailed the search must be. In hit-and-run cases, the outside and undercarriage of the car must be examined with care. Particular attention is paid to looking for any evidence resulting from a cross-transfer of evidence between the car and the victim—this includes blood, tissue, hair, fibers, and fabric impressions. Traces of paint or broken glass may be located on the victim. In cases of homicide, burglary, kidnapping, and so on, all areas of the vehicle, inside and outside, are searched with equal care for physical evidence.

Physical evidence can be anything from massive objects to microscopic traces. Often, many items of evidence are obvious in their presence, but others may be detected only through examination in the crime laboratory. For example, minute traces of blood may be discovered on garments only after a thorough search in the laboratory; or the presence of hairs and fibers may be revealed in vacuum sweepings or on garments only after close laboratory scrutiny. For this reason, it is important to collect *possible* carriers of trace evidence in addition to more discernible items. Hence, it may be necessary to take custody of all clothing worn by the participants in a crime. Each clothing item should be handled carefully and wrapped separately to avoid loss of trace materials. Critical areas of the crime scene should be vacuumed and the sweepings submitted to the laboratory for analysis. The sweepings from different areas must be collected and packaged separately. A portable vacuum cleaner equipped with a special filter attachment is suitable for this purpose (see Figure 2–4). Additionally, fingernail scrapings from individuals who were in contact may contain minute fragments of evidence capable of providing a link between assailant and victim. The undersurface of each nail is best scraped with a dull object such as a toothpick to avoid cutting the skin. These scrapings will be subjected to microscopic examination in the laboratory.

The search for physical evidence must extend beyond the crime scene to the autopsy room of a deceased victim. Here, the medical examiner or coroner will carefully examine the victim to establish a cause and manner of death. As a matter of routine, tissues and organs will be retained for pathological and toxicological examination. At the

Figure 2–4. Vacuum sweeper attachment, constructed of clear plastic in two pieces that are joined by a threaded joint. A metal screen is mounted in one half to support a filter paper to collect debris. The unit attaches to the hose of the vacuum sweeper. After a designated area of the crime scene is vacuumed, the filter paper is removed and retained for laboratory examination. *Courtesy* Sirchie Laboratories, Inc., Raleigh, N.C.

same time, arrangements must be made between the examiner and investigator to secure a variety of items that may be obtainable from the body for laboratory examination. The following are to be collected and sent to the forensic laboratory:

1. Victim's clothing
2. Fingernail scrapings
3. Head and pubic hairs
4. Blood (for typing purposes)
5. Vaginal, anal, and oral swabs (in sex-related crimes)
6. Recovered bullets from the body
7. Hand swabs from shooting victims (for gunshot residue analysis)

Once the body is buried, efforts at obtaining these items may prove difficult or futile. Furthermore, a lengthy time delay in obtaining many of these items will diminish or destroy their forensic value.

In recent years, many police departments have gone to the expense of purchasing and equipping "mobile crime laboratories" (see Figure 2–5) for their evidence technicians. However, the term *mobile crime laboratory* is a misnomer. These vehicles carry the necessary supplies to carry out the functions of a chemical laboratory. *Crime-scene search*

Figure 2–5. Evidence-collection vehicle. *Courtesy* Sirchie Laboratories, Inc., Raleigh, N.C.

vehicle would be a more appropriate but perhaps less dramatic name for such a vehicle.

COLLECT AND PACKAGE PHYSICAL EVIDENCE

Physical evidence must be handled and processed in a way that prevents any change from taking place between the time it is removed from the crime scene and the time it is received by the crime laboratory. Changes can arise through contamination, breakage, evaporation, accidental scratching or bending, or loss through improper or careless packaging.

The integrity of evidence is best maintained when the item is kept in its original condition as found at the crime site. Whenever possible, evidence should be submitted to the laboratory intact. Blood, hairs, fibers, soil particles, and other types of trace evidence should not normally be removed from garments, weapons, or other articles that bear them. Instead, the entire object is to be sent to the laboratory for processing. Of course, if evidence is adhering to an object in a precarious manner, good judgment is best exercised by removing and packaging the item. If evidence is found adhering to large structures, such as a door, wall, or floor, common sense must be used; remove the specimen with a forceps or other appropriate tool. In the case of a bloodstain, one has the option of either scraping the stain off the surface, transferring the stain to a moistened swab, or cutting out the area of the object bearing the stain.

Each different item or similar items collected at different locations must be placed in separate containers. Packaging evidence separately prevents damage through contact and prevents cross-contamination.

The well-prepared evidence collector will arrive at a crime scene with a large assortment of packaging materials and tools ready to encounter any type of situation. Forceps and similar tools may have to be used to pick up small items. Unbreakable plastic pill bottles with pressure lids are excellent containers for hairs, glass, fibers, and various other kinds of small or trace evidence. Alternatively, manila envelopes, screw-cap glass vials, or cardboard pillboxes are adequate containers for most trace evidence encountered at crime sites. Ordinary mailing envelopes should not be used as evidence containers because powders and fine particles will leak out of their corners. Small amounts of trace evidence can also be conveniently packaged in a carefully folded paper, using what is known as a "druggist fold." This consists of folding one end of the paper over one-third, then folding the other end (one-third) over that, and repeating the process from the other two sides. After being folded in this manner, the outside two edges are tucked into each other to produce a closed container that keeps the specimen from falling out.

Although pill bottles, vials, pillboxes, or manila envelopes are good universal containers for most trace evidence, two frequent finds at crime scenes warrant special attention. If bloodstained materials are stored in airtight containers, the accumulation of moisture may encourage the growth of mold, which can destroy the evidential value of blood. In these instances, wrapping paper, manila envelopes, or paper bags are recommended packaging materials (Figure 2–6). As a matter of routine, all items of clothing are to be air-dried and placed individually in separate paper bags to ensure a constant circulation of air through them. This will prevent the formation of mold and mildew. On the other hand, charred debris recovered from the scene of a suspicious fire must be sealed in an airtight container to prevent the evaporation of volatile petroleum residues. New paint cans or tightly sealed jars are recommended in such situations.

Figure 2–6. Paper bags are recommended evidence containers for objects suspected of containing blood and semen stains. Each object should be packaged in a separate bag. *Courtesy* Lightning Powder Co., Inc., Salem, Oreg.

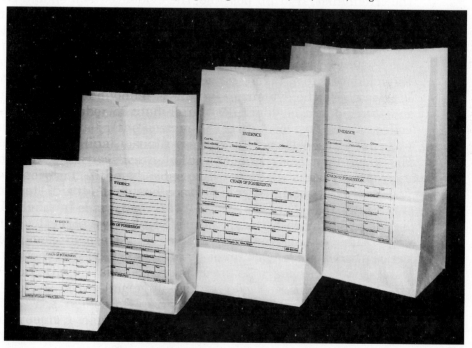

A detailed description of the proper collection and packaging of various types of physical evidence will be discussed in forthcoming chapters; additionally, most of this information is summarized in the evidence guide found in Appendix I.

MAINTAIN CHAIN OF CUSTODY

Continuity of possession, or the chain of custody, must be established whenever evidence is presented in court as an exhibit. Adherence to standard procedures in recording the location of evidence, marking it for identification, and properly completing evidence submission forms for laboratory analysis are the best guarantee that the evidence will withstand inquiries of what happened to it from the time of its finding to its presentation in court. This means that every person who handled or examined the evidence must be accounted for. Failure to substantiate the evidence's chain of custody may lead to serious questions regarding the authenticity and integrity of the evidence and the examinations rendered upon it.

All items of physical evidence should be carefully packaged and marked upon their retrieval at crime sites. This should be done with the utmost care to avoid destroying their evidential value or restricting the number and kind of examinations to which they may be subjected by the criminalist. If at all possible, the evidence itself should be marked for identification. Normally, the collector's initials and the date of collection are inscribed directly on the article. However, if the evidence collector is unsure of the necessity of marking the item itself, or has doubts as to where to mark it, it is best to omit this step. Where appropriate, the evidence is to be tagged for identification. Once an evidence container is selected for the evidence, whether it be box, bag, vial, or can, it also must be marked for identification. A minimum record would show the collector's initials, location of the evidence, and date of collection. If the evidence is turned over to another individual for care or delivery to the laboratory, this transfer must be recorded in notes and other appropriate forms. In fact, every individual who has occasion to possess the evidence must maintain a written record of its acquisition and disposition. Frequently, all of the individuals involved in the collection and transportation of the evidence may be requested to testify in court. Thus, to avoid confusion and to retain complete control of the evidence at all times, the chain of custody should be kept to a minimum.

OBTAIN CONTROLS

The examination of evidence, whether it is soil, blood, glass, hair, fibers, and so on, often requires comparison with a known standard or control. Although most investigators have little difficulty in recognizing and collecting relevant crime-scene evidence, few seem aware of the like necessity and importance of providing the crime lab with a thorough sampling of control materials. Such materials may be obtained from the victim, a suspect, or other sources. For instance, investigation of a hit-and-run incident might require the removal of control paint from a suspect vehicle. This will permit its comparison to paint recovered at the scene. Similarly, hair found at the crime scene will be of optimum value only when compared to control hairs removed from the suspect and victim. Likewise, bloodstained evidence must be accompanied by whole blood controls obtained from all relevant crime-scene participants. The quality and quantity of control specimens often determine the evidential value of crime-scene evidence, and these control specimens must be treated with equal care. The thorough collection and proper packaging of control specimens are the mark of a skilled investigator.

SUBMIT EVIDENCE TO THE LABORATORY

Evidence is usually submitted to the laboratory either by personal delivery or by mail shipment. The method of transmittal will usually be determined by the distance the submitting agency must travel to the laboratory and the urgency of the case. If personal delivery of the evidence is undertaken, the deliverer should be someone who is familiar with the case. This arrangement will facilitate any discussions that may ensue between laboratory personnel and the deliverer concerning specific aspects of the case.

If desired, most evidence can be conveniently shipped through the mails. However, postal regulations do restrict the shipment of certain chemicals and live ammunition and prohibit the mailing of explosives. In such situations, the laboratory must be consulted to determine the disposition of these substances. Care must also be exercised in the packaging of evidence in order to prevent breakage or other accidental destruction while it is in transit to the laboratory.

Most laboratories require that an evidence submission form accompany all evidence submitted. One such form is shown in Figure 2–7. It is essential that this form be properly completed. Its information will enable the laboratory analyst to make an intelligent and complete examination of the evidence. Particular attention should be paid to providing the laboratory with a brief description of the case history. This information will allow the examiner to analyze the specimens in a logical sequence and make the proper comparisons, and it will also facilitate the search for trace quantities of evidence.

The particular kind of examination requested for each type of evidence is to be delineated. However, it must be made clear that the

State of New Jersey
DEPARTMENT OF LAW AND PUBLIC SAFETY
DIVISION OF STATE POLICE

REQUEST FOR EXAMINATION OF EVIDENCE

Crime ___Rape & Murder_____ In County of ___Burlington_____ Lab. No. _____

Victim ___Mary F. Jones, w-f, age 34_____ Suspect ___George White, w-m, age 22___

Submitting Agency ___N. J. State Police, Troop C, Bordentown, N. J.___

Forward Replies to ___Capt. F. J. Smith, Commanding, Troop C, Princeton, N. J. 08540___

Invest. by ___DSG. J. F. Brown_____ Delivered by _____
SIGNATURE OF PERSON DELIVERING EVIDENCE

Brief History of Case: Victim found dead in bed, Apt. 9-A, Bordentown Arms Apts. Face of the victim bruised around cheekbones. Pink bedspread crumpled on floor next to bed. On night table one (1) prescription bottle containing two (2) blue pills (pharmacy check, prescription Amo-barbital). Bits of pink thread discovered in victim's mouth. Apt. door forced. Suspect was seen in the general area of Apt. 9-A. Pink threads on suspect's sweater. Screwdriver found in his pocket.

Examination Requested:
1. Nos. 1 & 2 - general toxicology for narcotics, poisons, alcohol.
2. No. 3 for pill content.
3. Compare threads, #4, removed from victim's mouth with fibers of bedspread #5.
4. Compare specimen #5 with #6 - threads adhering to sweater with fiber of bedspread.
5. Comparison, blade of #7 with mark on #8.
6. Nos. 9 through 19 for the presence of semen or stains.

List of Specimens:

1. Blood - 25 cc (Oxalated) from victim.
2. Urine - 20 cc from bladder of victim.
3. Prescription bottle containing two (2) blue pills, labeled "Bardly Pharmacy - Prescription #56789 - Dr. S. Johnson - Patient Mary F. Jones".
4. Four (4) strands of pink thread.
5. One (1) pink bedspread.
6. One (1) blue "Darwin" sweater with pink threads adhering to same - suspects.
7. One (1) five inch (5") "Handyman" screwdriver - suspects.
8. One (1) door latch from front door of apartment with possible toolmarks on same.
9. One (1) white bra - victims.
10. One (1) pair of white panties - victims.
11. One (1) housecoat, light blue - victims.
12. One (1) bed sheet, 72" x 108", white.
13. One (1) pillow case, white with blue design.
14. Rectal swab from victim.
15. Vaginal swab from victim.
16. Mouth swab from victim.
17. One (1) white "T" shirt - suspects.
18. One (1) pair of white "Jockey" shorts - suspects.
19. One (1) pair of light brown trousers - suspects.

NOTE: Photos of above scene and autopsy to be forwarded to Laboratory by Troop C Identification Bureau.

Figure 2-7. An example of a properly completed evidence submission form.
Courtesy New Jersey State Police.

analyst will not be bound to adhere strictly to the specific tests requested by the investigator. As the examination proceeds, new evidence may be uncovered, and as a result the complexity of the case may change. Furthermore, the analyst may find the initial requests to be incomplete or not totally relevant to the case. Finally, a list of items submitted for examination must be included on the evidence submission form. Each item is to be packaged separately and assigned a number or letter, which should be listed in an orderly and logical sequence on the form.

CRIME-SCENE SAFETY

The increasing spread of AIDS and hepatitis B has sensitized the law enforcement community to the potential health hazards that can exist at crime scenes. In reality, law enforcement officers have an extremely small chance of contracting AIDS or hepatitis at the crime scene. Both diseases are normally transmitted by the exchange of body fluids, such as blood, semen, vaginal and cervical secretions; intravenous drug needles and syringes; and the transfusion of infected blood products. The presence of blood and semen at crime scenes presents the investigator with biological specimens of unknown origin and the investigator has no way of gauging what health hazards they may contain. Therefore, caution and protection must be used at all times.

Fortunately, inoculation can easily prevent infection from hepatitis B in most people. Furthermore, the Federal Occupational Safety and Health Administration (OSHA) requires that law enforcement agencies offer the inoculations against hepatitis B to all officers who may have contact with body fluids while on the job, at no expense to the officer.

The International Association for Identification Safety Committee has proposed the following guidelines to protect investigators at crime scenes containing potentially infectious materials:

1. Forensic and crime-scene personnel may encounter potentially infectious materials, such as in the case of a homicide, where blood or body fluids may be localized to the area of the body, or dispersed throughout the crime scene. At such scenes, it is recommended that personnel wear a minimum of latex gloves (double gloved), and protective (Tyvek type) shoe covers. Where large contamination areas are concerned, it is recommended that liquid repellent coveralls (Tyvek or Kleengard suits) be utilized along with the gloves and shoe covers.

2. The use of a particle mask/respirator, goggles, or face shield is recommended in addition to the protective items listed in Section 1 when potentially infectious dust or mist may be encountered at the crime scene. This includes the collection of dried bloodstains by scraping, the

collection, folding, and preservation of garments which may be contaminated with blood or body fluids, especially if they are in a dried state, as well as the application of aerosol chemicals to bloodstains or prints for their detection and/or enhancement.

3. When processing and collecting evidence at a crime scene, personnel should be alert to sharp objects, knives, hypodermic syringes, razor blades, etc. In the event that such sharp objects are encountered and must be recovered as evidence, the items should be placed in an appropriate container and properly labeled. When conventional latent print powder techniques are used in or around areas contaminated with blood, a specific brush should be designated so that it can be subsequently decontaminated or appropriately disposed of after processing is complete. If latents are developed in or around blood contaminated areas, they preferably should be photographed, or lifted and placed in a sealed plastic bag. The sealed bag then should be affixed with an appropriate biohazard label.

   Evidence collected for transport should be packaged to maintain its integrity and to prevent contamination of personnel or personal items. Evidence contaminated with wet blood should be placed first in a paper bag and then temporarily stored in a red biohazard plastic bag for immediate transport to an appropriate drying facility.

4. When potentially infectious materials are present at a crime scene, personnel should maintain a red biohazard plastic bag for the disposal of contaminated gloves, clothing, masks, pencils, wrapping paper, etc. On departure from the scene, the biohazard bag must be taped shut and transported to an approved biohazardous waste pick-up site.

5. Note taking should be done while wearing uncontaminated gloves to avoid contamination of pens, pencils, notebook, paper, etc. Whenever pens or markers are used while marking and packaging contaminated evidence, they should be designated for proper disposal in a red biohazard bag prior to vacating the crime scene.

6. In the event that individual protective equipment becomes soiled or torn, it must be removed immediately. Personnel must then disinfect/decontaminate the potentially contaminated body areas using a recommended solution, such as a 10 percent bleach solution, or an antimicrobial soap or towelette. Once cleansing is completed, the area must be covered with clean, replacement protective equipment. On departure from the scene, this procedure should be repeated on any body area where contamination could have occurred.

7. Eating, drinking, smoking, and the application of makeup are prohibited at the immediate crime scene.

8. All nondisposable items, such as lab coats, towels, and personal clothing, that may be contaminated with potentially infectious material should be

placed in a yellow plastic bag, labeled "Infectious Linen," and laundered, at the expense of the employer, by a qualified laundry service. Personal clothing that may have been contaminated should never be taken home for cleaning.

LEGAL CONSIDERATIONS AT THE CRIME SCENE

In police work, there is perhaps no experience more exasperating or demoralizing than to watch valuable evidence excluded from use against the accused because of legal considerations. This situation most often arises from what is deemed to be an "unreasonable" search and seizure of evidence. Therefore, the removal of any evidence from a person or from the scene of a crime must be done in conformity with Fourth Amendment privileges:

> The right of the people to be secure in their persons, houses, papers, and effects, against unreasonable searches and seizure, shall not be violated, and no warrants shall issue, but upon probable cause, supported by oath or affirmation, and particularly describing the place to be searched, and the persons or things to be seized.

Since the 1960s, the Supreme Court has been particularly concerned with defining the circumstances under which the police can search for evidence in the absence of a court-approved search warrant. A number of allowances have been made to justify a warrantless search: (1) the existence of emergency circumstances, (2) the need to prevent the immediate loss or destruction of evidence, (3) a search of a person and property within the immediate control of the person provided it is made incident to a lawful arrest, and (4) a search made by consent of the parties involved. In cases other than the above, police must be particularly cautious about processing a crime scene without a search warrant. In 1978, the Supreme Court addressed this very issue and in so doing set forth guidelines for investigators to follow in determining the propriety of conducting a warrantless search at a crime scene. Significantly, the two cases decided on this issue related to homicide and arson crime scenes, both of which are normally subjected to the most intensive forms of physical evidence searches by police.

In the case of *Mincey* v. *Arizona*,[1] the Court dealt with the legality of a four-day search at a homicide scene. The case involved a police raid on the home of Rufus Mincey, who had been suspected of dealing

---

[1] 57 L. Ed. 2d 290 (1978).

in drugs. Under the pretext of buying drugs, an undercover police officer forced entry into Mincey's apartment and was killed in a scuffle that ensued. Without a search warrant, the police spent four days searching the apartment, recovering, among other things, bullets, drugs, and drug paraphernalia. These items were subsequently introduced as evidence at the trial. Mincey was convicted and on appeal contended that the evidence gathered from his apartment, without a warrant and without his consent, was illegally seized. The Court unanimously upheld Mincey's position, stating:

> We do not question the right of the police to respond to emergency situations. Numerous state and federal cases have recognized that the Fourth Amendment does not bar police officers from making warrantless entries and searches when they reasonably believe that a person within is in need of immediate aid. Similarly, when the police come upon the scene of a homicide they may make a prompt warrantless search of the area to see if there are other victims or if a killer is still on the premises. . . . Except for the fact that the offense under investigation was a homicide, there were no exigent circumstances in this case. . . . There was no indication that evidence would be lost, destroyed or removed during the time required to obtain a search warrant. Indeed, the police guard at the apartment minimized that possibility. And there is no suggestion that a search warrant could not easily and conveniently have been obtained. We decline to hold that the seriousness of the offense under investigation itself creates exigent circumstances of the kind that under the Fourth Amendment justify a warrantless search.

In *Michigan* v. *Tyler,*[2] a business establishment leased by Loren Tyler and a business partner was destroyed by fire. The fire was finally extinguished in the early hours of the morning; however, hampered by smoke, steam, and darkness, fire officials and police were prevented from thoroughly examining the scene for evidence of arson. The building was then left unattended until 8 A.M. of that day, when officials returned and began an inspection of the burned premises. During the morning search, assorted items of evidence were recovered and removed from the building. On three other occasions—4 days, 7 days, and 25 days after the fire—investigators reentered the premises and removed additional items of evidence. Each of these searches was made without a warrant or without consent, and the evidence seized was used to convict Tyler and his partner of conspiracy to burn real property and related offenses. The Supreme Court upheld the reversal of the conviction, holding the initial morning search to be proper but contending that evidence obtained from subsequent reentries to the scene was inadmissible:

---

[2]56 L. Ed. 2d 486 (1978).

We hold that an entry to fight a fire requires no warrant, and that once in the building, officials may remain there for a reasonable time to investigate the cause of a blaze. Thereafter, additional entries to investigate the cause of the fire must be made pursuant to the warrant procedures. . . .

The message from the Supreme Court is clear: When time and circumstances permit, obtain a search warrant before investigating and retrieving physical evidence at the crime scene.

REVIEW QUESTIONS

1. The term _____ encompasses all objects that can establish whether a crime has been committed or can provide a link between a crime and its victim or perpetrator.
2. Scientific evaluation of crime-scene evidence can usually overcome the results of a poorly conducted criminal investigation. (True, False)
3. The techniques of physical evidence collection require a highly skilled individual who must specialize in this area of investigation. (True, False)
4. All unauthorized personnel must be _____ from crime scenes.
5. Three methods for recording the crime scene are _____, _____, and _____.
6. The most important prerequisite for photographing a crime scene is to have it in an _____ condition.
7. Photographs of physical evidence must include overviews as well as _____ to record the details of objects.
8. An investigator need only draw a _____ sketch at the crime scene to show its dimensions and pertinent objects.
9. A detailed search of the crime scene for physical evidence must be conducted in a _____ manner.
10. Besides the more obvious items of physical evidence, possible _____ of trace evidence must be collected for detailed examination in the laboratory.
11. In cooperation with the medical examiner or coroner, what type of evidence retrieved from a deceased victim is to be submitted to the crime laboratory?
12. Whenever possible, trace evidence (is, is not) to be removed from the object that bears it.
13. Each item collected at the crime scene must be placed in a _____ container.

14. An ordinary mailing envelope is considered to be a good general-purpose evidence container. (True, False)
15. An airtight container (is, is not) recommended packaging material for bloodstained garments.
16. As a matter of routine, all items of clothing are to be _____ before packaging.
17. Charred debris recovered from the scene of an arson is best placed in a porous container. (True, False)
18. The possibility of future legal proceedings requires that a _____ be established with respect to the possession and location of physical evidence.
19. Most physical evidence collected at the crime site will require the accompanying submission of _____ material for comparison purposes.
20. In the case of *Mincey* v. *Arizona,* the Supreme Court restricted the practice of conducting a (an) _____ search at a homicide scene.
21. In the case of *Michigan* v. *Tyler,* the Supreme Court dealt with search and seizure procedures at a (an) _____ scene.

FURTHER REFERENCES

Fisher, Barry J., *Techniques of Crime Scene Investigation,* 5th ed. Boca Raton, Fla.: CRC Press, Inc., 1992.

Fox, Richard H., and Carl L. Cunningham, *Crime Scene Search and Physical Evidence Handbook.* Washington, D.C.: U.S. Government Printing Office, 1973.

Geberth, Vernon J., *Practical Homicide Investigation: Tactics, Procedures, and Forensic Techniques,* 3rd ed. Boca Raton, Fla.: CRC Press, Inc., 1996.

Goddard, Kenneth W., *Crime Scene Investigation.* Reston, Va.: Reston Publishing Company, 1977.

Handbook of Forensic Science. Washington, D.C.: U.S. Government Printing Office, 1994.

Osterburg, James W., and Richard H. Ward, *Criminal Investigation—A Method for Reconstructing the Past,* 2nd ed. Cincinnati, Ohio: Anderson Publishing Co., 1996.

Peterson, Joseph L., Steven Mihajlovic, and Michael Gilliand, *Forensic Evidence and the Police: The Effects of Scientific Evidence on Criminal Investigations.* Washington, D.C.: U.S. Government Printing Office, 1984.

Weston, Paul B., and Kenneth M. Wells, *Criminal Investigation,* 7th ed. Englewood Cliffs, N.J.: Prentice Hall, 1997.

CASE READING _____

THE ENRIQUE CAMARENA CASE:
A FORENSIC NIGHTMARE

Michael P. Malone

Special Agent
Laboratory Division
Federal Bureau of Investigation
Washington, D.C.

On February 7, 1985, U.S. Drug Enforcement Agency (DEA) Special Agent (SA) Enrique Camarena was abducted near the U.S. Consulate in Guadalajara, Mexico. A short time later, Capt. Alfredo Zavala, a DEA source, was also abducted from a car near the Guadalajara Airport. These two abductions would trigger a series of events leading to one of the largest investigations ever conducted by the DEA and would result in one of the most extensive cases ever received by the FBI Laboratory.

Throughout this lengthy investigation, unusual forensic problems arose that required unusual solutions. Eventually, numerous suspects were arrested, both in the United States and Mexico, which culminated in an 8-week trial held in U.S. District Court in Los Angeles, CA.

The Abduction

On February 7, 1985, SA Camarena left the DEA Resident Office to meet his wife for lunch. On this day, a witness observed a man being forced into the rear seat of a light-colored, compact car in front of the Camelot Restaurant and provided descriptions of several of the assailants. After some initial reluctance, Primer Comandante Pavon-Reyes of the Mexican Federal Judicial Police (MFJP) was put in charge of the investigation, and Mexican investigators were assigned to the case. Two known drug traffickers, Rafael Caro-Quintero and Ernesto Fonseca, were quickly developed as suspects. A short time later at the Guadalajara Airport, as Caro-Quintero and his men attempted to flee by private jet, a confrontation developed between Caro-Quintero's men, the MFJP and DEA Agents. After some discussion, Caro-Quintero and his men were permitted to board and leave. It was later learned that a 6-figure bribe had been paid to Pavon-Reyes to allow this departure.

_____

Reprinted from *FBI Law Enforcement Bulletin,* September 1989.

The Investigation

During February 1985, searches of several residences and ranches throughout Mexico proved fruitless, despite the efforts of the DEA task force assigned to investigate this matter and the tremendous pressure being applied by the U.S. Government to accelerate the investigation. High-level U.S. Government officials, as well as their Mexican counterparts, were becoming directly involved in the case. It is believed that because of this "heat," the Mexican drug traffickers and certain Mexican law enforcement officials fabricated a plan. According to the plan, the MFJP would receive an anonymous letter indicating that SA Camarena and Captain Zavala were being held at the Bravo drug gang's ranch in La Angostura, Michoacan, approximately 60 miles southeast of Guadalajara. The MFJP was supposed to raid the ranch, eliminate the drug gang and eventually discover the bodies of SA Camarena and Captain Zavala buried on the ranch. The DEA would then be notified and the case would be closed. Thus, the Bravo gang would provide an easy scapegoat.

During early March, MFJP officers raided the Bravo ranch before the DEA Agents arrived. In the resulting shootout, all of the gang members, as well as one MFJP officer, were killed. However, due to a mix-up, the bodies of SA Camarena and Captain Zavala were not buried on the Bravo ranch in time to be discovered as planned. The individuals paid to do this job simply left them by the side of a road near the ranch. It was later learned that certain Mexican law enforcement officials were paid a large sum of money to formulate and carry out this plan in order to obstruct and prematurely conclude the investigation.

Shortly after this shootout, a passer-by found two partially decomposed bodies, wrapped in plastic bags, along a road near the Bravo ranch. The bodies were removed and transported to a local morgue where they were autopsied. The DEA was then advised of the discovery of the bodies and their subsequent removal to another morgue in Guadalajara, where a second autopsy was performed.

On March 7, 1985, the FBI dispatched a forensic team to Guadalajara. They immediately proceeded to the morgue to identify the bodies and to process any evidence which might be present. After much bureaucratic delay from the local officials, they were finally allowed to proceed. The bodies were identified only as cadavers number 1 and number 2. It was apparent that each body had been autopsied and that both were in an advanced state of decomposition. Cadaver number 1 was quickly identified by the fingerprint expert as that of SA Camarena. Mexican officials would not allow the second body to be identified at this time; however, it was later identified through dental records as Captain Zavala.

The FBI forensic team requested permission to process the clothing, cordage, and burial sheet found with the bodies but the request was denied. However, they were allowed to cut small, "known" samples from these items and obtain hair samples from both bodies. Soil samples were also removed from the bodies and the clothing items.

A forensic pathologist from the Armed Forces Institute of Pathology was allowed to examine the body of SA Camarena. He concluded that SA Camarena's death was caused by blunt-force injuries. In addition, SA Camarena had a hole in his skull caused by a rod-like instrument. SA Camarena's body was then released to the American officials and immediately flown to the United States.

The next day, both FBI and DEA personnel proceeded to the Bravo ranch where the bodies were initially found. Because this site had been a completely uncontrolled crime scene, contaminated by both police personnel and onlookers, only a limited crime scene search was conducted. It was immediately noted that there was no grave site in the area, and that the color of the soil where the bodies had been deposited differed from the soil that had been removed from the bodies. Therefore, "known" soil samples from the drop site were taken to compare with soil removed from the victims. It was also noted that there were no significant body fluids at the "burial" site. This led the forensic team to conclude that the bodies had been buried elsewhere, exhumed and transported to this site.

The MFJP officials were later confronted with the evidence that the bodies had been relocated to the Michoacan area. This was one of the factors which led to a new, unilateral MFJP investigation. As a result, several suspects, including State Judicial Police Officers, were arrested and interrogated concerning the kidnapping of SA Camarena. Primer Comandante Pavon-Reyes was fired, and arrest warrants were issued for a number of international drug traffickers, including Rafael Caro-Quintero and Ernesto Fonseca.

In late March 1985, DEA Agents located a black Mercury Gran Marquis which they believed was used in the kidnapping or transportation of SA Camarena. The vehicle had been stored in a garage in Guadalajara, and a brick wall had been constructed at the entrance to conceal it. The vehicle was traced to a Ford dealership owned by Caro-Quintero. Under the watchful eye of the MFJP at the Guadalajara Airport, the FBI forensic team processed the vehicle for any hair, fiber, blood and/or fingerprint evidence it might contain.

During April 1985, the MFJP informed the DEA that they believed they had located the residence where SA Camarena and Captain Zavala had been held. The FBI forensic team was immediately dispatched to Guadalajara; however, they were not allowed to proceed to the residence, located at 881 Lope De Vega, until an MFJP forensic team had processed the residence and had removed all of the obvious evidence. The DEA was also informed that since the abduction of SA Camarena, all of the interior walls had been painted, the entire residence had recently been cleaned, and that a group of MFJP officers were presently occupying, and thereby contaminating, the residence.

On the first day after the arrival of the FBI forensic team, they surveyed and began a crime scene search of the residence and surrounding grounds. The residence consists of a large, two-story structure with a swimming pool, covered patio, aviary and tennis court surrounded by a common wall. The most logical place to hold a prisoner at this location would be in the small out-building located to the rear of the main residence. This out-building, designated as the "guest house," consisted of a small room, carpeted by a beige rug, with an adjoining bathroom. The entire room and bathroom were processed for hairs, fibers and latent fingerprints. The single door into this room was made of steel and reinforced by iron bars. It was ultimately determined by means of testimony and forensic evidence that several individuals interrogated and tortured SA Camarena in this room. In addition, a locked bedroom, located on the second floor of the main house, was also processed, and the bed linens were removed from a single bed. Known carpet samples were taken from every room in the residence.

A beige VW Atlantic, which fit the general description of the smaller vehicle noted by the person who witnessed SA Camarena's abduction, was parked under a carport at the rear of the residence. The VW Atlantic was also processed for hairs, fibers and fingerprints.

On the second day, a thorough grounds search was conducted. As FBI forensic team members were walking around the tennis court, they caught a glimpse of something blue in one of the drains. Upon closer inspection, it appeared to be a folded license plate, at the bottom of the drain. However, a heavy, iron grate covered the drain and prevented the plate's immediate retrieval.

When one of the FBI Agents returned to the main house to ask the MFJP officers for a crowbar, they became extremely curious and followed the Agent as he returned, empty handed, to the tennis court. By this time, a second Agent had managed to remove the grate by using a heavy-wire coat hanger. The license plate was retrieved, unfolded and photographed. The MFJP officers, all of whom were now at the tennis court, became upset at this discovery, and one of them immediately contacted his superior at MFJP headquarters, who ordered them to secure the license plate until the Assistant Primer Comandante arrived on the scene. After his arrival approximately 20 minutes later, he seized the license plate and would not allow the Americans to conduct any further searches.

However, by this time, five very large plastic bags of evidence had been recovered and were placed in the rear of a DEA truck. The evidence was quickly transported to the DEA vault in the U.S. Consulate.

After negotiations between the United States and Mexico, the MFJP did allow a second, final search of the residence. On June 24, 1985, a forensic team returned and processed the four remaining rooms on the first floor of the main house.

By this point in the investigation, an associate of Rafael Caro-Quintero had been arrested and interrogated by the MFJP. He stated that the bodies of two Americans, Albert Radelat and John Walker, who had been abducted and killed by Mexican drug traffickers, were buried on the south side of La Primavera Park, a large, primitive park west of Guadalajara. The bodies of Radelat and Walker were located and recovered. Soil samples taken from the surface of an area near their graves were similar in most respects to the soil recovered earlier from the bodies of SA Camarena and Captain Zavala.

In September 1985, DEA personnel went to La Primavera Park and sampled an area approximately 2 feet below the surface near the same site. This sample matched the soil samples from SA Camarena and Captain Zavala almost grain for grain, indicating that this site was almost certainly their burial site before they were relocated to the Bravo ranch.

Later that fall, after further negotiations between the U.S. and the Mexican governments, permission was finally granted for an FBI forensic team to process the evidence seized by the MFJP forensic team from 881 Lope De Vega the previous April. The evidence consisted of small samples the MFJP had taken of SA Camarena's burial sheet, a piece of rope used to bind SA Camarena, a portion of a pillowcase removed from bedroom number 3, a piece of unsoiled rope removed from the covered patio, and a laboratory report prepared by the MFJP Crime Laboratory. The remainder of the evidence had been destroyed for "health reasons."

In January 1986, a drug trafficker named Rene Verdugo, who was considered to be a high-ranking member of the Caro-Quintero gang, was apprehended and taken to San Diego, where he was arrested by the DEA. He was then transported to Washington, DC, where hair samples were taken. He refused to testify before a Federal grand jury investigating the Camarena case. Later that year, DEA personnel obtained hair samples in Mexico City from Sergio Espino-Verdin, a former federal comandante, who is believed to have been SA Camarena's primary interrogator during his ordeal at 881 Lope De Vega.

The Trial

In July 1988, the main trial of the murder, interrogation, and abduction of SA Camerena began in U.S. District Court in Los Angeles, CA. The forensic evidence presented in this trial identified 881 Lope De Vega as the site where SA Camarena had been held. [See Figure 1.] The evidence also strongly associated two Mexican citizens, Rene Verdugo and Sergio Espino-Verdin, with the "guest house" at 881 Lope De Vega. Several types of forensic evidence were used to associate SA Camarena with 881 Lope De Vega: Forcibly removed head hairs, found in the "guest house" and bedroom number 4, in the VW Atlantic and in the Mercury Gran Marquis, and two types of polyester rug fibers, a dark, rose-colored fiber and a light-colored fiber. [See Color Plates 1 and 2, following.] Fabric evidence was also presented, which demonstrated the similarities of color, composition, construction, and design between SA Camarena's burial sheet and the two pillowcases recovered from bedrooms number 3 and 5.

Based on this evidence associating SA Camarena and 881 Lope De Vega, the FBI Laboratory examiner was able to testify that SA Camarena was at this residence, as well as in the VW Atlantic and the Mercury Gran Marquis, and that he had been in a position such that his head hairs were forcibly removed. Captain Alfredo Zavala was also found to be associated with the "guest house" at 881 Lope De Vega. Light-colored nylon rug fibers, found on samples of his clothing taken at the second autopsy, matched the fibers from the "guest house" carpet.

A detailed model of the residence at 881 Lope De Vega was prepared by the Special Projects Section of the FBI Laboratory for the trial. [See Figure 2.] Over 20 trial charts were also prepared to explain the various types of forensic evidence. These charts proved invaluable in clarifying the complicated techniques and characteristics used in the examination of the hair, fiber, fabric and cordage evidence. [See Figure 3.]

Conclusion

The forensic pitfalls and problems in this case (i.e. destruction of evidence, contamination of crime scenes) were eventually resolved. In some cases, certain routine procedures had to be ignored or unconventional methods employed. However, in many instances, detailed trial testimony overcame the limitations of certain evidence, and eventually, almost all of the evidence introduced at the trial made a tremendous impact on the outcome of this proceeding. After an 8-week trial, conducted under tight security and involving hundreds of witnesses, all of the defendants were found guilty, convicted on all counts, and are currently serving lengthy sentences.

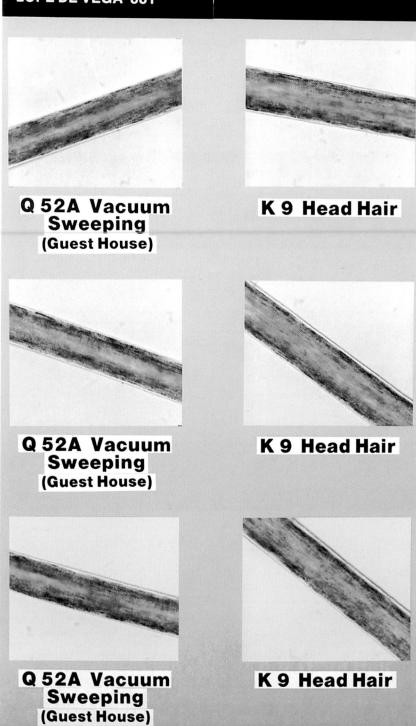

Color Plate 1. Trial chart showing hair comparisons between known Camarena hairs and hairs recovered from 881 Lope De Vega.

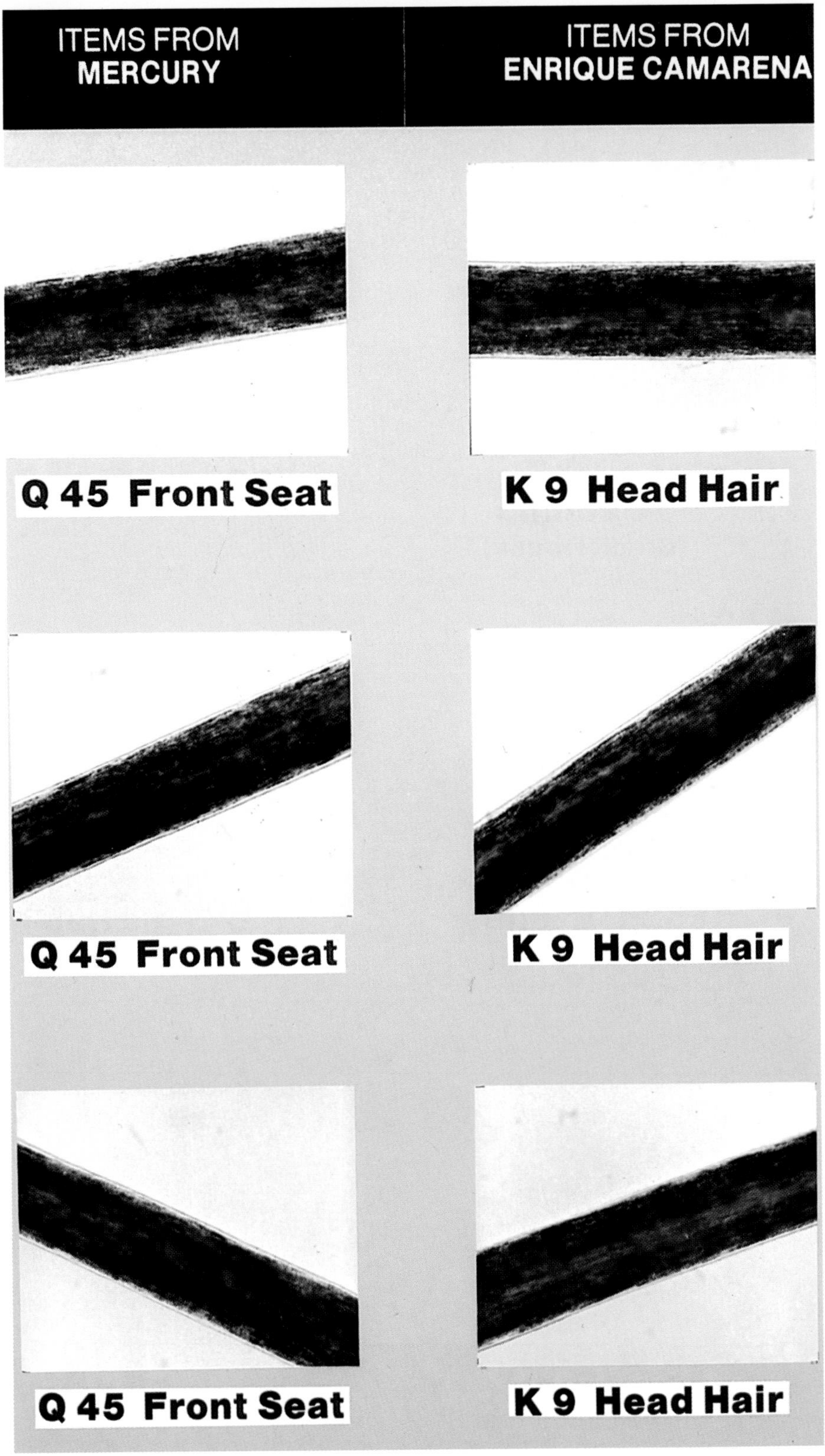
ITEMS FROM
MERCURY
ITEMS FROM
ENRIQUE CAMARENA
Q 45 Front Seat
K 9 Head Hair
Q 45 Front Seat
K 9 Head Hair
Q 45 Front Seat
K 9 Head Hair

Color Plate 2. Trial chart showing hair comparisons between Camarena hairs and hairs recovered from the Mercury Gran Marquis.

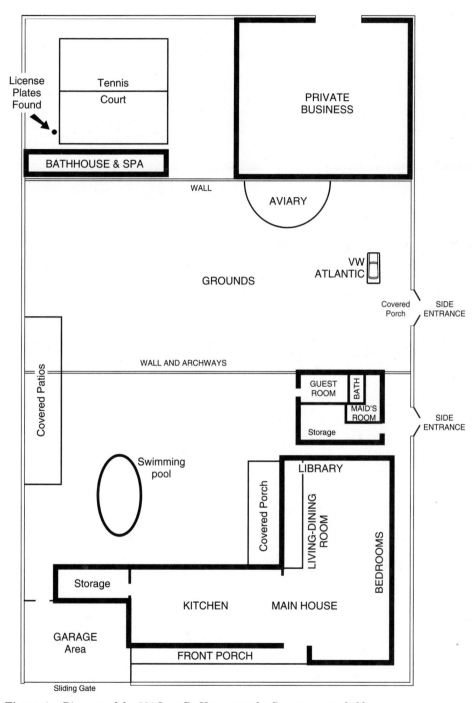

Figure 1. Diagram of the 881 Lope De Vega grounds. Camarena was held prisoner in the guest house.

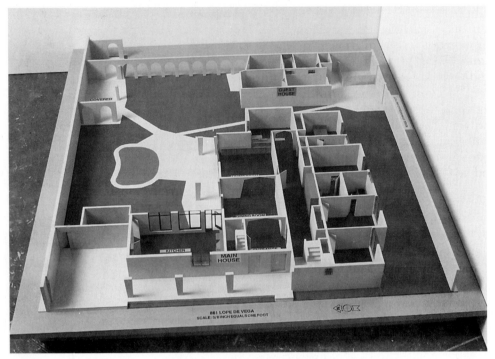

Figure 2.   A model of 881 Lope De Vega prepared as a trial exhibit.

CATEGORIES OF FORENSIC EVIDENCE
IN CAMARENA CASE

Type of Evidence Location	Hair	Carpet Fibers	Fabric Match	Cordage Match	Tape Match	Misc.
Mercury	**Camarena Head Hair**					**Blood on Floor Mat**
V.W. Atlantic	**Camarena Head Hair**					**Blood on Tissue**
Guest House	**Camarena Head Hair**	**Zavala Clothes** Nylon				
Bedroom #3		**Camarena Blindfold** Polyester	**Pillow Case** Camarena Burial Sheet			
Bedroom #4	**Camarena Head Hair**	**Camarena Blindfold & Burial Sheet** Polyester				
Bedroom #5			**Pillow Case** Camarena Burial Sheet			
Tennis Court						**License Plate** V.W./Merc.
Camarena Burial Sheet	**Camarena Head Hair**	**Bedroom #4** Polyester	**Pillow Case** Bedrooms #3 and #5			**Soil** La Primavera
Source— Blindfold/ Rope	**Camarena Head Hair**	**Bedrooms #3 and #4** Polyester			**Camarena Blindfold Tape**	
Camarena Burial Cordage				**Burial Rope** Rope from Covered Patio		
Zavala Clothing	**Zavala Head Hair**	**Guest House** Nylon				**Soil** La Primavera

Figure 3. Trial chart used to show association of Camarena and Zavala with various locations.

3 ▶ PHYSICAL EVIDENCE

It would be impossible to list all the objects that could conceivably be of importance to a crime; every crime scene obviously has to be treated on an individual basis, having its own peculiar history, circumstances, and problems. It is practical, however, to list those items whose scientific examination is likely to yield significant results in ascertaining the nature and circumstances of a crime. The investigator who is thoroughly familiar with the recognition, collection, and analysis of these items, as well as with laboratory procedures and capabilities, can make logical decisions when the uncommon and unexpected are encountered at the crime scene. Just as important, a qualified evidence collector cannot rely on collection procedures memorized from a pamphlet but must be able to make innovative, on-the-spot decisions at the crime scene.

COMMON TYPES OF PHYSICAL EVIDENCE

1. *Blood, Semen, and Saliva.* All suspected blood, semen, or saliva—liquid or dried, animal or human—present in a form to suggest a relation to the offense or persons involved in a crime. This category includes blood or semen dried onto fabrics or other objects, as well as cigarette butts that may contain saliva residues. These substances are subjected to serological and biochemical analysis for determination of identity and possible origin.

2. *Documents.* Any handwriting and typewriting submitted so that authenticity or source can be determined. Related items include paper, ink, indented writings, obliterations, and burned or charred documents.

3. *Drugs.* Any substance seized in violation of laws regulating the sale, manufacture, distribution, and use of drugs.

4. *Explosives.* Any device containing an explosive charge, as well as all objects removed from the scene of an explosion that are suspected to contain the residues of an explosive.

5. *Fibers.* Any natural or synthetic fiber whose transfer may be useful in establishing a relationship between objects and/or persons.

6. *Fingerprints.* All prints of this nature, latent and visible.

7. *Firearms and Ammunition.* Any firearm, as well as discharged or intact ammunition, suspected of being involved in a criminal offense.

8. *Glass.* Any glass particle or fragment that may have been transferred to a person or object involved in a crime. Windowpanes containing holes made by a bullet or other projectile are included in this category.

9. *Hair.* Any animal or human hair present that could link a person with a crime.

10. *Impressions.* This category includes tire markings, shoe prints, depressions in soft soils, and all other forms of tracks. Glove and other fabric impressions, as well as bite marks in skin or foodstuffs, are also included.

11. *Organs and Physiological Fluids.* Body organs and fluids are submitted for toxicology to detect possible existence of drugs and poisons. This category includes blood to be analyzed for the presence of alcohol and other drugs.

12. *Paint.* Any paint, liquid or dried, that may have been transferred from the surface of one object to another during the commission of a crime. A common example is the transfer of paint from one vehicle to another during an automobile collision.

13. *Petroleum Products.* Any petroleum product removed from a suspect or recovered from a crime scene. The most common examples are gasoline residues removed from the scene of an arson, or grease and oil stains whose presence may suggest involvement in a crime.

14. *Plastic Bags.* A polyethylene disposable bag such as a garbage bag may be evidential in a homicide or drug case. Examinations are conducted to associate a bag to a similar bag in the possession of a suspect.

15. *Powder Residues.* Any item suspected of containing firearm discharge residues.

16. *Serial Numbers.* This category includes all stolen property submitted to the laboratory for the restoration of erased identification numbers.

17. *Soil and Minerals.* All items containing soil or minerals that could link a person or object to a particular location. Common examples are soil imbedded in shoes and safe insulation found on garments.

18. *Tool Marks.* This category includes any object suspected of containing the impression of another object that served as a tool in a crime. For example, a screwdriver or crowbar could produce tool marks by being impressed into or scraped along a surface of a wall.

19. *Vehicle Lights.* Examination of vehicle headlights and taillights is normally conducted to determine whether a light was on or off at the time of impact.

20. *Wood and Other Vegetative Matter.* Any fragments of wood, sawdust, shavings, or vegetative matter discovered on clothing, shoes, or tools that could link a person or object to a crime location.

THE SIGNIFICANCE OF PHYSICAL EVIDENCE

The examination of physical evidence by a forensic scientist is usually undertaken for identification or comparison.

IDENTIFICATION

Identification has as its purpose the determination of the physical or chemical identity of a substance with as near absolute certainty as existing analytical techniques will permit. For example, the crime laboratory is frequently requested to identify the chemical composition of an illicit drug preparation that may contain heroin, cocaine, barbiturates, and so on. It may be asked to identify gasoline in residues recovered from the debris of a fire, or it may have to identify the nature of explosive residues—for example, dynamite or TNT. Also, the identification of blood, semen, hair, or wood would, as a matter of routine, include a determination for species origin. For example, did an evidential bloodstain originate from a human as opposed to a dog or cat? Each of these requests requires the analysis and ultimate identification of a specific physical or chemical substance to the exclusion of all other possible substances.

The process of identification first requires the adoption of testing procedures that give characteristic results for specific standard materials. Once these test results have been established, they may be permanently recorded and used repeatedly to prove the identity of suspect materials. For example, if one wants to ascertain that a particular suspect powder is heroin, the test results on the powder must be identical to those that have been previously obtained from a known heroin sample. Second, identification requires that the number and type of tests needed to identify a substance be sufficient to exclude all other substances. This means that the examiner must devise a specific analytical scheme that will eliminate all but one substance from consideration. Hence, if a conclusion is reached that a white powder contains heroin, the examiner's test results must have been comprehensive enough to have excluded all other drugs or, for that matter, all other substances from consideration.

Simple rules cannot be devised for defining what constitutes a thorough and foolproof analytical scheme. Each type of evidence obviously requires different tests, and each test has a different degree of specificity. Thus, one substance could conceivably be identified by one test, whereas another may require the combination of five or six different tests to arrive at an identification. In a science in which the practitioner has little or no control over the quality and quantity of the specimens received, a standard series of tests cannot encompass all possible problems and pitfalls. So, it is left to the forensic scientist to determine at what point the analysis can be concluded and the criteria for positive identification satisfied; for this, he or she must rely on knowledge gained through education and experience. Ultimately, the conclusion will have to be substantiated beyond any reasonable doubt in a court of law.

COMPARISON

A comparison analysis subjects a suspect specimen and a control specimen to the same tests and examinations for the ultimate purpose of determining whether or not they have a common origin. For example, the forensic scientist may assist in placing a suspect at a particular location by noting the similarities of a hair found at the crime scene to hairs removed from a suspect's head. Or a paint chip found on a hit-and-run victim's garment may have to be compared with paint removed from a vehicle suspected of being involved in the incident. The forensic comparison is actually a two-step procedure. First, combinations of select properties are chosen from the suspect and the control specimen for comparison. The question of which and how many properties are to be selected will obviously depend on the type of materials being examined. (This is a subject that will receive a good deal of discussion in forthcoming chapters.) The overriding consideration must be the ultimate evidential value of the conclusion. This brings us to the second objective. Once the examination has been completed, the forensic scientist must be prepared to render a conclusion with respect to the origins of the specimens. Do they or do they not come from the same source? Certainly if one or more of the properties selected for comparison do not agree, the analyst will not hesitate in concluding that the specimens are not the same and hence could not have originated from the same source. Suppose, on the other hand, that all the properties do compare and the specimens, as far as the examiner can determine, are indistinguishable. Does it logically follow that they come from the same source? Not necessarily so.

In order to comprehend the evidential value of a comparison, one must appreciate the role that probability has in ascertaining the origins of two or more specimens. Simply defined, probability is the frequency of occurrence of an event. If a coin is flipped 100 times, in theory we can expect heads to come up 50 times. Hence, the probability of the event (heads) occurring is 50 in 100. In other words, probability defines the odds at which a certain event will occur.

Individual Characteristics.   Evidence that can be associated with a common source with an extremely high degree of probability is said to possess individual characteristics. Examples of this are the matching ridge characteristics of two fingerprints, the comparison of random striation markings on bullets or tool marks, the comparison of irregular and random wear patterns in tire or footwear impressions, the comparison of handwriting characteristics, the fitting together of the irregular edges of broken objects in the manner of a jigsaw puzzle (Figure 3–1),

Figure 3–1. The body of a woman was found with evidence of beating about the head and a stablike wound in the neck. Her husband was charged with the murder. The pathologist found a knife blade tip in the wound in the neck. The knife blade tip was compared with the broken blade of a penknife found in the trousers pocket of the accused. Note that in addition to the fit of the indentations on the edges, there are scratch marks running across the blade tip corresponding in detail to those on the broken blade. *Courtesy* Centre of Forensic Sciences, Toronto, Canada.

or matching sequentially made plastic bags by striation marks running across the bags (see Figure 3–2). In all of these cases, it is not possible to state with mathematical exactness the probability that the specimens are of common origin; it can only be concluded that this probability is so high as to defy mathematical calculations or human comprehension. Furthermore, the conclusion of common origin must be substantiated by the practical experience of the examiner. For example, the French scientist Victor Balthazard has mathematically determined that the probability of two individuals having the same fingerprints is one out of 1×10^{60}, or 1 followed by 60 zeros. This probability value is so small as to exclude the possibility of any two individuals having the same fingerprints. This contention is also supported by the experience of fingerprint examiners who, after classifying millions of prints over the past 100 years, have never found any two to be exactly alike.

Figure 3–2.
The bound body of a young woman
was recovered from a river. Her head
was covered with a black polyethylene
trash bag (shown on the right). Among
the items recovered from one of
several suspects was a black
polyethylene trash bag (shown on the
left). A side-by-side comparison of the
two bags' extrusion marks and
pigment bands showed them to be
consecutively manufactured. This
information allowed investigators to
focus their attention on one suspect,
who ultimately was convicted of the
homicide. *Courtesy* George W.
Neighbor, New Jersey State Police.

Class Characteristics.   One of the disappointments awaiting the
investigator unfamiliar with the limitations of forensic science is the
frequent inability of the laboratory to relate physical evidence to a
common origin with a high degree of certainty. Evidence is said to possess class characteristics when it can be associated only with a group
and never with a single source. Here again probability is a determining factor. For example, if we were to compare two one-layer automobile paint chips of a similar color, the chance of their having originated
from the same car is not nearly as great as when we compare two
paint chips having *seven* similar layers of paint, not all of which were
part of the car's original color. The former will have class characteristics and could only be associated at best to one car model (which may
number in the thousands), whereas the latter may be judged to have
individual characteristics and to have a high probability of originating
from one specific car.

Blood offers another good example of evidence that has class characteristics. For example, two blood specimens are compared: Both are
found to be of human origin, and both are typed as A. The frequency of
occurrence in the population of type A blood is 26 percent—hardly
offering a basis for establishing the common origin of the stains. However, if other blood factors are also determined and are found to compare, the probability that the two bloods originated from a common
source increases.

For example, in the O. J. Simpson case, a bloodstain located at
the crime scene was found to contain a number of factors that compared to O. J.'s blood:

Blood Factors	Frequency
A	26%
EsD 1	85%
PGM 2+2–	2%

The product of all the frequencies shown in the table determines the probability that any one individual possesses such a combination of blood factors. In this instance, 0.44 percent or 1 in 200 would be expected to have this particular combination of blood factors. These bloodstain factors did not match either of the two victims, Nicole Brown-Simpson or Ronald Goldman, thus eliminating them as a possible source of the blood. Although the forensic scientist has still not individualized the bloodstains to one person, in this case, O. J. Simpson, data have been provided that will permit investigators and the courts to better assess the evidential value of the crime-scene stain.

One of the present weaknesses of forensic science is the inability of the examiner to assign exact or even approximate probability values to the comparison of most class physical evidence. For example, what is the probability that a nylon fiber originated from a particular sweater, or that a hair came from a particular person's head, or that a paint chip came from a suspect car involved in a hit-and-run accident? There are very few statistical data available from which to derive this information, and in a society that is increasingly dependent on mass-produced products, the gathering of such data is becoming an increasingly elusive goal. One of the primary endeavors of forensic scientists must be to create and update statistical databases for evaluating the significance of class physical evidence. Of course, when such information—for example, the population frequency of blood factors—is available, it is utilized; but for the most part, the forensic scientist must rely on personal experience when called upon to interpret the significance of class physical evidence.

Disappointment is often expressed when someone unfamiliar with the realities of modern criminalistics learns that most items of physical evidence retrieved at crime scenes cannot be linked definitively to a single person or object. Although efforts are always made to uncover physical evidence possessing individual characteristics—that is, fingerprints, tool marks, and bullets—the chances of finding class physical evidence are far greater. To deny or belittle the value of such evidence is to reject the potential role that criminalistics can play in a criminal investigation. In practice, criminal cases are fashioned for the courtroom around a collection of diverse elements, each pointing to the guilt or involvement of a party in a criminal act. Often, the majority of the evidence gathered is subjective in nature, prone to human error and bias. The believability of eyewitness accounts, confessions, and informant testimony can all be disputed, maligned, and subjected to severe attack and skepticism in the courtroom. Under these circumstances, errors in human judgment are often magnified to detract from the credibility of the witness.

The value of class physical evidence lies in its ability to provide corroboration of events with data that are, as nearly as possible, free of human error and bias. It is the thread that binds together other investigative findings that are more dependent on human judgments and, therefore, more prone to human failings. The fact that scientists have not yet learned to individualize many kinds of physical evidence only means that criminal investigators should not abdicate or falter in their pursuit of all investigative leads. However, the ability of scientists to achieve a high degree of success in evaluating class physical evidence does mean that criminal investigators can pursue their work with a much greater chance of success.

Admittedly, in most situations, the problem of trying to define the significance of an item of class evidence in exact mathematical terms is difficult if not impossible to solve. While class evidence is by its very nature not unique, our common experience tells us that meaningful items of physical evidence, such as those listed on pages 66–68, are extremely diverse in our environment. Select, for example, a colored fiber from an article of clothing and try to locate the exact same color on the clothing of individuals you randomly come in contact with, or select a car color and try to match it to other automobiles you see on local streets or roads. Furthermore, keep in mind that a forensic comparison actually goes beyond a mere color comparison and involves examining and comparing a variety of chemical and/or physical properties. The point to be made is that the chances are low of encountering two indistinguishable items of physical evidence at a crime scene that actually originated from different sources. Obviously, given these circumstances, only those objects that exhibit a significant amount of diversity in our environment are deemed appropriate for classification as physical evidence.

In the same way, when one is dealing with more than one type of class evidence, their collective presence may lead to an extremely high certainty that they originated from the same source. As the number of different objects linking an individual to a crime increases, the probability of involvement increases dramatically. A classic example of this situation can be found with evidence presented at the trial of Wayne Williams (see the case reading at the end of this chapter). Wayne Williams was charged with the murders of two individuals in the Atlanta, Georgia, metropolitan area; he was also linked to the murders of 10 other boys or young men. An essential element of the state's case involved the association of Williams with the victims through a variety of fiber evidence. Actually, 28 different types of fibers linked Williams to the murder victims, evidence that the forensic examiner characterized as "overwhelming."

In further evaluating the contribution of physical evidence, one cannot overlook one important reality in the courtroom: The weight or significance accorded physical evidence is a determination left entirely to the trier of fact, usually a jury of laypersons. Given the high esteem in which scientists are generally held by society and the infallible image created by books and television for forensic science, it is not hard to understand why scientifically evaluated evidence often takes on an aura of special reliability and trustworthiness in the courtroom. Often physical evidence, whether it be individual or class, is accorded great weight during jury deliberations and becomes a primary factor in reinforcing or overcoming lingering doubts about guilt or innocence. In fact, a number of jurists have already cautioned against giving carte blanche approval to admitting scientific testimony without first giving due consideration to its relevancy in a case. Given the potential weight of scientific evidence, failure to take proper safeguards may unfairly prejudice a case against the accused.

Physical evidence may also serve to exclude or exonerate a person from suspicion. For instance, if type A blood is linked to the suspect, all individuals that have types B, AB, and O blood can be eliminated from consideration. Because it is not possible to assess at the crime scene what value, if any, the scientist will find in the evidence collected, or what significance such findings will ultimately have to a jury, it is imperative that a thorough collection and scientific evaluation of physical evidence become a routine part of all criminal investigations.

Just when an item of physical evidence crosses the line that distinguishes class from individual is a most difficult question to answer and is often the source of heated debate and honest disagreement among forensic scientists. How many striations are necessary to individualize a mark to a single tool and no other? How many color layers will individualize a paint chip to a single car? How many ridge characteristics individualize a fingerprint, and how many handwriting characteristics will tie a person to a signature? These are all questions that defy simple solutions. It is the task of the forensic scientist to find as many characteristics as possible to compare one substance with another. The significance that is attached to the findings is a matter that is decided by the quality and composition of the evidence, the case history, and the examiner's experience. Ultimately, the conclusion can range from mere speculation to near certainty.

There are practical limits to the properties and characteristics the forensic scientist can select for comparison. Carried to the extreme, no two things in this world are alike in every detail. Modern analytical techniques have become so sophisticated and sensitive that the criminalist must be careful to define the limits of natural variation that exist among materials when interpreting the data gathered from a comparative analysis. For example, we will learn in the next chapter that two properties, density and refractive index, are best suited for comparing two pieces of glass. But the latest techniques that have been developed to measure these properties are so sensitive that they can even distinguish glass originating from a single pane of glass. Certainly, this goes beyond the desires of the criminalist who is just trying to determine if two glass particles originated from the same window. Similarly, if the surface of a paint chip is magnified 1600 times with a powerful scanning electron microscope, it is apparent that the fine details that are revealed could not be duplicated in any other paint chip. Under these circumstances, no two paint chips, even those coming from the same surface, could ever compare in the true sense of the word. Therefore, practicality dictates that such examinations be conducted at a less revealing, but more meaningful, magnification [see Figure 3–3 (a) and (b)].

Distinguishing evidential variations from natural variations is not always an easy task. Learning how to use the microscope and all the other modern instruments in a crime laboratory properly is one thing; gaining the proficiency needed to interpret the observations and data is another. As new crime laboratories are created and others expand to meet the requirements of the law enforcement community, many individuals are starting new careers in forensic science. They must be cautioned that merely reading relevant textbooks and journals is not and cannot be a substitute for experience in this most practical of sciences.

CRIME-SCENE RECONSTRUCTION

Previous discussions dealing with the processes of identification and comparison have stressed laboratory work routinely performed by forensic scientists. However, there is another dimension to the role that forensic scientists play during the course of a criminal investigation, that is, participating in a team effort to reconstruct events that have occurred prior, during, and subsequent to the commission of a crime. Reconstructing the circumstances of a crime scene entails a collaborative effort that includes experienced law enforcement personnel, medical examiners, and criminalists. All of the professionals contribute a unique perspective to develop the crime-scene reconstruction. Was there more than one person involved? How was the victim killed? Were there actions taken to cover up what actually took place? To

(a)

(b)

Figure 3–3. (a) Two-layer paint chip magnified 244 times with a scanning electron microscope. (b) The same paint chip as viewed at a magnification of 1600 times. Both photos *courtesy* Jeff Albright.

answer these questions, careful attention and logical thinking must be employed by all persons involved with the investigation.

The physical evidence left behind at a crime scene plays a crucial role in reconstructing the events that took place surrounding the crime. Although the evidence alone does not describe everything that happened, it can support or contradict accounts given by witnesses and/or suspects. Information obtained from physical evidence can also generate leads and confirm the reconstruction of a crime to a jury. The collection and documentation of physical evidence is the foundation of a reconstruction. **Reconstruction supports a likely sequence of events by the observation and evaluation of physical evidence, as well as statements made by witnesses and those involved with the incident.**

Law enforcement personnel must take the proper actions to enhance all aspects of the crime-scene search so as to optimize the crime-scene reconstruction. First, and of the utmost importance, is the security and protection of the crime scene. Protecting the scene is a continuous endeavor from the beginning to the end of the search. Evidence that can be invaluable to reconstructing the crime can be unknowingly altered or destroyed by people trampling through the scene, rendering the evidence useless. The issue of possible contamination of evidence will certainly be attacked during the litigation process and could make the difference between a guilty and not-guilty verdict.

Before processing the crime scene for physical evidence, the investigator should make a preliminary examination of the scene as it was left by the perpetrator. Each crime scene presents the investigator with its own set of circumstances. The investigator's experience and the presence or absence of physical evidence become critical factors in reconstructing a crime. The investigator captures the nature of the scene as a whole by performing an initial walk-through of the crime scene and contemplating the events that took place. Using the physical evidence available to the naked eye, he or she can hypothesize what occurred, where it occurred, and when it occurred. During the walk-through, it will be the investigator's task to document observations and formulate how the scene should ultimately be processed. As the collection of physical evidence begins, any and all observations should be recorded through photographs, sketches, and notes. By undertaking a careful collection of physical evidence and a thorough documentation of the crime scene, the investigator can begin to unravel the sequence of events that took place during the commission of the crime.

Often, reconstruction requires the involvement of a medical examiner or a criminalist. The positioning of the victim in a crime scene can often reveal pertinent information for the investigation. Trained medical examiners can examine the victim at a crime scene and determine if the body has been moved after death by evaluating the livor distribution within the body (see p. 20). For example, if livor has developed in areas other than those closest to the ground, the medical examiner can reason the victim was probably moved after death. Likewise, it can be determined if the victim was clothed subsequent to death since livor will not develop within areas of the body that are restricted by clothing. There are also special skills that a criminalist or trained crime-scene investigator can bring to the reconstruction of events that occurred during the commission of a crime. For example, the expertise of a criminalist utilizing a laser beam to plot the approximate bullet path in trajectory analysis can help determine the probable position of the shooter relative to that of the victim (see Figure 3–4). Other skills that a criminalist may employ during a crime-scene reconstruction analysis include blood spatter analysis (see pp. 379–381); determining the direction of impact of projectiles penetrating glass objects (see p. 117); locating gunshot residues deposited on victim's clothing for the purpose of estimating the distance of a shooter from a target (see pp. 479–483); and searching for primer residues deposited on the hands of a suspect shooter (see pp. 483–486).

Reconstruction is a team effort that involves putting together many different pieces of a puzzle (see Figure 3–5). The right connection has to be made between all the parts involved so as to portray the relationship between the victim, the suspect, and the crime scene. If successful, reconstruction can play a vital role in aiding a jury to arrive at an appropriate verdict.

Figure 3–4. A laser beam is used to determine the search area for the position of a shooter who has fired a bullet through a window and wounded a victim. The bullet path is determined by lining up the victim's bullet wound with the bullet hole present in the glass pane.

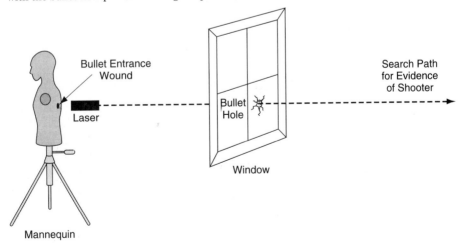

Figure 3–5.
Crime-scene reconstruction relies on the combined efforts of medical examiners, criminalists, and law enforcement personnel to recover physical evidence and to sort out the events surrounding the occurrence of a crime.

REVIEW QUESTIONS

1. The process of _____ determines a substance's physical or chemical identity with as near absolute certainty as existing analytical techniques will permit.

2. The number and type of tests needed to identify a substance must be sufficient to _____ all other substances from consideration.

3. A _____ analysis subjects a suspect and a control specimen to the same tests and examination for the ultimate purpose of determining whether they have a common origin.

4. _____ is the frequency of occurrence of an event.

5. Evidence that can be traced to a common source with an extremely high degree of probability is said to possess _____ characteristics.

6. Evidence associated with a group and not to a single source is said to possess _____ characteristics.

7. One of the major deficiencies of forensic science is the inability of the examiner to assign exact or approximate probability values to the comparison of most class physical evidence. (True, False)

8. The value of class physical evidence lies in its ability to provide _____ of events that is as nearly as possible free of human error and bias.

9. The _____ accorded physical evidence during a trial is left entirely to the trier of fact.

10. Physical evidence cannot be used to exclude or exonerate a person from suspicion of committing a crime. (True, False)

11. The distinction between individual and class evidence is always easy to make. (True, False)

12. Modern analytical techniques have become so sensitive that the forensic examiner must be aware of the _____ that exists among materials when interpreting the significance of comparative data.

13. A crime can accurately be reconstructed solely on the presence or absence of physical evidence. (True, False)

FURTHER REFERENCES

Kirk, Paul L., *Crime Investigation,* 2nd ed., John I. Thornton, ed. New York: Wiley & Sons, 1974.

Osterburg, James W., "The Evaluation of Physical Evidence in Criminalistics: Subjective or Objective Process?" *Journal of Criminal Law, Criminology and Police Science,* 60 (1969), 97.

Peterson, J. L., et al., "The Uses of and Effects of Forensic Science in the Adjudication of Felony Cases," *Journal of Forensic Sciences,* 32 (1987), 1730.

Walls, H. J., "What Is Reasonable Doubt? A Forensic Scientist Looks at the Law," in *Forensic Science,* Joseph L. Peterson, ed. New York: AMS Press, Inc., 1975.

CASE READING

FIBER EVIDENCE AND THE WAYNE WILLIAMS TRIAL

Harold A. Deadman

*Special Agent
Microscopic Analysis Unit
Laboratory Division
Federal Bureau of Investigation
Washington, D.C.*

On February 26, 1982, a Fulton County, Ga., Superior Court jury returned a verdict of "guilty as charged" on two counts of murder brought against Wayne Bertram Williams by a Fulton County grand jury in July 1981. Williams had been on trial since December 28, 1981, for the asphyxial murders of Nathaniel Cater and Jimmy Payne in

April and May of 1981. During the 8-week trial, evidence linking Williams to those murders and to the murders of 10 other boys or young men was introduced.

An essential part of this case, presented by the Fulton County District Attorney's Office, involved the association of fibrous debris removed from the bodies of 12 murder victims with objects from the everyday environment of Williams.

Fiber evidence has often been an important part of criminal cases, but the Williams trial differed from other cases in several respects. Fiber evidence has not played a significant role in any case involving a large number of murder victims. The victims whose deaths were charged to Williams were 2 of 30 black children and black young men who were reported missing or who had died under suspicious circumstances in the Atlanta area over a 22-month period beginning in July 1979. During the trial, fiber evidence was used to associate Williams with 12 of those victims.

Fiber evidence is often used to corroborate other evidence in a case—it is used to support other testimony and validate other evidence presented at a trial. This was not the situation in the Williams trial. Other evidence and other aspects of the trial were important but were used to support and complement the fiber evidence, not the usual order of things. The "hair and fiber matches" between Williams' environment and 11 of the 12 murder victims discussed at the trial were so significant that in the author's opinion, these victims were positively linked to both the residence and automobiles that were a major part of the world of Wayne Williams.

Another difference between this case and most other cases was the extremely large amount of publicity surrounding both the investigation of the missing and murdered children and the arrest and subsequent trial of Williams. Few other murder trials have received the attention that the Williams case received. . . .

It is often difficult to get an accurate picture from press reports of the physical evidence introduced at a trial and the significance of that evidence. This article will also set forth in some detail the fiber evidence that linked Williams to the murder victims.

By discussing only the fiber evidence introduced at the trial, many other aspects of the case against Williams are being neglected. Additional evidence dealing with Williams' motivations—his character and behavior, his association with several of the victims by eyewitness accounts, and his link to a victim recovered from a river in Atlanta— was also essential to the case. . . .

Reprinted in part from *FBI Law Enforcement Bulletin,* March and May 1984.

Development of Williams as a Murder Suspect

Before Wayne Williams became a suspect in the Nathaniel Cater murder case, the Georgia State Crime Laboratory located a number of yellowish-green nylon fibers and some violet acetate fibers on the bodies and clothing of the murder victims whose bodies had been recovered during the period of July 1979 to May 1981. The names of those victims were included on the list of missing and murdered children that was compiled by the Atlanta Task Force (a large group of investigators from law enforcement agencies in the Atlanta area). The yellowish-green nylon fibers were generally similar to each other in appearance and properties and were considered to have originated from a single source. This was also true of the violet acetate fibers. Although there were many other similarities that would link these murders together, the fiber linkage was notable since the possibility existed that a source of these fibers might be located in the future.

Initially, the major concern with these yellowish-green nylon fibers was determining what type of object could have been their source. This information could provide avenues of investigative activity. The fibers were very coarse and had a lobed cross-sectional appearance, tending to indicate that they originated from a carpet or a rug. The lobed cross-sectional shape of these fibers, however, was unique, and initially, the manufacturer of these fibers could not be determined. Photomicrographs of the fibers were prepared for display to contacts within the textile industry. On one occasion, these photomicrographs were distributed among several chemists attending a meeting at the research facilities of a large fiber producer. The chemists concurred that the yellowish-green nylon fiber was very unusual in cross-sectional shape and was consistent with being a carpet fiber, but again, the manufacturer of this fiber could not be determined. Contacts with other textile producers and textile chemists likewise did not result in an identification of the manufacturer.

In February 1981, an Atlanta newspaper article publicized that several different fiber types had been found on two murder victims. Following the publication of this article, bodies recovered from rivers in the Atlanta metropolitan area were either nude or clothed only in undershorts. It appeared possible that the victims were being disposed of in this undressed state and in rivers in order to eliminate fibers from being found on their bodies.[1]

---

[1]Prior to the publication of the February 11, 1981, newspaper article, one victim from the task force list, who was fully clothed, had been recovered from a river in the Atlanta area. In the 2 ½-month period after publication, the nude or nearly nude bodies of seven of the nine victims added to the task force list were recovered from rivers in the Atlanta area.

On May 22, 1981, a four-man surveillance team of personnel from the Atlanta Police Department and the Atlanta Office of the FBI was situated under and at both ends of the James Jackson Bridge over the Chattahoochee River in northwest Atlanta. Around 2:00 A.M., a loud splash alerted the surveillance team to the presence of an automobile being driven slowly off the bridge. The driver was stopped and identified as Wayne Bertram Williams.

Two days after Williams' presence on the bridge, the nude body of Nathaniel Cater was pulled from the Chattahoochee River, approximately 1 mile downstream from the James Jackson Parkway Bridge. A yellowish-green nylon carpet-type fiber, similar to the nylon fibers discussed above, was recovered from the head hair of Nathaniel Cater. When details of Williams' reason for being on the bridge at 2:00 A.M. could not be confirmed, search warrants for Williams' home and automobile were obtained and were served on the afternoon of June 3, 1981. During the late evening hours of the same day, the initial associations of fibers from Cater and other murder victims were made with a green carpet in the home of Williams. Associations with a bedspread from Williams' bed and with the Williams' family dog were also made at that time.

An apparent source of the yellowish-green nylon fibers had been found. It now became important to completely characterize these fibers in order to verify the associations and determine the strength of the associations resulting from the fiber matches. Because of the unusual cross-sectional appearance of the nylon fiber and the difficulty in determining the manufacturer, it was believed that this was a relatively rare fiber type, and therefore, would not be present in large amounts (or in a large number of carpets).

The Williams' Carpet

Shortly after Williams was developed as a suspect, it was determined the yellowish-green nylon fibers were manufactured by the Wellman Corporation. The next step was to ascertain, if possible, how much carpet like Williams' bedroom carpet had been sold in the Atlanta area— carpet composed of the Wellman fiber and dyed with the same dye formulation as the Williams' carpet. Names of Wellman Corporation customers who had purchased this fiber type, technical information about the fiber, and data concerning when and how much of this fiber type had been manufactured were obtained.

It was confirmed that the Wellman Corporation had, in fact, manufactured the fiber in Williams' carpet and that no other fiber manufacturer was known to have made a fiber with a similar cross section.

It was also determined that fibers having this cross-sectional shape were manufactured and sold during the years 1967 through 1974. Prior to 1967, this company manufactured only a round cross section; after 1974, the unusual trilobal cross section seen in Williams' carpet was modified to a more regular trilobal cross-sectional shape. A list of sales of that fiber type during the period 1967 through 1974 was compiled. . . .

Through numerous contacts with yarn spinners and carpet manufacturers, it was determined that the West Point Pepperell Corporation of Dalton, Ga., had manufactured a line of carpet called "Luxaire," which was constructed in the same manner as the Williams' carpet. One of the colors offered in the "Luxaire" line was called "English Olive," and this color was the same as that of the Williams' carpet (both visually and by the use of discriminating chemical and instrumental tests).

It was learned that the West Point Pepperell Corporation had manufactured the "Luxaire" line for a 5-year period from December 1970 through 1975; however, it had only purchased Wellman 181B fiber for this line during 1970 and 1971. In December 1971, the West Point Pepperell Corporation changed the fiber composition of the "Luxaire" line to a different nylon fiber, one that was dissimilar to the Wellman 181B fiber in appearance. Accordingly, "Luxaire" carpet, like the Williams' carpet, was only manufactured for a 1-year period. This change of carpet fiber after only 1 year in production was yet another factor that made the Williams' carpet unusual.

It is interesting to speculate on the course the investigation would have taken if the James Jackson Parkway Bridge had not been covered by the surveillance team. The identification of the manufacturer of the nylon fibers showing up on the bodies could still have occurred and the same list of purchasers of the Wellman fiber could have been obtained. The same contacts with the yarn and carpet manufacturers could have been made; however, there would not have been an actual carpet sample to display. It is believed that eventually the carpet manufacturer could have been determined. With a sample of carpet supplied by West Point Pepperell—which they had retained in their files for over 10 years—it would have been possible to conduct a house-by-house search of the Atlanta area in an attempt to find a similar carpet. Whether this very difficult task would have been attempted, of course, will never be known. A search of that type, however, would have accurately answered an important question that was discussed at the trial—the question of how many other homes in the Atlanta area had a carpet like the Williams' carpet. An estimation, to be discussed later, based on sales records provided by the West Point Pepperell Corporation indicated that there was a very low chance (1/7792) of finding a carpet like Williams' carpet by randomly selecting occupied residences in the Atlanta area.

Only the West Point Pepperell Corporation was found to have manufactured a carpet exactly like the Williams' carpet. Even though several manufacturers had gone out of business and could not be located, it was believed that considering the many variables that exist in the manufacture of carpet and the probable uniqueness of each carpet manufacturer's dye formulations, it would be extremely unlikely for two unrelated companies to construct a carpet or dye the carpet fibers in exactly the same way. A large number of other green fibers, visually similar in color to Williams' carpet, were examined. None was found to be consistent with fibers from the Williams' carpet.

Probability Determinations

To convey the unusual nature of the Williams' residential carpet, an attempt was made to develop a numerical probability—something never before done in connection with textile materials used as evidence in a criminal trial.[2] The following information was gathered from the West Point Pepperell Corporation:

1. West Point Pepperell reported purchases of Wellman 181B fiber for the "Luxaire" line during a 1-year period. The Wellman 181B fiber was used to manufacture "Luxaire" carpet from December 1970 until December 1971, at which time a new fiber type replaced that Wellman fiber.

2. In 1971, West Point Pepperell sold 5,710 square yards of English Olive "Luxaire" and "Dreamer" carpet to Region C (10 southeastern States which include Georgia). "Dreamer" was a line of carpet similar to "Luxaire" but contained a less dense pile. In order to account for the carpet manufactured during 1971, but sold after that time, all of the "Luxaire" English Olive carpet sold during 1972 to Region C (10,687 square yards) was added to the 1971 sales. Therefore, it was estimated that a total of 16,397 square yards of carpet containing the Wellman 181B fiber and dyed English Olive in color was sold by the West Point Pepperell Corporation to retailers in 10 southeastern States during 1971 and 1972. (In

---

[2]E. J. Mitchell and D. Holland, "An Unusual Case of Identification of Transferred Fibers," *Journal of the Forensic Science Society,* vol. 19, 1979, p. 23. This article describes a case in which carpet fibers transferred to a murder victim's body in England were traced back to the carpet manufacturer and finally to an automobile owned by the person who eventually confessed to the murder.

1979, existing residential carpeted floor space in the United States was estimated at 6.7 billion square yards.)[3]

3. By assuming that this carpet was installed in one room, averaging 12 feet by 15 feet in size, per house, and also assuming that the total sales of carpet were divided equally among the 10 southeastern States, then approximately 82 rooms with this carpet could be found in the State of Georgia.

4. Information from the Atlanta Regional Commission showed that there were 638,995 occupied housing units in the Atlanta metropolitan area in November 1981.[4] Using this figure, the chance of randomly selecting an occupied housing unit in metropolitan Atlanta and finding a house with a room having carpet like Williams' carpet was determined to be 1 chance in 7,792—a very low chance.

To the degree that the assumptions used in calculating the above probability number are reasonable, we can be confident in arriving at a valid probability number. . . .

The probability figures illustrate clearly that the Williams' carpet is, in fact, very uncommon. To enhance the figures even further, it is important to emphasize that these figures are based on the assumption that none of the carpet of concern had been discarded during the past 11 years. In fact, carpet of this type, often used in commercial settings, such as apartment houses, would probably have had a normal life span of only 4 or 5 years. . . .[5]

The Williams Trial

To any experienced forensic fiber examiner, the fiber evidence linking Williams to the murder victims was overwhelming. But regardless of the apparent validity of the fiber findings, it was during the trial that its true weight would be determined. Unless it could be conveyed meaningfully to a jury, its effect would be lost. Because of this, considerable

---

[3]This information was taken from a study by E. I. du Pont de Nemours & Co. concerned with the existing residential floor space with carpet in the United States. This study was reported in the marketing survey conducted by the Marketing Corporation of America, Westport, Conn.

[4]Information regarding the number of housing units in the Atlanta metropolitan area was obtained from a report provided by the Atlanta Regional Commission. The report, dated November 11, 1981, contained population and housing counts for counties, super districts, and census tracts in the Atlanta metropolitan area.

[5]Information about carpet similar to Williams' carpet was developed through contacts with carpet manufacturers and carpet salesmen in Georgia. It was determined that this type carpet was often installed in commercial settings, such as apartments, and in those settings, had an average life span of 4 to 5 years.

time was spent determining what should be done to convey the full significance of the fiber evidence. Juries are not usually composed of individuals with a scientific background, and therefore, it was necessary to "educate" the jury in what procedures were followed and the significance of the fiber results. In the Williams case, over 40 charts with over 350 photographs were prepared to illustrate exactly what the crime laboratory examiners had observed. . . .

Representatives of the textile fiber industry, including technical representatives from the Wellman and West Point Pepperell Corporations, were involved in educating the jury regarding textile fibers in general and helped lay the foundation for the conclusions of the forensic fiber examiners. The jury also was told about fiber analysis in the crime laboratory.

The trial, as it developed, can be divided into two parts. Initially, testimony was given concerning the murders of Nathaniel Cater and Jimmy Ray Payne, the two victims included in the indictment drawn against Williams in July 1981. Testimony was then given concerning Williams' association with 10 other murder victims.

The fiber matches made between fibers in Williams' environment and fibers from Victims Payne and Cater were discussed. The items from Williams' environment that were linked to either or both of the victims are shown in the center of the chart. (See Fig. 1.) Not only is

Figure 1.   Items from residence and station wagon of Wayne Williams that were found on Jimmy Ray Payne and Nathaniel Cater.

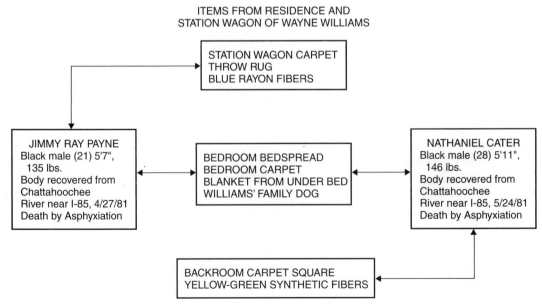

Payne linked to the Williams' environment by seven items and Cater linked by six items, but both of the victims are linked strongly to each other based on the fiber matches and circumstances surrounding their deaths.

In discussing the significance or strength of an association based on textile fibers, it was emphasized that the more uncommon the fibers, the stronger the association. None of the fiber types from the items in Williams' environment shown in the center of Figure 1 is by definition a "common" fiber type. Several of the fiber types would be termed "uncommon."

One of the fibers linking the body of Jimmy Ray Payne to the carpet in the 1970 station wagon driven by Williams was a small rayon fiber fragment recovered from Payne's shorts. Data were obtained from the station wagon's manufacturer concerning which automobile models produced prior to 1973 contained carpet made of this fiber type. These data were coupled with additional information from Georgia concerning the number of these models registered in the Atlanta metropolitan area during 1981. This allowed a calculation to be made relating to the probability of randomly selecting an automobile having carpet like that in the 1970 Chevrolet station wagon from the 2,373,512 cars registered in the Atlanta metropolitan area. This probability is 1 chance in 3,828, a very low probability representing a significant association.

Another factor to consider when assessing the significance of fiber evidence is the increased strength of the association when multiple fiber matches become the basis of the association. This is true if different fiber types from more than one object are found and each fiber type either links two people together or links an individual with a particular environment. As the number of different objects increases, the strength of an association increases dramatically. That is, the chance of randomly finding several particular fiber types in a certain location is much smaller than the chance of finding one particular fiber type.

The following example can be used to illustrate the significance of multiple fiber matches linking two items together. If one were to throw a single die one time, the chance or probability of throwing a particular number would be one chance in six. The probability of throwing a second die and getting that same number also would be one chance in six. However, the probability of getting 2 of the same numbers on 2 dice thrown simultaneously is only 1 in every 36 double throws—a much smaller chance than with either of the single throws. This number is a result of the product rule of probability theory. That is, the probability of the joint occurrence of a number of mutually independent events equals the product of the individual probabilities of each of the events (in this example—$\frac{1}{6} \times \frac{1}{6} = \frac{1}{36}$). Since numerous fiber types are in existence, the chance of finding one particular fiber type, other than a common type, in a specific randomly selected location is small. The chance then of finding several fiber types together in a specific location is the product of several small probabilities, resulting in an extremely small chance. . . .

However, no attempt was made to use the product rule and multiply the individual probability numbers together to get an approximation of the probability of finding carpets like Williams' residential carpet and Williams' automobile carpet in the same household. The probability numbers were used only to show that the individual fiber types involved in these associations were very uncommon. . . .[6]

In addition to the two probability numbers already discussed (bedroom and station wagon carpets), each of the other fiber types linking Williams to both Cater and Payne has a probability of being found in a particular location. The chance of finding all of the fiber types indicated on the chart [Fig. 1] in one location (seven types on Payne's body and six types on Cater's body) would be extremely small. Although an actual probability number for those findings could not be determined, it is believed that the multiple fiber associations shown on this chart are proof that Williams is linked to the bodies of these two victims, even though each fiber match by itself does not show a positive association with Williams' environment.

Studies have been conducted in England that show that transferred fibers are usually lost rapidly as people go about their daily routine.[7] Therefore, the foreign fibers present on a person are most often from recent surroundings. The fibrous debris found on a murder victim reflects the body's more recent surroundings, especially important if the body was moved after the killing. Accordingly, the victims' bodies in this particular case are not only associated with Williams but are apparently associated with Williams shortly before or after their deaths.

It was also pointed out during the trial that the locations of the fibers—on Payne's shorts and in Cater's head hairs and pubic hairs—were not those where one would expect to find fibrous debris transferred from an automobile or a house to victims who had been fully clothed.

---

[6]Joseph L. Peterson, ed. *Forensic Science* (New York: AMS Press, Inc., 1975), pp. 181–225. This collection of articles, dealing with various aspects of forensic science, contains five papers concerned with using statistics to interpret the meaning of physical evidence. It is a good discussion of probability theory and reviews cases where probability theory has been used in trial situations.

[7]C. A. Pounds and K. W. Smalldon, "The Transfer of Fibers between Clothing Materials During Simulated Contacts and Their Persistence During Wear," *Journal of the Forensic Science Society,* vol. 15, 1975, pp. 29–37.

Although from these findings it would appear that the victims were in the residence of Williams, there was one other location that contained many of the same fibers as those in the composition of various objects in his residence—Williams' station wagon. The environment of a family automobile might be expected to reflect, to some extent, fibers from objects located within the residence. This was true of the 1970 station wagon. With one exception, all of the fiber types removed from Payne and Cater, consistent with originating from items shown in the center of Figure 1, were present in debris removed by vacuuming the station wagon. The automobile would be the most logical source of the foreign fibers found on both Payne and Cater if they were associated with Williams shortly before or after their deaths. It should also be pointed out that two objects, the bedspread and the blanket, were portable and could have at one time been present inside the station wagon.

Both Payne and Cater were recovered from the Chattahoochee River. Their bodies had been in the water for several days. Some of the fibers found on these victims were like fibers in the compositions of the bedroom carpet and bedspread except for color intensity. They appeared to have been bleached. By subjecting various known fibers to small amounts of Chattahoochee River water for different periods of time, it was found that bleaching did occur. This was especially true with the carpet and bedspread fibers from Williams' bedroom.

Two crime laboratory examiners testified during the closing stages of the first part of the trial about Williams' association with Payne and Cater. They concluded that it was highly unlikely that any environment other than that present in Wayne Williams' house and car could have resulted in the combination of fibers and hairs found on the victims and that it would be virtually impossible to have matched so many fibers found on Cater and Payne to items in Williams' house and car unless the victims were in contact with or in some way associated with the environment of Wayne Williams.

After testimony was presented concerning the Payne and Cater cases, the Fulton County District Attorney's Office asked the court to be allowed to introduce evidence in the cases of 10 other victims whose murders were similar in many respects. Georgia law allows evidence of another crime to be introduced ". . . if some logical connection can be shown between the two from which it can be said that proof of the one tends to establish the other as relevant to some fact other than general bad character."[8] There need be no conviction for the other crime in order for details about that crime to be admissible.

---

[8]*Encyclopedia of Georgia Law,* vol. 11A (The Harrison Company, 1979), p. 70.

It was ruled that evidence concerning other murders could be introduced in an attempt to prove a "pattern or scheme" of killing that included the two murders with which Williams was charged. The additional evidence in these cases was to be used to help the jury ". . . decide whether Williams had committed the two murders with which he is charged."[9]

There were similarities between these additional victims and Payne and Cater. (See Fig. 2.) Although some differences can also be seen on this chart, the prosecution considered these differences to fit within the "pattern of killing" of which Payne and Cater were a part. The most important similarities between these additional victims were the fiber matches that linked 9 of the 10 victims to Williams' environment. The fiber findings discussed during the trial and used to associate Williams to the 12 victims were illustrated during the trial. (See Fig. 3.)

The 12 victims were listed in chronological order based on the dates their bodies were recovered. The time period covered by this chart, approximately 22 months, is from July 1979, until May 1981. During that time period, the Williams family had access to a large number of automobiles, including a number of rental cars. Three of these automobiles are listed at the top of Figure 3. If one or more of the cars was in the possession of the Williams family at the time a victim was found to be missing, the space under that car(s) and after the particular victim's name is shaded.

Four objects (including the dog) from Williams' residence are listed horizontally across the top of Figure 3, along with objects from three of his automobiles. An "X" on the chart indicates an apparent transfer of textile fibers from the listed object to a victim. Other objects from Williams' environment which were linked to various victims by an apparent fiber transfer are listed on the right side of the chart. Fiber types from objects (never actually located) that were matched to fiber types from one or more victims are also listed either at the top or on the right side of the chart. Fourteen specific objects and five fiber types (probably from five other objects) listed on this chart are linked to one or more of the victims. More than 28 different fiber types, along with the dog hairs, were used to link up to 19 objects from Williams' environment to 1 or more of the victims. Of the more than 28 fiber types from Williams' environment, 14 of these originated from a rug or carpet.

The combination of more than 28 different fiber types would not be considered so significant if they were primarily common fiber types.

---

[9]*The Atlanta Constitution*, "Williams Jury Told of Other Slayings," Sec. 1-A, 1/26/82, p. 25.

VICTIM'S NAME	DATE VICTIM MISSING	DAYS MISSING	BODY RECOVERY AREA	CAUSE OF DEATH	AGE	WEIGHT	HEIGHT
EVANS	7/25/79	3	WOODED AREA S.W. ATLANTA	PROBABLE ASPHYXIATION/ STRANGULATION	13	87 LBS.	5'4"
MIDDLEBROOKS	5/18/80	1	NEAR STREET S.E. ATLANTA	BLUNT TRAUMA TO HEAD	14	88 LBS.	4'10"
STEPHENS	10/9/80	1	NEAR STREET S.E. ATLANTA	ASPHYXIATION	10	120 LBS.	5'0"
GETER	1/3/81	33	WOODED AREA FULTON COUNTY	MANUAL STRANGULATION	14	130 LBS.	5'4"
PUE	1/22/81	1	NEAR HIGHWAY ROCKDALE CO.	LIGATURE STRANGULATION	15	105 LBS.	5'5"
BALTAZAR	2/6/81	7	NEAR HIGHWAY DEKALB CO.	LIGATURE STRANGULATION	12	125 LBS.	5'4"
BELL	3/2/81	31	SOUTH RIVER DEKALB CO.	ASPHYXIATION	16	100 BELL.	5'2"
ROGERS	3/30/81	10	NEAR STREET N.W. ATLANTA	ASPHYXIATION/ STRANGULATION	20	110 LBS.	5'3"
PORTER	4/10/81	1	NEAR STREET IN S.W. ATLANTA	STABBED	28	123 LBS.	5'7"
PAYNE	4/22/81	5	CHATTAHOOCHEE RIVER FULTON COUNTY	ASPHYXIATION	21	135 LBS.	5'7"
BARRETT	5/11/81	1	NEAR STREET DEKALB CO.	LIGATURE STRANGULATION (3 PUNCTURE WOUNDS)	17	125 LBS.	5'4"
CATER	5/21/81	3	CHATTAHOOCHEE RIVER FULTON COUNTY	ASPHYXIATION/ STRANGULATION	28	146 LBS.	5'11"

Figure 2. Chart used during the trial to show similarities between Payne and Cater and ten other murder victims.

Figure 3. Fiber findings discussed during the trial and used to associate Williams to the twelve victims.

NAME OF VICTIM	VIOLET-GREEN WILLIAMS' BEDSPREAD	GREEN CARPET WILLIAMS' BEDROOM	WILLIAMS' DOG DOG HAIRS	YELLOW BLANKET WILLIAMS' BEDROOM	BLUE RAYON FIBERS, DEBRIS TRUNK LINER FROM WILLIAMS' HOME	1978 PLYMOUTH CARPET	1979 FORD CARPET	1970 CHEVROLET CARPET	ADDITIONAL ITEMS FROM WILLIAMS' HOME, AUTOMOBILES OR PERSON
Alfred Evans	X	X			X				YELLOW NYLON
Eric Middlebrooks	X	X			X				FORD TRUNK LINER
Charles Stephens	X	X		X					YELLOW NYLON WHITE POLYESTER BACKROOM CARPET FORD TRUNK LINER
Lubie Geter	X	X				X			KITCHEN CARPET
Terry Pue	X	X							WHITE POLYESTER BACKROOM CARPET
Patrick Baltazar	X	X	X			X			YELLOW NYLON WHITE POLYESTER HEAD HAIR GLOVE JACKET PIGMENTED POLYPROPYLENE BACKROOM CARPET
Joseph Bell	X	X		X					
Larry Rogers	X	X	X			X			YELLOW NYLON PORCH BEDSPREAD
John Porter	X	X	X	X		X			PORCH BEDSPREAD
Jimmy Payne	X	X	X	X		X			BLUE THROW RUG
William Barrett	X	X	X			X			GLOVE
Nathaniel Cater	X	X	X			X			BACKROOM CARPET YELLOW-GREEN SYNTHETIC

In fact, there is only 1 light green cotton fiber of the 28 that might be considered common. This cotton fiber was blended with acetate fibers in Williams' bedspread. Light green cotton fibers removed from many victims were not considered or compared unless they were physically intermingled with violet acetate fibers which were consistent with originating from the bedspread. It should be noted that a combination of cotton and acetate fibers blended together in a single textile material, as in the bedspread, is in itself uncommon. . . .

The previous discussion concerning the significance of multiple fiber matches can be applied to the associations made in the cases of all the victims except Bell, but especially to the association of Patrick Baltazar to Williams' environment. Fibers and animal hairs consistent with having originated from 10 sources were removed from Baltazar's body. These 10 sources include the uncommon bedroom carpet and station wagon carpet. In addition to the fiber (and animal hair) linkage, two head hairs of Negroid origin were removed from Baltazar's body that were consistent with originating from the scalp area of Williams. Head hair matches were also very significant in linking Williams to Baltazar's body. In the opinion of the author, the association based upon the hair and fiber analyses is a positive association.

Another important aspect of the fiber linkage between Williams and these victims is the correspondence between the fiber findings and the time periods during which Williams had access to the three automobiles listed on the chart. Nine victims are linked to automobiles used by the Williams family. When Williams did not have access to a particular car, no fibers were recovered that were consistent with having originated from that automobile. Trunk liner fibers of the type used in the trunks of many late-model Ford Motor Company automobiles were also recovered from the bodies of two victims.

One final point should be made concerning Williams' bedroom and station wagon carpets where probability numbers had been determined. Fibers consistent with having originated from both of these "unusual" carpets were recovered from Payne's body. Of the nine victims who were killed during the time period when Williams had access to the 1970 station wagon, fibers consistent with having originated from both the station wagon carpet and the bedroom carpet were recovered from six of these victims.

The apparent bleaching of several fibers removed from the bodies of Payne and Cater was consistent with having been caused by river water. Several fibers similar to those from Payne and Cater were removed from many of the victims whose bodies were recovered on land. Consistent with the bleaching argument, none of the fibers from the victims found on land showed any apparent bleaching. The finding of many of the same fiber types on the remaining victims, who were recovered from many different locations, refutes the possibility that Payne's and Cater's bodies picked up foreign fibers from the river.

The fact that many of the victims were involved with so many of the same fiber types, all of which linked the victims to Williams' environment, is the basis for arguing conclusively against these fibers originating from a source other than Williams' environment.

It is hoped that this article has provided valuable insight concerning the use of fiber evidence in a criminal trial, has provided answers to questions from those in the law enforcement community about textile fiber evidence in general, and has presented convincing arguments to establish Wayne Williams' association with the bodies of the murder victims.

PHYSICAL PROPERTIES: GLASS AND SOIL

The forensic scientist must constantly determine those properties that impart distinguishing characteristics to matter, giving it a unique identity. The search for distinctive properties is a continuing one and ends only when the scientist has completely individualized a substance to one correct source. Properties are the identifying characteristics of substances. In this and succeeding chapters, we will examine properties that are most useful for characterizing soil, glass, and other physical evidence. However, before we begin this task, our understanding of the nature of properties can be made easier by classifying them into two broad categories: physical and chemical.

Physical properties describe a substance without reference to any other substance. For example, weight, volume, color, boiling point, and melting point are typical physical properties that can be measured for a particular substance without the necessity of altering the material's composition through a chemical reaction; they are associated only with the physical existence of that substance. **A chemical property describes the behavior of a substance when it reacts or combines with another substance.** For example, when wood burns, it chemically combines with oxygen in the air to form new substances; this transformation describes a chemical property of wood. In the crime laboratory, a routine procedure for determining the presence of heroin in a suspect specimen is to react it with a chemical reagent known as the

Marquis reagent. In the presence of heroin, the Marquis reagent turns purple. This color transformation thus becomes a chemical property of heroin and provides a convenient test for its identification.

Which physical and chemical properties the forensic scientist ultimately chooses to observe and measure will depend on the type of material that is being examined. Logic requires, however, that if the property can be assigned a numerical value, it must be one that relates to a standard system of measurement accepted throughout the scientific community.

THE METRIC SYSTEM

Although scientists throughout the world have been using the metric system of measurement for more than a century, the United States still uses the cumbersome "English system" to express length in inches or feet or yards; weight in ounces or pounds; and volume in pints or quarts. The inherent difficulty of this system is that no simple numerical relationship exists between the various units of measurement. For example, to convert inches to feet one must know that 1 foot is equal to 12 inches; the conversion of ounces to pounds requires the knowledge that 16 ounces is equivalent to 1 pound. In 1791, the French Academy of Science devised the simple system of measurement known as the metric system. This system uses a simple decimal relationship so that a unit of length, volume, or mass can be converted into a subunit by simply multiplying or dividing by a multiple of ten—for example, 10, 100, or 1000.

Even though the United States has not yet adopted the metric system, its system of currency is decimal and hence analogous to the metric system. The basic unit of currency is the dollar. A dollar is divided into 10 equal units called dimes, and each dime is further divided into 10 equal units of cents.

The metric system has basic units of measurement for length, mass, and volume; they are the meter, gram, and liter, respectively. These three basic units can be converted into subunits that are decimal multiples of the basic unit by simply attaching a prefix to the unit name. The following are common prefixes and their equivalent decimal value:

Prefix	Equivalent Value
deci	1/10 or 0.1
centi	1/100 or 0.01
milli	1/1000 or 0.001
micro	1/1,000,000 or 0.000001
nano	1/1,000,000,000 or 0.000000001
kilo	1000
mega	1,000,000

Hence, 1/10 or 0.1 of a gram is the same as a decigram (dg), 1/100 or 0.01 of a meter is equal to a centimeter (cm), and 1/1000 of a liter is a milliliter (ml). A metric conversion is carried out simply by moving the decimal point to the right or left and inserting the proper prefix to show the direction and number of places that the decimal point has been moved. For example, if the weight of a powder is 0.0165 gram, it may be more convenient to multiply this value by 100 and express it as 1.65 centigrams or by 1000 to show it as its equivalent value of 16.5 milligrams. Similarly, an object that weighs 264,450 grams may be expressed as 264.450 kilograms simply by dividing it by 1000. It is important to remember that in any of these conversions, the value of the measurement has not changed; 0.0165 gram is still equivalent to 1.65 centigrams, just as one dollar is still equal to 100 cents. We have simply adjusted the position of the decimal and shown the extent of the adjustment with a prefix.

One interesting aspect of the metric system is that volume can be defined in terms of length. A liter by definition is the volume of a cube, each side having a length of 10 centimeters. One liter is therefore equivalent to a volume of 10 cm × 10 cm × 10 cm, or 1000 cubic centimeters (cc). Thus, one-thousandth of a liter or one milliliter (ml) is equal to one cubic centimeter (cc) (see Figure 4–1). It is common for scientists to use the subunits ml and cc interchangeably to express volume.

At times, it may be necessary to convert units from the metric system into the English system, or vice versa (see Figure 4–2). In order to accomplish this, we must consult references that list English units and their metric equivalents. Some of the more useful equivalents follow:

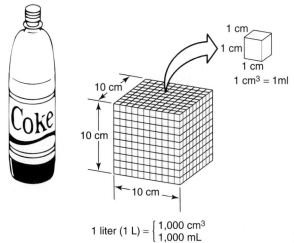

Figure 4–1.

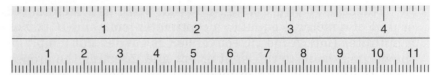

Figure 4–2. Comparison of the metric and English systems of length measurement; 2.54 centimeters = 1 inch.

1 inch = 2.54 centimeters
1 meter = 39.37 inches
1 pound = 453.6 grams
1 liter = 1.06 quarts
1 kilogram = 2.2 pounds

The general mathematical procedures for converting from one system to another can be illustrated by the conversion of 12 inches into centimeters. To change inches into centimeters, we need to know that there are 2.54 centimeters per inch. Hence, if we multiply 12 inches by 2.54 centimeters/inch (12 in × 2.54 cm/in.), the unit of inches will cancel out, leaving the product 30.48 cm. Similarly, applying the conversion of grams to pounds, 227 grams is equivalent to 227 gm × 1 lb/453.6 gm or 0.5 lb.

PHYSICAL PROPERTIES

TEMPERATURE

The determination of the physical properties of any material will often require the measurement of temperature. For instance, the temperatures at which a substance melts or boils are readily determinable characteristics that will help identify a substance. Temperature is a measure of heat intensity, or the hotness or coldness of a substance. Temperature is usually measured by causing a thermometer to come into contact with a substance. The familiar mercury-in-glass thermometer functions because mercury expands more than glass when heated and contracts more than glass when cooled. Thus, the length of the mercury column in the glass tube provides a measure of the surrounding environment's temperature. The construction of a temperature scale requires two reference points and a choice of units. The reference points most conveniently chosen are the freezing point and boiling point of water. The two most common temperature scales used are the Fahrenheit and Celsius (formerly called centigrade) scales.

The Fahrenheit scale is based on the assignment of the value 32°F to the freezing point of water and 212°F to its boiling point. The difference between the two points is evenly divided into 180 units.

Thus, a degree Fahrenheit is 1/180 of the temperature change between the freezing point and boiling point of water. The Celsius scale is derived by assigning the freezing point of water a value of 0°C and its boiling point a value of 100°C. A degree Celsius is thus 1/100 of the temperature change between the two reference points. Scientists in most countries use the Celsius scale to measure temperature. A comparison of the two scales is shown in Figure 4–3.

WEIGHT AND MASS

The force with which gravity attracts a body is called **weight.** If your weight is 180 pounds, this means that earth's gravity is pulling you down with a force of 180 pounds; on the moon, where the force

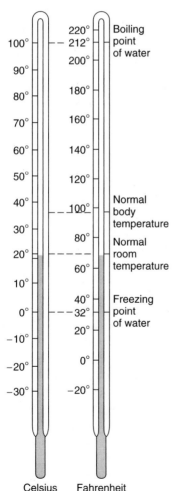

Figure 4–3.
Comparison of Celsius and Fahrenheit temperature scales.

of gravity is one-sixth that of earth, your weight would be 30 pounds.

Mass differs from weight because it refers to the amount of matter an object contains and is independent of its location on earth or any other place in the universe. The mathematical relationship between weight (w) and mass (m) is shown in Equation (4–1), where g is the acceleration imparted to a body by the force of gravity.

$$W = mg \qquad\qquad (4\text{–}1)$$

The weight of a body is seen to be directly proportional to its mass; hence, a large mass weighs more than a small mass.

In the metric system, it is always the mass of an object rather than its weight that is specified. The basic unit of mass is the gram. An object that has a mass of 40 grams on earth will have a mass of 40 grams anywhere else in this universe. Normally, however, the terms *mass* and *weight* are used interchangeably, and we often speak of the weight of an object when we really mean its mass.

The mass of an object is determined by comparing it against the known mass of standard objects. The comparison is confusingly called *weighing,* and the standard objects are called *weights (masses* would be a more correct term). The comparison is performed on a balance. The simplest type of balance for weighing is the equal-arm balance shown in Figure 4–4. The object to be weighed is placed on the left pan, and the standard weights are placed on the right pan; when the pointer between the two pans is at the center mark, the

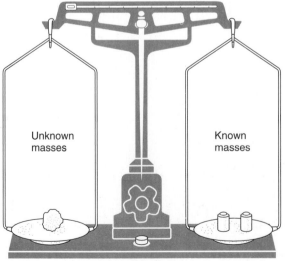

Unknown masses

Known masses

Figure 4–4.
The measurement of mass.

total mass on the right pan is equal to the mass of the object on the left pan.

The modern laboratory has progressed beyond the simple equal-arm balance, and either the top-loading balance or the single-pan analytical balance [Figure 4–5 (a) and (b)] is now likely to be used. The choice depends on the accuracy required and the amount of material being weighed. Each works on the same counterbalancing principle as the simple equal-arm balance, but the second pan, the one on which the standard weights are placed, is hidden from view within the balance's housing. Once the object whose weight is to be determined is placed on the visible pan, the operator selects the proper standard weights (also contained with the housing) by manually turning a set of knobs located on the front side of the balance. At the point of balance, the weights selected are automatically recorded on digital and optical readout scales. The top-loading balance can accurately weigh an object to the nearest 1 milligram or 0.001 gram; the analytical balance is

Figure 4–5.   (a) Top-loading balance. (b) Single-pan analytical balance. *Both courtesy* Mettler Instrument Corp., N.J.

(a)   (b)

even more accurate, weighing to the nearest tenth of a milligram or 0.0001 gram.

DENSITY

A most important physical property of matter with respect to the analysis of certain kinds of physical evidence is density. **Density is defined as mass per unit volume** [see Equation (4–2)].

$$\text{Density} = \frac{\text{mass}}{\text{volume}} \qquad (4\text{–}2)$$

Density is an intensive property of matter—that is, it is the same regardless of the size of a substance; thus, it is a characteristic property of a substance and can be used as an aid in identification. Solids tend to be more dense than liquids, and liquids more dense than gases. The densities of some common substances are shown in Table 4–1.

A simple procedure for determining the density of a solid is illustrated in Figure 4–6. First, the solid is weighed on a balance against

TABLE 4–1.
DENSITIES OF SELECT MATERIALS
(AT 20°C UNLESS OTHERWISE STATED)

Substance	Density (g/ml)
Solids	
Silver	10.5
Lead	11.5
Iron	7.8
Aluminum	2.7
Window glass	2.47–2.54
Ice (0°C)	0.92
Liquids	
Mercury	13.6
Benzene	0.88
Ethyl alcohol	0.79
Gasoline	0.69
Water at 4°C	1.00
Water	0.998
Gases	
Air (0°C)	0.0013
Chlorine (0°C)	0.0032
Oxygen (0°C)	0.0014
Carbon dioxide (0°C)	0.0020

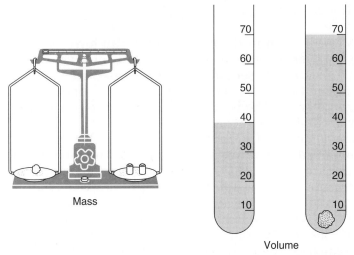

Figure 4–6. A simple procedure for determining the density of a solid is to first weigh it and then measure its volume by noting the volume of water it displaces.

known standard gram weights, and its mass is determined. The solid's volume is then determined from the volume of water it displaces. This is easily measured by filling a cylinder with a known volume of water (V_1), adding the object, and measuring the new water level (V_2). The difference $V_2 - V_1$ in ml is equal to the volume of the solid. Density can now be calculated from Equation (4–2) in grams per milliliter.

The volumes of gases and liquids vary considerably with temperature; hence, when determining density, it is important to control and record the temperature at which the measurements are made. For example, one gram of water occupies a volume of one milliliter at 4°C and thus has a density of 1.0 g/ml. However, as the temperature of water increases, its volume will expand. Therefore, at 20°C (room temperature) one gram of water will occupy a volume of 1.002 ml and will have a density of 0.998 g/ml.

The observation that a solid object will either sink, float, or remain suspended when immersed in a liquid is one that can be accounted for by the property of density. For instance, if the density of a solid is greater than the liquid medium in which it is immersed, the object will sink; if the solid has a density that is less than the liquid, it will float; and when the solid and liquid both have equal densities, the solid will remain suspended in the liquid medium. As we will shortly see, these observations provide the criminalist with a convenient technique for comparing the densities of solid objects.

REFRACTIVE INDEX

Light, as we will learn in the next chapter, can have the property of a wave. Lightwaves travel in air at a constant velocity of nearly 300,000,000 meters per second until they penetrate another medium, such as glass or water, at which point they are suddenly slowed, causing the rays to bend. The bending of a lightwave because of a change in velocity is called **refraction.**

    The phenomenon of refraction is apparent when we view an object that is immersed in a transparent medium; because we are accustomed to thinking that light travels in a straight line, we often forget to take refraction into account. For instance, suppose a ball is observed at the bottom of a pool of water; the light rays reflected from the ball will travel through the water and into the air to reach the eye. As the rays leave the water and enter the air, their velocity suddenly increases, causing them to be refracted. However, because of our assumption that light travels in a straight line, our eyes deceive us and make us think we see an object lying at a higher point than is actually the case. This phenomenon is illustrated in Figure 4–7.

    The ratio of the velocity of light in a vacuum to that in any medium determines the refractive index of that medium and is expressed as:

$$\text{Refractive index} = \frac{\text{velocity of light in vacuum}}{\text{velocity of light in medium}} \qquad (4\text{--}3)$$

For example, at 25°C the refractive index of water is 1.333. This means that light travels 1.333 times faster in a vacuum than it does in water at this temperature.

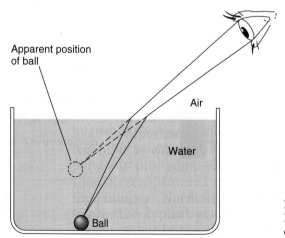

Apparent position of ball

Air

Water

Ball

Figure 4–7.
Light is refracted when it travels obliquely from one medium to another.

Like density, the refractive index is an intensive physical property of matter and will serve to characterize a substance. However, any procedure used to determine a substance's refractive index must be performed under carefully controlled temperature and lighting conditions, because the refractive index of a substance varies with its temperature and the frequency wavelength of light passing through it. Nearly all tabulated refractive indices are determined at a standard wavelength, usually 589.3 nanometers; this is the predominant wavelength emitted by sodium light and is commonly known as the sodium D light.

When a transparent solid is immersed in a liquid having a similar refractive index, light will not be refracted as it passes from the liquid into the solid. For this reason, the eye will not be able to distinguish the liquid-solid boundary, and the solid seems to disappear from view. This observation, as we will see, offers the forensic scientist a rather simple method for comparing the refractive indices of transparent solids.

Normally, a solid or a liquid would be expected to exhibit only one refractive index value for each frequency of light; however, many solids that are crystalline in nature will have two refractive indices whose values in part depend on the direction in which the light enters the crystal with respect to the crystal axis. **Solids that are crystalline have definite geometric forms because of the orderly arrangement of the fundamental particle of a solid, the atom.** In any type of crystal, the relative location and distance between its atoms are repetitive throughout the solid. Figure 4–8 shows the crystalline structure of sodium chloride, or ordinary table salt. Sodium chloride is an example of a cubic crystal in which each sodium atom is

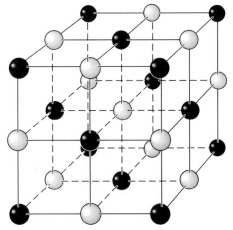

Figure 4–8.
Diagram of a sodium chloride crystal.
Sodium is represented by the black
spheres, chlorine by the white spheres.

surrounded by six chloride atoms and each chloride atom by six sodium atoms, except at the crystal surface. Not all solids are crystalline in nature; some, such as glass, have their atoms arranged randomly throughout the solid; these materials are known as **amorphous solids.**

Most crystals, excluding those that have cubic configurations, will refract a beam of light into two different light-ray components. This phenomenon is known as **double refraction** and can be illustrated by studying the behavior of the crystal calcite. When the calcite is laid on a printed page, the observer sees not one but two images of each word covered. The two light rays that give rise to the double image are refracted at different angles, and each has a different refractive index value. The indices of refraction for calcite are 1.486 and 1.658, and subtracting the two values yields a difference of 0.172; this difference is known as **birefringence.** Thus, the optical properties of crystals provide points of identification that will help characterize a crystal.

Many of us have at one time or another had the experience of holding a glass prism up toward the sunlight and watching it transform light into the colors of the rainbow. This observation serves to demonstrate that visible "white light" is not homogeneous but is actually composed of many different component colors. The process of separating light into component colors is called **dispersion.** The ability of a prism to disperse light into its component colors is explained by the property of refraction. Each color component of light, on passing through the glass, will be slowed to a speed slightly different from the others, thus causing each component to bend at a different angle as it emerges from the prism. As shown in Figure 4–9, the component colors of visible light extend from red to violet. We will learn in Chapter 5 that each color actually corresponds to a different range of frequencies or wavelengths of light. Dispersion thus separates light into its component frequencies and demonstrates that glass has a slightly different index of refraction for each frequency of light passing through it.

Figure 4–9.   Representation of the dispersion of light by a glass prism.

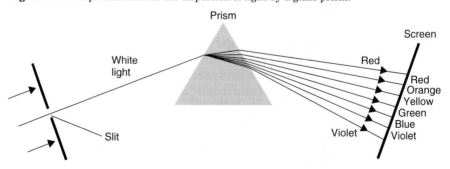

Now that we have investigated various physical properties of objects, we are ready to apply such properties to the characterization of two substances—glass and soil—that commonly must be examined by the criminalist.

COMPARING GLASS FRAGMENTS

Glass that is broken and shattered into fragments and minute particles during the commission of a crime can be used to place a suspect at the crime scene. For example, chips of broken glass from a window may be lodged in a suspect's shoes or garments during the act of a burglary, or particles of headlight glass found at the scene of a hit-and-run accident may offer clues that can confirm the identity of a suspect vehicle. All of these possibilities require the comparison of glass fragments found on the suspect, whether a person or vehicle, with the shattered glass remaining at the crime scene.

Glass is a hard, brittle, amorphous substance that is composed of silicon oxides mixed with various metal oxides. When sand is mixed with other metal oxides, melted at high temperatures, and then cooled to a rigid condition without crystallization, the product is glass. The main ingredient in ordinary glass is sand. By adding soda (Na_2CO_3) to the sand, its melting point and viscosity are both lowered, making it much easier to work. Lime (CaO) is added to the sand and soda mixture so that the "soda-lime" glass will not dissolve in water. The forensic scientist is often requested to analyze soda-lime glass, which is used for manufacturing most window and bottle glass. The common metal oxides found in this type of glass are sodium, calcium, magnesium, and aluminum. In addition, a wide variety of special glasses can be made by substituting in whole or in part other metal oxides for the silica, sodium, and calcium oxides. For example, automobile headlights and heat-resistant glass, such as Pyrex, are manufactured by adding boron oxide to the oxide mix. These glasses are therefore known as **borosilicates.**

Another type of glass that the reader may be familiar with is **tempered glass.** This glass is made stronger than ordinary window glass by introducing stress through rapid heating and cooling of the glass surfaces. When tempered glass breaks, it does not shatter but rather fragments or "dices" into small squares with little splintering. Because of this safety feature, tempered glass is used in the side and rear windows of automobiles made in the United States, as well as in the windshields of some foreign-made cars. The windshields of all cars manufactured in the United States are constructed from laminated glass. This glass derives its strength by sandwiching one layer of plastic between two pieces of ordinary window glass.

For the forensic scientist, the problem of glass comparison is one that depends on the need to find and measure those properties that will associate one glass fragment with another while minimizing or eliminating the possible existence of other sources. Needless to say, considering the prevalence of glass in our society, it is easy to develop an appreciation for the magnitude of this analytical problem. Obviously, glass will possess its greatest evidential value when it can be individualized to one source. Such a determination, however, can only be made when the suspect and crime-scene fragments are assembled and physically fitted together. Comparisons of this type will require piecing together irregular edges of broken glass as well as matching all irregularities and striations on the broken surfaces (see Figure 4–10). The possibility that two pieces of glass originating from different sources will fit exactly together is so unlikely as to exclude all other sources from practical consideration.

Unfortunately, the majority of glass evidence presented to the criminalist is either too fragmentary or too minute to permit a comparison of this type. In such instances, the search for individual properties has proven to be a fruitless one. For example, the general chemical composition of various window glasses within the capability of current analytical methods has so far been found to be relatively uniform among various manufacturers and thus offers no basis for

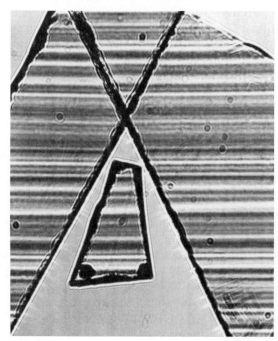

Figure 4–10.
Match of broken glass. Note that in addition to the physical fit of the edges, glass ream patterns are used to establish a relationship between the fragments. The normally invisible reams are visualized by focusing a point of light source on the glass so that it casts a shadow of the sample on photographic film. *Courtesy* Centre of Forensic Sciences, Toronto, Canada.

individualization. However, as more sensitive analytical techniques are developed, trace elements present in glass may prove to be distinctive and measurable characteristics.

At this time, the physical properties of density and refractive index are used most successfully for characterizing glass particles. However, these properties are class characteristics and as such will not provide the sole criteria for individualizing glass to a common source. They do, however, give the analyst sufficient data to evaluate the significance of a glass comparison, and the absence of comparable density and refractive index values will certainly serve to exclude glass fragments that originate from different sources.

It was previously indicated that a solid particle will either float, sink, or remain suspended in a liquid, depending on its density relative to the liquid medium. This knowledge gives the criminalist a rather precise and rapid method for comparing densities of glass. In a method known as **flotation,** a control glass particle is immersed in a liquid; a mixture of bromoform and bromobenzene may be used. The composition of the liquid is carefully adjusted by the addition of small amounts of bromoform or bromobenzene until the glass chip remains suspended in the liquid medium. At this point, the control glass and liquid each have the same density. Glass chips of approximately the same size and shape as the control are now added to the liquid for comparison. If both the unknown and the control particles remain suspended in the liquid, their densities are equal to each other and to that of the liquid.[1] Particles of different densities will either sink or float, depending on whether they are more or less dense than the liquid.

It is interesting to note that the density of a single sheet of window glass is not completely homogeneous throughout. It has a range of values that can differ by as much as 0.0003 g/ml. Therefore, in order to distinguish between the normal internal density variations of a single sheet of glass and those of glasses of different origins, it is advisable to let the comparative density approach but not exceed a sensitivity value of 0.0003 g/ml. The flotation method meets this requirement and can adequately distinguish glass particles that differ in density by 0.001 g/ml.

Once glass has been distinguished by a density determination, different origins are immediately concluded. Comparable density results, however, require the added comparison of refractive indices.

---

[1]As an added step, the analyst can determine the exact numerical density value of the particles of glass by transferring the liquid to a density meter. This instrument will electrically measure and calculate the liquid's density. See A. P. Beveridge and C. Semen, "Glass Density Measurement Using a Calculating Digital Density Meter," *The Canadian Society of Forensic Science Journal,* 12 (1979), 113.

This determination is best accomplished by an **immersion method.** For this, glass particles are immersed in a liquid medium whose refractive index is varied until it is equal to that of the glass particles. At this point, known as the **match point,** the observer will note the disappearance of the **Becke line** and minimum contrast between the glass and liquid medium. The Becke line is a bright halo that is observed near the border of a particle that is immersed in a liquid of a different refractive index. This halo disappears when the medium and fragment have similar refractive indices.

The refractive index of an immersion fluid is best varied by adjusting the temperature of the liquid. Temperature control is, of course, critical to the success of the procedure. One approach for carrying out this procedure is to heat the liquid in a special apparatus known as a **hot stage.** The glass is immersed in a high boiling liquid, usually a silicone oil, and heated at the rate of 0.2°C per minute until the match point is reached. Increasing the temperature of the liquid has a negligible effect on the refractive index of glass, while the liquid's index decreases at the rate of approximately 0.0004 per degree Celsius. The hot stage, as shown in Figure 4–11, is designed to be used in conjunction with a microscope, through which the examiner can observe the disappearance of the Becke line on minute glass particles that are illuminated with sodium D light or at other wavelengths of

Figure 4–11. Hot-stage microscope. *Courtesy* New Jersey State Police.

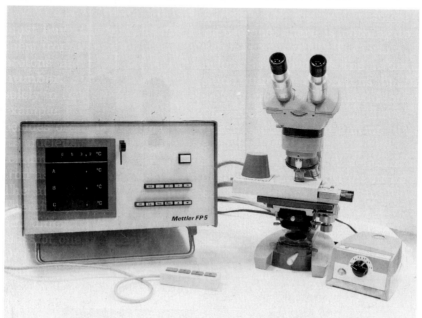

light. If all the glass fragments examined have similar match points, it can be concluded that they have comparable refractive indices (see Figure 4–12). Furthermore, the examiner can determine the refractive index value of the immersion fluid as it changes with temperature.

Figure 4–12.   Determination of the refractive index of glass. (a) Glass particles are immersed in a liquid of a much higher refractive index at a temperature of 77°C. (b) At 87°C the liquid still has a higher refractive index than the glass. (c) The refractive index of the liquid is closest to that of the glass at 97°C, as shown by the disappearance of the glass and the Becke lines. (d) At the higher temperature of 117°C, the liquid has a much lower index than the glass, and the glass is plainly visible. *Courtesy* Walter C. McCrone.

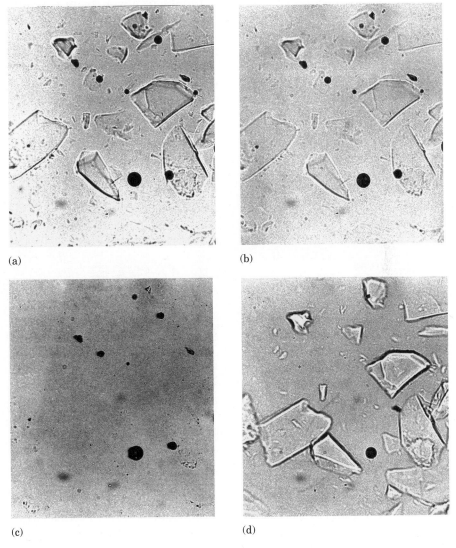

(a)

(b)

(c)

(d)

With this information, the exact numerical value of the glass refractive index can be calculated at the match point temperature.[2]

An automated approach for measuring the refractive index of glass fragments by temperature control using the immersion method with a hot stage is with the instrument known as GRIM 2[3] (see Figure 4–13). The GRIM 2 is a personal computer/video system designed to automate the measurements of the match temperature and refractive index for glass fragments. This instrument incorporates a video camera to view the glass fragments as they are being heated. As the immersion oil is heated or cooled, the contrast of the video image is measured continually until a minimum, the match point, is detected.

As with density, glass fragments removed from a single sheet of plate glass may not have a uniform refractive index value; instead, their values may vary by as much as 0.0002. Hence, for comparison purposes, the difference in refractive index between a control and questioned glass must exceed this value. This allows the examiner to differentiate between the normal internal variations present in a sheet of glass and those present in glasses that originate from completely different sources.

Figure 4–13.   An automated system for glass fragment identification.
Courtesy Foster and Freeman Limited, Worcestershire, U.K.

[2]A. R. Cassista and P. M. L. Sandercock, "Precision of Glass Refractive Index Measurements: Temperature Variation and Double Variation Methods, and the Value of Dispersion," *The Canadian Society of Forensic Science Journal*, 27 (1994), 203.

[3]Foster and Freeman Limited, 25 Swan Lane, Evesham, Worcestershire WRII 4PE, U.K.

A significant difference in either density or refractive index proves that the glasses examined do not have a common origin. But what if two pieces of glass exhibit comparable densities and comparable refractive indices? How certain can one be that they did, indeed, come from the same source? After all, there are untold millions of windows and other glass objects in this world. In order to provide a reasonable answer to this question, the FBI Laboratory has set about to collect density and refractive indices values from glass submitted to it for examination. What has emerged is a data bank correlating these values to their frequency of occurrence in the glass population of the United States. This collection is available to all forensic laboratories in the United States.

What this means is that once a criminalist has completed a comparison of glass fragments, he or she can correlate their density and refractive index values to their frequency of occurrence and can make a meaningful assessment as to the probability that the fragments were at one time from the same source. Figure 4–14 shows the distribution of refractive index values (measured with sodium D light) for nearly 1200 glasses analyzed by the FBI. The wide distribution of values clearly demonstrates that the refractive index is a highly distinctive property of glass and is thus useful for defining its frequency of occurrence and hence its evidential value. For example, a glass fragment having a refractive index value of 1.5290 is found in only 1 out of 1200 specimens, while glass with a value of 1.5180 occurs in 22 glasses out of 1200.

The distinction between tempered and nontempered glass particles can be made by slowly heating and then cooling the glass (a process known as *annealing*). The change in the refractive index value for tempered glass upon annealing is significantly greater when compared to nontempered glass and thus serves as a point of distinction.[4]

GLASS FRACTURES

Glass bends in response to any force that is exerted on any one of its surfaces; when the limit of its elasticity is reached, the glass fractures. Frequently, fractured window glass will reveal information that can be related to the force and direction of an impact; such knowledge may be useful for reconstructing events at a crime-scene investigation.

---

[4]A. R. Cassista and P. M. L. Sandercock, "Effects of Annealing on Toughened and Non-Toughened Glass," *The Canadian Society of Forensic Science Journal,* 27 (1994), 171.

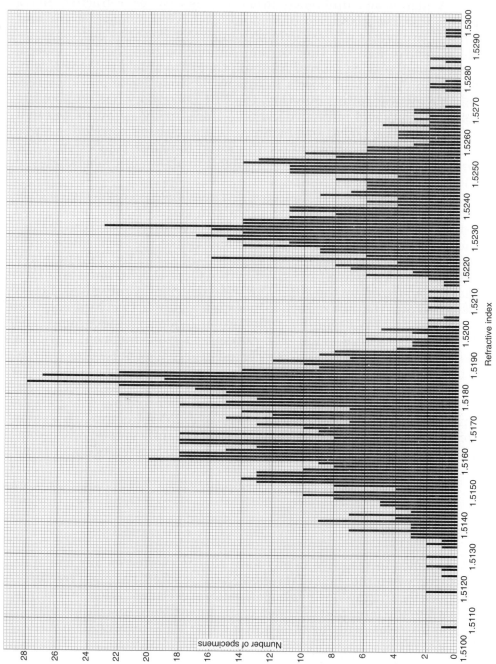

Figure 4-14. Frequency of occurrence of refractive index values (measured with sodium D light) for approximately 1200 flat glass specimens received by the FBI Laboratory. *Courtesy FBI Laboratory, Washington, D.C.*

The penetration of ordinary window glass by a projectile, whether it is a bullet or a stone, produces a familiar fracture pattern in which cracks both radiate outward and encircle the hole, as shown in Figure 4–15. The radiating lines are appropriately known as **radial fractures,** and the circular lines are termed **concentric fractures.**

Often it is difficult to determine just from the size and shape of a hole in glass whether it was made by a bullet or by some other projectile. For instance, a small stone thrown at a comparatively high speed against a pane of glass will often produce a hole very similar to that produced by a bullet. On the other hand, a large stone can completely shatter a pane of glass in a manner closely resembling the result of a close-range shot. However, in the latter instance, the presence of gunpowder deposits on the shattered glass fragments does point to damage caused by a firearm.

When it penetrates glass, a high-velocity projectile such as a bullet often leaves a round, crater-shaped hole that is surrounded by a nearly symmetrical pattern of radial and concentric cracks. The hole is inevitably wider at the exit side (Figure 4–16), and hence its examination is an important factor in determining the direction of impact. However, as the velocity of the penetrating projectile decreases, the irregularity of the shape of the hole and of its surrounding cracks increases, so that at some point the hole shape will provide no assistance for determining the direction of impact. At this time, information derived from an examination of the radial and concentric fracture lines may prove a useful alternative for determining the direction of impact.

When a force pushes on one side of a pane of glass, the elasticity of the glass permits it to bend in the direction of the force applied. Once the elastic limit is exceeded, the glass begins to crack. As shown in Figure 4–17, the first fractures form on the surface opposite that of the penetrating force, and these fractures develop into radial lines. The continued motion of the force places tension on the front surface

Figure 4–15.   Radial and concentric fracture lines in a sheet of glass. *Courtesy* New Jersey State Police.

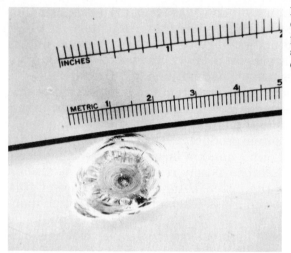

Figure 4–16.
Crater-shaped hole made by a pellet passing through glass. The upper surface is the exit side of the projectile. *Courtesy* New Jersey State Police.

of the glass, resulting in the formation of concentric cracks. An examination of the edges of the radial and concentric cracks frequently reveals. stress markings whose shape can be related to the side on which the window first cracked.

Stress marks, shown in Figure 4–18, are shaped like arches that are perpendicular to one glass surface and curved nearly parallel to the opposite surface. The importance of stress marks stems from the

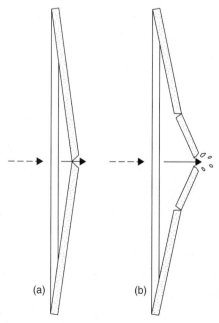

(a)   (b)

Figure 4–17.
Diagram showing the production of radial and concentric fractures in glass. (a) Radial cracks are formed first, commencing on the side of the glass opposite to the destructive force. (b) Concentric cracks occur afterward, starting on the same side as the force.

Figure 4–18.
Stress marks on the edge of a radial glass fracture. Arrow indicates direction of force. *Courtesy* New Jersey State Police.

observation that the perpendicular edge always faces the surface on which the crack originated. Thus, in examining the stress marks on the edge of a radial crack near the point of impact, the perpendicular end is always found to be located opposite the side from which the force of impact was applied. For a concentric fracture, the perpendicular end always faces the surface on which the force originated. A convenient way for remembering these observations is the 3R rule— **Radial cracks form a Right angle on the Reverse side of the force.** These facts will enable the examiner to determine readily the side on which a window was broken. Unfortunately, the absence of radial or concentric fracture lines prevents the above observations from being applied to broken tempered glass.

When there have been successive penetrations of glass, it is frequently possible to determine the sequence of impact by observing the existing fracture lines and their points of termination. **A fracture always terminates at an existing line of fracture.** In Figure 4–19, the fracture on the left preceded that on the right; we know this because the latter's radial fracture lines terminate at the cracks of the former.

COLLECTION AND PRESERVATION OF GLASS EVIDENCE

The gathering of glass evidence at the crime scene and from the suspect must be thorough if the examiner is to have any chance to individualize the fragments to a common source. If even the remotest possibility

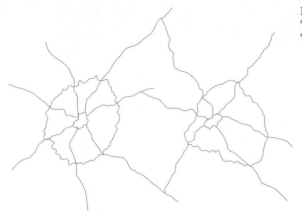

Figure 4–19.
Two bullet holes in a piece of glass.
The left hole preceded the right hole.

exists that fragments may be pieced together, every effort must be made to collect all the glass found. For example, collection of evidence at hit-and-run scenes must include all the broken parts of the headlight and reflector lenses. This evidence may ultimately prove to be an invaluable means of placing a suspect vehicle at the accident scene by actually matching the fragments with glass remaining in the headlight or reflector shell of the suspect vehicle. In addition, an examination of the headlight's filaments may resolve any questions regarding whether or not an automobile's headlights were on or off before the impact (see Figure 4–20).

When an individual fit is thought improbable, the evidence collector must submit all glass evidence found in the possession of the suspect along with a representative sample of broken glass remaining at the crime scene. This control glass should always be taken from any remaining glass in the window or door frames, as close as possible to the point of breakage. About one square inch of sample is usually adequate for this purpose. The glass fragments should be packaged in solid containers to avoid further breakage. If the suspect's shoes and/or clothing are to be examined for the presence of glass fragments, they should be individually wrapped in paper and transmitted to the laboratory. It is best that the field investigator avoid removing such evidence from garments unless it is thought absolutely necessary for its preservation.

When a determination of the direction of impact is desired, all broken glass must be recovered and submitted for analysis. Wherever possible, the exterior and interior surfaces of the glass must be indicated. In cases in which this is not immediately apparent, the presence of dirt, paint, grease, or putty may provide an indication as to the exterior surface of the glass.

Figure 4–20. Presence of oxides on the lower filament indicates the filament was hot when it was exposed to air. Thus, the filament must have been on prior to impact. *Courtesy* New Jersey State Police.

FORENSIC CHARACTERISTICS OF SOIL

There are many definitions for the term *soil;* however, for forensic purposes, soil may be thought of as including any disintegrated surface material, both natural and artificial, that lies on or near the earth's surface. Therefore, the forensic examination of soil is not only concerned with the analysis of naturally occurring rocks, minerals, vegetation, and animal matter—it also encompasses the detection of such manufactured objects as glass, paint chips, asphalt, brick fragments, and cinders, whose presence may impart soil with characteristics that will make it unique to a particular location. When this material is collected accidentally or deliberately in a manner that will associate it with a crime under investigation, it becomes valuable physical evidence.[5]

The value of soil as evidence rests with its prevalence at crime scenes and its transferability between the scene and the criminal. Thus, soil or dried mud found adhering to a suspect's clothing or shoes, or to an automobile, when compared to soil samples collected

---

[5]E. P. Junger, "Assessing the Unique Characteristics of Close-Proximity Soil Samples: Just How Useful Is Soil Evidence?" *Journal of Forensic Sciences,* 41 (1996), 27.

at the crime site, may provide associative evidence that can link a suspect or object to the crime scene. As with most types of physical evidence, forensic soil analysis is comparative in nature; soil found in the possession of the suspect must be carefully collected to be compared to soil samplings from the crime scene and the surrounding vicinity. However, one should not rule out the value of soil even if the site of the crime has not been ascertained. For instance, a person or object containing small amounts of soil may be found far from the actual site of a crime. A geologist having knowledge of local geology, and with the aid of geological maps, may be able to direct police to the general vicinity where the soil was originally picked up and the crime committed.

Most soils can be differentiated and distinguished by their gross appearance. A side-by-side visual comparison of the color and texture of soil specimens is easy to perform and provides a sensitive property for distinguishing soils that originate from different locations. It is important to remember that the color of soil is darker when it is wet; therefore, color comparisons must always be made when all the samples are dried under identical laboratory conditions. It is estimated that there are nearly 1100 distinguishable soil colors; hence, the comparison of color offers a logical first step in a forensic soil comparison.

Low-power microscopic examination of soil will reveal the presence of plant and animal materials as well as of artificial debris. Further high-power microscopic examination will aid in the characterization of minerals and rocks present in earth materials. Although this approach to the forensic identification of soil requires the expertise of an investigator trained in geology, it can provide the most varied and significant points of comparison between soil samples. Only through a careful examination and comparison of the minerals and rocks naturally present in soil can one take advantage of the large number of variations that exist between soils and thus add to the evidential value of a positive comparison.[6] A mineral is a naturally occurring crystal, and like any other crystal, its physical properties—for example, color, geometric shape, density, and refractive index or birefringence—are most useful for identification. More than 2200 minerals are known to exist; however, most of these are so rare that the forensic geologist will usually encounter only about 40 of the more common ones. Rocks are composed of a combination of minerals and therefore exist in thousands of varieties on the earth's surface. Their identification is usually made by characterizing their mineral content and grain size.

---

[6]W. J. Graves, "A Mineralogical Soil Classification Technique for the Forensic Scientist," *Journal of Forensic Sciences,* 24 (1979), 323.

Considering the vast variety of minerals and rocks and the possible occurrence of artificial debris that may be present in soil, the forensic geologist is presented with many points of comparison between two or more specimens. The number of comparative points and their frequency of occurrence must all be taken into consideration before similarity between specimens can be concluded and the probability of common origin judged.

Rocks and minerals are not only present in earth materials but also used to manufacture a wide variety of industrial and commercial products. For example, it is not uncommon to find that the tools and garments of an individual suspected of breaking into a safe will contain traces of safe insulation. Safe insulation may be made from a wide combination of mineral mixtures that can provide significant points of identification. Similarly, building materials, such as brick, plaster, and concrete blocks, are combinations of minerals and rocks that can easily be recognized and compared microscopically to similar minerals found on the breaking and entering suspect.

Many forensic laboratories presently rely on the **density-gradient tube technique** to compare soil specimens. Typically, glass tubes 6 to 10 millimeters in diameter and from 25 to 40 centimeters in length are filled with layers of two liquids mixed in varying proportions so that each layer has a different density value. For example, tetrabromoethane (density 2.96 g/ml) and ethanol (density 0.789 g/ml) may be mixed so that the ratios of the two liquids in each layer are such that each successive layer has a lower density than the preceding one, from the bottom to the top of the tube. The simplest gradient tube may have from six to ten layers, in which the bottom layer is pure tetrabromoethane and the top layer is pure ethanol, with corresponding variations of concentration in the layers between these two extremes. When soil is added to the density-gradient tube, its particles will sink to the portion of the tube that has a density of equal value; the particles will remain suspended in the liquid at this point. In this way, a density distribution pattern of soil particles can be obtained and compared to other specimens treated in a similar manner (Figure 4–21). This procedure is used by many crime laboratories to compare soil evidence. However, there is evidence that this test is far from definitive, in that many soils collected from different locations yield similar density distribution patterns.[7] At best, the density-gradient test has been shown to be useful for comparing soils when it's used in combination with other tests.

---

[7]K. Chaperlin and P. S. Howarth, "Soil Comparison by the Density Gradient Method—A Review and Evaluation," *Forensic Science International,* 23 (1983), 161–77.

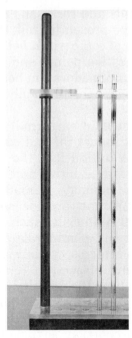

Figure 4–21.
A soil comparison by density-gradient
tubes. *Courtesy* Philadelphia Police
Dept. Laboratory.

The ultimate forensic value of soil evidence depends on its variation at the crime scene. If, for example, soil is indistinguishable for miles surrounding the location of a crime, with the methods used in the examination, it will have limited value in associating soil found on the suspect with that particular site. Significant conclusions relating the suspect to a particular crime-scene location through a soil comparison may be made when variations in soil composition occur every 10 to 100 yards from the crime site. However, even when such variations do exist, it is usually not possible for the forensic geologist to individualize soil to any one location unless an unusual combination of rare minerals, rocks, or artificial debris can be located.

Up to this time, there have been no statistically valid forensic studies on the variability of soil evidence. A pilot study recently conducted in southern Ontario, Canada, seems to indicate that this part of Canada has soil showing extensive diversity. It was found that the probability is smaller than 1 in 50 of finding two soils that are indistinguishable in both color and mineral properties but that originate in two different locations separated by a distance on the order of 1000 feet. Based on these preliminary results, similar diversity may be expected in the northern United States, Canada, northern Europe, and much of the former Soviet Union. However, such probability values can only serve as a general indication of the variation of soil within these geographical areas. It must be emphasized that each crime scene must be evaluated separately to establish its own soil variation probabilities.

COLLECTION AND PRESERVATION OF SOIL EVIDENCE

The importance of establishing the variation of soil at the crime-scene area must be given primary consideration when the evidence collector gathers soil specimens. For this reason, control soils are to be collected at various intervals within a 100-yard radius of the crime scene, as well as at the site of the crime, for comparison to the questioned soil. Additionally, soil specimens should also be collected at all possible alibi locations that the suspect may claim. It is important that the specimens gathered be representative of the soil that was removed by the suspect. In most cases, this means that only the top-surface layer of soil will be picked up during the commission of a crime. Thus, control specimens must be removed from the surface without digging too deeply into the unrepresentative subsurface layers. A quantity of soil equal to approximately a tablespoon or two is all that is required by the laboratory for a thorough comparative analysis. All specimens collected should be packaged in individual containers, such as plastic vials. Each vial should be marked to indicate the location at which the sampling was made.

Soil found on a suspect must be carefully preserved for analysis. If it is found adhering to an object, as in the case of soil on a shoe, the investigator must not remove it. Instead, each object should be individually wrapped in paper, with the soil intact, and transmitted to the laboratory. Similarly, no effort should be made to remove loose soil adhering to garments; these items should be carefully wrapped individually in paper bags and sent to the laboratory for analysis. Care must be taken that all particles that may accidentally fall off the garment during transportation will remain within the paper bag.

When a lump of soil is found, it should be collected and preserved intact. For example, an automobile tends to collect and build up layers of soil under fenders, body, and so on. In some situations, the impact of an automobile with another object may jar some of this soil loose. Once the suspect car has been apprehended, a comparison of the soil left at the scene with soil remaining on the automobile may help establish that the car was present at the accident scene. In these situations, separate samples are collected from under all the fender and frame areas of the vehicle; care is taken to remove the soil in lump form in order to preserve the order in which the soil was deposited onto the car. Undoubtedly, during the normal use of an automobile, soil will be picked up from numerous locations over a period of months and years. This layering effect may serve to impart soil with greater variation, and hence greater evidential value, than that which is normally associated with loose soil.

The prevalence of glass and soil in our environment makes them common types of physical evidence at crime scenes. Their proper collection and preservation by the criminal investigator will help ensure that a proper scientific examination can support investigative conclusions placing a suspect or object at the crime scene. Equally important is that glass and soil, like other types of physical evidence, when properly collected and examined may serve to exonerate the innocent from involvement in a crime.

REVIEW QUESTIONS

1. A _____ property describes the behavior of a substance without reference to any other substance.
2. A _____ property is one that describes the behavior of a substance when it reacts or combines with another substance.
3. The _____ system of measurement was devised by the French Academy of Science in 1791.
4. The basic units of measurement for length, mass, and volume in the metric system are the _____, _____, and _____, respectively.
5. A centigram is equivalent to _____ of a gram.
6. A milliliter is equivalent to _____ liter.
7. 0.2 grams is equivalent to _____ milligrams.
8. One cubic centimeter (cc) is equivalent to one _____.
9. One meter is slightly longer than a yard. (True, False)
10. The equivalent of one pound in grams is _____.
11. A liter is slightly larger than a quart. (True, False)
12. _____ is a measure of a substance's heat intensity.
13. There are _____ degrees Fahrenheit between the freezing and boiling points of water.
14. There are _____ degrees Celsius between the freezing and boiling points of water.
15. The amount of matter an object contains determines its _____.
16. The simplest type of balance for weighing is the _____.

17. Mass per unit volume defines the property of _____.
18. If an object is immersed in a liquid of greater density, it will (sink, float).
19. The bending of a lightwave because of a change in velocity is called _____.
20. The physical property of _____ is determined by the ratio of the velocity of light in a vacuum to light's velocity in a substance.
21. Solids having an orderly arrangement of their constituent atoms are crystalline. (True, False)
22. Solids that have their atoms randomly arranged are said to be _____.
23. The crystal calcite has two indices of refraction. The difference between these two values is known as _____.
24. The process of separating light into its component colors or frequencies is known as _____.
25. A hard, brittle, amorphous substance composed mainly of silicon oxides is _____.
26. Glass that can be physically pieced together has _____ characteristics.
27. The two most useful physical properties of glass for forensic comparisons are _____ and _____.
28. Comparing the relative densities of glass fragments is readily accomplished by a method known as _____.
29. When glass is immersed in a liquid of similar refractive index, its _____ will disappear, and minimum contrast between the glass and liquid will be observed.
30. The exact numerical density and refractive indices of glass can be correlated to _____ in order to assess the evidential value of the comparison.
31. The fracture lines radiating outward from a crack in glass are known as _____ fractures.
32. A crater-shaped hole in glass is (narrower, wider) on the side where the projectile entered the glass.
33. It is easy to determine from the size and shape of a hole in glass whether it was made by a bullet or some other projectile. (True, False)
34. Stress marks on the edge of a radical crack are always perpendicular to the edge of the surface on which the impact force originated. (True, False)
35. A fracture line (will, will not) terminate at an existing line fracture.

36. The vast majority of soils have indistinguishable color and texture. (True, False)
37. Naturally occurring crystals commonly found in soils are _____.
38. A comparison of the density of soil particles is readily accomplished through the use of _____ tubes.
39. The ultimate value of soil as evidence is dependent on its variation at the crime scene. (True, False)

FURTHER REFERENCES

Dolan, D. N., "Vehicle Lights and Their Use as Evidence," *Journal of the Forensic Science Society,* 11 (1971), 69–82.

Dudley, R. J., and K. Smalldon, "The Evaluation of Methods for Soil Analysis under Simulated Scenes of Crime Conditions," *Forensic Science International,* 12 (1978), 49–60.

Fisher, Barry J., *Techniques of Crime Scene Investigation,* 5th ed. New York: Elsevier Science Publishing Co., 1992.

Hickman, D. A., "Linking Criminals to the Scene of the Crime with Glass Analysis," *Analytical Chemistry,* 56 (1984), 844A–52A.

McJunkins, Steven P., and John I. Thornton, "Glass Fracture Analysis—A Review," *Forensic Science,* 2 (1973), 1–27.

Miller, Elmer T., "Forensic Glass Comparisons," in *Forensic Science Handbook,* R. Saferstein, ed. Englewood Cliffs, N.J.: Prentice Hall, 1982.

Murray, Raymond C., "Forensic Examination of Soil," in *Forensic Science Handbook,* R. Saferstein, ed. Englewood Cliffs, N.J.: Prentice Hall, 1982.

———, and John C. F. Tedrow, *Forensic Geology,* 2nd ed. Englewood Cliffs, N.J.: Prentice Hall, 1992.

Ojena, S. M., and P. R. De Forest, "Precise Refractive Index Determination by the Immersion Method, Using Phase Contract Microscopy and the Mettler Hot Stage," *Journal of the Forensic Science Society,* 12 (1973), 315–29.

5 ORGANIC ANALYSIS

In the previous chapter, some physical properties were described and used to characterize glass and soil evidence. Before we can apply other physical properties, as well as chemical properties, to the identification and comparison of evidence, we need to gain an insight into the composition of matter. Beginning with knowledge of the fundamental building block of all substances—the element—it will be convenient for us to classify all evidence as either organic or inorganic. The procedures used to measure the properties associated with each class are distinctly different and merit separate chapters for their description. In later chapters, we will continually return to these procedures as we discuss the examination of the various kinds of physical evidence. This chapter will be devoted, in large part, to reviewing a variety of techniques and instruments that have become the indispensable tools of the forensic scientist for examining organic evidence.

ELEMENTS AND COMPOUNDS

Matter is anything that has a mass and occupies space. As we examine the world that surrounds us and consider the countless variety of materials that we encounter, we must consider it one of humankind's most remarkable accomplishments to have discovered the concept of the atom to explain the composition of all matter. This search had its earliest contribution from the ancient Greek philosophers, who suggested air, water, fire, and earth as matter's fundamental building blocks. It culminated with the development of the atomic theory and the discovery of matter's simplest identity, the **element.**

An element is the simplest substance known and provides the building block from which all matter is composed. At present, 110 elements have been identified (see Table 5–1); of these, 89 occur naturally on earth, and the remainder have been created in the laboratory. In Figure 5–1, all the elements are listed by name and symbol in a form that has become known as the **periodic table.** This table is most useful to chemists because it systematically arranges elements with similar chemical properties in the same vertical row or group.

For convenience, chemists have chosen letter symbols to represent the elements. Many of these symbols come from the first letter of the element's English name—for example, carbon (C), hydrogen (H), and oxygen (O). Others are two-letter abbreviations of the English name—calcium (Ca), zinc (Zn). Some of the symbols are derived from the first letters of Latin or Greek names. Thus, the symbol for silver, Ag, comes from the Latin name *argentum,* copper, Cu, from the Latin *cuprium,* and helium, He, from the Greek name *helios.*

The smallest particle of an element that can exist and still retain its identity as that element is the atom. When we write the symbol C we mean one atom of carbon; the chemical symbol for carbon dioxide, CO_2, signifies one atom of carbon combined with two atoms of oxygen. When two or more elements are combined to form a substance, as with carbon dioxide, there is created a new substance, different in its physical and chemical properties from its elemental components. This new material is called a **compound.** Compounds contain at least two elements. Considering that there are 89 natural elements, it is not difficult to imagine the large number of possible elemental combinations that may exist to form compounds. Not surprisingly, over six million known compounds have already been identified.

Just as the atom is the basic particle of an element, the molecule is the smallest unit of a compound. Thus, a molecule of carbon dioxide is represented by the symbol CO_2, and a molecule of table salt is symbolized by NaCl, representing the combination of one atom of the element sodium (Na) with one atom of the element chlorine (Cl).

As we look around us and view the materials that comprise our home planet, Earth, it becomes an awesome task even to attempt to estimate the number of different kinds of matter that exist. A much more logical approach is to classify matter according to the physical form it takes. These forms are called **physical states.** There are three such states: **solid, liquid,** and **gas (vapor).** A solid is rigid and

TABLE 5–1.
LIST OF ELEMENTS WITH THEIR SYMBOLS
AND ATOMIC MASSES

Element	Symbol	Atomic Mass[a] (amu)	Element	Symbol	Atomic Mass[a] (amu)
Actinium	Ac	(227)	Neon	Ne	20.179
Aluminum	Al	26.9815	Neptunium	Np	237.0482
Americium	Am	(243)	Nickel	Ni	58.71
Antimony	Sb	121.75	Niobium	Nb	92.9064
Argon	Ar	39.948	Nitrogen	N	14.0067
Arsenic	As	74.9216	Nobelium	No	(259)
Astatine	At	(210)	Osmium	Os	190.2
Barium	Ba	137.34	Oxygen	O	15.9994
Berkelium	Bk	(247)	Palladium	Pd	106.4
Beryllium	Be	9.01218	Phosphorus	P	30.9738
Bismuth	Bi	208.9806	Platinum	Pt	195.09
Boron	B	10.81	Plutonium	Pu	(244)
Bromine	Br	79.904	Polonium	Po	(209)
Cadmium	Cd	112.40	Potassium	K	39.102
Calcium	Ca	40.08	Praseodymium	Pr	140.9077
Californium	Cf	(251)	Promethium	Pm	(145)
Carbon	C	12.011	Protactinium	Pa	231.0359
Cerium	Ce	140.12	Radium	Ra	226.0254
Cesium	Cs	132.9055	Radon	Rn	(222)
Chlorine	Cl	35.453	Rhenium	Re	186.2
Chromium	Cr	51.996	Rhodium	Rh	102.9055
Cobalt	Co	58.9332	Rubidium	Rb	85.4678
Copper	Cu	63.546	Ruthenium	Ru	101.07
Curium	Cm	(247)	Samarium	Sm	105.4
Dysprosium	Dy	162.50	Scandium	Sc	44.9559
Einsteinium	Es	(254)	Selenium	Se	78.96
Erbium	Er	167.26	Silicon	Si	28.086
Europium	Eu	151.96	Silver	Ag	107.868
Fermium	Fm	(257)	Sodium	Na	22.9898
Fluorine	F	18.9984	Strontium	Sr	87.62
Francium	Fr	(223)	Sulfur	S	32.06
Gadolinium	Gd	157.25	Tantalum	Ta	180.9479
Gallium	Ga	69.72	Technetium	Tc	98.9062
Germanium	Ge	72.59	Tellurium	Te	127.60
Gold	Au	196.9665	Terbium	Tb	158.9254
Hafnium	Hf	178.49	Thallium	Tl	204.37
Helium	He	4.00260	Thorium	Th	232.0381
Holmium	Ho	164.9303	Thulium	Tm	168.9342
Hydrogen	H	1.0080	Tin	Sn	118.69
Indium	In	114.82	Titanium	Ti	47.90
Iodine	I	126.9045	Tungsten	W	183.85
Iridium	Ir	192.22	Unnilennium	Une	(266?)
Iron	Fe	55.847	Unnilhexium	Unh	(263)
Krypton	Kr	83.80	Unniloctium	Uno	(265)
Lanthanum	La	138.9055	Unnilpentium	Unp	(262)
Lawrencium	Lr	(260)	Unnilquadium	Unq	(261)
Lead	Pb	207.2	Unnilseptium	Uns	(261)
Lithium	Li	6.941	Unununium	Uun	(272)
Lutetium	Lu	174.97	Uranium	U	238.029
Magnesium	Mg	24.305	Vanadium	V	50.9414
Manganese	Mn	54.9380	Xenon	Xe	131.30
Mendelevium	Md	(258)	Ytterbium	Yb	173.04
Mercury	Hg	200.59	Yttrium	Y	88.9059
Molybdenum	Mo	95.94	Zinc	Zn	65.57
Neodymium	Nd	144.24	Zirconium	Zr	91.22

[a]Based on the assigned relative atomic mass of C = exactly 12; parentheses denote the mass number of the isotope with the longest half-life.

Group

Period	IA	IIA	IIIB	IVB	VB	VIB	VIIB	VIII	VIII	VIII	IB	IIB	IIIA	IVA	VA	VIA	VIIA	O
1	1 H																	2 He
2	3 Li	4 Be											5 B	6 C	7 N	8 O	9 F	10 Ne
3	11 Na	12 Mg											13 Al	14 Si	15 P	16 S	17 Cl	18 Ar
4	19 K	20 Ca	21 Sc	22 Ti	23 V	24 Cr	25 Mn	26 Fe	27 Co	28 Ni	29 Cu	30 Zn	31 Ga	32 Ge	33 As	34 Se	35 Br	36 Kr
5	37 Rb	38 Sr	39 Y	40 Zr	41 Nb	42 Mo	43 Tc	44 Ru	45 Rh	46 Pd	47 Ag	48 Cd	49 In	50 Sn	51 Sb	52 Te	53 I	54 Xe
6	55 Cs	56 Ba	57 La a	72 Hf	73 Ta	74 W	75 Re	76 Os	77 Ir	78 Pt	79 Au	80 Hg	81 Tl	82 Pb	83 Bi	84 Po	85 At	86 Rn
7	87 Fr	88 Ra	89 Ac b	104 Unq	105 Unp	106 Unh	107 Uns	108 Uno	109 Une	110 Uun								

a Lanthanide series	58 Ce	59 Pr	60 Nd	61 Pm	62 Sm	63 Eu	64 Gd	65 Tb	66 Dy	67 Ho	68 Er	69 Tm	70 Yb	71 Lu
b Actinide series	90 Th	91 Pa	92 U	93 Np	94 Pu	95 Am	96 Cm	97 Bk	98 Cf	99 Es	100 Fm	101 Md	102 No	103 Lr

Figure 5–1.   The periodic table.

132

therefore has a definite shape and volume. A liquid also occupies a specific volume, but its fluidity causes it to take the shape of the container in which it is residing. A gas has neither a definite shape nor volume, and it will completely fill any container into which it is placed.

Substances can change from one state to another. For example, as water is heated, it is converted from a liquid form into a vapor. At a high enough temperature (100°C), water boils and is rapidly changed into steam. Similarly, at 0°C, water solidifies or freezes into ice. Under certain conditions, some solids can be converted directly into a gaseous state. For instance, a piece of dry ice (solid carbon dioxide) left standing at room temperature will quickly form carbon dioxide vapor and disappear. This change of state from a solid to a gas is called **sublimation.**

In each of these examples, it is important to recognize that no new chemical species are formed; matter is simply being changed from one physical state to another. Water, whether it is in the form of liquid, ice, or steam, remains chemically H_2O. Simply, what has been altered are the attractive forces that exist between the water molecules. In a solid, these forces are very strong, and the molecules are held closely together in a rigid state. In a liquid, the attractive forces are not as strong, and the molecules have more mobility. Finally, in the vapor state, there are no longer appreciable attractive forces between the molecules; thus, they are permitted to move in any and all directions at will.

Chemists are forever combining different substances, no matter whether they are in the solid, liquid, or gaseous states, hoping to create new and useful products. Our everyday observations should make it apparent that not all attempts at mixing matter can be productive. For instance, oil spills testify to the fact that oil and water do not mix. **Whenever a situation exists in which substances can be distinguished by a visible boundary, different phases are said to exist.** Thus, oil floating on water is an example of a two-phase system. The oil and water each constitute a separate liquid phase, clearly distinct from each other. Similarly, when sugar is first added to water, it will not dissolve, and there exist two distinctly different phases, the solid sugar and the liquid water. However, after stirring, all the sugar will dissolve, leaving just one liquid phase.

SELECTING AN ANALYTICAL TECHNIQUE

Now that the basic components of matter have been defined, the proper selection of analytical techniques that will allow the forensic scientist to identify or compare matter can best be understood by categorizing all substances into one of two broad groups: **organics** and **inorganics.**

Organic substances contain the element carbon, commonly in combination with one or more of the following elements: hydrogen, oxygen, nitrogen, sulfur, phosphorus, chlorine, and bromine. Inorganic substances encompass all other known chemical substances. Each of these two broad groups has properties that are quite distinctive and characteristic. Thus, once the analyst has determined whether a material is organic or inorganic, the properties to be measured and the choice of analytical techniques to be used will generally be the same for all materials falling into each group.

Another consideration in selecting an analytical technique is the need for either a **qualitative** or a **quantitative** determination. The former relates just to the identity of the material, whereas the latter requires the determination of the percentage combination of the components of a mixture. Hence, a qualitative identification of a powder may reveal the presence of heroin and quinine, whereas a quantitative analysis may conclude the presence of 10 percent heroin and 90 percent quinine. Obviously, a qualitative identification must precede any attempt at quantitation, for little value is served by attempting to quantitate a material without first determining its identity. Essentially, a qualitative analysis of a material will require the determination of numerous properties using a variety of analytical techniques. On the other hand, a quantitative measurement is usually accomplished by the precise measurement of a single property of the material.

Most of the evidence currently received by crime laboratories requires the identification of organic compounds. These compounds may include substances such as commonly abused drugs (e.g., alcohol, marijuana, heroin, amphetamines, and barbiturates), synthetic fibers, petroleum products, paint binders, and high-order explosives. As we have already observed, organic compounds are composed of a combination of a relatively small number of elements that must include carbon; fortunately, the nature of the forces or bonds that exist between these elements is such that the resultant compounds can readily be characterized by their absorption of light. The study of the absorption of light by chemical substances, known as **spectrophotometry,** serves as a basic tool for the characterization and identification of organic materials. Although spectrophotometry is most applicable to organic analysis, its optimum utilization requires that a material be in a relatively pure state. Because the purity of physical evidence is almost always beyond the control of the criminalist, this criterion often is not met. For this reason, the analytical technique of **chromatography** is widely applied for the analysis of physical evidence. **Chromatography is a means of separating and tentatively**

identifying the components of a mixture. We will discuss both of these techniques in this chapter.

CHROMATOGRAPHY

THEORY OF CHROMATOGRAPHY

Chromatography as a technique for purifying substances is particularly useful for analyzing the multicomponent specimens that are frequently received in the crime laboratory. For example, illicit drugs sold on the street are not manufactured to meet government labeling standards; instead, they may be diluted with practically any material that is at the disposal of the drug dealer in order to increase the quantity of the product that is made available to prospective customers. Hence, the task of identifying an illicit drug preparation would be an arduous one without the aid of chromatographic methods to first separate the mixture into its components.

The theory of chromatography has as its basis the observation that chemical substances have a tendency to partially escape into the surrounding environment when dissolved in a liquid or when absorbed on a solid surface. This is best illustrated by a gas dissolved in a beaker of water kept at a constant temperature. It will be convenient for us to characterize the water in the beaker as the liquid phase and the air above it as the gas phase. If the beaker is covered with a bell jar, as shown in Figure 5–2, some of the gas molecules (represented by the dark balls) will escape from the water into the surrounding enclosed air. The molecules remaining behind are said to be in the liquid phase; those molecules that have found their way into the air are said to be in the gas phase. As the gas molecules continue their escape

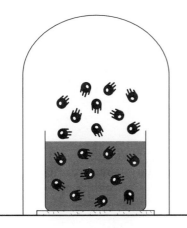

Figure 5–2.
Evaporation of a liquid.

into the surrounding air, they will begin to accumulate above the water; here, random motion will carry some of them back into the water. Eventually, a point will be reached at which the number of molecules leaving the water will be equal to the number returning. At this time, the liquid and gas phases are said to be in **equilibrium.** If the temperature of the water is increased, the equilibrium state will readjust itself to a point where more gas molecules will move into the gas phase.

This behavior was first observed in 1803 by a British chemist, William Henry. His explanation of this phenomenon, known appropriately as Henry's Law, may be stated as follows: *When a volatile chemical compound is dissolved in a liquid and is brought to equilibrium with air, there is a fixed ratio between the concentration of the volatile compound in air and its concentration in the liquid, and this ratio remains constant for a given temperature.*

The distribution or partitioning of a gas between the liquid and gas phases is determined by the solubility of the gas in the liquid. The higher its solubility, the greater the tendency of the gas molecules to remain in the liquid phase. If two different gases are simultaneously dissolved in the same liquid, each will reach a state of equilibrium with the surrounding air independently of the other. For example, as shown in Figure 5–3, gas A (black balls) and gas B (white balls) are both dissolved in water. At equilibrium, gas A has a greater number of its molecules dissolved in the water as compared to B. This is so because A is more soluble in water than B.

Now return to the concept of chromatography. In Figures 5–2 and 5–3, both phases—liquid and gas—were kept stationary; that is, they were not moving. During a chromatographic process, this is not the case; instead, one phase is always made to move continuously in one direction over a stationary or fixed phase. For example, in Figure 5–3, showing the two gases A and B dissolved in water, chromatography

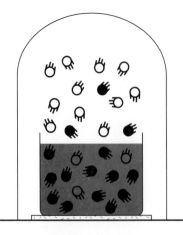

Figure 5–3.
At equilibrium, there are more gas A molecules (black balls) than gas B molecules (white balls) in the liquid phase.

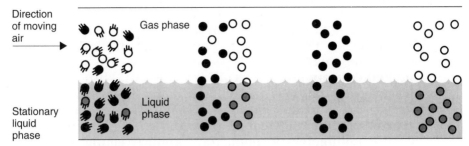

Direction of moving air →

Gas phase

Stationary liquid phase

Liquid phase

Figure 5–4. In this illustration of chromatography, the molecules represented by the white balls have a greater affinity for the upper phase and hence will be pushed along at a faster rate by the moving air. Eventually, the two sets of molecules will separate from each other, completing the chromatographic process.

will occur only when the air is forced to move continuously in one direction over the water. Because B has a greater percentage of its molecules in the moving gas phase as compared to A, its molecules will travel over the liquid at a faster pace than those of A. Eventually, when the moving phase has advanced a reasonable distance, B will become entirely separated from A and the chromatographic process will be complete. This process is illustrated in Figure 5–4.

Simply, we can think of chromatography as being analogous to a race between chemical compounds. At the starting line, all the participating substances are mixed together; however, as the race progresses, those materials that have a preference for the moving phase will slowly pull ahead of those substances that prefer to remain in the stationary phase. Finally, at the completion of the race, all the participants will be separated, each crossing the finish line at different times.

The different types of chromatographic systems that can exist are as varied as the possible number of stationary and moving-phase combinations that can be devised. However, three chromatographic processes—gas chromatography (GC), high-performance liquid chromatography (HPLC), and thin-layer chromatography (TLC)—are found to be most applicable for solving many of the analytical problems encountered in the crime laboratory.

GAS CHROMATOGRAPHY (GC)

Gas chromatography (GC) separates mixtures on the basis of their distribution between a stationary liquid phase and a moving gas phase. This technique is widely utilized because of its ability to resolve a highly complex mixture into its components within a time period that is usually measured in minutes.

In gas chromatography, the moving phase is actually a gas called the **carrier gas,** which flows through a column constructed of stainless steel or glass. The stationary phase is a thin film of liquid contained within the column. Two types of columns are in current use: the **packed column** and the **capillary column.** With the packed column, the stationary phase is a thin film of liquid that is fixed onto small granular particles packed into the column. This column is usually constructed of stainless steel or glass and is 2 to 6 meters in length and about 3 millimeters in diameter. Capillary columns are composed of glass and are much longer than packed columns—15 to 60 meters in length. These types of columns are very narrow, ranging from 0.25 to 0.75 millimeter in diameter. Capillary columns can be made narrower than packed columns since their stationary liquid phase is actually coated as a very thin film directly onto the column's inner wall. In any case, as the carrier gas flows through the packed or capillary column, it carries along with it the components of a mixture that have been injected into the column. Those components having a greater affinity for the moving gas phase will travel through the column at a faster rate as compared to those having a greater affinity for the stationary liquid phase. Eventually, after the mixture has traversed the length of the column, it will emerge separated into its components.

A simplified scheme of the gas chromatograph is shown in Figure 5–5. The operation of the instrument can be summed up briefly as

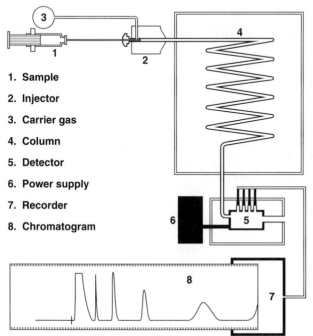

1. Sample
2. Injector
3. Carrier gas
4. Column
5. Detector
6. Power supply
7. Recorder
8. Chromatogram

Figure 5–5.
Basic gas chromatography. Gas chromatography permits the rapid separation of complex mixtures into individual compounds and allows identification and quantitative determination of each compound. As shown, a sample is introduced by a syringe (1) into a heated injection chamber (2). A constant stream of nitrogen gas (3) flows through the injector, carrying the sample into the column (4), which contains a thin film of liquid. The sample is separated in the column, and the carrier gas and separated components emerge from the column and enter the detector (5). Signals developed by the detector activate the recorder (7), which makes a permanent record of the separation by tracing a series of peaks on the chromatograph (8). The time of elution identifies the component present, and the peak area identifies the concentration. *Courtesy* Varian Instruments, Calif.

follows: A gas stream, the so-called carrier gas, is fed into the column at a constant rate. The carrier gas is chemically inert and is generally nitrogen or helium. The sample under investigation is injected as a liquid into a heated injection port with a syringe, where it is immediately vaporized and swept into the column by the carrier gas. The column itself is heated in an oven in order to keep the sample in a vapor state as it travels through the column. In the column, the components of the sample travel in the direction of the carrier gas flow at speeds that are determined by their distribution between the stationary and moving phases. Assuming that the analyst has selected the proper liquid phase and has made the column long enough, the components of the sample will be completely separated as they emerge from the column.

As each component emerges from the column, it enters a detector. One type of detector uses a flame to ionize the emerging chemical substance, thus generating an electrical signal. The signal is recorded onto a strip-chart recorder as a function of time. This written record of the separation is called a **chromatogram.** A gas chromatogram is a plot of the recorder response (vertical axis) versus time (horizontal axis). A typical chromatogram will show a series of peaks, each peak corresponding to one component of the mixture. The time required for a component to emerge from the column from the time of its injection into the column is known as the **retention time.** This serves as a useful identifying characteristic of a material. Figure 5–6 (a) shows the chromatogram of two barbiturates; each barbiturate has tentatively been identified by comparing its retention time to those of known barbiturates, shown in Figure 5–6 (b). (See Appendix IV for chromatographic conditions.) However, because it is always possible that other substances may have comparable retention times under similar chromatographic conditions, gas chromatography cannot be considered an absolute means of identification. Conclusions derived from this technique must be confirmed by other testing procedures.

Gas chromatography has an added advantage in that it is extremely sensitive and can yield quantitative results. The amount of substance passing through the GC detector is proportional to the peak area recorded; therefore, by chromatographing a known concentration of a material and comparing it to the unknown, the amount of the sample may be determined by proportion. Gas chromatography has sufficient sensitivity to detect and quantitate materials at the nanogram (0.000000001 gram or 1×10^{-9} gram) level.[1]

---

[1]For ease of handling large or small numbers, the power of ten notion is quite useful and simple. The power of ten expresses the number of places that the decimal point must be moved. If it is positive, the decimal point is moved to the right; if it is negative, the decimal point is moved to the left. Thus, to express 1×10^{-9} as a number, the decimal point is simply moved nine places to the left of 1.

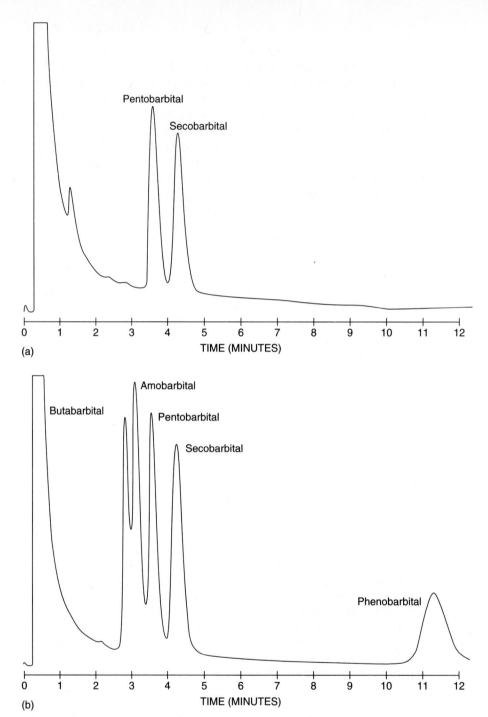

Figure 5–6. (a) An unknown mixture of barbiturates is identified by comparing its retention times to (b), a known mixture of barbiturates. *Courtesy* Varian Instruments, Calif.

An important extension of the application of gas chromatography to forensic science is the technique of **pyrolysis gas chromatography.** Many solid materials commonly encountered as physical evidence—for example, paint chips, fibers, and plastics—cannot be readily dissolved in a solvent for injection into the gas chromatograph. Thus, under normal conditions these substances cannot be subjected to gas chromatographic analysis. However, materials such as these can be heated or pyrolyzed to high temperatures (500–1000°C) so that they will decompose into numerous gaseous products. Pyrolyzers have been designed to permit these gaseous products to enter the carrier gas stream where they flow into and through the GC column. The pyrolyzed material can then be characterized by the pattern produced by its chromatogram or **pyrogram.** As an example, Figure 5–7 illustrates the pyrogram of a paint chip. The complexity of the paint pyrogram in essence serves as a "fingerprint" of the material and gives the examiner many points to compare with other paints that are analyzed in a similar fashion.

Figure 5–7. Pyrogram of a GM automobile paint. *Courtesy* Varian Instruments, Calif.

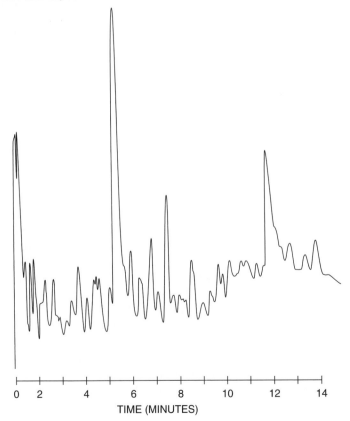

TIME (MINUTES)

HIGH-PERFORMANCE LIQUID CHROMATOGRAPHY (HPLC)

As was previously mentioned, a chromatographic system requires having a moving phase and a stationary phase in contact with each other. In the previous section, gas chromatography was described. Here, the stationary phase is a thin film and the moving phase a gas. However, by changing the nature of these phases, one can create different forms of chromatography. One form finding increasing utility in crime laboratories is high-performance liquid chromatography (HPLC). Its moving phase is a liquid that is pumped under through a column filled with fine solid particles. In one form of HPLC, the surfaces of these solid particles are chemically treated and act as the stationary phase. As the liquid moving phase is being pumped through the column, a sample is injected into the column. As the liquid carries the sample through the column, different components are retarded to different degrees, depending on their interaction with the stationary phase. This leads to a separation of the different components making up the sample mixture.

The major advantage of HPLC is that the entire process takes place at room temperature. With GC, the sample must first be vaporized and made to travel through a heated column. Hence, any materials sensitive to high temperatures may fail to survive their passage through the column. In such situations, the analyst may turn to HPLC as the method of choice. Organic explosives are generally heat sensitive and are therefore more readily separated by HPLC. Likewise, heat-sensitive drugs, such as LSD, lend themselves to analysis by HPLC.

THIN-LAYER CHROMATOGRAPHY (TLC)

The technique of thin-layer chromatography (TLC) incorporates a solid stationary phase and a moving liquid phase to effect the separation of the constituents of a mixture. A thin-layer plate is prepared by coating a glass plate with a thin film of a granular material. Commonly, silica gel or aluminum oxide is used. This granular material serves as the solid stationary phase and is usually held in place on the plate with a binding agent such as plaster of Paris. If the sample to be analyzed is a solid, it must first be dissolved in a suitable solvent and a few microliters of the solution spotted with a capillary tube onto the granular surface near the lower edge of the plate. A liquid sample may be applied directly to the plate in the same manner. The plate is then placed upright into a closed chamber that contains a selected liquid, with care that the liquid does not touch the sample spot.

The liquid will slowly begin to rise up the plate by capillary action. It is the rising liquid that serves as the moving phase in thin-layer chromatography. As it moves past the sample spot, the components of the sample will become distributed between the stationary solid phase and the moving liquid phase. Those components with the greatest affinity for the moving phase will travel up the plate at a faster speed as compared to those that have greater affinity for the stationary phase. When the liquid front has moved a sufficient distance (usually 10 cm), the development is complete, and the plate is removed from the chamber and dried (see Figure 5–8).

Because most compounds are colorless, no separation will be noticed after development unless the materials are *visualized*. To accomplish this, the plates are placed under ultraviolet light, revealing those materials that fluoresce as bright spots on a dark

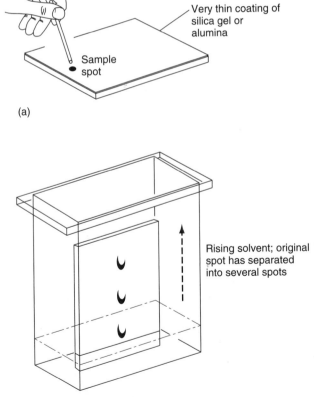

(a)

Very thin coating of silica gel or alumina

Sample spot

(b)

Rising solvent; original spot has separated into several spots

Figure 5–8.
(a) In thin-layer chromatography, a liquid sample is spotted onto the granular surface of a gel-coated plate. (b) The plate is placed into a closed chamber that contains a liquid. As the liquid rises up the plate, the components of the sample will distribute themselves between the coating and the moving liquid. The mixture is separated, with substances having a greater affinity for the moving liquid traveling up the plate at a faster speed.

background. When a fluorescent dye has been incorporated into the solid phase, nonfluorescent substances appear as dark spots against a fluorescent background when exposed to the ultraviolet light. A second method of visualization is accomplished when the plate is sprayed with a chemical reagent that reacts with the separated substances and causes them to form colored spots. Figure 5–9 shows the chromatogram of a marijuana extract that has been separated into its components by TLC and visualized by having been sprayed with a chemical reagent.

Once the components of a sample have been separated, their identification must follow. For this, the questioned sample must be

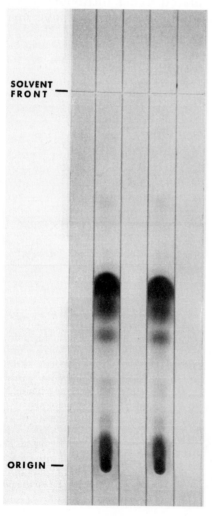

SOLVENT
FRONT —

ORIGIN —

Figure 5–9.
Chromatogram of a marijuana extract.

developed alongside an authentic or standard sample on the same TLC plate. If both the standard and the unknown are found to travel the same distances up the plate from their origins, they can tentatively be identified as being the same. For example, a sample suspected of containing heroin and quinine is chromatographed alongside known heroin and quinine standards, as shown in Figure 5–10. A confirmation of the identity of the suspect material is made by comparing the migration distances of the heroin and quinine standards against those of the components of the unknown material. If the distances are the same, a tentative identification can be made. However, it must be cautioned that such an identification cannot be considered definitive, for the possibility always exists that numerous other substances can

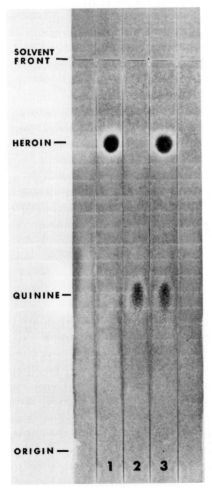

Figure 5–10.
Chromatograms of known heroin (1) and quinine (2) standards alongside suspect sample (3).

migrate the same distance up the plate when chromatographed under similar conditions. Thus, thin-layer chromatography cannot by itself provide an absolute identification; it must be utilized in conjunction with other testing procedures to prove absolute identity.

The distance a spot has traveled up a thin-layer plate can be assigned a numerical value known as the R_f **value.** This value is defined as the distance traveled by the component divided by the distance traveled by the moving liquid phase. For example, in Figure 5–10 the moving phase was allowed to travel 10 centimeters up the plate before the plate was removed from the tank. After visualization, the heroin spot moved 8 centimeters, and this has an R_f value of 0.8; the quinine migrated 4 centimeters and has a R_f value of 0.4.

There are literally thousands of possible combinations of liquid and solid phases that can be chosen from in thin-layer chromatography. Fortunately, years of research have produced much published data relating to the proper selection of TLC conditions for separating and identifying specific classes of substances—for example, drugs, dyes, and petroleum products. These references, along with the personal experiences of the analyst, will aid in the proper selection of TLC conditions for specific problems.

Thin-layer chromatography is a powerful tool for solving many of the analytical problems presented to the forensic scientist. The method is both rapid and sensitive; moreover, less than 100 micrograms of suspect material are required for the analysis. In addition, the equipment necessary for TLC work has minimal cost and space requirements. And numerous samples can be analyzed simultaneously on one thin-layer plate. The principal application of this technique is the detection and identification of components in complex mixtures.

ELECTROPHORESIS

Electrophoresis is somewhat related to thin-layer chromatography in that it separates materials according to their migration rates on a stationary solid phase. However, it does not utilize a moving liquid phase to move the material; instead, an electrical potential is placed across the stationary medium. The nature of this medium can vary; most forensic applications call for a starch or agar gel coated onto a glass plate. Under these conditions, only substances that possess an electrical charge will migrate across the stationary phase (see Figure 5–11). The technique is particularly useful for separating and identifying complex biochemical mixtures. In forensic science, electrophoresis finds its most successful application in the characterization of proteins and DNA in dried blood.

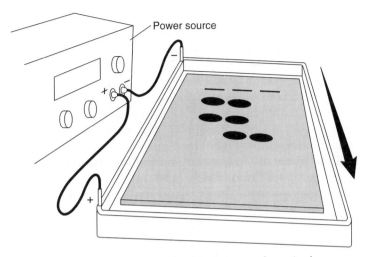

Figure 5–11.   Electrophoresis separates mixtures of proteins by forcing them to migrate across a gel-coated plate under the influence of an electrical potential. Due to variations in charge and size, proteins will move across the plate at different speeds.

Because many of the substances in blood carry an electrical charge, they can be separated and identified by electrophoresis. Forensic serologists have developed several electrophoretic procedures for characterizing dried blood. Many enzymes present in blood are actually composed of distinct proteins that can be separated by electrophoresis on starch gel. These proteins will migrate on the plate at speeds that vary according to their electrical charge and size. After completion of the electrophoresis run, the separated proteins are stained with a suitable developing agent for visual observation. In this manner, characteristic band patterns are obtained that are related to the enzyme type present in the blood. Likewise, mixtures of DNA fragments can be separated by gel electrophoresis by taking advantage of the fact that the rate of movement of DNA across a gel-coated plate will depend on the molecule's size. Smaller DNA fragments will move at a faster rate along the plate than will the larger DNA fragments. This technique will be discussed in further detail in Chapters 12 and 13.

SPECTROPHOTOMETRY

THEORY OF LIGHT

We have already seen that when white light passes through a glass prism, it is dispersed into a continuous spectrum of colors. This phenomenon demonstrates the fact that white light is not homogeneous but is actually composed of a range of colors that extends from red through violet. Similarly, the observation that a substance has a color is also consistent with this description of white light. For example, when light is passed through a red glass, all the component colors of light are absorbed by the glass except for red, which passes through or is transmitted by the glass. Likewise, one can determine the color of an opaque object by observing its ability to absorb some of the component colors of light while reflecting others back to the eye. Color is thus a visual indication of the fact that objects absorb certain portions of visible light and transmit or reflect others. Scientists have long recognized this phenomenon and have learned to characterize different chemical substances by the type and quantity of light they absorb.

To understand why materials absorb light, one must first comprehend the nature of light. Two simple models have been developed to explain light's behavior. **The first model describes light as a continuous wave; the second depicts it as a stream of discrete energy particles.** Together, these two very different descriptions can explain all of the observed properties of light; but by itself, no one model can explain all the facets of the behavior of light.

The wave concept depicts light as having an up-and-down motion of a continuous wave, as shown in Figure 5–12. Several terms are used to describe such a wave. The distance between two consecutive crests

Figure 5–12. The frequency of the lower wave is twice that of the upper wave.

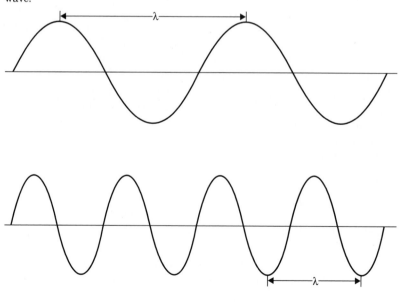

(or one trough to the next trough) is called the **wavelength;** the Greek *lambda* (λ) is used as its symbol, and the unit of nanometers is frequently used to express its value. The number of crests (or troughs) passing any one given point in a unit of time is defined as the **frequency** of the wave. Frequency is normally designated by the letter f and is expressed in cycles per second (cps). The speed of light in a vacuum is a universal constant at 300,000,000 meters per second and is designated by the symbol c. Frequency and wavelength are inversely proportional to one another, as shown by the relationship expressed in Equation (5–1).

$$f = \frac{c}{\lambda} \qquad\qquad (5–1)$$

Actually, visible light is only a small part of a large family of radiation waves known as the **electromagnetic spectrum.** All electromagnetic radiations travel at the speed of light (c) and are distinguishable from one another only by their different wavelengths or frequencies. (Figure 5–13 illustrates the various types of electromagnetic radiations in the order of decreasing frequency.) Hence, the only property that distinguishes X-rays from radio waves is the different frequencies the two types of waves possess. Similarly, the range of colors that comprise the visible spectrum can be correlated with frequency. For instance, the lowest frequencies of visible light are red in color, with those waves having a somewhat lower frequency falling into the invisible infrared region. The highest frequencies of visible light are violet in color, and those radiations having a somewhat higher frequency extend into the invisible region. No definite boundaries exist between any colors or regions of the electromagnetic spectrum; instead, each region is composed of a continuous range of frequencies, each blending into the other.

Ordinarily, light in any region of the electromagnetic spectrum is a collection of waves possessing a range of wavelengths. Under normal circumstances, this light will be composed of waves that are all out of step with each other (incoherent light). However, it is now possible for scientists to produce light that has all its waves pulsating in unison

Figure 5–13. Electromagnetic spectrum.

Electromagnetic spectrum

Gamma rays	X rays	Ultraviolet rays	Visible light	Infrared rays	Microwave rays	Radio rays

Decreasing frequency ⟶
Increasing wavelength ⟶

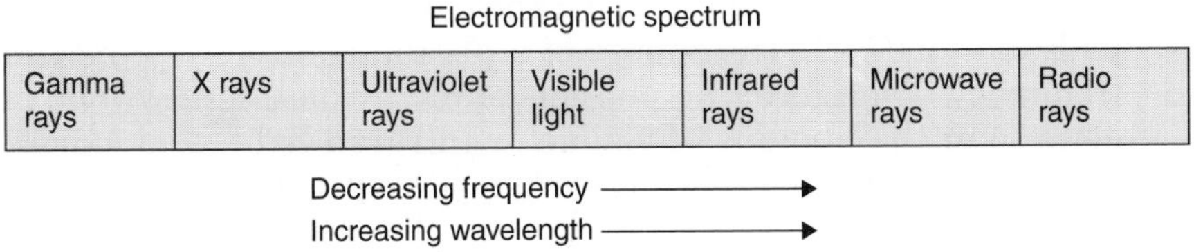

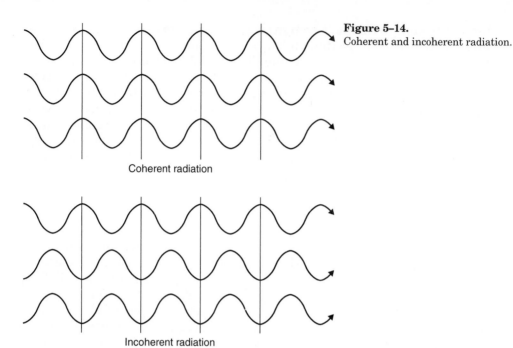

Figure 5–14.
Coherent and incoherent radiation.

Coherent radiation

Incoherent radiation

(see Figure 5–14). This is called **coherent light** or **laser** (*l*ight *a*mplification by the *s*imulated *e*mission of *r*adiation). Light in this form is very intense and can be focused on a very small area. Laser beams can be focused down to pinpoints that are so intense that they can zap microscopic holes in a diamond.

As long as electromagnetic radiation is moving through space, its behavior can be described as that of a continuous wave; however, once radiation is absorbed by a substance, the model of light as a stream of discrete particles must be invoked to best describe its behavior. Here, light is depicted as consisting of energy particles that are known as **photons.** Each photon has a definite amount of energy associated with its behavior. This energy is related to the frequency of light, as shown by Equation (5–2):

$$E = hf \tag{5–2}$$

where E specifies the energy of the photon, f is the frequency of radiation, and h is a universal constant called *Planck's constant*. As shown by Equation (5–2), the energy of a photon is directly proportional to its frequency. Therefore, the photons of ultraviolet light will be more energetic than the photons of visible or infrared light, and exposure to the more energetic photons of X-rays presents more danger to human health than exposure to the photons of radio waves.

ABSORPTION OF ELECTROMAGNETIC RADIATION

Just as a substance can absorb visible light to produce color, many of the invisible radiations of the electromagnetic spectrum are likewise absorbed. This absorption phenomenon is the basis for spectrophotometry, an important analytical technique in chemical identification. Spectrophotometry measures the quantity of radiation that a particular material absorbs as a function of wavelength or frequency.

We have already observed in the description of color that an object will not absorb all the visible light it is exposed to; instead, it will selectively absorb some of the component frequencies and will reflect or transmit others. Similarly, the absorption of other types of electromagnetic radiation by chemical substances is also found to be selective. The key questions that must be asked are: Why does a particular substance absorb only at certain frequencies and not at others? And, are these frequencies predictable? The answers are not simple ones. Scientists find it most difficult to predict with certainty all the frequencies at which any one substance will absorb in a particular region of the electromagnetic spectrum. What is known, however, is that a chemical substance will absorb photons of radiation that have a frequency that corresponds to an energy requirement of the substance, as defined by Equation (5–2). Different materials have different energy requirements and therefore absorb at different frequencies. What is most important to the analyst is that these absorbed frequencies are measurable, and they can be used to characterize a material.

The selective absorption of a substance is measured by an instrument called the **spectrophotometer.** It produces a graph or **absorption spectrum** that depicts the absorption of light as a function of wavelength or frequency. The absorption of ultraviolet (UV), visible, and infrared (IR) radiations is particularly applicable for obtaining qualitative data pertaining to the identification of organic substances.

Absorption at a single wavelength or frequency of light is not 100 percent complete—there will be some radiation transmitted or reflected by the material. Just how much radiation a substance will absorb is defined by a fundamental relationship known as Beer's Law, Equation (5–3):

$$A = kc \qquad (5\text{–}3)$$

Here, A symbolizes the absorption or the quantity of light taken up at a single frequency, c is the concentration of the absorbing material, and k is a proportionality constant. From this relationship, it is seen that the quantity of light absorbed at any frequency is directly proportional to the concentration of the absorbing species; the more material you have, the more radiation it will absorb. By defining the relationship between absorbance and concentration, Beer's Law permits spectrophotometry to be used as a technique for quantification.

THE SPECTROPHOTOMETER

The spectrophotometer is the instrument used to measure and record the absorption spectrum of a chemical substance. The basic components of a simple spectrophotometer are the same regardless of whether it is designed to measure the absorption of UV, visible, or IR radiation. These components are illustrated diagrammatically in Figure 5–15. They include (1) a radiation source, (2) a monochromator or frequency selector, (3) a sample holder, (4) a detector to convert electromagnetic radiation into an electrical signal, and (5) a recorder to produce a record of the signal.

The choice of a source will vary with the type of radiation desired. For visible radiation, an ordinary tungsten bulb provides a convenient source of radiation. In the UV region, a hydrogen or deuterium discharge lamp is normally used, and a heated molded rod containing a mixture of rare-earth oxides is a good source of IR light.

The function of the monochromator is to select a single wavelength or frequency of light from the source. In some inexpensive spectrophotometers, this may be accomplished when the light is caused to pass through colored glass filters that will remove all radiation from the beam except for a desired range of wavelengths. More precise spectrophotometers may employ a prism or diffraction grating to disperse radiation into its component wavelengths or frequencies.[2]

Figure 5–15.   Parts of a simple spectrophotometer.

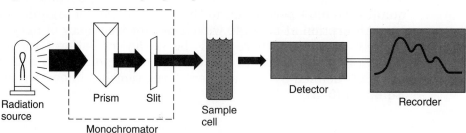

---

[2]A diffraction grating is made by scratching many thousands of parallel lines on a transparent surface such as glass. As light passes through the narrow spacings between the lines, it spreads out and produces a spectrum similar to that formed by a prism.

The desired wavelength is obtained when the dispersed radiation is focused onto a narrow slit that permits only selected radiations to pass through.

Currently, most laboratory infrared spectrophotometers use the concept of Fourier transform analysis to measure the wavelengths of light at which a material will absorb in the infrared spectrum. This approach does not make use of any dispersive elements that select single wavelengths or frequencies of light emitted from a source; instead, the heart of a Fourier transform infrared spectrometer (FT-IR) is the Michelson interferometer. The interferometer uses a beam-splitting prism and two mirrors, one movable and one stationary, to direct light toward a sample. As the wavelengths pass through the sample and reach a detector, they are all measured simultaneously. A mathematical operation, the Fourier transform method, is used to decode the measured signals and record the wavelength data. These Fourier calculations are rapidly carried out by a computer. In a matter of seconds, a computer-operated FT-IR instrument can produce an infrared absorption pattern compatible to one generated by a prism instrument.

Sample preparation varies with the type of radiation being studied. Absorption spectra in the UV and visible regions are usually obtained from samples that have been dissolved in an appropriate solvent. Because the cells holding the solution must be transparent to the light being measured, glass cells are used in the visible region and quartz cells in the ultraviolet region. Practically all substances absorb in some region of the IR spectrum, so sampling techniques must be modified to measure absorption in this spectral region; special cells made out of sodium chloride or potassium bromide are commonly utilized because they will not absorb light over a wide range of the IR portion of the electromagnetic spectrum.

The detector measures the quantity of radiation that passes through the sample by converting it to an electrical signal. UV and visible spectrophotometers employ photoelectric tube detectors. A signal is generated when the photons strike the tube surface to produce a current that is directly proportional to the intensity of the light transmitted through the sample. When this signal is compared to the intensity of light that is transmitted to the detector in the absence of an absorbing material, the absorbance of a substance can be determined at each wavelength or frequency of light selected. The signal from the detection system is then fed into a recorder, which plots absorbance as a function of wavelength or frequency. Modern spectrophotometers are designed to trace an entire absorption spectrum automatically.

ULTRAVIOLET, VISIBLE, AND INFRARED SPECTROPHOTOMETRY

Ultraviolet (UV) and visible spectrophotometry measure the absorbance of UV and visible light as a function of wavelength or frequency. For example, the UV absorption spectrum of heroin shows a maximum absorption band at a wavelength of 278 nanometers (Figure 5–16). From this it can readily be seen that the simplicity of a UV spectrum facilitates its use as a tool for determining a material's probable identity. For instance, a white powder may have a UV spectrum comparable to heroin and therefore may be tentatively identified as such. (Fortunately, sugar and starch, common diluents of heroin, do not absorb UV light.) However, this technique will not provide for a definitive result; the possibility always exists that there are other drugs or materials that have a UV absorption spectrum similar to that of heroin. But this lack of specificity does not diminish the value of the technique, for the analyst has quickly eliminated thousands of other possible drugs from consideration and can now proceed to conduct other confirmatory tests, such as thin-layer or gas chromatography, to complete the identification.

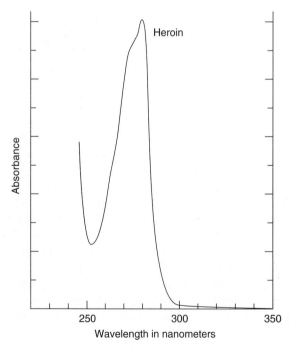

Figure 5–16.
Ultraviolet spectrum of heroin.

In contrast to the simplicity of a UV spectrum, absorption in the infrared region provides a far more complex pattern. Figure 5–17 (a) and (b) depicts the IR spectra of heroin and secobarbital. Here, the absorption bands are so numerous that each spectrum can provide enough characteristics to identify a substance specifically. **Different materials always have distinctively different infrared spectra; each IR spectrum is therefore equivalent to a "fingerprint" of that substance and no other.** This technique is one of the few tests available to the forensic scientist that can be considered specific in itself for identification. The IR spectra of thousands of organic compounds have been collected, indexed, and cataloged to serve as invaluable references for identifying organic substances.

MASS SPECTROMETRY (MS)

In a previous section, the operation of the gas chromatograph was discussed. This instrument is one of the most important tools to be found in a crime laboratory. Its ability to separate the components of a complex mixture is unsurpassed. However, gas chromatography (GC) does suffer one important drawback—that is, its inability to produce a specific identification. A forensic chemist cannot unequivocally state the identification of a substance based solely on a retention time as determined by the gas chromatograph. Fortunately, by coupling the gas chromatograph to a mass spectrometer this problem has largely been overcome.

The separation of a mixture's components is first accomplished on the gas chromatograph. A direct connection between the GC column and the mass spectrometer then allows each component to flow into the spectrometer as it emerges from the gas chromatograph. In the mass spectrometer, the material enters a high-vacuum chamber where a beam of high-energy electrons is aimed at the sample molecules. The electrons collide with the molecules, causing them to lose electrons and to acquire a positive charge (commonly called **ions**). These positively charged molecules or ions are very unstable or are formed with excess energy and almost instantaneously decompose into numerous smaller fragments. The fragments then pass through an electric or magnetic field, where they are separated according to their masses. **The unique feature of mass spectrometry is that under carefully controlled conditions, no two substances produce the same fragmentation pattern.** In essence, one can think of this pattern as a "fingerprint" of the substance being examined (see Figure 5–18).

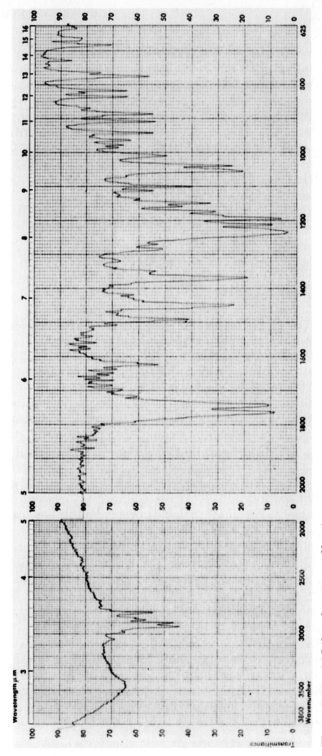

Figure 5–17. (a) Infrared spectrum of heroin.

156

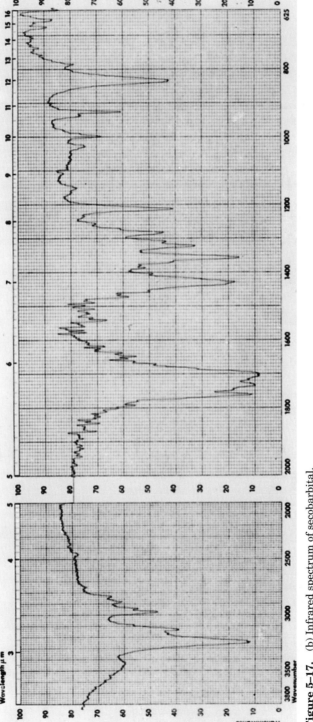

Figure 5-17. (b) Infrared spectrum of secobarbital.

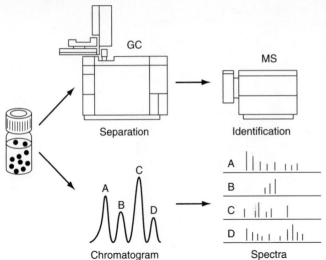

Figure 5–18.
How GC/MS works. Left to right, the sample is separated into its components by the gas chromatograph, and then the components are ionized and identified by characteristic fragmentation patterns of the spectra produced by the mass spectrometer. *Courtesy Hewlett Packard, Palo Alto, Calif.*

Figure 5–19. (a) Mass spectrum of heroin. (b) Mass spectrum of cocaine.

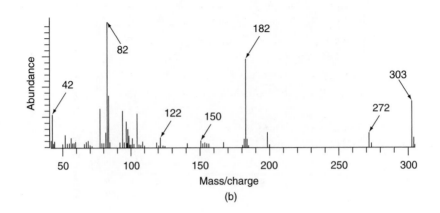

The technique thus provides a specific means for identifying a chemical structure. It is also sensitive to minute concentrations. At present, mass spectrometry finds its widest application in areas relating to the identification of drugs; however, further research is expected to yield significant applications with respect to the identification of other types of physical evidence. Figure 5–19 illustrates the mass spectra of heroin and cocaine; here, each line represents a fragment of a different mass (actually the ratio of mass to charge), and the line height reflects the relative abundance of each fragment. Note how different the fragmentation patterns of heroin and cocaine are. Each mass spectrum is unique to each drug and therefore serves as a specific test for identifying that substance.

The combination of the gas chromatograph and mass spectrometer is further enhanced when a computer is added to the system. The integrated gas chromatograph/mass spectrometer/computer system provides the ultimate in speed, accuracy, and sensitivity. With the ability to record and store in its memory several hundred mass spectra, such a system can detect and identify substances present in only one-millionth-of-a-gram quantities. Furthermore, the computer can be programmed to compare an unknown spectrum against a comprehensive library of mass spectra stored in its memory. The advent of personal-sized computers and microcircuitry has made it possible to design mass spectrometer systems that can fit on a small table. Such a unit is pictured in Figure 5–20 (a) and (b).

REVIEW QUESTIONS

1. Anything that has mass and occupies space is defined as _____.

2. The basic building blocks of all substances are the _____.

3. The number of elements known today is _____.

4. An arrangement of elements by similar chemical properties is accomplished in the _____ table.

5. An _____ is the smallest particle of an element that can exist.

6. Substances composed of two or more elements are called _____.

7. A _____ is the smallest unit of a compound formed by the union of two or more atoms.

8. The physical state that retains a definite shape and volume is a _____.

9. A gas (has, has no) definite shape or volume.

Figure 5–20.   (a) A table-top mass spectrometer. *Courtesy* Hewlett Packard, Palo Alto, Calif.

Figure 5–20.   (b) Diagram of a table-top mass spectrometer. (1) The sample is injected into a heated inlet port, and a carrier gas sweeps it into the column. (2) The GC column separates the mixture into its components. (3) In the ion source, a filament wire emits electrons that strike the sample molecules, causing them to fragment as they leave the GC column. (4) The quadrupole, consisting of four rods, separates the fragments according to their mass. (5) The detector counts the fragments passing through the quadrupole. The signal is small and must be amplified. (6) The data system is responsible for total control of the entire GC/MS system. It detects and measures the abundance of each fragment and displays the mass spectrum. *Courtesy* Hewlett Packard, Palo Alto, Calif.

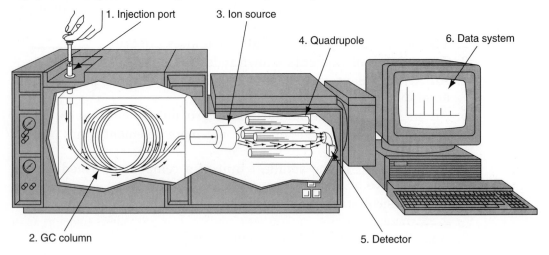

10. During the process of _____, solids will go directly to the gaseous state, bypassing the liquid state.

11. The attraction forces between the molecules of a liquid are (more, less) than those in a solid.

12. Different _____ are separated by definite visible boundaries.

13. Carbon-containing substances are classified as _____.

14. _____ substances encompass all non–carbon-containing materials.

15. A _____ analysis describes the identity of a material, and a _____ analysis relates to a determination of the quantity of a substance.

16. The study of the absorption of light by chemical substances is known as _____.

17. The separation of a mixture's components can be accomplished utilizing the technique of _____.

18. Henry's Law describes the distribution of a volatile chemical compound between its liquid and gas phases. (True, False)

19. The (higher, lower) the solubility of a gas in a liquid, the greater will be its tendency to remain dissolved in that liquid.

20. In order for chromatography to occur, one phase must be made to move continuously in one direction over a stationary phase. (True, False)

21. A technique that separates mixtures on the basis of their distribution between a stationary liquid phase and a moving gas phase is _____.

22. The time required for a substance to travel through the gas chromatographic column is a useful identifying characteristic known as _____.

23. Solid materials that are not readily dissolved in solvents for injection into the gas chromatograph can be _____ into numerous gaseous products prior to entering the gas chromatograph.

24. A major advantage of high-performance liquid chromatography is that the entire process takes place at _____ temperature.

25. A technique that utilizes a moving liquid phase and a stationary solid phase to separate mixtures is _____.

26. Since most chemical compounds are colorless, the final step of the thin-layer development usually requires that they be _____ by spraying with a chemical reagent.

27. The distance a spot has traveled up a thin-layer plate can be assigned a numerical value known as the _____ value.

28. Thin-layer chromatography yields the positive identification of a material. (True, False)

29. The migration of materials along a stationary phase under the influence of an electrical potential describes the technique of _____.

30. Color is a usual indication that substances selectively absorb light. (True, False)

31. The distance between two successive identical points on a wave is known as _____.

32. Frequency and wavelength are directly proportional to one another. (True, False)

33. Light, X-rays, and radio waves are all members of the _____ spectrum.

34. Red light is (higher, lower) in frequency than violet light.

35. Light that has all its waves pulsating in unison is called a _____.

36. One model of light depicts it as consisting of energy particles known as _____.

37. The energy of a light particle (photon) is directly proportional to its frequency. (True, False)

38. Red light is (more, less) energetic than violet light.

39. The selective absorption of electromagnetic radiation by materials (can, cannot) be used as an aid for identification.

40. The amount of radiation a substance will absorb is directly proportional to its concentration as defined by _____ Law.

41. The _____ is the instrument used to measure and record the absorption spectrum of a chemical substance.

42. The function of the _____ is to select a single frequency of light emanating from the spectrophotometer's source.

43. An (ultraviolet, infrared) absorption spectrum provides a unique "fingerprint" of a chemical substance.

44. The technique of _____ exposes molecules to a beam of high-energy electrons in order to fragment them.

45. A mass spectrum is normally considered to be a specific means for identifying a chemical substance. (True, False)

FURTHER REFERENCES

Saferstein, Richard, "Forensic Applications of Mass Spectrometry," in *Forensic Science Handbook,* R. Saferstein, ed. Englewood Cliffs, N.J.: Prentice Hall, 1982.

Smith, R. N., "Forensic Applications of High-Performance Liquid Chromatography," in *Forensic Science Handbook,* R. Saferstein, ed. Englewood Cliffs, N.J.: Prentice Hall, 1982.

Stafford, David T., "Forensic Capillary Gas Chromatography," in *Forensic Science Handbook,* Vol. 2, R. Saferstein, ed. Englewood Cliffs, N.J.: Prentice Hall, 1988.

Suzuki, Edward M., "Forensic Applications of Infrared Spectroscopy," in *Forensic Science Handbook,* Vol. 3, R. Saferstein, ed. Englewood Cliffs, N.J.: Prentice Hall, 1993.

Tebbett, I. ed., *Gas Chromatography in Forensic Science.* Chichester, West Sussex, England: Ellis Horwood, 1992.

INORGANIC ANALYSIS

INTRODUCTION

In the previous chapter, analytical techniques were described for characterizing a class of matter known as organics. Generally, these materials contain the element carbon in their chemical composition. Although organic substances do constitute a substantial portion of the physical evidence submitted to crime laboratories, the element carbon does not appear among the earth's most abundant elements. It is perhaps rather surprising to observe that about three-quarters of the weight of the earth's crust is composed of only two elements—oxygen and silicon. In fact, only 10 elements make up approximately 99 percent of the earth's crust (see Table 6–1). The remaining elements may be considered almost as impurities, although exceedingly important ones. Carbon, the element that is a constituent of most chemical compounds, comprises less than 0.1 percent of the earth's crust.

Considering these facts, it is certainly reasonable to expect that non–carbon-containing substances—that is, inorganics—will be encountered as physical evidence at crime scenes. One only has to consider the prevalence of metallic materials, such as iron, steel, copper, and aluminum, in our society to understand the possibilities of finding tools, coins, weapons, and metal scrapings at crime scenes.

TABLE 6–1.
ELEMENTAL ABUNDANCE
AS PERCENTAGES IN THE EARTH'S CRUST

Element	Percentage by Weight
Oxygen	47.3
Silicon	27.7
Aluminum	7.9
Iron	4.5
Calcium	3.5
Sodium	2.5
Potassium	2.5
Magnesium	2.2
Titanium	0.5
Hydrogen	0.2
Other elements	1.2

Less well known, but perhaps almost as significant to the criminalist, are the utilization of inorganic chemicals as pigments in paints and dyes, the incorporation of inorganics into explosive formulations, and the prevalence of inorganic poisons such as mercury, lead, or arsenic.

To appreciate fully the role that inorganic analysis has in forensic science, we must first examine its application to the basic objectives of the crime laboratory—the identification and comparison of physical evidence. The identification of inorganic evidence is exemplified by a typical request to examine an explosive formulation suspected of containing the inorganic chemical potassium chlorate, or perhaps to examine a poisonous powder thought to be arsenic. In each case, the forensic scientist must perform tests that will ultimately determine the specific chemical identity of the suspect materials to the exclusion of all others. Only after tests are completed and their results found to be identical to tests previously recorded for a known potassium chlorate or a known arsenic can a valid conclusion as to the chemical identity of the evidence be reached.

However, in a situation that requires a comparison of two or more objects in order to ascertain their common origin, a different problem is presented to the analyst. For example, a criminalist may be requested to determine whether or not a piece of brass pipe found in the possession of a suspect compares to a broken pipe found at the crime scene. The condition of the two pipes might not allow for their comparison by the physical fitting together of broken edges. Under these circumstances, the only alternative will be to attempt a comparison through chemical analysis. Here, it is not enough for the analyst to conclude that both pipes are alike because they are brass (an alloy of copper and zinc). After all, hundreds of thousands of brass pipes are known to exist, a situation that is hardly conducive to proving that these two particular pipes were at one time a single unit. The examiner must go a step further to try and distinguish these pipes from all others. Although this may not be possible, a comparison of the pipes' trace elements—that is, elements present in small quantities—will provide a meaningful criterion for at least increasing the probability that the two pipes originated from the same source.

Considering the fact that most of our raw materials originate from the earth's crust, it is not surprising to observe that they are rarely obtained in pure form; instead, they include numerous elemental impurities that usually have to be eliminated through industrial processing. However, in most cases it is not economically feasible to completely exclude all such minor impurities, especially in light of the fact that their presence will have no effect on the appearance or performance of the final product. For this reason, we find that many of our manufactured products, and even most natural materials, contain small quantities of elements present in concentrations of less than 1 percent. For the criminalist, the presence of **trace elements** is particularly useful because they provide "invisible" markers that may establish the source of a material or at least provide additional points for comparison. Table 6–2 illustrates how two types of brass alloys can readily be distinguished by their elemental composition. Similarly, the comparison of trace elements present in paint or other types of metallic specimens

TABLE 6–2.
ELEMENTAL ANALYSIS OF BRASS ALLOYS

Element	High-Tensile Brass (percentage)	Manganese Brass (percentage)
Copper	57.0	58.6
Aluminum	2.8	1.7
Zinc	35.0	33.8
Manganese	2.13	1.06
Iron	1.32	0.90
Nickel	0.48	1.02
Tin	0.64	1.70
Lead	0.17	0.72
Silicon	0.08	Nil

Source: R. L. Williams, "An Evaluation of the SEM with X-Ray Microanalyzer Accessory for Forensic Work," in *Scanning Electron Microscopy/1971,* O. Johari and I. Corvin, eds. (Chicago: IIT Research Institute, 1971), p. 541.

may provide particularly meaningful data with respect to source or origin. Forensic investigators have examined the evidential value of trace elements known to be present in hair, soil, fibers, and glass, as well as in all types of metallic objects. One illustrative example of this application occurred with the examination of the bullet and bullet fragments recovered after the assassination of President Kennedy.

EVIDENCE IN THE ASSASSINATION OF PRESIDENT KENNEDY

Ever since President Kennedy was killed in 1963, questions have lingered about whether or not Lee Harvey Oswald was part of a conspiracy to assassinate the president or, as the Warren Commission concluded, a lone assassin. In arriving at their conclusions, the Warren Commission reconstructed the crime as follows: Oswald fired three shots from behind the president while positioned in the Texas School Book Depository building. The president was struck by two bullets, with one bullet totally missing the president's limousine. One bullet hit the president in the back, exited from his throat, and then went on to strike Governor Connally, who was sitting in a jump seat in front of the president. The bullet hit Connally first in his back, then exited from his chest, struck his right wrist, and then temporarily lodged in his left thigh. This bullet was later found in the governor's stretcher at the hospital. A second bullet in the skull fatally wounded the president.

In a room at the Texas School Book Depository, a 6.5-mm Mannlicher-Carcano military rifle was found with Oswald's palm print on it. Also found were three spent 6.5-mm Western Cartridge Co./ Mannlicher-Carcano (WCC/MC) cartridge cases. Oswald, an employee of the Book Depository, had been seen there that morning and also a few minutes after the assassination, disappearing soon thereafter. He was apprehended a few miles away from the Depository nearly two hours after the shooting.

Critics of the Warren Commission have long argued that evidence exists for proving Oswald did not act alone. Eyewitness accounts and acoustical data interpreted by some experts have been used to advocate the contention that someone else fired at the president from a region in front of the limousine (the so-called grassy knoll). Furthermore, it is argued that the Warren Commission's reconstruction of the crime relied on the assumption that only one bullet caused both the president's throat wound and Connally's back wound. Critics contend that such damage would have deformed and mutilated a bullet. Instead, the recovered bullet showed some flattening, no deformity, and only about 1 percent weight loss.

In 1977, at the request of the U.S. House of Representatives Select Committee on Assassinations, the bullet taken from Connally's stretcher along with bullet fragments recovered from the car and various wound areas were examined for trace element levels.

Lead alloys used for the manufacture of bullets contain an assortment of trace elements. For example, antimony is often added to lead as a hardening agent; copper, bismuth, and silver are other trace elements commonly found in bullet lead. In this case, the bullet and bullet fragments were compared for their antimony and silver content. Previous studies had amply demonstrated that the levels of these two elements are particularly important for characterizing WCC/MC bullets. Bullet lead from this type of ammunition ranges in antimony concentration from 20 to 1200 parts per million (ppm) and 5 to 15 ppm in silver content.

As can be seen in Table 6–3, the samples designated Q1 and Q9 (the Connally stretcher bullet and fragments from Connally's wrist, respectively) are indistinguishable from one another in antimony and silver content. The samples Q2, Q4, 5, and Q14 (Q4, 5 being fragments from Kennedy's brain, and Q2 and Q14 being fragments recovered from two different areas in the car) also are indistinguishable in antimony and silver content but are different from Q1 and Q9.

The conclusions derived from studying these results are:

1. There is evidence of only two bullets—one of a composition of 815 ppm antimony and 9.3 ppm silver, the other of a composition of 622 ppm antimony and 8.1 ppm silver.

TABLE 6–3.

ANTIMONY AND SILVER CONCENTRATIONS IN THE KENNEDY ASSASSINATION BULLETS

Sample	Silver (parts per million)[a]	Antimony (parts per million)	Sample Description
Q1	8.8 ± 0.5	833 ± 9	Connally stretcher bullet
Q9	9.8 ± 0.5	797 ± 7	Fragments from Connally's wrist
Q2	8.1 ± 0.6	602 ± 4	Large fragment from car
Q4, 5	7.9 ± 0.3	621 ± 4	Fragments from Kennedy's brain
Q14	8.2 ± 0.4	642 ± 6	Small fragments found in car

[a]One part per million equals 0.0001%.

Source: Reprinted with permission from V. P. Guinn, "JFK Assassination: Bullet Analyses," *Analytical Chemistry,* 51 (1979), 484A. Copyright 1979, American Chemical Society.

2. Both bullets have a composition highly consistent with WCC/MC bullet lead, although other sources cannot entirely be ruled out.

3. The bullet found in the Connally stretcher also damaged Connally's wrist. The absence of bullet fragments from the back wounds of Kennedy and Connally prevented any effort at linking these wounds to the stretcher bullet.

None of these conclusions can totally verify the Warren Commission's reconstruction of the assassination, but the results are at least consistent with the Commission's findings.

The analyses on the Kennedy assassination bullets were performed by the technique of neutron activation analysis. The remainder of this chapter will be devoted to describing this and other techniques currently used for the examination of inorganic physical evidence.

THE EMISSION SPECTRUM OF ELEMENTS

We have already observed that organic molecules can readily be characterized by their selective absorption of ultraviolet, visible, or infrared radiations. Equally significant to the analytical chemist is the knowledge that the elements will also selectively absorb and emit light. These observations form the basis of two important analytical techniques designed to determine the elemental composition of materials—**emission spectroscopy** and **atomic absorption spectrophotometry.**

The statement that elements emit light should not come as a total surprise, for one need only observe the common tungsten incandescent lightbulb or the glow of a neon light to confirm this observation. When the light emitted from a bulb or from any other light source is passed through a prism, it is separated into its component colors or frequencies. The resulting display of colors is called an **emission spectrum.**

When sunlight or the light from an incandescent bulb is passed through a prism, we have already observed that a range of rainbow colors is produced. This emission spectrum is called a **continuous spectrum** because all the colors merge or blend into one another to form a continuous band. However, not all light sources produce such a spectrum. For example, if the light from a sodium lamp or a mercury arc lamp or a neon light was passed through a prism, the resultant spectrum would consist not of a continuous band but of several individual colored lines separated by dark spaces. Here, each line represents a definite wavelength or frequency of light that is separate and distinct from all others present in the spectrum. This type of spectrum is called a **line spectrum.** Figure 6–1 shows the line spectra of three elements.

Hydrogen

Helium

Mercury

Figure 6–1.   Some characteristic emission spectra.

It is important to realize that heated matter in a solid or liquid state produces a continuous spectrum that is not very indicative of its composition. However, if this same matter is vaporized and "excited" by exposure to high temperature, each element present will emit light that is composed of select frequencies that are characteristic of the element. This spectrum is in essence a "fingerprint" of an element and offers itself as a very practical method of identification. Sodium vapor, for example, always shows the same line spectrum, which differs from the spectrum of all other elements.

An **emission spectrograph** is an instrument used to obtain and record the line spectra of elements. Essentially, this instrument requires a means for vaporizing and exciting the atoms of elements so that they emit light, a means for separating this light into its component frequencies, and a means of recording the resultant spectrum. A simple emission spectrograph is depicted in Figure 6–2.

Excitation of the specimen under investigation is accomplished when it is inserted between two carbon electrodes through which a direct current arc is passed. The arc produces a sufficient amount of heat to vaporize and excite the specimen's atoms. The resultant emitted light is collected by a lens and is focused onto a prism that disperses it into component frequencies. The separated frequencies are then directed toward a photographic plate, where they are recorded as line images. Normally, a specimen consists of numerous elements; hence, the typical emission spectrum contains many lines. Each element present in the spectrum can be identified when it is compared to

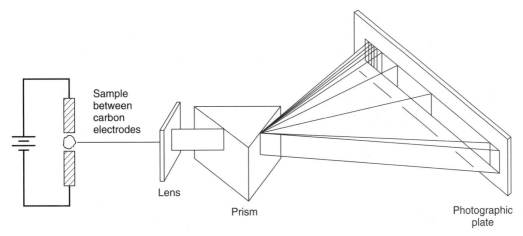

Figure 6–2. Parts of a simple emission spectrograph.

a standard chart that shows the position of the principal spectral lines of all the elements. However, the more common situation in forensic analysis simply requires a rapid comparison of the elemental composition of two or more specimens. This can readily be accomplished when the emission spectra are matched line for line, an approach illustrated in Figure 6–3. Here, the emission spectra of two paint chips are shown to be comparable.

ATOMIC ABSORPTION SPECTROPHOTOMETRY

When an atom is vaporized, it will absorb many of the same frequencies of light that it emits in an excited state. The selective absorption of light by atoms is the basis for a technique known as **atomic absorption spectrophotometry.** A simple atomic absorption spectrophotometer is illustrated in Figure 6–4.

Figure 6–3. A comparison of paint chips 1 and 2 by emission spectrographic analysis. A line-for-line comparison shows that both paints have the same elemental composition.

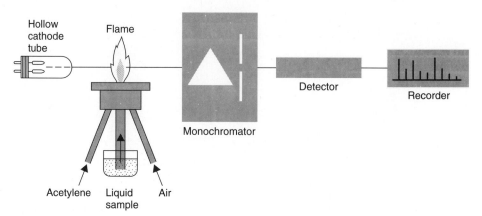

Figure 6–4. Parts of a simple flame atomic absorption spectrophotometer.

In atomic absorption spectrophotometry, the specimen is heated to a temperature that is hot enough to vaporize its atoms while leaving a substantial number of atoms in an unexcited state. Normally, the specimen is inserted into an air-acetylene flame to achieve this temperature. The vaporized atoms are then exposed to radiation emitted from a light source. In practice, the technique achieves great specificity by using as its radiation source a discharge tube made of the very same element being analyzed in the specimen. When the discharge lamp is turned on, it emits only those frequencies of light that are present in the emission spectrum of the element. Likewise, the sample will absorb these frequencies only when it contains this very same element. Therefore, if one wanted to determine the presence of the element antimony in a specimen, the atomic absorption spectrophotometer would have to be fitted with a discharge lamp that is constructed of antimony. Under these conditions, the sample will absorb light only when it contains antimony.

Once the radiation has passed through the sample, a monochromator, consisting of a prism or a diffraction grating and a slit, isolates the desired radiation frequency and transmits it to a detector. The detector converts the light into an electrical signal, the intensity of which is recorded on a strip-chart recorder.

The absorption of light by the element of interest is the phenomenon that is being measured in atomic absorption spectrophotometry. The concentration of the absorbing element will be directly proportional to the quantity of the light absorbed. The higher the concentration of the element, the more light absorbed. For this reason, atomic absorption spectroscopy has its most useful application in providing an accurate determination of an element's concentration in a sample. Furthermore, the technique is sufficiently sensitive as to find wide application in detecting and quantitating elements that are present at trace levels. However, the technique does have one drawback, in that the analyst can determine only one element at a time, each time having to select the proper lamp to match the particular element under investigation.

Although atomic absorption spectrophotometry has been utilized for chemical analysis since 1955, it has not yet found wide application for solving forensic problems. However, a modification in the design of the instrument promises to change this situation. By substituting a heated graphite furnace or a heated strip of metal (tantalum) for the flame, analysts have succeeded in achieving a more efficient means of atomic volatilization and as a result have produced a substantial increase in the sensitivity of the technique. Many elements can now be detected at levels that approach one-trillionth of a gram.

The high sensitivity of "flameless" atomic absorption now equals or surpasses that of any known analytical procedure. Considering the relative simplicity and low cost of the technique, atomic absorption spectrophotometry has become an attractive method for detecting and measuring the smallest levels of trace elements present in physical evidence.

THE ORIGIN OF EMISSION AND ABSORPTION SPECTRA

Any proposed theory that attempts to explain the origin of emission and absorption spectra must relate to the fundamental structure of the element—the atom. Scientists now know that the atom is composed of even more elementary particles that are collectively known as **subatomic particles.** The most important subatomic particles are the **proton, electron,** and **neutron.** The masses of the proton and neutron are each about 1837 times the mass of an electron. The proton is a particle with a positive electrical charge; the electron has a negative charge equal in magnitude to that of the proton; and the neutron is a neutral particle having neither a positive nor a negative charge. The properties of the proton, neutron, and electron are summarized in the following table:

Particle	Symbol	Relative Mass	Electrical Charge
Proton	P	1	+1
Neutron	n	1	0
Electron	e	1/1837	-1

A popular descriptive model of the atom, and the one that will be adopted for the purpose of this discussion, pictures an atom as consisting of electrons orbiting around a central nucleus—an image that is analogous to our solar system, in which the planets revolve around the sun.[1] The nucleus of the atom is composed of positively charged protons and neutrons that have no charge. Because the atom has no net electrical charge, the number of protons must always be equal to the number of negatively charged electrons in orbit around the nucleus.

With this knowledge, we can now begin to describe the atomic structure of the elements; for example, hydrogen has a nucleus consisting of one proton and no neutrons, and it has one orbiting electron. Helium has a nucleus comprised of two protons and two neutrons, with two electrons in orbit around the nucleus (see Figure 6–5).

The behavior and properties that distinguish one element from another must be related to those differences that exist in the atomic structure of each element. One such distinction resides in the fact that each element possesses a different number of protons. This number is called the **atomic number** of the element. As we look back at the periodic table illustrated in Figure 5–1, we see that the elements are numbered consecutively. Those numbers represent the atomic number or number of protons associated with each element. **An element is therefore a collection of atoms, all having the same number of protons.** Thus, each atom of hydrogen has 1 and only 1 proton; each atom of helium has 2 protons; each atom of silver has 47 protons; and each atom of lead has 82 protons in its nucleus.

To explain the origin of atomic spectra, our attention must now focus on the orbiting electrons of the atom. As electrons move around the nucleus, they are confined to a path of flight from which they cannot stray. This orbital path is associated with a definite amount of energy and is therefore called an **energy level.** Each element has its

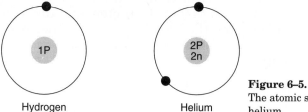

Hydrogen   Helium

Figure 6–5.
The atomic structures of hydrogen and helium.

---

[1]Actually, the electrons are moving so rapidly around the nucleus as to be best visualized as being in the form of an electron cloud spread out over the surface of the atom.

own set of characteristic energy levels located at varying distances from the nucleus. Some of these levels are occupied by electrons; others are empty.

An atom will be in its most stable state when all of its electrons are positioned in their lowest possible energy orbitals in the atom. When an atom absorbs energy, such as heat or light, its electrons are pushed into higher energy orbitals. In this condition, the atom is in an **excited state.** However, because energy levels have fixed values, only a definite amount of energy can be absorbed in moving an electron from one level to another. This is a most important observation, for it means that atoms will absorb only a definite value of energy, and all other energy values will be excluded. In atomic absorption spectrophotometry, a photon of light interacts with an electron, causing it to jump into a higher orbital, as shown in Figure 6–6(a). A specific frequency of light is required to effect this transition, and its energy must correspond to the exact energy difference between the two orbitals involved in the transition. This energy difference is expressed by the relationship $E = hf$, where E represents the energy difference between the two orbitals, f is the frequency of absorbed light, and h is a universal constant called Planck's constant. Any energy value that is more or less than this difference will not affect the transition. Hence, an element is selective in the frequency of light it will absorb, and this selectivity is determined by the electron energy levels each element possesses.

In the same manner, if atoms are exposed to intense heat, enough energy will be generated to push electrons into higher unoccupied energy orbitals. Normally, the electron will not remain in this excited state for long, and it will quickly fall back to its original energy level. As the electron falls back, it will have to release energy. An emission spectrum testifies to the fact that this energy loss comes about in the form of light emission [see Figure 6–6(b)]. The frequency of light emitted will again be determined by the relationship $E = hf$, where E is the energy difference between the upper and lower energy levels, and f is the frequency of emitted light. Because each element has its own characteristic set of energy levels, each will emit a unique set of frequency values. The emission spectrum thus provides us with a "picture" of the energy levels that surround the nucleus of each element.

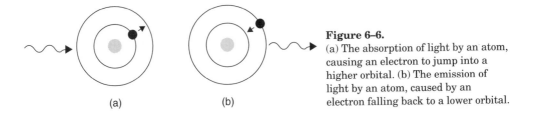

(a)   (b)

Figure 6–6.
(a) The absorption of light by an atom, causing an electron to jump into a higher orbital. (b) The emission of light by an atom, caused by an electron falling back to a lower orbital.

Thus, we see that as far as atoms are concerned, energy is a two-way street. Energy can be put into the atom while at the same time energy is given off; what goes in must come out. The chemist has the option of studying the atom using either approach. Atomic absorption spectrophotometry carefully measures the value and amount of light energy going into the atom; emission spectroscopy collects and measures the various light energies given off. The end result is the same; atoms are identified by the existence of characteristic energy levels.

NEUTRON ACTIVATION ANALYSIS

Once scientists realized that it was possible to change the number of subatomic particles in the atom's nucleus, the unleashing of a new source of energy—nuclear energy—was inevitable. This energy has proven so awesome in its power that the very survival of civilization will depend on our ability to refrain from using its destructive forces. Today, of course, this threat does not obscure the fact that controlled nuclear energy promises to be a source of power capable of relieving our dependency on the earth's dwindling reserves of fossil fuels. For the chemist, nuclear chemistry provides a new tool for identifying and quantitating the elements.

Until now, our discussion of subatomic particles has been limited to the proton and electron. However, in order to understand the principles of nuclear chemistry, we must look at the other important subatomic particle, the neutron. Although the atoms of a single element must have the same number of protons, there is nothing to prevent them from having different numbers of neutrons. The total number of protons and neutrons in a nucleus is known as the **atomic mass number.** Atoms having the same number of protons but differing solely in the number of neutrons they possess are called **isotopes.** For example, the element hydrogen actually consists of three isotopes; besides ordinary hydrogen, which has one proton and no neutrons in its nucleus, two other isotopes exist, deuterium and tritium. Deuterium (or heavy hydrogen) also has one proton but contains one neutron as well. Tritium has one proton and two neutrons in its nucleus. The atomic structures of these isotopes are shown in Figure 6–7. Therefore, all the isotopes of hydrogen have an atomic number of one but differ in their atomic mass numbers. Hydrogen has an atomic mass of one, deuterium a mass of two, and tritium a mass of three. Ordinary hydrogen makes up 99.98 percent of all the hydrogen atoms found in nature.

Like hydrogen, most elements are known to have two or more isotopes. The element tin, for example, has as many as 10 isotopes. Many

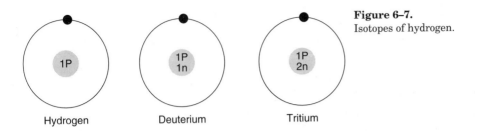

Figure 6–7.
Isotopes of hydrogen.

of these isotopes are quite stable, and for all intents and purposes, the isotopes of any one element have indistinguishable properties. Others, however, are not as stable and will decompose with time by a process known as **radioactive decay.** Radioactivity is the emission of radiation that accompanies the spontaneous disintegration of unstable nuclei. Radioactivity is actually composed of three types of radiation: **alpha rays, beta rays,** and **gamma rays.**

Alpha rays have proven to be positively charged particles, each having a mass approximately four times that of a hydrogen atom. These particles are known to be helium atoms stripped of their orbiting electrons. Beta rays are actually electrons, and the gamma rays are electromagnetic radiations similar to X-rays but of a higher frequency and energy (refer to the electromagnetic spectrum in Figure 5–13). Fortunately, the vast majority of naturally occurring isotopes are not radioactive, and those that do exist—that is, radium, uranium, and thorium—are found in such small quantities in the earth's crust that their radioactivity presents no hazard to human survival.

The existence of isotopes would be of little importance to the forensic chemist were it not for the fact that scientists have mastered the techniques for synthesizing radioactive isotopes. If the only distinction between isotopes of an element is the number of neutrons each possesses, is it not reasonable to assume that by bombarding atoms with neutrons, some neutrons will be captured to make new isotopes? This is exactly what takes place in a nuclear reactor. A nuclear reactor is simply a source of neutrons that can be used for bombarding the atoms of a specimen, thereby creating radioactive isotopes. When a neutron is captured by the nucleus of an atom, a new isotope is formed with one additional neutron. In this state, the nuclei are said to be activated, and many will immediately begin to decompose by emitting radioactivity.

To identify the activated isotope, it is necessary to measure the energy of the gamma rays emitted as radioactivity. The gamma rays of each element can be associated with a characteristic energy value. Furthermore, once the element has been identified, its concentration can be measured by the intensity of its gamma ray radiation; intensity

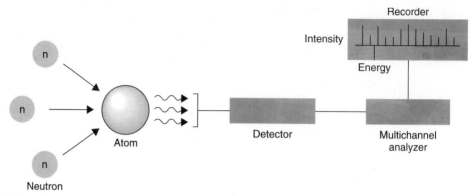

Figure 6–8. The neutron activation process requires the capture of a neutron by the nucleus of an atom. The new atom is now radioactive and emits gamma rays. A detector permits the identification of the radioactive atoms present by measuring the energies and intensities of the gamma rays emitted.

is directly proportional to the concentration of the element in a specimen. The technique of bombarding specimens with neutrons and measuring the resultant gamma ray radioactivity is known as **neutron activation analysis.** The process is depicted in Figure 6–8.

The major advantage of neutron activation analysis is that it provides a nondestructive method for identifying and quantitating trace elements. A median detection sensitivity of one-billionth of a gram (one nanogram) makes neutron activation analysis one of the most sensitive methods available today for the quantitative detection of many elements. Further, neutron activation has the capability to perform a simultaneous analysis for 20 to 30 elements. A major drawback to the technique is its expense. Only a handful of crime laboratories have access to a nuclear reactor; in addition, sophisticated analyzers are needed to detect and discriminate gamma ray emissions.

As far as forensic analysis is concerned, neutron activation has been employed for characterizing the trace elements present in metals, drugs, paint, soil, gunpowder residues, and hair. A typical illustration of its application occurred during the investigation of a theft of copper telegraphic wires in Canada. Four lengths of copper wire (A_1, A_2, A_3, A_4) found at the scene of the theft were compared by neutron activation with a length of copper wire (B) seized at a scrap yard and suspected of being stolen. All were bare, single-stranded wire with the same general physical appearance and a diameter of 0.28 centimeter. Prior experiments had revealed that significant variations could be expected in the concentration levels of the trace elements selenium, gold, antimony, and silver for wires originating from different sources.

TABLE 6–4.
CONCENTRATION OF TRACE ELEMENTS
IN COPPER WIRE

	Selenium	*Gold*	*Antimony*	*Silver*
Control Wire				
A$_1$	2.4	0.047	0.16	12.7
A$_2$	3.5	0.064	0.27	17.2
A$_3$	2.6	0.050	0.20	13.3
A$_4$	1.9	0.034	0.21	12.6
Suspect Wire				
B	2.3	0.042	0.15	13.0

Note: Average concentration measured in parts per million.

Source: R. K. H. Chan, "Identification of Single-Stranded Copper Wires by Nondestructive Neutron Activation Analysis," *Journal of Forensic Sciences,* 17 (1972), 93. Reprinted by permission of the American Society for Testing and Materials, copyright 1972.

A comparison of these elements present in the wire involved in the theft was undertaken. After exposing the wires to neutrons in a nuclear reactor, neutron activation analysis revealed a match between A$_1$ and B that was well within experimental error (see Table 6–4). The findings suggested a common origin of control and suspect wires.

X-RAY DIFFRACTION

Until now, we have discussed methods for detecting and identifying the elements. Emission spectroscopy, atomic absorption, and neutron activation analysis tell us what elements are present in a particular substance, but they do not provide any information as to how the elements are combined into compounds. One way of eliciting this information is to aim a beam of X-rays at a crystal and to study how the X-rays interact with the atoms that comprise the substance under investigation. This technique is known as **X-ray diffraction.**

X-ray diffraction can be applied only to the study of solid, crystalline materials—that is, solids having a definite and orderly arrangement of their atoms. For example, sodium chloride (common table salt), pictured in Figure 4–8, is crystalline. Fortunately, many substances, including 95 percent of all inorganic compounds, are crystalline in nature and hence are identifiable by X-ray diffraction analysis. The atoms in a crystal can be thought of as being composed of a series of parallel planes. As the X-rays penetrate the crystal, a portion of the beam is reflected by each of the atomic planes. As the reflected beams leave the crystal's planes, they combine with one another to

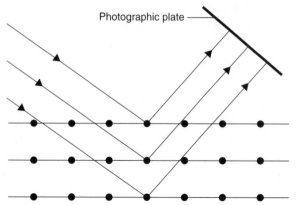

Photographic plate

Figure 6–9.
A beam of X-rays being reflected off the atomic planes of a crystal. The diffraction patterns that are formed are recorded on photographic film. These patterns are unique for each crystalline substance.

form a series of light and dark bands known as a **diffraction pattern.** Every compound is known to produce its own unique diffraction pattern, thus giving analysts a means for "fingerprinting" compounds.

A diagram depicting the X-ray diffraction process is illustrated in Figure 6–9. Diffraction patterns for potassium nitrate and potassium chlorate, two common constituents of homemade explosives, are shown in Figure 6–10 (a) and (b). A comparison of a questioned specimen with a known X-ray pattern is a rapid and specific way of proving chemical identity.

One drawback to X-ray diffraction is its lack of sensitivity. The technique is suitable for identifying the major constituents of a mixture, but it often fails to detect the presence of substances comprising less than 5 percent of a mixture. For this reason, the forensic chemist must resort to more sensitive techniques—that is, emission spectroscopy, atomic absorption, and neutron activation analysis—if there is a need to identify the trace elements that may be present.

Figure 6–10.   (a) X-ray diffraction pattern for potassium nitrate. (b) X-ray diffraction pattern for potassium chlorate.

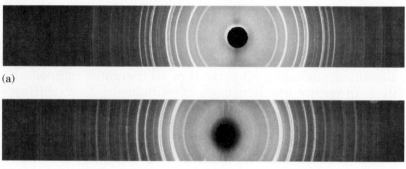

(a)

(b)

REVIEW QUESTIONS _____

1. The elements _____ and _____ make up 75 percent of the weight of the earth's crust.

2. Only _____ elements make up about 99 percent of the weight of the earth's crust.

3. The presence of _____ elements in materials provides useful "invisible" markers when comparing physical evidence.

4. The knowledge that elements selectively _____ and _____ light provides the basis for important analytical techniques designed to detect the presence of elements in materials.

5. An _____ is a display of colors or frequencies emitted from a light source.

6. A continuous spectrum consists of a blending of colors. (True, False)

7. A _____ spectrum shows distinct frequencies or wavelengths of light.

8. A line spectrum of an element (is, is not) characteristic of the element.

9. Matter in a solid or liquid state will produce an emission spectrum that is characteristic of its composition. (True, False)

10. The _____ is an instrument used to obtain and record the line spectrum of elements.

11. Excitation of a specimen can be accomplished when it is inserted between two _____ electrodes.

12. The selective absorption of light by atoms is the basis for a technique known as _____.

13. The composition of the discharge lamp (does, does not) have to be taken into consideration when performing an analysis by atomic absorption for a particular element.

14. One advantage of atomic absorption analysis is that it can simultaneously detect 20 to 30 elements. (True, False)

15. Three important subatomic particles of the atom are the _____, _____, and _____.

16. The proton and electron (are, are not) of approximately equal mass.

17. A proton imparts the nucleus of an atom with a _____ charge.

18. The number of protons (is, is not) always equal to the number of electrons in orbit around the nucleus of an atom.

19. Each atom of the same element always has the same number of _____ in its nucleus.

20. The number of protons in the nucleus of an atom is called the _____.

21. Each element has its own characteristic set of energy levels. (True, False)
22. To move an electron from one energy level to the next requires a definite amount of energy. (True, False)
23. As an electron falls back from a higher to a lower energy level, it emits _____.
24. The total number of protons and neutrons present in a nucleus is known as the _____.
25. Atoms differing only in the number of neutrons present in their nuclei are called _____.
26. Deuterium has the greatest number of protons of all the isotopes of hydrogen. (True, False)
27. Radioactivity is composed of the following emissions: _____, _____, and _____.
28. Beta particles are identical to _____.
29. Electromagnetic radiations similar to X-rays but of a higher energy are _____.
30. A nuclear reactor is a source of _____.
31. The technique of bombarding specimens with neutrons and measuring the resultant gamma ray emissions is known as _____.
32. As X-rays are reflected off a material's surface, they will form a series of light and dark bands known as a _____.
33. X-ray diffraction patterns are obtained from (crystalline, amorphous) substances.

FURTHER REFERENCES

Guinn, V. P., "NAA of Bullet-Lead Evidence Specimens in Criminal Cases," *Journal of Radioanalytical Chemistry,* 72 (1982), 645–63.

Krishnan, S. S., "Merits and Demerits of Forensic Activation Analysis When Compared to Other Analysis Methods," *Journal of Radioanalytical Chemistry,* 15 (1973), 165–72.

————, *An Introduction to Modern Criminal Investigation with Basic Laboratory Techniques.* Springfield, Ill.: Charles C Thomas, Publisher, 1978.

Singhal, S. P., "Atomic Absorption Spectroscopy in Forensic Chemistry," *The Canadian Society of Forensic Science Journal,* 7 (1974), 7.

Willard, H. H., L. L. Merritt, J. A. Dean, and F. A. Settle, Jr., *Instrumental Methods of Analysis,* 7th ed. New York: Wadsworth Publishing Co., 1988.

7 THE MICROSCOPE

A microscope is an optical instrument that uses a lens or a combination of lenses to magnify and resolve the fine details of an object. The earliest methods for examining physical evidence in crime laboratories relied almost solely on the microscope to study the structure and composition of matter. Even the advent of modern analytical instrumentation and techniques in recent years has done little to diminish the usefulness of the microscope for forensic analysis. If anything, the development of the powerful scanning electron microscope promises to add a new dimension to forensic science heretofore unattainable within the limits of the ordinary light microscope.

The earliest and simplest microscope was the single lens commonly referred to as a *magnifying glass*. The handheld magnifying glass makes things appear larger than they are because of the way light rays are refracted, or bent, in passing from the air into the glass and back into the air. The magnified image is observed by looking through the lens, as shown in Figure 7–1. Such an image is known as a **virtual image;** it can be seen only by looking through a lens and cannot be viewed directly. This is distinguished from a **real image,** which can be seen directly, like the image that is projected onto a motion picture screen.

The ordinary magnifying glass can achieve a magnification of about five to ten times. Higher magnifying power is obtainable only with a **compound microscope,** constructed of two lenses mounted at

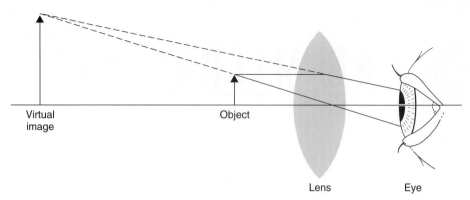

Figure 7–1. The passage of light through a lens, showing how magnification is obtained.

each end of a hollow tube. The object to be magnified is placed under the lower lens, called the **objective lens,** and the magnified image is viewed through the upper lens, known as the **eyepiece lens.** As shown in Figure 7–2, the objective lens forms a real, inverted, and magnified image of the object. The eyepiece, acting just like a simple magnifying glass, further magnifies this image into a virtual image, which is what is seen by the eye. The combined magnifying power of both lenses can produce an image magnified up to 1500 times.

The optical principles of the compound microscope are incorporated into the basic design of different types of light microscopes. Those microscopes found most applicable for examining forensic specimens are:

1. The compound microscope
2. The comparison microscope
3. The stereoscopic microscope
4. The polarizing microscope
5. The microspectrophotometer

After descriptions of these five microscopes, we will talk about a completely different approach to microscopy, the scanning electron microscope (SEM). This instrument focuses a beam of electrons instead of visible light onto the specimen to produce a magnified image. The principle and design of this microscope permit magnifying powers as high as 100,000 times.

THE COMPOUND MICROSCOPE

The parts that collectively comprise the compound microscope are illustrated in Figure 7–3(a). Basically, this microscope consists of a mechanical system, which supports the microscope, and an optical

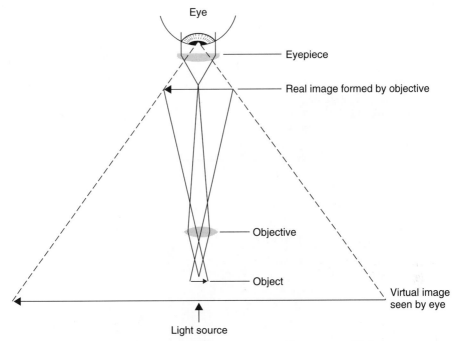

Figure 7–2. The principle of the compound microscope. The passage of light through two lenses forms the virtual image of the object seen by the eye.

system. The latter illuminates the object under investigation and passes the light through a series of lenses to form an image of the specimen on the retina of the eye. The optical path of light through a compound microscope is shown in Figure 7–3(b).

The mechanical system is composed of six parts:

Base. The support upon which the instrument rests.

Arm. A C-shaped upright structure, hinged to the base, that supports the microscope and acts as a handle for carrying.

Stage. The horizontal plate on which the specimens are placed for study. The specimens are normally mounted on glass slides that are held firmly in place on the stage by means of spring clips.

Body Tube. A cylindrical hollow tube on which the objective and eyepiece lenses are mounted at opposite ends. This tube merely serves as a corridor through which light passes from one lens to another.

Coarse Adjustment. This knob serves to focus the microscope lenses on the specimen by raising and lowering the body tube.

Fine Adjustment. The movements effected by this knob are similar to those of the coarse adjustment but are of a much smaller magnitude.

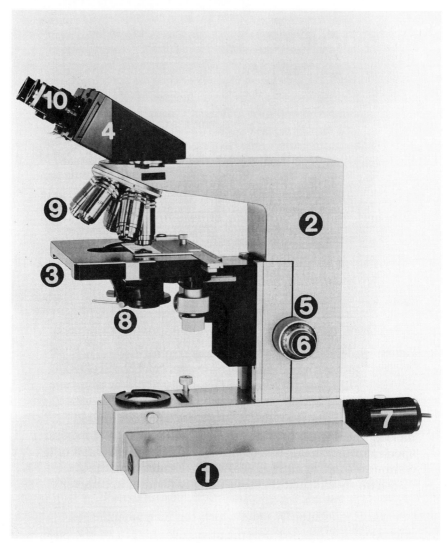

Figure 7–3. (a) Parts of the compound microscope: (1) base, (2) arm, (3) stage, (4) body tube, (5) coarse adjust, (6) fine adjust, (7) illuminator, (8) condenser, (9) objective lens, and (10) eyepiece lens. *Courtesy* E. Leitz, Inc., Rockleigh, N.J.

The optical system is made up of four parts:

> *Illuminator.* Most modern microscopes use artificial light supplied by a lightbulb to illuminate the specimen being examined. If the specimen is transparent, the light is directed up toward and through the specimen stage from an illuminator built into the base of the microscope. This is known as **transmitted illumination.** When the object is opaque—that

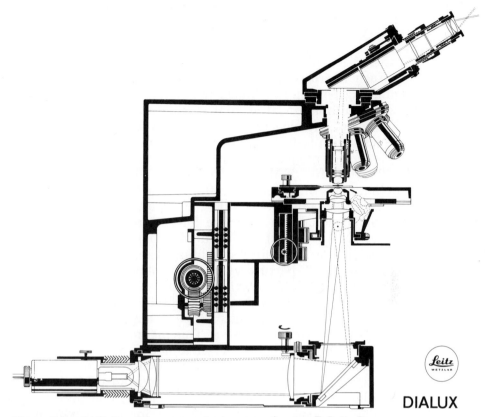

DIALUX

Figure 7–3. (b) Optics of the compound microscope. *Courtesy* E. Leitz, Inc., Rockleigh, N.J.

is, not transparent—the light source must be placed above the specimen so that it can be reflected off the specimen's surface and into the lens system of the microscope. This type of illumination is known as **vertical** or **reflected illumination.**

Condenser. The condenser collects light rays from the base illuminator and concentrates them on the specimen. The simplest condenser is known as the **Abbé condenser.** It consists of two lenses held together in a metal mount. The condenser also includes an iris diaphragm that can be opened or closed to control the amount of light passing into the condenser.

Objective Lens. This is the lens positioned closest to the specimen. To facilitate changing from one objective lens to another, several objectives are mounted on a revolving nosepiece or turret located above the specimen. Most microscopes are **parfocal,** meaning that when the microscope is focused with one objective in position, the other objective can be rotated into place by revolving the nosepiece while the specimen remains very nearly in correct focus.

Eyepiece or Ocular Lens. This is the lens closest to the eye. A microscope having only one eyepiece is **monocular;** one constructed with two eyepieces (one for each eye) is **binocular.**

Each microscope lens is inscribed with a number signifying its magnifying power. The image that is viewed by the microscopist will have a total magnification that is equal to the product of the magnifying power of the objective and eyepiece lenses. For example, an eyepiece lens with a magnification of 10 times (10×) used in combination with an objective lens of 10 times will have a total magnification power of 100 times (100×). Most forensic work will require a 10× eyepiece in combination with either a 4×, 10×, 20×, or 45× objective. The respective magnifications will be 40×, 100×, 200×, and 450×.

In addition, each objective lens is inscribed with its numerical aperture (N.A.). The ability of an objective lens to resolve details into separate images instead of one blurred image is directly proportional to the numerical aperture value of the objective lens. For example, an objective lens of N.A. 1.30 can separate details that are twice as close as compared to a lens with an N.A. of 0.65. The maximum useful magnification of a compound microscope is approximately 1000 times the N.A. of the objective being used. This magnification is sufficient to permit the eye to see all the detail that can be resolved. Any effort to increase the total magnification beyond this figure will yield no additional detail and is referred to as **empty magnification.**

Although a new student of the microscope may be tempted to immediately choose the highest magnifying power available to view a specimen, the experienced microscopist realizes that a number of important factors must be weighed before the selection of magnifying power is made. A first consideration must be the size of the specimen area, or the **field of view,** that the examiner wishes to study. As magnifying power increases, the field of view decreases. Thus, it is best to first select a low magnification in which a good general overall view of the specimen is seen and to switch later to a higher power in which a smaller portion of the specimen can be viewed in more detail.

The **depth of focus** is also a function of magnifying power. After a focus has been achieved on a specimen, the depth of focus defines the thickness of that specimen. Areas lying above and below this region will be blurred and can be viewed only when the focus is readjusted. Depth of focus decreases as magnifying power increases.

THE COMPARISON MICROSCOPE

Forensic microscopy often requires a side-by-side comparison of specimens. This kind of examination can best be performed with a comparison microscope, such as the one pictured in Figure 7–4. Basically, the

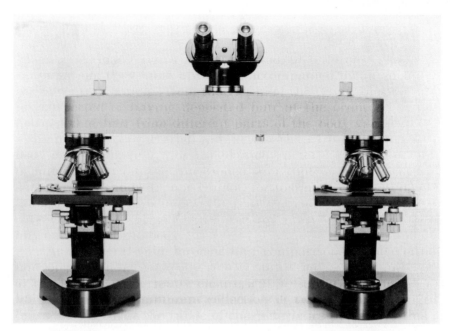

Figure 7–4. The comparison microscope—two independent objective lenses joined together by an optical bridge. *Courtesy* E. Leitz, Inc., Rockleigh, N.J.

comparison microscope is two compound microscopes combined into one unit. The unique feature of its design is that it uses a bridge incorporating a series of mirrors and lenses to join two independent objective lenses into a single binocular unit. When a viewer looks through the eyepiece lenses of the comparison microscope, a circular field, equally divided into two parts by a fine line, is observed. The specimen mounted under the left-hand objective is seen in the left half of the field, and the specimen under the right-hand objective is observed in the right half of the field. It is important that the optical characteristics of the objective lenses be closely matched to assure that both specimens are seen at equal magnification and with minimal but identical lens distortions.

Figure 7–5 shows the striation markings on two bullets that have been placed under the objective lenses of a comparison microscope. Modern firearms examination began with the introduction of the comparison microscope, with its ability to give the firearms examiner a side-by-side magnified view of bullets. Bullets that are fired through the same rifle barrel will display comparable rifling markings on their surfaces. By matching the majority of striations present on each bullet, a conclusion that both bullets traveled through the same barrel is justified.

Figure 7–5. Photomicrograph taken through a comparison microscope. On the left are the striation markings on the test-fired bullet, fired through the suspect weapon. On the right are the markings of the crime-scene bullet. *Courtesy* Laboratoire de l'Identité Judicaire, Paris.

THE STEREOSCOPIC MICROSCOPE

The details that characterize the structures of many types of physical evidence do not always require examination under very high magnifications. For such specimens, the stereoscopic microscope has proven quite adequate, providing magnifying powers that range from 10× to 125×. This microscope has the advantage of presenting a distinctive three-dimensional image of an object. Also, whereas the image formed by a compound microscope is inverted, the stereoscopic microscope is made more convenient for use by the placement of erecting prisms in its light path, permitting the formation of a right-side-up image. The stereoscopic microscope, shown in Figure 7–6, is actually two monocular compound microscopes properly spaced and aligned to present a three-dimensional image of a specimen to the viewer, who looks through both eyepiece lenses.

The stereoscopic microscope is undoubtedly the most frequently used and versatile microscope found in the crime laboratory. Its wide field of view and great depth of focus make it an ideal instrument for locating trace evidence that may be present in debris, garments, weapons, or tools. Furthermore, its potentially large **working distance** (the distance between the objective lens and the specimen) makes it quite applicable for the microscopic examination of big, bulky

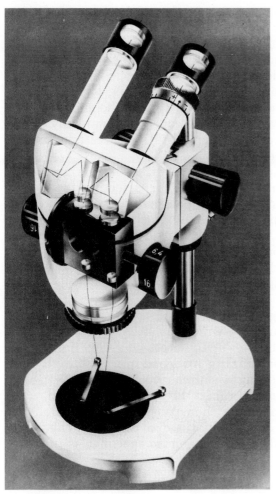

Figure 7–6. A schematic diagram of a stereoscopic microscope. This microscope is actually two separate monocular microscopes, each having its own set of lenses except for the lowest objective lens, which is common to both microscopes. *Courtesy* Wild Heerbrugg Ltd., Switzerland.

items. When fitted with vertical illumination, the stereoscopic microscope becomes the primary tool for characterizing physical evidence as diverse as paint, soil, gunpowder residues, and marijuana.

THE POLARIZING MICROSCOPE

It will be recalled from the discussion in Chapter 5 that light's wave-like motion in space can be invoked to explain many facets of its behavior. The waves that comprise a beam of light can be pictured as vibrating in all directions perpendicular to the direction in which the light is traveling. However, it is a familiar observation that when a beam of light passes through certain types of specially fabricated crystalline substances, it emerges vibrating in only one plane. Light that is confined to a single plane of vibration is said to be **plane-polarized.** The device that polarizes light in this manner is called a **polarizer.** A common example of this phenomenon is the passage of sunlight through Polaroid sunglasses. By transmitting light vibrating in the vertical plane only, these sunglasses will have the effect of eliminating or reducing light glare. Most glare consists of partially polarized light that has been reflected off horizontal surfaces and thus is vibrating in a horizontal plane.

Because polarized light appears no different to the eye from ordinary light, special means must be devised for detecting it. This is accomplished simply by placing a second polarizing crystal, called an **analyzer,** in the path of the polarized beam. As shown in Figure 7–7, if the polarizer and analyzer are aligned parallel to each other, the polarized light will pass through and be seen by the eye. If, on the other hand, the polarizer and analyzer are set perpendicular to one another, or are "crossed," no light will penetrate, and the result will be total darkness or extinction.

In this manner, the design of a compound or stereoscopic microscope can be modified to be outfitted with a polarizer and analyzer so as to be capable of allowing the viewer to detect polarized light. Such a microscope is known as a **polarizing microscope.** Essentially, the polarizer is placed between the light source and the sample stage to polarize the light before it passes through the specimen. The polarized light penetrating the specimen must then pass through an analyzer before it reaches the eyepiece and finally the eye. Normally, the polarizer and analyzer are "crossed" so that when no specimen is in place,

Figure 7–7. Polarization of light.

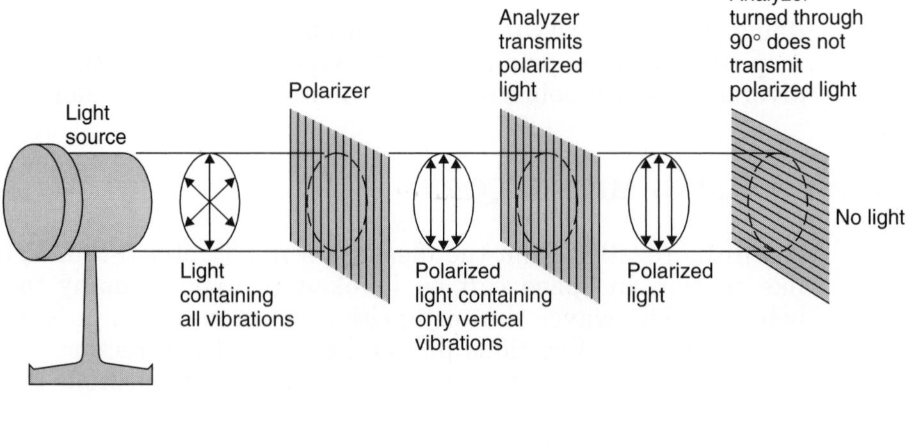

the field appears dark. However, the effect of introducing a specimen that polarizes light will be to reorient the polarized light, allowing it to pass through the analyzer. This result produces vivid colors and intensity contrasts that make the specimen readily distinguishable.

The most obvious and important applications of this microscope relate to studying materials that polarize light. For example, as we learned in Chapter 4 (see p. 108), many crystalline substances are birefringent; that is, they will split a beam of light into two light-ray components of different refractive index values. What makes this observation particularly relevant to our discussion of the polarizing microscope is that both light beams are polarized at right angles to one another. With this knowledge, polarizing microscopy has found wide application for the examination of birefringent minerals present in soil. By utilizing the immersion method (see p. 112) and selecting the proper immersion liquids, a refractive index corresponding to each plane of polarized light can be determined. Thus, when a mineral is viewed under polarized light in a liquid that matches one of its refractive indices, the Becke line will no longer be visible. This information, plus observations on crystal color and form, and so on, makes it possible for the microscopist to identify the mineral. Similarly, criminalists take advantage of the fact that many synthetic fibers are birefringent in order to characterize them with a polarizing microscope.

THE MICROSPECTROPHOTOMETER

From a practical point of view, few instruments present in a crime laboratory can match the versatility of the microscope. The microscope's magnifying power is an indispensable necessity for searching and locating minute traces of physical evidence. Once located, many items of physical evidence may be characterized by a microscopic examination of their morphological features. Likewise, the microscope can be used to study how light interacts with the material under investigation, or it can be used to observe the effects that other chemical substances are having on such evidence. Each of these features will allow an examiner to better characterize and identify physical evidence. Recently, by linking it to a computerized spectrophotometer, a new dimension has been added to the capability of the microscope. This combination has given rise to a new instrument called the **microspectrophotometer.**

In many respects, this is an ideal marriage from the forensic scientist's viewpoint. In Chapter 5, we saw how a chemist can take advantage of the selective absorption of light by materials in order to characterize them. In particular, light in the ultraviolet, visible, and infrared regions of the electromagnetic spectrum has proved most helpful for this purpose. Unfortunately, in the past, forensic chemists were unable to take full advantage of the capabilities of spectrophotometry for examining trace evidence, as most spectrophotometers are not well suited for examining the very small particles frequently encountered as evidence. However, with the development of the microspectrophotometer, a forensic analyst can now view a particle under a microscope while, at the same time, a beam of light is directed at the particle in order to obtain its absorption spectrum. Depending on the type of light employed, an examiner can acquire either a visible or an IR spectral pattern of a substance being viewed under the microscope. The obvious advantage of this approach is to provide the forensic scientist with added information that will characterize trace quantities of evidence. A microspectrophotometer designed to measure the uptake of visible light by materials is shown in Figure 7–8.

The visual comparison of color is usually one of the first steps in examining paint, fiber, and ink evidence. Such comparisons are easily

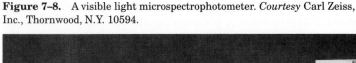

Figure 7–8. A visible light microspectrophotometer. *Courtesy* Carl Zeiss, Inc., Thornwood, N.Y. 10594.

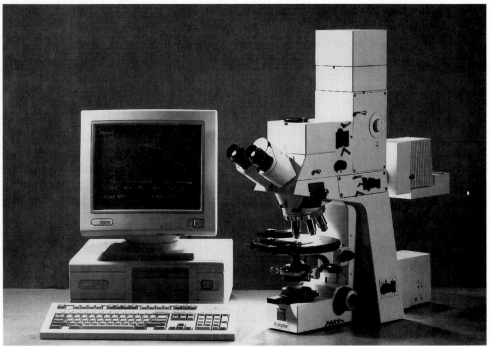

obtained using a comparison microscope. Now, with the use of the microspectrophotometer, not only can the color of materials be compared visually but, at the same time, an absorption spectrum can be plotted for each item under examination to display the exact wavelengths at which it absorbs in the visible light spectrum. Occasionally, colors that appear similar by visual examination will show significant differences in their absorption spectra. An example of this approach is shown in Figure 7–9, where the microspectrophotometer is utilized to distinguish counterfeit and authentic currency by comparing the spectral patterns of inked lines on currency.

Another emerging technique in forensic science is the utilization of the infrared microspectrophotometer for the examination of fibers and paints. The "fingerprint" IR spectrum (see p. 155) is unique for each chemical substance. Therefore, if such a spectrum can be obtained from either a fiber or a paint chip, it will allow the analyst to better identify and compare the type of chemicals from which these materials are manufactured. With a microspectrophotometer, a forensic analyst can view a substance through the microscope and at the same time have the instrument plot the infrared absorption spectrum for that material.

THE SCANNING ELECTRON MICROSCOPE (SEM)

All the microscopes described thus far utilize light coming off the specimen to produce a magnified image. The scanning electron microscope is, however, a special case in the family of microscopes (see Figure 7–10). Here, the image formation is produced by aiming a beam of electrons onto the specimen and studying electron emissions on a closed TV circuit. The beam of electrons is emitted from a hot tungsten filament and is focused by means of electromagnets onto the surface of the specimen. This primary electron beam causes the emission of electrons from the elements that make up the upper layers of the specimen. The emitted electrons are collected, and the amplified signal is displayed on a cathode-ray or TV tube. By scanning the primary electron beam across the specimen's surface in synchronization with the cathode-ray tube, it is possible to convert the emitted electrons into an image of the specimen for display on the cathode-ray tube.

The major attractions of the SEM image are its high magnification, high resolution, and great depth of focus. In its usual mode, the SEM has a magnification that ranges from 10× to 100,000×. Its depth of focus is some 300 times better than optical systems at similar

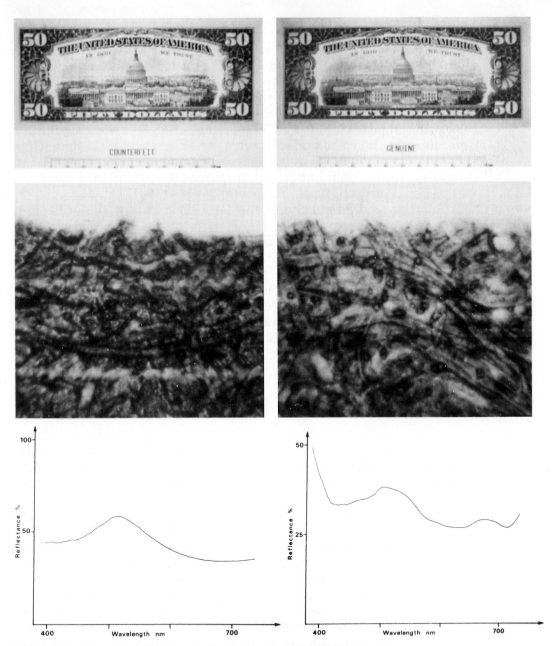

Figure 7–9. Two $50 bills are shown at top; one is genuine and the other is counterfeit. Below each bill is a microphotograph of an inked line present on each bill. Each line was examined under a visible light microspectrophotometer. As shown, the visible absorption spectrum of each line is readily differentiated, thus allowing the examiner to distinguish a counterfeit bill from genuine currency. *Courtesy* Peter W. Pfefferli, forensic scientist, Lausanne, Switzerland.

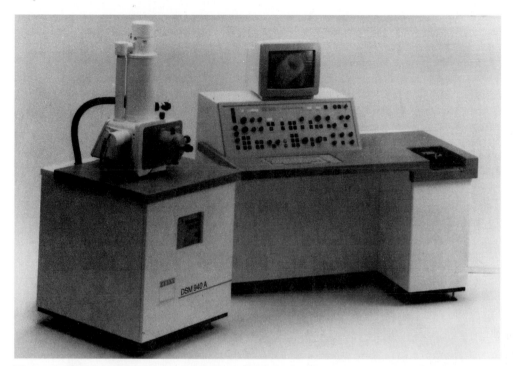

Figure 7–10.   A scanning electron microscope. *Courtesy* Carl Zeiss, Inc.,
Thornwood, N.Y. 10594.

magnifications, and the resultant picture is almost stereoscopic in
appearance. Its great depth of field and magnification are exemplified
by the magnification of cystolithic hair on the marijuana leaf as shown
in Figure 7–11.

Another facet of scanning electron microscopy has been the use of
X-ray production as a means of determining the elemental composition
of the specimen under examination. X-rays are generated when the
electron beam of the scanning electron microscope strikes a target.
When the SEM is coupled to an X-ray analyzer, the emitted X-rays can
be sorted according to their energy values and used to build up a picture of the elemental distribution in the specimen. Because each element emits X-rays of characteristic energy values, the X-ray analyzer
can identify the elements present in a specimen. Furthermore, the element's concentration can be determined by measuring the intensity of
the X-ray emission.

One application of scanning electron microscopy has been as a
tool for determining whether or not a suspect has recently fired a gun.
In this case, an attempt is made to remove any gunshot particles that
may be remaining on a shooter's hands by lifting them off with a piece

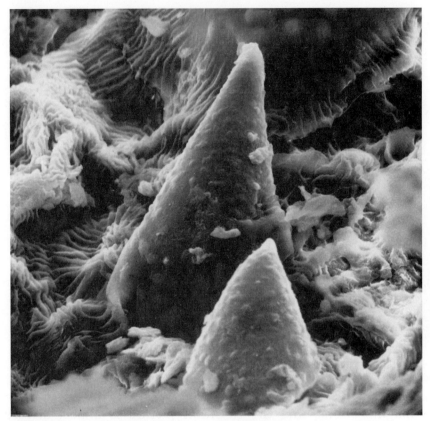

Figure 7–11. The cystolithic hairs of the marijuana leaf, as viewed with a scanning electron microscope (800×). *Courtesy* Jeff Albright.

of adhesive tape. The tape is then examined under the SEM for the presence of particles that may have originated from the bullet primer. These particles can be characterized by their size, shape, and elemental composition. As shown in Figure 7–12, when the sample of gunshot residue is exposed to a beam of electrons from the scanning electron microscope, X-rays are emitted. These X-rays are passed into a detector, where they are converted into electrical signals. These signals are sorted and displayed according to the energies of the emitted X-rays. Through the use of this technique, the elements lead, antimony, and barium, frequently found in most primers, can be rapidly detected and identified.

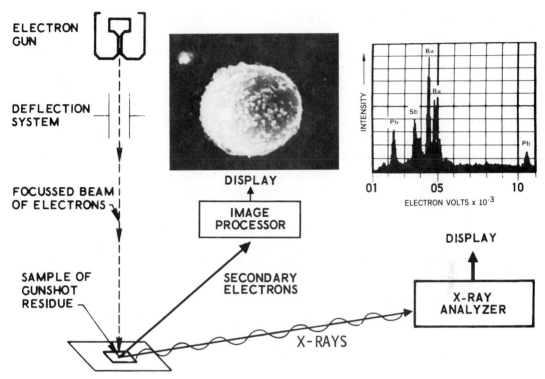

Figure 7–12. A schematic diagram of a scanning electron microscope displaying the image of a gunshot residue particle. Simultaneously, an X-ray analyzer detects and displays X-ray emissions from the elements lead (Pb), antimony (Sb), and barium (Ba) present in the particle. *Courtesy* Aerospace Corp., El Segundo, Calif.

REVIEW QUESTIONS

1. A microscope uses a combination of _____ to magnify an image.
2. A type of image that cannot be viewed directly is called a _____ image.
3. A _____ microscope consists of two lenses mounted at each end of a hollow tube.
4. The lens closest to the specimen is called the _____ .
5. The lens nearest the viewer's eye is called the _____.
6. The image seen through a compound microscope is (virtual, real).
7. The coarse and fine adjustments are part of the microscope's mechanical system. (True, False)

8. A transparent specimen is viewed through a microscope using _____ light.

9. An opaque object requires _____ illumination for viewing with a microscope.

10. A _____ collects light rays from the base illuminator and concentrates them on the specimen.

11. A microscope that remains in focus regardless of which objective lens is rotated into place is _____.

12. A microscope having only one eyepiece is monocular; one having two eyepieces is _____.

13. Each microscope lens is inscribed with a number signifying its _____.

14. An eyepiece lens of 10× used in combination with an objective lens of 20× will have a total magnification power of _____.

15. The ability of an objective lens to resolve details into separate images is directly proportional to its _____.

16. The size of the specimen area in view is known as the _____.

17. As magnification increases, the field of view (increases, decreases).

18. The thickness of a specimen in view is known as the _____.

19. The depth of focus (increases, decreases) with increasing magnification.

20. A side-by-side view of two specimens is best obtained with the _____ microscope.

21. A bridge is used to join two independent objective lenses into a single binocular unit to form a comparison microscope. (True, False)

22. Two monocular compound microscopes properly spaced and aligned describe the _____ microscope.

23. The stereoscopic microscope is the least frequently used microscope in a typical crime laboratory. (True, False)

24. The stereoscopic microscope offers a large _____ between the objective lens and the specimen.

25. Light confined to a single plane of vibration is said to be _____.

26. If a polarizer and analyzer are placed (perpendicular, parallel) to each other, no light will penetrate.

27. The _____ microscope allows a viewer to detect polarized light.

28. Crystals that are _____ will produce two planes of polarized light, each perpendicular to the other.

29. By utilizing the _____, one can view a particle under a microscope while at the same time a beam of light is directed at the particle in order to obtain its absorption spectrum.

30. The _____ microscope focuses a beam of electrons on a specimen to produce an image.

31. When a beam of electrons strikes a specimen, _____ are emitted whose energies correspond to elements present in the specimen.

FURTHER REFERENCES

Bartick, E. G., and M. W. Tungol, "Infrared Microscopy and Its Forensic Applications," in *Forensic Science Handbook,* Vol. 3, R. Saferstein, ed. Englewood Cliffs, N.J.: Prentice Hall, 1993.

De Forest, Peter R., "Foundations of Forensic Microscopy," in *Forensic Science Handbook,* R. Saferstein, ed. Englewood Cliffs, N.J.: Prentice Hall, 1982.

McCrone, W. C., "Forensic Microscopy," in *Forensic Science,* 2nd ed., G. Davies, ed. Washington, D.C.: American Chemical Society, 1986.

McCrone, Walter C., and John G. Delly, *The Particle Atlas,* Vol. 1, 2nd ed. Ann Arbor, Mich.: Ann Arbor Science Publishers, 1973.

McCrone, Walter C., Lucy B. McCrone, and John G. Delly, *Polarized Light Microscopy.* Ann Arbor, Mich.: Ann Arbor Science Publishers, 1978.

Olson, Larry A., "Color Comparison in Questioned Document Examination Using Microspectrophotometry," *Journal of Forensic Sciences,* 31 (1986), 1330.

Palenik, Skip, "Microscopy and Microchemistry of Physical Evidence," in *Forensic Science Handbook,* Vol. 2, R. Saferstein, ed. Englewood Cliffs, N.J.: Prentice Hall, 1988.

Petraco, N., and P. R. De Forest, "A Guide to the Analysis of Forensic Dust Specimens," in *Forensic Science Handbook,* Vol. 3, R. Saferstein, ed. Englewood Cliffs, N.J.: Prentice Hall, 1993.

Schlueter, Gene E., and Walter E. Gumpertz, "The Stereomicroscope— Instrumentation and Techniques," *American Laboratory,* 8 (1979), 61.

Taylor, M. E., "Scanning Electron Microscopy in Forensic Science," *Journal of the Forensic Science Society,* 13 (1973), 269.

CASE READING

MICROSCOPIC TRACE EVIDENCE—
THE OVERLOOKED CLUE
ARTHUR KOEHLER—WOOD DETECTIVE

Skip Palenik

Walter C. McCrone Associates Inc.

. . . Arthur Koehler . . . wood technologist and chief of the division of silvicultural relations at the U.S. Forest Products Laboratory in Madison, Wisconsin, . . . was born on June 4, 1885 in Mishicot, Wisconsin. His father was a carpenter and young Koehler grew up on a farm with a love of both wood and fine tools. This love naturally led him into forestry and he received a B.S. degree in the subject from the University of Michigan in 1911. . . . Upon graduation he went to work for the U.S. Forest Service in Washington, D.C., and three years later obtained a post at the U.S. Forest Products Laboratory where he served in various capacities until his retirement.

Although his primary responsibilities lay in wood identification and the correlation of microscopic wood structure and end use, Koehler also began to build a reputation as a wood detective after his success in obtaining evidence from wood fragments which were submitted to the laboratory in several cases of local importance. . . . The case which thrust Koehler into the limelight of international publicity, however, was the Lindbergh kidnapping case in which he, by the most painstaking work, traced the kidnap ladder back to the lumberyard from which its constituent parts had been purchased.

Sometime between the hours of 8 and 10 P.M. on the night of March 1, 1932, a kidnapper climbed into the nursery of the newly completed home of Charles and Anne Lindbergh in Hopewell, New Jersey, and abducted their infant son. The only clues left behind were a few indistinct muddy footprints, a ransom note in the nursery, a homemade ladder and a chisel found a short distance from the house. Scarcely two months later, on May 12, the dead body of the child was found, half buried in the woods, about a mile from the Lindbergh home. One of the most intensive manhunts in U.S. history ensued, but failed to uncover any trace of the kidnapper or the ransom money which had been paid.[1]

Reprinted in part from *The Microscope*, vol. 31, no. 1 (1983), pp. 1–14. Copyright 1982 by McCrone Research Institute, Inc., and reprinted by permission of the copyright owner.

Shortly after the news of the kidnapping broke in the press Koehler wrote a letter to Colonel Lindbergh offering his services to help with the investigation of the ladder. He never received a reply (which was not surprising considering the flood of mail which arrived at the Lindbergh home in the weeks following the kidnap). He was not entirely surprised though when his boss, Carlyle P. Winslow, placed before him some slivers of the ladder with the request that the wood be accurately identified.[2] This Koehler did, noting in his report the presence of golden brown, white and black wool fibers which he speculated might be from clothing worn by the kidnapper. That was the last he heard about the ladder for almost a year. During this time it was carried around the country (carefully wrapped in a wool blanket) to various experts including specialists at the National Bureau of Standards.[3] However, after a year of investigation the authorities were no closer to arresting a suspect than they were the day after the crime.

It was almost a year after the kidnapping when Koehler was asked by the head of the U.S. Forest Service, Major Robert Y. Stuart, to travel to Trenton to give the ladder an in-depth examination. Discussions between Colonel Norman Schwarzkopf, who headed the New Jersey State Police (and the kidnap investigation), and Major Stuart had convinced Colonel Schwarzkopf that the ladder might still yield clues about its maker if Koehler were given a chance to examine it thoroughly. Schwarzkopf wasn't too certain about Koehler's ability ("Wasn't he the one who identified the blanket fibers on the wood we sent him?" he asked) but felt he had nothing to lose.

For the first time, Koehler saw the ladder (Figure 1). He was immediately struck by the fact that, although it was cleverly contrived, it was shamefully constructed. Instead of rungs it had cleats, which had been carelessly mortised with a dull chisel. A dull hand plane had been used needlessly in some places and a handsaw had been drawn carelessly across some of the boards.

Alone for four days, Koehler studied the ladder in the police training school in Wilburtha. He then returned to the Forest Products Laboratory with the ladder and closed himself up in a private laboratory with the best optical equipment available.[4] He began by completely dissecting the ladder into its component parts. Each piece was numbered. The cleats were labeled 1 (bottom) through 11 (top). The rails were numbered starting from 12 (bottom left) to 17 (right-hand top). . . . Each mark was noted and indexed. After probing with microscopes, calipers and a variety of lighting and photographic techniques, the ladder slowly began to give up its secrets.

The sheer number of observations, facts and deductions about the origin of the ladder (and its producer) made by Koehler are truly

Figure 1.   The ladder used in the kidnapping of the Lindbergh baby.

staggering. We are concerned here only with those facts and observations which (1) allowed the parts to be traced and (2) described the carpenter and the previous environment of the ladder. The results were presented not as the subject of a single report but of daily letters to the director of the laboratory. As certain aspects were revealed they were pursued until the object could be traced no further. The most pertinent observations and deductions are listed and described below.

1. Microscopical examination showed four types of wood were used (Table 1). North Carolina pine is a trade name for wood from the southern yellow pine group which grows in commercial stands in the Southern U.S. along the Gulf of Mexico and along the Eastern Seaboard up into New Jersey and southern New York.[5] Douglas fir and Ponderosa pine grow in the Western U.S. and Birch is found throughout the country.[6]

TABLE 1.

WOODS USED IN KIDNAP LADDER

CLEATS

      1–10 Ponderosa pine

             1 × 6-inch boards ripped lengthwise into strips 2¾ inches wide to make cleats.

        11 Douglas fir

             Grain matched bottom of rail 15.

SIDE RAILS

      12, 13—North Carolina pine. Second growth. Cut from one board originally 14 feet long. Dressed to 3¾ inches in width. Both dressed on same planer.

      14, 15—Douglas fir

             Dressed on two different planers.

        16—North Carolina pine

             Narrowed from a wider board as indicated by handsaw and hand-planer marks on edges.

        17—Douglas fir

             Dressed on different planers than 14 and 15.

DOWEL PINS

        Birch

---

2. Rails 12 and 13 showed faint marks which gave information about the planer in the mill where the wood was dressed. . . . Figure 2 shows the operation of a mill planer in diagrammatic form. Defects in the cutters allowed the number of knives in the cutters to be determined by counting cutter marks between defect marks. Eight cutter heads dressed the wide surface and six heads the edges. . . .

The lumber went through the planer at a rate of 0.93 inches per complete revolution of the top and bottom cutter heads and 0.86 inches per revolution of the cutter heads that dressed the edges. This was determined by the distance of identical cuts made by a defective knife on each surface. . . .[7] Using the fact that the cutters in mill planers are usually driven at 3600 revolutions per minute it was possible to calculate the speed at which the wood passed into the planer as 258 feet per minute for the edge and 279 feet per minute for the board surfaces. The difference in the speed of the horizontal and vertical heads indicated that the planer was belt driven.

3. Rail 16 had four nail holes made by old fashioned square cut 8-penny nails. The holes had no connection with the construction of the ladder and therefore indicated prior use. The nail holes were clean and free from rust indicating inside use. This was confirmed by the general appearance of the rail which, although sapwood, showed no sign of exposure to the weather for any length of time since it was bright and

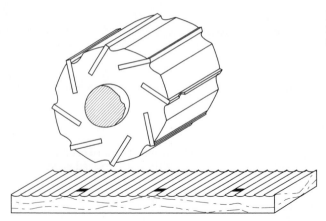

Figure 2. Detail of a cutter head illustrating how a defect allowed the number of knives to be determined.

unchecked. Therefore, it must have been nailed down indoors. Since it was low-grade lumber it would not have been used for finish purposes, but for rough construction. The spacing of the nails at 16 and 32 inches was considered significant and the suggestion was made that the rail came from the interior of a barn, garage or attic.

After an initial, futile attempt to trace the birch dowels, Koehler set out to try and trace the North Carolina rails (numbers 12 and 13). Although North Carolina pine grew in a large region it would not be profitable to ship it far, and since the ladder had turned up in New Jersey he felt certain that it had been milled somewhere in the Atlantic States. Using the Southern Lumberman's Directory, a list of 1598 planing mills from Alabama to New York was compiled. A confidential letter from Colonel Schwarzkopf and a two-page description written by Koehler were sent off to all of the mills on the list.

Of all the letters sent, only 25 mills reported having planers which matched the specifications outlined in the letter. Two were immediately excluded since they didn't dress lumber of the requisite size. Samples of 1 × 4-inch wood were requested from each of the remaining 23 mills. A sample received from the M. G. and J. J. Dorn mill of McCormick, South Carolina, showed exactly the marks Koehler was looking for.

A visit to the mill showed that the particular spacing was due to a pulley which had been purchased in September of 1929. The records of the mill showed that forty-six carloads of 1 × 4 had been shipped north of the Potomac River in the time between the purchases of the pulley and the kidnapping. . . . After personally visiting the final destination of each of the shipments, Koehler and Detective Bornmann finally arrived at a Bronx firm, the National Lumber and Millwork Company. Although the entire shipment had long before been sold, the foreman remembered that some storage bins had been built from some of the wood. The wood matched that from the ladder perfectly (Figures 3 and 4). Examination of wood from shipments before and after the Bronx carload showed that the belt on the planer had been changed and the knife sharpened. This meant that this shipment was the only one from which the two particular rails from the attic could have come. Whoever built the ladder had purchased part of the wood here!

Koehler was unprepared for the foreman's answer to his request to see the sales records. They had none. They had started selling cash and carry sometime before the Dorn shipment arrived and had no records. Although he had failed to come up with the carpenter's name, the authorities at least now knew the region where the kidnapper lived and bought his wood for the ladder.

Koehler went back to his laboratory and, undaunted, started tracing the Douglas fir rails. At the time a suspect was arrested, he had succeeded in tracing one of the boards to a mill in Bend, Oregon, and another to Spokane, Washington. With the arrest of Richard Hauptmann on September 19, 1934, . . . his role in the case changed from an investigative to a comparative one. In Hauptmann's garage a variety of tools were found whose markings could be compared with those from the ladder. Comparative micrographs of marks made with Hauptmann's plane and plane marks on the ladder showed that his plane was used to plane the cleats (Figure 5). Finally, one of the investigators searching the attic of the suspect's home found that a board had been sawed out of the floor (Figure 6). Koehler's examination showed that the nail holes in the floor joists and the ladder rail (No. 16)

Figure 3.   Comparison of knife marks from mill planer on edges of 1 × 4-inch pine from two shipments from the Dorn mill and a ladder rail.

Figure 4. Comparison of knife marks on upper surface of ladder rail and North Carolina pine board located in shipment to the National Lumber and Millwork Company.

Figure 5. Comparison of defect marks in Hauptmann's hand plane with marks on cleats (runs) from the ladder.

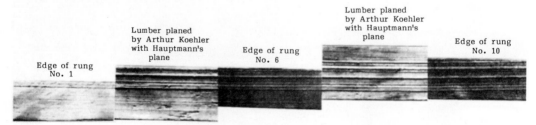

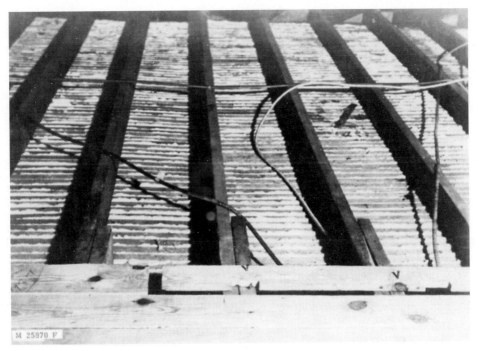

M 25970 F

Figure 6.   Rail 16 fitted into its original position in Hauptmann's attic.

aligned perfectly. A detailed analysis of the grain and wood itself showed that rail 16 and the section of board remaining in the attic were originally all one piece (Figures 7 and 8).

Richard Bruno Hauptmann was convicted and sentenced to death in a sensational trial. Although, in retrospect, there may have been many errors and a good deal of prejudice in the trial itself, the professionalism and objectiveness of Arthur Koehler still stand as an example of science at its best in the service of the law. . . .

Figure 7.   Composite photograph by Koehler showing comparison of end grain (growth rings) in board from attic and rail 16.

Board from
attic floor

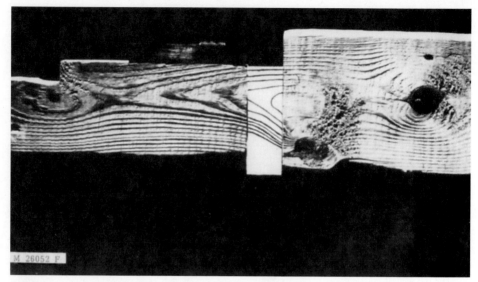

Figure 8.   Construction by Koehler showing probable grain pattern of missing piece between attic board and rail 16.

Acknowledgement

The author gratefully acknowledges the invaluable assistance of Dr. Regis Miller and Donna Christensen of the Forest Products Laboratory in Madison, Wisconsin, for making available documents and photographs which were necessary to this article. Additional thanks are due Jame Gerakaris of McCrone Associates for preparing the drawings of the ladder and mill planer.

References

1. Waller, George. *Kidnap; The Story of the Lindbergh Case.* Dial Press, New York, 1961.
2. Koehler, Arthur. "Who Made That Ladder?" as told to Boyden Sparkes. *The Saturday Evening Post,* 297, p. 10, April 20, 1935.
3. Saylor, Charles, Proffer. "Optical Microscopy as Used in Unorthodox Ways," *SPIE,* 104, Multi-disciplinary Microscopy, 31–33, 1977.
4. Koehler, Arthur. *The Saturday Evening Post,* 297, p. 84, April 20, 1935.
5. Isenberg, Irving. *Pulpwoods of the United States and Canada.* Institute of Paper Chemistry, Appleton, pp. 19–22, 1951.
6. Christensen, Donna. Wood Technology and the Lindbergh Kidnap Case. Report, May 1971.
7. Koehler, Arthur. "Techniques Used in Tracing the Lindbergh Kidnapping Ladder," *Am. J. Police Science,* 27, 5 (1937).

◆8 Hairs, fibers, and paint

The trace evidence that is transferred between individuals and objects during the commission of a crime will, if recovered, often corroborate other evidence developed during the course of an investigation. Although in most cases physical evidence cannot by itself provide for a positive identification of a suspect, laboratory examination may narrow the origin of such evidence to a group that includes the suspect. Utilizing many of the instruments and techniques described in the previous three chapters, the crime laboratory has developed a variety of procedures for comparing and tracing the origins of physical evidence. It will be the purpose of this and forthcoming chapters to apply these techniques to the analysis of the types of physical evidence most often encountered at crime scenes. We will begin with a discussion of hairs, fibers, and paint.

MORPHOLOGY OF HAIR

Hair is encountered as physical evidence in a wide variety of crimes. However, any review of the forensic aspects of hair examination must start with the observation that it is not yet possible to individualize a human hair to any single head or body. Over the years, criminalists have tried in vain to find a way to isolate the physical and chemical properties of hair that could serve as individual characteristics of identity. One by one these efforts have repeatedly failed to uncover any one property that remains consistent with time and is uniform throughout the head or body. It is a testimony to hair's reluctance to yield distinctive chemical properties that its color and structure, or morphology, still remain its most characteristic forensic features.

This is not to imply that hair has no value as physical evidence. On the contrary, when it is properly collected at the crime scene and its submission to the laboratory is accompanied by an adequate number of controls, hair can provide strong corroborative evidence for placing an individual at a crime site.

Hair is an appendage of the skin that grows out of an organ known as the **hair follicle.** The length of a hair extends from its root or bulb embedded in the follicle, continues into a shaft, and terminates at a tip end. It is the shaft, which is composed of three layers—the **cuticle, cortex,** and **medulla**—that is subjected to the most intense examination by the forensic scientist (see Figure 8–1).

Figure 8–1.   Cross section of skin showing hair growing out of a tubelike structure called the follicle.

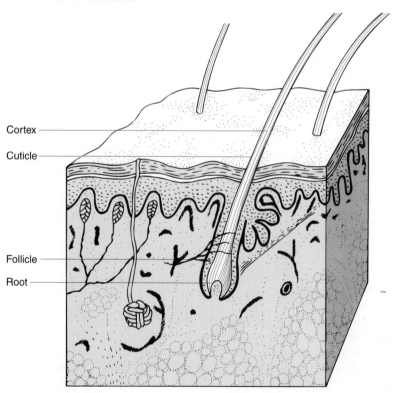

Cortex

Cuticle

Follicle

Root

Cuticle.   Two of the features that make hair a good subject for establishing individual identity are its resistance to chemical decomposition and its ability to retain structural features over a long period of time. Much of this resistance and stability is attributed to the cuticle or outside covering of the hair. The cuticle is formed by overlapping scales that always point toward the tip end of each hair. The scales are formed from specialized cells that have hardened *(keratinized)* and flattened in progressing from the follicle. The scales of most animal hair can best be described as having the appearance of shingles on a roof. Although the scale pattern is not a useful characteristic for individualizing human hair, the variety of patterns formed by animal hair makes it an important feature for species identification. Figure 8–2 shows the scale patterns of some animal hairs and of a human hair as viewed by the scanning electron microscope. Another method of studying the scale pattern of hair is to make a cast of its surface. This is readily done by embedding the hair in a soft medium, such as clear nail polish or softened vinyl. When the medium has hardened, the hair is removed, and there remains a clear, distinct impression of the hair's cuticle, ideal for examination with a compound microscope.

Cortex.   Contained within the protective layer of the cuticle is the cortex. The cortex is actually made up of spindle-shaped cortical cells that are aligned in a regular array, parallel to the length of the hair. The cortex derives its major forensic importance from the fact that it is embedded with the pigment granules that impart hair with color. It is the color, shape, and distribution of these granules that provide the criminalist with important points of comparison between the hairs of different individuals.

The structural features of the cortex are examined microscopically after the hair has been mounted in a liquid medium that has a refractive index closely matched to that of the hair. Under these conditions, the amount of light reflected off the hair's surface is minimized, and the amount of light penetrating the hair is optimized.

Medulla.   The medulla is a collection of cells having the appearance of a central canal running through a hair. In many animals, this canal is a most predominant feature, occupying more than half of the hair's diameter. The **medullary index** measures the diameter of the medulla relative to the diameter of the hair shaft and is normally expressed as a fraction. For humans, the index generally has a value less than $\frac{1}{3}$; for most other animals, the value is $\frac{1}{2}$ or greater.

It is important to stress that the presence and appearance of the medulla vary from individual to individual and even between hairs of a given individual. Not all hairs have medullae, and when they do exist,

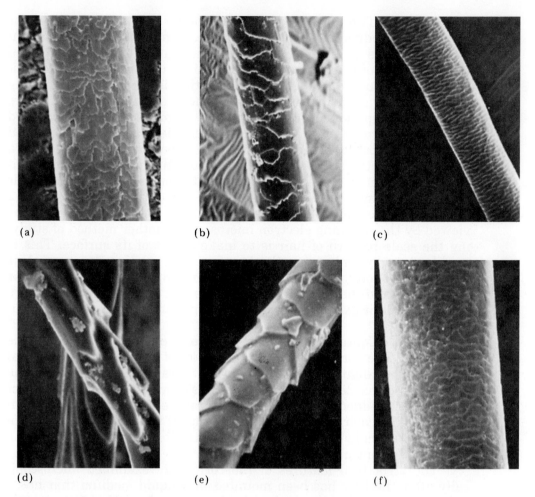

Figure 8–2.   Scale patterns of various types of hair. (a) Human head hair (600x); (b) dog (1250x); (c) deer (120x); (d) rabbit (300x); (e) cat (2000x); (f) horse (450x). *Courtesy* International Scientific Instruments, Mountain View, Calif., and New Jersey State Police.

the degree of medullation can vary. In this respect, medullae may be classified as being continuous, interrupted, fragmented, or absent (see Figure 8–3). Human head hairs generally exhibit no medullae or have fragmented ones; they rarely show continuous medullation. One noted exception is the Mongoloid race, who usually have head hairs with continuous medullae. Also, most animals have medullae that are either continuous or interrupted.

Another interesting feature of the medulla is its shape. Humans, as well as many animals, have medullae that give a nearly cylindrical

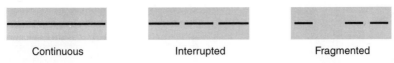

Continuous   Interrupted   Fragmented

Figure 8–3. Medulla patterns.

appearance. Other animals exhibit medullae that have a patterned shape. For example, the medulla of a cat can best be described as resembling a string of pearls, whereas members of the deer family show a medullary structure consisting of spherical cells occupying the entire hair shaft. Figure 8–4 illustrates medullary sizes and forms for a number of common animal hairs and a human head hair.

IDENTIFICATION AND COMPARISON OF HAIR

Most often when hair evidence is present in a criminal case, the prime purpose for its examination in a crime laboratory is to establish whether the hair is human or animal in origin, or to determine whether human hair retrieved at a crime scene compares with hair that is known to have come from a particular individual. Although the distinction of animal hair from human hair can normally be accomplished with little difficulty, the problem of human hair comparisons is one that must be undertaken with extreme caution and with an awareness of hair's tendency to exhibit variable morphological characteristics, not only from one person to another but also within a single individual.

A careful microscopic examination of hair will reveal morphological features that can distinguish human hair from the hair of animals. The hair of various animals also differs in structure to such an extent that the examiner may often be able to identify the species of animal from which the hair originated. It is important, however, that before such a conclusion is reached, the examiner has access to a comprehensive collection of reference standards and the accumulated experience of hundreds of prior hair examinations. Scale structure, medullary index, and medullary shape are features that are particularly important in hair identification.

The most common request that is made of the laboratory when hair is used as forensic evidence is to determine whether or not hair recovered at the crime scene compares to hair removed from a suspect. In most cases, such a comparison relates to hair obtained from the scalp or pubic area. Ultimately, the evidential value of the comparison will depend on the degree of probability with which the examiner can associate the questioned hair to a particular individual.

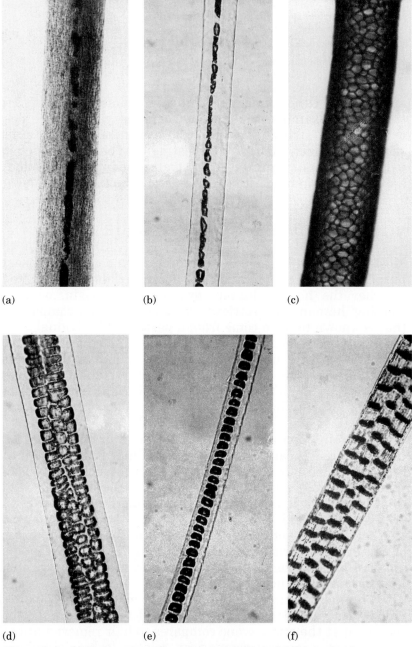

(a)   (b)   (c)

(d)   (e)   (f)

Figure 8–4.   Medulla patterns for various types of hair. (a) Human head hair (450×); (b) dog (450×); (c) deer (100×); (d) rabbit (450×); (e) cat (450×); (f) mouse (450×). All *courtesy* Linda Jankowski.

In making a hair comparison, a comparison microscope is an invaluable tool that allows the examiner to view the questioned and known hair together, side by side. Any variations in the microscopic characteristics will thus be readily observed. Because hair from any part of the body exhibits a range of characteristics, it is necessary to have an adequate number of known hairs that are representative of all its features when making a comparison.

In comparing hair, the criminalist is particularly interested in matching the color, length, and diameter. Other important features are the presence or absence of a medulla and the distribution, shape, and color intensity of the pigment granules present in the cortex. A microscopic examination may also be able to distinguish dyed or bleached hair from natural hair. A dyed color will often be present in the cuticle as well as throughout the cortex. Bleaching, on the other hand, tends to remove pigment from the hair and to give it a yellowish tint. If there has been a growth of hair since it was last bleached or dyed, the natural-end portion will be quite distinct in color. An estimate of the time since dyeing or bleaching can be made because hair is known to grow at a rate of approximately one centimeter per month. Other significant but less frequent features may be observed in hair. For example, morphological abnormalities may be present due to certain diseases or deficiencies. Also, the presence of fungal and nit infections can serve to further link a hair specimen to a particular individual.

Hair is class evidence, and thus it is not possible, except in rare instances, to determine that a questioned hair sample came from a particular individual to the exclusion of all others. In seeking to define how closely a particular hair can be associated with an individual, the examiner must to a large extent rely on experience. Each case will have to be evaluated on its own merits. A study conducted by the laboratory of the Royal Canadian Mounted Police offers an interesting insight into the evidential value of a hair comparison.[1] One hundred different individuals were asked to submit a sample of 80 to 100 hairs randomly selected from various regions of the scalp. From these, depending on the homogeneity of the sample, 6 to 11 mutually dissimilar hairs were selected to represent the range of length, coarseness, and color present in the 80 to 100 hairs. The representative hairs were then mounted individually on glass slides and compared to one another, utilizing a comparison microscope. A total of 861 hairs from the 100 individuals were compared in this manner.

---

[1] B. D. Gaudette and E. S. Keeping, "An Attempt at Determining Probabilities in Human Scalp Hair Comparison," *Journal of Forensic Sciences,* 19 (1974), 599.

By use of a card coding system, it was possible to record 366,630 hair comparisons between the 861 hairs. As a result, it was estimated that if one human head hair found at the scene of a crime is found to be similar to a representative hair from a suspect's head, the odds against it originating from another person are about 4500 to 1.[2] Another study conducted along the same lines revealed that the odds against two similar pubic hairs originating from two different individuals are about 800 to 1.[3] Because Negroid and Mongoloid hairs exhibit less variation in many of their characteristics, it is expected that these odds would be somewhat less for persons of these racial origins.

Until more definitive probability data are acquired, a final assessment of the significance of any hair comparison will depend almost entirely on the experience and judgment of the examiner. However, these initial studies have confirmed what many forensic scientists have long suspected—hair, when accompanied by a thorough collection of control specimens, can be highly distinctive evidence for personal identification.

A number of questions may be asked to further ascertain the present status of forensic hair examinations.

Can the body area of a hair be determined?   Normally, little difficulty is experienced in ascertaining the body area of those hairs commonly submitted to crime laboratories. For example, scalp hairs generally show little diameter variation and have a more uniform distribution of pigment color when compared to other body hairs. Pubic hairs are short and curly, with wide variations in shaft diameter, and usually have continuous medullae. Beard hairs are coarse, normally triangular in cross section, and have blunt tips acquired from cutting or shaving.

Can the racial origin of hair be determined?   In many instances, the examiner can distinguish hair originating from members of different races; this is especially true of Caucasian and Negroid head hair. Negroid hairs are normally kinky, containing dense, unevenly distributed pigments. Caucasian hairs are usually straight or wavy, with

---

[2]A modified approach for the Gaudette and Keeping study has been reported by R. A. Wickenheiser and D. G. Hepworth, "Further Evaluation of Probabilities in Human Scalp Comparisons," *Journal of Forensic Sciences,* 35 (1990), 1323. This study supports the findings of Gaudette and Keeping and finds the odds of 4500 to 1 to be very conservative.

[3]B. D. Gaudette, "Probabilities and Human Pubic Hair Comparisons," *Journal of Forensic Sciences,* 21 (1976), 514.

very fine to coarse pigments that are more evenly distributed when compared to Negroid hair. Sometimes a cross-sectional examination of hair may aid in the identification of race. Cross sections of hair from Caucasians are oval to round in shape, whereas cross sections of Negroid hair are flat to oval in shape. However, it must be emphasized that all of these observations are general in nature, with many possible exceptions. The criminalist must approach the determination of race from hair with caution and a good deal of experience.

Can the age and sex of a hair be determined? The age of an individual cannot be learned from a hair examination with any degree of certainty except with infant hair. Infant hairs are fine, are short in length, have fine pigment, and are rudimentary in character. Although the presence of dye or bleach on the hair may offer some clue to sex, present hair styles make these characteristics less valuable than they were in the past. Currently, a number of researchers are making good progress in studies aimed at determining the sex origin of human hair. Most of this research has concentrated on using techniques for identifying genetic substances in human cells. However, at this time sexual discrimination of hair cells is not considered to be a routine forensic technique.

Is it possible to determine if hair was forcibly removed from the body? A microscopic examination of the hair root *may* establish whether the hair has fallen out or has been pulled out of the skin. A hair root found to have follicular tissue (root sheath cells) adhering to it, as shown in Figure 8–5, is indicative of a hair that has been pulled

Figure 8–5. Head hair forcibly removed, with follicular tissue attached. *Courtesy* New Jersey State Police.

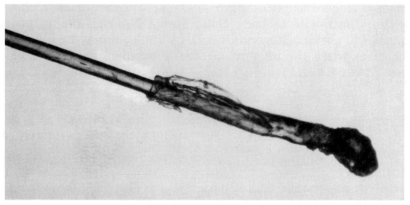

out either by another person or by brushing or combing. Hair naturally falling off the body will show a bulbous-shaped root free of any adhering tissue. However, the absence of sheath cells cannot always be relied upon for correctly judging whether or not hair has been forcibly pulled from the body. It has been demonstrated that in some cases the root of a hair may be devoid of any adhering tissue even when it has been pulled from the body. Apparently, an important consideration is how quickly the hair is pulled out of the head. Hairs pulled quickly from the head are much more likely to have sheath cells as compared to hairs that have been removed slowly from the scalp.[4]

Are efforts being made to individualize human hair?   The current approach for the examination of hair specimens still relies primarily on morphological characteristics. However, there are good reasons to believe that major breakthroughs are near in applying genetic typing technology to the individualization of human hair. As we will learn in Chapter 13, forensic scientists are starting to isolate and characterize individual variations in DNA (deoxyribonucleic acid), the basic chemical structure of our genes. This work has served as a basis for identifying individuals through their DNA makeup. One group of researchers has demonstrated the feasibility of recovering DNA from hair and typing a segment of the DNA molecule.[5] This method utilizes a technique called polymerase chain reaction (PCR) to amplify the small amount of DNA found in the human hair root or in follicular tissue adhering to a pulled hair. PCR will be discussed in greater detail in Chapter 13. The actual DNA typing success rate for single hairs has been shown to be in the area of 34 percent for case samples.[6]

In 1996, the FBI initiated a program to compare human head and pubic hairs through DNA analysis. The type of DNA analyzed in these cases is known as mitochondrial DNA. Mitochondrial DNA are located within the nuclei of body cells. This DNA is transmitted only from mother to child. Mitochondrial DNA analysis may be applied in forensic cases when the amount of DNA present is very small or degraded (see Appendix III).

---

[4]L. A. King, R. Wigmore and J. M. Twibell, "The Morphology and Occurrence of Human Hair Sheath Cells," *Journal of the Forensic Science Society,* 22 (1982), 267.

[5]R. Higuchi et al., "DNA Typing from Single Hairs," *Nature,* 332 (1988), 543.

[6]E. Blake et al., "Polymerase Chain Reaction (PCR) Amplification and Human Leukocyte Antigen (HLA)—DQ alpha Oligonucleotide Typing on Biological Evidence Samples. Casework Experience," *Journal of Forensic Sciences,* 37 (1992), 700.

COLLECTION OF HAIR EVIDENCE

When questioned hairs are submitted to a forensic laboratory for examination, they must always be accompanied by an adequate number of control samples from the victim of the crime and from individuals suspected of having deposited hair at the crime scene. We have learned that hair from different parts of the body varies significantly in its physical characteristics. Likewise, hair from any one area of the body also can have a wide range of characteristics. For this reason, it is imperative that the questioned and control hairs come from the same area of the body; one cannot, for instance, compare head hair to pubic hair. It is also important that the collection of control hair be carried out in a way to ensure a representative sampling of hair from any one area of the body.

As a general rule, forensic hair comparisons involve either head hair or pubic hair. The collection of 50 full-length hairs from all areas of the scalp will normally ensure a representative sampling of head hair. Likewise, a minimum collection of two dozen full-length pubic hairs should cover the range of characteristics present in this portion of the body. In rape cases, care must first be taken to comb the pubic area with a clean comb to remove all loose foreign hair present before the victim is sampled for control hair. The comb is to be packaged in a separate envelope.

Because a hair may show variation in color and other morphological features over its entire length, the entire hair length is collected. This requirement is best accomplished by either pulling the hair out of the skin or clipping it at the skin line.

As a matter of routine, hair samples are collected from the victim(s) of suspicious death during an autopsy. As the autopsy may occur early in an investigation, the need for hair controls may not always be apparent. However, one should never rule out the possible involvement of hair evidence in subsequent investigative findings. Failure to make this simple collection at an opportune time may result in complicated legal problems at a later date.

TYPES OF FIBERS

Just as hair left at a crime scene can serve as identification, the same logic can reasonably be extended to the fibers that comprise our fabrics and garments. Fibers may become important evidence in incidents that involve personal contact—such as homicide, assault, or sexual offenses—in which cross-transfers may occur between the clothing of suspect and victim. Similarly, it is not uncommon to find that the force of impact between a hit-and-run victim and a vehicle leaves fibers, threads, or even whole pieces of clothing adhering to parts of the vehicle. Fibers may also become fixed in screens or glass broken in the course of a breaking-and-entering attempt.

Regardless of where and under what conditions fibers are recovered, their ultimate value as forensic evidence will depend on the criminalist's ability to narrow their origin to a limited number of sources or even to a single source. Unfortunately, the mass production of our garments and fabrics has served to limit the value of fiber evidence in this respect, and it is only under the most unusual circumstances that the recovery of fibers at a crime scene will provide individual identification with a high degree of certainty.

For centuries, humans were dependent on natural sources derived from plants and animals for textile fibers. Early in the twentieth century, the first manufactured fiber—rayon—became a practical reality, followed in the 1920s by the introduction of cellulose acetate. Since the late 1930s, scientists have produced literally dozens of new fibers. In fact, the development of fibers, fabrics, finishes, and other textile-processing techniques has made greater advances since 1900 than in the four to five thousand years of recorded history before the twentieth century. Today, such varied items as clothing, carpeting, drapes, wigs, and even artificial turf attest to the predominant role that manufactured fibers have come to play in our culture and environment.

For the purpose of discussing the forensic examination of fibers, it will be convenient to classify them into two broad groups: **natural** and **man-made.**

NATURAL FIBERS

Natural fibers are derived in whole from animal or plant sources. Animal fibers comprise the majority of the natural fibers encountered in crime laboratory examinations. These include hair coverings from such animals as sheep (wool), goats (mohair, cashmere), camels, llamas, alpacas, and vicuñas; fur fibers include those obtained from animals such as mink, rabbit, beaver, and muskrat.

Any discussion of the forensic examination of animal fibers will merely restate procedures developed in the previous section for the forensic examination of animal hairs. The identification and comparison of such fibers will rely solely on a microscopic examination of color and morphological characteristics. Again, a sufficient number of control specimens must be examined to establish the range of fiber characteristics that comprise the suspect fabric.

By far the most prevalent plant fiber is cotton. However, the wide use of undyed white cotton fibers in clothing and other fabrics has made its evidential value almost meaningless, although the presence of dyed cotton in a combination of colors has, in some cases, served to enhance its evidential significance. The microscopic view of cotton fiber shown in Figure 8–6 reveals its most distinguishing feature—a ribbonlike shape with twists at irregular intervals.

MAN-MADE FIBERS

Beginning with the introduction of rayon in 1911 and the development of nylon in 1939, man-made fibers have increasingly replaced natural fibers in garments and fabrics. Today, such fibers are marketed under hundreds of different trademark names. To reduce consumer confusion, the U.S. Federal Trade Commission has approved "generic" or family names for the grouping of all man-made fibers. Many of these generic classes are produced by several manufacturers and are sold under a confusing variety of trademark names. For example, in the United States, polyesters are marketed under names that include Dacron®, Fortrel®, and Kodel®. In England, polyesters are called Terylene®. Table 8–1 lists major generic fibers and their tradenames.

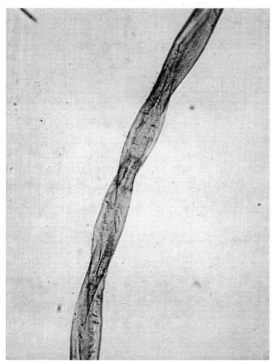

Figure 8–6.
Photomicrograph of cotton fiber (450×). *Courtesy* Linda Jankowski.

TABLE 8–1.
MAJOR GENERIC FIBERS

Major Generic Fibers and Tradenames			Characteristics
ACETATE Celebrate Chromspun Estron			Luxurious feel and appearance; wide range of colors and lusters; excellent drapability and softness; relatively fast-drying; shrink-, moth-, and mildew-resistant.
ACRYLIC Acrilan Bi-Loft Creslan Du-Rel	Fi-lana Orlon Pil-Trol So-Lara	Zefkrome Zefran	Soft and warm, wool-like, lightweight; retains shape; resilient; quick-drying; resistant to moths, sunlight, oil, and chemicals.
ARAMID Kevlar Nomex			No melting point; highly flame-resistant; high strength; high resistance to stretch; maintains its shape and form at high temperatures.
MODACRYLIC SEF			Soft, resilient, abrasion- and flame-resistant; quick-drying; resists acids and alkalies; retains shape.
NYLON A.C.E. Anso Antron Blue "C" Cadon Cantrece Capima	Caplana Carprolan Captiva Compet Cordura Crepeset Cumuloft	Hydrofil No Shock Patina Shareen Shimmereen Tolaram Ultron	Vivana WorryFree Zefsport Zefstat Zeftron
			Exceptionally strong, supple, abrasion-resistant; lustrous; easy to wash. Resists damage from oil and many chemicals. Resilient; low in moisture absorbency.
OLEFIN Alpha Essera Genesis Marquesa Lana	Marquesa Lana ST Marvess Patlon III Spectra	Synera Trace Tolaram	Unique wicking properties that make it very comfortable. Abrasion-resistant; quick-drying; resistant to deterioration from chemicals, mildew, perspiration, rot, and weather; sensitive to heat; soil resistant; strong; very lightweight. Excellent colorfastness.

Fiber	Trade Names	Characteristics
POLYESTER A.C.E. Ceylon Comfort Fiber Compet Dacron E.S.P. Fortrel	Golden Glow Golden Touch Hollofil Kodaire Kodel KodOfill KodOsoff	MicroSpun Pentron Premafill Plump Premafill Soft Silky Touch Spunnese Strialine	Tolaram Trevira Trevira Finesse Trevira Micronesse Ultra Touch Universe	Strong, resistant to stretching and shrinking; resistant to most chemicals; quick-drying; crisp and resilient when wet or dry; wrinkle- and abrasion-resistant; retains heat-set pleats and creases; easy to wash.
PBI PBF Arozole				Highly flame-resistant. Outstanding comfort factor combined with thermal and chemical stability properties. Will not burn or melt. Low shrinkage, when exposed to flame.
RAYON Beau-Grip Courtaulds Rayon Zantrel				Highly absorbent; soft and comfortable; easy to dye; versatile; good drapability.
SPANDEX Lycra				Can be stretched 500 percent without breaking; can be stretched repeatedly and recover original length; lightweight; stronger, more durable than rubber; resistant to body oils.
SULFAR Ryton				High-performance fibers with excellent resistance to harsh chemicals and high temperatures. Excellent strength retention in adverse environments; flame-retardant; nonconductive.
VINYON Hoechst Celanese				Softens at low temperature; high resistance to chemicals; nontoxic.

Source: American Fiber Manufacturers Assoc. Inc., Washington, D.C.

The first machine-made fibers were manufactured from raw materials that were derived from cotton or wood pulp. These materials are processed, and pure cellulose is extracted from them. Depending on the type of fiber that is desired, the cellulose may be chemically treated and dissolved in an appropriate solvent before it is forced through the small holes of a spinning jet or spinnerette to produce the fiber. Fibers manufactured from natural raw materials in this manner are classified as **regenerated fibers** and commonly include rayon, acetate, and triacetate, all of which are produced from regenerated cellulose.

Most of the fibers presently manufactured are produced solely from synthetic chemicals and are therefore classified as **synthetic fibers.** These include nylons, polyesters, and acrylics. The creation of synthetic fibers became a reality only when scientists developed a method of synthesizing long-chained molecules called **polymers.**

In 1930, chemists discovered an unusual characteristic of one of the polymers under investigation. It was found that when a glass rod in contact with viscous material in a beaker was slowly pulled away, the substance adhered to the rod and formed a fine filament that hardened as soon as it entered the cool air. Furthermore, it was observed that the cold filaments could be stretched several times their extended length to produce a flexible, strong, and attractive fiber. The first synthetic fiber was to be improved upon and marketed as nylon. Since then, fiber chemists have successfully synthesized new polymers and have developed more efficient methods for manufacturing them. These efforts have produced a multitude of synthetic fibers.

THE POLYMER

The polymer is the basic chemical substance of all synthetic fibers. Indeed, an almost unbelievable array of household, industrial, and recreational products are manufactured from polymers; these include plastics, paints, adhesives, and synthetic rubber. Polymers exist in countless forms and varieties and with the proper treatment can be made to assume different chemical and physical properties.

As we have already observed, chemical substances are composed from basic structural units called **molecules.** The molecules of most materials are composed of just a few atoms; for example, water, H_2O, has 2 atoms of hydrogen and 1 atom of oxygen. The heroin molecule, $C_{21}H_{23}O_5N$, contains 21 atoms of carbon, 23 atoms of hydrogen, 5 atoms of oxygen, and 1 atom of nitrogen. Polymers, on the other hand, are formed by linking together a large number of molecules, so that it is not unusual for a polymer to contain thousands or even millions of atoms. This is why polymers are often referred to as **macromolecules,** or "big" molecules.

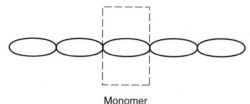

Monomer

Figure 8–7.
The chain-link model of a segment of a polymer molecule. The actual molecule may contain as many as several million monomer units or links.

Simply, a polymer can be pictured as resembling a long, repeating chain, with each link representing the basic structure of the polymer (see Figure 8–7). The repeating molecular units in the polymer, called **monomers,** are joined together end to end, so that on a greatly enlarged scale, thousands upon thousands are linked together to form a long chain. What makes polymer chemistry so fascinating is the countless varieties of possibilities that exist for linking different molecules together. By simply varying the chemical structure of the basic molecules, or monomers, and by devising numerous ways to weave them together, chemists have created polymers that exhibit different properties. It is this versatility that enables polymer chemists to synthesize glues, plastics, paints, and fibers.

It would be a mistake to give the impression that all polymers are synthesized in the chemical laboratory. Indeed, this is far from true, for nature has produced polymers that humans have not yet been able to copy. For example, the proteins that form the basic structure of animal hairs, as well as of all living matter, are polymers, composed of thousands of amino acids linked together in a highly organized arrangement and sequence. Similarly, cellulose, the basic ingredient of wood and cotton, and starch are both natural polymers built by the combination of several thousand carbohydrate monomers, as shown in Figure 8–8. Hence, the synthesis of manufactured fibers merely represents an extension of chemical principles that nature has successfully utilized to produce hair and vegetable fibers.

Figure 8–8. Starch and cellulose are natural carbohydrate polymers consisting of a large number of repeating units or monomers.

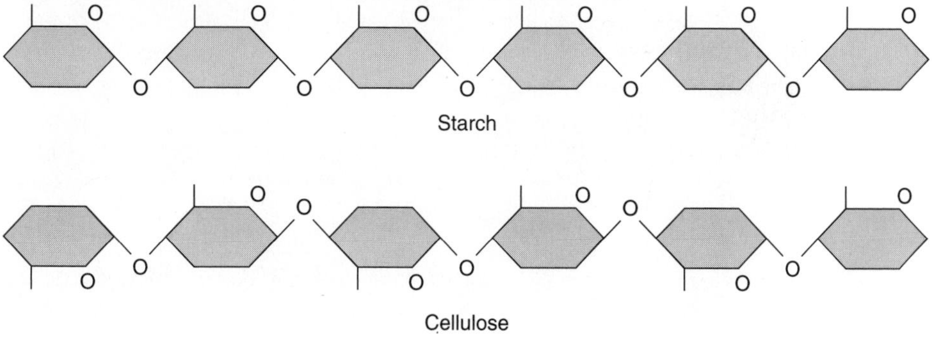

Starch

Cellulose

IDENTIFICATION AND COMPARISON OF MAN-MADE FIBERS

The evidential value of fibers is related to the criminalist's ability to trace their origin. Obviously, if the examiner is presented with fabrics that can be exactly fitted together at their torn edges, it is a virtual certainty that the fabrics were of common origin. Such a fit is demonstrated in Figure 8–9 for a piece of fabric that was removed from a vehicle suspected of involvement in a hit-and-run fatality. The exact fit with the remains of the victim's trousers resulted in the direct implication of the car's driver in the incident.

However, a more common case finds the criminalist presented with a very limited number of fibers for identification and comparison. Generally, in these situations, the possibilities for obtaining a physical match are nonexistent, and the examiner must resort to a side-by-side comparison of the control and crime-scene fibers.

The first and most important step in the examination will be a microscopic comparison for color and diameter utilizing a comparison microscope (pp. 188–89). Unless there is agreement between these two characteristics, there would be little reason to suspect a match. Other morphological features that could be present to

Figure 8–9.   A piece of fabric found on a suspect hit-and-run vehicle inserted into the torn trousers of the victim. *Courtesy* New Jersey State Police.

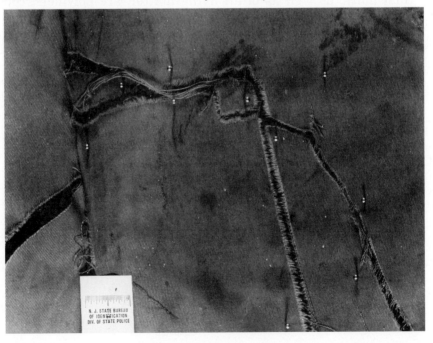

aid in the comparison are lengthwise striations on the surface of some fibers and the pitting of the fiber's surface with delustering particles (usually titanium dioxide) added in the manufacturing process to reduce shine (Figure 8–10). The shape of a fiber through a cross-sectional view may also assist in characterizing the fiber.[7] In the previously discussed Wayne Williams case (pp. 87–96), it was unusually shaped yellow-green fibers discovered on a number of the murder victims that ultimately were linked to a carpet in the home of Wayne Williams. This fiber proved to be a key element in proving the guilt of Williams. A photomicrograph of this unusually shaped fiber is shown in Figure 8–11.

Figure 8–10. Photomicrographs of synthetic fibers. (a) Cellulose triacetate (450×). (b) Nylon embedded with titanium dioxide particles (450×). *Courtesy* Linda Jankowski.

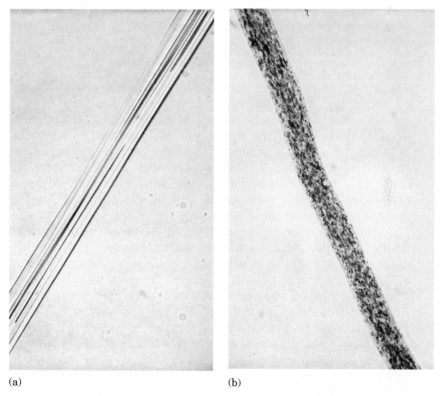

(a)   (b)

---

[7]S. Palenki and C. Fitzsimons, "Fiber Cross-Sections: Part I," *Microscope,* 38 (1990), 187.

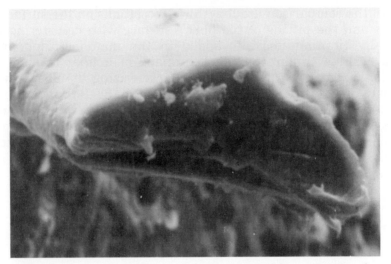

Figure 8–11. A scanning electron photomicrograph of the cross section of a nylon fiber removed from a sheet used to transport the body of a murder victim. The fiber, associated with a carpet in Wayne Williams's home, was manufactured in 1971 in relatively small quantities. *Courtesy* Federal Bureau of Investigation, Washington, D.C.

Although two fibers may seem to have the same color when they are viewed under the microscope, there may actually exist compositional differences in the dyes that were applied to them during their manufacture. In fact, most textile fibers are impregnated with a mixture of dyes selected to obtain a desired shade or color. The significance of a fiber comparison is enhanced when the forensic examiner can show that the questioned and control fibers actually have the same dye composition. The visible light microspectrophotometer (pp. 193–195) is a convenient way for analysts to compare the colors of fibers through spectral patterns. This technique is not limited by sample size, as a fiber as small as one millimeter or less in length can be examined by this type of microscope. The examination is nondestructive and is carried out on fibers simply mounted on a microscope slide. A more detailed analysis of the fiber's dye composition can be obtained through a chromatographic separation of the dye constituents. To accomplish this, small strands of fibers are compared for dye content by first extracting the dye off each fiber with a suitable solvent and then spotting the dye solution onto a thin-layer chromatography plate. The dye components of the questioned and control fibers are separated on the thin-layer plate and compared side by side for similarity.[8]

---

[8]D. K. Laing et al., "The Standardisation of Thin-Layer Chromatographic Systems for Comparisons of Fibre Dyes," *J. Forensic Science Society,* 30 (1990), 299.

Once this phase of the analysis is complete, and before any conclusion can be reached that two or more fibers compare, both must be shown to have the same chemical composition. In this respect, tests are performed to confirm that all the fibers involved belong to the same broad generic class. Additionally, the comparison will be substantially enhanced if it can be demonstrated that all the fibers belong to the same subclassification within their generic class. For example, when we speak of nylon, we must remember that there are at least four different types of nylon available in commercial and consumer markets. These include nylon 6, nylon 6–10, nylon 11, and nylon 6–6. Although all types of nylon have many properties in common, each may differ in physical shape, appearance, and dyeability owing to modifications in basic chemical structure. Similarly, a recent study of over 200 different samples of acrylic fibers revealed that they could actually be divided into 24 distinguishable groups on the basis of their polymeric structure and microscopic characteristics.[9]

Textile chemists have devised numerous tests for determining the class of a fiber. However, unlike the textile chemist, the criminalist frequently does not have the luxury of having a substantial quantity of fabric to work with and must therefore select those tests that will yield the most information with the least amount of material. Only a single fiber may be available for analysis, and often this may amount to no more than a minute strand recovered from a fingernail scraping of a homicide or rape victim.

A most useful physical property of fibers, from the criminalist's point of view, arises out of the knowledge that many manufactured fibers exhibit double refraction or birefringence (see p. 108). Synthetic fibers are manufactured by melting a polymeric substance or dissolving it in a solvent and then forcing it through the very fine holes of a spinnerette. The polymer emerges as a very fine filament, with its molecules aligned parallel to the length of the filament (see Figure 8–12). Just as the regular arrangement of atoms produces a crystal, so will the regular arrangement of the fiber's polymers cause crystallinity in the finished fiber. It is the crystallinity that makes a fiber stiff and strong and is responsible for its exhibiting the optical property of double refraction.

Light passing through a synthetic fiber emerges polarized, perpendicular and parallel to the length of the fiber. Depending on the class of fiber, each polarized plane of light will have a characteristic index of refraction. This value can be determined by immersing the fiber in a fluid that has a comparable refractive index and observing

[9]M. C. Grieve, "Another Look at the Classification of Acrylic Fibres, using FTIR Microscopy," *Science & Justice*, 35 (1995), 179.

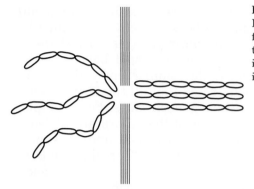

Figure 8–12.
In the production of manufactured
fibers, the bulk polymer is forced
through small holes to form a filament
in which all the polymers are aligned
in the same direction.

the disappearance of the Becke line under a polarizing microscope.
Table 8–2 lists the two refractive indices of some common classes of
fibers, along with their birefringence. The virtue of this technique is
that a single fiber, microscopic in size, can be analyzed in a nondestructive manner.

The polymers that comprise a manufactured fiber, just as in any
other organic substance, will selectively absorb infrared light in a
characteristic pattern. Infrared spectrophotometry thus provides a
rapid and reliable method for identifying the generic class, and in
some cases the subclasses, of fibers. The infrared microspectropho-

TABLE 8–2.
REFRACTIVE INDICES OF COMMON
TEXTILE FIBERS

	Refractive Index		
Fiber	*Parallel*	*Perpendicular*	*Birefringence*
Acetate	1.478	1.477	0.001
Triacetate	1.472	1.471	0.001
Acrylic	1.524	1.520	0.004
Nylon			
Nylon 6	1.568	1.515	0.053
Nylon 6–6	1.582	1.519	0.063
Polyester			
Dacron	1.710	1.535	0.175
Kodel	1.642	1.540	0.102
Modacrylic	1.536	1.531	0.005
Rayon			
Cuprammonium rayon	1.552	1.520	0.032
Viscose rayon	1.544	1.520	0.024

Note: The listed values are for specific fibers, which explain the highly precise values
given. In identification work, such precision is not practical; values within 0.02 or 0.03 of those
listed will suffice.

tometer combines a microscope with an infrared spectrophotometer (see p. 195). Such a combination makes possible the infrared analysis of a small single-strand fiber while it is being viewed under a microscope.[10]

Case Reading
Fatal Vision Revisited

Dr. Jeffrey MacDonald was convicted in 1979 of murdering his wife and two young daughters. The events surrounding the crime and the subsequent trial were recounted in Joe McGinniss's best-selling book, *Fatal Vision.* The focus of MacDonald's defense was that intruders entered his home and committed these violent acts. Eleven years after this conviction, MacDonald's attorneys filed a petition for a new trial claiming the existence of "critical new" evidence.

The defense asserted that wig fibers found on a hair brush in the MacDonald residence were evidence that an intruder dressed in a wig entered the MacDonald home on the day of the murder. Subsequent examination of this claim by the FBI Laboratory focused on a blond fall frequently worn by MacDonald's wife. Fibers removed from the fall were shown to clearly match fibers on the hair brush. The examination included the use of the infrared microspectrophotometry for the purpose of demonstrating that the suspect wig fibers were chemically identical to fibers found in the composition of the MacDonald fall (see Figure 8–13). Hence, while wig fibers were found at the crime scene, the source of these fibers could be accounted for—they came from Mrs. MacDonald's fall.

Another piece of evidence cited by MacDonald's lawyers was the existence of a bluish-black woolen fiber found on the body of Mrs. MacDonald. The claim was that this fiber compared to a bluish-black woolen fiber recovered from the club that was used to assault her. These wool fibers were central to MacDonald's defense that the "intruders" were wearing dark-colored clothing. Initial examination showed that the fibers were microscopically indistinguishable. However, the FBI also compared the two wool fibers by visible light microspectrophotometry. Comparison of their spectra clearly showed that their dye compositions differ, suggesting no evidence of outside

---

[10]M. W. Tungol et al., "Analysis of Single Polymer Fibers by Fourier Transform Infrared Microscopy: The Results of Case Studies," *Journal of Forensic Sciences,* 36 (1992), 1027.

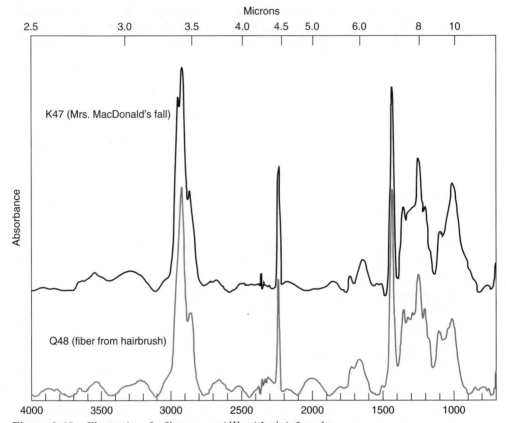

Figure 8–13. Illustration of a fiber comparison with an infrared spectrophotometer. The infrared spectrum of a fiber from Mrs. MacDonald's fall compares to a fiber recovered from a hair brush in the MacDonald home. These fibers were identified as modacrylics, the most common type of synthetic fiber used in the manufacture of human hair goods. *Courtesy* S. A. Michael Malone, FBI Laboratory, Washington, D.C.

intruders (see Figure 8–14). Ultimately, the U.S. Supreme Court denied the merits of MacDonald's petition for a new trial.[11]

Once it has been determined that there is a fiber match, the question of the significance of such a finding is bound to be raised. In reality, there is no analytical technique that will permit the criminalist to

[11]*Source:* B. M. Murtagh and M. P. Malone, "Fatal Vision Revisited," *The Police Chief,* June 1993, 15.

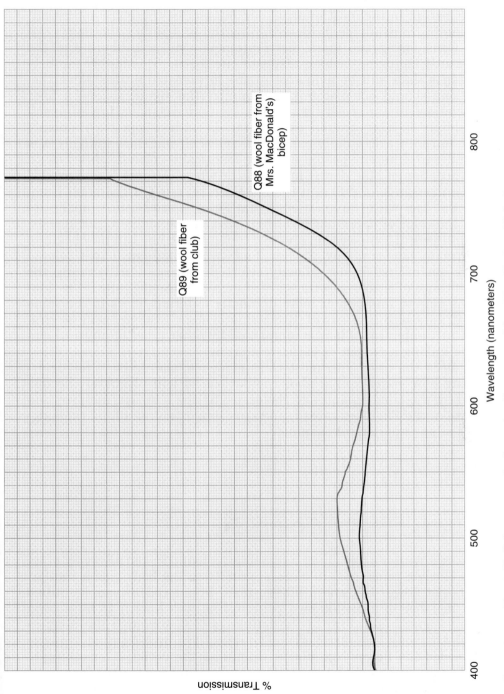

Figure 8–14. The visible light spectrum for the woolen fiber recovered from Mrs. MacDonald's body is clearly different from that of the fiber recovered from the club used to assault her. *Courtesy S. A. Michael Malone, FBI Laboratory, Washington, D.C.*

associate a fiber strand definitively to any single garment. Furthermore, except in the most unusual circumstances, there are no statistical databases available for determining the probability of a fiber's origin. Considering the mass distribution of synthetic fibers and the constantly changing fashion tastes of our society, it is highly unlikely that such data will be available in the foreseeable future. Nevertheless, one should not discount or minimize the significance of a fiber association. In our society, there exists an enormous variety of fibers. By simply looking around at individuals with whom we randomly come in contact on a daily basis, it becomes obvious how unlikely it is to find two different people wearing identically colored fabrics (with the exception of blue denim materials or white cottons). There are literally thousands of different-colored fibers in our environment. Combine this fact with the knowledge that forensic scientists compare not only the color of fibers but also their size, shape, microscopic appearance, chemical composition, and dye content, and one can now begin to appreciate how unlikely it is to find two indistinguishable colored fibers emanating from randomly selected sources. Furthermore, the significance of a fiber association will increase dramatically if the analyst is able to link two or more distinctly different fibers to the same object. Likewise, the associative value of fiber evidence will be dramatically enhanced if it is accompanied by other types of physical evidence linking a person or object to a crime.

As is the case with most class evidence, the decision for determining how significant a fiber comparison is will ultimately be dictated by the circumstances of the cases; by the location, number, and nature of the fibers examined; and most important of all, by the judgment of an experienced examiner.

Case Reading

On a cold winter's day . . . , a female was found in the alleyway of an East Harlem tenement. In close proximity to the body was a California florist flower box and a plastic liner. The decedent was identified as a member of a well-known church. She was known to have been selling church literature in the buildings that surround the alley in which the body was discovered. The detectives investigating the case forwarded the flower box, plastic liner, and the decedent's clothing to the forensic science laboratory. On the box and liner were found tan wool fibers, red acrylic fibers, and navy blue wool fibers (all identified by polarized light microscopy). The three types of questioned fibers were compared microscopically with the decedent's clothing. All three were found to be consistent in all respects to the textile fibers composing the decedent's clothing (tan wool overcoat, navy blue wool/polyester blend slacks, and red acrylic sweater), thereby associating the woman with the flower box and liner. In addition light blue nylon rug fibers and several brown-colored rabbit hairs were found on the box and liner. Similar light blue nylon rug fibers and rabbit hairs, as well as red colored nylon rug fibers, were found on the decedent's tan wool overcoat. Neither the rabbit hairs nor the nylon rug fibers could be associated with the victim's environment (her clothing or residence).

All this information was conveyed to the field investigators. Upon further inquiry in the neighborhood, the investigating officers learned the identification of a man who had, the day after the body was discovered, sold a full-length, brown-colored, rabbit hair coat to a local man. The investigators obtained the rabbit hair coat from the purchaser. The hair composing the coat was compared microscopically to the questioned rabbit hairs found on the victim's wool coat and the flower box liner. The specimens of questioned rabbit hair were found to be consistent in all physical and microscopic characteristics to the rabbit hair composing the suspect's coat. Armed with this information, the police now had probable cause to obtain a search warrant for the suspect's apartment.

In the suspect's apartment two rugs were found. One was colored light blue and the other was red in color; both rugs were composed of nylon fibers. Samples of each rug were collected by the crime-scene unit and forwarded to the forensic science laboratory for comparison with the questioned rug fibers found on the victim's clothing, the flower box, and plastic liner. Both the questioned and known rug fibers were found to be consistent in all respects. The presence of light blue nylon rug fibers, red nylon rug fibers, and brown-colored rabbit hairs on the flower box, plastic liner, and woman's clothing enabled the author to make associations between the woman, flower box, and liner found in the alleyway with the suspect and his apartment. . . .

Further inquiry about the suspect was made in the neighborhood by the investigating officers. A witness was located who stated he saw the suspect carrying a large California flower box a day or two before the body was discovered.

From the evidence it was theorized that the woman was killed in the suspect's apartment, placed in the flower box, brought up to the roof of the building in which the defendant resided, and thrown off the building into the alley below. On the basis of all of this evidence, the suspect was arrested, indicted, and tried for murder in the second degree. After two trials, at which extensive testimony (three days) about the trace evidence was given by the author, the defendant was found guilty of murder in the second degree and subsequently sentenced to life imprisonment.[12]

COLLECTION OF FIBER EVIDENCE

As criminal investigators have become more aware of the potential contribution of trace physical evidence to the success of their investigation, they have placed greater emphasis on conducting thorough crime-scene searches for evidence of forensic value. Their skill and determination at carrying out these tasks will be tested when it comes to the collection of fiber-related evidence. Fiber evidence can be associated with virtually any type of crime. It's the kind of evidence that will not usually be seen with the naked eye and thus can be easily overlooked by someone not specifically looking for it. For the investigator committed to optimizing the laboratory's chances for locating minute strands of fibers, the task becomes one of identifying and preserving potential "carriers" of fiber evidence. Relevant articles of clothing should be packaged carefully in paper bags. Each article must be placed in a separate bag to avoid the possibility of cross-contamination of evidence. Scrupulous care must be taken to prevent articles of clothing from different people or from different locations from coming into contact. Such articles must not even be placed on the same surface prior to their packaging. Likewise, carpets, rugs, and bedding are to be folded carefully to protect areas suspected of containing fibers. Car seats should be carefully covered with polyethylene sheets to protect fiber evidence, and knife blades should be covered to protect adhering fibers. If a body is thought to have been wrapped at one time in a blanket or carpet, adhesive tape lifts of exposed body areas may reveal fiber strands.

Occasionally, it may be necessary for the field investigator to remove a fiber from an object, particularly if the possibility exists that loosely adhering fibrous material will be lost in transit to the laboratory. These fibers must be removed with a clean forceps and placed in a small sheet of paper, which, after folding and labeling, can be placed inside another container. Again, scrupulous care must be taken to avoid fibers collected from different objects or from different locations from coming into contact.

---

[12]Reprinted in part by permission of the American Society of Testing and Materials from N. Petraco, "Trace Evidence—The Invisible Witness," *Journal of Forensic Sciences,* 31 (1986), 321. Copyright 1986.

In the laboratory, the search for fiber evidence on clothing and other relevant objects, as well as in debris, is a time-consuming and tedious process. The search will test the skill and patience of the examiner. The crime-scene investigator can reduce this task to manageable proportions by collecting only relevant items for examination. It is essential from the onset of an investigation that the crime-scene investigator pinpoint areas where a likely transfer of fiber evidence occurred and then take necessary measures to ensure the proper collection and preservation of these materials.

FORENSIC EXAMINATION OF PAINT

Our environment is literally surrounded with millions of objects whose surfaces are painted. Thus, it is not surprising to observe that paint, in one form or another, is one of the most prevalent types of physical evidence received by the crime laboratory. Paint as physical evidence is perhaps most frequently encountered in hit-and-run and burglary cases. For example, a chip of dried paint or a paint smear may be transferred to the clothing of a hit-and-run victim on impact with an automobile, or paint smears could be transferred onto a tool during the commission of a burglary. Obviously, there exist numerous possibilities and situations under which a transfer of paint from one surface to another could impart an object with an identifiable forensic characteristic.

In most circumstances, the criminalist will be required to compare two or more paints for the ultimate purpose of establishing their common origin. Through such a comparison, it may be possible, for example, to associate an individual or a vehicle with the crime site. However, the criminalist need not be confined to comparisons alone. Crime laboratories can often provide valuable assistance in identifying the color, make, and model of an automobile by examining small quantities of paint recovered at an accident scene. Such requests, normally made in connection with hit-and-run cases, can lead to the apprehension of the responsible vehicle.

Paint spread onto a surface will dry into a hard film that can best be described as consisting of pigments and additives suspended in a binder. Pigments impart color and hiding (or opacity) to paint and are usually mixtures of different inorganic and organic compounds added to the paint by the manufacturer to produce specific colors and properties. The binder provides the support medium for the pigments and additives and is a polymeric substance. Paint is thus composed of a binder and pigments, as well as other additives, all dissolved or dispersed in a suitable solvent. After the paint has been applied to a surface, the solvent evaporates, leaving behind a hard polymeric binder and any pigments that were suspended in it.

One of the most common types of paint examined in the crime laboratory involves finishes emanating from automobiles. One interesting aspect that is helpful in forensic characterization of automotive paint is the knowledge that manufacturers apply a variety of coatings to the body of an automobile. This knowledge adds significant diversity to automobile paint and contributes to the forensic significance of forensic automobile paint comparisons. The automotive finishing system for steel usually consists of at least four organic coatings:

Electrocoat Primer. The first layer applied to the steel body of a car is the electrocoat primer. The primer, consisting of epoxy-based resins, is electroplated onto the steel body of the automobile to provide corrosion resistance. The resulting coating is uniform in appearance and thickness. The color of these electrodeposition primers range from black to gray.

Primer Surfacers. Originally responsible for corrosion control, the surfacer is the layer of coating that usually follows the electrocoat layer and is applied before the basecoat. Primer surfacers are epoxy-modified polyesters. The function of this layer today is to completely smooth out and hide any seams or imperfections because it is on this surface that the colorcoat will be applied. This layer is highly pigmented. Color pigments are used so as to minimize color contrast between primer and topcoats. For example, a light gray primer may be used under pastel shades of a colored topcoat, or a red oxide may be used under a dark-colored topcoat.

Basecoat. The next layer of paint on a car is the basecoat or colorcoat. This is the layer that provides the color and aesthetics of the finish and therefore represents the "eye appeal" of the finished automobile. The integrity of this layer is dependent on its ability to resist the elements of weather, UV radiation, and acid rain. Most commonly, an acrylic-based polymer comprises the binder system of basecoats. Interestingly, the choice of automotive pigments is dictated by toxic and environmental concerns. Thus, the uses of lead and chrome and other heavy metal pigments have been abandoned in favor of organic-based pigments. There is also a growing trend toward pearl luster or mica pigments. Mica pigments are coated with layers of metal oxide to generate interference colors. Also, the addition of aluminum flakes to automotive paint will impart a metallic look to the paint's finish.

Clearcoats. An unpigmented clearcoat is applied to improve gloss, durability, and appearance. Presently, most clearcoats are acrylic-based, but polyurethane clearcoats are increasing in popularity. These topcoats provide outstanding etch resistance and appearance.

The microscope has traditionally been and remains the most important instrument for locating and comparing paint specimens. When one considers the thousands upon thousands of paint colors and shades that are known to exist, it is quite understandable why color, more than any other property, imparts paint with its most distinctive forensic characteristics. Questioned and known specimens are best compared side by side under a stereoscopic microscope for color, surface texture, and color layer sequence.

The importance of layer structure for evaluating the evidential significance of paint evidence cannot be overemphasized. When paint specimens possess colored layers that match with respect to number and sequence of colors, the examiner can begin to think confidently in terms of relating the paints to a common origin. How many layers must be matched before the criminalist can conclude that the paints come from the same source? There is no one accepted criterion. Much depends on the uniqueness of each layer with respect to its color and texture, as well as the frequency with which the particular combination of colors under investigation is observed to occur. Because there are at present no books or journals that have compiled this type of information, the criminalist is left to his or her own experience and knowledge when making this decision.

Unfortunately, the vast majority of the paint specimens presented to the criminalist will not have a layer structure of sufficient complexity to allow them to be individualized to a single source, nor is it common to have paint chips that can be physically fitted together to prove common origin, as shown in Figure 8–15. However, the diverse chemical composition of modern paints does provide for additional points of comparison between specimens. Specifically, a thorough comparison of paint must include a chemical analysis of either the paint's pigments or its binder composition, or both.

The wide variation in binder formulations provides particularly significant information with respect to the forensic comparison of automobile finishes. What is more important is the knowledge that paint manufacturers make automobile finishes in hundreds of varieties; this is most helpful to the criminalist who is trying to associate a paint chip to one car as distinguished from the thousands of similar models that have been produced in any one year. For instance, there are over 100 automobile production plants in the United States. Each can use one paint supplier for a particular color or vary suppliers during a model year. Although a paint supplier must maintain strict quality control over a paint's color, the batch formulation of any paint binder can vary, depending on the availability and cost of basic ingredients.

Pyrolysis gas chromatography has proven to be a particularly invaluable technique for distinguishing most paint formulations. Here,

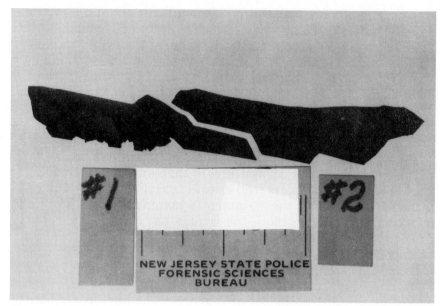

Figure 8–15.   Paint chip 1 was recovered from the scene of a hit-and-run. Paint chip 2 was obtained from the suspect vehicle. *Courtesy* New Jersey State Police.

paint chips as small as 20 micrograms are decomposed by heat into numerous gaseous products and are sent through a gas chromatograph. As shown in Figure 8–16, the polymer chain is decomposed by a heated filament, and the resultant products are swept into and through a gas chromatograph column. What emerge and are recorded are the separated decomposition products of the polymer. It is the pattern of this chromatogram or "pyrogram" that distinguishes one polymer from another. What results is a pyrogram that is sufficiently detailed to reflect chemical makeup of the binder. Figure 8–17 illustrates how the patterns produced by paint pyrograms can differentiate acrylic enamel paints removed from two different automobiles. Infrared spectrophotometry is still another analytical technique used to provide the analyst with information about the binder composition of paint.[13] Binders will selectively absorb infrared radiation to yield a spectrum that is highly characteristic of a paint specimen.

---

[13]P. G. Rodgers et al., "The Classification of Automobile Paint by Diamond Window Infrared Spectrophotometry, Part I: Binders and Pigments," *The Canadian Society of Forensic Science Journal,* 9 (1976), 1. Also, T. J. Allen, "Paint Sample Presentation for Fourier Transform Infrared Microscopy," *Vibration Spectroscopy,* 3 (1992), 217.

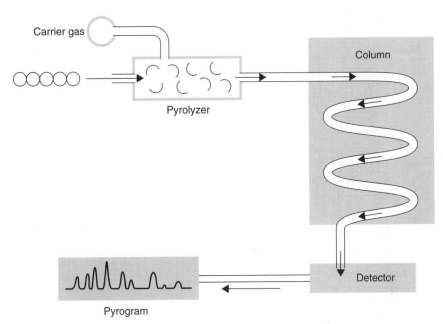

Carrier gas

Column

Pyrolyzer

Detector

Pyrogram

Figure 8–16. Schematic diagram of pyrolysis gas chromatography.

The elements that comprise the inorganic pigments of paints can be identified by any one of a variety of techniques—emission spectroscopy, neutron activation analysis, X-ray diffraction, and X-ray spectroscopy (pp. 197–98). The emission spectrograph, for instance, can simultaneously detect 15 to 20 elements in most automobile paints. Some of these elements are relatively common to all paints and have little forensic value; others are less frequently encountered and provide excellent points of comparison between paint specimens (see Figure 6–3).

Once a paint comparison is completed, the task of assessing the significance of the finding begins. How certain can one be that two similar paints did indeed come from the same surface? For instance, to a casual observer, countless identically colored automobiles are seen on our roads and streets. If this is the case, what value is a comparison of a paint chip from a hit-and-run scene to paint removed from a suspect car? From previous discussions it should be apparent that far more is involved in paint comparison than matching surface paint colors. Paint layers present beneath a surface layer offer valuable points of comparison. Furthermore, forensic analysts are capable of detecting subtle differences in paint binder formulations, as well as major or minor differences in the elemental composition of paint. Obviously, to the naked eye these properties cannot be discerned.

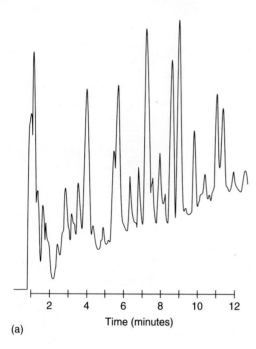

(a)

Figure 8–17.
Paint pyrograms of acrylic enamel
paints. (a) Paint from a Ford model.
(b) Paint from a Chrysler model.
Courtesy Varian Instruments, Calif.

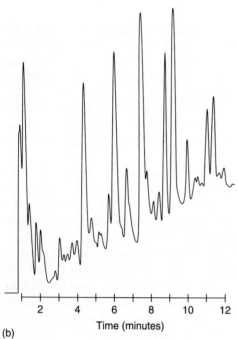

(b)

The significance of a paint comparison was convincingly demonstrated from data gathered at the author's laboratory. Paint chips, randomly taken from 500 vehicles located in a local wreck yard, were compared by layer structure, solvent tests, pyrolysis gas chromatography, and X-ray spectroscopy. All were distinguishable except for eight pairs. In statistical terms, these results signify that if a crime-scene paint and a paint control removed from a suspect car compare by the previously discussed tests, the odds against the crime-scene paint originating from another randomly chosen vehicle are approximately 16,000 to 1. Obviously, this type of evidence is bound to forge a strong link between the suspect car and the crime scene.

It is often requested of crime laboratories to identify the make and model of a car from a very small amount of paint left behind at a crime scene. Such information is frequently of use in a search for an unknown car involved in a hit-and-run incident. Often, the questioned paint can be identified when its color is compared to color chips representing the various makes and models of manufactured cars. However, in many cases, it is not possible to state the exact make or model of the car in question, since any one paint color can be found on more than one car model. For instance, General Motors may use the same paint color for several production years on cars in their Cadillac, Buick, Oldsmobile, Pontiac, and Chevrolet lines.

Color charts for automobile finishes are available from various paint manufacturers and refinishers. Starting with the 1974 model year, the Law Enforcement Standards Laboratory at the National Bureau of Standards collected and disseminated to crime laboratories auto paint color samples from U.S. domestic passenger cars. This collection was distributed by Collaborative Testing Services, McLean, Virginia, up through 1991.

Case Reading

In the early morning hours . . . atop a lonely roof garage on the westside of Manhattan, three men were found murdered. Each man had been shot once in the back of the head. A light-colored van was seen speeding away from the scene. Hours later, in a secluded alley street on the lower east side of Manhattan, the body of a fully clothed woman was found lying face down by two dog walkers. The woman had been killed in the same manner as the men on the roof garage.

The condition of the woman's body, and other evidence, made it apparent that she had been shot at the garage, and then transported to the alley.

An eyewitness to the incident stated that he saw a man shoot a woman and place her in a light-colored van. The gunman then chased down the three men who were coming to the woman's aid, and shot each one of them. Days later, the prime suspect to the killings was arrested in Kentucky, in a black-colored van.

Numerous items of evidence (over 100) were collected from the van, and forwarded to the New York City police laboratory for examination. Among the items of evidence forwarded were three sets of vacuum sweepings from the van's interior.

An autopsy of the woman produced several items of trace evidence that were removed from the victim and forwarded to the author for microscopic examination. The woman's clothing was also received by the author for trace analysis.

A prime question that arose during the investigation was: could the woman's body, which had been placed in a light-colored van at the garage, and later left in an alley on the lower east side, be associated with the black van recovered over 1000 km (600 miles) away from the scene? Microscopic analysis and comparison of the trace evidential materials found on the victim and inside the van made this association possible.

Listed in Table 1 are all the items of similar trace materials that both the victim and the van had in common.

Microscopic comparisons of the questioned human head hair present on the victim's clothing were made with known samples. Ten of the brown-colored and gray-colored Caucasian head hairs from the victim's blazer were consistent in microscopic characteristics to the defendant's known head hair sample. One chemically treated head hair found on the victim was consistent in microscopic characteristics to the known head hair sample obtained from the defendant's wife. One forcibly removed, brown-colored, Caucasian head hair that was found on the rear door of the van's interior by the Kentucky state police was found to be consistent in all characteristics with the decedent's known head hair sample.

Microscopic comparisons of the white- and brown/white-colored dog hair from the victim's clothing, and the van's interior, were made with known samples of dog hair obtained from a dog owned by the defendant's nephew, the van's previous owner. The questioned dog hairs were found to be consistent with the hair from the nephew's dog.

The white seed that was recovered from the victim's mouth by the medical examiner, and the white seed that was found in the van's sweepings by the author, were forwarded to an internationally known botanist for identification and comparison. During the trial, the botanist testified that the two seeds were identical in all respects, and

TABLE 1.
ITEMS OF SIMILAR TRACE EVIDENCE THAT
WERE RECOVERED FROM BOTH THE VICTIM
AND THE VAN'S INTERIOR

	Source	
Trace Evidence	*Victim*	*Van*
White seed	mouth	sweepings
Paint chips	hair and wool blazer	sweepings and floor
gray metallic/black		
Sawdust	hair, blazer, and sheet	sweepings and misc. items
Glass fragments	wool blazer and sheet	sweepings and misc. items
clear		
amber		
green		
Cellophane	wool blazer	floor
Urethane foam	wool blazer	sweepings, misc. items, and foam mattress
Blue olefin	skirt	floor
plastic		
Dog hair	wool blazer	sweepings and misc. items
brown/white		
white		
Human hair	wool blazer	hair brush, sweepings, and misc. items
brown		
gray		

that although he could not identify the seed, both were either from the same species of plant, *if not the same plant,* probably a rare wild flower.

Sixteen gray metallic/black-colored paint chips from the victim and her clothing were compared to the gray metallic/black-colored paint removed from the van. Samples from the questioned and known sources were examined and compared by microscopic, chemical, and instrumental means. All of the paint specimens from the van and from the victim were found to be similar in all respects.

The remaining items of trace evidence from the victim and the van were examined and compared microscopically, and where necessary, by chemical and instrumental methods. Each of the remaining types of trace evidence from the victim was found to be similar to its counterpart from the van.

Blue- and black-colored flakes of acrylic paint were found in the van's sweepings, and on the suspect's sneakers. No blue- or black-colored paint flakes were found on the victim and her clothing. During a crime scene search of the defendant's residence in New Jersey, a large quantity of blue- and black-colored acrylic paint was found in the garage. It was apparent from the evidence present in the defendant's garage that a large rectangular shaped object had recently been painted with blue- and black-colored paint. The blue and black paint flakes from all the sources and the known blue (undercoat) and black (topcoat) paint from the van were compared by microscopic, chemical, and instrumental means. All the samples of paint were found to be consistent in every respect.

At the trial, extensive testimony concerning the collection, examination, identification, and comparison of the trace evidence from the victim and the van was given by the author, over a two-day period. When questioned about the source of the trace evidence found on the victim and her clothing, the author stated unequivocally that the trace evidence on the victim was from the defendant's van. On the basis of this evidence and other circumstantial evidence, the defendant was found guilty of all charges and sentenced to 100 years in prison.[14]

COLLECTION AND PRESERVATION OF PAINT EVIDENCE

As has already been noted, paint chips are most likely to be found on or near persons or objects involved in hit-and-run incidents. The recovery of loose paint chips from a garment or from the road surface must be done with the utmost care to keep the paint chip intact. Paint chips may be picked up with a tweezers or scooped up with a piece of paper. Paper druggist folds and glass or plastic vials make excellent containers for paint. If the paint is smeared or embedded in garments or objects, the investigator should not attempt to remove it; instead, it is best to package the whole item carefully and send it on to the laboratory for examination.

When a transfer of paint occurs in hit-and-run situations, such as to the clothing of a pedestrian victim, uncontaminated control paint must always be collected from an undamaged area of the vehicle for comparison in the laboratory. It is particularly important that the collected paint be close to the area of the car that was suspected of being in contact with the victim. This is necessary because other portions of the car may have faded or been repainted. Control samples are always removed so as to include all the paint layers down to the bare metal. This is best accomplished by removing a painted sec-

---

[14]Reprinted by permission of the American Society of Testing and Materials from N. Petraco, "Trace Evidence—The Invisible Witness," *Journal of Forensic Sciences*, 31 (1986), 321. Copyright 1986.

tion with a clean scalpel or knife blade. Samples ¼-inch square are sufficient for laboratory examination. Each paint sample should be separately packaged and marked as to the exact location of its recovery. When a cross-transfer of paint occurs between two vehicles, again all the layers, including the foreign as well as the underlying original paints, must be removed from each vehicle. A control sample from an adjacent undamaged area of each vehicle must also be taken in such cases. Carefully wipe the blade of any knife or scraping tool used before collecting each sample. This step will avoid cross-contamination of paints.

Tools used to gain entry into buildings or safes often contain traces of paints as well as other substances such as wood, safe insulation, and so on. Care must be taken that this type of trace evidence is not lost. It is preferable that the scene investigator avoid making any attempt to remove the paint, choosing instead to package the tool for laboratory examination. Control paint should be collected from all surfaces suspected of having been in contact with the tool. Again, all layers of paint must be included in the sample.

In some cases in which the tool has left its impression on a surface, control paint is collected from an uncontaminated area adjacent to the impression. No attempt is to be made to collect the paint from the impression itself. If this is done, the impression may be permanently altered and its evidential value lost.

REVIEW QUESTIONS _____

1. Hair is an appendage of the skin, growing out of an organ known as the _____ .
2. The three layers that comprise the hair shaft are _____ , _____, and _____ .
3. The scales of most animal hairs can be described as having the appearance of shingles on a roof. (True, False)
4. The _____ contains the pigment granules that impart color to hair.
5. The central canal running through many hairs is known as the _____ .
6. The diameter of the medulla relative to the diameter of the hair shaft is the _____ .
7. Human hair generally has a medullary index of less than _____; the hair of most animals has an index of _____ or greater.

8. Human head hairs generally exhibit (continuous, absent) medullae.

9. If a medulla exhibits a patterned shape, the hair is (human, animal) in origin.

10. A single hair (can, cannot) be individualized to one person.

11. In making hair comparisons, it is best to view the hairs side by side under a _____ microscope.

12. _____ hairs are short and curly, with wide variation in shaft diameter.

13. It (is, is not) possible to determine the time when hair was last bleached or dyed.

14. The age and sex of hair can be determined through an examination of its morphological features. (True, False)

15. Hair forcibly removed from the body (always, often) has follicular tissue adhering to its root.

16. Currently, it is possible for DNA typing to provide for the near individualization of a single hair. (True, False)

17. A minimum collection of _____ full-length hairs will normally ensure a representative sampling of head hair.

18. A minimum collection of _____ full-length pubic hairs is recommended to cover the range of characteristics present in this region of the body.

19. _____ fibers are derived totally from animal or plant sources.

20. The most prevalent natural plant fiber is _____.

21. Regenerated fibers, such as rayon and acetate, are manufactured by chemically treating cellulose and passing it through a spinnerette. (True, False)

22. Fibers manufactured solely from synthetic chemicals are classified as _____.

23. Polyester was the first synthetic fiber. (True, False)

24. _____ are composed of a large number of atoms arranged in repeating units.

25. The basic unit of the polymer is called the _____.

26. _____ are polymers composed of thousands of amino acids linked together in a highly organized arrangement and sequence.

27. A first step in the forensic examination of fibers will be the comparison of color and diameter. (True, False)

28. The microspectrophotometer employing _____ light is a convenient way for analysts to compare the colors of fibers through spectral patterns.

29. The dye components removed from fibers can be separated and compared by _____ chromatography.

30. Synthetic fibers possess the physical property of _____ because they are crystalline.

31. The microspectrophotometer employing _____ light provides a rapid and reliable method for identifying the generic class of a single fiber.

32. Normally, fibers possess (individual, class) characteristics.

33. The two most important components of dried paint from the criminalist's point of view are the _____ and the _____.

34. The most important physical property of paint relating to a forensic comparison is _____ .

35. Paints can be individualized to a single source only when they have a sufficiently detailed _____.

36. The _____ layer provides corrosion resistance for the automobile.

37. "Eye appeal" of the automobile comes from the _____ layer.

38. Pyrolysis gas chromatography is a particularly valuable technique for characterizing paint's (binder, pigments).

39. Emission spectroscopy can be used to identify the (inorganic, organic) components of paint's pigments.

40. Paint samples removed for examination must always include all the paint layers. (True, False)

FURTHER REFERENCES

Bisbing, R. E., "The Forensic Identification and Association of Human Hair," in *Forensic Science Handbook,* R. Saferstein, ed. Englewood Cliffs, N.J.: Prentice Hall, 1982.

Fong, W., "Analytical Methods for Developing Fibers as Forensic Science Proof: A Review with Comments," *Journal of Forensic Sciences,* 34 (1989), 295.

Gaudette, B. D., "The Forensic Aspects of Textile Fiber Examination," in *Forensic Science Handbook,* Vol. 2, R. Saferstein, ed. Englewood Cliffs, N.J.: Prentice Hall, 1988.

Grieve, M. C., "Fibers and Forensic Science—New Ideas, Developments, and Techniques," *Forensic Science Review,* 6 (1994), 60.

Hicks, J. W., *Microscopy of Hair: A Practical Guide and Manual.* Washington, D.C.: U.S. Government Printing Office, 1977.

Petraco, N., and P. R. De Forest, "A Guide to the Analysis of Forensic Dust Specimens," in *Forensic Science Handbook,* Vol. 3, R. Saferstein, ed. Englewood Cliffs, N.J.: Prentice Hall, 1993.

Porter, J., and C. Fouweather, "An Appraisal of Human Head Hair as Forensic Evidence," *Journal of the Society of Cosmetic Chemists,* 26 (1975), 299.

Proceedings of the International Symposium on the Analysis and Identification of Polymers. Washington, D.C.: U.S. Government Printing Office, 1985.

Proceedings of the International Symposium on Forensic Hair Comparisons. Washington, D.C.: U.S. Government Printing Office, 1987.

Robertson, J., ed., *Forensic Examination of Fibres.* Basingstoke, Hants, England: Taylor & Francis, 1992.

Saferstein, R., "Forensic Aspects of Analytical Pyrolysis," in *Pyrolysis and GC in Polymer Analysis,* S. A. Lieberman and E. J. Levy, eds. New York: Marcel Dekker, 1985.

Thornton, J. I., "Forensic Paint Examination," in *Forensic Science Handbook,* R. Saferstein, ed. Englewood Cliffs, N.J.: Prentice Hall, 1982.

◆ DRUGS

A drug can be defined as a natural or synthetic substance that is used to produce physiological or psychological effects in humans or other higher-order animals. However, this colorless clinical definition does not really tell us what drugs are; in their modern context, drugs mean something different to each person. To some, drugs are a necessity for sustaining and prolonging life; to others, drugs provide an escape from the pressures of life; and to some, they are a means of ending it.

Considering the wide application and acceptance of drugs in our society, it was perhaps inevitable that a segment of our population would abuse their use. During the 1960s, succeeding waves of hallucinogens, amphetamines, and barbiturates found their way out of laboratories, pharmacies, and medicine chests and into the streets. During this decade, marijuana became the most widely used illicit drug in the United States, and alcohol consumption continued to rise—today 90 million Americans drink alcohol regularly, and 10 million of these are hopelessly addicted or have severe problems in coping with their drinking habits. In the 1970s, heroin addiction emerged as a national problem, and today the United States is in the midst of an epidemic spread of cocaine abuse.

Drug abuse has grown from a problem generally associated with members of the lower end of the social-economic ladder to one that cuts across all social and ethnic classes of society. Today, 23 million people in the United States are users of illicit drugs. Of these, there are about a half-million heroin addicts and nearly six million users of cocaine.

In the United States, the epidemic proportions of illegal drug use have produced a situation that finds more than 75 percent of the evidence now being evaluated in crime laboratories to be drug-related. The deluge of drug specimens has forced the expansion of existing crime laboratories and the creation of new ones. For many concerned forensic scientists, the crime laboratory's preoccupation with drug evidence represents a serious distraction from time that could be devoted to the evaluation of evidence related to homicides and other types of serious crimes. However, few can deny that the increasing caseloads associated with drug evidence have provided the major, and often the sole, justification for the expansion of forensic laboratory services. Unquestionably, this expansion has had the effect of increasing the overall analytical capabilities of crime laboratories.

DRUG DEPENDENCE

In assessing the potential danger of drugs, society has become particularly conscious of their effects on human behavior. In fact, the first drugs to be regulated by law in the early years of the twentieth century were those deemed to have "habit-forming" properties. The early laws were aimed primarily at controlling opium and its derivatives, cocaine, and later marijuana. Today, it is known that the ability of a drug to induce dependence after repeated use is submerged in a complex array of physiological and social factors.

Dependence on drugs exists in numerous patterns and in all degrees of intensity, depending on the nature of the drug, the route of administration, the dose, the frequency of administration, and the individual's rate of metabolism. Furthermore, nondrug factors play an equally crucial role in determining the behavioral patterns associated with drug use. The personal characteristics of the user, his or her expectations about the drug experience, society's attitudes and possible responses, as well as the setting in which the drug is used, are all major determinants of drug dependence.

The question of how to define and measure a drug's influence on the individual and the danger it poses for society is difficult to assess. To this end, the nature and significance of drug dependence must be considered from two overlapping points of view: One relates to the interaction of the drug with the individual, and the second has to do with the drug's impact on society. It will be useful when discussing the nature of the drug experience to approach the problem from two distinctly different aspects of human behavior—**psychological dependence** and **physical dependence.**

The common denominator that characterizes all types of repeated drug use is the creation of a psychological dependence for continued use of the drug. In this context, it is important to discard the unrealistic image that all drug users are hopeless "addicts" who are social dropouts. The fact is that most users present quite a normal appearance and remain both socially and economically integrated in the life of the community.

The reasons why some people abstain from drugs while others become moderately or heavily involved are difficult if not impossible to answer. Unquestionably, psychological needs arise from numerous personal and social factors that inevitably stem from the individual's desires to create a sense of well-being and to escape from reality. In some cases, the individual may be seeking relief from personal problems or stressful situations, or he or she may be trying to sustain a physical and emotional state that permits an improved level of performance. Whatever the reasons, it is the existence of underlying psychological needs and the desire to fulfill them that create a conditioned pattern of drug abuse.

The intensity of the psychological dependence associated with a drug's use is difficult to define and to a large extent depends on the nature of the drug used. For drugs such as alcohol, heroin, amphetamines, barbiturates, and cocaine, there is a significant likelihood that continued use will result in a high degree of involvement. Others, such as marijuana and codeine, appear to have a considerably lower potential for the development of psychological dependence. However, this is not to imply that the repeated abuse of drugs deemed to have a low potential for psychological dependency is safe or will always produce low psychological dependence. The fact is that we have no precise way of measuring or predicting the impact of drug abuse on the individual. Even if a system could be devised for controlling the many possible variables affecting a user's response, the unpredictability of the human personality would still have to be contended with; for it is the personal inadequacies of the drug user that represent the underlying motivation for drug use.

Our general knowledge of alcohol consumption should warn us of the fallacy of generalizing when attempting to describe the danger of drug abuse. Obviously, not all drinkers of alcohol are psychologically addicted to the drug; most are "social" drinkers who drink in reasonable amounts and on an irregular basis. Certainly, there are many who have progressed beyond this stage and who consider alcohol a necessary crutch for dealing with life's stresses and anxieties. However, a wide range of behavioral patterns does exist among alcohol abusers, and to a large extent the determination of the degree of psychological dependency must be made on an individual basis. Likewise, it would be fallacious to generalize that all users of marijuana can at worst develop a low degree of dependency on the drug. A wide range of factors also influence marijuana's effect, and heavy users of the drug do expose themselves to the danger of developing a high degree of psychological dependency.

Where emotional well-being is the primary motive leading to repeated and intensive use of a drug, certain drugs, when taken in sufficient dose and frequency, are capable of producing physiological changes that encourage their continued use. Once the user abstains from such a drug, severe physical illness follows. It is the desire to avoid this **withdrawal sickness** or **abstinence syndrome** that ultimately causes physical dependence, or addiction. Hence, for the addict who is accustomed to receiving large doses of heroin, the thought of abstaining and encountering body chills, vomiting, stomach cramps, convulsions, insomnia, pain, and hallucinations serves as a powerful inducement for continued drug use.

Interestingly, some of the more widely abused drugs have little or no potential for creating physical dependence. Drugs such as marijuana, LSD, and cocaine do create strong anxieties when their repeated use is discontinued; however, no medical evidence exists to attribute these discomforts to physiological reactions that accompany withdrawal sickness. On the other hand, the use of alcohol, heroin, and barbiturates can result in the development of physical dependency.

Physical dependency develops only when the drug user adheres to a regular schedule of drug intake; that is, the interval between doses must be short enough so that the effects of the drug never wear off completely. For example, the interval between injections of heroin for the drug addict probably does not exceed six to eight hours. Beyond this time the addict begins to experience the uncomfortable symptoms of withdrawal. It is well known that many users of heroin avoid taking the drug on a regular basis for fear of becoming physically addicted to its use. Similarly, the risk of developing physical dependence on alcohol becomes greatest when the consumption is characterized by a continuing pattern of daily use in large quantities.

Table 9–1 categorizes some of the more commonly abused drugs according to their effect on the body and summarizes their tendency to produce psychological dependency and to induce physical dependency with repeated use.

The social impact of drug dependence is directly related to the extent with which the user has become preoccupied with the drug. Here, the most important element to consider is the extent to which

TABLE 9–1.
THE POTENTIAL OF SOME COMMONLY ABUSED
DRUGS TO PRODUCE DEPENDENCY WITH
REGULAR USE

Drug	Psychological Dependence	Physical Dependence
Narcotics		
Morphine	High	Yes
Heroin	High	Yes
Methadone	High	Yes
Codeine	Low	Yes
Depressants		
Barbiturates (short-acting)	High	Yes
Barbiturates (long-acting)	Low	Yes
Alcohol	High	Yes
Methaqualone (Quaalude)	High	Yes
Meprobamate (Miltown, Equanil)	Moderate	Yes
Diazepam (Valium)	Moderate	Yes
Chlordiazepoxide (Librium)	Moderate	Yes
Stimulants		
Amphetamines	High	?
Cocaine	High	No
Caffeine	Low	No
Nicotine	High	Yes
Hallucinogens		
Marijuana	Low	No
LSD	Low	No
Phencyclidine (PCP)	High	No

drug use has become interwoven in the fabric of the user's life. The more frequently the drug satisfies the person's need, the greater is the likelihood of his or her preoccupation with its use, with a consequent neglect of individual and social responsibilities. Personal health, economic relationships, and family obligations may all suffer as the drug-seeking behavior increases in frequency and intensity and dominates the individual's life. The extreme of drug dependence may lead to behavior that has serious implications for the public's safety, health, and welfare.

Drug dependence in its broadest sense involves much of the world's population. As a result, there must be a complex array of individual, social, cultural, legal, and medical factors that ultimately influence society's decision to prohibit or to impose strict controls on a drug's distribution and use. Invariably, society must weigh the beneficial aspects of the drug against the ultimate harm its abuse will do to the individual and to society as a whole. Obviously, there are many forms of drug dependence that do not carry adverse social conse-quences, as illustrated by the widespread use of such drug-containing substances as tobacco and coffee. Although the heavy and prolonged use of these drugs may eventually damage body organs and result in injury to an individual's health, there is no evidence that they result in antisocial behavior, even upon prolonged or excessive use. Hence, society is willing to accept the widespread use of these substances.

We are certainly all aware of the disastrous failure in the United States to prohibit the use of alcohol during the 1920s and the current debate on whether or not marijuana should be legalized. Each of these issues emphasizes that the balance between individual desires and needs and society's concern with the consequences of drug abuse is a delicate one; moreover, it is one that is continuously subject to change and reevaluation.

NARCOTIC DRUGS

The term **narcotic** is derived from the Greek word *narkotikos,* which implies a state of lethargy or sluggishness. Pharmacologists actually classify narcotic drugs as substances that bring relief from pain and produce sleep. Unfortunately, "narcotic" has come to be popularly asso-ciated with any drug that is socially unacceptable. As a consequence of this incorrect usage, many drugs are improperly called narcotics. Fur-thermore, this confusion has produced legal definitions that are at variance with the pharmacological actions of many drugs. For exam-ple, until the early 1970s, most drug laws in the United States incor-rectly designated marijuana as a narcotic substance; even at the pre-sent time, many drug-control laws in the United States, including the federal law, classify cocaine as a narcotic drug. Pharmacologically, cocaine is actually a powerful central nervous system stimulant, pos-sessing properties opposite to those normally associated with the depressant effects of a narcotic.

Narcotic drugs are analgesics—that is, they relieve pain by exert-ing a depressing action on the central nervous system. The regular use of a narcotic drug will invariably lead to physical dependence, with all its dire consequences. The source of most analgesic narcotics is opium, a gummy, milky juice exuded through a cut made in the unripe pod of the poppy *(Papaver somniferium),* a plant grown mostly in parts of Asia. Opium is brownish in color and has a morphine content that can range from 4 to 21 percent.

Although morphine is readily extracted from opium, for reasons that are not totally known most addicts prefer to use one of its deriv-atives, heroin. Heroin is made rather simply by reacting morphine with acetic anhydride or acetyl chloride (see Figure 9–1). Heroin's high solubility in water makes its street preparation for intravenous administration rather simple, for it is only by injection that heroin's effects are almost instantaneously felt and with maximum sensitivity. To prepare the drug for injection, the addict frequently dissolves it in a small quantity of water in a spoon. The process can be speeded up by heating the spoon over a candle or several matches. The solution is then drawn into a syringe or eyedropper for injection beneath the skin. Figure 9–2 shows some of the paraphernalia typically associated with heroin's street administration.

Besides being a powerful analgesic, heroin produces a "high" that is accompanied by drowsiness and a deep sense of well-being; however, the effect is of short duration, generally lasting only three to four hours.

The content of a typical heroin bag is an excellent example of the uncertainty attached to buying illicit drugs. For many years into the 1960s and early 1970s, the average bag contained 15 to 20 percent heroin. Currently, the average purity of heroin obtained in the illicit U.S. market is approximately 35 percent. The addict rarely knows or cares what comprises the other 65 percent or so of the material.

Figure 9–1. The opium poppy and its derivatives. Shown are the poppy plant, crude and smoking opium, codeine, heroin, and morphine. *Courtesy* Drug Enforcement Administration, Washington, D.C.

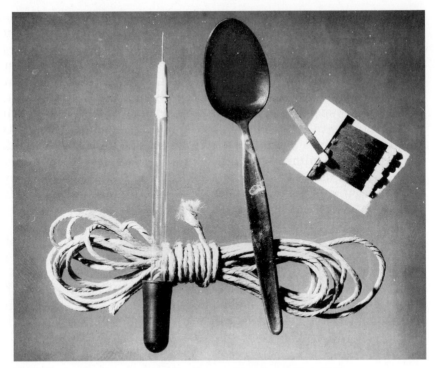

Figure 9–2. Heroin paraphernalia. *Courtesy* New Jersey State Police.

Traditionally, quinine has been the most common diluent of heroin. Like heroin, it has a bitter taste and was probably originally used to obscure the actual potency of a heroin preparation for those who wished to taste-test the material before buying it. Other diluents commonly added to heroin are starch, lactose, procaine (Novocain), and mannitol.

Codeine is also present in opium, but it is usually prepared synthetically from morphine. It is commonly used as a cough suppressant in cough syrup. Codeine, only one-sixth as strong as morphine, is not an attractive street drug for addicts.

There are a number of narcotic drugs that are not derived from opium or morphine. However, because they too have the same physiological effects on the body as the opium narcotics, they are commonly referred to as "opiates." Methadone is perhaps the best known of the synthetic opiates. In the 1960s, scientists discovered that a person receiving methadone periodically in oral doses of 80 to 120 milligrams a day would not get high if he or she then took heroin or morphine. Clearly, although methadone is a narcotic pharmacologically related to heroin, its administration appears to eliminate the addict's desire for heroin while producing minimal side effects. Critics of the controversial methadone maintenance programs claim that methadone is just substituting one narcotic drug for another, and supporters argue that this is the only known treatment for keeping the addict off heroin and offering some hope for eventual abstention from narcotics.

Another synthetic narcotic beginning to receive close scrutiny by legal authorities is propoxyphene, first marketed in 1957 under the trade name of Darvon. This drug is normally prescribed for the relief of moderate pain; however, evidence of its abuse and increasing incidences of propoxyphene overdoses have sparked investigations regarding the drug's usefulness and whether steps are warranted to restrict its availability as a prescription drug.

HALLUCINOGENS

Hallucinogens are drugs that can cause marked alterations in normal thought processes, perceptions, and moods. Perhaps the most popular and controversial member of this class of drugs is marijuana.

MARIJUANA

Marijuana easily qualifies as the most widely used illicit drug in the United States today. For instance, more than 43 million Americans have tried marijuana, according to the latest surveys, and almost half that number may be regular users. Marijuana refers to a preparation derived from the plant *Cannabis*. Most botanists believe there is only one species of the plant, *Cannabis sativa L*. The marijuana preparation normally consists of crushed leaves mixed in varying proportions with the plant's flower, stem, and seed. The plant secretes a sticky resin that is known as *hashish*. The resinous material can also be extracted from the plant by soaking in a solvent such as alcohol. On the illicit drug market, hashish usually appears in the form of compressed vegetation containing a high percentage of resin. A potent form of marijuana is known as *sinsemilla*. This is made from the unfertilized flowering tops of the female *Cannabis* plants, attained by removal of all male plants from the growing field at the first sign of their appearance. It follows that the production of sinsemilla requires a great deal of attention and care, and the plant is therefore cultivated on small plots.

Marijuana and its related products have been in use legally and illegally for almost three thousand years. The first reference to the medical use of marijuana is in a pharmacy book written about 2737 B.C.

by the Chinese Emperor Shen Nung, who recommended it for "female weakness, gout, rheumatism, malaria, beriberi, constipation and absent-mindedness." In China, at that time and even today, the marijuana or hemp plant was also a major source of fiber for the production of rope. Marijuana's mood-altering powers probably did not receive wide attention until about 1000 B.C., when it became an integral part of Hindu culture in India. After A.D. 500, marijuana began creeping westward, and references to it began to appear in the Persian and Arabian literature.

The plant was probably brought to Europe by Napoleon's soldiers returning from Egypt in the early years of the nineteenth century. In Europe, the drug excited the interests of many physicians who foresaw its application for the treatment of a wide range of ailments. At this time, it also found some use as a painkiller and mild sedative. In later years, these applications were to be either forgotten or ignored.

Marijuana was first introduced into the United States around 1920. The weed was smuggled by Mexican laborers across the border into Texas. American soldiers also brought the plant in from the ports of Havana, Tampico, and Veracruz. Although its use was confined to a small segment of the population, its popularity quickly spread from the border and Gulf states into most of the major U.S. cities. By 1937, 46 states and the federal government had laws prohibiting the use or possession of marijuana. Under most of these laws, marijuana was subject to the same rigorous penalties applicable to morphine, heroin, and cocaine and was often erroneously designated a "narcotic."

Marijuana is a weed that grows wild under most climatic conditions. The plant grows to a height of 5 to 15 feet and is characterized by an odd number of leaflets on each leaf. Normally, each leaf contains five to nine leaflets, all having serrated or saw-tooth edges, as shown in Figure 9–3.

It wasn't until 1964 that scientists isolated the chemical substance largely responsible for the hallucinogenic properties of marijuana. This substance is known as **tetrahydrocannabinol,** or **THC.** Its discovery has allowed researchers to measure the potency of marijuana preparations and has permitted studies related to measuring the effect of marijuana's potency on individuals. It has also been found that the THC content of *Cannabis* varies in different parts of the plant, generally decreasing in the following sequence: resin, flowers, and leaves. Little THC is found in the stem, roots, or seeds. The potency and resulting effect of the drug fluctuate, depending on the relative proportion of these plant parts in the marijuana mixture.

The potency of marijuana will depend on its form. Marijuana in the form of loose vegetation has an average THC content of about 1.5 percent. The more potent sinsemilla form averages about 3.5 to 4 percent in THC content, while hashish preparations average about 3.5

Figure 9–3.
The marijuana leaf. *Courtesy* Drug
Enforcement Administration,
Washington, D.C.

percent. Another form of hashish is known as "liquid hashish" or "hashish oil." Hashish in this form is normally a viscous substance, dark green in color and having the consistency of tar (see Figure 9–4). Liquid hashish is produced by efficiently extracting the THC-rich resin from the marijuana plant with an appropriate solvent. The liquid hashish so far discovered has varied between 20 and 65 percent in THC content. Because of its extraordinary potency, one drop of the material can make a "high." Ordinarily, a drop is placed on a regular cigarette or on a marijuana cigarette before smoking.

Any study that relates to marijuana's effect on humans must take the potency of the marijuana preparation into consideration. An interesting insight into the relationship between dosage level and marijuana's pharmacological effect was presented in the first report of the National Commission of Marijuana and Drug Abuse:

> At low, usual "social" doses the user may experience an increased sense of well-being; initial restlessness and hilarity followed by a dreamy, carefree state of relaxation; alteration of sensory perceptions including expansion of space and time; and a more vivid sense of touch, sight, smell, taste and sound; a feeling of hunger, especially a craving for sweets; and subtle changes in thought formation and expression. To an

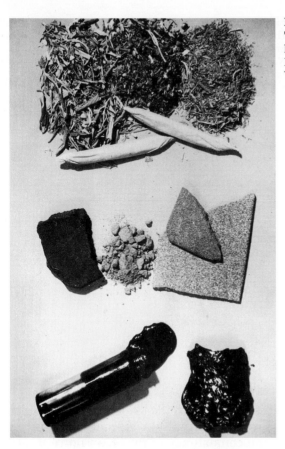

Figure 9–4.
Top to bottom: marijuana vegetation, hashish, and liquid hashish. *Courtesy* Drug Enforcement Administration, Washington, D.C.

unknowing observer, an individual in this state of consciousness would not appear noticeably different from his normal state.

At higher, moderate doses these same reactions are intensified but the changes in the individual would still be scarcely noticeable to an observer. . . . At very high doses, psychotomimetic phenomena may be experienced. These include distortion of body image, loss of personal identity, sensory and mental illusions, fantasies and hallucinations.[1]

There is no current evidence that experimental or intermittent use causes physical or psychological harm. Marijuana does not cause physical dependency. However, the risk of harm lies instead in the heavy, long-term use of the drug, particularly of the more potent preparations. The heavy user can develop a strong psychological

---

[1]*Marijuana—A Signal of Misunderstanding* (Washington, D.C.: U.S. Government Printing Office, 1972), p. 56.

dependence on the drug. Marijuana's long-term effects on the health of people who use it are still largely unknown.

There is accumulating evidence that marijuana has potential medical uses. Two promising areas of research are marijuana's reduction of excessive eye pressure in glaucoma and the lessening of nausea caused by powerful anticancer drugs. There are also suggestions that marijuana might be useful as a muscle relaxant.

OTHER HALLUCINOGENS

There are a substantial number of substances of widely varying chemical compositions that have become part of the drug culture because of their hallucinogenic properties. These include lysergic acid diethylamide (LSD), dimethoxymethylamphetamine (STP), dimethyltryptamine (DMT), mescaline, phencyclidine (PCP), and psilocybin. Of this family of drugs, LSD is the most potent and differs little from the other drugs except for the greater intensity of its induced reactions and side effects.

LSD is synthesized from lysergic acid, a substance derived from ergot, which is a type of fungus that attacks certain grasses and grains. Its hallucinogenic effects were first described by the Swiss chemist Albert Hofmann after he accidentally ingested some of the material in his laboratory in 1943. The drug is very potent; as little as 25 micrograms is enough to start vivid visual hallucinations that may last for about 12 hours. The drug also produces marked changes in mood, leading to laughing or crying at the slightest provocation. Feelings of anxiety and tension almost always accompany LSD's use. Although physical dependence does not develop with continued use, the individual user may be prone to flashbacks and psychotic reactions even after use is discontinued.

The possibility of LSD causing chromosome damage in the children of users has been explored. At present, there is no medical evidence to substantiate this claim; however, this issue has received so much publicity that undoubtedly many have stopped experimenting with the drug for fear of maiming future offspring.

In recent years, abuse of phencyclidine, commonly called PCP, has grown to alarming proportions. Because this drug can be synthesized by rather simple chemical processes, it is manufactured surreptitiously for the illicit market in so-called clandestine laboratories (see Figure 9–5). These laboratories range from large, sophisticated operations to small labs located in an individual's garage or bathroom. Small-time operators normally have little or no training in chemistry and employ "cookbook" methods to synthesize the drug. Some of the

Figure 9–5.
Scene from a clandestine drug laboratory. *Courtesy* Drug Enforcement Administration, Washington, D.C.

more knowledgeable and experienced operators have been able to achieve clandestine production levels that approach a commercial level of operation.

Phencyclidine is often mixed with other drugs, such as LSD or amphetamine, and is sold as a powder ("Angel Dust"), capsule, or tablet, or as a liquid sprayed on plant leaves. The drug is smoked, ingested, or sniffed.

Following oral intake of moderate doses (1–6 milligrams), the user first experiences feelings of strength and invulnerability, along with a dreamy sense of detachment. However, the user soon becomes unresponsive, confused, and agitated. Depression, irritability, feelings of isolation, audio and visual hallucinations, and sometimes paranoia accompany PCP's use. Severe depression, tendencies toward violence, and suicide accompany long-term daily use of the drug. In some cases, the PCP user will experience sudden schizophrenic behavior days after the drug has been taken.

Methylenedioxymethamphetamine, also known as MDMA or Ecstasy, has gained worldwide attention as the latest "designer drug." Ecstasy is a synthetic, mind-altering drug that exhibits many hallucinogenic and amphetamine-like effects. Ecstasy was originally patented as an appetite suppressant and was later discovered to bring about feelings of happiness and relaxation. Recreational drug users find that Ecstasy enhances self-awareness and decreases inhibitions. However, severe adverse reactions, some with fatal side effects, have been reported. Ecstasy is known to increase the heart rate and blood pressure; produce muscle tension, teeth grinding, and nausea; and cause psychological difficulties such as confusion, severe anxiety, and paranoia episodes.

DEPRESSANTS

ALCOHOL (ETHYL ALCOHOL)

Many people tend to overlook the fact that alcohol is a drug; as such, its major behavioral effects derive from its depressant action on the central nervous system. In the United States, the alcohol industry annually produces over one billion gallons of spirits, wine, and beer for which 90 million consumers pay nearly $40 billion. Unquestionably, these and other statistics support the fact that alcohol is the most widely used and abused drug in the world today.

The behavioral patterns of alcohol intoxication are varied and depend in part on such factors as social setting, amount consumed, and the personal expectation of the individual with regard to alcohol. When alcohol enters the body's bloodstream, it quickly travels to the brain, where it acts to suppress the brain's control of thought processes and muscle coordination.

Low doses of alcohol tend to inhibit the mental processes of judgment, memory, and concentration. The drinker's personality becomes expansive, and he or she exudes confidence. When taken in moderate doses, alcohol has been found to reduce coordination substantially, inhibit orderly thought processes and speech patterns, and slow down reaction times. Under these conditions, the ability to walk or drive becomes noticeably impaired. In the next chapter, we will examine in greater detail the relationship between alcohol blood levels and driving ability. Higher doses of alcohol may cause the user to become highly irritable and emotional; displays of anger and crying are not uncommon. Extremely high doses may cause an individual to lapse into unconsciousness or even into a comatose state that may be a prelude to a fatal depression of circulatory and respiratory functions.

BARBITURATES

Barbiturates are commonly referred to as "downers" because they relax, create a feeling of well-being, and produce sleep. Like alcohol, barbiturates act on the central nervous system to suppress its vital functions. Collectively, barbiturates can be described as derivatives of barbituric acid, which was first synthesized by a German chemist, Adolf Von Bayer, over 100 years ago. Twenty-five barbiturate derivatives are currently used in medical practice in the United States; however, only five—amobarbital, secobarbital, phenobarbital, pentobarbital, and butabarbital—seemingly suffice for most present-day medical applications. Slang terms for "barbs" usually stem from the color of the capsule or tablet (e.g., "yellow jackets," "blue devils," and "reds").

Normally, barbiturate users take these drugs by mouth. The average sedative dose is about 10 to 70 milligrams. When taken in this fashion, the drug enters the blood through the walls of the small intestine. Some barbiturates, such as phenobarbital, are absorbed more slowly than others and are therefore classified as long-acting barbiturates. Undoubtedly, it is the slow action of phenobarbital that accounts for its low incidence of abuse. Apparently, barbiturate abusers prefer the faster acting ones—secobarbital, pentobarbital, and amobarbital.

When taken in prescribed amounts, barbiturates are relatively safe, but in instances of extensive and prolonged use, physical dependence can develop. However, this happens only when the total daily intake of the drug significantly exceeds the normal therapeutic level prescribed by a physician. This means that patients can, for example, take barbiturates daily for sedative purposes or as an aid to sleep without developing physical dependence. However, for individuals who deliberately resort to maintaining high levels of barbiturate use, cessation will produce a withdrawal syndrome more severe than that caused by any other drug. This may result in insomnia, muscle spasms, delirium, and convulsions. Consequently, withdrawal must be conducted under close medical supervision if the likelihood of death is to be minimized.

Since the early 1970s, a new nonbarbiturate depressant, methaqualone (Quaalude), has appeared on the illicit scene. Methaqualone is a powerful sedative and muscle relaxant that possesses many of the depressant properties of barbiturates. Its initial popularity before 1973 probably stemmed from the fact that the drug was not controlled by U.S. federal law or by most of the states. However, since this time the drug has been placed under strict control, causing the incidence of its abuse to decline.

TRANQUILIZERS

In the past 35 years, there has been a dramatic growth in the use of tranquilizers. Although tranquilizers can be considered depressants, they do differ from barbiturates in the extent of their actions on the central nervous system. Generally, these drugs produce a relaxing tranquility without impairment of high-thinking facilities or the inducement of sleep. "Major tranquilizers" like reserpine and chlorpromazine have been successfully used to reduce the anxieties and tensions of mental patients.

There is a group of so-called mild tranquilizers commonly prescribed to deal with the everyday tensions of many healthy people. These drugs include meprobamate (Miltown), chlordiazepoxide (Librium), and diazepam (Valium). There is medical evidence to show that these drugs produce psychological and physical dependency with repeated and high levels of usage. For this reason, the widespread prescribing of tranquilizers as a means of overcoming the pressures and tensions of life has worried many who fear the creation of a legalized drug culture.

"GLUE SNIFFING"

Since the early 1960s, the practice of sniffing materials containing volatile solvents (airplane glue or model cement, for example) has grown in popularity. Within recent years, another dimension has been added to the problem with the increasing number of incidents involving the sniffing of aerosol gas propellants such as freon. All materials used in sniffing contain volatile or gaseous substances that are primarily central nervous system depressants.

Although toluene seems to be the most popular solvent to sniff, there are others that can produce comparable physiological effects. These chemicals include naphtha, methyl ethyl ketone, gasoline, and trichloroethylene.

The usual immediate effects of sniffing are a feeling of exhilaration and euphoria combined with slurred speech, impaired judgment, and double vision. Finally, the user may experience drowsiness and stupor, with these depressant effects slowly wearing off as the user returns to a normal state. Most experts believe that users become physiologically dependent on the effects achieved by sniffing. There is, however, little evidence to suggest that the practice of solvent inhalation is addictive. But sniffers do expose themselves to the danger of liver, heart, and brain damage from the chemicals they have inhaled. Even worse, sniffing of some solvents, particularly halogenated hydrocarbons, is accompanied by a significant risk of death.

STIMULANTS

AMPHETAMINES

Amphetamines are a group of synthetic drugs that stimulate the central nervous system. They are commonly referred to in the terminology of the drug culture as "uppers" or "speed." Ordinary therapeutic doses of 5 to 20 milligrams per day, taken orally, provide a feeling of well-being and increased alertness that is followed by a decrease in fatigue and a loss of appetite. However, these apparent benefits of the drug are accompanied by restlessness and instability or apprehension, and once the drug effects wear off, depression may set in.

In the United States, the most serious form of amphetamine abuse stems from the intravenous injection of amphetamine or its chemical derivative methamphetamine. The desire for a more intense amphetamine experience is the primary motive for this route of administration. The initial sensation of a "flash" or "rush," followed by an intense feeling of pleasure, constitutes the principal appeal of the intravenous route for the "speed freak." During a "speed binge," the individual may inject 500 to 1000 milligrams of amphetamines every 2 to 3 hours. Users have reported experiencing a euphoria that produces hyperactivity, with a feeling of clarity of vision as well as hallucinations. As the effect of the amphetamines wears off, the individual lapses into a period of exhaustion and may sleep continuously for one or two days. Following this, the user often experiences a prolonged period of severe depression, lasting from days to weeks.

A new smokable form of methamphetamine known as "ice" is reported to be in heavy demand in some areas of the United States. Ice is prepared by a slow evaporation of a methamphetamine solution to produce large, crystal-clear "rocks." Like crack cocaine, ice is smoked and produces effects similar to those of crack cocaine, but the effects last for a longer period of time. Once the effects of ice wear off, users often become depressed and may sleep for days. Chronic users exhibit violent destructive behavior and acute psychosis similar to paranoid schizophrenia.

The repeated use of amphetamines does lead to a strong psychological dependency, which encourages their continued administration. At this time, there is some disagreement among medical specialists as to whether the repeated use of amphetamines does create physical dependence. Several investigators are of the opinion that the prolonged sleep, chronic fatigue, and sensation of hunger that follow the repeated administration of amphetamines constitute withdrawal sickness.

In light of the reduced production quotas that have been imposed on amphetamine manufacturers by U.S. government regulations, an increasing percentage of the amphetamines sold on the illicit market is being synthesized in clandestine drug laboratories.

Drugs that have pharmacological properties similar to those of amphetamines, but that are chemically unrelated, are also being increasingly abused. These include phenmetrazine and phendimetrazine, two drugs commonly prescribed for weight control.

COCAINE

Between 1884 and 1887, Sigmund Freud created something of a sensation in European medical circles by describing his experiments with a new drug. What he reported was a substance of seemingly limitless potential as a source of "exhilaration and lasting euphoria" that permitted "intensive mental or physical work [to be] performed without fatigue. . . . It is as though the need for food and sleep was completely banished."

The object of Freud's enthusiasm was cocaine, a drug stimulant extracted from the leaves of *Erythroxylon coca,* a plant grown in the Andes Mountains of South America and tropical Asia (see Figure 9–6). At one time, cocaine had wide medical application as a local painkiller or anesthetic. However, this function has now been largely replaced by other drugs—namely, procaine and lidocaine. Cocaine is also a powerful stimulant to the central nervous system, and its effects resemble those caused by the amphetamines—namely, increased alertness and vigor, accompanied by the suppression of hunger, fatigue, and boredom. Most commonly, cocaine is sniffed or "snorted" and is absorbed into the body through the mucous membranes of the nose.

One form of cocaine that has gained widespread popularity in the drug culture is known as "crack." The process used to make crack is simple. Ordinary cocaine is mixed with baking soda and water into a solution that is then heated in a pot. This material is then dried and

Figure 9–6.
Coca leaves and illicit forms of cocaine. *Courtesy* Drug Enforcement Administration, Washington, D.C.

broken into tiny chunks that dealers sell as crack rocks. Crack is free-base cocaine and is sufficiently volatile to be smoked, usually in glass pipes. Crack, like cocaine that is snorted, produces a feeling of euphoria by stimulating a pleasure center in the base of the brain, in an area connected to nerves that are responsible for emotions. Cocaine stimulates this pleasure center to a far greater degree than it would ever normally be stimulated. The result is euphoria—a feeling of increased energy, of being mentally more alert, of feeling really good. The faster the cocaine level rises in the brain, the greater the euphoria, and the surest way to obtain a fast rise in the brain's cocaine level is to smoke crack. Inhaling the cocaine vapor gets a large wallop of the drug to the brain in less than 15 seconds—about as fast as injecting it and much faster than snorting it. The dark side of crack, however, is that the euphoria fades quickly as cocaine levels drop, leaving the user feeling depressed, anxious, pleasureless. The desire to return to a euphoric feeling is so intense that crack users quickly develop a habit for the drug that is almost impossible to overcome. Only a small percentage of crack abusers can ever be cured of this drug habit.

In the United States, cocaine abuse is on the rise. Cocaine generates confidence and produces increased alertness, giving a false illusion that one is doing well at an assigned task. However, some regular users of cocaine report accompanying feelings of restlessness, irritability, and anxiety. Cocaine used chronically or at high doses can have toxic effects. Cocaine-related deaths are a result of cardiac arrest or seizures followed by respiratory arrest. Many people are apparently using cocaine to improve their ability to work and to keep going when tired. Another reason for the popularity of the drug is its reputation for being harmless. Actually, this reputation is untrue. While there is no evidence of physical dependency accompanying cocaine's repeated use, abstention from cocaine after prolonged use does bring on severe bouts of mental depression, which produce a very strong compulsion to resume the drug's use. In fact, laboratory experiments with animals have demonstrated that cocaine produces the strongest psychological compulsions for continued use of all the commonly abused drugs.

The United States spends millions of dollars annually in attempting to control the cultivation of the coca leaf in various South American countries and to prevent cocaine trafficking into the United States. Three-quarters of the cocaine smuggled into the United States is refined at clandestine laboratories located in Colombia. The profits are astronomical. Peruvian farmers may be paid $200 for enough coca leaves to make one pound of cocaine. The refined cocaine will be worth $1000 when it leaves Colombia and will sell at retail in the United States for up to $20,000.

ANABOLIC STEROIDS

Anabolic steroids are synthetic compounds that are chemically related to the male sex hormone testosterone. Testosterone has two different effects on the body. It promotes the development of secondary male characteristics (androgen effects), and it accelerates muscle growth (anabolic effects). Efforts to promote muscle growth and to minimize the hormone's androgenic effects have led to the synthesis of numerous anabolic steroids. However, it has not yet been possible to develop a steroid free of the accompanying harmful side effects of an androgen drug.

Incidence of steroid abuse first received widespread public attention when it became known that both amateur and professional athletes were using these substances to enhance their performance. Interestingly, current research on male athletes given anabolic steroids has generally found little or, at best, marginal evidence of enhanced strength or performance. While the full extent of anabolic steroid abuse by the general public is not fully known, there is a sufficient concern on the part of the U.S. government to warrant regulating the availability of these drugs to the general population and to severely punish individuals for illegal possession and distribution of anabolic steroids. In 1991, anabolic steroids were classified as controlled dangerous substances, and the Drug Enforcement Administration was given enforcement power to prevent their illegal use and distribution.

Anabolic steroids are usually taken by individuals who are unfamiliar with the harmful medical side effects. Liver cancer and other liver malfunctions have been linked to steroid use. These drugs also cause masculinizing effects on females, infertility, and diminished sex drive in males. For teenagers, anabolic steroids result in premature halting of bone growth before reaching full height. Anabolic steroids can also cause unpredictable effects on mood and personality, leading to unprovoked acts of anger and destructive behavior. Depression is also a frequent side effect of anabolic steroid abuse.

DRUG-CONTROL LAWS

Although the previous sections have attempted to classify drugs according to their physiological effects on the body, for practical purposes of law enforcement, the legal community requires a thorough knowledge of drug classification and definitions as they are delineated by drug laws. As may often happen, the medical and legal definitions or classifications of a drug bear little resemblance to one another. The provisions of drug laws are of particular interest to the criminalist, for they may impose specific analytical requirements on a drug analysis. For example, the severity of a penalty associated with the manufacture, distribution, possession, and use of a drug may depend on the weight of the drug or its concentration in a mixture. In such cases, the chemist's report must contain all information that is needed to properly charge a suspect under the provisions of the existing law.

The provisions of any drug-control law are an outgrowth of national and local law enforcement requirements and customs, as well as the result of moral and political philosophies. These factors have combined to produce a wide spectrum of national and local drug-control laws. Although their detailed discussion is beyond the intended scope of this book, a brief description of the U.S. federal law known as the Controlled Substances Act will serve to illustrate a legal drug-classification system that has been created to prevent and control drug abuse. The fact that many states have modeled their own drug-control laws after this act represents an important step in establishing uniform drug-control laws throughout the United States.

CONTROLLED SUBSTANCES ACT

The federal law establishes five schedules of classification (to be outlined later) for controlled dangerous substances on the basis of a drug's potential for abuse, potential for physical and psychological dependence, and medical value. This classification system is extremely flexible in that the U.S. Attorney General has the authority to add, delete, or reschedule a drug as more information becomes available. In addition, controlled dangerous substances listed in schedules I and II are subject to manufacturing quotas set by the attorney general. For example, some 8 billion doses of amphetamines were manufactured in the United States in 1971. In 1972, production quotas were established reducing amphetamine production approximately 80 percent below 1971 levels.

The criminal penalties for the unauthorized manufacture, sale, or possession of controlled dangerous substances are related to the schedules as well. The most severe penalties are associated with drugs listed in schedules I and II. For example, for drugs included in schedules I and II, a first offense is punishable by up to 20 years in prison and/or a fine of up to $1 million for an individual or up to $5 million for other than individuals. Table 9–2 summarizes the control mechanisms and penalties for each schedule of the Controlled Substances Act.

Schedule I.   Schedule I drugs are deemed to have a high potential for abuse, have no currently accepted medical use in the United

States, and/or lack accepted safety for use in treatment under medical supervision. Drugs controlled under this schedule include heroin, marijuana, methaqualone, and LSD.

Schedule II.   Schedule II drugs have a high potential for abuse, a currently accepted medical use or a medical use with severe restrictions, and a potential for severe psychological or physical dependence. Schedule II drugs include opium and its derivatives not listed in schedule I, cocaine, methadone, phencyclidine (PCP), most amphetamine preparations, and most barbiturate preparations containing amobarbital, secobarbital, and pentobarbital. Dronabinol, the synthetic equivalent of the active ingredient in marijuana, has been placed in schedule II in recognition of its growing medical uses in treating glaucoma and chemotherapy patients.

Schedule III.   Schedule III drugs have a potential for abuse less than those in schedules I and II, have a currently accepted medical use in the United States, and have a potential for low or moderate physical dependence or high psychological dependence. Schedule III controls, among other substances, all barbiturate preparations (except phenobarbital) not covered under schedule II and certain codeine preparations. Anabolic steroids were added to this schedule in 1991.

Schedule IV.   Schedule IV drugs have a low potential for abuse relative to schedule III drugs and have a current medical use in the United States; and their abuse may lead to limited dependence relative to schedule III drugs. Drugs controlled in this schedule include propoxyphene (Darvon), phenobarbital, and tranquilizers such as meprobamate (Miltown), diazepam (Valium), and chlordiazepoxide (Librium).

Schedule V.   Schedule V drugs must show low abuse potential, have medical use in the United States, and have less potential for producing dependence than schedule IV drugs. Schedule V controls certain opiate drug mixtures that contain nonnarcotic medicinal ingredients.

The Controlled Substances Act also includes a provision stipulating that an offense involving a controlled substance analog, a chemical substance substantially similar in chemical structure to a controlled substance, shall trigger penalties as if it were a controlled substance listed in schedule I. This section is designed to combat the proliferation of so-called **designer drugs.** Designer drugs are substances that are chemically related to some controlled drugs and are pharmacologically very potent. These substances are manufactured by skilled

TABLE 9–2.

CONTROL MECHANISMS OF THE CONTROLLED SUBSTANCES ACT

Schedule	Registration	Record Keeping	Manufacturing Quotas	Distribution Restrictions	Dispensing Limits
I	Required	Separate	Yes	Order forms	Research use only
II	Required	Separate	Yes	Order forms	Rx: written; no refills
III	Required	Readily retrievable	No *but* Some drugs limited by schedule II quotas	Records required	Rx: written or oral; with medical authorization, refills up to 5 times in 6 months
IV	Required	Readily retrievable	No *but* Some drugs limited by schedule II quotas	Records required	Rx: written or oral; with medical authorization, refills up to 5 times in 6 months
V	Required	Readily retrievable	No *but* Some drugs limited by schedule II quotas	Records required	Over-the-counter (Rx drugs limited to MD's order)

individuals in clandestine laboratories, with the knowledge that their products will not be covered by the schedules of the Controlled Substances Act. For instance, the compound fentanyl is a powerful narcotic that is commercially marketed for medical use and is also listed as a controlled dangerous substance. This drug is about 100 times as potent as morphine. Currently, there are a number of substances chemically related to fentanyl that have been synthesized by underground chemists and sold on the street. The first such substance encountered was sold under the street name "China White." These drugs have been responsible for more than 100 overdose deaths in Cal-

Import-Export		Security	Manufacturer/ Distributor Reports to Drug Enforcement Administration	Criminal Penalties for Individual Trafficking (First Offense)
Narcotic	*Nonnarcotic*			
Permit	Permit	Vault/safe	Yes	0–20 years/ $1 million
Permit	Permit	Vault/safe	Yes	0–20 years/ $1 million
Permit	Declaration	Secure storage area	Yes, Narcotic	0–5 years/ $250,000
			No, Nonnarcotic	
Permit	Declaration	Secure storage area	Manufacturer only, Narcotic	0–3 years/ $250,000
			No, Nonnarcotic	
Permit to import Declaration to export	Declaration	Secure storage area	Manufacturer only, Narcotic	0–1 year/ $100,000
			No, Nonnarcotic	

Source: Drug Enforcement Administration.

ifornia and nearly 20 deaths in western Pennsylvania. As designer drugs, such as China White, are identified and linked to drug abuse, they have been placed in appropriate schedules.

Recent changes in the Controlled Substances Act reflect an effort to decrease the prevalence of clandestine drug laboratories designed to manufacture controlled substances. The act now regulates the manufacture and distribution of precursors, the chemical compounds used by clandestine drug laboratories to synthesize drugs of abuse. Targeted precursor chemicals are listed in the definition section of the Controlled Substances Act. Severe penalties are provided for a person who possesses a listed precursor chemical with the intent to manufacture a controlled substance or who possesses or distributes a listed chemical knowing, or having reasonable cause to believe, that the listed chemical will be used to manufacture a controlled substance. In addition, precursors to PCP, amphetamines, and methamphetamines are enumerated specifically in schedule II, making them subject to regulation in the same manner as other schedule II substances.

DRUG IDENTIFICATION

One only has to look into the evidence vaults of crime laboratories to appreciate the assortment of drug specimens that confront the criminalist. The presence of a huge array of powders, tablets, capsules, vegetable matter, liquids, pipes, cigarettes, cookers, and syringes is testimony to the vitality and sophistication of the illicit drug market. If outward appearance is not evidence enough of the difficult analytical chore facing the forensic chemist, consider the complexity of the drug preparations themselves. Usually these contain active drug ingredients of unknown origin and identity as well as additives—for example, sugar, starch, and quinine—that dilute their potency and stretch their value on the illicit marketplace. Do not forget that illicit dealers are not hampered by governmental regulations that ensure the quality and consistency of a product.

When a forensic chemist picks up a drug specimen for analysis, anything can be expected to be found, and all contingencies must be prepared for. The analysis must leave no room for error, for its results will have a direct bearing on the process of determining the guilt or innocence of a defendant. There is no middle ground in drug identification—either the specimen is a specific drug or it is not—and once a positive conclusion is drawn, the chemist must be prepared to support and defend the validity of the results in a court of law.

The challenge or difficulty of forensic drug identification comes in selecting analytical procedures that will ensure a specific identification of a drug. Presented with a substance of unknown origin and composition, the forensic chemist must develop a plan of action that will ultimately yield the drug's identity. This plan, or scheme of analysis, is divided into two phases. First, faced with the prospect that the unknown substance may be any one of a thousand or more commonly encountered drugs, the analyst must employ **screening tests** to reduce these possibilities to a small and manageable number. This objective is often accomplished by subjecting the material to a series of color tests that will produce characteristic colors for the more commonly encountered illicit drugs. Even if these tests should produce negative results, their value lies in having excluded drugs from further consideration.

Once the number of possibilities has been substantially reduced, the second phase of the analysis must be devoted to pinpointing and confirming the drug's identity. In an era in which crime laboratories are receiving voluminous quantities of drug evidence, it would certainly be impractical to subject a drug to all the chemical and instrumental tests that are at the disposal of the modern criminalist. Indeed, it is more realistic to look on these techniques as constituting a large analytical arsenal. It is up to the chemist, aided by training and experience, to choose tests that will most conveniently furnish the identity of a particular drug.

In many instances, forensic chemists will use a specific test (e.g., infrared spectrophotometry and mass spectrometry) to identify a drug substance to the exclusion of all other known chemical substances. In some cases, the analytical scheme will consist of a series of nonspecific or presumptive tests. Each test in itself is insufficient to prove the drug's identity; however, the proper analytical scheme will encompass a combination of test results that are characteristic of one and only one chemical substance—the drug under investigation. Furthermore, experimental evidence must exist to confirm that the probability of any other substance responding in an identical manner to the scheme selected is so small as to be beyond any reasonable scientific certainty.

There are several tests that forensic chemists normally rely on to comprise a routine drug-identification scheme. These are color tests, microcrystalline tests, chromatography, spectrophotometry, and mass spectrometry.

COLOR TESTS

Many drugs yield characteristic colors when brought into contact with specific chemical reagents. Not only do these tests provide a useful indicator of a drug's presence, but they are also utilized by investigators in the field to examine materials suspected of containing a drug.[2] However, it must be emphasized that color tests are useful for screening purposes only and are never taken as conclusive identification of unknown drugs.

Five primary color test reagents are listed and described next:

1. *Marquis* (2 percent formaldehyde in sulfuric acid). The reagent turns purple in the presence of heroin and morphine and most opium

---

[2]Field test color kits for drugs can be purchased from various commercial manufacturers.

derivatives. Marquis will also become orange-brown when mixed with amphetamines and methamphetamines.

2. *Dillie-Koppanyi* (1 percent cobalt acetate in methanol is first added to the suspect material, followed by 5 percent isopropylamine in methanol). This is a valuable screening test for barbiturates, in whose presence the reagent turns violet-blue in color.

3. *Duquenois-Levine* (solution A is a mixture of 2 percent vanillin and 1 percent acetaldehyde in ethyl alcohol; solution B is concentrated hydrochloric acid; solution C is chloroform). This is a valuable color test for marijuana, performed by adding solutions A, B, and C, respectively, to the suspect vegetation. A positive result is shown by a purple color in the chloroform layer.

4. *Van Urk* (1 percent solution of *p*-dimethylaminobenzaldehyde in 10 percent concentrated hydrochloric acid and ethyl alcohol). Reagent turns blue-purple in the presence of LSD. However, owing to the extremely small quantities of LSD in illicit preparations, this test is difficult to conduct under field conditions.

5. *Scott Test* (solution A is 2 percent cobalt thiocyanate dissolved in water and glycerine [1:1]; solution B is concentrated hydrochloric acid; solution C is chloroform). This is a color test for cocaine. A powder containing cocaine will turn solution A blue. Upon addition of B, the blue color is transformed to a clear pink color. Upon addition of C, if cocaine is present, the blue color reappears in the chloroform layer.

MICROCRYSTALLINE TESTS

A technique considerably more specific than color tests is the microcrystalline test. Here, a drop of a chemical reagent is added to a small quantity of the drug on a microscopic slide. After a short time, a chemical reaction ensues, producing a crystalline precipitate. It is the size and shape of the crystals, under microscope examination, that are highly characteristic of the drug. Crystal tests for heroin are illustrated in Figure 9–7(a) and (b).

Over the years, analysts have developed hundreds of crystal tests to characterize the most commonly abused drugs. These tests are rapid and often do not require the isolation of a drug from its diluents; however, because diluents can sometimes alter or modify the shape of the crystal, the examiner must develop experience in interpreting the results of the test.

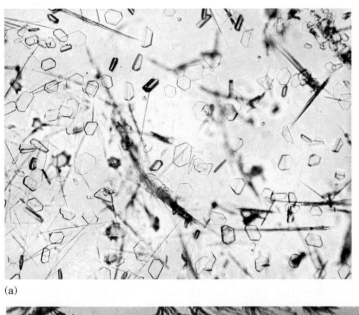

(a)

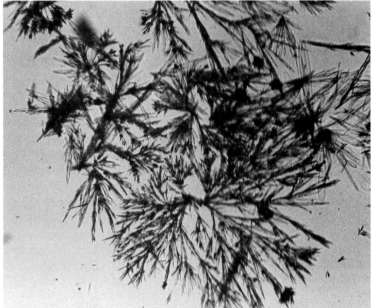

(b)

Figure 9–7. (a) A photomicrograph of heroin crystals in the presence of 10% sodium acetate. (b) A photomicrograph of heroin crystals in the presence of mercuric iodine.

It is important to note that most color and crystal tests are largely empirical—that is, scientists do not fully understand why they produce the results that they do. From the forensic chemist's point of view, this is not important. The fact is that when the tests are properly chosen and are used in proper combination, their results constitute an analytical scheme that is characteristic for one and only one drug.

CHROMATOGRAPHY

The techniques of thin-layer and gas chromatography are especially well suited to the needs of the drug analyst, because they separate drugs from their diluents while providing for their tentative identification. The basic principles of these techniques have already been described in Chapter 5.

Because chromatography requires a comparison of either R_f or retention-time values between questioned and known drugs, the analyst must have some clue as to the identity of the illicit material before utilizing these techniques. Hence, in a typical drug analysis, chromatography accompanies and complements color and crystal tests.

SPECTROPHOTOMETRY

The selective absorption of light by drugs in the UV and IR regions of the electromagnetic spectrum provides a valuable technique for characterizing drugs. The ultraviolet spectrum is not conclusive for the positive identification of a drug, because other materials may very well produce an indistinguishable spectrum. Nevertheless, UV spectrophotometry is often a useful technique for establishing the *probable* identity of a drug. For example, if an unknown substance yields a UV spectrum that resembles amphetamine (see Figure 9–8), thousands of substances are immediately eliminated from consideration, and efforts can now begin to identify the material from a relatively small number of possibilities. A comprehensive collection of UV drug spectra will give the analyst a ready index that can rapidly be searched in order to tentatively identify a drug or, failing that, to at least exclude certain drugs from consideration.

Infrared spectrophotometry is one of the few analytical techniques available to the chemist that can specifically identify a substance. The pattern of an infrared spectrum is unique for each compound and can thus be thought of as being analogous to a "fingerprint" of the compound. The combination of preliminary screening tests with a final verification by infrared spectrophotometry offers an ideal

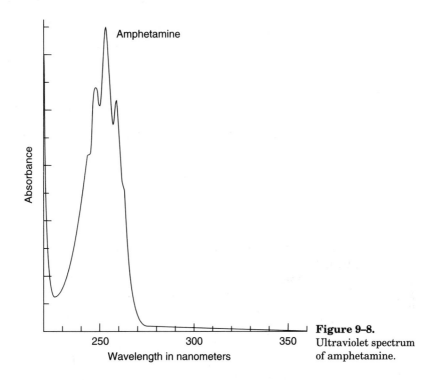

Figure 9–8.
Ultraviolet spectrum
of amphetamine.

approach to drug identification. Unfortunately, the technique does present some problems to the criminalist because the substance to be identified must be as pure as possible. This requirement often necessitates employing lengthy purification steps to prepare the sample for IR analysis. The IR spectra of heroin and secobarbital were shown in Figure 5–17.

MASS SPECTROMETRY

The technique of chromatography is particularly suited for analyzing drugs of abuse, since it can readily separate a drug from other substances that may be present in the drug preparation. Chromatography does, however, suffer from the drawback of not being able to provide the analyst with a specific identification of the material under investigation. This deficiency has been overcome by linking the gas chromatograph to a mass spectrometer (see discussion on pp. 155–159) to yield a very powerful combination known as **gas chromatography/mass spectrometry (GC/MS).** As a sample emerges from the gas chromatograph, it immediately enters the mass spectrometer. Here, the sample is exposed to high-energy electrons, which cause the sample molecules to fragment or break apart. With few exceptions, no two substances fragment in the same fashion; hence, this fragmentation pattern serves as a "fingerprint" of a chemical substance. The fragmentation patterns of heroin and cocaine were shown in Figure 5–19.

With data obtained from a GC/MS determination, a forensic analyst can, with one instrument, separate the components of a complex drug mixture and then unequivocally identify each substance present in the mixture (see Figure 5–18).

THE IDENTIFICATION OF MARIJUANA

Enforcement of laws prohibiting the sale and use of marijuana presently accounts for a high percentage of drug arrests in the United States. Any trial or hearing involving a seizure of marijuana requires an identification of the material before the issue of guilt or innocence can be decided.

Unlike most other drugs received by the crime laboratory, marijuana *(Cannabis sativa L.)* possesses botanical features that impart identifiable characteristics. Because the vast majority of marijuana specimens consist of small leaf fragments, their identification must be partially based on botanical features observed under the microscope by a trained expert. This approach is further augmented with a chemical test that will independently confirm the findings of the botanical examination.

The identification of marijuana by microscopic methods depends largely on observing short hairs having the shape of "bear claws" on the upper side of the leaf (see SEM photo in Figure 7–11). These hairs are known as **cystolithic hairs.** Further verification of the identity of marijuana is confirmed by the presence of longer, nonglandular hairs on the opposite side of the leaf.

The Duquenois-Levine color test, described on page 280, has been found to be a highly but not totally specific test for marijuana. However, when used in combination with a botanical examination, the results constitute a specific identification of marijuana. In addition, situations may arise in which the analyst is unable to obtain a microscopic identification of the marijuana leaf, as in the case of hashish or hashish oil. Here, the color test has to be supplemented by another examination, preferably thin-layer chromatography. This method involves separating chemical constituents found in the suspect resin on a thin-layer plate. The separated components are compared on the same plate to those obtained from a known marijuana extract, as shown in Figure 5–9. In this manner, a positive TLC comparison, when used in conjunction with the Duquenois-Levine color test, constitutes a specific identification for marijuana.

COLLECTION AND PRESERVATION OF DRUG EVIDENCE

The preparation of drug evidence for submission to the crime laboratory is normally a relatively simple task, accomplished with minimal precautions in the field. The field investigator has the responsibility of ensuring that the evidence is properly packaged and labeled for delivery to the laboratory. Considering the countless forms and varieties of drug evidence seized, it is not practical to prescribe any single packaging procedure for fulfilling these requirements. Generally, common sense is the best guide in such situations, keeping in mind that the package must prevent the loss of the contents and/or cross-contamination between specimens. Often, the original container in which the drug was seized will suffice to meet these requirements. Specimens suspected of containing volatile solvents, such as those involved in glue-sniffing cases, must be packaged in an airtight container to prevent evaporation of the solvent.

All packages must be marked with information that is sufficient to ensure identification by the officer in future legal proceedings and to establish the chain of custody.

To aid the drug analyst, it would be helpful if the investigator could supply any background information that may relate to a drug's identity. In some instances, analysis time is markedly reduced when this information is at the disposal of the chemist. For the same reason, the results of drug-screening tests used in the field must also be transmitted to the laboratory. However, although these tests indicate the presence of a drug and may help the officer establish probable cause to search and arrest a suspect, they do not offer conclusive evidence of a drug's identity.

REVIEW QUESTIONS _____

1. Underlying emotional factors are the primary motives leading to the repeated use of a drug. (True, False)
2. Drugs such as alcohol, heroin, amphetamines, barbiturates, and cocaine can lead to a (high, low) degree of psychological dependence with repeated use.

3. The development of (psychological, physical) dependence on a drug is shown by withdrawal symptoms such as convulsions when the user stops taking the drug.

4. Abuse of barbiturates can lead to physical dependency. (True, False)

5. The repeated use of LSD will lead to physical dependency. (True, False)

6. Physical dependency develops only when the drug user adheres to a _____ schedule of drug intake.

7. Narcotic drugs are _____ that exert a _____ action on the central nervous system.

8. _____ is a gummy, milky juice exuded through a cut made in the unripe pod of the opium poppy.

9. The primary constituent of opium is _____.

10. _____ is a chemical derivative of morphine made by reacting morphine with acetic anhydride.

11. Methadone is classified as a narcotic drug, even though it is not derived from opium or morphine. (True, False)

12. Drugs that cause marked alterations in normal thought processes, perceptions, and mood are called _____.

13. _____ is the sticky resin extracted from the marijuana plant.

14. The active ingredient of marijuana largely responsible for its hallucinogenic properties is _____.

15. The potency of a marijuana preparation depends on the proportion of the various plant parts in the mixture. (True, False)

16. A marijuana preparation having the highest THC content is _____.

17. LSD is a chemical derivative of _____. This chemical is obtained from the ergot fungus that grows on certain grasses and grains.

18. The drug phencyclidine is often manufactured for the illicit market in _____ laboratories.

19. Alcohol (stimulates, depresses) the central nervous system.

20. _____ are called "downers" because they depress the actions of the central nervous system.

21. Phenobarbital is an example of a (short-, long-) acting barbiturate.

22. _____ is a powerful sedative and muscle relaxant that possesses many of the depressant properties of barbiturates.

23. _____ are drugs used for the relief of anxiety and tension without inducing sleep.

24. Glue sniffing stimulates the central nervous system. (True, False)
25. _____ are a group of synthetic drugs that stimulate the central nervous system.
26. The most severe form of amphetamine abuse stems from its (oral, intravenous) administration.
27. An increasing percentage of amphetamines available on the illicit market originate from _____ drug laboratories.
28. _____ is extracted from the leaf of the coca plant.
29. Traditionally, cocaine is _____ into the nostrils.
30. Cocaine is a powerful central nervous system depressant. (True, False)
31. _____ steroids are designed to promote muscle growth but have harmful side effects.
32. The federal drug control law is known as _____.
33. Federal law establishes _____ schedules of classification for the control of dangerous drugs.
34. Drugs that have no accepted medical use are placed in schedule _____.
35. Librium and Valium are listed in schedule _____.
36. Color tests are used to identify drugs conclusively. (True, False)
37. The _____ color test turns purple in the presence of heroin.
38. The _____ color test turns orange-brown in the presence of amphetamines.
39. The Duquenois-Levine test is a valuable color test for _____.
40. The _____ test is a widely used color test for cocaine.
41. _____ tests tentatively identify drugs by the size and shape of crystals formed when the drug is mixed with specific reagents.
42. _____ provides a means of separating drugs from their diluents while making a tentative identification.
43. The pattern of an _____ absorption spectrum is unique for each drug and thus is a specific test for identification.
44. The gas chromatograph, in combination with the _____, can separate the components of a drug mixture and then unequivocally identify each substance present in the mixture.
45. The microscopic identification of marijuana largely depends on observing short hairs on the leaf known as _____ hairs.
46. All packages containing drugs must be marked for identification by the police officer before being sent to the laboratory in order to maintain the _____.

FURTHER REFERENCES

Dal Cason, T. A., R. Fox, and R. S. Frank, "Investigations of Clandestine Drug Manufacturing Laboratories," *Analytical Chemistry,* 52 (1980), 804A.

Henderson, G. L., "Designer Drugs: Past History and Future Prospects," *Journal of Forensic Science,* 33 (1988), 569.

Hofmann, Fredrick G., *A Handbook on Drug and Alcohol Abuse,* 2nd ed. New York: Oxford University Press, 1983.

Klein, M., A. V. Kruegel, and S. P. Sobol, eds., *Instrumental Applications in Forensic Drug Chemistry.* Washington, D.C.: U.S. Government Printing Office, 1979.

Lowry, W. T., and James C. Garriott, *Forensic Toxicology: Controlled Substances and Dangerous Drugs.* New York: Plenum Press, 1979.

Moffat, A. E., et al., eds., *Clarke's Isolation and Identification of Drugs,* 2nd ed. London: Pharmaceutical Press, 1986.

Proceedings of the International Symposium on the Forensic Aspects of Controlled Substances. Washington, D.C.: U.S. Government Printing Office, 1989.

Siegel, J. A., "Forensic Identification of Controlled Substances," in *Forensic Science Handbook,* Vol. 2, R. Saferstein, ed. Englewood Cliffs, N.J.: Prentice Hall, 1988.

Thornton, J. I., and G. R. Nakamura, "The Identification of Marijuana," *Journal of the Forensic Science Society,* 12 (1972), 461.

FORENSIC TOXICOLOGY

It is no secret that in spite of the concerted effort that law enforcement agencies are making to prevent the distribution and sale of illicit drugs, thousands die every year from the intentional or unintentional administration of drugs, and many more innocent lives are lost as a result of the erratic and frequently uncontrollable behavior of individuals who are under the influence of drugs. Thus, one should not automatically attribute these occurrences to the wide proliferation of illicit drug markets. For example, in the United States alone, drug manufacturers produce enough barbiturates and tranquilizers each year to provide every man, woman, and child with about 40 pills. All the statistical and medical evidence presently available shows ethyl alcohol, a legal over-the-counter drug, to be the most heavily abused drug in Western countries. In the United States, nearly 17,500 automobile deaths, 40 percent of all traffic deaths, are alcohol-related, with a rate of injury requiring hospital treatment exceeding two million persons per year. This death toll of human beings on the road, as well as the untold damage to life, limb, and property, is testimony in itself to the dangerous consequences of alcohol abuse.

At a time when the uncontrolled use of drugs has become a worldwide problem affecting all segments of society, the role of the toxicologist has taken on new and added significance. Toxicologists are charged with the responsibility for detecting and identifying the presence of drugs and poisons in body fluids, tissues, and organs. Their services are not just required in such legal institutions as crime laboratories and medical examiners' offices; they also reach into hospital laboratories—where the possibility of identifying a drug overdose may represent the difference between life and death—and into various health facilities responsible for monitoring the intake of drugs and other toxic substances. Primary examples include blood tests performed on children exposed to leaded paints, or the analysis of the urine of addicts enrolled in methadone maintenance programs.

The role of the forensic toxicologist is limited to matters that pertain to violations of criminal law. However, the assignment of the responsibility for performing toxicological services in a criminal justice system does vary considerably throughout the United States. In those systems that have a crime laboratory independent of the medical examiner, this responsibility may reside with one or the other, or may be shared by both. Some systems, however, take advantage of the expertise residing in governmental health department laboratories and assign to them this role. Nevertheless, it is a fact that whatever facility is ultimately assigned this work, its caseload will reflect the prevailing popularity of the drugs that are abused in the community. In most cases, this means that the forensic toxicologist must expect to be confronted with numerous requests relating to the determination of the presence of alcohol in the body.

TOXICOLOGY OF ALCOHOL

THE FATE OF ALCOHOL IN THE BODY

The subject of the analysis of alcohol immediately confronts us with the primary objective of forensic toxicology—the detection and isolation of drugs in the body for the express purpose of determining their influence on human behavior. In the case of alcohol, however, the problem is further complicated by practical considerations. The predominant role of the automobile in our society has mandated the imposition of laws designed to protect the public from the drinking driver. In practice, this has meant that toxicologists have had to devise rapid and specific procedures for measuring the degree of alcohol intoxication. The methods utilized must be suitably designed to test hundreds of thousands of motorists annually without causing them undue physical harm or unreasonable inconveniences, while at the same time providing reliable diagnoses that can be supported and defended within the framework of the legal system.

Alcohol, or ethyl alcohol, is a colorless liquid normally diluted with water and consumed as a beverage. Logically, the most obvious measure of intoxication would be the amount of liquor a person has consumed. Unfortunately, most arrests are made after the fact, when such information is not available to legal authorities; furthermore, even if these data could be collected, numerous related factors, such as body weight and the rate of alcohol's absorption into the body, are so extremely variable that it would be impossible to prescribe uniform standards that would yield reliable alcohol intoxication levels.

Like any other depressant, alcohol has its principal effect on the central nervous system, particularly the brain. The extent of the depression is proportional to the concentration of alcohol within the nerve cells. The nerve functions most susceptible to the action of alcohol are found in the surface areas of the forebrain. Later, as the subject absorbs alcohol to a greater extent, the functions of the central and rear portions of the brain are affected. The nerve functions that are most resistant, and that are the last to fail, are those centered in the brain's medulla, which regulates such vital functions as respiration and heart activity.

Theoretically, if one wanted a true determination of the quantity of alcohol that was impairing normal body functions, it would be best to remove a portion of brain tissue and perform a direct analysis on it for alcohol content. For obvious reasons, this cannot be done on living subjects. Consequently, toxicologists have concentrated their efforts on the blood, for it is the blood that provides the medium for circulating alcohol throughout the body, carrying it to all tissues, including the brain. Fortunately, experimental evidence supports this approach and shows blood-alcohol concentration to be directly proportional to the concentration of alcohol in the brain. From the medicolegal point of view, blood-alcohol levels have become the accepted standard for relating alcohol intake to its effect on the body.

Alcohol appears in the blood within minutes after it has been taken by mouth and slowly increases in concentration while it is being absorbed from the stomach and the small intestine into the bloodstream. When all the alcohol has been absorbed, a maximum alcohol level is reached in the blood, and the postabsorption period begins. Then the alcohol concentration slowly decreases until a zero level is again reached.

There are many factors that determine the rate at which alcohol is absorbed into the bloodstream. These include the total time taken to consume the drink, the alcohol content of the beverage, the amount consumed, and the quantity and type of food that may be present in the stomach at the time of drinking. With so many variables, it is difficult to predict just how long the absorption process will require. For example, beer is absorbed more slowly than is an equivalent concentration of alcohol in water. This is apparently because of the carbohydrates present in beer. Also, alcohol consumed on an empty stomach is absorbed faster than an equivalent amount of alcohol taken when there is food in the stomach. The longer the total time required for complete absorption to occur, the lower will be the peak alcohol concentration in the blood (see Figure 10–1). Depending on a combination of factors, maximum blood-alcohol concentration may not be reached until two or three hours have elapsed from the time of consumption. However, under normal social drinking conditions, it takes anywhere from 30 to 90 minutes from the time of the final drink until the absorption process is completed.

During the absorption phase, alcohol slowly enters the body's bloodstream and is carried to all parts of the body. When the absorption period is completed, the alcohol will become distributed uniformly throughout the watery portions of the body—that is, throughout about two-thirds of the body volume. Fat, bones, and hair are low in water content and therefore contain little alcohol, whereas alcohol concentration in the rest of the body is fairly uniform. Hence, if blood is not available, as may be the case in some postmortem situations, a medical

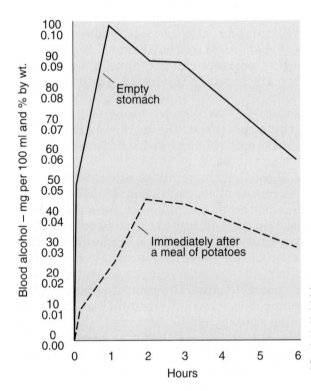

Figure 10–1.
Blood-alcohol concentrations after ingestion of 2 ounces of pure alcohol mixed in 8 ounces of water (equivalent to about 5 ounces of 80-proof vodka). *Source:* U.S. Dept. of Transportation, Washington, D.C.

examiner always has the option of selecting a water-rich organ or fluid—for example, brain, cerebrospinal fluid, or vitreous humor—for determining the body's alcohol content to a reasonable degree of accuracy.

As the alcohol is circulated by the bloodstream, the body proceeds at once to begin the task of eliminating its presence. Elimination is accomplished through two mechanisms—**oxidation** and **excretion.** Nearly all the alcohol (95 to 98 percent) consumed is eventually oxidized to carbon dioxide and water. Oxidation takes place almost entirely in the liver. Here, in the presence of the enzyme alcohol dehydrogenase, the alcohol is converted into acetaldehyde and then to acetic acid. The acetic acid is subsequently oxidized in practically all parts of the body to carbon dioxide and water.

The remaining portion of alcohol is excreted unchanged in the breath, urine, and perspiration. Most significantly, extensive experimental evidence has verified that the amount of alcohol exhaled in the breath is in direct proportion to the concentration of alcohol in the blood. This observation has had a tremendous impact on the technology and procedures used for blood-alcohol testing. The development of instruments to reliably measure breath for its alcohol content has made possible the testing of millions of persons in a rapid, safe, and convenient manner.

The fate of alcohol in the body is therefore relatively simple—namely, absorption into the bloodstream, distribution throughout the body's water, and finally, elimination by oxidation and excretion. The elimination or "burn-off" rate of alcohol varies in different individuals; 0.015 percent w/v per hour seems to be an average value once the absorption process is complete.[1] However, it must be emphasized that this figure is an average that may vary by as much as 30 percent between individuals.

ALCOHOL IN THE CIRCULATORY SYSTEM

The extent to which an individual may be under the influence of alcohol is usually determined by measuring the quantity of alcohol present in the blood system. Normally, this is accomplished in one of two ways: (1) by direct chemical analysis of the blood for its alcohol content; and (2) by measurement of the alcohol content of the breath and a subsequent relating of this value to blood-alcohol concentration. In either

---

[1] In the United States, laws that define blood-alcohol levels almost exclusively use the unit percent weight per volume—% w/v. Hence, 0.015% w/v is equivalent to 0.015 grams of alcohol per 100 milliliters of blood, or 15 milligrams of alcohol per 100 milliliters of blood.

case, the significance and meaning of the results can better be understood when the movement of alcohol through the circulatory system is studied.

Humans, like all vertebrates, have a closed circulatory system, which consists basically of a heart and numerous arteries, capillaries, and veins. An **artery** is a blood vessel carrying blood away from the heart, and a **vein** is a vessel carrying blood back toward the heart. **Capillaries** are tiny blood vessels that interconnect the arteries with the veins. It is across the thin walls of the capillaries that the exchange of materials between the blood and the other tissues takes place. A schematic diagram of the circulatory system is shown in Figure 10–2.

Let us now proceed to trace the movement of alcohol through the human circulatory system. After alcohol is ingested, it moves down the esophagus into the stomach. About 20 percent of the alcohol is absorbed through the stomach walls into the portal vein of the blood system. The remaining alcohol passes into the blood through the walls of the small intestine. Once in the blood, the alcohol is carried to the liver, where the process of its destruction starts as the blood (carrying

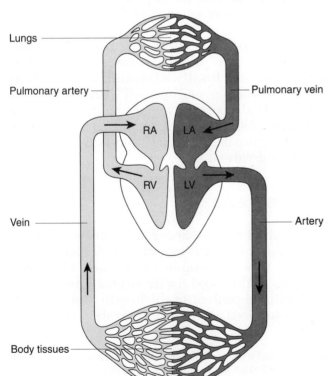

Lungs

Pulmonary artery — — Pulmonary vein

RA   LA

RV   LV

Vein — — Artery

Body tissues —

Figure 10–2.
Simplified diagram of the human
circulatory system. Dark vessels
contain oxygenated blood; light vessels
contain deoxygenated blood.

the alcohol) moves up to the heart. The blood enters the upper right chamber of the heart, called the right atrium (or auricle), and is forced into the lower right chamber of the heart, known as the right ventricle. Having returned to the heart from its circulation through the tissues, the blood at this time contains very little oxygen and much carbon dioxide. Consequently, the blood must be pumped up to the lungs, through the pulmonary artery, to be replenished with oxygen.

It is in the lungs that the respiratory system bridges with the circulatory system so that oxygen can enter the blood and carbon dioxide can leave it. As shown in Figure 10–3(a), the pulmonary artery branches into capillaries lying in close proximity to tiny pear-shaped sacs called **alveoli.** There are about 250 million alveoli in the lungs, all located at the ends of the bronchial tubes. The bronchial tubes themselves connect into the windpipe (trachea), which leads up to the

Figure 10–3.   (a) Gas exchange in the lungs. Blood flows from the pulmonary artery into vessels that lie close to the walls of the alveoli sacs. Here the blood gives up its carbon dioxide and absorbs oxygen. The oxygenated blood leaves the lungs via the pulmonary vein and returns to the heart.

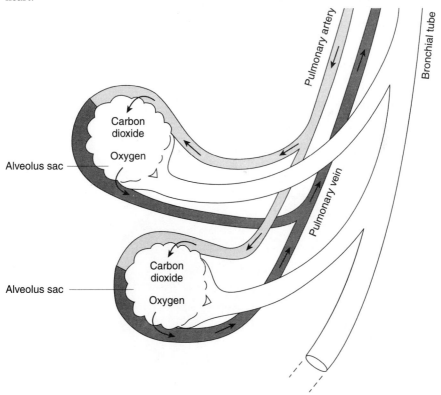

mouth and nose [see Figure 10–3(b)]. It is at the surface of the alveolar sacs that blood flowing through the capillaries comes in contact with fresh oxygenated air in the sacs. A rapid exchange now proceeds to take place between the fresh air in the sacs and the spent air in the blood. Oxygen passes through the walls of the alveoli into the blood while carbon dioxide is discharged from the blood into the air; see Figure 10–3(a). If, while this exchange is taking place, alcohol or any other volatile substance happens to be in the blood, it too will pass into the alveoli. During the act of breathing, the carbon dioxide and alcohol are expelled through the nose and mouth, and the alveoli sacs are replenished with fresh oxygenated air breathed into the lungs, thus allowing the process to begin all over again.

The distribution of alcohol between the blood and alveolar air is very much analogous to the example of a gas dissolved in an enclosed beaker of water, as described on page 136. Here again, one can use Henry's Law to explain how the alcohol will divide itself between the air and blood. Henry's Law may now be restated as follows: **When a**

Figure 10–3. (b) The respiratory system. The trachea connects the nose and mouth to the bronchial tubes. The bronchial tubes divide into numerous branches that terminate in the alveoli sacs in the lungs.

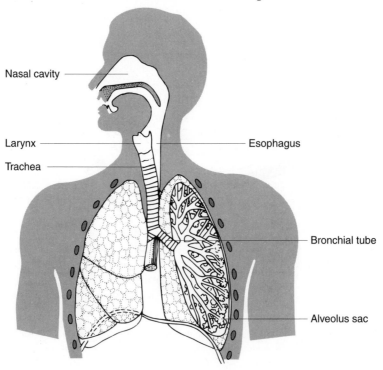

volatile chemical (alcohol) is dissolved in a liquid (blood) and is brought to equilibrium with air (alveolar breath), there is a fixed ratio between the concentration of the volatile compound (alcohol) in air (alveolar breath) and its concentration in the liquid (blood), and this ratio is constant for a given temperature.

The temperature at which the breath leaves the mouth is normally 34°C. **At this temperature, experimental evidence has shown that the ratio of alcohol in the blood to alcohol in alveoli air is approximately 2100 to 1. In other words, 1 milliliter of blood will contain nearly the same amount of alcohol as 2100 milliliters of alveolar breath. Henry's Law thus becomes a basis for relating breath to blood-alcohol concentration.**

Now let's return to the circulating blood. After emerging from the lungs, the oxygenated blood is rushed back to the upper left chamber of the heart (left atrium) by the pulmonary vein. When the left atrium contracts, it forces the blood through a valve into the left ventricle, which is the lower, left chamber of the heart. The left ventricle then pumps the freshly oxygenated blood into the arteries, which carry the blood to all parts of the body. Each of these arteries, in turn, branches into smaller arteries, which eventually connect with the numerous tiny capillaries embedded in the tissues. Here, the alcohol moves out of the blood and into the tissues. The blood then runs from the capillaries into tiny veins that fuse to form larger and larger veins. These veins eventually lead back to the heart to complete the circuit.

During the period of absorption, the concentration of alcohol in the arterial blood will be considerably higher than the concentration of alcohol in the venous blood. One typical study revealed a subject's arterial blood-alcohol level to be 41 percent higher than the venous level 30 minutes after the last drink.[2] This difference is thought to exist because of the rapid diffusion of alcohol into the body tissues from venous blood during the early phases of absorption. Because the administration of a blood test requires drawing venous blood from the arm, this test is clearly to the advantage of a subject who may still be in the absorption stage. However, once absorption is complete, the alcohol will become equally distributed throughout the blood system.

A breath test reflects the alcohol concentration in the pulmonary artery. Breath-test results obtained during the absorption phase may be higher than results obtained from a simultaneous direct analysis of venous blood. However, the former are more reflective of

---

[2]R. B. Forney et al., "Alcohol Distribution in the Vascular System: Concentrations of Orally Administered Alcohol in Blood from Various Points in the Vascular System and in Rebreathed Air During Absorption," *Quarterly Journal of Studies on Alcohol*, 25 (1964), 205.

the concentration of alcohol reaching the brain and therefore more accurately reflect the effects of alcohol on the subject. Again, once absorption is complete, the difference between a blood test and a breath test should be minimal.

BREATH-TEST INSTRUMENTS

From a practical point of view, the idea of drawing blood from a vein to test motorists suspected of being under the influence of alcohol simply does not provide a convenient method for monitoring alcoholic drivers. The need to have the suspect transported to a location where a medically qualified person can draw blood would be a costly and time-consuming operation, considering the hundreds of tests that the average police department must conduct every year. Thus, breath analysis serves a very useful purpose in providing an easily obtainable specimen along with a rapid and accurate result.

One breath-testing instrument that has become widely employed for testing individuals suspected of being under the influence of alcohol is known as the Breathalyzer. The Breathalyzer was first developed in 1954 by R. F. Borkenstein, who at that time was a captain in the Indiana State Police. Although it has since undergone several modifications, the basic theory and design of the instrument have not changed. The Breathalyzer and an accompanying schematic diagram of its parts are illustrated in Figure 10–4(a) and (b).

Figure 10–4.
(a) The Breathalyzer. *Courtesy* Smith & Wesson Electronics Co., Pittsburgh, Pa.

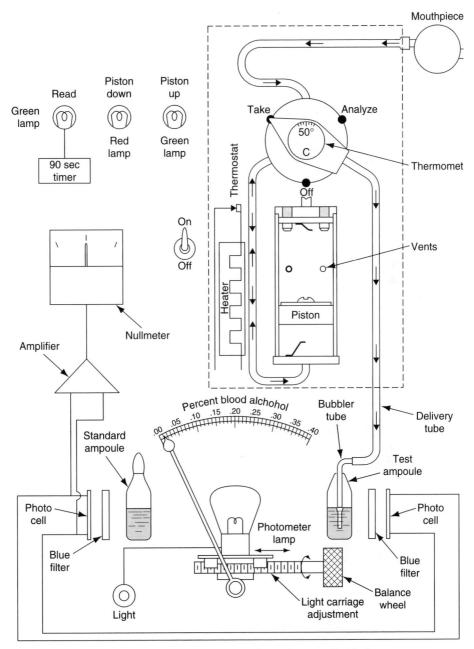

Figure 10–4. (b) Schematic diagram of a Breathalyzer. *Courtesy* Smith & Wesson Electronics Co., Pittsburgh, Pa.

Simply, the Breathalyzer is a device for collecting and measuring the alcohol content of alveolar breath. When the valve is in the TAKE position, the subject is required to blow into a mouthpiece that leads into a metal cylinder. As the subject is blowing, the pressure of the exhaled breath raises a piston to a height that exposes two vent holes near the top of a heated cylinder. When the last breath has been expired, the piston settles down to a predetermined position, covering the vent holes and trapping the last portion of air (alveolar breath) in the cylinder. The amount of breath collected in this manner is 52.5 milliliters, or 1/40 of 2100 milliliters.[3] We have already seen that the amount of alcohol contained within 2100 milliliters of alveolar breath approximates that within 1 milliliter of blood. Hence, in essence, the Breathalyzer is designed to measure alcohol concentration present in 1/40 of a milliliter of blood.

When the valve is placed in the ANALYZE position, the piston drops, causing the trapped sample of alveolar air to pass into a glass ampoule that contains 3 milliliters of 0.025 percent potassium dichromate and 0.025 percent silver nitrate in sulfuric acid and water. Any alcohol present in the breath immediately dissolves in the dichromate solution and is oxidized to acetic acid. In the oxidation process, potassium dichromate is also destroyed. It is the extent of this destruction that is measured by the Breathalyzer and is related to the quantity of alcohol passed into the ampoule.

Basically, the Breathalyzer is a spectrophotometer (see Chapter 5) that has been specially designed to measure the absorption of light passing through the potassium dichromate solution at a single wavelength. To better understand its operation, let's examine what is happening in the ampoule when alcohol is converted to acetic acid. Whenever a chemical reaction takes place between two or more substances, chemists use a chemical equation as a shorthand method to describe the changes taking place. The equation serves two purposes. It identifies the participants, and it describes the quantitative aspects of the reaction.

The following equation depicts the chemical reaction taking place in the ampoule:

$$2K_2Cr_2O_7 \quad + \quad 3C_2H_5OH \quad + \quad 8H_2SO_4 \qquad \rightarrow$$

| potassium dichromate | ethyl alcohol | sulfuric acid | yields |

---

[3]Actually, the collection cylinder is designed to hold 56.5 milliliters of breath. This is because having left the mouth at 34°C, the breath will expand when heated to 50°C in the cylinder. Furthermore, added breath is needed to compensate for the air that remains in the delivery tube leading to the test ampoule.

$$2Cr_2(SO_4)_3 \;+\; 2K_2SO_4 \;+\; 3CH_3COOH \;+\; 11\,H_2O$$

chromium   potassium   acetic   water
sulfate   sulfate   acid

From this chemical equation, we can see that there is always a fixed relationship between the number of potassium dichromate molecules reacting with the alcohol. Two molecules of potassium dichromate always combine with three molecules of ethyl alcohol. Hence, by determining the amount of potassium dichromate consumed, one has an indirect way of determining the quantity of alcohol that was originally present. Silver nitrate is also present in the Breathalyzer ampoule; however, this substance acts only as a catalyst to speed up the rate of reaction between potassium dichromate and ethyl alcohol. As a catalyst, silver nitrate undergoes no net change itself during the reaction.

Potassium dichromate is yellow in color and is known to absorb visible light in the wavelength region of 420 nanometers. In accordance with Beer's Law (see page 151, $A = kc$, the quantity of light absorbed by potassium dichromate is directly proportional to its concentration. As the reaction proceeds, the concentration and hence the light absorbance of potassium dichromate will diminish in proportion to the amount of alcohol consumed. **The Breathalyzer indirectly determines the quantity of alcohol consumed by measuring the absorption of light by potassium dichromate before and after its reaction to alcohol.**

Because the Breathalyzer determines alcohol concentration by measuring a change in light absorption, its operation entails two measurements. First, referring to the schematic diagram in Figure 10–4(b), the light source is positioned somewhere between a test ampoule and a sealed standard ampoule, both having a similar chemical composition, so that the intensity of the light passing through each is the same. At this time, there will be an equal electrical signal coming from each of the photocells located behind the ampoules, as shown by a "zero" reading on the null meter. The light source is mechanically connected to a pointer that is located above a scale calibrated to read directly in blood-alcohol percentage. The pointer is now manually set to read "zero." The filters incorporated into the design of the Breathalyzer will allow only a narrow band of wavelengths in the region of 420 nanometers to pass through the ampoules and reach the photocells.

The captured alveolar air is now bubbled into the test ampoule in the manner previously described, and the operator must wait 90 seconds for the chemical reaction to be complete. If alcohol was present in the breath, its oxidation to acetic acid will be accompanied by a corresponding decline in the potassium dichromate concentration, and this in turn will be reflected by a decrease in light absorption in the test ampoule. To compensate for this decrease, the operator must move the light source away from the test ampoule toward the standard ampoule in order to return the null meter to a "zero" reading. When the light source is moved to its new position, the pointer moves a distance that reflects the blood-alcohol percentages as read off the scale.

It is well recognized that almost the only volatile substances encountered in significant concentrations in the blood or breath of subjects operating a motor vehicle are acetone, acetaldehyde, methanol, isopropyl alcohol, and paraldehyde. Acetone, which might be present on the breath of an untreated diabetic, does not give a test result under the reaction conditions of the Breathalyzer. Isopropyl alcohol and paraldehyde have a distinct odor that can be recognized on the breath. However, it must be emphasized that all of these interfering substances are highly toxic, and their presence in the blood in concentrations sufficient to give an apparent blood-alcohol reading of 0.04 to 0.05 percent w/v would be associated with severe poisoning or death.

Recent technology has made possible the incorporation of new operational and design concepts into breath-testing instruments. Emphasis is currently being placed on automating the breath-testing procedure to minimize the chance of operator error and to use breath testers free of any chemical reagents. In particular, breath testers that operate on the principle of infrared light absorption are becoming increasingly popular within the law enforcement community.

An evidential testing instrument that incorporates the principle of infrared light absorption is shown in Figure 10–5. In principle, these instruments operate no differently from the spectrophotometers described on pp. 152–153. If alcohol is present in the subject's breath, it will be captured in the instrument's breath chamber. As shown in Figure 10–6, a beam of infrared light is aimed through the chamber. A filter is used to select a wavelength of infrared light at which alcohol

Figure 10–5.
An infrared breath-testing instrument—the Intoxilyzer 5000.
Courtesy Federal Signal Corp., Park Forest South, Ill.

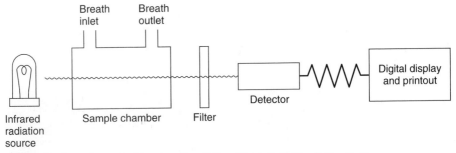

Figure 10–6.   Schematic diagram of an infrared breath-testing instrument.

will absorb. As the infrared light passes through the chamber, it will interact with the alcohol and cause the light to decrease in intensity. The decrease in light intensity is measured by a photoelectric detector that gives a signal proportional to the concentration of alcohol present in the captured breath sample. This information is processed by an electronic microprocessor, and the percent blood-alcohol concentration is displayed on a digital readout. Also, the blood-alcohol level is printed on a card to produce a permanent record of the test result. Most infrared breath testers aim a second infrared wavelength beam into the same chamber in order to check for the presence of acetone in the breath.

FIELD SOBRIETY TESTING

When a police officer suspects that an individual is under the influence of alcohol, an opportunity is usually provided to conduct a series of preliminary tests prior to ordering the suspect to submit to an evidential breath or blood test. **These preliminary or field sobriety tests are normally performed to ascertain the degree of the suspect's physical impairment and whether or not an evidential test is justified.** Field sobriety tests usually consist of a series of psychophysical tests and a preliminary breath test (if such devices are authorized and available for use). A portable, handheld, roadside breath tester is shown in Figure 10–7. This device, about the size of a pack of cigarettes, weighs 5 ounces and uses a fuel cell to measure the alcohol content of a breath sample. The fuel cell absorbs the alcohol from the breath sample, oxidizes it, and produces an electrical current proportional to the breath-alcohol content. This instrument can provide up to 3000 tests before the fuel cell needs replacement. Breath-test results obtained with devices such as those shown in Figure 10–7 must be considered preliminary and nonevidential in nature. They

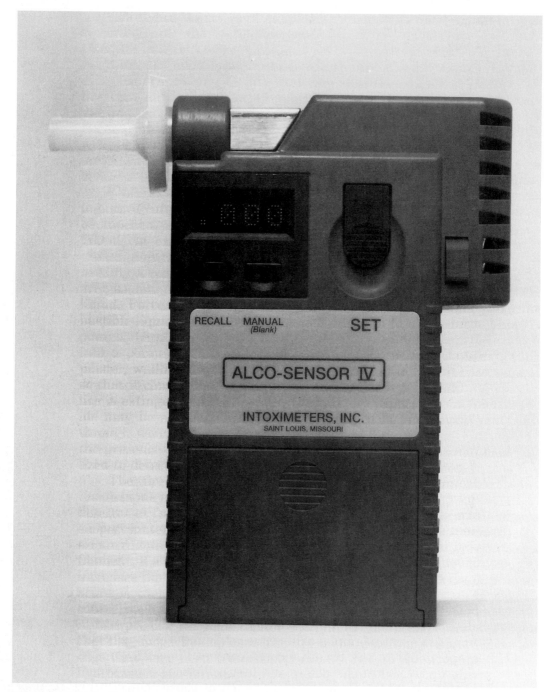

Figure 10–7.   The Alco-Sensor IV. *Courtesy* Intoximeters, Inc., St. Louis, Mo.

should serve only to establish probable cause for requiring an individual to submit to a more thorough breath or blood test.

Horizontal gaze nystagmus, walk and turn, and the one-leg stand constitute a series of reliable and effective psychophysical tests. Horizontal gaze nystagmus refers to an involuntary jerking of the eye as it moves to the side. A person experiencing nystagmus is usually unaware that the jerking is happening and is unable to stop or control it. The subject being tested is asked to follow a penlight or some other object with his or her eye as far to the side as it can go. The more intoxicated the person is, the less the eye has to move toward the side before jerking or nystagmus begins. Usually, when a person's blood-alcohol concentration is in the range of 0.10 percent, the jerking will begin before the eyeball has moved 45 degrees to the side (see Figure 10–8). Higher blood-alcohol concentration will cause jerking at smaller angles. Also, if the suspect has taken a drug that also causes nystagmus (e.g., phencyclidine, barbiturates, and other depressants), then one would expect that the nystagmus onset angle might occur much earlier than would be expected from alcohol alone.

Walk and turn and the one-leg stand are divided-attention tasks, testing the subject's ability to comprehend and execute two or more simple instructions at one time. The ability to understand and simultaneously carry out more than two instructions is significantly affected by increasing blood-alcohol levels. Walk and turn requires the suspect to maintain balance while standing heel-to-toe and at the same time listening to and comprehending the test instructions. During the walking stage, the suspect must walk a straight line, touching heel-to-toe for nine steps, then turn around on the line and repeat the process. The one-leg stand requires the suspect to maintain balance while standing with heels together listening to the instructions. During the balancing stage, the suspect must stand on one foot while holding the other foot several inches off the ground for 30 seconds; simultaneously, the suspect must count out loud during the 30-second time period.

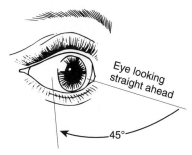

Figure 10–8.

THE ANALYSIS OF BLOOD FOR ALCOHOL

Gas chromatography offers the toxicologist the most widely used approach for determining alcohol levels in blood. When proper gas chromatographic conditions are used, alcohol can be separated from other volatiles that may be present in blood. By comparing the resultant alcohol peak area to ones obtained with known blood-alcohol standards, the investigator can calculate the alcohol level with a high degree of accuracy (see Figure 10–9).

Another procedure developed for alcohol analysis involves the oxidation of alcohol to acetaldehyde. This reaction is carried out in the presence of the enzyme alcohol dehydrogenase and a coenzyme nicotinamide-adenine dinucleotide (NAD). As the oxidation proceeds, NAD is converted into another chemical species, NADH. The extent of this conversion is measured spectrophotometrically and is related to alcohol concentration. This approach to blood-alcohol testing is normally associated with instruments used in a clinical or hospital setting. On the other hand, forensic laboratories normally utilize gas chromatography for determining blood-alcohol content.

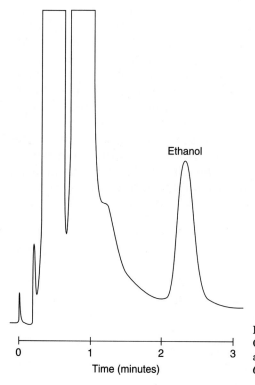

Ethanol

0   1   2   3

Time (minutes)

Figure 10–9.
Gas chromatogram showing ethyl alcohol (ethanol) in whole blood.
Courtesy Varian Instruments, Calif.

COLLECTION AND PRESERVATION OF BLOOD

Blood must always be drawn under medically accepted conditions by a qualified individual. It is important that before the suspect's skin is penetrated with a sterile needle or lancet, a nonalcoholic disinfectant be applied. This procedure will negate any argument that an alcoholic disinfectant may have inadvertently contributed to a falsely high blood-alcohol result. Nonalcoholic disinfectants such as aqueous benzalkonium chloride (Zepiran), aqueous mercuric chloride, or povidone-iodine (Betadine) are recommended for this purpose.

Once blood is removed from an individual, its preservation will be best ensured when it has been sealed in an airtight container after an anticoagulant and a preservative have been added. The blood should be stored in a refrigerator until delivery to the toxicology laboratory. The addition of an anticoagulant, such as EDTA or potassium oxalate, will prevent clotting; and a preservative, such as sodium fluoride, will inhibit the growth of microorganisms capable of destroying alcohol.

One study performed to determine the stability of alcohol in blood, removed from living individuals, found that the most significant factors affecting alcohol's stability in blood are storage temperature, the presence of a preservative, and the time of storage.[4] It is worth noting that not a single blood specimen examined showed an increase in alcohol level with time. Failure to keep the blood refrigerated or to add sodium fluoride resulted in a substantial decline in alcohol concentration. Longer storage times also reduced blood-alcohol levels. Hence, failure to adhere to all or any of the proper preservation requirements for blood will work to the benefit of the suspect and to the detriment of society.

The collection of postmortem blood samples for alcohol determination requires added precautions as compared to collection from living subjects. Ethyl alcohol may be generated in a *deceased individual* as a result of bacterial action. Therefore, it is best to collect a number of blood samples from different body sites. For example, blood may be removed from the heart and from the femoral (leg) and cubital (arm) veins. Each sample should be placed in a clean, airtight container containing an anticoagulant and sodium fluoride preservative and should be refrigerated. It is expected that blood-alcohol levels attributed solely to alcohol consumption would result in nearly similar results for all blood samples collected from the same person. Alternatively, the collection of vitreous humor and urine is recommended. It

---

[4]G. A. Brown et al., "The Stability of Ethanol in Stored Blood," *Analytica Chemica Acta,* 66 (1973), 271.

has been demonstrated that vitreous humor and urine usually do not suffer from postmortem ethyl alcohol production to any significant extent.

ALCOHOL AND THE LAW

Constitutionally, every state in the United States is charged with the responsibility of establishing and administering statutes regulating the operation of motor vehicles. Although it might be expected that such an arrangement would encourage diverse laws defining permissible blood-alcohol levels, this has not been the case. Both the American Medical Association and the National Safety Council have been able to exert considerable influence in convincing the states to establish uniform and reasonable blood-alcohol standards.

Between 1939 and 1964, 39 states and the District of Columbia enacted legislation that followed the recommendations of the American Medical Association and the National Safety Council in specifying that a person having a blood-alcohol concentration in excess of 0.15 percent w/v was to be considered under the influence of alcohol.[5] However, continued experimental studies have since shown that there is a clear correlation between drinking and driving impairment for blood-alcohol levels much below 0.15 percent w/v. As a result of these studies, in 1960 the American Medical Association and in 1965 the National Safety Council recommended lowering the presumptive level at which an individual was considered to be under the influence of alcohol to 0.10 percent w/v. All the states, as well as the District of Columbia, and most possessions of the United States have compiled with this recommendation. In fact, all states have now established *per se* laws, meaning that any individual meeting or exceeding a defined blood-alcohol level (usually 0.10 percent) shall be deemed to be intoxicated. No other proof of alcohol impairment is necessary. As shown in Figure 10–10, one is about 4 times more likely to become involved in an automobile accident at the 0.08 percent level as compared to a sober individual. At the 0.15 percent level, the chances are 25 times greater for involvement in an automobile accident as compared to a sober driver. The reader may *estimate* the relationship of blood-alcohol levels to body weight and the quantity of 80-proof liquor consumed by referring to Figure 10–11.

The trend toward lowering the impairment level continues; in 1972, the Committee on Alcohol and Drugs of the National Safety

---

[5]0.15% w/v is equivalent to 0.15 grams of alcohol per 100 milliliters of blood, or 150 milligrams per 100 milliliters.

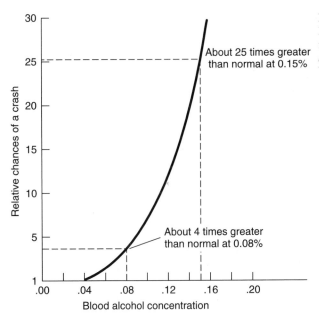

Figure 10–10.
Diagram of increased driving risk in relation to blood-alcohol concentration. *Source:* U.S. Dept. of Transportation, Washington, D.C.

About 25 times greater than normal at 0.15%

About 4 times greater than normal at 0.08%

Relative chances of a crash

Blood alcohol concentration

Council suggested that a blood concentration of 0.08 percent w/v indicates impairment in driving performance. In 1992, the U.S. Department of Transportation (DOT) recommended that states adopt 0.08 percent blood-alcohol concentration as the legal measure of drunk driving. This recommendation would apply only to noncommercial drivers. DOT has already set the maximum allowable blood-alcohol concentration for commercial truck and bus drivers at 0.04 percent.

Several Western countries have also set 0.08 percent w/v as the blood level above which it is an offense to drive a motor vehicle. Those countries include Canada, France, Italy, Switzerland, and the United Kingdom. Finland, Ireland, Japan, the Netherlands, and Norway have a 0.05 percent limit. Australian states have adopted either 0.08 percent or 0.05 percent blood-alcohol concentration levels. Sweden has lowered its blood-alcohol concentration limit to 0.02 percent.

In order to prevent a person's refusal to take a test for alcohol intoxication on the constitutional grounds of self-incrimination, the National Highway Traffic Safety Administration recommended an "implied consent" law. By 1973, all the states had complied with this recommendation. In accordance with this statute, the operation of a motor vehicle on a public highway automatically carries with it the stipulation that the driver will have the choice of either submitting to a test for alcohol intoxication if requested or be subject to loss of

How to Tell What Your Blood Alcohol Level Is After Drinking

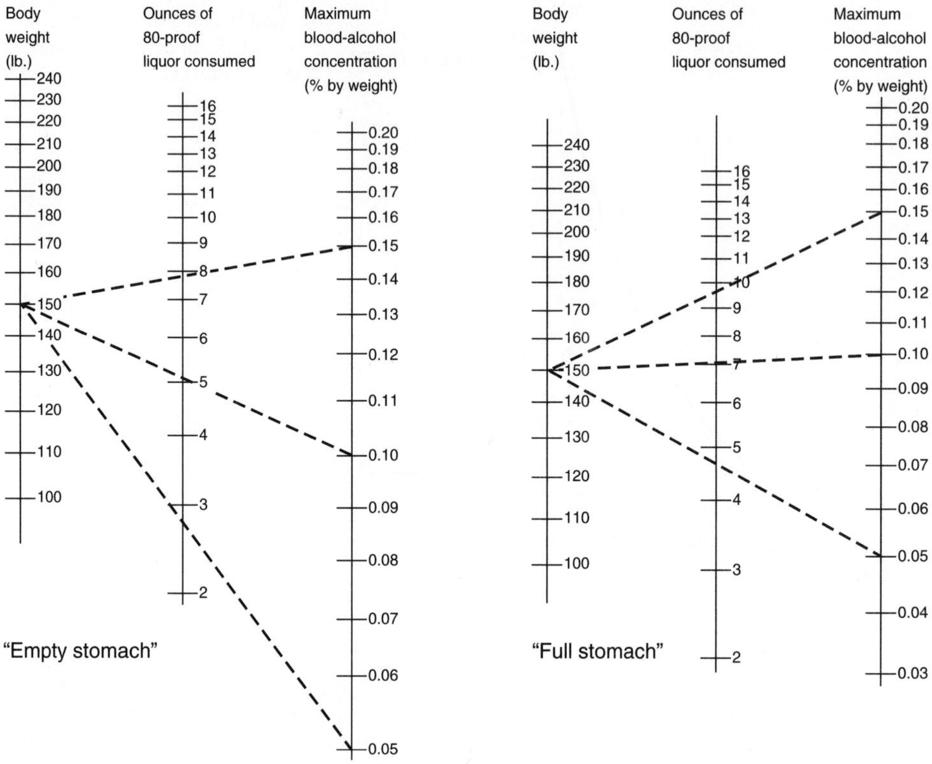

Body weight (lb.)	Ounces of 80-proof liquor consumed	Maximum blood-alcohol concentration (% by weight)	Body weight (lb.)	Ounces of 80-proof liquor consumed	Maximum blood-alcohol concentration (% by weight)

"Empty stomach"

"Full stomach"

Figure 10–11. To use this diagram, lay a straightedge across your weight and the number of ounces of liquor you've consumed on an empty or full stomach. The point where the edge hits the right-hand column is your maximum blood-alcohol level. The rate of elimination of alcohol from the bloodstream is approximately 0.015 percent per hour. Therefore, to calculate your actual blood-alcohol level, subtract 0.015 from the number indicated on the right-hand column for each hour from the start of drinking.

the license for some designated period—usually six months to one year.

The leading case relating to the constitutionality of collecting a blood specimen for alcohol testing, as well as for obtaining other types of physical evidence from a suspect without consent, is *Schmerber* v. *California*.[6] While being treated at a Los Angeles hospital for injuries sustained in an automobile collision, Schmerber was arrested on a charge of having driven under the influence of alcohol. A blood sample was subsequently obtained from Schmerber

---

[6]384 U.S. 757 (1966).

by a physician at the direction of the police, over the objection of the defendant. On appeal to the U.S. Supreme Court, the defendant argued that his privilege against self-incrimination had been violated by the introduction of the results of the blood test at his trial. The Court ruled against the defendant, reasoning that the Fifth Amendment only prohibits compelling a suspect to give "testimonial" evidence that may prove to be self-incriminating; furnishing "physical" evidence, such as fingerprints, photographs, measurements, and blood samples, the Court ruled, was protection not afforded by the Fifth Amendment.

The Court also addressed the question of whether Schmerber was subjected to an unreasonable search and seizure by the taking of a blood specimen without a search warrant. The Court upheld the blood removal, reasoning in this case that the police were confronted with an emergency situation. By the time police officials would have obtained the warrant, the blood levels would have declined significantly as a result of natural body elimination processes. In effect, the evidence would have been destroyed. The Court also emphasized that the blood specimen was taken in a medically accepted manner and without unreasonable force.

It must be emphasized that this opinion in no way condones the warrantless taking of blood for alcohol or drug testing under all circumstances. The reasonableness of actions a police officer may take to compel an individual to yield evidence can be judged only on a case-by-case basis.

THE ROLE OF THE TOXICOLOGIST

Once the forensic toxicologist ventures beyond the analysis of alcohol, he or she immediately confronts an encyclopedic maze of drugs and poisons. Only a cursory discussion of the problems and handicaps imposed on the toxicologist is enough to develop a sense of appreciation for the accomplishments and ingenuity of the scientists who occupy this branch of forensic science. The toxicologist is originally presented with body fluids and/or organs and is normally requested to examine them for the presence of drugs and poisons. If he or she is fortunate, which is not often, some clue as to the type of toxic substance present may develop from the victim's symptoms, a postmortem pathological examination, an examination of the victim's personal effects, or the nearby presence of empty drug containers or house chemicals. Without such supportive information, the toxicologist is forced into using general screening procedures with the hope of narrowing thousands of possibilities to one.

If this task in itself does not seem monumental, consider that the toxicologist is not dealing with drugs at the concentration levels found in powders and pills. By the time a drug specimen reaches the toxicology laboratory, it has been dissipated and distributed throughout the body. Where the drug analyst may have gram or milligram quantities of material to work with, the toxicologist must be satisfied with nanogram or at best microgram amounts, and these are only acquired after careful extraction from body fluids and organs.

Furthermore, the body is an active chemistry laboratory, and no one can appreciate this observation more than a toxicologist. Few substances enter and completely leave the body in the same chemical state. The drug that is injected is not always the substance extracted from the body tissues. Therefore, a thorough understanding of how the body alters or metabolizes the chemical structure of a drug is essential in ultimately detecting the presence of a drug. It would, for example, be a futile and frustrating effort on the part of any toxicologist to undertake an exhaustive search for heroin in the human body. This drug is almost immediately metabolized to morphine on entering the bloodstream. Even with this information, the search may still prove impossible unless the examiner is also aware of the fact that only a small percentage of morphine is excreted unchanged in urine. For the most part, morphine becomes chemically bonded to body carbohydrates before its elimination in urine. Thus, the successful detection of morphine requires that its extraction be planned in accordance with a knowledge of its chemical fate in the body.

Last, when and if the toxicologist has surmounted all these obstacles and has finally detected, identified, and quantitated a drug or poison, he or she must be prepared to assess the substance's toxicity. Unfortunately, there is very little published information relating to the toxic levels of most drugs. Even when such data are available, their interpretation must be predicated on the assumption that the victim's physiological behavior is in agreement with that experienced by the subjects of previous studies. In some cases, such an assumption may not be entirely valid without knowing the subject's case history. No experienced toxicologist would be terribly surprised to find an individual walking around with a toxic level of a drug that would have killed most others.

Toxicology is made infinitely easier once it is recognized that the toxicologist's capabilities are directly dependent on the input received from the attending physician, medical examiner, and police investigator. It is a tribute to forensic toxicologists, who must often labor under conditions that do not afford such cooperation, that they can achieve the high level of proficiency that they do.

Generally, with a deceased person, the medical examiner is in a position to make the necessary decisions regarding what biological specimens must be shipped to the toxicology laboratory for analysis. However, the living person suspected of being under the influence of a drug presents a completely different problem, and there are few options available. When possible, both blood and urine are to be taken from any suspected drug user. The entire urine void is to be collected and submitted for toxicological analysis. Preferably, two consecutive voids should be collected in separate specimen containers. When a licensed physician or registered nurse is available, a sample of blood should also be collected. The amount of blood taken is dependent on the type of examination to be conducted. Comprehensive toxicological tests for drugs and poisons can conveniently be carried out on a minimum of 10 cc of blood. A determination solely for the presence of alcohol will require much less—approximately 5 cc of blood. However, it must be emphasized that many therapeutic drugs, such as tranquilizers and barbiturates, when taken in combination with a small, nonintoxicating amount of alcohol, will produce behavioral patterns resembling alcohol intoxication. For this reason, it is particularly important that the toxicologist be given an adequate amount of blood so he or she will have the option of performing a comprehensive analysis for drugs in cases of low alcohol concentrations.

TECHNIQUES USED IN TOXICOLOGY

For the toxicologist, the upsurge in drug use and abuse has meant that the overwhelming majority of fatal and nonfatal toxic agents are drugs. Not surprisingly, a relatively small number of drugs—namely, those discussed in Chapter 9—comprise nearly all the toxic agents encountered. Of these, alcohol and cocaine normally account for 90 percent or more of the drugs encountered in a typical toxicology laboratory.

Like the drug analyst, the toxicologist must devise an analytical scheme that will successfully detect, isolate, and specifically identify a toxic substance. In doing so, the first chore will be to selectively remove and isolate drugs and other toxic agents from the biological materials submitted as evidence. Because drugs do constitute a large portion of the toxic materials found, a good deal of effort will necessarily have to be devoted to their extraction and detection. The procedures used are numerous, and their description is too detailed for inclusion in an introductory text such as this is intended to be. We can best understand the underlying principle of drug extraction by observing that a very large number of drugs fall into the categories of **acids** and **bases.**

Although there are a number of definitions for these two classes, a reasonably simple one states that an acid is a compound that sheds a hydrogen ion (or a hydrogen atom minus its electron) with reasonable ease. Conversely, a base is a molecule that can pick up a hydrogen ion shed by an acid. The idea of acidity and basicity can be expressed in terms of a simple numerical value that relates to the concentration of the hydrogen ion (H^+) in a liquid medium such as water. Chemists use what is called the **pH scale** to do this. This scale runs from 0 to 14:

$$pH = 0 \quad 1 \quad 2 \quad 3 \quad 4 \quad 5 \quad 6 \quad 7 \quad 8 \quad 9 \quad 10 \quad 11 \quad 12 \quad 13 \quad 14$$

$\leftarrow$ Increasing acidity — Neutral — Increasing basicity $\rightarrow$

Normally, water is neither acid nor basic—in other words, it is neutral, with a pH of 7. However, when an acidic substance—for example, sulfuric acid or hydrochloric acid—is added to the water, it adds excess hydrogen ions, and the pH value becomes less than 7. The lower the number, the more acidic the water. Similarly, when a basic substance—for example, sodium hydroxide or ammonium hydroxide—is added to water, it removes hydrogen ions, thus making water basic. The more basic the water, the higher its pH value.

By controlling the pH of a water solution into which blood, urine, or tissues are dissolved, the toxicologist can conveniently control the type of drug that will be recovered. For example, acid drugs are easily extracted from an acidified water solution (pH less than 7) with organic solvents such as chloroform. Similarly, basic drugs are readily removed from a basic water solution (pH greater than 7) with organic solvents. This relatively simple approach gives the toxicologist a general technique for extracting and categorizing drugs. Some of the more commonly encountered drugs may be classified as follows:

Acid Drugs	*Basic Drugs*
Barbiturates	Phencyclidine
Acetylsalicylic acid (aspirin)	Methadone
	Amphetamines
	Cocaine

Once the specimen has been extracted and divided into acidic and basic fractions, the toxicologist can proceed to identify the drugs present. The strategy used for identifying abused drugs entails a two-step approach: **screening** and **confirmation** (see Figure 10–12). A screening test is normally employed to provide the analyst with quick

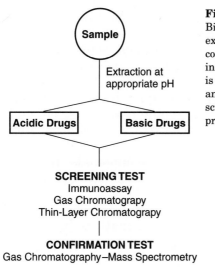

Figure 10–12.
Biological fluids and tissues are extracted for acidic and basic drugs by controlling the pH of a water solution in which they are dissolved. Once this is accomplished, the toxicologist will analyze for drugs by utilizing screening and confirmation test procedures.

insight into the likelihood that a specimen contains a drug substance. This test is designed to allow a toxicologist to examine a large number of specimens within a short period of time for a wide range of drugs. Any positive results arising from a screening test are considered to be tentative at best and must be verified with a confirmation test.

The three most widely used screening tests are thin-layer chromatography (TLC), gas chromatography (GC), and immunoassay. The techniques of GC and TLC have already been described on pp. 137–140 and 142–146, respectively. Immunoassay has proven to be a useful screening tool in toxicology laboratories. Its principles are very different from any of the analytical techniques we have discussed so far. Suffice it to say at this point that immunoassay is based on specific drug antibody reactions. We will learn about this concept in Chapter 12. The primary advantage of immunoassay is its ability to detect small concentrations of drugs in body fluids and organs. In fact, this technique provides the best approach for detecting the low drug levels normally associated with the smoking of marijuana.

The necessity of eliminating the possibility that a positive screening test may in fact be due to a substance's having a close chemical structure to an abused drug requires the toxicologist to follow up a positive screening test with a confirmation test. Because of the potential impact of the results of a drug finding on an individual, only the most conclusive confirmation procedures should be used. **Gas chromatography/mass spectrometry is generally accepted as**

the confirmation test of choice. The combination of gas chromatography and mass spectrometry provide the toxicologist with a one-step confirmation test of unequaled sensitivity and specificity (see pp. 155–159). As shown in Figure 10–13, the sample is separated into its components by the gas chromatograph. When the separated sample component leaves the column of the gas chromatograph, it enters the mass spectrometer, where it is bombarded with high-energy electrons. This bombardment causes the sample to break up into fragments, producing a fragmentation pattern or mass spectrum for each sample. For most compounds, the mass spectrum represents a unique "fingerprint" pattern that can be used for identification.

Currently, there is a tremendous interest in drug-testing programs conducted not only in criminal matters but for industry and government as well. Urine testing for drugs is becoming common for job applicants and employees in the workplace. Likewise, the U.S. military has an extensive drug urine-testing program for its members. Many of the urine-testing programs currently in existence rely on the services of private laboratories to perform the required analyses. In any case, when the consequences of such an analysis form the basis for actions to be taken against an individual, it is essential that both a screening and confirmation test be incorporated into the testing protocol to ensure the integrity of the laboratory's conclusions.

These days, the forensic toxicologist only occasionally encounters a group of poisons known as "heavy metals." These include arsenic, bismuth, antimony, mercury, and thallium. To screen for many of these metals, the investigator may dissolve the suspect body fluid or tissue in a hydrochloric acid solution and insert a copper strip into the solution (the Reinsch test). The appearance of a silvery or dark coating on the copper is indicative of the presence of a heavy metal. Such a

Figure 10–13. The combination of the gas chromatograph and the mass spectrometer enables forensic toxicologists to separate the components of a drug mixture and provides for the specific identification of a drug substance.

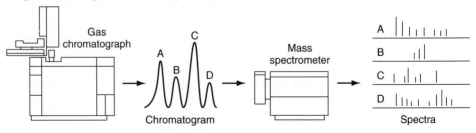

finding must be confirmed by the use of analytical techniques suitable for inorganic analysis—namely, atomic absorption spectrophotometry, emission spectroscopy, or X-ray diffraction.

Carbon monoxide still represents one of the most common poisons encountered in a forensic laboratory. When carbon monoxide enters the human body, it is primarily absorbed by the red blood cells, where it combines with hemoglobin to form carboxyhemoglobin. An average red blood cell contains about 280 million molecules of hemoglobin. It is with hemoglobin that oxygen normally combines, allowing the blood to transport the oxygen throughout the body. However, if a high percentage of the hemoglobin combines with carbon monoxide, not enough is left to carry sufficient oxygen to the tissues, and death by asphyxiation follows shortly.

There are two basic methods for measuring the concentration of carbon monoxide in the blood. Spectrophotometric methods can examine the visible spectrum of blood to determine the relative amount of carboxyhemoglobin to oxyhemoglobin or total hemoglobin; or a volume of blood can be treated with a reagent to liberate the carbon monoxide, which is then measured by gas chromatography.

The amount of carbon monoxide in blood is generally expressed as "percent saturation." This actually represents the extent to which the available hemoglobin has been converted to carboxyhemoglobin. The transition from normal or occupational levels of carbon monoxide to toxic levels is not sharply defined. It depends, among other things, on the age, health, and general fitness of each individual. In a healthy middle-aged individual, a carbon monoxide blood saturation greater than 50 to 60 percent is considered fatal. However, in combination with alcohol or other depressants, fatal levels may be significantly lower. For instance, a carbon monoxide saturation of 35 to 40 percent may prove fatal in the presence of a blood-alcohol concentration of 0.20 percent w/v. Interestingly, chain smokers may have a carbon monoxide level of 8 to 10 percent from the carbon monoxide in cigarette smoke.

Inhalation of automobile fumes is a relatively common way to commit suicide. A garden or vacuum cleaner hose is often used to connect the tailpipe with the vehicle's interior, or the engine is allowed to run in a closed garage. A level of carbon monoxide sufficient to cause death accumulates in 5 to 10 minutes in a closed single-car garage.

The level of carbon monoxide in the blood of a victim found dead at the scene of a fire is of significance in ascertaining whether or not foul play has occurred. The presence of high levels of carbon monoxide in the blood is proof that the victim breathed the combustion products of the fire and was therefore alive when the fire began. Many attempts at covering up a murder by setting fire to a victim's house or car have been uncovered in this manner.

THE SIGNIFICANCE OF TOXICOLOGICAL FINDINGS

Once a drug is found and identified, the toxicologist is called upon to assess its influence on the behavior of the individual under examination. The task of interpreting the results of a toxicology find is one of the more difficult chores facing the toxicologist. We have already seen that many of the world's countries have created laws designating a specific blood-alcohol level at which an individual is presumed to be under the influence of alcohol. These levels were established as a result of numerous studies carried out over a period of years to measure the effects of alcohol levels on driving performance. However, no such legal guidelines are available to the toxicologist who must offer an opinion as to how a drug other than alcohol affects an individual's performance or physical state.

For many drugs, blood concentration levels can readily be determined and can be used to *estimate* the pharmacological effects of the drug on the individual. For a deceased person, drug levels present in various body organs and tissues can be ascertained to provide additional information about the individual's state at the time of death. However, before conclusions can be drawn about drug-induced behavior, other factors must also be taken into consideration. These include the age, physical condition, and tolerance of the drug user. With the prolonged use of a drug, an individual may become less responsive to a drug's effects and may be able to tolerate blood-drug concentrations that would normally be fatal to the casual drug user. Therefore, knowledge of an individual's history of drug use is very important in evaluating drug concentrations found by the toxicologist. Another consideration may be additive or synergistic effects provided by the interaction of two or more drugs. The combination of two or more drugs may produce a highly intoxicated or comatose state, even though none of the drugs alone is present at high or toxic levels. The combination of alcohol with barbiturates or narcotics is a common example of a potentially lethal drug combination.

The concentration of a drug present in urine is a poor indicator of how extensively an individual's behavior or state is influenced by the drug. Urine is formed outside the body's circulatory system, and consequently drug levels can build up in it over a relatively long period of time. In fact, some drugs are found in the urine one to three days after they have been taken and long after their effects on the user have disappeared. Nevertheless, the value of this information should not be discounted. Urine drug levels, like blood levels, are best used by law enforcement authorities and the courts to corroborate other investigative and medical findings pertaining to an individual's condition. Hence, for the individual who is arrested for suspicion of being under the influence of a drug, a toxicologist's determinations will supplement the observations of the arresting officer, including the results of balance and coordination tests performed on the suspect at the time of apprehension. For a deceased person, the ultimate responsibility for establishing a cause of death rests with the medical examiner or coroner. However, before a conclusive determination is made, the examining physician is dependent on the skills of the forensic toxicologist to demonstrate the presence or absence of a drug or poison in the tissues or body fluids of the deceased. It is only through the combined efforts of the toxicologist and the medical examiner (or coroner) that society can be assured that death investigations will achieve high professional and legal standards.

THE DRUG RECOGNITION EXPERT

While the recognition of alcohol-impaired performance is an expertise generally accorded to police officers by the courts, the problem of recognizing drug-induced intoxication is much more difficult and generally lies outside the area of expertise normally accorded to police officers. During the 1970s, the Los Angeles Police Department developed and tested a series of clinical and psychophysical examinations that a trained police officer could use to identify and differentiate between types of drug impairment. This program has evolved into a national program to train police as "drug recognition experts." Normally, a three- to five-month training program is required to certify an officer as a drug recognition expert (DRE).

The DRE program incorporates standardized methods for examining suspects to determine whether they have taken one or more drugs. The process followed by the DRE is systematic and standard; and to ensure that each subject has been tested in a routine fashion, each DRE must complete a standard Drug Influence Evaluation form (see Figure 10–14). The entire drug evaluation requires approximately 30 to 40 minutes to perform. The components of the twelve-step process are summarized in Table 10–1.

The DRE evaluation process can suggest the presence of the following seven broad categories of drugs:

DRUG INFLUENCE EVALUATION

PAGE _____ OF _____
DR NUMBER:
EVALUATOR:
CONTROL #:
BOOKING #:

ARRESTEE'S NAME (Last, First, MI) | AGE | SEX | RACE | ARRESTING OFFICER (Name, Badge, District)

DATE EXAMINED/TIME/LOCATION | BREATH RESULTS: □ Refused | CHEMICAL TEST □ Both Tests
RESULTS | Instrument | □ Urine □ Blood Refused

MIRANDA WARNING GIVEN: □ Yes □ No
Given by:

What have you eaten today? | When? | What have you been drinking? How much? | Time of last drink?

Time now? | When did you last sleep? How long? | Are you sick or injured? □ Yes □ No | Are you diabetic or epileptic? □ Yes □ No

Do you take insulin? □ Yes □ No | Do you have any physical defects? □ Yes □ No | Are you under the care of a doctor/dentist? □ Yes □ No

Are you taking any medication or drugs? □ Yes □ No | ATTITUDE | COORDINATION

SPEECH | BREATH | FACE

CORRECTIVE LENS: □ None □ Glasses □ Contacts, if so □ Hard □ Soft | Eyes: □ Normal □ Bloodshot □ Watery | Blindness: □ None □ R. Eye □ L. Eye | Tracking: □ Equal □ Unequal

PUPIL SIZE: □ Equal □ Unequal (explain) | HGN Present: □ Yes □ No | Able to follow stimulus: □ Yes □ No | Eyelids: □ Normal □ Droopy

PULSE & TIME | HGN | Right Eye | Left Eye | Vertical Nystagmus? □ Yes □ No | ONE LEG STAND:
1. ___/___ | Lack of Smooth Pursuit | | | Convergence Right Eye Left Eye
2. ___/___ | Max. Deviation
3. ___/___ | Angle of Onset

BALANCE EYES CLOSED | WALK AND TURN TEST | Cannot keep balance ___
Starts too soon ___ 1st Nine 2nd Nine
Stops Walking
Misses Heel-Toe | L R □ □ Sways while balancing
Steps off Line | □ □ Uses arms to balance
Raises Arms | □ □ Hopping
Actual Steps Taken | □ □ Puts foot down

INTERNAL CLOCK: ___ Estimated as 30 sec. | Describe Turn | Cannot do Test (explain) | Type of Footwear

○ Right △ Left | PUPIL SIZE | Room Light | Darkness | Indirect | Direct | NASAL AREA
Draw lines to spots touched | Left Eye
| Right Eye | | | | | ORAL CAVITY
| HIPPUS □ Yes □ No | REBOUND DILATION □ Yes □ No | Reaction to Light

② ④ ⑤ ① ③ ⑥ | RIGHT ARM | LEFT ARM

BLOOD PRESSURE: ___/___ | TEMP °
MUSCLE TONE: □ Near Normal □ Flacid □ Rigid
Comments: | ATTACH PHOTOS OF FRESH PUNCTURE MARKS

What medicine or drug have you been using? | How much? | Time of use? | Where were the drugs used? (Location)

DATE/TIME OF ARREST | TIME DRE NOTIFIED | EVAL START TIME | TIME COMPLETED

OFFICER'S SIGNATURE | DISTRICT | ID NUMBER | REVIEWED BY

Figure 10–14.   Drug Influence Evaluation Form.

TABLE 10–1.

**COMPONENTS OF THE DRUG
RECOGNITION PROCESS**

1. *The Breath Alcohol Test.* By obtaining an accurate and immediate measurement of the suspect's blood-alcohol concentration, the drug recognition expert (DRE) can determine whether alcohol may be contributing to the suspect's observable impairment and whether the concentration of alcohol is sufficient to be the sole cause of that impairment.

2. *Interview with the Arresting Officer.* Spending a few minutes with the arresting officer often enables the DRE to determine the most promising areas of investigation.

3. *The Preliminary Examination.* This is a structured series of questions, specific observations, and simple tests that provide the first opportunity to examine the suspect closely. It is designed to determine if the suspect is suffering from an injury or from another condition unrelated to drug consumption. It also affords an opportunity to begin assessing the suspect's appearance and behavior for signs of possible drug influence.

4. *The Eye Examination.* Certain categories of drugs induce nystagmus, an involuntary, spasmodic motion of the eyeball. Nystagmus is an indicator of drug-induced impairment. The inability of the eyes to converge toward the bridge of the nose also indicates the possible presence of certain types of drugs.

5. *Divided Attention Psychophysical Tests.* These tests check balance and physical orientation and include the Walk and Turn, One-Leg Stand, the Romberg Balance, and the Finger-to-Nose.

6. *The Vital Signs Examinations.* Precise measurements of blood pressure, pulse rate, and body temperature are taken. Certain drugs will elevate these signs; others will depress them.

7. *Dark Room Examinations.* The size of the suspect's pupils in room light, near-total darkness, indirect light, and direct light is checked. Some drugs cause the pupils to either dilate or constrict.

8. *Examination for Muscle Rigidity.* Certain categories of drugs cause the muscles to become hypertense and quite rigid. Others may cause the muscles to relax and become flaccid.

9. *Examination for Injection Sites.* Users of certain categories of drugs routinely or occasionally inject their drugs. Evidence of needle use may be found on veins along the neck, arms, and hands.

10. *Suspect's Statements and Other Observations.* The next step is to attempt to interview the suspect concerning the drug or drugs he or she has ingested. Of course, the interview must be conducted in full compliance of the suspect's constitutional rights.

11. *Opinions of the Evaluator.* Using the information obtained in the previous 10 steps, the DRE is able to make an informed decision about whether or not the suspect is impaired by drugs and, if so, what category or combination of categories is the probable cause of the impairment.

12. *The Toxicological Examination.* The DRE should obtain a blood or urine sample from the suspect for laboratory analysis in order to secure scientific, admissible evidence to substantiate his or her conclusions.

1. Central nervous system depressants
2. Central nervous system stimulants
3. Hallucinogens
4. Phencyclidine
5. Inhalants
6. Narcotic analgesics
7. Cannabis

It must be recognized that the DRE program is not designed to be a substitute for toxicological testing. The toxicologist can often determine that a suspect has a particular drug in his or her body. But the toxicologist often cannot infer with reasonable certainty that the suspect was impaired at a specific time. On the other hand, the DRE can supply credible evidence that the suspect was impaired at a specific time and that the nature of the impairment was consistent with a particular family of drugs. But the DRE program usually cannot determine which specific drug was ingested. In reality, what is required to prove drug intoxication is a coordinated effort and the production of competent data from both the DRE and the forensic toxicologist.

REVIEW QUESTIONS

1. The most heavily abused drug in the Western world is
   _____.
2. Toxicologists are employed only by crime laboratories. (True, False)
3. The amount of alcohol present in the blood (is, is not) directly proportional to the concentration of alcohol in the brain.
4. Blood levels have become the accepted standard for relating alcohol intake to its effect on the body. (True, False)
5. Alcohol consumed on an empty stomach is absorbed (faster, slower) than an equivalent amount of alcohol taken when there is food in the stomach.
6. Under normal drinking conditions, alcohol concentration in the blood peaks in _____ to _____ minutes.
7. In the postabsorption period, alcohol is distributed uniformly among the _____ portions of the body.
8. Elimination of alcohol from the body is accomplished by _____ and _____.

9. Ninety-five to 98 percent of the alcohol is _____ to carbon dioxide and water.

10. The oxidation of alcohol takes place almost entirely in the _____.

11. The amount of alcohol exhaled in the _____ is directly proportional to the concentration of the alcohol in the blood.

12. Alcohol is eliminated from the blood at an average rate of _____ percent w/v.

13. Alcohol is absorbed into the blood from the _____ and _____.

14. An _____ carries blood away from the heart; a _____ carries blood back to the heart.

15. The _____ artery carries deoxygenated blood from the heart to the lungs.

16. Alcohol passes from the blood capillaries into the _____ sacs located in the lungs.

17. One milliliter of blood will contain the same amount of alcohol as approximately _____ milliliters of alveolar breath.

18. During the period when alcohol is being absorbed into the blood, the alcohol concentration in venous blood will be (higher, lower) than that in arterial blood.

19. In a Breathalyzer ampoule, the ethyl alcohol reacts with _____ in a fixed ratio.

20. The Breathalyzer measures the (absorption, emission) of light by potassium dichromate before and after its reaction with alcohol.

21. Silver nitrate is present in a Breathalyzer ampoule as a _____ to speed up the rate of reaction.

22. Alcohol can be separated from other volatiles present in blood and can be quantitated by the technique of _____.

23. Breath testers that operate on the principle of _____ light absorption of alcohol are becoming increasingly popular with the law enforcement community.

24. Portable, handheld, roadside breath testers for alcohol provide evidential test results. (True, False)

25. Usually, when a person's blood-alcohol concentration is in the range of 0.10 percent, horizontal gaze nystagmus will begin before the eyeball has moved _____ degrees to the side.

26. When drawing blood for alcohol testing, the suspect's skin must first be wiped with a _____ disinfectant.

27. Failure to add a preservative, such as sodium fluoride, to blood removed from a living person may lead to a(n) (decline, increase) in alcohol concentration.

28. Most states have established _____ percent w/v as the impairment limit for blood-alcohol concentration.

29. In the case of _____, the Supreme Court ruled that the taking of nontestimonial evidence, such as a blood sample, was not in violation of a suspect's Fifth Amendment privileges.

30. Heroin is changed upon entering the body into _____.

31. The body fluids _____ and _____ are both desirable for the toxicological examination of a living person suspected of being under the influence of a drug.

32. A large number of drugs can be classified chemically as _____ and _____.

33. Water having a pH value (less, greater) than 7 is basic.

34. Barbiturates are classified as _____ drugs.

35. Drugs are extracted from body fluids and tissues by carefully controlling the _____ of the medium in which the sample has been dissolved.

36. The technique of _____ is based on specific drug antibody reactions.

37. It is essential that both _____ and _____ tests be incorporated into the drug-testing protocol of a toxicology laboratory to ensure the correctness of the laboratory's conclusions.

38. The gas _____ will combine with hemoglobin in the blood to form carboxyhemoglobin, thus interfering with the transportation of oxygen in the blood.

39. The amount of carbon monoxide present in blood is usually expressed as _____.

40. Blood levels of drugs can alone be used to draw definitive conclusions about the effects of a drug on an individual. (True, False)

41. The interaction of alcohol and barbiturates in the body can produce a _____ effect.

42. The level of a drug present in the urine is by itself a (good, poor) indicator of how extensively an individual is affected by a drug.

43. Urine and blood drug levels are best used by law enforcement authorities and the courts to _____ other investigative and medical findings pertaining to an individual's condition.

44. The _____ program incorporates standardized methods for examining suspects to determine if they have taken one or more drugs.

FURTHER REFERENCES

Benjamin, David M., "Forensic Pharmacology," in *Forensic Science Handbook,* Vol. 3, R. Saferstein, ed. Englewood Cliffs, N.J.: Prentice Hall, 1993.

Caplan, Y. H., "The Determination of Alcohol in Blood and Breath," in *Forensic Science Handbook,* R. Saferstein, ed. Englewood Cliffs, N.J.: Prentice Hall, 1982.

Garriott, James C., ed., Medicolegal Aspects of Alcohol, 3rd ed. Tucson, AZ: Lawyers & Judges Publishing Company, 1996.

Hawks, R. L., and C. N. Chiang, eds., *Urine Testing for Drugs of Abuse.* Washington, D.C.: U.S. Government Printing Office, 1986.

Jones, A. W., "Enforcement of Drink-Driving Laws by Use of 'Per Se' Legal Alcohol Limits: Blood and/or Breath Concentration as Evidence of Impairment," *Alcohol, Drugs and Driving,* 4 (1988), 99.

Karch, Steven B., *The Pathology of Drug Abuse,* 2nd ed. Boca Raton, Fla.: CRC Press, 1996.

Moffat, A. E., et al., eds., *Clarke's Isolation and Identification of Drugs,* 2nd ed. London: Pharmaceutical Press, 1986.

Proceedings of the International Symposium on Driving under the Influence of Alcohol and/or Drugs. Washington, D.C.: U.S. Government Printing Office, 1987.

FORENSIC ASPECTS OF ARSON AND EXPLOSION INVESTIGATIONS

Arson and explosions often present the criminal investigator with complex and difficult circumstances to investigate. Normally, these incidents are committed at the convenience of a perpetrator who has thoroughly planned the criminal act and has left the crime scene long before any official investigation is launched. Furthermore, proof of the commission of the offense is rendered more difficult to obtain because of the extensive destruction that frequently dominates the crime scene. The contribution of the criminalist is only one aspect of a comprehensive and difficult investigative process that must establish a motive, the *modus operandi,* and a suspect.

In practice, the criminalist's function is a rather limited one; usually he or she is expected only to detect and identify relevant chemical materials collected at the scene and to reconstruct and identify ignitors or detonating mechanisms. Although a chemist can identify trace amounts of gasoline or kerosene in debris, there is no scientific test that will determine whether or not an arsonist has used a pile of rubbish or paper to start a fire. Furthermore, a fire can have many accidental causes, including faulty wiring, overheated electric motors, improperly cleaned and regulated heating systems, and cigarette smoking—and these usually leave no chemical traces. Thus, the final determination as to the cause of a fire or explosion must take numerous factors into consideration and requires an extensive on-site investigation. The ultimate determination must be made by an investigator whose training and knowledge have been augmented by the practical experiences of fire and explosion investigation.

THE CHEMISTRY OF FIRE

Humankind's early search to explain the physical concepts underlying the behavior of matter always bestowed a central and fundamental role on fire. To ancient Greek philosophers, fire was one of the four basic elements from which all matter was derived. The alchemist thought of fire as an instrument of transformation, to be used for changing one element into another. One ancient recipe expresses its mystical power as follows:

> Now the substance of cinnabar is such that the more it is heated, the more exquisite are its sublimations. Cinnabar will become mercury, and passing through a series of other sublimations, it is again turned into cinnabar, and thus it enables man to enjoy eternal life.

Today, we know of fire not as an element of matter but as a transformation process during which oxygen is united with some other substance to produce noticeable quantities of heat and light (a flame). Therefore, any insight into why and how a fire is initiated and sustained must begin with the knowledge of the fundamental chemical reaction of fire—**oxidation.**

A simple description of oxidation is one that has oxygen combining with other substances to produce new products. Thus, we may write the chemical equation for the burning of methane gas, a major component of natural gas, as follows:

$$CH_4 \quad + \quad 2O_2 \quad \longrightarrow \quad CO_2 \quad + \quad 2H_2O$$

$$\text{methane} \qquad \text{oxygen} \quad \text{yields} \quad \text{carbon} \qquad \text{water}$$
$$\text{dioxide}$$

However, not all oxidation proceeds in the manner that one associates with fire. For example, oxygen combines with many metals to form oxides. Thus, iron forms a red-brown iron oxide, the familiar rust, as follows:

$$4Fe \quad + \quad 3O_2 \quad \longrightarrow \quad 2Fe_2O_3$$

$$\text{iron} \qquad \text{oxygen} \quad \text{yields} \quad \text{iron oxide}$$

Yet chemical equations do not give us a complete insight into the oxidation process. Other factors must be taken into consideration if we are to understand all the implications of oxidation or, for that matter, any other chemical reaction. We know that when methane unites with oxygen, it burns; but the mere mixing of methane and oxygen will not produce a fire, nor, for example, will gasoline burn when it is simply exposed to air. However, light a match in the presence of any one of these fuel-air mixtures (assuming proper proportions) and you have an instant fire. What are the reasons behind these differences? Why do some oxidations proceed with the outward appearances that we associate with a fire while others do not? Why do we need a match to initiate some oxidations while others proceed at room temperature? The explanation lies in a fundamental but abstract concept—**energy.**

Energy can be defined as the capacity for doing work. Energy takes many forms, such as heat energy, electrical energy, mechanical energy, nuclear energy, light energy, and chemical energy. For example, when methane is burned, the stored chemical energy in methane is converted to energy in the form of heat and light. This heat may be used to boil water or to provide high-pressure steam to turn a turbine. This is an example of converting chemical energy to heat energy to mechanical energy. The turbine can then be used to generate electricity, involving a transformation from mechanical to electrical energy. Electrical energy may then be used to turn a motor. In other words, energy can enable work to be done; heat is energy.

The quantity of heat from a chemical reaction comes from the breaking and formation of chemical bonds. Methane is a molecule composed of one carbon atom bonded with four hydrogen atoms:

$$\begin{array}{c} H \\ | \\ H- C -H \\ | \\ H \end{array}$$

An oxygen molecule forms when two atoms of the element oxygen bond:

$$O = O$$

In chemical changes, atoms are not lost but are merely redistributed during the chemical reaction; thus, the products of methane's oxidation will be carbon dioxide:

$$O = C = O$$

and water:

$$H - O - H$$

This rearrangement, however, means that the bonds holding the atoms together must be broken and new bonds formed. We now have arrived at a fundamental observation in our dissection of a chemical reaction—that molecules must absorb energy to break apart their chemical bonds, and that they will liberate energy when their bonds are reformed. The amount of energy needed to break a bond and the quantity of energy liberated when a bond is formed are characteristic of the type of chemical bond involved. Hence, a chemical reaction involves a change in energy content; energy is going in and energy is given off. The quantities of energies involved are different for each reaction and are determined by the participants of the chemical reaction.

All oxidation reactions, including the combustion of methane, are examples of reactions in which more energy is liberated than what is required to break the various bonds. This excess energy is liberated as heat and often as light and is known as the **heat of combustion.** Such reactions are said to be **exothermic.** Table 11–1 summarizes the heats of combustion of a few of the more important fuels from the standpoint of fire investigation.

Although we will not be concerned with them, there are reactions that require more energy than what they will eventually liberate. These reactions are known as **endothermic** reactions.

TABLE 11–1.
HEATS OF COMBUSTION OF FUELS

Fuel	Heat of Combustion[a]
Crude oil	19,650 BTU/gal
Diesel fuel	19,550 BTU/lb
Gasoline	19,250 BTU/lb
Methane	995 BTU/cu ft
Natural gas	128–1868 BTU/cu ft
Octane	121,300 BTU/gal
Wood	7500 BTU/lb
Coal—bituminous	11,000–14,000 BTU/lb
Anthracite	13,351 BTU/lb

[a]*BTU (British thermal unit) is defined as the quantity of heat required to raise the temperature of 1 pound of water 1°F at or near its point of maximum density.*

Source: John D. DeHaan, *Kirk's Fire Investigation,* 2nd ed. (Englewood Cliffs, N.J.: Prentice Hall, 1983).

It is apparent from these considerations that all reactions require an energy input to start them. We can perhaps think of this requirement as an invisible energy barrier that has been erected between the reactants and the products of a reaction (see Figure 11–1). The higher this barrier, the more energy will be required to initiate the reaction. Where does this initial energy come from? There are many sources of energy; however, for the purpose of this discussion it will be necessary to look at only one—heat.

The energy barrier that exists in the conversion of iron to rust is a relatively small one, and it can be surmounted with the help of heat energy present in the surrounding environment at normal outdoor temperatures. Not so for methane or gasoline; here, the energy barriers are quite high, and a high temperature must be applied to start the oxidation of these fuels. Hence, before any fire can result, the temperature of these fuels must be raised to a value that will allow the heat energy input to exceed the energy barrier. Table 11–2 shows that this temperature, known as the **ignition temperature,** is quite high for common fuels. Once the combustion starts, a sufficient amount of heat is liberated to keep the reaction going by itself. In essence, the fire becomes a chain reaction, absorbing a portion of its own liberated heat in order to generate even more heat. The fire will continue to burn until either the supply of oxygen or the fuel is exhausted.

Normally, an ordinary lighted match provides a convenient ignitor of fuels. However, the fire investigator must also consider other potential sources of ignition—for example, electrical discharges, sparks, and chemicals—while reconstructing the initiation of a fire. All of these sources have temperatures in excess of what is needed to meet the ignition temperature requirement of most fuels.

Although the liberation of energy explains many important features of oxidation, it does not offer a complete explanation for all the characteristics of the reaction. Obviously, although all oxidations liberate energy, they are not all accompanied by the presence of a flame; witness the oxidation of iron to rust. There is, therefore, one other important consideration that must be taken into account before our

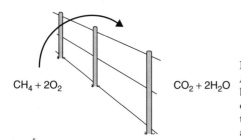

Figure 11–1.
An energy barrier must be hurdled before reactants such as methane and oxygen can combine with one another to form the products of carbon dioxide and water.

TABLE 11–2.

**IGNITION TEMPERATURES OF SOME
COMMON FUELS**

Fuel	Ignition Temperature °F
Acetone	1000
Benzene	1045
Fuel oil #2	495
Gasoline	495
Kerosene (fuel oil #1)	445
n-Octaine	428
Petroleum ether	550
Turpentine	488

Source: John D. DeHaan, *Kirk's Fire Investigation,* 3rd ed. (Englewood
Cliffs, N.J.: Prentice Hall, 1991).

understanding of oxidation and fire is complete. **This additional factor is the rate or speed at which the reaction takes place.**

Simply, we can picture a chemical reaction, such as oxidation, taking place when molecules combine or collide with one another. Essentially, the faster the molecules move, the greater the number of collisions taking place between them and the faster the rate of reaction. There are many factors that influence the rate at which these collisions take place. In our description of fire and oxidation, we need be concerned with only two: the physical state of the fuel and temperature.

A fuel will achieve a reaction rate with oxygen sufficient to produce a flame only when it is in the gaseous state, for it is only in this state that molecules can collide frequently enough to support a flaming fire. This remains true even though the fuel that may be feeding the flame is a solid such as wood, paper, cloth, or plastic, or a liquid such as gasoline or kerosene. How then does a liquid or solid maintain a gaseous reaction? In the case of a liquid fuel, the temperature must be high enough to vaporize the fuel. The vapor that forms burns when it mixes with oxygen and combusts as a flame. The **flash point** is the *lowest* temperature at which a liquid gives off sufficient vapor to form a mixture with air that will support combustion. Once the flash point is reached, the fuel can be ignited by some outside source of temperature to start a fire. The ignition temperature is always considerably higher than the flash point. For example, gasoline has a flash point of –50°F; however, it takes an ignition temperature of 495°F to start a gasoline fire. With a solid fuel, the process of generating vapor is more complex. Wood, or any other solid fuel, will burn only when it is exposed to heat that is hot enough to decompose the solid into gaseous products. This chemical breakdown of solid material is known as **pyrolysis.** It is the numerous gaseous products of pyrolysis that combine with oxygen to produce a fire. Here again, fire can be described as a chain reaction. A match or other source of heat initiates the pyrolysis of the solid fuel, the gaseous products react with oxygen in the air to produce heat and light, and this heat in turn is used to pyrolyze more solid fuel into volatile gases.

As we have seen from our discussion about a gaseous fuel, air (oxygen) and sufficient heat are the basic ingredients of a flaming fire. There is also one other consideration—the gas fuel–air mix. Gaseous fuel and air will burn only if their composition lies within certain limits. If the fuel concentration is too low (lean) or too great (rich), combustion will not occur. The concentration range between the upper and lower limits is called the **flammable range.** For example, the flammable range for gasoline is 1.3 to 6.0 percent.

Although a flaming fire will be supported only by a gaseous fuel, there are instances in which a fuel can burn without the presence of a flame. Witness the burning cigarette or the red glow of hot charcoals. These are examples of a phenomenon known as **glowing combustion** or **smouldering.** Here, combustion is taking place on the surface of a solid fuel in the absence of heat sufficiently high enough to pyrolyze the fuel. Interestingly, this phenomenon generally ensues long after the flames have gone out. Wood, for example, tends to burn with a flame until all of its pyrolyzable components have been expended; however, wood's carbonaceous residue will continue to smoulder long after the flame has extinguished itself.

We may now consider the conversion of iron to rust as an example of an extremely slow oxidation process, a situation that exists because of the inability of the iron atoms to achieve a gaseous state. For this reason, the combination of oxygen with iron to produce rust is restricted to the surface area of the metal exposed to air, a limitation that severely reduces the rate of reaction. On the other hand, the reaction of methane and oxygen is an example of oxidation in which all the reactants are in the gaseous state. Hence, this reaction proceeds at a rapid rate, as reflected by the production of noticeable quantities of heat and light (a flame).

Most typically, the rate of a chemical reaction increases when the temperature is raised. The magnitude of the increase in rate with temperature varies from one reaction to another and also from one temperature range to another. For most reactions, a 10°C (18°F) rise in temperature doubles or triples the reaction rate. This observation explains in part why burning is so rapid. As the fire spreads, it raises the temperature of the fuel-air mixture, thus increasing the rate of reaction; this in turn generates more heat, again increasing the rate of reaction. It is only when the fuel or oxygen is depleted that this vicious cycle will come to a halt.

One rather interesting phenomenon that is often invoked by arson suspects as being the cause of a fire is **spontaneous combustion.** Actually, the conditions under which spontaneous combustion can develop are rather limited and in fact rarely account for the cause of a fire. Spontaneous combustion is the result of a natural heat-producing process in poorly ventilated containers or areas. For example, hay stored in barns provides an excellent growing medium for bacteria whose activities will generate heat. If the hay is not properly ventilated, the heat will build to a level that will support other types of heat-producing chemical reactions in the hay. Eventually, as the heat rises, the ignition temperature of hay is reached, spontaneously setting off a fire.

Another known example of spontaneous combustion involves the ignition of improperly ventilated containers containing rags soaked with certain types of highly unsaturated oils, such as linseed oil. It is conceivable that heat will build up to the point of ignition as a result of a slow heat-producing chemical oxidation between the air and the oil. Of course, storage conditions will have to encourage the accumulation of the heat over a prolonged period of time. However, spontaneous combustion will not occur with hydrocarbon lubricating oils, and it is not expected to occur with most of the fats and oils that are found in a household.

Until now we have referred only to oxidation reactions that rely on air as the sole source of oxygen. However, we need not restrict ourselves to this type of situation. For example, explosives are substances that undergo a rapid exothermic oxidation reaction, with the production of large quantities of gases. It is this sudden buildup of gas pressure that constitutes the nature of an explosion. Detonation occurs so rapidly that oxygen in the air cannot participate in the reaction; thus, many explosives must have their own source of oxygen. Chemicals that supply oxygen are known as **oxidizing agents.** One such agent is found in black powder, a low explosive, which is composed of a mixture of the following chemical ingredients:

75% potassium nitrate (KNO_3)

15% charcoal (C)

10% sulfur (S)

In this combination, oxygen containing potassium nitrate acts as an oxidizing agent for the charcoal and sulfur fuels. As heat is applied to black powder, oxygen is liberated from potassium nitrate and simultaneously combines with charcoal and sulfur to produce heat and gases (symbolized by ↑), as represented in the following chemical equation:

$$3C \;+\; S \;+\; 2KNO_3 \;\rightarrow\; 3CO_2\uparrow \;+\; N_2\uparrow \;+\; K_2S + heat$$

carbon   sulfur   potassium   yields   carbon   nitrogen   potassium
nitrate   dioxide   sulfide

Some explosives have their oxygen and fuel components combined within one molecule. For example, nitroglycerin, the major constituent of dynamite, has a chemical structure that combines carbon, hydrogen, nitrogen, and oxygen:

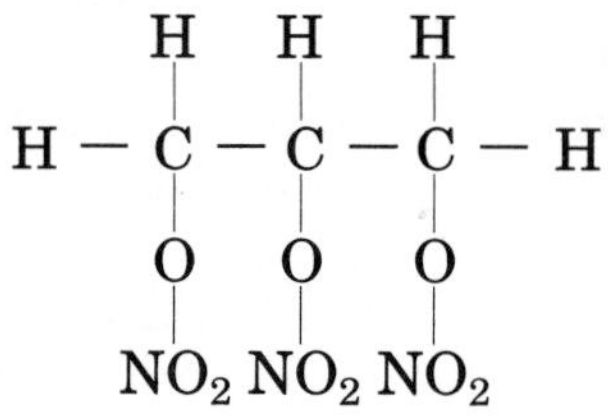

$$
\begin{array}{ccccccc}
 & H & & H & & H & \\
 & | & & | & & | & \\
H - & C & - & C & - & C & - H \\
 & | & & | & & | & \\
 & O & & O & & O & \\
 & | & & | & & | & \\
 & NO_2 & & NO_2 & & NO_2 &
\end{array}
$$

When nitroglycerin detonates, large quantities of energy are released as the molecule decomposes, and the oxygen recombines to produce large volumes of carbon dioxide, nitrogen, and water.

In summary, three requirements must be satisfied if combustion is to be initiated and sustained:

1. A fuel must be present.
2. Oxygen must be available in sufficient quantity to combine with the fuel.
3. Heat must be applied to initiate the combustion, and sufficient heat must be generated to sustain the reaction.

SEARCHING THE FIRE SCENE

It is important that the arson investigator begin examining a fire scene for signs of arson as soon as the fire has been extinguished. Time is constantly working against the arson investigator. Experience has shown that most arsons are started with petroleum-based accelerants such as gasoline or kerosene. If any petroleum residues remain after the fire is extinguished, they may evaporate within a matter of hours if not within a few days. Furthermore, safety and health conditions may necessitate that cleanup and salvage operations begin as quickly as possible. Once this occurs, it will be impossible to conduct a meaningful investigation of the fire scene.

The necessity to begin an *immediate* investigation of the circumstances surrounding a fire even takes precedence over the requirement to obtain a search warrant to enter and search the premises. The Supreme Court, in explaining its position on this issue, stated in part:

> Fire officials are charged not only with extinguishing fires, but with finding their causes. Prompt determination of the fire's origin may be necessary to prevent its recurrence, as through the detection of continuing dangers such as faulty wiring or a defective furnace. Immediate investigation may also be necessary to preserve evidence from intentional or accidental destruction. And, of course, the sooner the officials complete their duties, the less will be their subsequent interference with the privacy and the recovery efforts of the victims. For these reasons, officials need no warrant to remain in a building for a reasonable time to investigate the cause of a blaze after it has been extinguished. And if the warrantless entry to put out the fire and determine its cause is constitutional, the warrantless seizure of evidence while inspecting the premises for these purposes also is constitutional. . . .
>
> In determining what constitutes a reasonable time to investigate, appropriate recognition must be given to the exigencies that confront officials serving under these conditions, as well as to individuals' reasonable expectations of privacy.[1]

A search of the fire scene must focus on finding the fire's origin, for it is this area that will prove most productive in any search for an accelerant or ignition device. In a search to determine the specific point of origin of a fire, the investigator may uncover some telltale signs of arson. For instance, there may be evidence of separate and unconnected fires or the use of "streamers" to spread the fire from one area to another. For example, the arsonist may have spread a trail of gasoline or paper to cause the fire to move rapidly from one room to another. Additionally, the presence of containers capable of holding an accelerant or the finding of an ignition device ranging in sophistication from a candle to a time-delay device certainly will arouse suspicions of an arson-caused fire. Simultaneously with these efforts, investigators should look for signs of breaking and entering and theft, and they should begin interviewing any eyewitnesses to the fire.

---

[1] *Michigan* v. *Tyler,* 56 L. Ed. 2d 486 (1978).

There are no fast and simple rules for identifying a fire's origin. Normally, a fire has a tendency to move in an upward direction, and thus the probable origin will most likely be located closest to the lowest point that shows the most intense characteristics of burning. However, there are many factors that can contribute to the deviation of a fire from normal behavior. Prevailing drafts and winds; secondary fires due to collapsing floors and roofs; the physical arrangement of the burning structure; stairways and elevator shafts; holes in the floor, wall, or roof; and the effects of the firefighter in suppressing the fire are all factors that the knowledgeable fire investigator must consider before determining conclusive findings.

Once located, the point of origin should be protected as necessary to permit careful investigation. As at any crime scene, nothing should be touched or moved before notes, sketches, and photographs are taken. An examination must also be made for possible accidental causes, as well as for evidence of arson. The most common materials used by an arsonist to assure the rapid spread and intensity of a fire are gasoline and kerosene or, for that matter, any volatile flammable liquid. Fortunately, only under the most ideal conditions will combustible liquids be entirely consumed during a fire. When the liquid is poured over a large area, it is highly likely that a portion of it will seep into a porous surface, such as cracks in the floor, upholstery, rags, plaster, wallboards, or carpet, where enough of it remains unchanged so that it can be detected in the crime laboratory. In addition, when a fire is extinguished with water, the rate of evaporation of volatile fluids may be slowed down, because water cools and covers materials through which the combustible liquid may have soaked. Fortunately, the presence of water does not interfere with laboratory methods utilized to detect and characterize flammable liquid residues.

The fire investigator's search for traces of flammable liquid residues may be aided by the use of a highly sensitive portable vapor detector or "sniffer" (see Figure 11–2). This device can rapidly screen suspect materials for the presence of volatile residues by sucking in the air surrounding the questioned sample. The air is passed over a heated filament; if a combustible vapor is present, it oxidizes and immediately increases the temperature of the filament. The rise in filament temperature is then registered as a deflection on the detector's meter. Of course, such a device is not a conclusive test for a flammable vapor, but it does provide the investigator with an excellent screening device for checking suspect samples at the fire scene. Another approach is to use dogs that have been trained and conditioned to recognize the odor of hydrocarbon accelerants.

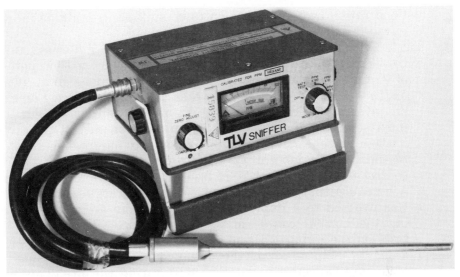

Figure 11–2. Portable hydrocarbon detector. *Courtesy* New Jersey State Police.

COLLECTION AND PRESERVATION OF ARSON EVIDENCE

As a matter of routine, two to three quarts of ash and soot debris must be collected at the point of origin of a fire when arson is suspected. The collection should include all porous materials and all other substances thought likely to contain flammable residues. These include such things as wood flooring, rugs, upholstery, and rags. Specimens are to be immediately packaged in airtight containers so no loss can occur through evaporation. New, clean paint cans with friction lids are good containers, as they are low cost, airtight, and unbreakable and are available in a variety of sizes. Wide-mouthed glass jars are also useful for packaging suspect specimens, provided that they contain airtight lids. Cans and jars should be filled one-half to two-thirds full, leaving an air space in the container above the debris. If need be, large bulky samples will have to be cut to size at the scene so that they will fit into available containers. Plastic polyethylene bags are not suitable for packaging specimens because they react with hydrocarbons and will permit volatile hydrocarbon vapors to be depleted. However, polyester-polyolefin bags distributed by Kapak

Corporation have been shown to be suitable containers for debris collected from the scenes of fire.[2]

It is important that the collection of all materials suspected of containing volatile liquids be accompanied by a thorough sampling of similar but uncontaminated control specimens from another area of the fire scene. This is known as *substrate control*. For example, if an investigator collects carpeting at the point of origin, he or she must sample the same carpet from another part of the room, where it can be reasonably assumed that no flammable substance was placed. In the laboratory, the criminalist will check the substrate control to be sure that it is free of any flammables. This procedure will reduce the possibility and subsequent argument that the carpet was exposed to a flammable liquid such as a cleaning solution during the normal course of its maintenance. In addition, laboratory tests on the unburned control material may have to be performed in order to help analyze the breakdown products arising from the material's exposure to intense heat during the fire. This is because, on occasion, common materials such as plastic floor tiles, carpet, linoleum, and adhesives can produce volatile hydrocarbons when they are burned. Under some circumstances, these breakdown products could be mistaken for an accelerant.

Needless to say, fluids found in open bottles or cans must be collected and sealed. Even when such containers appear to be empty, the investigator is wise to seal and preserve them in case they contain trace amounts of liquids or vapors. At the same time, a thorough search of the scene should be undertaken for ignitors. The most common ignitor is the match. Normally, the match is completely consumed during a fire and is impossible to locate. However, there have been cases in which, by force of habit, matches have been extinguished and tossed aside only to be recovered later by the investigator. This evidence may prove valuable if the criminalist can successfully fit the match to a book found in the possession of a suspect, as shown in Figure 11–3. There are, in addition, many other types of devices that an arsonist can construct to start a fire. These might include a burning cigarette, firearms, ammunition, a mechanical match striker, electrical sparking devices, and a "Molotov cocktail." Relatively complex mechanical devices are much more likely to survive the fire for later discovery. The broken glass and wick of the Molotov cocktail, if recovered, must be preserved as well.

One important piece of evidence that is not to be overlooked by arson investigators is the clothing of the suspect perpetrator. If this

---

[2]W. D. Kinard and C. R. Midkiff, "Arson Evidence Container Evaluation: II. New Generation Kapak Bags," *Journal of Forensic Sciences,* 36 (1991), 1714.

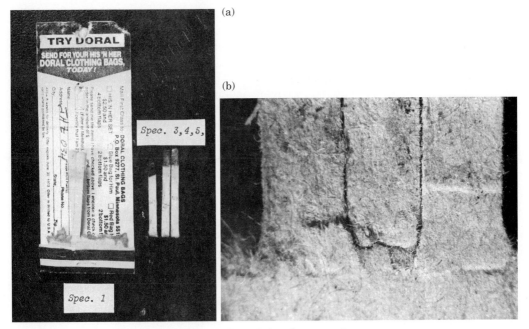

Figure 11–3. Three matches (Spec. 3, 4, 5) discarded at the scene of an arson are each shown to fit into a matchbook (Spec. 1) found in the suspect's possession. Such evidence provides a strong link between the crime scene and the suspect. *Courtesy* New Jersey State Police.

individual is arrested within a few hours of initiating the fire, residual quantities of the accelerant may still be present in the clothing. As we will see in the next section, the forensic laboratory can detect extremely small quantities of accelerant materials, making the examination of a suspect's clothing a feasible investigative approach. Each item of clothing should be placed in a separate airtight container, preferably a new, clean paint can.

The arson investigator must also be aware that hydrocarbon accelerants present in soil and vegetation can rapidly be degraded by bacterial action. Freezing samples containing soil or vegetation has been shown to be an effective way to prevent this degradation.

ANALYSIS OF FLAMMABLE RESIDUES

Criminalists are nearly unanimous in judging the gas chromatograph to be the most sensitive and reliable instrument for detecting and characterizing flammable residues. The vast majority of arsons are initiated by petroleum distillates such as gasoline and kerosene; these liquids are actually composed of a complex mixture of hydrocarbons. Basically, the gas chromatograph separates the hydrocarbon components and produces a chromatographic pattern characteristic of a particular petroleum product.

The easiest way to recover accelerant residues from fire-scene debris is to heat the airtight container in which the sample is sent to the laboratory. When the container is heated, any volatile residue present in the debris will be driven off and will be trapped in the container's enclosed air space. The vapor or "headspace" is removed with a syringe, as shown in Figure 11–4. When the vapor is injected into the gas chromatograph, it is separated into its components, and each peak is recorded on the chromatogram. The identity of the volatile residue is determined when the pattern of the resultant chromatogram is compared to patterns produced by known petroleum products. For example, in Figure 11–5, a gas chromatographic analysis of debris recovered from a fire site shows a chromatogram similar to a known gasoline standard, thus proving the presence of gasoline. In the absence of any recognizable pattern, the individual peaks can be identified when the investigator compares their retention times to known hydrocarbon standards (e.g., hexane, benzene, toluene, and xylenes).

One major disadvantage of the "headspace" technique described earlier is that the size of the syringe limits the volume of vapor that

Figure 11–4.
Removal of vapor from an enclosed container prior to gas chromatographic analysis. *Courtesy* New Jersey State Police.

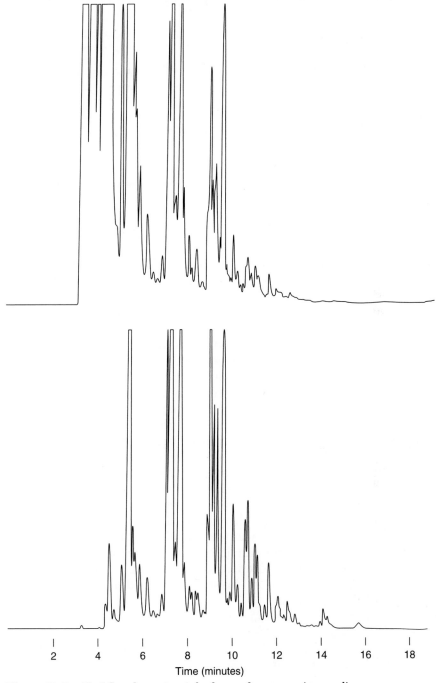

Time (minutes)

Figure 11–5. (Top) Gas chromatograph of vapor from a genuine gasoline sample. (Bottom) Gas chromatograph of vapor from debris recovered at a fire site. Note the similarity of the known gasoline to vapor removed from the debris. *Courtesy* New Jersey State Police.

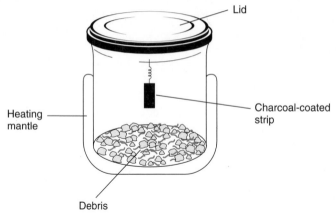

Figure 11–6.
Apparatus for accelerant recovery by vapor concentration. The vapor in the enclosed container is exposed to charcoal, a chemical absorbent, where it is trapped for later analysis.

can be removed from the container and injected into the gas chromatograph. In order to overcome this deficiency, many crime laboratories have begun to augment the "headspace" technique with a method called **vapor concentration.** One setup for accomplishing this analysis is shown in Figure 11–6. Here, a charcoal-coated Teflon strip, similar to what is used in environmental monitoring badges, is placed within the container holding the debris that has been collected from the fire scene.[3] The container is then heated to about 60°C for about one hour. At this temperature, a significant quantity of accelerant will vaporize into the container airspace. The charcoal will absorb the accelerant vapor that it comes in contact with. In this manner, over a short period of time, a significant quantity of the accelerant will be trapped and concentrated onto the charcoal strip. Once the heating procedure is complete, the analyst will remove the charcoal strip from the container and recover the accelerant from the strip by washing it with a small volume of solvent (carbon disulfide). The solvent will then be injected into the gas chromatograph for analysis. The major advantage of using vapor concentration in conjunction with gas chromatography is its extreme sensitivity. By absorbing the accelerant into a charcoal strip, the forensic analyst can increase the sensitivity of accelerant detection at least a hundredfold over the conventional headspace technique.

Once an accelerant has been identified as being present at a fire scene, the question of where that accelerant originated may become an issue in the investigation. Gas chromatography has been shown to play a useful role in helping forensic scientists ascertain the origin of

---

[3]W. R. Deitz, "Improved Charcoal Packaging for Accelerant Recovery by Passive Diffusion," *Journal of Forensic Sciences,* 36 (1991), III.

gasoline. By comparing select gas chromatographic peaks from a liquid gasoline or partially evaporated gasoline sample recovered from the fire scene to a gasoline of known origin, a forensic analyst *may* be able to demonstrate that sufficient similarity exists between the samples.[4] This will lead to the conclusion that the specimens *could have* a common origin. If an investigator wants the crime laboratory to undertake a comparative analysis in order to pinpoint a gasoline sample to a particular gas station, it is important that the criminalist be supplied with known gasoline samples from all local and suspect stations for comparison to the unknown. These specimens must be collected as quickly as possible in order to minimize the possibility that the gasoline composition at the pumps will be altered by fresh gasoline deliveries.

In one illustrative case, fire investigators were able to pinpoint the origin of a house fire to a bundle of gasoline-soaked newspapers. Samples from the interior of the newspaper bundle were taken as evidence, along with a partially filled one-gallon gasoline can from the trunk of the suspect's car. As seen in Figure 11–7, the gas chromatograph of gasoline in the one-gallon can recovered from the trunk of the suspect's automobile was very similar to the gas chromatograph of gasoline recovered from the newspaper bundle. The test results led to the conclusion that the gasoline from the newspapers could have originated from the one-gallon can and provided investigators with additional evidence linking the suspect to the commission of the arson.

At present, it's not possible to determine the exact brand name of a gasoline sample by gas chromatography or any other technique. Fluctuating gasoline markets and exchange agreements among the various oil companies precludes this possibility.

TYPES OF EXPLOSIVES

The ready accessibility of potentially explosive laboratory chemicals, dynamite, and, in some countries, an assortment of military explosives has provided the criminal element of society with a very lethal weapon. Although worldwide politically motivated bombings have received considerable publicity, it is a fact that in the United States the vast majority of bombing incidents are perpetrated by isolated individuals rather than by organized terrorists. Unfortunately for

---

[4]D. C. Mann, "Comparison of Automotive Gasolines Using Capillary Gas Chromatography I: Comparison Methodology," *Journal of Forensic Sciences,* 32 (1987), 606. D. C. Mann, "Comparison of Automotive Gasolines Using Capillary Gas Chromatography II: Limitation of Automotive Gasoline Comparisons in Casework," *Journal of Forensic Sciences,* 32 (1987), 616.

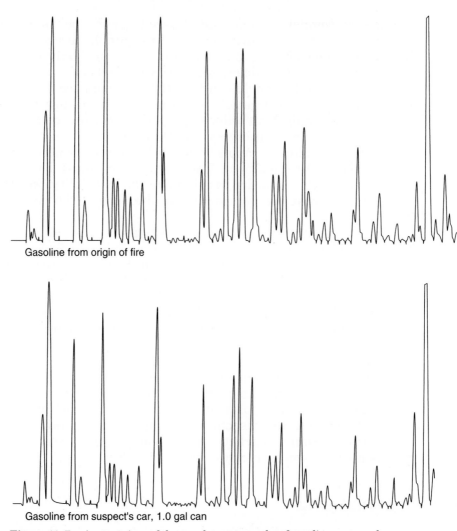

Gasoline from origin of fire

Gasoline from suspect's car, 1.0 gal can

Figure 11–7. A comparison of the gas chromatographs of gasoline recovered from fire debris to a liquid gasoline found in the suspect's car. Note the similarity of the chromatograms indicating that both gasolines could have come from the same source. *Courtesy* Dale C. Mann, Washington State Patrol Crime Laboratory.

society, explosives have become attractive weapons to be used by the criminal bent on revenge, the destruction of commercial operations, or just plain mischief.

Most bombing incidents that confront police agencies today involve the use of homemade explosives and incendiary devices. The design of such weapons is limited only by the imagination and ingenuity of the bomber. Like arson investigation, bomb investigation requires the close cooperation of a group of highly specialized individuals trained and experienced in bomb disposal, bomb-site investigation, forensic analysis, and criminal investigation. To the criminalist falls the responsibility of detecting and identifying explosive chemicals recovered from the crime scene as well as identifying the detonating mechanisms. It is this special responsibility that will concern us for the remainder of this chapter.

Like fire, an explosion is the product of combustion accompanied by the creation of gases and heat. However, the distinguishing characteristic of an explosion is the rapid rate at which the reaction proceeds. It is the sudden buildup of expanding gas pressure at the origin of the explosion that produces the violent physical disruption of the surrounding environment. Consider, for example, the effect of confining an explosive charge to a relatively small, closed container. Upon detonation, the explosive almost instantaneously produces large volumes of gases that begin to exert enormously high pressures on the interior walls of the container. In addition, the heat energy released by the explosion serves to expand the gases, causing them to push on the walls with an even greater force. If we could observe the effects of an exploding lead pipe in slow motion, we would first see the pipe's walls stretch and balloon under pressures as high as several hundred tons per square inch. Finally, the walls would fragment and fly outward in all directions. It is this flying debris or shrapnel that constitutes a great danger to life and limb in the immediate vicinity of this kind of an explosion.

Upon release from confinement, the gaseous products of the explosion suddenly expand and compress layers of surrounding air as they move outward from the origin of the explosion. This blast effect, or outward rush of gases, at a rate that may be as high as 7000 miles per hour creates an artificial gale that can overthrow walls, collapse roofs, and disturb any object in its path. If a bomb is sufficiently powerful, the more serious damage will be inflicted by the blast effect rather than by fragmentation debris.

The speed at which explosives decompose varies greatly from one to another and permits their classification as high and low explosives. In the low explosive, this speed is called the **speed of deflagration** (burning). This is characterized by a very rapid oxidation producing heat, light, and a subsonic pressure wave. In the high explosive, it is called the **speed of detonation.** Detonation refers to the creation of a supersonic shock wave within the explosive charge. This shock wave causes the chemical bonds of the explosive charge to break apart leading to the new instantaneous buildup of heat and gases.

Low explosives, such as black and smokeless powders, decompose relatively slowly at rates that vary up to 1000 meters per second. Because of their slow burning rates, they produce a propelling or throwing action that makes them suitable as propellants for ammunition or skyrockets. However, the danger of this group of explosives must not be underestimated, for when any one of them is confined to a relatively small container, it can explode with a force as lethal as any known explosive. High explosives include dynamite, TNT, PETN, and RDX. They detonate almost instantaneously at rates from 1000 to 8500 meters per second, producing a smashing or shattering effect on their target.

LOW EXPLOSIVES

The most widely used explosives in the low-explosive group are black powder and smokeless powder. The popularity of these two explosives is enhanced by their accessibility to the public. Both are available in any gun store, and black powder can easily be made from ingredients purchased at any chemical supply house as well. Black powder is a relatively stable mixture of potassium or sodium nitrate, charcoal, and sulfur. Unconfined, it merely burns; it is, in fact, used as a medium for carrying a flame to an explosive charge. A safety fuse usually consists of black powder wrapped in a fabric or plastic casing. When ignited, a sufficient length of fuse will burn at a rate slow enough to allow an individual adequate time to leave the site of the pending explosion. Black powder, like any other low explosive, becomes explosive and lethal only when it is confined.

Actually, the only ingredients required for a low explosive are fuel and a good oxidizing agent. Thus, the oxidizing agent potassium chlorate, for example, when it is mixed with sugar, produces a popular and accessible explosive mix. When it is confined to a small container—for example, a pipe—and ignited by the flame of a safety fuse, this mixture can explode with a force equivalent to a stick of 40 percent dynamite. Some other commonly encountered ingredients that may be combined with chlorate to produce an explosive are carbon, sulfur, starch, phosphorous, and magnesium filings. Chlorate mixtures may also be ignited by the heat generated from a chemical reaction. For instance, sufficient heat can be generated to initiate combustion when concentrated sulfuric acid comes in contact with a sugar-chlorate mix.

The safest and most powerful low explosive is smokeless powder. This explosive usually consists of nitrated cotton or nitrocellulose (single-base powder) or nitroglycerin mixed with nitrocellulose (double-base powder). The powder is manufactured in a variety of grain sizes and shapes, depending on the desired application.

Another form of low explosive is created when a considerable quantity of natural gas escapes into a confined area and mixes with a sufficient amount of air. If ignited, this mixture will result in simultaneous combustion, with the sudden production of large volumes of gases and heat. In a building, walls are forced outward by the expanding gases, causing the roof to fall into the interiors, and objects are thrown outward and scattered in erratic directions with no semblance of pattern.

Mixtures of air and a gaseous fuel will explode or burn only within a limited concentration range. For example, the concentration limits for methane in air range from 5.3 to 13.9 percent. In the presence of too much air, the fuel will become too diluted and will not respond to efforts to ignite it; on the other hand, if the fuel becomes too concentrated, ignition will be prevented because there is not enough oxygen to support the combustion. Mixtures at or near the upper concentration limit ("rich" mixtures) will explode; however, some gas will remain unconsumed because there is not enough oxygen to complete the combustion. As air rushes back into the origin of the explosion, it combines with the residual hot gas and a fire is produced that is characterized by a "whoosh" sound. Often this fire may prove to be more destructive than the explosion that preceded it. Mixtures near the lower end of the limit ("lean" mixtures) generally cause an explosion without accompanying damage due to fire.

HIGH EXPLOSIVES

The sensitivity of a high explosive provides a convenient basis for its classification into two groups. The first group, **initiating explosives,** are ultrasensitive to heat, shock, or friction, and under normal conditions will detonate violently instead of burning. For this reason, they are used to detonate other explosives through a chain reaction and are often referred to as **primers.** Initiating explosives provide the major ingredient of a blasting cap and include lead azide, lead styphnate, and mercury fulminate. Because of their extreme sensitivity, these explosives are rarely used as the main charge of a homemade bomb.

The second group, **noninitiating explosives,** are relatively insensitive to heat, shock, or friction, and will normally burn rather than detonate if they are ignited in small quantities in the open air. This group comprises the majority of high explosives used for commercial and military blasting. Some common examples of noninitiating explosives are dynamite, TNT (trinitrotoluene), PETN (pentaerythritol tetranitrate), RDX (cyclotrimethylenetrinitramine), and tetryl (2,4,6-trinitrophenylmethylnitramine).

It is an irony of history that the prize most symbolic of humanity's search for peace—the Nobel Peace Prize—should bear the name of the developer of one of our most lethal discoveries—dynamite. In 1867, the Swedish chemist Alfred Nobel, searching for a method to desensitize nitroglycerin, found that when kieselguhr, a variety of diatomaceous earth, absorbed a large portion of nitroglycerin, it became far less sensitive but still retained its explosive force. Nobel later decided to use pulp as an absorbent because kieselguhr was a heat-absorbing material. Thus, pulp dynamite was the beginning of what is now known as the straight dynamite series, the gradations of which are specified according to the percentage of nitroglycerin used. These dynamites are used when a quick shattering action is desired. Present-day straight dynamites also include sodium nitrate, which serves to furnish oxygen for complete combustion, along with a small percentage of a stabilizer—for example, calcium carbonate. The strength rating of a straight dynamite is designated by the weight percentage of nitroglycerin in the formula; a 40-percent straight dynamite contains 40 percent, a 60-percent grade contains 60 percent, and so forth. However, the concept that the actual blasting power developed by different strengths is in direct proportion to the percent markings is erroneous. Actually, a 60-percent straight dynamite, rather than being three times as strong as a 20-percent, is only one and one-half times as strong.

In recent years, nitroglycerin-based dynamite has all but disappeared from the industrial explosive market. Commercially, these explosives have been replaced mainly by **ammonium nitrate–based explosives,** that is, *water gels, emulsions,* and *ANFO* explosives. These explosives mix oxygen-rich ammonium nitrate with a fuel to form a low-cost and very stable explosive. Typically, water gels have a consistency resembling that of set gelatin or gel-type toothpaste. They are characterized by their water-resistant nature and are employed for all types of blasting under wet conditions. These explosives are based on formulations of ammonium nitrate and sodium nitrate gelled with a natural polysaccharide such as guar gum. Commonly, a combustible material such as aluminum is mixed into the gel to serve as the explosive's fuel.

Emulsion explosives differ from gels in that they consist of two distinct phases, an oil phase and a water phase. In these emulsions, a droplet of a supersaturated solution of ammonium nitrate is surrounded by a hydrocarbon serving as a fuel. A typical emulsion consists of water, one or more inorganic nitrate oxidizers, oil, and emulsifying agents. Commonly, emulsions contain micron-sized glass, resin, or ceramic spheres known as microspheres or microballons. The size of these spheres controls the explosive's sensitivity and detonation velocity.

Ammonium nitrate soaked in fuel oil is an explosive known as ANFO. Such commercial explosives are inexpensive and safe to handle and have found wide applications in blasting operations in the mining industry. The availability of ammonium nitrate in the form of fertilizer makes a readily obtainable ingredient for homemade explosives. Indeed, in an incident related to the 1993 bombing of New York City's World Trade Center, the FBI arrested five men during a raid on their hideout in New York City, where they were mixing a "witches' brew" of fuel oil and an ammonium nitrate–based fertilizer.

No discussion of high explosives would be complete without a mention of military high explosives. In many countries outside the United States, the accessibility of high explosives to terrorist organizations makes them very common constituents of homemade bombs. RDX is the most popular and powerful of the military explosives. This explosive is often encountered in the form of a pliable plastic of dough-like consistency known as *composition C–4* (a U.S. military designation).

TNT was produced and used on an enormous scale during World War II and may be considered the most important military bursting charge explosive. Alone or in combination with other explosives, it has found wide application in shells, bombs, grenades, demolition explosives, and propellant compositions. Interestingly, military "dynamite" contains no nitroglycerin but is actually composed of a mixture of RDX and TNT. Like other military explosives, TNT is rarely encountered in bombings in the United States.

PETN is used by the military in TNT mixtures for small-caliber projectiles and grenades. Commercially, the chemical is used as the explosive core in detonating fuse or primacord. Instead of the slower burning safety fuse, a detonating fuse is often used to interconnect a series of explosive charges so that they will detonate simultaneously.

Unlike low explosives, bombs made of high explosives must be detonated by an initiating explosion. In most cases, detonators are blasting caps composed of copper or aluminum cases filled with lead azide as an initiating charge and PETN or RDX as a detonating charge. Blasting caps can be initiated by means of a burning safety fuse or by an electrical current (see Figure 11–8).

Homemade bombs camouflaged in packages, suitcases, and the like are for the most part usually initiated with an electrical blasting cap wired to a battery. An unlimited number of switching-mechanism designs have been devised for setting off these devices; favored are clocks and mercury switches. There are certain situations in which

Figure 11–8.
Blasting caps. The left and center caps
are initiated by an electrical current;
the right cap is initiated by a safety
fuse.

individual bombers prefer to employ outside electrical sources. For instance, most automobile bombs are detonated when the ignition switch of a car is turned on.

COLLECTION AND ANALYSIS OF EXPLOSIVES

The single most important step in the detection and analysis of explosive residues is the collection of appropriate samples from the explosion scene. Invariably, undetonated residues of the explosive remain at the site of the explosion. The ultimate detection and identification of these explosives in the laboratory will depend on the bomb-scene investigator's skill and ability to recognize and sample the areas most likely to contain such materials.

The most obvious characteristic of a high or a contained low explosive is the presence of a crater at the origin of the blast. Once the crater has been located, all loose soil and other debris must immediately be removed from the interior of the hole and preserved for laboratory analysis. Other good sources of explosive residues are objects located near the origin of detonation. Wood, insulation, rubber, or other soft materials that are readily penetrated often collect traces of the explosive. However, nonporous objects in close proximity to the blast must not be overlooked. For instance, experience has shown that residues can be located on the surfaces of metal objects found near the site of an explosion. Material blown away from the blast's origin should also be recovered because it, too, may retain explosive residues.

The entire area must be systematically searched with great care to recover any trace of a detonating mechanism or any other item foreign to the explosion site. Wire-mesh screens are best utilized for sifting through debris. In pipe-bomb explosions, particles of the explosive are frequently found adhering to the pipe cap or to the pipe threads, as a result of either being impacted into the metal by the force of the explosion or being deposited in the threads during the construction of the bomb. **One approach for screening objects for the presence of explosive residues in the field or the laboratory is the EGIS® system.**[5] This portable detection machine uses a vacuum to collect vapors from surfaces suspected of containing explosive residues. A high-speed gas chromatograph separates the components of the vapor. Used as a screening tool, this method rapidly detects a full range of explosives, even at low detection levels. However, all results need to be verified through confirmatory tests. The EGIS machine is capable of detecting plastic explosives, as well as commercial and military explosives.

All materials collected for examination by the laboratory must be placed in sealed containers and labeled with all pertinent information. Soil and other soft loose materials are best stored in metal containers or plastic bags. Debris and articles collected from different areas are to be packaged in separate containers. If the evidence is packaged in plastic bags, do not place these bags in close proximity to each other. It has been demonstrated that some explosives can diffuse through plastic and contaminate nearby containers. Sharp-edged objects should not be allowed to pierce the sides of a plastic bag. It is best to place these types of items in metal containers.

When the bomb-scene debris and other material arrive in the laboratory, everything is first examined microscopically so that particles

---

[5]Thermedics Detection, Inc., 220 Mill Road, Chelmsford, Mass. 01824-4178.

of unconsumed explosive can be detected. Portions of the recovered debris and detonating mechanism, if found, are carefully viewed under a low-power stereoscopic microscope in a painstaking effort to locate particles of the explosive. Black powder and smokeless powder are relatively easy to locate in debris because of their characteristic shapes and colors (see Figure 11–9). However, dynamite and other high explosives present the microscopist with a much more difficult task and often have to be detected by other means.

Following microscopic examination, the recovered debris is thoroughly rinsed with acetone. The high solubility of most explosives in acetone will assure their quick removal from the debris. Once collected, the acetone extract is concentrated and analyzed utilizing color spot tests, thin-layer chromatography, high-performance liquid chromatography (see p. 142), and gas chromatography–mass spectrometry (see pp. 155–159). The presence of an explosive will be indicated by a well-defined spot on a TLC plate with an R_f value corresponding to a known explosive—for example, nitroglycerin, RDX, or PETN. The high sensitivity of high-performance liquid chromatography (HPLC) also makes it very useful for the analysis of trace evidence of explosives. The HPLC operates at room temperature and hence will not cause explosives, many of which are temperature sensitive, to decompose during their analysis. When a water-gel explosive containing ammonium nitrate or a low explosive is suspected, the debris should be

Figure 11–9. Samples of smokeless powders. *Courtesy* Bureau of Alcohol, Tobacco, and Firearms, U.S. Treasury Dept., Washington, D.C.

rinsed with water so that water-soluble substances (e.g., nitrates and chlorates) will be extracted.

Table 11–3 lists a number of simple color tests the examiner can perform on the acetone and water extracts in order to screen for the presence of organic and inorganic explosives, respectively.

When sufficient quantities of explosives are recoverable, confirmatory tests may be performed by either infrared spectrophotometry or X-ray diffraction. The former produces a unique "fingerprint" pattern for an organic explosive, as shown by the IR spectrum of RDX in Figure 11–10. The latter provides a unique diffraction pattern for inorganic substances, as exemplified by the diffraction patterns for potassium nitrate and potassium chlorate, shown in Figure 6–10 (p. 180).

An explosive "taggant" program has been proposed to further enhance a bomb-scene investigator's chances of recovering useful evidence at a postexplosion scene. Under this proposal, tiny color-coded chips, the size of sand grains, would be added to commercial explosives during their manufacture. Some of these chips would be expected to survive an explosion and be capable of recovery at explosion scenes. To aid in their recovery, the chips are made both fluorescent and magnetic sensitive. Hence, taggants can be searched for at the explosion site with the use of magnetic tools and ultraviolet light.

TABLE 11–3.
COLOR SPOT TESTS
FOR COMMON EXPLOSIVES

Substance	*Griess*[a]	*Diphenylamine*[b]	*Alcoholic KOH*[c]
		Reagent	
Chlorate	No color	Blue	No color
Nitrate	Pink to red	Blue	No color
Nitrocellulose	Pink	Blue-black	No color
Nitroglycerin	Pink to red	Blue	No color
PETN	Pink to red	Blue	No color
RDX	Pink to red	Blue	No color
TNT	No color	No color	Red
Tetryl	Pink to red	Blue	Red-violet

[a]*Griess reagent: Solution 1—Dissolve 1 g sulfanilic acid in 100 ml of 30% acetic acid. Solution 2—Dissolve 0.5 g N-(1-napthyl) ethylenediamine in 100 ml of methyl alcohol. Add solutions 1 and 2 and a few milligrams of zinc dust to the suspect extract.*

[b]*Diphenylamine reagent: Dissolve 1 g diphenylamine in 100 ml concentrated sulfuric acid.*

[c]*Alcoholic KOH reagent: Dissolve 10 g of potassium hydroxide in 100 ml of absolute alcohol.*

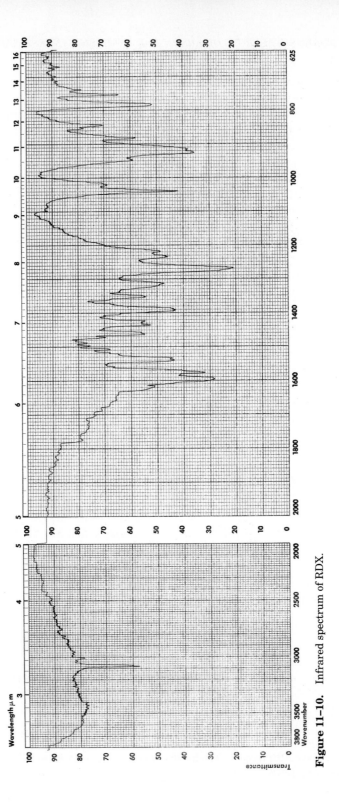

Figure 11–10. Infrared spectrum of RDX.

354

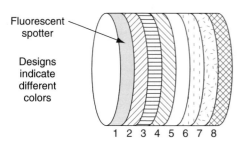

Fluorescent spotter

Designs indicate different colors

1 2 3 4 5 6 7 8

Figure 11–11.
Cross section of a taggant. The color sequence of the recovered taggant is observed with the aid of a low-power microscope. The colors are then matched to a color code to yield vital information about the plant of manufacture, production lot, and purchasers of the explosive material.

The taggant chip is arranged in a color sequence that indicates where the explosive was made and when it was produced (see Figure 11–11). With this knowledge, upon recovery the explosive can be traced through its distribution chain to its final legal possessor. The taggant colors are readily observed and are read with the aid of a low-power microscope.

At present, there are no plans to institute a taggant program in the United States. While some European countries are considering the adoption of explosives taggants, it is extremely doubtful that taggants will be found in any significant number of bombing incidents in the foreseeable future.

Case Reading
The Search: The TWA Plane Crash

Three weeks after the Atlantic Ocean swallowed a flaming Boeing 747, investigators continue to explore a prevailing theory that the downfall of Trans World Airlines Flight 800 was caused by a bomb. But their complicated mission is made all the more complex by the very water in which much of the plane rests.

Investigators say they are still concerned that the extended submersion in saltwater might have an effect on telltale chemical traces that a bomb would have left on airplane aluminum, plastic containers, luggage—and anything else from the jumbo jet's front end, where, investigators theorize, the explosion that downed the aircraft took place. More than 80 percent of the airplane remains scattered on the ocean floor, 120 feet down.

Their worry has heightened the sense of urgency in recovering debris from the water, said Joseph Cantamessa Jr., an F.B.I. special agent in charge. "It's the reason we have been so impatient about getting the evidence in the lab for testing."

Christopher Ronay, the former head of the Federal Bureau of Investigation's explosives unit and now president of the Institute of Makers of Explosives in Washington, D.C., said investigators have cause for concern. "Your explosive residue," he said, "adheres to all sorts of materials—to carpet fibers and upholstery and plastics, and it can be trapped in the surface material through all sorts of means. And certainly water washes away some kinds of residues."

But the July 17 explosion of Flight 800, which killed all 230 people on board, remains a puzzle in many pieces. As Mr. Ronay and others point out, the airplane may or may not have been brought down by a bomb. And if a bomb was the cause, the explosive material could have been one of several kinds. And depending on the kind of explosive, ocean water could either wash away the chemical residue or have little effect.

Dr. Jesse L. Beauchamp, a chemistry professor at the California Institute of Technology in Pasadena, said: "It goes without saying that any traces of explosives that were present on wreckage would likely be partially removed—not entirely removed—by continued exposure to saltwater. But it depends on the type of explosives."

Mr. Ronay, who helped coordinate the bureau's successful investigation into the fatal explosion of Pan Am Flight 103 over Lockerbie, Scotland, in 1988, expressed confidence in the F.B.I. laboratory's sophisticated equipment and in Tom Thurman, his successor as chief of the explosives unit and the case agent in the Lockerbie investigation.

Mr. Thurman and his team of forensic specialists have been examining the recovered airplane debris at a hangar in Calverton, L.I. In general they are concentrating on two avenues of inquiry: finding any explosive's chemical residue, and searching for pockmarks, tearing and other signs found on items that were near the explosion, often called "witness material."

In an explosion, a chemical reaction transforms the explosive material into gas. But some of that material is merely scattered, albeit in microscopic fragments. And that is what the forensic investigator seeks.

"There's almost always some residue," said Dr. Jimmie Oxley, a professor of chemistry at the University of Rhode Island. "And you look for something abnormal in the chemical analysis, something that shouldn't be there."

Dr. Oxley, who is a consultant to the F.B.I. and the Bureau of Alcohol, Tobacco and Firearms, said that investigators undoubtedly are rinsing airplane parts with an organic solvent to see if there is organic material that would not normally be present. "If you found traces of a military explosive such as RDX, which is not water soluble, it would have no reason for possibly being there," she said. "So now you have positive evidence."

But the ocean presents another variable. "On the other hand, if you never find anything at all, you can't draw any conclusions," Dr. Oxley said. "Now you've got to look at a lot of other things. There are explosive materials that could have been used that are water soluble. There is ammonium nitrate fuel oil, which is water soluble except for the oil. And this stuff has been bathing down there for a long time."

Even in the case of ammonium nitrate fuel oil, or ANFO, the material used in last year's deadly bombing of a Federal building in Oklahoma City, the investigators would expect to find traces of insoluble materials used to detonate the mixture.

Investigators in Calverton are using tools such as a gas chromatograph, which separates organic components, and a mass spectrometer, which identifies each component by its molecular weight. But Mr. Ronay said that more in-depth analysis is being done at the F.B.I. laboratory in Washington where, he said, there are specific instruments to use on specific explosives.

"Their equipment is so sensitive that it can track material in parts per trillion," he said. "I don't think a shark can smell blood in the water to that degree."

Still, Mr. Ronay acknowledged the difficulty that his former colleagues face. "It's such a big, big project," he said. "And you might never find the right piece."

That would force investigators to focus on the other avenue of inquiry—the hunt for a specific kind of tear in metal, or the pitting in a piece of luggage that might have been near the source of an explosion.

"If they never find the residue, the experts will probably characterize the damage and make some estimates regarding the kind of explosive that was used," Mr. Ronay said. "But if you find residue, you don't need to guess."[6]

REVIEW QUESTIONS

1. The absence of chemical residues always rules out the possibility of arson. (True, False)
2. The combination of oxygen with other substances to produce new chemical products is called _____.

---

[6]Dan Barry, "Saltwater's Ill Effects Depend on Bomb Type," *New York Times,* August 7, 1996, p. B–5. Copyright © 1996 by the New York Times Company. Reprinted by permission.

3. All oxidation reactions produce noticeable quantities of heat and light. (True, False)

4. _____ is the capacity for doing work.

5. Burning methane for the purpose of heating water to produce steam in order to drive a turbine is an example of converting _____ energy to _____ energy.

6. The quantity of heat evolved from a chemical reaction arises out of the _____ and _____ of chemical bonds.

7. Molecules must (absorb, liberate) energy to break their bonds and will (absorb, liberate) energy when their bonds are reformed.

8. All oxidation reactions (absorb, liberate) heat.

9. Reactions that liberate heat are said to be _____.

10. Excess heat energy liberated by an oxidation reaction is called the _____.

11. A chemical reaction in which heat is absorbed from the surroundings is said to be _____.

12. All reactions require an energy input to start them. (True, False)

13. The minimum temperature at which a fuel will burn is known as the _____ temperature.

14. A fuel will achieve a sufficient reaction rate with oxygen to produce a flame only when it is in the (gaseous, liquid) state.

15. The lowest temperature at which a liquid fuel will produce enough vapor to burn is the _____.

16. _____ is the chemical breakdown of a solid material to gaseous products.

17. _____ is a phenomenon in which a fuel will burn without the presence of a flame.

18. The rate of a chemical reaction (increases, decreases) as the temperature rises.

19. _____ describes a fire caused by a natural heat-producing process.

20. Oxidizing agents supply _____ to a chemical reaction.

21. Three ingredients of black powder are _____, _____, and _____.

22. An immediate search of a fire scene can commence without obtaining a search warrant. (True, False)

23. A search of the fire scene must focus on finding the fire's _____.

24. The probable origin of a fire will most likely be located closest to the lowest point that shows the most intense characteristics of burning. (True, False)

25. The collection of debris at the origin of a fire should include all (porous, nonporous) materials.

26. _____ containers must be used to package all materials suspected of containing hydrocarbon residues.

27. The most sensitive and reliable instrument for detecting and characterizing flammable residues is the (gas chromatograph, infrared spectrophotometer).

28. The identity of a volatile petroleum residue is determined by the (size, pattern) of its gas chromatogram.

29. The major advantage of using the vapor concentration technique in combination with gas chromatography is its extreme sensitivity for detecting volatile residues from fire-scene evidence. (True, False)

30. If two gasolines compare by gas chromatographic analysis, it can be concluded that they (definitely, could have) come from the same source.

31. The criminalist (can, cannot) identify gasoline residues by brand name.

32. Rapid combustion accompanied by the creation of large volumes of gases describes an _____.

33. Explosives that decompose at relatively slow rates are classified as _____ explosives.

34. _____ explosives detonate almost instantaneously to produce a smashing or shattering effect.

35. The most widely used low explosives are _____ and _____.

36. A low explosive becomes explosive and lethal only when it is _____.

37. Air and a gaseous fuel will burn when mixed at any concentration range. (True, False)

38. High explosives can be classified either as _____ or _____ explosives.

39. The blasting power of different dynamite strengths (is, is not) in direct proportion to the weight percentage of nitroglycerin.

40. The most common commercial explosives incorporate the chemical ammonium nitrate. (True, False)

41. The most widely used explosive in the military is _____.

42. The explosive core in detonating cord is _____.

43. A high explosive is normally detonated by an _____ explosive contained within a blasting cap.

44. An obvious characteristic of a high explosive is the presence of a _____ at the origin of the blast.

45. The single most important step in the detection of explosive residues is the _____ of appropriate samples from the explosion scene.

46. Unconsumed explosive residues may be detected in the laboratory through a careful _____ examination of the debris.

47. Debris recovered from the site of an explosion is routinely rinsed with _____ in an attempt to recover high-explosive residues.

48. Once collected, the acetone extract is initially analyzed by _____, _____, and _____.

49. The technique of _____ produces a unique absorption spectrum for an organic explosive.

50. The technique of _____ provides a unique diffraction pattern for the identification of the inorganic constituents of explosives.

FURTHER REFERENCES _____

Bertsch, Wolfgang, "Chemical Analysis of Arson Debris—Was It Arson?" *Analytical Chemistry,* 68 (1996), 541A.

Camp, Michael J., "Analytical Techniques in Arson Investigation," *Analytical Chemistry,* 52 (1980), 422A.

DeHaan, John D., *Kirk's Fire Investigation,* 3rd ed. Englewood Cliffs, N.J.: Prentice Hall, 1991.

Fultz, M. L., and J. D. DeHaan, "Gas Chromatography in Arson and Explosive Analysis," in *Gas Chromatography in Forensic Science,* I. Tebbett, ed. Basingstoke, Hants, England: Taylor & Francis, 1992.

Midkiff, C. R., "Arson and Explosive Investigation," in *Forensic Science Handbook,* R. Saferstein, ed. Englewood Cliffs, N.J.: Prentice Hall, 1982.

NFPA 921 Guide for Fire and Explosion Investigations, 1995 Edition. Quincy, Ma.: National Fire Protection Association, 1995.

Washington, W. D., and C. R. Midkiff, "Explosive Residues in Bombing Scene Investigations. New Technology Applied to Their Detection and Identification," in *Forensic Science,* 2nd ed., G. Davies, ed. Washington, D.C.: American Chemical Society, 1986.

Yinon, J., and S. Zitrin, *Modern Methods and Applications in Analysis of Explosives.* West Sussex, England: John Wiley & Sons Ltd., 1993.

FORENSIC SEROLOGY

In 1901, Karl Landsteiner announced one of the most significant discoveries of this century—the typing of blood—a finding that 29 years later was to earn for him a Nobel Prize. For years before the new century, physicians had attempted to transfuse blood from one individual to another. Their efforts often ended in failure because the transfused blood had a tendency to coagulate in the body of the recipient, causing instantaneous death. It was Landsteiner who first recognized that all human blood was not the same; instead, he found blood to be distinguishable by its group or type. Out of Landsteiner's work came the classification system that we presently call the A-B-O system. Now for the first time physicians had the key for properly matching the blood of a donor to a correct recipient. One blood type cannot be mixed with a different blood type without disastrous consequences. This discovery of course had important implications for blood transfusion and the millions of lives it has since saved. Meanwhile, Landsteiner's findings had opened up a completely new field of research in the biological sciences. Now, others were to pursue the identification of additional characteristics that could further differentiate blood. By 1937, the Rh factor in blood was demonstrated, and shortly thereafter, numerous blood factors or groups were discovered. At present, more than 100 different blood factors have been shown to exist. However, of all these, the ones belonging to the A-B-O system are still by far the most important for properly matching a donor and recipient for a transfusion.

The intriguing aspect of all these findings, as far as forensic science is concerned, is that in theory no two individuals, except for identical twins, can be expected to have the same combination of blood factors. In other words, blood factors are controlled genetically and have the potential of being a highly distinctive feature for personal identification. What makes this observation so relevant is the high frequency of occurrence of bloodstains at crime scenes, especially crimes of the most serious nature—that is, homicides, assaults, and rapes. Consider, for example, the situation in which a transfer of blood takes place between the victim and assailant during a struggle; that is, the victim's blood is transferred to the suspect's garment or vice versa. If, as has been suggested, the criminalist can individualize human blood by identifying all of its known factors, the result could be evidence of the strongest kind for linking the suspect to the crime scene.

Unfortunately, we must separate theory from reality. The problem of identifying most blood factors in whole blood is in itself a difficult task; however, in the crime laboratory the task is further complicated by the fact that practically all blood evidence is received in the form of dried stains. As blood dries, some of its characteristic blood factors are destroyed; and as the stain continues to age, the destruction slowly extends to most of the other factors. Even a task as relatively simple as determining the A-B-O classification of blood becomes much more difficult when applied to dried bloodstains.

During the past two decades, the individualization of dried blood has become one of the most exciting and promising research areas in forensic science. As forensic serologists pursue the detection and identification of various blood characteristics, their ability to associate a bloodstain to a particular individual with a known degree of probability has increased dramatically. The fact is that the individualization of bloodstains now has become a distinct possibility—but one that can be achieved only through the willingness of crime laboratories to commit time, brainpower, and money to unravel the mysteries of blood.

This chapter focuses on the substantial progress forensic scientists have made using select antigens, enzymes, and proteins for the purpose of linking various types of biological materials to a particular person. The next chapter is devoted to discussing the recent breakthroughs forensic scientists have achieved in associating blood and semen stains to a single individual through the characterization of **deoxyribonucleic acid (DNA).**

THE NATURE OF BLOOD

ANTIGENS AND ANTIBODIES

The word *blood* actually refers to a highly complex mixture of cells, enzymes, proteins, and inorganic substances. The fluid portion of blood is called **plasma.** Plasma is composed principally of water and accounts for 55 percent of blood content. Suspended in the plasma are solid materials consisting chiefly of cells—that is, red blood cells (erythrocytes), white blood cells (leukocytes), and platelets. The solid portion of blood accounts for 45 percent of its content. Blood clots when a protein in the plasma known as *fibrin* traps and enmeshes the red blood cells. If one were to remove the clotted material, a pale yellowish liquid known as **serum** would be left.

Obviously, considering the complexity of blood, any discussion of its function and chemistry would have to be an extensive one, extending beyond the scope of this text. It is certainly far more relevant at this point to concentrate our discussion on those blood components that are directly pertinent to the forensic aspects of blood identification—the red blood cells and the blood serum.

Functionally, red blood cells transport oxygen from the lungs to the body tissues and in turn remove carbon dioxide from tissues by transporting it back to the lungs, where it is exhaled. However, for reasons unrelated to the red blood cell's transporting mission, there resides on the surface of each cell millions of characteristic chemical structures called **antigens.** It is these antigens that impart blood-type characteristics to the red blood cells. Blood antigens are grouped into systems depending on their relationship to each other. More than 15 blood antigen systems have been identified to date; of these, the A-B-O and Rh systems are the most important.

If an individual is type A, this simply indicates that each red blood cell has A antigens located on its surface; similarly, all type B persons have B antigens; and the red blood cells of type AB contain both A and B antigens. Type O persons will have neither A nor B antigens on their cells. Hence, it is the presence or absence of the A and B antigens on the red blood cells that determines a person's blood type in the A-B-O system.

Another important blood antigen has been designated as the Rh factor, or D antigen. Those people having the D antigen are said to be *Rh positive;* those not having this antigen are *Rh negative.* In routine blood banking, it is the presence or absence of the three antigens—A, B, and D—that must be determined in testing for the compatibility of the donor and recipient.

Serum is important because it contains certain proteins known as **antibodies. The fundamental principle of blood typing is that for every antigen, there exists a specific antibody.** Each antibody symbol contains the prefix *anti,* followed by the name of the antigen for which it is specific. Hence, anti-A is specific only for A antigen, anti-B for B antigen, and anti-D for D antigen. The serum-containing antibody is referred to as the **antiserum,** meaning a serum that reacts against something (antigens).

An antibody will react only with its specific antigen and no other. Thus, if serum containing anti-B is added to red blood cells carrying the antigen B, the two will immediately combine, causing the antibody to attach itself to the cell. Antibodies are normally *bivalent*—that is, they have two reactive sites. This means that each antibody can simultaneously be attached to antigens located on two different red blood cells. This creates a vast network of cross-linked cells usually seen as clumping or **agglutination** (see Figure 12–1).

Let's look a little more closely at this phenomenon. In normal blood, shown in Figure 12–2 (a), antigens on red blood cells and antibodies can coexist without destroying each other because the antibodies present are not specific toward any of the antigens. However, suppose a foreign serum added to the blood introduces a new antibody. The occurrence of a specific antigen–antibody reaction will immediately cause the red blood cells to link together, or agglutinate, as shown in Figure 12–2(b).

Evidently, nature has taken this situation into account, for when we examine the serum of type A blood, we find anti-B and no anti-A. Similarly, type B blood contains only anti-A, type O blood has both anti-A and anti-B, and type AB blood contains neither anti-A nor anti-B. The antigen and antibody components of normal blood are summarized in the following table:

Blood Type	Antigens on Red Blood Cells	Antibodies in Serum
A	A	Anti-B
B	B	Anti-A
AB	AB	Neither anti-A nor anti-B
O	Neither A nor B	Both anti-A and anti-B

The reasons for the fatal consequences of mixing incompatible blood during a transfusion should now be quite obvious. For example, the transfusion of type A blood into a type B patient will cause the natural anti-A in the blood of the type B patient to react promptly with the incoming A antigens, resulting in agglutination. In addition, the incoming anti-B of the donor will react with the B antigens of the patient.

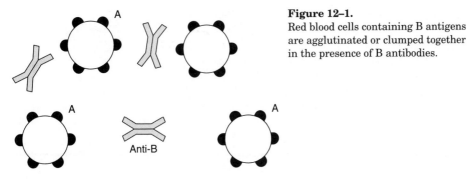

Figure 12–1.
Red blood cells containing B antigens
are agglutinated or clumped together
in the presence of B antibodies.

Red blood cells containing A antigens
will not combine with B antibodies

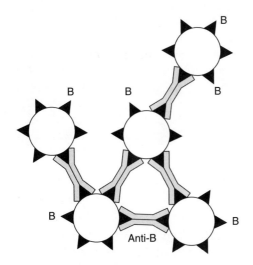

Red blood cells containing B antigens
are agglutinated or clumped together
in the presence of B antibodies

BLOOD TYPING

The term **serology** is used to describe a broad scope of laboratory
tests that utilize specific antigen and serum antibody reactions. The
most widespread application of serology is the typing of whole blood
for its A-B-O identity. In determining the A-B-O blood type, only two
antiserums are needed—anti-A and anti-B. For routine blood typing,
both of these antiserums are commercially available.

Table 12–1 summarizes how the identity of each of the four blood
groups is established when the blood is tested with anti-A and anti-B

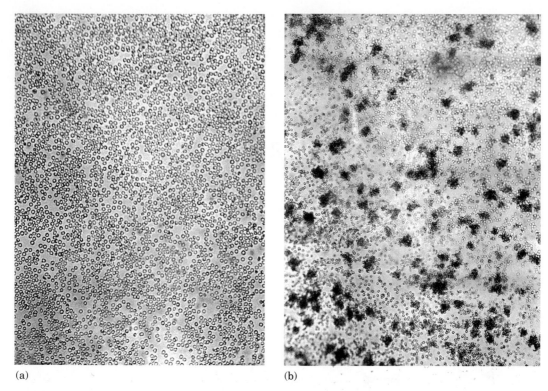

(a)   (b)

Figure 12–2. (a) Microscopic view of normal and red blood cells (225×).
(b) Microscopic view of agglutinated red blood cells (225×). *Courtesy* Linda
Jankowski.

serum. Blood of type A will be agglutinated by anti-A serum; blood of
type B will be agglutinated by anti-B serum; AB blood will be agglutinated by both anti-A and anti-B; and blood of type O will not be agglutinated by either the anti-A or anti-B serum.

TABLE 12–1.

**IDENTIFICATION OF BLOOD
WITH KNOWN ANTISERUM**

Anti-A Serum + Whole Blood	Anti-B Serum + Whole Blood	Antigen Present	Blood Type
+	−	A	A
−	+	B	B
+	+	A and B	AB
−	−	Neither A nor B	O

Note: + shows agglutination; − shows absence of agglutination.

The identification of natural antibodies present in blood offers another route to the determination of blood type. Testing blood for the presence of anti-A and anti-B requires using red blood cells that have known antigens. Again, these cells are commercially available. Hence, when A cells are added to a blood specimen, agglutination will occur only in the presence of anti-A. Similarly, B cells will agglutinate only in the presence of anti-B. All four A-B-O types can be identified in this manner by testing blood with known A and B cells, as summarized in Table 12–2.

The population distribution of blood types varies with location and race throughout the world. In the United States, a typical distribution is as follows:

O	A	B	AB
43%	42%	12%	3%

IMMUNOASSAY TECHNIQUES

The concept of a specific antigen–antibody reaction is one that is finding application in other areas unrelated to the blood typing of individuals. Most significantly, this approach has been extended to the detection of drugs in blood and urine. Antibodies that are capable of reacting with drugs do not naturally exist; however, they can be produced in animals such as rabbits by first combining the drug with a protein and injecting this combination into the animal. This drug-protein complex now acts as an antigen stimulating the animal to produce antibodies (see Figure 12–3). The recovered blood serum of the animal will now contain antibodies that are specific or nearly specific toward the drug.

TABLE 12–2.
IDENTIFICATION OF BLOOD
WITH KNOWN CELLS

A Cells + Blood	B Cells + Blood	Antibody Present	Blood Type
+	−	Anti-A	B
−	+	Anti-B	A
+	+	Both anti-A and anti-B	O
−	−	Neither anti-A nor anti-B	AB

Note: + shows agglutination; − shows absence of agglutination.

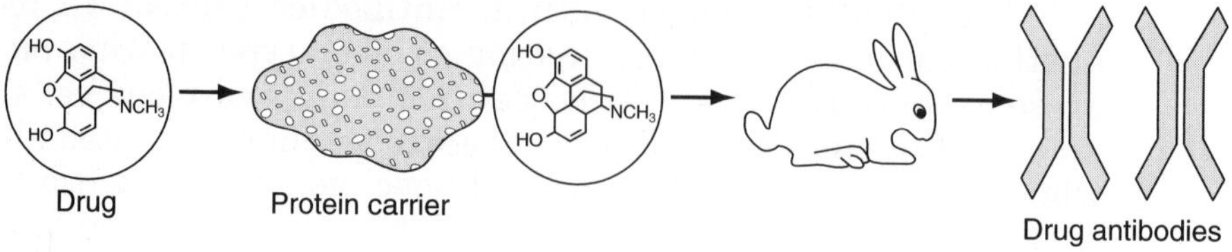

Figure 12–3.

There are at present a number of immunological assay techniques commercially available for detecting drugs through an antigen–antibody reaction. One such technique, the enzyme-multiplied immunoassay technique (EMIT), has gained widespread popularity among toxicologists because of its speed and high sensitivity for detecting drugs in urine. A typical EMIT analysis begins by adding to a subject's urine antibodies that will bind to the drug being measured. For example, if someone's urine is being checked for the presence of methadone, one would add methadone antibodies to the urine. Any methadone drug present in the urine will immediately combine with these antibodies. Then enzyme-labeled methadone drug is added to the urine. Methadone antibodies that did not interact with the methadone drug will now combine with the enzyme-labeled methadone. The quantity of enzyme-labeled methadone left uncombined is then measured, and this value is related to the concentration of methadone drug originally present in the urine.

One of the most frequent uses of the EMIT technique in forensic laboratories has been for screening the urine of suspected marijuana smokers. In marijuana, THC is considered the primary pharmacologically active agent (see page 262). In order to facilitate its elimination, the body converts THC to a series of substances or metabolites that are more readily excreted. The major THC metabolite found in urine is a substance called *THC-9-carboxylic acid.* It is against this metabolite that antibodies are prepared for testing by the EMIT technique. Normally, the urine of marijuana smokers will contain THC-9-carboxylic acid in a very small quantity (less than one-millionth of a gram); however, this is a level that is readily detected by the EMIT procedure.

The greatest problem associated with marijuana's detection in urine is interpretation. While smoking marijuana will result in the detection of THC metabolite, it is very difficult to determine when the individual actually used marijuana. In individuals who smoke marijuana frequently, detection is possible within 2 to 5 days after the last use of the drug. However, some individuals may yield positive results up to 10 days after the last use of marijuana.

Though EMIT is presently a popular immunoassay technique in forensic laboratories, there are other immunoassay procedures commercially available. For example, radioimmunoassay (RIA) uses drugs that are labeled with radioactive tags. Whether an analyst is using an enzyme tag as in EMIT or a radioactive tag as in RIA, one must be cautioned that immunoassay techniques are not totally specific for any drug. Substances having a chemical structure similar to the drug in question may cross-react with the antibody to give a false positive reaction. Hence, positive immunoassay tests must always be confirmed by another reliable analytical procedure. The issue of specificity, along with other questions relating to the reliability of RIA, was raised during the murder trial of Dr. Mario E. Jascalevich, which is described in detail on pages 26–35.

FORENSIC CHARACTERIZATION OF BLOODSTAINS

The criminalist must be prepared to answer the following questions when examining dried blood: (1) Is it blood? (2) From what species did the blood originate? (3) If the blood is of human origin, how closely can it be associated to a particular individual?

The determination of blood is best made by means of a preliminary color test. For many years, the most commonly used test for this purpose was the **benzidine color test;** however, because benzidine has been identified as a known carcinogen, its use has generally been discontinued, and the chemical phenolphthalein is usually substituted in its place (this test is also known as the **Kastle-Meyer color test**).[1] Both the benzidine and Kastle-Meyer color tests are based on the observation that blood hemoglobin possesses peroxidase-like activity. Peroxidases are enzymes that accelerate the oxidation of several classes of organic compounds by peroxides. When a bloodstain, phenolphthalein reagent, and hydrogen peroxide are all mixed together, the blood's hemoglobin will cause the formation of a deep pink color.

The Kastle-Meyer test is not a specific test for blood; there are some vegetable materials, for instance, that may turn Kastle-Meyer pink. These substances include potatoes and horseradish. However, it is unlikely that such materials will be encountered in criminal situations, and thus from a practical point of view, a positive Kastle-Meyer test is highly indicative of blood.

---

[1]M. Cox, "A Study of the Sensitivity and Specificity of Four Presumptive Tests for Blood," *Journal of Forensic Sciences,* 36 (1991), 1503.

Another important presumptive identification test for blood is the **luminol test.**[2] Unlike the benzidine and Kastle-Meyer tests, the reaction of luminol with blood results in the production of light rather than color. By spraying luminol reagent onto a suspect item, large areas can be quickly screened for the presence of bloodstains. The sprayed objects must be located in a darkened area while being viewed for the emission of light (luminescence).

The luminol test is extremely sensitive—it is capable of detecting bloodstains diluted up to 10,000 times. For this reason, spraying large areas such as carpets, walls, flooring, or the interior of a vehicle may reveal blood traces or patterns that would have gone unnoticed under normal lighting conditions (see Figure 12–4). Because luminol is known to destroy many important blood factors necessary for the forensic characterization of blood, its use should be limited only to seeking out blood invisible to the naked eye.

The identification of blood can be made more specific if microcrystalline tests are performed on the material. There are several tests available; the two most popular ones are the Takayama and Teichmann tests. Both of these depend on the addition of specific chemicals to the blood so that characteristic crystals with hemoglobin derivatives will be formed. The criminalist must be cautioned that crystal tests are far less sensitive than color tests for blood identification and are more susceptible to interferences from contaminants that may be present in the stain.

Once the stain has been characterized as blood, the serologist will have to determine whether the stain is of human or animal origin. For this purpose, the standard test used is the **precipitin test.** Precipitin tests are based on the fact that when animals (usually rabbits) are injected with human blood, antibodies are formed that react with the invading human blood to neutralize its presence. The investigator can recover these antibodies by bleeding the animal and isolating the blood serum. This serum will contain antibodies that specifically react with human antigens. For this reason, the serum is known as **human antiserum.** In the same manner, by injecting rabbits with the blood of other known animals, virtually any kind of animal antiserum can be produced. Currently, antiserums are commercially available for humans and for a variety of commonly encountered animals—for example, dogs, cats, and deer.

A number of techniques have been devised for performing precipitin tests on bloodstains. The classic method is to layer an extract of

---

[2]The luminol reagent is prepared by mixing 0.1 g 3-amino-phthalhydrazide and 5.0 g sodium carbonate in 100 ml of distilled water. Before use, 0.7 g of sodium perborate is added to the solution.

(a)

(b)

Figure 12–4. (a) A section of a linoleum floor photographed under normal light. This floor was located in the residence of a missing person. (b) Same section of the floor shown in (a) after spraying with luminol. A circular pattern was revealed. It was concluded that the circular blood pattern was left by the bottom of a bucket carried about during the cleaning up of the blood. A small clump of sponge, blood, and hair was found near where this photograph was taken. *Courtesy* North Carolina State Bureau of Investigation.

the bloodstain on top of the human antiserum in a capillary tube. Human blood, or for that matter, any protein of human origin in the extract, will react specifically with antibodies present in the antiserum, as indicated by the formation of a cloudy ring or band at the interface of the two liquids (see Figure 12–5).

Another method, called **gel diffusion,** takes advantage of the fact that antibodies and antigens will diffuse or move toward one another on an agar gel–coated plate. Here, the extracted bloodstain and the human antiserum are placed in separate holes opposite each other on the gel. If the blood is of human origin, a line of precipitation will form where the antigens and antibodies meet. Similarly, the antigens and antibodies can be induced to move toward one another under the influence of an electrical field. In the **electrophoretic method** (see pp. 146–147), an electrical potential is applied to the gel medium; a specific antigen–antibody reaction will be denoted by a line of precipitation formed between the hole containing the blood extract and the hole containing the human antiserum (see Figure 12–6).

The precipitin test is very sensitive and requires only a small amount of blood for testing. Human bloodstains dried for as long as 10

Figure 12–5.

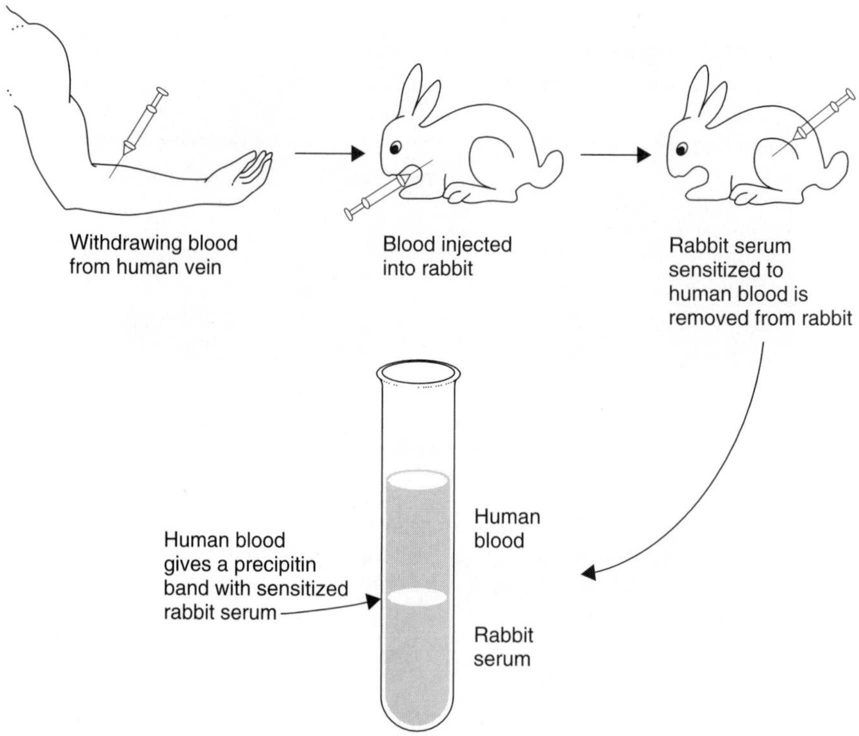

Withdrawing blood from human vein

Blood injected into rabbit

Rabbit serum sensitized to human blood is removed from rabbit

Human blood gives a precipitin band with sensitized rabbit serum

Human blood

Rabbit serum

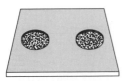 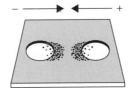 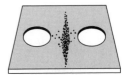

| Antigen and antibody are added to their respective wells | Antigen and antibody are being moved toward each other | Antigen and antibody have formed a visible precipitin line in the gel between the wells |

Figure 12–6.

to 15 years and longer may still give a positive precipitin reaction. Even extracts of tissue from mummies four to five thousand years old have given positive reactions with this test. Furthermore, experience has shown that human bloodstains diluted by washing in water and left with only a faint color may still yield a positive precipitin reaction (see Figure 12–7).

Once it has been determined that the bloodstain is of human origin, an effort must be made to associate or disassociate the stain with a particular individual. In this situation, however, the forensic serologist is severely limited to only those blood factors that survive the drying and aging processes. Stains also vary considerably in purity and quantity, all of which makes the analysis of dried blood much more complex than the analysis of whole blood. Until recently, existing procedures permitted the typing of bloodstains only by the A-B-O system; however, extensive research efforts have now made the characterization

Figure 12–7. Results of the precipitin test of dilutions of human serum up to 1 in 4096 against a human antiserum. A reaction is visible for blood up to 1 in 256. *Courtesy* Millipore Biomedica, Acton, Mass.

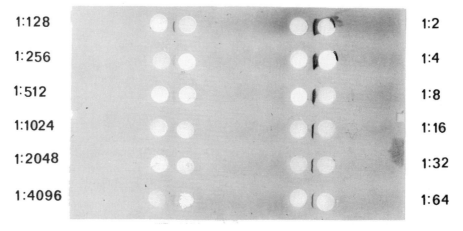

of some blood enzymes and proteins feasible for routine dried-blood analysis.

In the earlier description of whole-blood typing, it was noted that the identification of A and B antigens was easily accomplished by directly reacting the blood with anti-A and anti-B serums. This identity of the antigens present was confirmed by visually observing the clumping or agglutination of the red blood cells. Unfortunately, one cannot use the same approach in dried-blood typing, because red blood cells rupture on drying, leaving no cells in the stain to be agglutinated. However, although the cells may have disintegrated, the antigens present on their surfaces remain intact and are still identifiable by indirect means.

TYPING OF DRIED STAINS

The **absorption-elution technique** is the current method of choice for the indirect typing of bloodstains. As illustrated in Figure 12–8, the procedure consists of four steps:

Figure 12–8.   The absorption-elution technique for typing dried bloodstains.

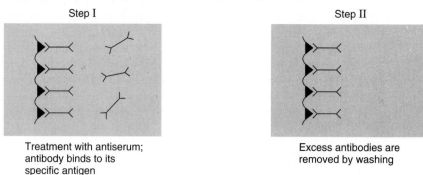

Step I

Treatment with antiserum;
antibody binds to its
specific antigen

Step II

Excess antibodies are
removed by washing

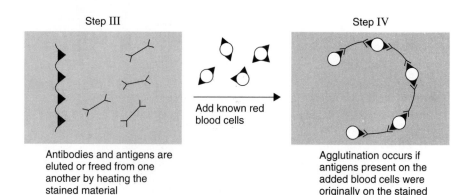

Step III

Antibodies and antigens are
eluted or freed from one
another by heating the
stained material

Add known red
blood cells

Step IV

Agglutination occurs if
antigens present on the
added blood cells were
originally on the stained
material as well

Step I: The antiserum is placed on the bloodstained material, allowing sufficient time for the antibodies to combine with their specific antigens.

Step II: The unreacted serum is removed by being washed off the blood-stained material.

Step III: Once an antibody combines with an antigen, it is possible to break the complex apart by a process known as **elution.** To do this, the stained material must be heated at 56°C. This allows the antibody–antigen bond to break, freeing both.

Step IV: When the eluted antibodies are combined with known red blood cells so that the presence or absence of agglutination can be observed, they can be identified. The identification of A-B-O type by the absorption-elution technique is summarized in Table 12–3.

This technique is sufficiently sensitive to type stains on a thread of fiber that is one-half inch in length. In addition, stains as old as 11 years have been typed by the absorption-elution procedure.

There are other antigens present in dried blood that can in theory be identified in the same manner as A and B antigens. However, in practice, most forensic laboratories find these antigens difficult to characterize in a reliable fashion from routine case specimens and prefer to concentrate their efforts on identifying select enzymes and proteins recovered from dried bloodstains. Additionally, a number of forensic science laboratories have developed, or are in the process of developing, capabilities for characterizing DNA in blood. This technology will be discussed in greater detail in the next chapter.

Secretors. The antigens of the A-B-O system are not confined exclusively to the red blood cells. Approximately 80 percent of individuals are classified as secretors—which means that their blood-type antigens

TABLE 12–3.

**IDENTIFICATION OF BLOOD TYPES
BY THE ABSORPTION-ELUTION TECHNIQUE**

Bloodstains Tested with			
Anti-A + A Cells	*Anti-B + B Cells*	*Antigen Present on Stain*	*Blood Type*
+	–	A	A
–	+	B	B
+	+	Both A and B	AB
–	–	Neither A nor B	O

Note: + shows agglutination; – shows absence of agglutination.

are found in high concentration in most body fluids (e.g., saliva, semen, vaginal secretions, and gastric juice) as well as in blood. In fact, saliva and semen have a higher concentration of A and B antigens than does blood. The value of this observation in criminal investigation is obvious. It is possible, for example, to type semen stains on the clothing of a victim of a sexual attack, or even the saliva deposited on the butt of a cigarette. The A-B-O typing of solid tissue, such as muscle or skin, is also possible.

BLOOD ENZYMES AND PROTEINS

In addition to the A and B antigens discussed earlier, there are other substances found in the red blood cell that are becoming increasingly important for the individualization of bloodstains. These substances are called **enzymes.** Enzymes are proteins that have important functions in regulating many of the body's chemical reactions. Forensic serologists are particularly interested in enzymes that exist in different forms, or are **polymorphic.** These enzymes can actually be separated into protein components called iso-enzymes.

Let's look at one such enzyme, PGM, in order to understand its importance to the forensic serologist. The iso-enzymes of PGM (phosphoglucomutase) can be separated from one another by electrophoresis (see pp. 146–147). What is interesting and most important about this separation is the observation that all persons do not have the same PGM iso-enzymes. Actually, as shown in Figure 12–9, there are three common variations or types of PGM: PGM 1, PGM 2-1, and PGM 2. These variations are distributed unevenly throughout the population: PGM 1 is present in approximately 58 percent of the population; PGM 2-1 is in 36 percent; and PGM 2 is in 6 percent. Thus, the identification of the PGM type in a dried bloodstain provides the forensic serologist with added statistical information with which to reduce the number of possible sources of the bloodstain.

A number of years after the discovery of the three PGM variants just described, it was observed that these variants could actually be further subtyped by more refined electrophoretic techniques. Thus, instead of three PGM types, forensic scientists can now identify 10 common PGM variants. This discovery has allowed forensic analysts to further narrow the possible sources of a bloodstain. For example, whereas PGM 2-1 is present in 36 percent of the population, its subtypes PGM 2 + 1 +, 2 + 1 −, 2 − 1 +, and 2 − 1 − are found in approximately 25 percent, 5 percent, 4 percent, and 2 percent, respectively, of the population.

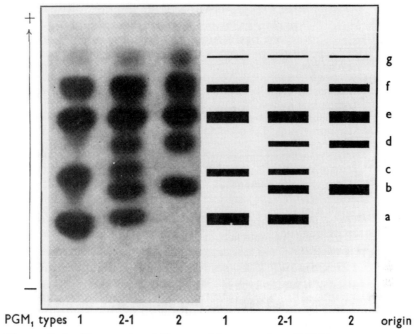

Figure 12–9.   Photograph and diagram of the separation of PGM iso-
enzymes accomplished by electrophoresis. PGM can be grouped into one of
three types—1, 2-1, and 2—according to band patterns. Reproduced from
Harry Harris, *The Principles of Human Biochemical Genetics,* 2nd ed. (New
York: North-Holland Publishing Co., 1975), p. 61.

Apparently, there are numerous polymorphic enzymes in red
blood cells that provide potential markers for determining blood origin. Also, a number of polymorphic proteins have been found to exist
in blood serum. However, from a practical point of view, only those
enzymes and proteins that are capable of surviving the drying and
aging processes are of any value to the forensic serologist.

Because antigens, enzymes, and proteins occur independently of
each other, the probability of a dried bloodstain having a particular
combination of these factors is determined by the product of their distribution in the population. For example, if a bloodstain is found to be
type A, then it can be concluded that such a stain could have originated from approximately 42 percent of the population. Now, if it is
also determined that this stain contains PGM 1, then its origin can be
narrowed to 24 percent of the population (42% × 58% = 24%). Obviously, the more factors a serologist can find in a stain, the smaller will
be its frequency of occurrence in a population. Hence, forensic
researchers have made extensive efforts at uncovering blood factors
that are identifiable in bloodstains (see Table 12–4).

TABLE 12–4.

**BLOOD ENZYMES AND PROTEINS USED
TO DISCRIMINATE BLOODSTAINS**

Blood Factor	Abbreviation
Adenosine deaminase	ADA
Adenylate kinase	AK
Carbonic anhydrase II	CA II
Erythrocyte acid phosphatase	EAP
Esterase D	EsD
Glucose-6-Phosphate dehydrogenase	G6PD
Glyoxylase I	GLO I
Group-specific component	Gc
Haptoglobin	Hp
Peptidase A	Pep A
Phosphoglucomutase	PGM
6-Phosphogluconate dehydrogenase	6PGD
Transferrin	Tf

Using only the most common type of the A-B-O system and the most common types of many of the polymorphic systems cited earlier, one would get:

Grouping System	Type	Frequency (approx.)
ABO	O	43%
ADA	1	90%
AK	1	91%
EAP	BA	43%
EsD	1	79%
GLO I	2-1	52%
Gc	1	50%
Hp	2-1	49%
PGM	1+1+	41%
6PGD	A	96%
Tf	CC	98%

The product of these frequencies $(0.43 \times 0.90 \times 0.91 \ldots$ etc.) shows that nearly 0.6 percent of the population will have this combination of blood types. Since the vast majority of people are expected to have less common types for at least some of these blood group systems, their frequency of occurrence will be far less than 0.6 percent. For instance, using the grouping systems in the previous table, the author's blood is found in only 0.04 percent of the population. Certainly, by expanding its ability to go beyond the A-B-O system, the crime laboratory has taken a significant step toward individualizing human blood and in so doing has dramatically enhanced the value of bloodstain evidence.

STAIN PATTERNS OF BLOOD

The crime-scene investigator must not overlook the fact that the location, distribution, and appearance of bloodstains and splatters may be useful for interpreting and reconstructing the events that must have occurred to have produced the bleeding. A thorough analysis of the significance of the position and shape of blood patterns with respect to their origin and trajectory is exceedingly complex and requires the services of an examiner who is experienced in such determinations. Most important, the interpretation of bloodstain patterns necessitates carefully planned control experiments utilizing surface materials comparable to those found at the crime scene.

An in-depth study of this subject has been published by Herbert L. MacDonell.[3] Many of MacDonell's observations and conclusions have important implications for any investigator who seeks to trace the direction, dropping distance, and angle of impact of a bloodstain. Some of them can be summarized as follows:

1. Surface texture is of paramount importance in the interpretation of bloodstain patterns, and correlations between standards and unknowns are valid only if identical surfaces are used. In general, the harder and less porous the surface, the less splatter results. The effect of surface is shown in Figure 12–10.

2. The direction of travel of blood striking an object may be discerned by the stain's shape. The pointed end of a bloodstain always faces its direction of travel. In Figure 12–11, the bloodstain pattern was produced by several droplets of blood that were traveling from left to right before striking a flat level surface.

3. It is possible to determine the impact angle of blood on a flat surface by measuring the degree of circular distortion of the stain. A drop of blood striking a surface at right angles gives rise to a nearly circular stain; as the angle decreases, the stain becomes elongated in shape. This progressive elongation is evident in Figure 12–12.

4. The origin of a bloodspatter in a two-dimensional configuration can be established by drawing straight lines through the long axis of several individual bloodstains. The intersection or point of convergence of the lines represents the point from which the blood emanated (see Figure 12–13).

An example of the utility of blood spatter formations in performing crime-scene reconstruction is illustrated in Color Plates 3 and 4

---

[3]Herbert L. MacDonell, *Bloodstain Patterns* (Corning, N.Y.: Laboratory of Forensic Science, 1993).

(a)

(b)

Figure 12–10. (a) Bloodstain from a single drop of blood that struck a plastic wall tile after falling 42 inches. (b) Bloodstain from a single drop of blood that struck a heavy, irregular-textured wallpaper after falling 42 inches. Reprinted from Herbert L. MacDonell, *Flight Characteristics and Stain Patterns of Human Blood* (Washington, D.C.: U.S. Government Printing Office, 1971), pp. 36–37.

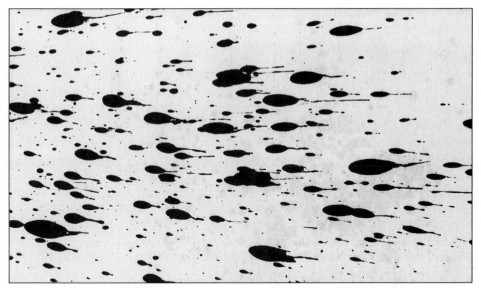

Figure 12–11. This bloodstain pattern was produced by droplets of blood that were traveling from left to right. Reprinted from Herbert L. MacDonell, *Flight Characteristics and Stain Patterns of Human Blood* (Washington, D.C.: U.S. Government Printing Office, 1971), p. 66.

and in Figure 12–14. This case relates to an elderly male who was found lying dead on his living room floor. He had been beaten about the face and head, then stabbed in the chest and robbed. The reconstruction of bloodstains found on the interior front door and the adjacent wall documented that the victim was beaten about the face with a fist and struck on the back of the head with his cane. A suspect was apprehended three days later and found to have an acute fracture of the right hand. When confronted with the bloodstain evidence, the suspect admitted striking the victim, first with his fist, then with a cane, and finally stabbing him with a kitchen knife. The suspect pled guilty to three first-degree felonies.

PRESERVATION OF BLOOD EVIDENCE

Before the collection of blood evidence begins, it is important that the bloodstains be photographed close up and that their location relative to the entire crime scene be recorded through notes, sketches, and photographs. If it is determined that the shape and position of bloodstains may provide information about the circumstances of the crime, an expert must immediately be dispatched to the location for an on-the-spot evaluation of the blood evidence. The significance of the position

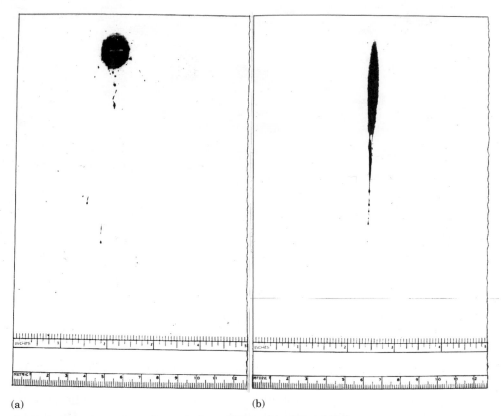

(a)   (b)

Figure 12–12.   (a) Pattern of a single drop of human blood that fell 42
inches and struck hard, smooth cardboard at 60 degrees. (b) Pattern of a
single drop of human blood that fell 42 inches and struck hard, smooth
cardboard at 10 degrees. Reprinted from Herbert L. MacDonell, *Flight
Characteristics and Stain Patterns of Human Blood* (Washington, D.C.: U.S.
Government Printing Office, 1971), pp. 44, 49.

and shape of bloodstains can best be ascertained when the expert has
an on-site overview of the entire crime scene and can better reconstruct
the movements of the individuals involved. No attempt should be made
to disturb the blood pattern before this phase of the investigation is
completed.

The evidence collector must handle all body fluids and biologically
stained materials with a minimum amount of personal contact. All
body fluids must be assumed to be infectious; hence, wearing disposable latex gloves while handling the evidence is required. Latex gloves
will also significantly reduce the possibility that the evidence collector
will contaminate the evidence.

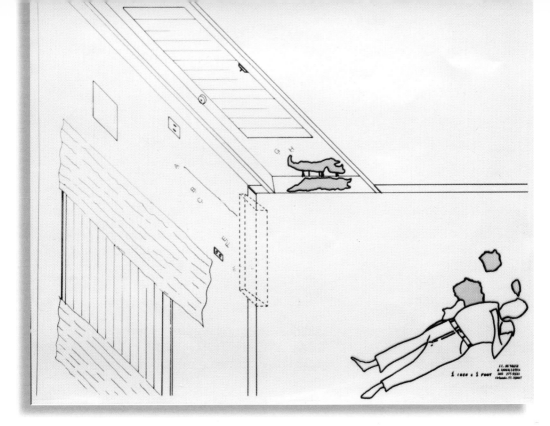

(a) Three-dimensional diagram illustrating bloodstain patterns that were located, documented, and reconstructed. Also see Figure 12–14 (a–c).

(b) Crime scene photograph of bloodstained areas.

Color Plate 3
Reconstructive photographs, bloodstain patterns, and graphic illustrations courtesy of Judith Bunker, J.L. Bunker & Associates, Ococee, Florida. Scene photographs courtesy of Sarasota County Sheriff's Department, Sarasota, Florida.

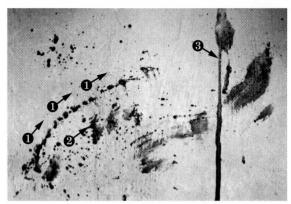

(c) Detail photograph of bloodstains on the wall adjacent to the interior door. Positions of impact spatter from blows that were inflicted to victim's face are indicated in Figure 12–14(a). Arrows no. 1 point to cast-off pattern directed left to right as blood was flung from perpetrator's fist while inflicting blows. Arrow no. 2 points to three repetitive transfer impression patterns directed left to right as the perpetrator's bloodstained hand contacted the wall as the fist blows were being inflicted upon the victim. Arrow no. 3 points to blood flow from the victim's wounds as he slumped against the wall.

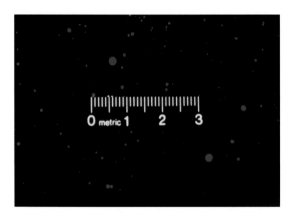

(d) Laboratory test pattern showing impact spatter. Size and shape of stains demonstrate forceful impact 90 degrees to target.

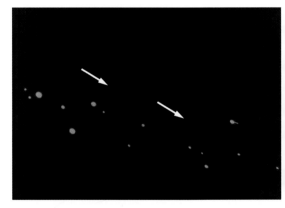

(e) Laboratory test pattern illustrating cast-off pattern directed left to right from a right overhand swing.

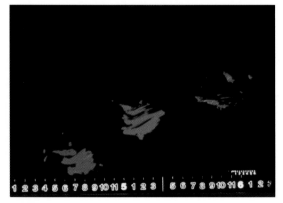

(f) Laboratory test pattern showing repetitive transfer impression pattern produced by a bloodstained hand moving left to right across the target.

(g) Laboratory test patterns illustrating vertical flow patterns. Left pattern represents stationary source; right pattern produced by left-to-right motion.

Color Plate 4

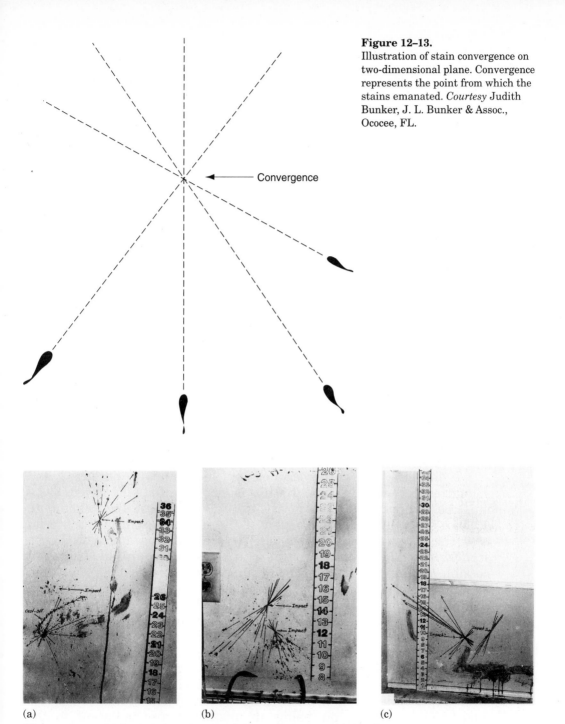

Figure 12–13.
Illustration of stain convergence on
two-dimensional plane. Convergence
represents the point from which the
stains emanated. *Courtesy* Judith
Bunker, J. L. Bunker & Assoc.,
Ococee, FL.

Convergence

(a)   (b)   (c)

Figure 12–14. (a) Convergence of impact spatter patterns associated with
beating by fist. (b) Convergence of impact spatter associated with victim falling
to the floor while bleeding from the nose. (c) Convergence of impact spatter
associated with victim while face down at the door, being struck with cane.

Blood has great evidential value when a transfer between victim and suspect can be demonstrated. For this reason, all clothing from both victim and suspect should be collected and sent to the laboratory for examination. This procedure must be followed even when the presence of blood on a garment does not appear obvious to the investigator. Laboratory search procedures are far more revealing and sensitive than any that can be conducted at the crime scene. In addition, blood should also be searched for in the less than obvious places. For example, the criminal may have wiped his or her hands on materials not readily apparent to the investigator. Efforts must be made to find towels, handkerchiefs, or rags that may have been used and then hidden. Attention should be given to examining floor cracks or other crevices that may have trapped a quantity of blood.

Wet blood can be typed much more quickly and easily in the laboratory than dried blood. If a sufficient quantity of liquid blood is found at the scene, it may be collected with a medicine dropper, placed in a glass tube, and kept refrigerated until submission to the laboratory. When the quantity of moist blood is insufficient to be preserved in this manner, it is best to allow the material to thoroughly air-dry out of the presence of direct sunlight or heat. The packaging of blood-stained evidence in plastic or airtight containers must be avoided, because the accumulation of residual moisture could contribute to the growth of blood-destroying bacteria and fungi. **Each stained article should be packaged separately in a paper bag or in a well-ventilated box.**

If feasible, the entire stained article should be packaged and submitted for examination. If this is not possible, the dried blood must be scraped off the surface with a disposable scalpel blade onto a clean sheet of paper. A portion of the unstained surface material near the recovered stain must likewise be removed and placed in a separate package. This is known as a **substrate control.** If it's not possible or feasible to remove the unstained surface material, then an apparently uncontaminated area close to the questioned stain should be swabbed with a clean cotton swab moistened with distilled water and the swab submitted to the laboratory. The forensic examiner will use the unstained material or swab as a control to confirm that the results of the tests performed were brought about by the stain and not by the material on which it was deposited. An alternative procedure is to absorb the dried blood onto a clean swab or filter paper dampened with distilled water. When stains are recovered in this manner, swabbing an unstained area adjacent to the stained area with clean, moistened cotton or filter paper is also necessary to provide the laboratory with a proper substrate control. All packages containing biological evidence should be refrigerated or stored in a cool location out of direct sunlight until delivery to the laboratory.

In previous sections of this chapter, the identification of select antigens, enzymes, and proteins in blood have been described. A human bloodstain will attain its full forensic value only when an analyst can compare each of these blood factors to whole-blood specimens collected from victims and suspects. For this purpose, at least 7 cc of whole blood should be drawn from individuals by a qualified medical person. The blood sample should be collected in a sterile vacuum tube. The addition of a preservative and anticoagulant should be avoided, as it may interfere with some of the blood grouping tests performed in the laboratory. The blood must be kept refrigerated (do not freeze) while awaiting transportation to the laboratory.

The next chapter discusses the characterization of DNA in blood for the purpose of linking a bloodstain to a particular individual. When a whole-blood specimen is collected for the purpose of comparing its DNA type to an evidential bloodstain, a minimum of 7 cc of blood should be taken. The whole blood is to be placed in a tube containing the anticoagulant EDTA (ethylenediamine tetraacetic acid). In addition to serving as an anticoagulant, EDTA inhibits the activity of enzymes that act to degrade DNA. Prior to delivery to the laboratory, the tubes should be refrigerated, but not frozen.

As we will learn in the next chapter, forensic scientists are capable of detecting extremely small quantities of DNA. With increased sensitivity comes a greater chance that accidental contamination can be detected in crime scene evidence. Contamination can occur by introducing foreign DNA into a stain while collecting it, or there can be a transfer of DNA when items of evidence are in contact with each other.

There are some relatively simple steps that crime scene investigators can take in order to minimize the possible occurrence of contamination of biological evidence:

1. Always wear disposable latex gloves when collecting biological evidence;

2. Always collect a substrate control for subsequent laboratory examination;

3. Pick up small items of evidence such as cigarette butts and stamps with clean forceps. Forceps should be cleaned with distilled water or alcohol between each use; and

4. Always package each item of evidence in its own well-ventilated container.

PRINCIPLES OF HEREDITY

TRANSMISSION OF OUR TRAITS

All of the antigens and polymorphic enzymes and proteins that have been described in previous sections are genetically controlled traits. That is, they are inherited from parents and become a permanent feature of a person's biological makeup from the moment he or she is conceived. Determining the identity of these traits, then, not only provides us with a picture of how one individual agrees or differs from another, but gives us an insight into the basic biological substances that determine our overall makeup as human beings and the mechanism by which they are transmitted from one generation to the next.

The transmission of hereditary material is accomplished by means of microscopic units called **genes.** The gene is the basic unit of heredity. Each gene by itself or in concert with other genes controls the development of a specific characteristic in the new individual; the genes determine the nature and growth of virtually every body structure.

The genes are positioned on **chromosomes,** threadlike bodies that appear in the nucleus of every body cell. All human cells contain 46 chromosomes, mated in 23 pairs. The only exceptions are the human reproductive cells, the egg and sperm, which contain only 23 unmated chromosomes. During fertilization, a sperm and egg combine so that each contributes chromosomes to form the new cell **(zygote).** Hence, the new individual begins life properly mated with 23 chromosome pairs. Because the genes are positioned on the chromosomes, the new individual inherits genetic material from each parent.

Actually, two dissimilar chromosomes are involved in the determination of sex. The egg cell always contains a long chromosome known as the **X chromosome;** but the sperm cell may contain either a short one, known as the **Y chromosome,** or a long X one. When an X-carrying sperm fertilizes an egg, the new cell is XX and develops into a female. A Y-carrying sperm produces an XY fertilized egg and develops into a male. Because it is the contribution of the sperm cell that ultimately determines the nature of the chromosome pair, we can say that the father biologically determines the sex of the child.

Just as chromosomes come together in pairs, so do the genes they bear. The position a gene occupies on a chromosome is its **locus.** Genes that govern a given characteristic are similarly positioned on the chromosomes inherited from the mother and father. Thus, a gene for eye color on the mother's chromosome will be aligned with a gene for eye color on the corresponding chromosome inherited from the father. Alternative forms of genes that influence a given characteristic and are aligned with one another on a chromosome pair are known as **alleles.** Another rather simple example of allele genes in humans is that of blood types belonging to the A-B-O system. Inheritance of the A-B-O type is best described by a theory that utilizes three genes designated A, B, and O.

A gene pair made up of two similar genes—for example, AA and BB—is said to be **homozygous;** and a gene pair made up of two different genes—AO, for example—is said to be **heterozygous.** If the chromosome inherited from the father carried the A gene and the chromosome inherited from the mother carried the same gene, the offspring would have an AA combination. Similarly, if one chromosome contained the A gene and the other had the O gene, the genetic makeup of the offspring would be AO.

When an individual inherits two similar genes from his or her parents, there is no problem in determining the blood type of that person. Hence, an AA combination will always be type A, a BB type B, and an OO type O. However, when two different genes are inherited, one gene will be dominant. It can be said that the A and B genes are **dominant** and that the O gene is always **recessive**—that is, its characteristics remain hidden. For instance, with an AO combination, A is always dominant over O, and the individual will be typed as A. Similarly, a BO combination is typed as B. In the case of AB, the genes are codominant, and the individual's blood type will be AB. The recessive characteristics of O will appear only when both recessive genes are present. Hence, the combination OO is typed simply as O.

A pair of allele genes together constitutes the **genotype** of the individual. However, there is no laboratory test known that can determine an individual's ABO genotype. For example, a person's outward characteristic, or **phenotype,** may be that of type A, but this does not tell us whether his or her genotype is AA or AO. The genotype can be determined only by studying the family history of the individual. If the genotypes of both parents are known, that of their possible offspring can be forecast.

An easy way of figuring this out is by constructing a so-called Punnet square. To do this, write along a horizontal line the two genes of the male parent, and in the vertical column the two kinds of female genes present, as shown. In our example, we'll assume the male parent is type O and therefore has to be an OO genotype; the female parent is type AB and can only be AB genotype:

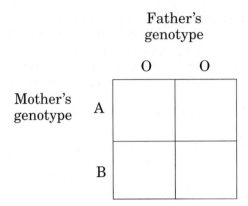

Next, write in each box the corresponding gene contributed from the female and then from the male. The result will be that the squares contain all the possible genotype combinations that the parents can produce in their offspring:

	O	O
A	AO	AO
B	BO	BO

Hence, in this case, 50 percent of the offspring are likely to be AO and the other 50 percent BO. These are the only genotypes possible from this combination. Because O is recessive, 50 percent of the offspring will probably be type A and 50 percent type B. **From this example, we can see that no blood group gene can appear in a child unless it is present in at least one of the parents.**

In the same way, the genotypes of parents determine the identity of all blood group systems as well as the polymorphic enzymes and proteins of their offspring. For example, an individual whose blood carries the enzyme EAP-BA has two allelic genes determining this trait. One gene corresponds to EAP-B, the other to EAP-A. When paired, these genes are codominant.

PATERNITY TESTING

Although the genotyping of blood factors has useful applications for studying the transmittance of blood characteristics from one generation to the next, it actually has no direct relevance to criminal investigations. It does, however, have important implications in disputed paternity cases, which are normally encountered in civil, not criminal, courts.

Many cases of disputed paternity can be resolved when the suspected parents and the offspring are related according to their blood-group systems. For instance, in the previous example, had the child been type AB, the suspected father would have been cleared. A type O father and a type AB mother cannot have a type AB child. On the other hand, if the child had been type A or type B, the most that could be said is that the suspect *may* have been the father; this does not mean that he is in fact the father. Obviously, there are many other males who also have type O blood. Of course, the more blood group systems that are tested, the better the chances of excluding an innocent male from involvement. Conversely, if no discrepancies are found between offspring and suspect father, the more certain one can be that the suspect is indeed the father.

In fact, routine paternity testing involves characterizing blood factors other than A-B-O. For example, the HLA (human leukocyte antigen) test relies on identifying a complex system of antigens that exists on white blood cells. If a suspect cannot be excluded as fathering a child after this test is performed, the chances are better than 90 percent that he is the father. These odds can be raised to more than 95 percent by combining the HLA test with A-B-O and haptoglobin blood typing.[4] Many paternity testing laboratories are currently implementing DNA test procedures that can raise the odds of paternity beyond 99 percent.

FORENSIC CHARACTERIZATION OF SEMEN

A great number of cases received in a forensic laboratory involve sexual offenses, making it necessary to examine exhibits for the presence of seminal stains.

The normal male releases 2.5 to 6 milliliters of seminal fluid during an ejaculation. Each milliliter contains 100 million or more sper-

---

[4]P. I. Terasaki et al., "Ninety-Five Percent Probability of Paternity with HLA, ABO and Haptoglobins," *Forensic Science International,* 12 (1978), 227.

matozoa, the male reproductive cells. The forensic examination of articles for seminal stains can actually be considered a two-step process. First, before any tests can be conducted, the stain must be located. Considering the number and soiled condition of outergarments, undergarments, and possible bed clothing submitted for examination, this may in itself prove to be an arduous task. Once located, the stain will have to be subjected to tests that will prove its identity; possibly, it may even be tested for the blood type of the individual from whom it originated.

Often, seminal stains are readily visible on a fabric because they exhibit a stiff, crusty appearance. However, reliance on such appearance for locating the stain is at best unreliable and is useful to a criminalist only when the stain is present in a rather obvious area. Certainly, if the fabric has been washed or contains only minute quantities of semen, visual examination of the article will offer little chance of detecting the stain. The best way to locate and at the same time characterize a seminal stain is to perform the **acid phosphatase color test.**

Acid phosphatase is an enzyme that is secreted by the prostate gland into seminal fluid. Its concentrations in seminal fluid are up to 400 times greater than those found in any other body fluid. Its presence can easily be detected when it comes in contact with an acidic solution of sodium alphanaphthylphosphate and Fast Blue B dye.

The utility of the acid phosphatase test is apparent when it becomes necessary to search numerous garments or large fabric areas for seminal stains. If a filter paper is simply moistened with water and rubbed lightly over the suspect area, acid phosphatase, if present, will be transferred to the filter paper. Then, when a drop or two of the sodium alphanaphthylphosphate and Fast Blue B solution are placed on the paper, the appearance of a purple color will be indicative of the acid phosphatase enzyme. In this manner, any fabric or surface can be systematically searched for seminal stains. If it is necessary to search extremely large areas—for example, a bed sheet or carpet—the article can be tested in sections, narrowing the location of the stain with each successive test. A negative reaction can be interpreted as meaning the absence of semen. Although some vegetable and fruit juices (e.g., cauliflower and watermelon), fungi, contraceptive creams, and vaginal secretions do give a positive response to the acid phosphatase test, none of these substances normally reacts with the speed of seminal fluid. A reaction time of less than 30 seconds is considered a strong indication of the presence of semen.

Other tests for semen involve the detection of choline and spermine. Since choline and spermine are also present in other biological materials and since neither of these components is unique to semen, the finding of either or both of them is only an indication of the possi-

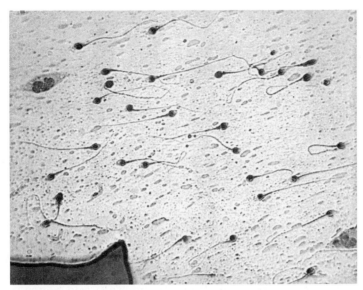

Figure 12–15. Photomicrograph of human spermatozoa (420×).
Courtesy Linda Jankowski.

ble presence of semen. Procedures for the identification of choline and spermine utilize microcrystalline tests. The Florence test for choline uses potassium triiodide, and the Barberio test for spermine uses picric acid as the crystallizing reagents.

Semen can be unequivocally identified by the presence of spermatozoa. When spermatozoa are located through a microscope examination, the stain is definitely identified as having been derived from semen. Spermatozoa are slender, elongated structures 50 to 70 microns long, each with a head and a thin flagellate tail (see Figure 12–15). The criminalist can normally locate them by immersing the stained material in a small volume of water. Rapid stirring of the liquid will transfer any spermatozoa present into the water. A drop of the water is dried onto a microscope slide, then stained and examined under a compound microscope at a magnification of approximately 400×.

Considering the extremely large number of spermatozoa found in seminal fluid, one would think the chance of locating one would be very good; however, this is not always true. One reason is that spermatozoa are extremely brittle when dry and easily disintegrate if the stain is washed or when the stain is rubbed against another object, as can frequently happen in the handling and packaging of this type of evidence. Furthermore, sexual crimes may involve males who have an abnormally low sperm count, a condition known as **oligospermia,** or they may involve individuals who have no spermatozoa at all in their seminal fluid **(aspermia).** Significantly, aspermatic individuals are increasing in numbers due to the increasing popularity of vasectomies.

Often in forensic laboratories, analysts will be placed in the situation of examining stains or swabs that they suspect contain semen (because of the presence of acid phosphatase) but that yield no detectable spermatozoa. How, then, can one unequivocally prove the presence of semen? The solution to this problem came with the discovery in the 1970s of a protein called **p30** or **Prostate Specific Antigen (PSA).** Under the analytical conditions employed in forensic laboratories, p30 is unique to seminal plasma. When p30 is isolated and injected into a rabbit, it will stimulate the production of antibodies (anti-p30). The sera collected from these immunized rabbits can now be used to test suspected semen stains.

As shown in Figure 12–16, the stain extract is placed in one well of an electrophoretic plate and the anti-p30 in an opposite well. When an electric potential is applied, the antigens and antibodies will move toward each other. The formation of a visible line midway between the two wells shows the presence of p30 in the stain and hence proves that the stain was seminal in nature.

Once the material under examination is proven to be semen, the next endeavor will be to attempt to associate the semen as closely as possible to a single individual. Initial efforts in this area begin with a possible A-B-O blood group determination. We have already observed that nearly 80 percent of the population are secretors having high concentrations of their blood-type antigens in most body fluids. Hence, for a substantial segment of the male population, seminal fluid and/or stains can yield the identity of an individual's blood type. Often, this information can provide important corroborative evidence that supports a suspect's involvement in a sexual assault. Likewise, such an identification can serve to exonerate someone unjustly accused of committing such a crime. However, the determination of blood type from

– ⟶ ⟵ +

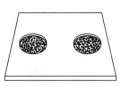 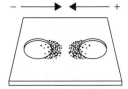 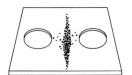

| Semen extract and anti-p30 are added to their respective wells | Antigen and antibody are being moved toward each other | Formation of a visible precipitation line midway between the wells shows the presence of p30 in the stain and proves the stain is seminal in nature |

Figure 12–16.

semen is not without its problems, especially under conditions that normally accompany a sexual assault. Often, the semen stains found on the victim's garments will be mixed with sweat and/or vaginal secretions. Since it is just as probable for a female victim to secrete her blood-type antigens as it is for the male suspect, it becomes important to establish whether the victim and suspect are both secretors and their respective blood types. This information can readily be obtained in the laboratory by a determination of the concentration levels of A, B, and H antigens present in saliva. The saliva of secretors will yield higher levels of blood antigens than that of nonsecretors. Naturally, if both the victim and suspect are secretors having the same blood type, the examiner must be especially cautious in typing a seminal stain, taking special care to make sure that the stain is free of any possible contaminants.

As with blood, forensic serologists have been successful in finding polymorphic enzymes in semen. Unfortunately, the list of readily identifiable enzymes in semen stains is far shorter than it is for blood. Two enzymes which lend themselves to ready detection in semen stains are PGM and Pep A. One major impact of DNA typing (see Chapter 13) will be the association of seminal material to a single individual with a high degree of certainty. Likewise, this technology will serve to exonerate many of those wrongfully accused of the crime of sexual assault.

COLLECTION OF RAPE EVIDENCE

The finding of seminal constituents in a rape victim is important evidence for substantiating the fact that sexual intercourse has taken place, but their absence does not necessarily mean that a rape did not occur. Physical injuries such as bruises or bleeding tend to confirm the fact that a violent assault did take place. Furthermore, there is a distinct possibility that the forceful physical contact between victim and assailant will result in a transfer of physical evidence—that is, blood, semen, hairs, and fibers. The presence of such physical evidence will help forge a vital link in the chain of circumstances surrounding a sexual crime.

To protect this kind of evidence, all the outer- and undergarments from the involved parties should be carefully removed and packaged separately in paper (not plastic) bags. Place a clean bed sheet on the floor and lay a clean paper sheet over it. The victim must remove her shoes before standing on the paper. Have the party disrobe while standing on the paper in order to collect any loose foreign material falling from the clothing. Collect each piece of clothing as it is removed and place in separate paper bags in order to avoid cross-contamination of physical evidence. Carefully fold the paper sheet so that all foreign materials will be contained inside.

If it is deemed appropriate, bedding, or the object upon which the assault took place, should be submitted to the laboratory for processing. Items suspected of containing seminal stains must be handled carefully. Folding an article through the stain may cause it to flake off, as will rubbing the stained area against the surface of the packaging material. If, under unusual circumstances, it is not possible to transport the stained article to the laboratory, the stained area should be cut out and submitted with an unstained piece as a substrate control.

In cases relating to the typing of seminal stains, laboratory submissions must include saliva so that the secretor status of both the suspect and victim can be determined. To obtain saliva, the individuals in question should be asked to thoroughly saturate a clean piece of filter paper with saliva. The saliva should then be air-dried out of direct sunlight or heat. The donor should not have anything in his or her mouth for 25 minutes before giving this sample—this includes gum, cigarettes, cigars, and the like. In addition, a sample of whole blood from both victim and suspect should be obtained for blood typing.

The fact that individuals may secrete their blood-type antigens in body fluids can be a double-edged sword for the careless investigator. By needlessly touching the suspect area, the investigator may inadvertently transfer his or her own blood type to the stain through the medium of perspiration. In this respect, it is exceedingly important that stained articles be handled with care, minimizing direct personal contact. It is important that the evidence collector wear disposable latex gloves when such evidence must be touched.

The rape victim must be subjected to a medical examination as soon as possible after the assault. At this time, the appropriate items of physical evidence are collected by trained personnel. It is to be expected that evidence collectors will have an evidence-collection kit that has been disseminated by the local crime laboratory (see Figure 12–17).

The following items of physical evidence are to be collected:

1. *Pubic combings.* Place a paper towel under the buttocks and comb pubic area for loose or foreign hairs.
2. *Pubic hair controls.* Pull out 15 to 20 full-length hairs from the pubic area.
3. *Vaginal swabs and smear.* Using two swabs simultaneously, carefully swab the vaginal area and let them air-dry before packaging. Using two additional swabs, repeat swabbing procedure and smear the swabs onto separate microscope slides, allowing them to air-dry before packaging.
4. *Rectal swabs and smear.* To be taken when warranted by case history. Using two swabs simultaneously, swab the rectal canal, smearing one of the swabs onto a microscope slide. Allow both samples to air-dry before packaging.

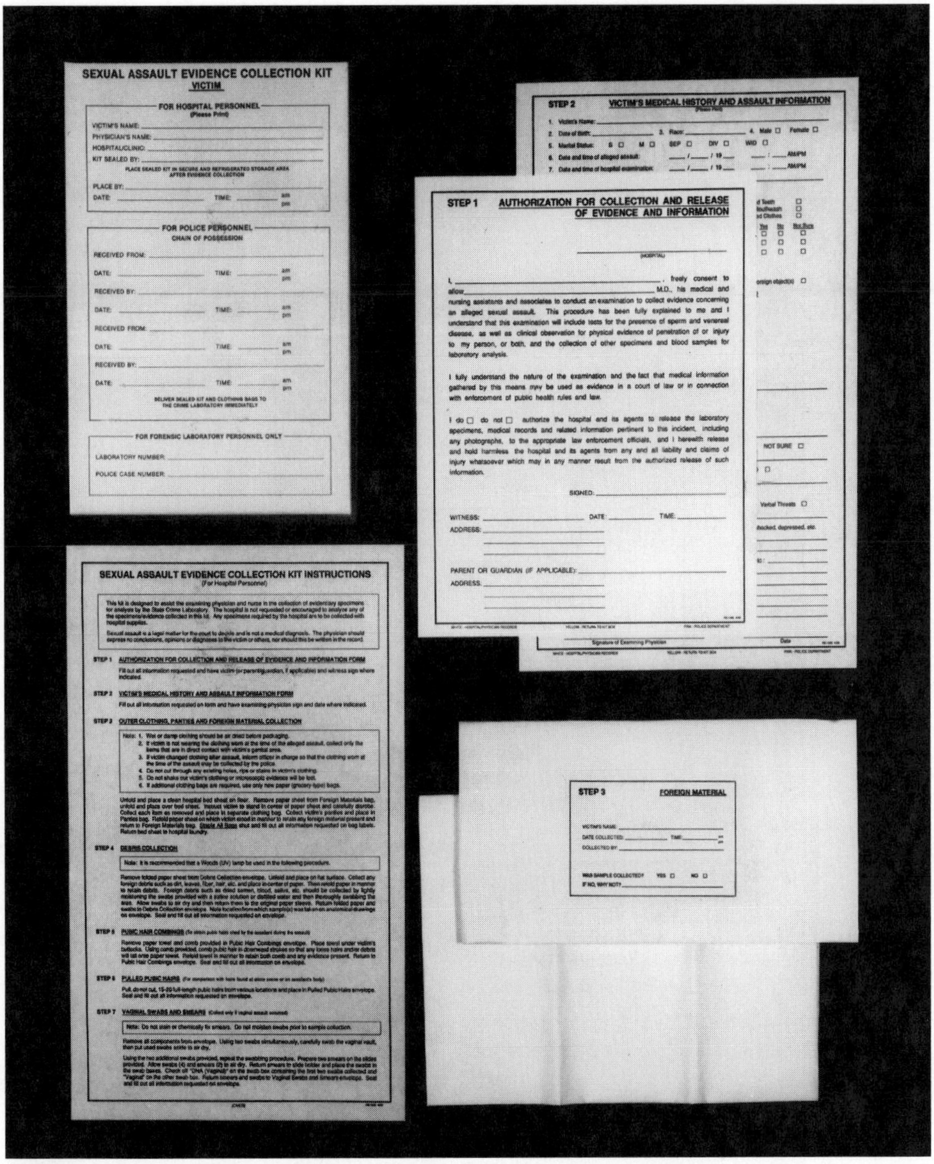

Figure 12–17. (a) Victim rape collection kit showing the kit envelope, kit instructions, medical history and assault information forms, and foreign materials collection bag. *Courtesy* of Tri-Tech, Inc., Southport, N.C.

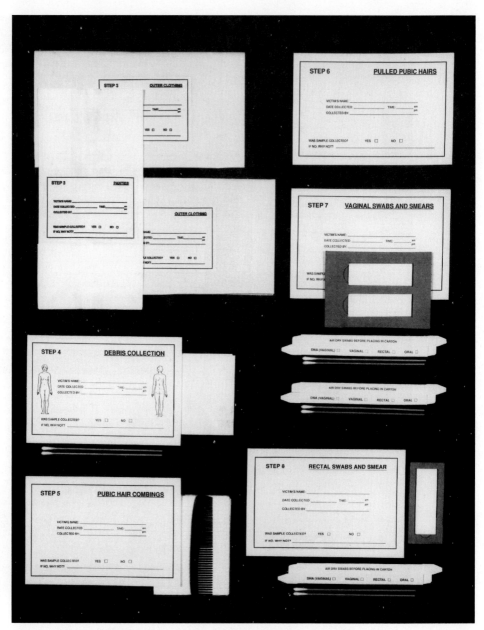

Figure 12–17. (b) Victim rape collection kit showing collection bags for outer clothing, underpants, debris, pubic hair combings, pubic hair controls, vaginal swabs, and rectal swabs. *Courtesy* of Tri-Tech, Inc., Southport, N.C.

5. *Oral swabs and smear.* To be taken if oral-genital contact occurred. Use two swabs simultaneously to swab the buccal area and gum line. Using both swabs, prepare one smear slide. Allow both swabs and the one smear to air-dry before packaging.

6. *Pulled head hairs.* Pull a minimum of 5 full-length hairs from each of the following scalp locations: center, front, back, left side, and right side. It is recommended that a total of at least 50 hairs be pulled and submitted to the laboratory.

7. *Saliva sample.* Obtain as described earlier.

8. *Blood sample.* Collect a minimum of 7 milliliters in a vacuum tube that does not contain either a preservative or an anticoagulant. If DNA typing is to be pursued, also collect a minimum of 7 milliliters in a vacuum tube containing the anticoagulant EDTA.

9. *Fingernail scrapings.* Scrape the undersurface of the nails with a dull object over a piece of clean paper to collect debris. Use separate paper, one for each hand.

10. *All clothing.* Package as described earlier.

If a suspect is apprehended, the following items are routinely collected:

1. *All clothing.* Items believed to have been worn at the time of assault.

2. *Pubic hair combings.*

3. *Pulled head and pubic hair controls.*

4. *Saliva and blood samples.*

The persistence of seminal constituents in the vagina may become a factor when trying to ascertain the time of an alleged sexual attack. While the presence of spermatozoa in the vaginal cavity provides evidence of intercourse, important information regarding the time of sexual activity can be obtained from the knowledge that motile or living sperm *may* generally survive up to 4 to 6 hours in the vaginal cavity of a living person. However, a successful search for motile sperm requires that a microscopic examination of a vaginal smear be conducted immediately after it is taken from the victim.

A more extensive examination of vaginal collections is later made at a forensic laboratory. Nonmotile sperm *may* be found in a living female for up to three days after intercourse and occasionally up to six days. However, intact sperm (sperm with tails) are rarely found 16 hours after intercourse but have been found as late as 72 hours after intercourse. The likelihood of finding seminal acid phosphatase in the vaginal cavity markedly decreases with time following intercourse, with little chance of identifying this substance 48 hours after intercourse.[5] Hence, taking into consideration the possibility of the prolonged persistence of both spermatozoa and acid phosphatase in the vaginal cavity after intercourse, investigators should seek information to determine when and if voluntary sexual activity last occurred prior to the sexual assault. This information will be useful for evaluating the significance of a find of these seminal constituents in the female victim. Blood and saliva samples are to be taken as described earlier from any consensual partner having sex with the victim within 72 hours of the assault.

Another significant indicator of recent sexual activity is p30. At appropriate concentration levels, this protein usually is not found in the vaginal cavity beyond 8 hours following intercourse.[6]

REVIEW QUESTIONS

1. Karl Landsteiner discovered that blood can be classified by its _____.

2. No two individuals, except for identical twins, can be expected to have the same combination of blood types or antigens. (True, False)

3. _____ is the fluid portion of unclotted blood.

4. The liquid that separates from the blood when a clot is formed is called the _____.

5. _____ transport oxygen from the lungs to the body tissues and carry carbon dioxide back to the lungs.

6. On the surface of the red blood cells are chemical substances called _____. It is these substances that impart blood-type characteristics to the cells.

7. Type A individuals have _____ antigens located on the surface of their red blood cells.

8. Type O persons have (both, neither) A and B antigens on their cells.

9. It is the presence or absence of the _____ and _____ antigens on the red blood cells that determines a person's blood type in the A-B-O system.

---

[5]Anne Davies and Elizabeth Wilson, "The Persistence of Seminal Constituents in the Human Vagina," *Forensic Science,* 3 (1974), 45.

[6]N. A. Stubbings and P. J. Newall, "An Evaluation of Gamma-Glutamyl Transpeptidase (GGT) and p30 Determinations for the Identification of Semen on Postcoital Vaginal Swabs," *Journal of Forensic Sciences,* 30 (1985), 604.

10. The D antigen is also known as the _____ antigen.

11. Serum contains proteins known as _____, which destroy or inactivate antigens.

12. An antibody will react with (any, only a specific) antigen.

13. Agglutination describes the clumping together of red blood cells by the action of an antibody. (True, False)

14. Type B blood contains _____ antigens and anti-_____ antibodies.

15. Type AB blood has (both, neither) anti-A (and, nor) anti-B.

16. A drug-protein complex can be injected into an animal to cause the formation of specific _____ for that drug.

17. The term _____ describes the study of antigen–antibody reactions.

18. Type AB blood will (be, not be) agglutinated by both anti-A and anti-B serum.

19. Type B red blood cells will agglutinate when added to type (A, B) blood.

20. Type A cells will agglutinate when added to type (AB, O) blood.

21. An immunological assay technique currently being used to detect the presence of minute quantities of drugs in blood and urine is _____.

22. The distribution of type A blood in the United States is approximately (42, 15) percent.

23. The distribution of type AB blood in the United States is approximately (12, 3) percent.

24. (All, Most) blood hemoglobin has peroxidase-like activity.

25. For many years, the most commonly used color test for identifying blood was the _____ color test.

26. _____ reagent reacts with blood, causing it to luminesce.

27. Blood can be characterized as being of human origin by the _____ test.

28. Antigens and antibodies (can, cannot) be induced to move toward one another under the influence of an electrical field.

29. The _____ technique is the current method of choice for the indirect typing of bloodstains.

30. Approximately _____ percent of the population are classified as secretors.

31. _____ are proteins that have important functions in regulating many of the body's chemical reactions.

32. Enzymes that exist in different forms in a population are (polymorphic, monomorphic).

33. Protein and enzyme components can be separated and typed by the technique of _____.

34. The shape of bloodstains may provide useful information regarding the direction, dropping distance, and angle of impact of splattered blood. (True, False)

35. Small amounts of blood are best submitted to a crime laboratory in a (wet, dry) condition.

36. Airtight packages make the best containers for blood-containing evidence. (True, False)

37. The basic unit of heredity is the _____.

38. Genes are positioned on threadlike bodies called _____.

39. All cells in the human body, except the reproductive cells, have _____ pairs of chromosomes.

40. The sex of an offspring is always determined by the (mother, father).

41. Genes that influence a given characteristic and are aligned with one another on a chromosome pair are known as _____.

42. When a pair of allelic genes are identical, they are said to be (homozygous, heterozygous).

43. A (phenotype, genotype) is an observable characteristic of an individual.

44. The combination of genes present in the cells of an individual is called the _____.

45. A gene (will, will not) appear in a child when it is present in one of the parents.

46. A type B person may have the genotype _____ or the genotype _____.

47. A type AB mother and type AB father will have offspring of what possible genotypes?

48. A type AB mother and type AB father will have offspring of what possible phenotypes?

49. The _____ color test is used to locate and characterize seminal stains.

50. Semen is unequivocally identified by the microscopic appearance of _____.

51. Males having a low sperm count suffer from a condition known as (oligospermia, aspermia).

52. The protein _____ is unique to seminal plasma.

53. The blood type of a male secretor (can, cannot) be determined from a seminal stain.
54. If the typing of seminal stains is desired by an investigator, (saliva, urine) from the suspect and victim must be submitted to the laboratory.
55. Seminal constituents may remain in the vagina for up to six days after intercourse. (True, False)

FURTHER REFERENCES

Baechtel, F. S., "The Identification and Individualization of Semen Stains," in *Forensic Science Handbook,* Vol. 2, R. Saferstein, ed. Englewood Cliffs, N.J.: Prentice Hall, 1988.

Baird, J. B., "The Individuality of Blood and Bloodstains," *The Canadian Society of Forensic Science Journal,* 11 (1978), 83.

Eckert, W. G., and S. H. James, *Interpretation of Bloodstain Evidence at Crime Scenes.* Boca Raton, Fla.: CRC Press, Inc., 1989.

Melvin, Joseph R., Jr. et al., "Paternity Testing," in *Forensic Science Handbook,* Vol. 2, R. Saferstein, ed. Englewood Cliffs, N.J.: Prentice Hall, 1988.

Proceedings of a Forensic Science Symposium on the Analysis of Sexual Assault Evidence. Washington, D.C.: U.S. Government Printing Office, 1984.

Proceedings of the International Symposium on Forensic Immunology. Washington, D.C.: U.S. Government Printing Office, 1987.

Proceedings of the International Symposium on the Forensic Applications of Electrophoresis. Washington, D.C.: U.S. Government Printing Office, 1985.

Sensabaugh, G. F., "Biochemical Markers of Individuality," in *Forensic Science Handbook,* R. Saferstein, ed. Englewood Cliffs, N.J.: Prentice Hall, 1982.

Whitehead, P. H., "A Historical Review of the Characterization of Blood and Secretion Stains in the Forensic Laboratory—Part One: Bloodstains," *Forensic Science Review,* 5 (1993), 35.

Dna: a new forensic science tool

The discovery of **deoxyribonucleic acid,** or DNA, the deciphering of its structure, and the decoding of its genetic information were turning points in our understanding of the underlying concepts of inheritance. Now, with incredible speed, as molecular biologists are unraveling the basic structure of genes, we are able to create new products through genetic engineering and develop diagnostic tools and treatments for genetic disorders. Up until recently, these developments were of seemingly peripheral interest to forensic scientists. All that changed when, in 1985, what started out as a more or less routine investigation into the structure of a human gene led to the discovery that portions of the DNA structure of certain genes are as unique to each individual as fingerprints. Alec Jeffreys and his colleagues at Leicester University, England, who were responsible for these revelations, named the process for isolating and reading these DNA markers "DNA fingerprinting." As researchers uncover new approaches and variations to the original Jeffreys technique, the term **DNA typing** has come to be applied to describe this new technology. This discovery caught the imagination of the forensic science community; for it has long been the ambition of forensic scientists to link with certainty the origin of biological evidence such as blood, semen, hair, or tissue to a single individual. Although conventional testing procedures have gone a long way in narrowing the source of biological materials, individualization remains an elusive goal. Now DNA typing has brought forensic science to the brink of this goal. The technique is still new, but in the few years since its introduction, DNA typing has become part of the routine in many public crime laboratories and has been made available to interested parties through the services of a number of skilled private laboratories. In the United States, courts have overwhelmingly admitted DNA evidence and accepted the reliability of its scientific underpinnings.

WHAT IS DNA?

Inside each of 60 trillion cells in the human body are strands of genetic material called **chromosomes.** Arranged along the chromosomes, like beads on a thread, are nearly 100,000 genes. **The gene is the fundamental unit of heredity. It instructs the body cells to make proteins that determine everything from hair color to our susceptibility to diseases.** Each gene is actually composed of DNA specifically designed to carry out a single body function. Interestingly, although DNA was first discovered in 1868, scientists were slow in understanding and appreciating its fundamental role in inheritance. Painstakingly, researchers developed evidence that DNA was probably the substance by which genetic instructions are passed from one generation to the next. But the major breakthrough in comprehending how DNA works didn't occur until the early 1950s, when two researchers, James Watson and Francis Crick, deduced the structure of DNA. It turns out that DNA is an extraordinary molecule skillfully designed to carry out the task of controlling the genetic traits of all living cells, plant and animal.

Before examining the implications of Watson and Crick's discovery, let's see how DNA is constructed. DNA is a **polymer.** As we learned in Chapter 8 (pp. 226–227), a polymer is a very large molecule made by linking together a series of repeating units. In this case, the units are known as **nucleotides.** A nucleotide is composed of a sugar molecule, a phosphorous-containing group, and a nitrogen-containing molecule called a **base.**

Figure 13–1 shows how nucleotides can be strung together to form a DNA strand. In this figure, *S* designates the sugar component, which is joined together with a phosphate group to form the backbone of the DNA strand. Projecting from the backbone are the bases. The key to understanding how DNA works is to appreciate the fact that there are only four types of bases associated with DNA: adenine, cytosine, guanine, and thymine. To simplify our discussion of DNA, we will designate each of these bases by the first letter of their names. Hence,

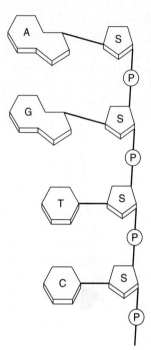

Figure 13–1.
How nucleotides can be linked together to form a DNA strand. *S* designates the sugar component, which is joined with phosphate groups (*P*) to form the backbone of DNA. Projecting from the backbone are four bases: *A*, adenine; *G*, guanine; *T*, thymine; and *C*, cytosine.

A will stand for adenine, *C* will stand for cytosine, *G* will stand for guanine, and *T* will represent thymine. Again, notice in Figure 13–1 how the bases project from the backbone of DNA. Also, although this figure shows a DNA strand of four bases, keep in mind that in theory there is no limit to the length of the DNA strand; in fact, a DNA strand can be composed of a long chain having millions of bases.

The information just discussed was well known to Watson and Crick by the time they set about to detail the structure of DNA. Their efforts led to the discovery that the DNA molecule is actually composed of two DNA strands coiled into a **double helix.** This can be thought of as resembling two wires twisted around one another. As these researchers manipulated scale models of DNA strands, they realized that the only way the bases on each strand could be properly aligned with one another in a double-helix configuration was to place base *A* opposite *T* and *G* opposite *C*. Watson and Crick had solved the puzzle of the double helix and presented the world with a simple but elegant picture of DNA (see Figure 13–2).

The only arrangement possible in the double-helix configuration was the pairing of bases *A* to *T* and *G* to *C*, a concept that has become known as **base pairing.** Although *A-T* and *G-C* pairs are always required, there are no restrictions on how the bases are to be

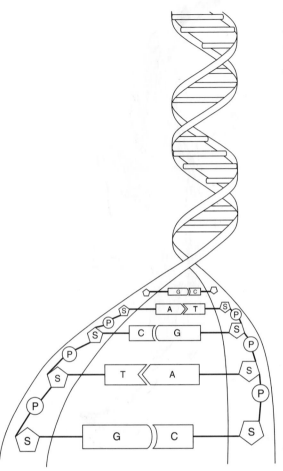

Figure 13–2.
A representation of a DNA double helix. Notice how bases *G* and *C* pair with one another, as do bases *A* and *T*. This is the only arrangement in which two DNA strands can align with one another in a double-helix configuration.

sequenced on a DNA strand. Thus, one can observe the sequences *T-A-T-T* or *G-T-A-A* or *G-T-C-A*. When these sequences are joined together with their opposite number in a double-helix configuration, they pair as follows:

TATT	*GTAA*	*GTCA*
| | | |	| | | |	| | | |
ATAA	*CATT*	*CAGT*

Any base can follow another on a DNA strand, which means that the possible number of different sequence combinations is staggering! Consider that the average human chromosome has DNA containing

100 million base pairs. All the human chromosomes taken together contain about 3 billion base pairs. From these numbers, we can begin to appreciate the diversity of DNA and hence the diversity of living organisms. DNA is like a book of instructions. The alphabet used to create the book is simple enough: *A, T, G,* and *C.* The order in which these letters are arranged defines the role and function of a DNA molecule.

DNA AT WORK

The inheritable traits that are controlled by DNA arise out of its ability to direct the production of complex molecules called **proteins.** Proteins are actually made by linking together a combination of **amino acids.** Although many thousands of proteins are known to exist, they can all be derived from a combination of up to 20 known amino acids. It's the sequence of amino acids in a protein chain that will determine the shape and function of the protein. Let's look at one example: The protein hemoglobin is found in our red blood cells. It's responsible for carrying oxygen to our body cells and for removing carbon dioxide from these cells. One of the four amino acid chains comprising "normal" hemoglobin is shown in Figure 13–3(a). Studies of individuals afflicted with sickle-cell anemia show that this inheritable disorder arises from the presence of "abnormal" hemoglobin in the red blood cells of afflicted persons. An amino acid chain for "abnormal" hemoglobin is shown in Figure 13–3(b). Note that the sole difference between "normal" and "abnormal" or sickle-cell hemoglobin arises from the substitution of one amino acid for another in the protein chain.

The genetic information that determines the amino acid sequence for every protein manufactured in the human body is stored in DNA in a genetic code that relies on the sequence of bases along the DNA strand. The alphabet of DNA is simple—*A, T, G,* and *C*—but the key to deciphering the genetic code is to know that each amino acid is coded by a sequence of **three bases.** Thus, the amino acid alanine is coded by the combination *C-G-T;* the amino acid aspartate is coded by the combination *C-T-A;* and the amino acid phenylalanine is coded by the combination *A-A-A.* With this code in hand, we can now see how the amino acid sequence in a protein chain is determined by the structure of DNA. Consider the DNA segment

-C-G-T-C-T-A-A-A-A-C-G-T-

The triplet code contained within this segment translates into

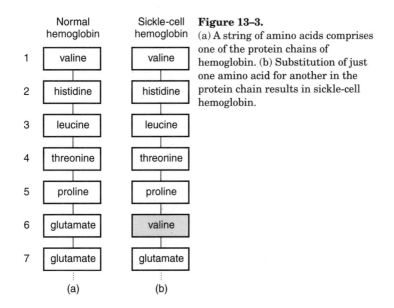

	Normal hemoglobin	Sickle-cell hemoglobin
1	valine	valine
2	histidine	histidine
3	leucine	leucine
4	threonine	threonine
5	proline	proline
6	glutamate	valine
7	glutamate	glutamate
	(a)	(b)

Figure 13–3.
(a) A string of amino acids comprises one of the protein chains of hemoglobin. (b) Substitution of just one amino acid for another in the protein chain results in sickle-cell hemoglobin.

$$[\text{-}C\text{-}G\text{-}T]--[C\text{-}T\text{-}A]--[A\text{-}A\text{-}A]--[C\text{-}G\text{-}T]$$

alanine aspartate phenylalanine alanine

or the protein chain

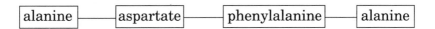

| alanine | aspartate | phenylalanine | alanine |

Interestingly, this code is not restricted to humans. Almost all living cells studied to date use the same genetic code as the language of protein synthesis.[1]

If we go back and look at the difference between "normal" and sickle-cell hemoglobin (see Figure 13–3), we see that the latter is formed by substituting one amino acid (valine) for another (glutamate). Within the DNA segment that codes for the production of normal hemoglobin, the letter sequence is

$$\text{-}[C\text{-}C\text{-}T]\text{-}[G\text{-}A\text{-}G]\text{-}[G\text{-}A\text{-}G]\text{-}$$

proline glutamate glutamate

---

[1]Instructions for assembling proteins are actually carried from DNA to another region of the cell by ribonucleic acid (RNA). It's RNA that is directly involved in the assembly of the protein utilizing the genetic code it received from DNA.

Individuals afflicted with sickle-cell disease carry the sequence

$$-[C\text{-}C\text{-}T]\text{-}[G\text{-}T\text{-}G]\text{-}[G\text{-}A\text{-}G]-$$
proline   valine glutamate

Thus, we see that a single base or letter change (T has been substituted for A in valine) is the underlying cause of sickle-cell anemia, demonstrating the delicate chemical balance between health and disease in the human body.

As scientists unravel the base sequences of DNA, they are obtaining a greater appreciation for the roles that proteins play in the chemistry of life. Already the genes responsible for hemophilia, Duchenne muscular dystrophy, and Huntington's disease have been located. Once scientists have isolated a disease-causing gene, they can determine the protein that the gene has directed the cell to manufacture. By studying these proteins—or the absence of them—scientists will be able to design a treatment for genetic disorders.

Currently, many scientists have given their support to a 15-year, $200-million-a-year project to determine the order of bases on all 23 pairs of human chromosomes (also called the **human genome**). Knowing where on a specific chromosome DNA codes for the production of a particular protein are will be useful for diagnosing and treating genetic diseases. This information will be crucial for understanding the underlying causes of cancer. Also, comparing the human genome with that of other organisms will help us understand the role and implications of evolution.

REPLICATION OF DNA

Once the double-helix structure of DNA was discovered, it became apparent how DNA duplicated itself prior to cell division. The concept of base pairing in DNA suggests the analogy of positive and negative photographic film. Each strand of DNA in the double helix has the same information; one can make a positive print from a negative or a negative from a positive. DNA replication begins with the unwinding of the DNA strands in the double helix. Each strand is then exposed to a collection of free nucleotides. Letter by letter, the double helix is recreated as the nucleotides are assembled in the proper order, as dictated by the principle of base pairing (i.e., A with T and G with C). The result is the emergence of two identical copies of DNA where before there was only one (see Figure 13–4). A cell can now pass on its genetic identity when it divides.

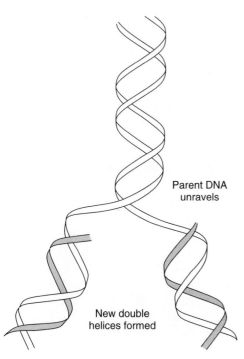

Figure 13–4.
Replication of DNA. The strands of the original DNA molecule are separated, and two new strands are assembled. The new strands are shown with shading.

Parent DNA unravels

New double helices formed

Many enzymes and proteins are involved in the process of unwinding the DNA strands, keeping the two DNA strands apart, and assembling the new DNA strands. For example, DNA **polymerases** are enzymes that assemble a new DNA strand in the proper base sequence determined by the original or parent DNA strand. DNA polymerases also "proofread" the growing DNA double helices for mismatched base pairs, which are replaced with correct bases.

Until recently, the phenomenon of DNA replication appeared to be only of academic interest to forensic scientists interested in DNA for identification purposes. However, this changed when researchers were able to perfect the technology of using DNA polymerases to copy a DNA strand located outside a living cell. This new laboratory technique is known as **PCR** (polymerase chain reaction). Small quantities of DNA or broken pieces of DNA found in crime-scene evidence can be copied with the aid of a DNA polymerase. The copying process can be accomplished in an automated fashion using a DNA Thermal Cycler (see Figure 13–5). Each cycle of the PCR technique results in a doubling of the DNA, as shown in Figure 13–4. Within a matter of a few hours, 30 cycles can multiply DNA a millionfold. Once DNA copies are in hand, they can be analyzed by any of the methods of modern molecular biology. The ability to multiply small bits of DNA opens new and

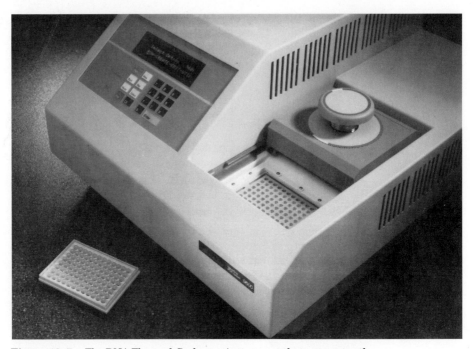

Figure 13–5. The DNA Thermal Cycler, an instrument that automates the rapid and precise temperature changes required to copy a DNA strand. Within a matter of hours, DNA can be multiplied a millionfold. *Courtesy* Perkin-Elmer, Norwalk, Conn.

exciting avenues for forensic scientists to explore. It means that sample size is no longer a limitation in characterizing DNA recovered from crime-scene evidence.

RECOMBINANT DNA: CUTTING AND SPLICING DNA

The relationship between the base letters on a DNA strand and the type of protein specified for manufacture by the sequence of these letters is called the **genetic code.** Once a particular DNA site has been identified as controlling the production of a certain protein, it may be desirable for molecular biologists to take advantage of the natural chemical-producing abilities of the DNA site. This undertaking has given rise to the technology known as **recombinant DNA.**

Recombinant DNA relies on the ability of certain chemicals, known as **restriction enzymes,** to cut DNA into fragments that can later be incorporated into another DNA strand. Restriction enzymes can be thought of as highly specialized scissors that cut a DNA molecule when it recognizes a specific sequence of bases. At present, more than 150 restriction enzymes are commercially available. Thus, molecular biologists have a great deal of flexibility in choosing the portion of a DNA strand they wish to cut out. Once a portion of the DNA strand has been cut out with the aid of a restriction enzyme, the next step in the recombinant DNA process is to insert the isolated DNA segment into a foreign DNA strand (normally, bacterium DNA is selected). Many types of bacteria contain DNA shaped in the form of a circle. A restriction enzyme is used to cut open the circular DNA; then the foreign DNA is spliced in to reform the circle (see Figure 13–6). The

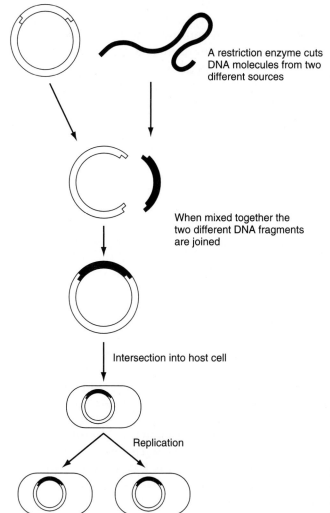

A restriction enzyme cuts
DNA molecules from two
different sources

When mixed together the
two different DNA fragments
are joined

Intersection into host cell

Replication

Figure 13–6.
The joining of DNA from two different
sources via recombinant DNA
technology.

newly fashioned DNA is reintroduced into the bacterial cells. As the bacteria multiply rapidly in their usual fashion, copies of altered DNA are passed on to all descendants.

The commercial implications of recombinant DNA technology are enormous. For example, the gene that produces human growth hormone has been introduced into goldfish and carp, and the gene that produces growth hormone in rainbow trout has been introduced into carp. In each case, the gene-altered fish have grown significantly faster and larger than their natural relatives. If altered bacteria are infused with the DNA segment that makes human insulin, for example, the bacteria will make human insulin. Because bacteria multiply so rapidly, it isn't long before significant amounts of insulin can be recovered and used to treat diabetes. In this manner, other naturally occurring substances can be produced in commercial quantities for the treatment of human ailments. Likewise, plant genetic engineering holds promise for increasing global food production.

DNA TYPING

RESTRICTION FRAGMENT LENGTH POLYMORPHISMS (RFLP)

Geneticists concerned with the technology of recombinant DNA are usually interested in finding and reproducing DNA segments that control protein synthesis. However, not all the letter sequences in DNA code for the production of proteins. Portions of the DNA molecule contain sequences of letters that are repeated numerous times. The origin and significance of these "tandem repeats" is a mystery, but to forensic scientists they offer a means of distinguishing one individual from another through **DNA typing.** Let's examine some DNA strands with regions of repeating base sequences. Figure 13–7 illustrates a portion of a pair of chromosomes. Note that each chromosome is composed of two DNA strands wrapped in a double-helix configuration. On each chromosome there exists a region that contains the repeating base sequence *T-A-G.* Note that there's an important distinction between the two chromosomes; the chromosome on the left has three repeating sequences of *T-A-G,* while the one on the right has two repeating sequences of *T-A-G.* As with any genetic trait, these repeating sequences were inherited from the parents. In this example, one parent contributed the chromosome containing the three repeating sequences, and the other parent passed on the chromosome containing the two repeating sequences.

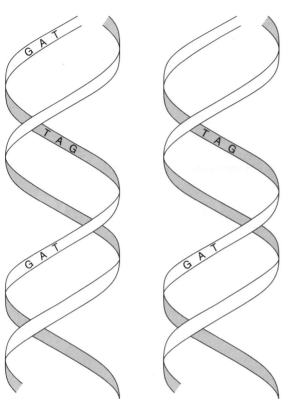

Figure 13–7.
Intertwined strands of DNA representing segments of two chromosomes. Note that the chromosome segment on the left contains three repeating sequences of *T-A-G,* while the chromosome segment on the right has two repeating sequences of *T-A-G.*

The key to understanding DNA typing lies in the knowledge that within the world's population there are numerous possibilities for the number of times a particular sequence of base letters can repeat themselves on a DNA strand. The possibilities become even greater when one deals with two chromosomes, each containing different lengths of repeating sequences. In DNA typing, restriction enzymes are used to cut up chromosomes into hundreds of fragments, some containing repeating sequences from the DNA molecule. In our example, shown in Figure 13–7, the chromosome pair, when cut, will yield two different fragment lengths of *T-A-G.* Length differences associated with DNA strands are called **restriction fragment length polymorphisms (RFLPs).** Once the DNA molecules have been cut up by the restriction enzyme, the resulting fragments must be sorted out. This is accomplished by separating the fragments by electrophoresis (pp. 146–147). DNA from various sources, cut up by restriction enzymes, are placed in separate lanes on an electrophoretic gel and subjected to an electric field. During the electrophoretic process, the DNA fragments will migrate across a gel-coated plate. The smaller DNA fragments will move at a faster rate along the plate than will the larger fragments. Once the electrophoresis process is completed, the double-stranded fragments of DNA are chemically treated so that the strands separate from each other. The fragments are then transferred to a nylon membrane in much the same way as one would transfer an ink line onto a blotter. This transfer process is called **Southern blotting,** named after its developer, Edward Southern. In order to visualize the separated RFLPs, the nylon sheet is treated with radioactively labeled probes containing a base sequence complementary to the RFLPs being identified (a process called **hybridization**). In our example, we aim to identify RFLPs composed of a repeating string of letters spelling *T-A-G.* Hence, the appropriate probes would have the complementary letter sequence, *A-T-C,* as shown in the following diagram, so that the probes can specifically bind to the desired RFLP. (Note: The asterisk designates a radioactive label.)

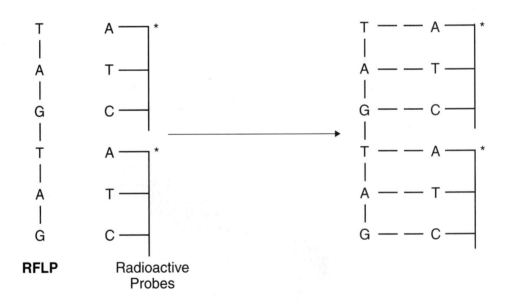

RFLP   Radioactive
                  Probes

Next, the nylon sheet is placed against X-ray film and exposed for several days. The radioactive decay products strike the film. When the film is processed, bands appear where the radioactive probes stuck to the fragments on the nylon sheet. The length of each fragment is determined by running known DNA fragment lengths alongside the test specimens and comparing the distances they migrated across the plate. The entire DNA typing process is depicted in Figure 13–8.

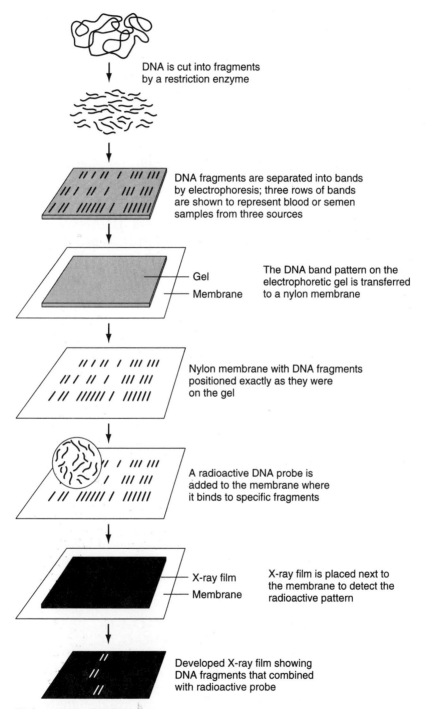

Figure 13–8.   The DNA typing process.

A typical DNA fragment pattern will show two bands (one RFLP from each chromosome). When comparing the DNA fragment patterns of two or more specimens, one merely looks for a match between the band sets. For example, in Figure 13–9, DNA extracted from a crime-scene semen stain matches the DNA recovered from the suspect's whole blood. The DNA pattern obtained from the victim's blood was completely different from that of the suspect. Although only a limited number of people in a population would have the same DNA fragment pattern as the suspect, this test in itself cannot be used to individualize the stain to the suspect. But by using additional DNA probes, each of which recognizes different repeating DNA segments (other than *T-A-G*), a high degree of discrimination or even near individualization can be achieved. For example, if each probe selected yielded a DNA type having a frequency of occurrence of one in a hundred in a population, then four different probes would have a combined frequency of one in a hundred million (1/100 × 1/100 × 1/100 × 1/100).

POLYMERASE CHAIN REACTION (PCR)

While RFLP DNA typing has gained wide acceptance in the forensic science community, a second technique, polymerase chain reaction (PCR), has emerged as a viable DNA typing technique. PCR offers the possibility of increased sensitivity, as little as one-billionth of a gram of DNA is required for analysis. This is fifty times less than what is normally required for RFLP analysis. Consequently, PCR can characterize DNA extracted from small quantities of blood, semen, saliva, and hair. Also, PCR can yield useful information from degraded DNA samples that often fail RFLP analysis.

PCR is the outgrowth of knowledge gained from an understanding of how DNA strands naturally replicate within a cell. The most important feature of PCR is knowing that an enzyme called *DNA polymerase* can be directed to synthesize a specific region of DNA. In a relatively straightforward manner, PCR can be used to repeatedly duplicate or amplify a strand of DNA many millions of times. As an example, let's consider a segment of DNA that we want to duplicate by PCR:

*-G-T-C-T-C-C-T-T-**C-C-A-G**-*
*-**C-A-G-A**-G-G-A-A-G-G-T-C-*

In order to perform PCR on this DNA segment, short sequences of DNA on each side of the region of interest must be identified. In the example shown above, the short sequences are designated by boldface

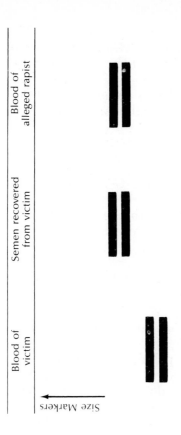

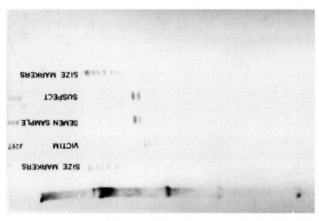

Figure 13–9. The DNA pattern extracted from a crime-scene semen stain matches the DNA recovered from the suspect's whole blood. *Courtesy Lifecodes Corp., Elmsford, N.Y.*

417

letters in the DNA segment. These short DNA segments must be available in a pure form known as a **primer** if the PCR technique is going to work.

The first step in the PCR process is to heat the DNA strands to about 94°C. At this temperature, the double-stranded DNA molecules separate completely:

-G-T-C-T-C-C-T-T-C-C-A-G-

-C-A-G-A-G-G-A-A-G-G-T-C-

The second step is to add the primers to the separated strands and allow the primers to combine or hybridize with the strands by lowering the test-tube temperature.

-G-T-C-T-C-C-T-T-C-C-A-G-
C-A-G-A

C-C-A-G
-C-A-G-A-G-G-A-A-G-G-T-C-

The third step is to add the DNA polymerase and a mixture of free nucleotides (*G,A,T,C*) to the separated strands. The polymerase enzyme directs the rebuilding of a double-stranded DNA molecule, extending the primers by adding the appropriate bases, one at a time, resulting in the production of two complete pairs of double-stranded DNA segments.

-G-T-C-T-C-C-T-T-C-C-A-G-
C-A-G-A-G-G-A-A-G-G-T-C-

-G-T-C-T-C-C-T-T-C-C-A-G
-C-A-G-A-G-G-A-A-G-G-T-C-

This completes the first cycle of the PCR technique, and the outcome is a doubling of the number of DNA strands—that is, from one to two. The cycle of heating, cooling, and strand rebuilding is then repeated resulting again in a doubling of the DNA strands. Upon completion of the second cycle, four double-stranded DNA molecules will have been created from the original double-stranded DNA sample. Typically, 25 to 30 cycles are carried out to yield over one million copies of the original DNA molecule. Each cycle takes less than two minutes to perform.

From the forensic scientist's viewpoint, PCR offers two distinct advantages. First, it can amplify minute quantities of DNA, thus overcoming the limited sample-size problem often associated with crime-scene evidence. Second, the amplification process of PCR can create a large quantity of DNA for genetic typing purposes. With high numbers of DNA molecules, the technology for performing the DNA typing operation can be greatly simplified when compared, for example, to RFLP.

The first commercial and validated PCR-based genetic marker system available for forensic science work was the HLA DQ alpha system, now called DQA1. The DQA1 gene contains a significant number of variants whose identification had originally proven valuable in the areas of tissue typing for transplantation purposes and in the study of immune system diseases. The current PCR typing system for DQA1 can distinguish 28 DQA1 types that range in frequency of occurrence for the U.S. Caucasian population from approximately 1 percent to 11 percent.

The PCR process for typing DQA1 is illustrated in Figure 13–10. In practice, the analysis for DQA1 types is far less complicated than the previously described RFLP procedure (see Figure 13–8). First, the DNA is extracted from the sample. Primer, DNA polymerase, and free nucleotides (A,T,G,C) are then added to the extract, and the mixture is subjected to heating and cooling cycles in a thermal cycle (see Figure 13–5). Once this amplification process is completed, the DNA sample is added to select areas of a nylon strip. The strip is commercially prepared and affixed with a series of probes that are complementary to DQA1 variants. When the amplified DNA is placed onto the strip, DQA1 genes will hybridize to their complementary probes embedded in the strip. The hybridized DNA is visualized as a blue dot on the strip, and the DQA1 type is readily obtained by reading the pattern of dots on the strip.

The frequency of occurrence of a DQA1 type in a population is far greater than frequencies typically obtained through the RFLP technique, and thus the technique is not as discriminating. However, a second commercial PCR typing kit known as Polymarker (PM) has recently become available. This kit allows a forensic analyst to type five additional genetic markers and when used in combination with DQA1 will typically produce frequency of occurrences in the range of 1/5000. Furthermore, the extraordinary sensitivity of PCR allows forensic analysts to characterize small quantities of DNA that could never be detected by RFLP. For instance, PCR has been applied to the identification of DQA1 types in hair and in saliva residues found on envelopes, stamps, and cigarette butts.

SHORT TANDEM REPEATS (STR)

The latest method of DNA typing, short tandem repeat (STR) analysis, may just prove to be the most useful technique of all. Not only does this process have the potential for a higher discrimination than RFLP

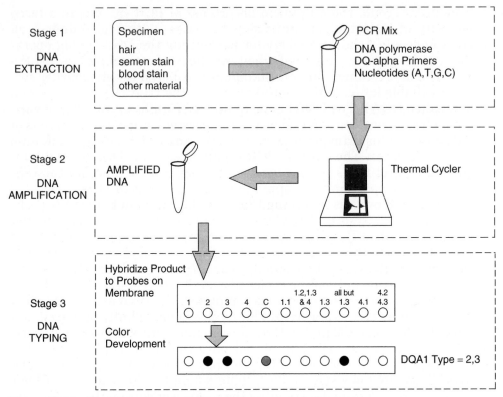

Figure 13–10. The PCR process for typing blood, semen, and other
materials for DQA1 is a three-stage process. The DQA1 type is obtained by
reading the dot pattern on a nylon strip. *Courtesy* Perkin-Elmer, Forster City,
Calif.

DNA typing, but it also reduces the amount of time to obtain results
from a sample and requires a sample size smaller than that needed for
the current RFLP methods.

**STRs are locations (loci) on the chromosome that contain
short sequence elements that repeat themselves within the
DNA molecule.** They serve as helpful markers for identification
because they are found in great abundance throughout the human
genome. What is important to appreciate is that the repeating
sequence is relatively short in length, 3 to 7 bases, and that the
entire strand of an STR is also very short, less than 400 bases in
length. This means that STRs are much less susceptible to degradation and may often be recovered from bodies or stains that have been
subject to extreme decomposition. In order to understand the utility
of STRs in forensic science, let's look at one commonly used STR

known as HUMTH01. This DNA segment contains the repeating sequence *A-A-T-G*. There have been seven HUMTH01 variants identified in the human genome. These variants contain five through eleven repeats of *A-A-T-G*. Figure 13–11 illustrates two such HUMTH01 variants, one containing six repeats and the other containing eight repeats of *A-A-T-G*.

During a forensic examination, HUMTH01 is extracted from biological materials and amplified by PCR in the same manner that was described on pp. 416–419. The ability to copy an STR means that extremely small amounts of the molecule can be detected and analyzed. Once the STRs have been copied or amplified, they are separated on an electrophoretic gel. By examining the distance the STR has migrated on the electrophoretic plate, one can determine the number of *A-A-T-G* repeats that exist in the STR. Every person has two STR types for HUMTH01, each inherited from one parent. Thus, for example, one may find in a semen stain HUMTH01 with six repeats and eight repeats. This combination of HUMTH01 is found in approximately 3.5 percent of the population.

What makes STRs so attractive to forensic scientists is that there are hundreds of different types of STRs found in human genes. The more STRs one can characterize, the smaller will be the percentage of

Figure 13–11. Variants of the short tandem repeat, HUMTH01. The upper DNA strand contains 6 repeats of the sequence AATG; the lower DNA strand contains 8 repeats of the sequence AATG.

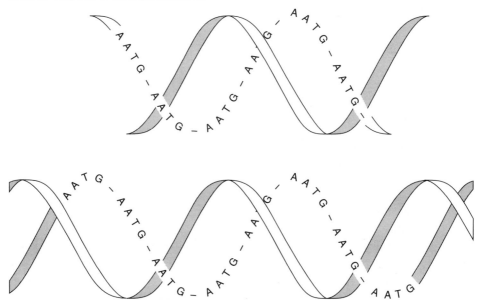

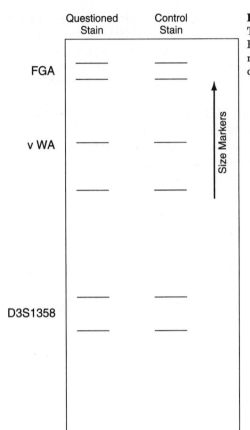

Figure 13–12.
Triplex system containing three loci: FGA, vWA, and D3S1358, indicating a match between the questioned and the control stains.

the population from which these STRs can emanate. This gives rise to the concept of **multiplexing.** Using the technology of PCR, one can simultaneously extract and amplify a combination of different STRs. For example, one system on the commercial market is the STR Blue kit.[2] This kit provides the necessary materials for the coamplification and detection of three STRs—D3S1358, vWA, and FGA **(triplexing).** The design of the system ensures that the size of the STRs does not overlap, thereby allowing each marker to be viewed clearly on an electrophoretic gel (see Figure 13-12). The combination of these STRs typically produces a frequency of occurrence of about 1 in 5000. Used in conjunction with DQA1 and Polymarker, the combination of these methods provides an impressive frequency of occurrence of about 1 in 25,000,000!

---

[2]Perkin Elmer, 850 Lincoln Centre Drive, Foster City, Calif. 94404.

DNA typing, whether it's RFLP or PCR, has become an essential and basic investigative tool in the law enforcement community. The technology has progressed at a rapid rate and in only a few years has surmounted numerous legal challenges to become vital evidence for resolving violent crimes and sex offenses. DNA evidence is impartial, implicating the guilty and exonerating the innocent. Significantly, about one-third of the examinations conducted by the FBI Laboratory have excluded suspects identified by police as the source of DNA evidence collected from the crime scene. In a number of well-publicized cases, DNA evidence has exonerated individuals who have been wrongly convicted and imprisoned for the commission of a crime (see Figure 13–13).

The FBI policy for accepting evidence for DNA testing is contained in Appendix III.

Case Reading
Outrage: The O. J. Simpson Verdict[3]

To distill this case down to its irreducible minimum (and temporarily ignoring all the other evidence pointing inexorably to Simpson's guilt), if your blood is found at the murder scene, as Simpson's was conclusively proved to be by DNA tests, that's really the end of the ball game. There is nothing more to say. (And in this case, not only was Simpson's blood found at the murder scene, but the victims' blood was found inside his car and home.) I mean, to deny guilt when your blood is at the murder scene is the equivalent of a man being caught by his wife *in flagrante* with another woman and saying to her (quoting comedian Richard Pryor), "Who are you going to believe? Me or your lying eyes?"

At the crime scene there were five blood drops leading away from the slain bodies of Nicole Brown Simpson and Ronald Goldman toward the rear alley, four of which were immediately to the *left* of bloody size-12 shoe prints (Simpson's shoe size). This indicated, of course, that the killer had been wounded on the left side of his body. And the morning after the murders, Simpson was observed by the police to be wearing a bandage on his left middle finger. When the bandage was removed that afternoon, it was seen that he had a deep cut on the knuckle of the finger.

---

[3]*Source:* Vincent Bugliosi, *OUTRAGE: The Five Reasons Why O. J. Simpson Got Away with Murder.* Copyright © 1996 by Vincent Bugliosi. Reprinted by permission of W. W. Norton & Company, Inc.

DNA Frees Convicted Rapist After 9 Years

By LISA W. FODERARO
Special to The New York Times

GREEN HAVEN, N.Y., July 31 — Charles Dabbs was convicted in 1984 of raping a distant cousin two years earlier in a darkened alley — the outcome of a trial that basically pitted his word against hers for lack of any conclusive scientific evidence.

Since then, he has maintained he was innocent from the cell where he is imprisoned here in Dutchess County.

Today, a State Supreme Court judge in White Plains overturned Mr. Dabbs's conviction, basing his decision on recent DNA tests that Mr. Dabbs struggled for two years to have performed. The tests showed that the semen on the victim's underpants was someone else's.

'A Case Long Remembered'

The reversal is one of the first times that DNA analysis was applied retroactively to evidence in a case that predated the introduction of genetic testing in criminal trials. "Perhaps," Judge Nicholas Colabella said, "this will be a case long remembered for the proposition that courts must be ever-vigilant to correct a wrong, if there is a wrong here."

But Mr. Dabbs, who is to be released from prison on Thursday, is not concerned about making legal history so much as he is about removing from his life the label of rapist. The 36-year-old man admits to a variety of crimes over his lifetime from burglary to drug dealing but rape, he said, is not one of them.

"I've been raised by females — aunts and grandmothers," Mr. Dabbs said in an interview at the prison last week. "We were always taught to have a little more respect for women. What hurt me the most is that I had an aunt who died last week, and she hasn't spoken to me in nine years. Her last words in 1982 were, 'How could you do that?'"

The Westchester District Attorney's office chose not to oppose Mr. Dabbs's lawyer's motion to throw out the conviction. But even with the dismissal of the conviction, the indictment against Mr. Dabbs stands, and now prosecutors must decide whether to retry him. In court today, an assistant district attorney, Joseph M. Latino, told the judge about the interview that prosecutors had on Tuesday with the victim. "Despite the results of the tests, she is still adamant that Mr. Dabbs is the rapist," Mr. Latino said. "She said, 'I know he did it; he knows he did it,' and basically that's her position."

Legal experts predicted that the Dabbs case would give impetus to other requests to have DNA tests applied to old evidence.

"All over the land, prosecutors are going to wake up with agonizing headaches," said James E. Starrs, a professor of forensic science at George Washington University. "There is a gathering storm to loose the jailhouse doors by having evidence re-tested with DNA analysis. It's a last-ditch stand. It can't hurt since they're already convicted."

In an interview last week, Mr. Dabbs told how he ended up in the maximum-security state prison here. It began on Sept. 13, 1982, when the police came to a friend's home where he was eating breakfast to arrest him. An outstanding charge from 1980 for selling drugs, combined with the first-degree rape charge, landed him in jail where he spent a year and a half awaiting the two trials. He was eventually convicted of both crimes and given two consecutive sentences totaling 18½ to 25 years. Without the rape conviction, he would have been eligible for parole three years ago and released unconditionally last August.

Life as a Crime Spree

At a hearing last Friday, Mr. Dabb's lawyer, Andrew M. Micek, who did not represent him at the rape trial, pointed out some inconsistencies in the victim's testimony. For instance, the victim had testified that she knew her attacker was Mr. Dabbs because of his missing front teeth, Mr. Micek told the judge, but Mr. Dabbs possessed all of his teeth at the time.

Immediately after his conviction, Mr. Dabbs began his campaign to clear his name. "I always thought guys who raped were sick," he said. "You can buy sex. Why take it?"

But Mr. Dabbs talks candidly about his life as a long crime spree.

Born in Brooklyn and raised by his grandparents in Peekskill, N.Y., he said he was first arrested at age 9 for starting a fire. He was kicked out of the

A lab uses rape evidence saved for 9 years.

seventh grade, he said, for assaulting the principal. By age 14, he had tried heroin, he said, and throughout his 20's he robbed and burglarized stores, drug dealers and gambling houses to support a drug habit. In the mid-1970's, he served two years in prison on a drug-sale charge.

Along the way, he said, he gave up drugs and started to pull his life together, receiving a high school equivalency diploma and briefly attending college, Mr. Dabbs said. But eventually, he would succumb to drugs and crime.

Long Legal Crusade

But the rape charge seems to have provided Mr. Dabbs's life with a focus. He said he had passed up many opportunities to use drugs in prison. Instead, he has spent hours in the law library, engineering an unsuccessful appeal in 1988 before the Appellate Division of State Supreme Court in Brooklyn and crusading more recently for the DNA tests.

Justice Colabella ordered the tests performed last November. This month, the Lifecodes Corporation in Valhalla, N.Y., said the semen on the underpants, stored by Westchester County in a freezer, did not come from Mr. Dabbs.

Mr. Dabbs first heard about the use of DNA tests in criminal trials in 1987 — the year in which they were first used. Though there have been challenges, the analysis of a suspect's DNA, known as genetic fingerprinting, has become an accepted method of identifying the source of blood, semen, hair and skin. He wrote to the Federal Bureau of Investigation and Lifecodes for information. He also persuaded a New Jersey-based organization, Centurion Ministries, to help him finance the tests.

Crucial to the outcome was a 1980 decision by Westchester County, unlike most jurisdictions, to save evidence from all criminal trials in a giant freezer — even after all appeals had run out. It turned out that the underpants had been discarded, but the swatch of material with the semen stain was there.

In recent days, Mr. Dabbs has reflected on what nine years behind bars had wrought. "This gave me a chance to regroup," he said. "I think about all the guys I grew up with who are either dead, insane or on crack. With the type of life style I was leading, I could have achieved all of the above."

"It's going to be hard," he continued. "I know there are going to be things I want that I can't have as quickly as I had in the past. I think I've acquired enough discipline in here though. You don't learn too much in here, but the one thing you do learn is patience."

Last week as he awaited the judge's decision, Mr. Dabbs said he was trying not to get ahead of himself. "Not until I step out the door," he said, "will I be confident that this is over."

Figure 13-13. Copyright © 1991 by The New York Times Company. Reprinted by permission.

DNA (deoxyribonucleic acid) is the genetic material found in all human cells that carries the coded messages of heredity unique (with the exception of identical twins) to each individual. DNA, then, is our genetic fingerprint. Each of the approximately 100 trillion cells in a human body contains twenty-three pairs of chromosomes—one of each pair coming from one's father, the other from the mother—which contain DNA molecules. In criminal cases, DNA can be extracted from samples of blood, semen, saliva, skin, or hair follicles found at a crime scene and then compared to DNA drawn from a suspect to determine if there is a "match." DNA testing is a new forensic science, first used in Great Britain in 1985 and in the United States in 1987.

DNA tests on all five blood drops and on three bloodstains found on the rear gate at the crime scene showed that all of this blood belonged to Simpson. Two DNA tests were used, PCR (polymerase chain reaction) and RFLP (restrictive fragment length polymorphism). The PCR test is less precise than the RFLP, but can be conducted on much smaller blood samples as well as samples that have degenerated ("degraded") because of bacteria and/or exposure to the elements. PCR tests were conducted on four out of the five blood drops. Three showed that only one out of 240,000 people had DNA with the markers found in the sample. (A marker is a gene that makes up one portion of the DNA molecule, and the more markers in the sample, the more comparison tests can be conducted, and hence the greater the exclusion of other humans.) The fourth blood drop had markers which one out of 5200 people could have. Simpson was one of these people. The fifth blood drop had sufficient markers for an RFLP test, and showed that only one out of 170 million people had DNA with those markers. Again, Simpson's blood did. The richest sample was on the rear gate, and an RFLP test showed that only one out of 57 *billion* people had those markers. Simpson was one of them. In other words, just on the blood evidence alone, there's only a one out of 57 billion chance that Simpson is innocent. Fifty-seven billion is approximately ten times the current population of the entire world.

Now I realize that Igor in Kiev, Gino in Naples, Colin down Johannesburg way, and Kartac on Pluto might have the same DNA as O. J. Simpson. If you're a skeptic I wouldn't blame you if you checked to see if Igor, Gino, Colin, or Kartac was in Brentwood on the night of the murders, used to beat Nicole within an inch of her life, had blood all over his car, driveway, and home on the night of the murders, had no alibi, and, if charged with the murders, would refuse to take the witness stand to defend himself. Who knows—maybe Simpson isn't the murderer after all. Maybe Igor or one of the others is. You should definitely check this out. And while you're checking it out, someone should be checking you into the nearest mental ward.

To elaborate on the irreducible minimum mentioned earlier, there are only three possible explanations other than guilt for one's blood being found at the murder scene, and all three are preposterous on their face. One is that Simpson left his blood there on an earlier occasion. When Simpson was interrogated by LAPD detectives on the afternoon after these murders, he said he had not cut himself the last time he was at the Bundy address a week earlier. But even without that, how can one believe that on some prior occasion Simpson bled, not just on the Bundy premises, but at the precise point on the premises where the murders occurred? In fact, so far-fetched is this possibility that even the defense attorneys, whose stock-in-trade during the trial was absurdity, never proffered it to the jury.

And here, not only was Simpson's blood found at the murder scene, but there were the four drops of Simpson's blood found just to the left of the killer's bloody shoe prints leaving the murder scene. If there is someone who isn't satisfied even by this, I would suggest that this book is perhaps not for you, that you think about pursuing more appropriate intellectual pursuits, such as comic strips. When I was a kid, one of my favorites was *Mandrake the Magician*. You might check to see if Mandrake is still doing his thing.

The second possibility is that Simpson cut himself while killing Ron Goldman and Nicole Brown in self-defense—that is, either Ron or Nicole or both together unleashed a deadly assault on Simpson, and he either took out a knife he had on his own person or wrested Ron's or Nicole's knife away, and stabbed the two of them to death. This, of course, is just too insane to talk about. Again, even the defense attorneys, who apparently possess the gonads of ten thousand elephants, never suggested this possibility. It should be added parenthetically that if such a situation had occurred, Simpson wouldn't have had any reason to worry, since self-defense is a justifiable homicide, a complete defense to murder.

The third and final possibility is that the LAPD detectives planted Simpson's blood not just at the murder scene but to the left of the bloody shoe prints leaving the scene. This is not as insane a proposition as the first two, but only because there are degrees of everything in life. It is still an insane possibility, and if any reader is silly enough to believe that the LAPD detectives decided to frame someone they believed to be innocent of these murders (Simpson) and actually planted his blood all over the murder scene (and, of course, planted the victims' blood in Simpson's car and home), again, this book is probably not for that reader. This book is for people who are very angry that a brutal murderer is among us—with a smile on his face, no less—and want to know how this terrible miscarriage of justice could have occurred. . . .

Let me point out to those who believe in the "possible" existence of either of the aforementioned three innocent possibilities for Simpson's blood being found at the murder scene, that the prosecution only has the burden of proving guilt beyond a *reasonable* doubt, not beyond all possible doubt. So it isn't necessary to have all possible doubts of guilt removed from one's mind in order to reach a conclusion of guilt. Only reasonable doubts of guilt have to be removed. Of course, in this case, *no* doubt remains of Simpson's guilt. . . .

There perhaps is no better example of the phenomenon of people seeing what they expect to see working to the prosecution's very definite disadvantage than the situation with one of the defense's expert witnesses, Dr. Henry Lee. Lee, director of the Connecticut State Forensic Science Laboratory, is reputed to be the preeminent dean of American forensic scientists, the "top forensic sleuth," as it were. But I think we all know by now how suspect reputations can be, and if Lee's testimony in the Simpson case is any indication at all of his abilities, he is nothing short of incompetent. At best, he's an example of how Mark Twain once described an expert: "Just some guy from out of town." The problem is that the jury couldn't see through the bloated reputation of Dr. Lee, and the prosecution, in its summation, never exposed Lee so the jurors could see the emperor without his clothing on.

There were two particular areas in which Lee's testimony, if believed by the jury, was very damaging to the prosecution. One, he testified that he found four small bloodstains on a paper bindle enclosing seven cotton swatches containing blood removed from one of the blood drops (Item 47) to the left of a bloody shoe print leaving the Bundy murder scene (later identified as Simpson's blood by DNA testing). Lee couldn't figure out how the blood could have leaked onto the paper when the swatches had been left out to dry overnight prior to their being packaged. The fact that there was no assurance the blood on all seven swatches had dried completely by the time they were wrapped, or that the subsequently frozen swatches did not leak the blood later in the summer when they were thawed out for DNA testing, or that there was not some other innocent explanation (in virtually every case there are questions, the innocent answers to which are simply never learned) did not deter Lee from saying there was "something wrong," a term that resonated with the jurors during their deliberations. The implication the defense sought to convey, of course, was that the answer lay in evil LAPD conspirators who crept into the LAPD lab in the middle of the night and planted and tampered with the blood evidence.

Lee also testified that he found three key "imprints" on the terracotta walkway at the crime scene which he himself photographed when he went to the scene on June 25, 1994. They did not match the many size-12 Bruno Magli bloody shoe prints at the scene which the prosecutors said belonged to Simpson. One was definitely a shoe print, he testified, one was a "parallel line imprint," and the other he simply called an "imprint." The latter two "could be" shoe prints, he said, raising the inference of a second assailant. This, of course, challenged the prosecution's position that Simpson was the lone killer, and hence challenged their conception of the entire case against him.

Lee also found bloody "parallel line imprint" patterns on the envelope found at the murder scene containing the glasses belonging to Nicole's mother which she had left at the Mezzaluna restaurant earlier in the evening and which Ron Goldman was returning when he was murdered, on a small, triangular piece of paper near the bodies, and on Ron Goldman's jeans. Lee testified that all of these imprints could possibly be partial shoe prints, and since he concluded they were not from the Bruno Maglis or Ron Goldman's shoes, the defense suggested they came from the shoe of the second assailant.

But William Bodziak, the FBI's senior expert on shoe prints, and the former chairman of the footwear and tire section of the International Association for Identification, later debunked all of Lee's conclusions. Bodziak told me he went back to the Bundy crime scene with copies of photographs Lee had taken on June 25 to examine the shoe print and the other two imprints on the walkway which Lee said "could be" shoe prints. What he found was astonishing. With blown-up color photographs, he pointed out to the jury that one of the imprints (the parallel line one) on the walkway Lee had photographed and testified to was actually tool (trowel) marks made by the workers in the laying of the cement years earlier, and the other imprint was a shoe print from one of these workers which was a permanent indentation in the concrete (ridges, depressions) that Bodziak felt with his own hands.

As to the bloody "parallel line imprint" patterns on the envelope, paper, and jeans Lee had suggested could possibly have come from the shoes of a second assailant, Bodziak said that none of them were shoe prints. The parallel line imprints on the right leg of Ron Goldman's blue jeans were too erratic to be shoe prints and also had no borders representing the edge of any heel or sole. They appeared to be consistent with having been made by a swiping or brushing motion against the jeans by a sleeve from Goldman's long-sleeved shirt, which was thick and roughly textured. Bodziak testified that he found a "striking similarity between the ribbed design on the shirt [taken from test impressions]" and the bloody imprint on the shirt. (FBI special agent Douglas Deedrick, an expert on fiber evidence, had previously testified that the bloody imprint on the jeans appeared to have come from fiber such as that on Goldman's shirt.) As to the small ("half the size of one's thumb") bloody imprint on the envelope, it too was not a part of a shoe print, again having no borders, being too erratic, and the patterns being so fine and small as to be uncharacteristic of any shoe sole or heel Bodziak had ever seen. Bodziak testified that the parallel lines were consistent with a "fabric" pattern, and could have come from the jeans or shirt of Goldman. Bodziak also testified that the bloody imprint on the piece of paper wasn't a shoe print, and even if it had been, it would have had to come from the shoe of a tiny child.

Lee demonstrated further incompetence in the forensic technique he employed to reach his conclusions. He made no test impressions of Ron Goldman's Levi jeans and shirt (although photographs were taken of the small piece of paper, the LAPD criminalists did not collect it). This was shocking to Bodziak. He testified: "You could look at the fabric on my sleeves with a magnifying glass, but because of its three-dimensional quality, you could not determine what the exact pattern would look like in a test impression. It is absolutely essential to make test impressions for comparison purposes. It is the *only* way that you can make a valid comparison."

Lee, stung and wounded by the obvious repudiation of his conclusions by the FBI's shoe print expert (Lee's specialty is not shoe prints), told reporters from his laboratory in Connecticut that although he stuck to his conclusions, "I'm sorry I ever got involved in the Simpson case," and said he would probably resist any defense subpoena to return to Los Angeles to defend himself and his conclusions.

As it turned out, he didn't have to defend or rehabilitate himself. His reputation was enough for the jury, which should have been skeptical of every single one of his conclusions once his shoe print and imprint testimony was proved to be claptrap. The foreperson of the jury, Armanda Cooley, said in the book she coauthored on the case, *Madam Foreman:* "Dr. Henry Lee was a very impressive gentleman. Highly intelligent, *world-renowned.* I had a lot of respect for Dr. Lee." Lee's discredited testimony hadn't lessened his stature in Cooley's mind one iota. Juror Lionel (Lon) Cryer told the *Los Angeles Times* right after the verdict that the jury viewed Lee as "the most credible witness" of all at the trial. Cryer repeated Lee's statement that "there was something wrong," saying the jury took these words back to the jury room with them. "Dr. Lee had a lot of impact on a lot of people," he added.

THE COMBINED DNA INDEX SYSTEM

Perhaps the most significant investigative tool to emanate from a DNA typing program will allow crime laboratories to compare DNA types recovered from crime-scene evidence to those of convicted sex offenders and other criminals. This capability will be of tremendous value to investigators in cases in which the police have not been able to identify a suspect. Over 40 states have legislatively mandated the collection of DNA samples from convicted offenders and the establishment of DNA databases for law enforcement purposes. The federal DNA Identification Act of 1994 provides $40 million for a five-year program for state and local forensic laboratories. The act also authorizes the FBI to create a national DNA Identification Index for law enforcement purposes. This national system, known as the Combined DNA Index System (CODIS), allows forensic laboratories to store and match DNA records from convicted offenders and crime-scene evidence. The FBI Laboratory is now in the process of taking these state databases and molding them into a national computerized network. This computerized system will facilitate the exchange of DNA typing data between police agencies in the investigation of sexual assaults and other violent crimes. The CODIS concept has already had a significant impact on police investigations in various states as exemplified by the following.[4]

> **Minnesota:** In 1991, Minnesota was the first state to identify a suspect in the absence of any other investigative information by matching DNA profiles. An unknown suspect's DNA profile obtained from evidence in a rape/murder was matched against Minnesota's database of convicted offenders, then containing 1200 DNA profiles, and the suspect was identified. This case was soon followed by another in which a rape suspect was identified by matching rape evidence to the state's DNA database. Minnesota's Bureau of Criminal Apprehension laboratory in St. Paul also determined that DNA profiles from 18 rape cases established the existence of two unknown suspects. Significantly, two suspects originally arrested in these cases were eliminated through DNA testing. By linking cases which could be associated, police identified two other suspects whose DNA profiles were linked to crime-scene evidence.
>
> **Florida:** A test release of CODIS software linked a November 1991 rape case in Miami, in which police were unable to develop a suspect, with a man convicted in 1993 of sexual assault in Orlando. Several aspects of this case are noteworthy. First, the matching DNA profiles were developed in different DNA laboratories: the Metro-Dade laboratory in Miami and the Florida Department of Law Enforcement (FDLE) laboratory in Tallahassee, thus highlighting the power of

---

[4]*Crime Laboratory Digest*, 20 (1993), 51.

national DNA testing standards to ensure comparability of results between crime laboratories. Second, the suspect's movement from Miami to Orlando demonstrates that serial offenders do not always operate in the same locale. Third, the match was made at the FDLE laboratory in Tallahassee where Florida's state DNA database is administered, thereby demonstrating the power of a statewide DNA database. In another case, the Metro-Dade crime laboratory solved a rape case having no suspect by linking its DNA evidence to another rape in which a suspect was identified; the suspect pled guilty to both rapes. Two other rapes in south Florida were linked through DNA profiles, thereby assisting police by focusing their ongoing investigations.

Virginia: The Virginia Department of Forensic Services identified a suspect in a rape case from January 1993 by matching crime-scene evidence to DNA profiles stored in the state's DNA database. The suspect's DNA sample was taken upon his imprisonment in March 1993, following his conviction in a different rape case. Until August, when the crime laboratory in Richmond matched the DNA samples, police had no suspect. This was the first time a rape charge in Virginia was initiated solely because of investigative information developed by linking DNA profiles stored in the state database. Police found the suspect in the Arlington County jail where he was being held on unrelated drug charges.

REVIEW QUESTIONS _____

1. The fundamental unit of heredity is the _____.
2. Each gene is actually composed of _____, specifically designed to carry out a single body function.
3. A _____ is a very large molecule made by linking together a series of repeating units.
4. A _____ is composed of a sugar molecule, a phosphorous-containing group, and a nitrogen-containing molecule called a base.
5. DNA is actually a very large molecule made by linking together a series of _____ to form a natural polymer.
6. How many different bases are associated with the makeup of DNA?
7. Watson and Crick demonstrated that DNA is composed of two strands coiled into the shape of a _____.

8. The structure of DNA requires the pairing of base *A* to _____ and base *G* to _____.

9. The base sequence *T-G-C-A* can be paired with the base sequence _____ in a double-helix configuration.

10. The inheritable traits that are controlled by DNA arise out of DNA's ability to direct the production of _____.

11. _____ are derived from a combination of up to 20 known amino acids.

12. The production of an amino acid is controlled by a sequence of how many bases on the DNA molecule?

13. Enzymes known as DNA polymerase assemble new DNA strands into a proper base sequence during replication. (True, False)

14. DNA can be copied outside a living cell. (True, False)

15. Recombinant DNA relies on the ability of chemicals known as _____ to cut DNA into fragments.

16. All the letter sequences in DNA code for the production of proteins. (True, False)

17. In DNA typing, restriction enzymes are used to cut out (repeating, random) sequences from the DNA molecule.

18. In DNA typing, restriction enzymes are used to cut out sequences of DNA having different (widths, lengths).

19. DNA fragments can be sorted out according to their size by the technique of _____.

20. In the DNA typing process, DNA fragments are transferred to a nylon membrane by a process called _____ blotting.

21. In the DNA typing process, a radioactively labeled probe is used to visualize the separated DNA fragments. (True, False)

22. The probe complementary to the base sequence *T-A-G* has the letter sequence _____.

23. In DNA typing, a typical DNA pattern will show (two, three) bands.

24. Specimens amenable to DNA typing are blood, semen, body tissues, and hair. (True, False)

25. The current PCR typing system for DQAI can distinguish _____ DQAI types ranging in frequency from 1 percent to 11 percent.

26. Short DNA segments containing repeating sequences of three to seven bases are called _____.

27. The concept of (CODIS, multiplexing) involves the simultaneous detection of more than one DNA marker.

FURTHER REFERENCES

Coleman, H., and E. Swenson, *DNA in the Courtroom: A Trial Watcher's Guide.* Seattle, Wash.: GeneLex Corp., 1994.

DNA Technology in Forensic Science. Washington, D.C.: National Academy Press, 1992.

Evaluation of Forensic DNA Evidence. Washington, D.C.: National Academy Press, 1996.

Inman, K., and N. Rudin, *An Introduction to Forensic DNA Analysis.* Boca Raton, Fla.: CRC Press, Inc., 1997.

Kobilinsky, L., "Deoxyribonucleic Acid Structure and Function—A Review," in *Forensic Science Handbook,* Vol. 3, R. Saferstein, ed. Englewood Cliffs, N.J.: Prentice Hall, 1993.

Sensabaugh, G. F., and E. T. Blake, "DNA Analysis in Biological Evidence: Application of the Polymerase Chain Reaction," in *Forensic Science Handbook,* Vol. 3, R. Saferstein, ed. Englewood Cliffs, N.J.: Prentice Hall, 1993.

Waye, J. S., and R. M. Fourney, "Forensic DNA Typing of Highly Polymorphic VNTR Loci," in *Forensic Science Handbook,* Vol. 3, R. Saferstein, ed. Englewood Cliffs, N.J.: Prentice Hall, 1993.

CASE READINGS

TOMMIE LEE ANDREWS V. STATE OF FLORIDA

Through 1986, some 23 incidents of prowling, breaking into women's homes, and attempted assaults or rapes were committed in Orlando, Florida; police suspected that the perpetrator was the same man in all cases. On February 21, 1987, a 27-year-old woman was assaulted in the early-morning hours while her two children slept in the room next door. The victim was awakened when someone jumped on top of her and held what felt like a straight-edge razor to her neck. The intruder, whom the victim could identify only as a strong, black male, held his hand over her mouth, told her to keep quiet, and threatened to kill her if she saw his face. The victim struggled with the intruder and was cut on her face, neck, legs, and feet. A sleeping bag was wrapped around her head, and she was beaten and raped repeatedly. The police found two fingerprints on the window screen the perpetrator had removed to enter the house. Shortly after the rape, police arranged to have a swab taken from the victim in an effort to recover the perpetrator's semen.

The following month, police received a call reporting a prowler in the southeast section of the city. A responding patrol car saw a car speeding away from the area. The officer followed the car for miles before the suspect sped around a sharp corner and crashed into a utility pole. The driver was identified as Tommie Lee Andrews.

The following morning, a victim of an earlier rape, Nancy Hodge, identified Andrews as her assailant. He was charged with sexual battery, aggravated battery, and armed burglary. Andrews was also charged with the rape of the young mother attacked in February. On November 3, 1987, Andrews stood trial for the February rape.

A crime-scene technician testified that on the morning following the crime, one of the windows of the victim's house was open, and the screen was missing. The victim had testified that this window had been broken previously and was held together with wire from a coat hanger. A screen was found on the ground, and fingerprints were lifted from it. A fingerprint expert testified that two of the prints lifted from the screen matched Tommie Lee Andrews's right index and middle fingers.

A crime laboratory analyst testified that an examination of the victim revealed the presence of semen in the victim's vagina. Serological testing established that the semen originated from a type O secretor. Andrews was determined to be an O secretor. The victim's blood type was that of an O nonsecretor. The analyst concluded that although the semen found in the victim's vagina could have come from Andrews, the possibility existed that the type O reading from the semen could also have come from the victim's blood picked up by the swab. Over objection, the state presented DNA typing evidence linking Andrews to the crime. The DNA test compared Andrews's DNA structure, as found in his blood, with the DNA structure of the victim's blood and the DNA found in the semen on the vaginal swab taken from the victim shortly after the attack. In court, an expert testified that Andrews's DNA matched that of the semen and that the population frequency of Andrews's DNA type was 1 in 10 billion. On November 6, the jury returned a guilty verdict and sentenced Andrews to 22 years. Andrews thus became one of the first individuals in the United States to be convicted of a crime with the help of DNA.

The examination of semen recovered from a vaginal swab collected within an hour of the Hodge rape also revealed a DNA type consistent with that of Andrews. Again, a geneticist was able to testify during the Hodge trial that this DNA type occurred in only 1 in 10 billion. A jury again convicted Andrews. Added to the 22 years he had received in the other rape trial, Andrews was served with a 100-year sentence.

SIGNS OF THE TIMES: DNA STARS
IN VIRGINIA LEGAL FIRMAMENT

There ought to be a Hall of Fame for law enforcement officers. If there were, Detective Joe Horgas of the Arlington County, Virginia, police would be in the front and center rank of those first to be enrolled. Without a flicker of a doubt, but for the law enforcement perspicacity and pluck of Detective Horgas, Timothy Spencer would still be on the Virginia streets burglarizing, raping and murdering in the serial way that had become his signature.

Horgas was assigned to investigate the death of Susan Tucker, 44, who was found in bed, trussed up and nude, in her Arlington home after the 1987 Thanksgiving Day weekend. The condition of her body indicated that Mrs. Tucker had been dead for some few days.

A broken downstairs window evidenced a burglar's entry. The autopsy revealed that Mrs. Tucker had been raped or sodomized or both. Her husband was proved to have been out of the country preparing for a relocation of the family to England. There were no eyewitnesses to the crime or to any peepers, leerers or gawkers in the neighborhood of Mrs. Tucker's residence. Detective Horgas had a detective's Gordian knot to unwind.

Horgas catalogued the various features of the Tucker murder that seemed distinctive. The breaking and the entry, the private home, the lone woman, the tying up of the victim, the rape were all suggestive of a pattern which Horgas recalled from a number of unsolved burglary-rapes committed in Arlington County in 1983. But the 1983 crimes had, unaccountably, ceased late in January 1984.

The 1983 crimes had two additional elements: the offender had been masked and armed with a knife. Horgas decided to chance fate by tacking these ingredients onto the profile he was formulating of the Tucker murderer.

Checking and rechecking proceeded apace with police departments in other areas of Virginia. A Richmond rape-murder in early September 1987 had many of the features of the Tucker killing and the Richmond killer was still at large.

Horgas consulted the F.B.I.'s Violent Criminal Apprehension Program to press his inquiries nationwide employing the profile that he thought best fit the Tucker murderer. But all leads were futile dead ends until Horgas zeroed in on the dates that appeared most hauntingly telltale.

In January 1984, the burglary-rapes ended in Arlington County and in September 1987 they recommenced in Richmond, or so his best

---

Reprinted in part from J. E. Starrs, *The Scientific Sleuthing Newsletter,* 12, no. 3 (1988), 3.

investigative speculations led him to surmise. Where was the culprit during that period? The F.B.I. had already informed Horgas that serial rapists do not spontaneously renounce their marauding ways. So his rapist must have been, somewhere and somehow, disabled from engaging in his favorite nefarious pastime.

Horgas honed in on the records of persons incarcerated in the Virginia state prison system during the three and a half years in question. And eventually but not inevitably, after the fashion of the tireless labors of the F.B.I., which revealed the fingerprint card of the murderer of Martin Luther King Jr., Horgas came upon a person who had been sentenced to prison after an Alexandria burglary conviction in late January 1984. And this confinement followed by scant days the cessation of the unknown burglar-rapist's depredations.

Further checking disclosed that this same convicted burglar had been paroled to a half-way house in Richmond just two weeks before the unsolved Richmond burglary-rape-murder had occurred. As further evidence that the trail was blazing hot, Horgas learned that the parolee in question had been on a weekend furlough from his Richmond half-way house both when the Richmond and the Arlington murders had been perpetrated.

The pattern seemed too compelling to be coincidental and sufficiently probative for the issuance of an Arlington bench warrant for the arrest of Timothy Spencer for burglary, a crime that Spencer had been convicted of committing six times before in his twenty-six years of life.

With the arrest of Spencer in Richmond by Horgas, the case against him as the Tucker murderer took more precise and persuasive shape, indeed by leaps and bounds. Spencer made statements incriminating to himself as he and Horgas travelled the one hundred miles from Richmond to Arlington. (No "Christian burial speech" induced these disclosures.) Scientific analyses of hair, glass, and semen pointed accusingly at Spencer. And the DNA typing evidence set at one in 135 million the chance that a black other than Spencer deposited the biological samples at the Tucker crime scene. The DNA typing became the sword and buckler of the prosecution's case.

On July 15, 1988, a day signed by Cancer but, more appropriately, within the dawning of the age of DNA typing, a jury of eight women and four men convicted Timothy Spencer of rape and capital murder in the killing of Susan Tucker.

CHAPTER

14 FINGERPRINTS

HISTORY OF FINGERPRINTING

Since the beginnings of criminal investigation, police have sought an infallible means of human identification. The first systematic attempt at personal identification was devised and introduced by a French police expert, Alphonse Bertillon, in 1883. The Bertillon system relied on a detailed description *(portrait parlé)* of the subject, combined with full-length and profile photographs and a system of precise body measurements known as **anthropometry.**

The use of anthropometry as a method of identification rested on the premise that the dimensions of the human bone system remained fixed from the age of twenty until death. Skeleton sizes were thought to be so extremely diverse that no two individuals could have exactly the same measurements. Bertillon recommended the routine taking of eleven measurements of the human anatomy. These included height, reach, width of head, and length of the left foot.

For two decades, this system was considered the most accurate method of identification. It was only in the first years of the new century that police began to appreciate and accept a system of identification based on the classification of finger ridge patterns known as **fingerprints.** Today, the fingerprint is the pillar of modern criminal identification.

Evidence exists that the Chinese used the fingerprint to sign legal documents as far back as three thousand years ago. However, whether this practice was performed for ceremonial custom or as a means of personal identity remains a point of conjecture lost to history. In any case, the examples of fingerprinting in ancient history are ambiguous, and the few that do exist certainly did not contribute to the development of fingerprinting techniques as we know them today.

Several years before Bertillon began work on his system, William Herschel, an English civil servant stationed in India, started the practice of requiring natives to sign their contracts with the imprint of a right hand that had been pressed against a stamp pad. The motives for Herschel's requirement remain unclear; it is debatable whether he envisioned fingerprinting as a means of personal identification or just as a method for utilizing the Hindu custom that a trace of bodily contact was more binding than a signature on a contract. In any case, he did not publish anything about his activities until after a Scottish physician, Henry Fauld, working in a hospital in Japan, published his views on the potential application of fingerprinting to personal identification.

In his communication to a specific publication in 1880, Fauld suggested that skin ridge patterns could be important for the identification of criminals. He related an incident about a thief who left his fingerprint on a whitewashed wall, and how in comparing these prints with those of a suspect, he found that they were quite different. A few days later another suspect was found whose fingerprints compared with those on the wall. When confronted with this evidence, the individual confessed to the crime.

Fauld was convinced that fingerprints furnished infallible proof of identification. He even offered to set up at his own expense a fingerprint bureau at Scotland Yard to test the practicality of the method. But his offer was rejected in favor of the Bertillon system. This decision was reversed less than two decades later.

It was the extensive research into fingerprinting conducted by another Englishman, Francis Galton, that provided the needed impetus that made police agencies aware of its potential application. In 1892, Galton published his classic textbook *Finger Prints,* the first book of its kind on the subject. In his book, he discussed the anatomy of fingerprints and suggested methods for recording them. Galton also proposed assigning fingerprints to three pattern types—loops, arches, and whorls. Most importantly, the book convincingly demonstrated that no two prints were identical and that an individual's prints remained unchanged from year to year. At Galton's insistence, the British government adopted fingerprinting as a supplement to the Bertillon system.

The next step in the development of fingerprint technology was the creation of classification systems capable of filing many thousands of prints in a logical and searchable sequence. Dr. Juan Vucetich, an Argentinian police officer fascinated by Galton's work, devised a workable concept in 1891. His classification system has been refined over the years and is still widely used today in most Spanish-speaking countries. In 1897, another classification system was proposed by an Englishman, Sir Edward Richard Henry. Four years later, Henry's system was adopted by Scotland Yard. Today, most English-speaking countries, including the United States, use some version of Henry's classification system to file fingerprints.

Early in the twentieth century, Bertillon's measurement system was beginning to fall into disfavor. It was becoming apparent that its results were highly susceptible to error, particularly when the measurements were taken by persons who were not thoroughly trained. The method was dealt its most severe and notable setback in 1903 when a convict, Will West, arrived in Fort Leavenworth Prison. A routine check of the prison files startlingly revealed that a William West, already in the prison, could not be distinguished from the new prisoner by body measurements or even by photographs. In fact, the two men looked just like twins, and their measurements were practically the same. Subsequently, fingerprints of both prisoners clearly distinguished them.

In the United States, the first systematic and official use of fingerprints for personal identification was adopted by the New York City Civil Service Commission in 1901. Here, the method was used for certifying all civil service applications. Several American police officials received instruction in fingerprint identification at the 1904 World's Fair in St. Louis from representatives of Scotland Yard. After the fair and the Will West incident, fingerprinting began to be used in earnest in all major cities of the United States. In 1924, the fingerprint records of the Bureau of Investigation and Leavenworth Prison were merged to form the nucleus of the identification records of the new Federal Bureau of Investigation. Presently, the FBI has the largest collection of fingerprints in the world. By the beginning of World War I, England and practically all of Europe had adopted fingerprinting as their primary method of identifying criminals.

FUNDAMENTAL PRINCIPLES
OF FINGERPRINTS

*FIRST PRINCIPLE: A FINGERPRINT IS
AN INDIVIDUAL CHARACTERISTIC; NO TWO
FINGERS HAVE YET BEEN FOUND TO POSSESS
IDENTICAL RIDGE CHARACTERISTICS*

The acceptance of fingerprint evidence by the courts has always been predicated on the assumption that no two individuals have identical fingerprints. Early fingerprint experts consistently referred to Galton's calculation, showing the possible existence of 64 billion different fingerprints, to support this contention. Later, researchers questioned the validity of Galton's figures and attempted to devise mathematical models to better approximate this value. However, no matter what mathematical model one refers to, the conclusions are always the same: The probability for the existence of two identical fingerprint patterns in the world's population is extremely small.

Not only is this principle supported by theoretical calculations, but just as importantly, it is verified by the millions upon millions of individuals who have had their prints classified over the past 90 years—no two have ever been found to be identical.

The individuality of a fingerprint is not determined by its general shape or pattern but by a careful study of its **ridge characteristics** (also known as **minutiae**). It is the identity, number, and relative location of characteristics, such as those illustrated in Figure 14–1, that impart individuality to a fingerprint. If two prints are to compare, they

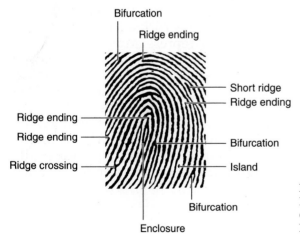

Figure 14–1.
Fingerprint ridge characteristics.
Courtesy Police Science Services,
Niles, Ill.

will have to reveal characteristics that not only are identical but have the same relative location to one another in a print. In a judicial proceeding, a point-by-point comparison must be demonstrated by the expert, using charts similar to the one shown in Figure 14–2, in order to prove the identity of an individual.

If an expert were asked to compare the characteristics of the complete fingerprint, no difficulty would be encountered in completing such an assignment; there are as many as 150 individual ridge characteristics on the average fingerprint. However, in practice the vast majority of the prints recovered at crime scenes are partial impressions, showing only a segment of the entire print. Under these circumstances, the expert has to be prepared to compare only a small number of ridge characteristics from the recovered print to a known recorded print. For years, experts have debated the question of just how many ridge comparisons are necessary before two fingerprints can be identified as being the same. Numbers that range from 8 to 16 have been suggested as being sufficient to meet the criteria of individuality.

Figure 14–2.   A fingerprint exhibit illustrating the matching ridge characteristics between the crime-scene print and an inked impression of one of the suspect's fingers. *Courtesy* New Jersey State Police.

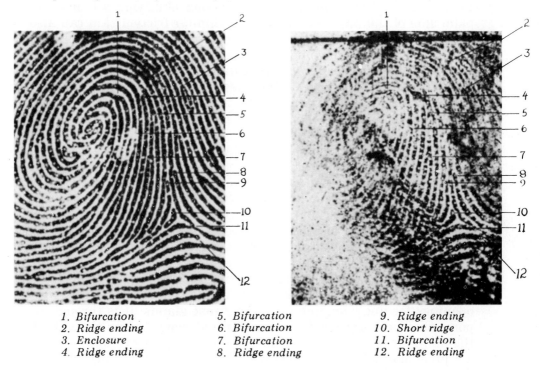

1. *Bifurcation*	5. *Bifurcation*
2. *Ridge ending*	6. *Bifurcation*
3. *Enclosure*	7. *Bifurcation*
4. *Ridge ending*	8. *Ridge ending*

9. *Ridge ending*
10. *Short ridge*
11. *Bifurcation*
12. *Ridge ending*

However, the difficulty that arises in establishing such a minimum is that no comprehensive statistical study has ever been undertaken to determine the frequency of occurrence of different ridge characteristics and their relative locations. Until such a study is undertaken and completed, no meaningful guidelines can be established for defining the uniqueness of a fingerprint.

In 1973, the International Association for Identification, after a three-year study of this question, concluded that "no valid basis exists for requiring a predetermined minimum number of friction ridge characters which must be present in two impressions in order to establish positive identification." Hence, the final determination must be based on the experience and knowledge of the expert, with the understanding that others may profess honest differences of opinion on the uniqueness of a fingerprint if the question of minimal number of ridge characteristics exists.

SECOND PRINCIPLE: A FINGERPRINT WILL REMAIN UNCHANGED DURING AN INDIVIDUAL'S LIFETIME

Fingerprints are a reproduction of friction skin ridges found on the palm side of the fingers and thumbs. Similar friction skin can also be found on the surface of the palms and soles of the feet. Apparently, these skin surfaces have been designed by nature to provide our bodies with a firmer grasp and a resistance to slippage. A visual inspection of friction skin reveals a series of lines corresponding to hills (ridges) and valleys (grooves). It is the shape and form of the skin ridges that one sees as the black lines of an inked fingerprint impression.

Actually, skin is composed of layers of cells. Those nearest the surface make up the outer portion of the skin known as the **epidermis,** and the inner skin is known as the **dermis.** As one looks at a cross section of skin (see Figure 14–3), a boundary of cells separating the epidermis and dermis is noted. It is the shape of this boundary, made up of **dermal papillae,** that determines the form and pattern of the ridges on the surface of the skin. Once the dermal papillae develop in the human fetus, the ridge patterns will remain unchanged throughout life except to enlarge during growth.

Each skin ridge is populated by a single row of pores that are the openings for ducts leading from the sweat glands. It is through these pores that perspiration is discharged and deposited on the surface of the skin. Once the finger touches a surface, perspiration, along with oils that may have been picked up by touching the hairy portions of

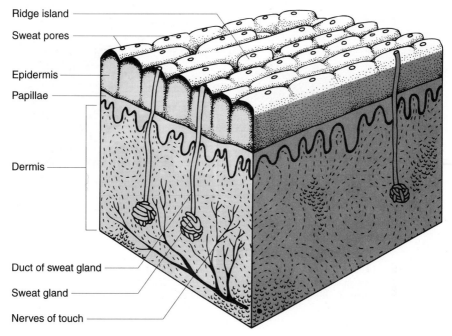

Ridge island
Sweat pores
Epidermis
Papillae
Dermis
Duct of sweat gland
Sweat gland
Nerves of touch

Figure 14–3. Cross section of human skin.

the body, is transferred onto that surface, thereby leaving an impression of the finger's ridge pattern (a fingerprint). Prints deposited in this manner are invisible to the eye and are commonly referred to as **latent** or **hidden fingerprints.**

Although it is impossible to change one's fingerprints, there has been no lack of effort on the part of some criminals to obscure them. If an injury reaches deeply enough into the skin and damages the dermal papillae, a permanent scar will form. However, for this to happen, such a wound would have to penetrate 1 to 2 millimeters beneath the skin's surface. Indeed, efforts at intentionally scarring the skin can only be self-defeating, for it would be totally impossible to obliterate all the ridge characteristics on the hand, and the presence of permanent scars merely provides new characteristics for identification.

Perhaps the most publicized attempt at obliteration was that of the notorious gangster John Dillinger, who tried to destroy his own fingerprints by applying a corrosive acid to them. Prints taken at the morgue after he was shot to death, compared with fingerprints recorded at the time of a previous arrest, proved that his efforts had been fruitless (see Figure 14–4).

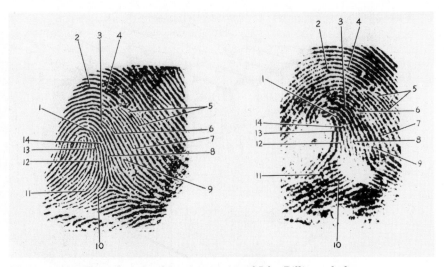

Figure 14–4. The right index finger impression of John Dillinger, before scarification on the left and afterward on the right. Comparison is proved by the 14 matching ridge characteristics. *Courtesy* Institute of Applied Science, New York.

THIRD PRINCIPLE: FINGERPRINTS HAVE GENERAL RIDGE PATTERNS THAT PERMIT THEM TO BE SYSTEMATICALLY CLASSIFIED

All fingerprints are divided into three classes on the basis of their general pattern: **loops, whorls,** and **arches.** Sixty to 65 percent of the population has loops, 30 to 35 percent has whorls, and about 5 percent has arches. These three classes form the basis for all ten-finger classification systems presently in use.

A typical loop pattern is illustrated in Figure 14–5. A loop must have one or more ridges entering from one side of the print, recurving, and exiting from the same side. If the loop opens toward the little finger, it is called an **ulnar loop;** if it opens toward the thumb, it is a

Figure 14–5.
Loop pattern.

radial loop. The pattern area of the loop is surrounded by two diverging ridges known as **type lines.** The ridge point nearest the type-line divergence is known as the **delta.** To many, a fingerprint delta resembles the silt formation that builds up as a river flows into the entrance of a lake—hence, the analogy to the geological formation known as a delta. All loops must have one delta. The **core,** as the name suggests, is the approximate center of the pattern.

Whorls are actually divided into four distinct groups, as shown in Figure 14–6: plain, central pocket loop, double loop, and accidental. All whorl patterns must have type lines and a minimum of two deltas. A plain whorl and a central pocket loop have at least one ridge that makes a complete circuit. This ridge may be in the form of a spiral, oval, or any variant of a circle. If an imaginary line is drawn between the two deltas contained within these two patterns, and if the line touches any one of the spiral ridges, the pattern is a plain whorl. If no such ridge is touched, the pattern is a central pocket loop.

As the name implies, the double loop is made up of two loops combined into one fingerprint. Any print classified as an accidental either contains two or more patterns (not including the plain arch) or is a pattern not covered by other categories. Hence, an accidental may consist of a combination loop and plain whorl or loop and tented arch.

Arches, the least common of the three general patterns, are subdivided into two distinct groups: plain arches and tented arches, shown in Figure 14–7. The plain arch is the simplest of all fingerprint patterns; it is formed by ridges entering from one side of the print and exiting on the opposite side. Generally, these ridges tend to rise in the center of the pattern, forming a wavelike pattern. The tented arch is similar to the plain arch except that instead of rising smoothly at the center, there is a sharp upthrust or spike, or the ridges meet at an angle that is less than 90 degrees.[1] Arches do not have type lines, deltas, or cores.

Figure 14–6. Whorl patterns.

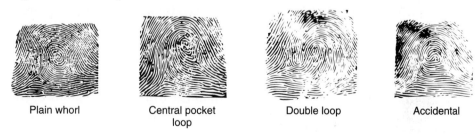

| Plain whorl | Central pocket loop | Double loop | Accidental |

---

[1]A tented arch is also any pattern that resembles a loop but lacks one of the essential requirements for classification as a loop.

Plain   Tented

Figure 14–7. Arch patterns.

With a knowledge of basic fingerprint pattern classes, we may now begin to develop an appreciation for fingerprint classification systems. However, the subject is far more complex than can be described in a textbook of this nature. The student seeking a more detailed treatment of the subject would do well to consult the references cited at the end of the chapter.

CLASSIFICATION OF FINGERPRINTS

The original Henry system, as it was adopted by Scotland Yard in 1901, converted ridge patterns on all ten fingers into a series of letters and numbers arranged in the form of a fraction. However, the system as it was originally designed could only accommodate files of up to 100,000 sets of prints; thus, as collections grew in size, it became necessary to expand the capacity of the classification system. In the United States, the FBI, faced with the problem of filing ever-increasing numbers of prints, expanded its classification capacity by modifying and adding additional extensions to the original Henry system. These modifications are collectively known as the FBI system and are used by most agencies in the United States today.

THE PRIMARY CLASSIFICATION

Although we will not discuss all of the different divisions of the FBI system, a description of just one part, the primary classification, will provide an interesting insight into the process of fingerprint classification.

The primary classification is part of the original Henry system and provides the first classification step in the FBI system. Using this classification alone, all of the fingerprint cards in the world could be divided in 1024 groups. The first step in obtaining the primary classification is to pair up fingers, placing one finger in the numerator of a fraction, the other in the denominator. The fingers are paired in the following sequence:

$$\frac{R.\ Index}{R.\ Thumb} \qquad \frac{R.\ Ring}{R.\ Middle} \qquad \frac{L.\ Thumb}{R.\ Little} \qquad \frac{L.\ Middle}{L.\ Index} \qquad \frac{L.\ Little}{L.\ Ring}$$

The presence or absence of the whorl pattern is the basis for the determination of the primary classification. If a whorl pattern is found on any finger of the first pair, it is assigned a value of 16; on the second pair, a value of 8; on the third pair, a value of 4; on the fourth pair, a value of 2; and on the last pair, a value of 1. Any finger having an arch or loop pattern is assigned a value of 0.

After values for all ten fingers are obtained in this manner, they are totaled, and 1 is added to both the numerator and denominator. The fraction thus obtained is the primary classification. As an example, if the right index and right middle fingers are whorls and all the others are loops, the primary classification is:

$$\frac{16 + 0 + 0 + 0 + 0 + 1}{0 + 8 + 0 + 0 + 0 + 1} = \frac{17}{9}$$

Approximately 25 percent of the population falls into the 1/1 category; that is, all their fingers have either loops or arches.

A fingerprint classification system cannot in itself unequivocally identify an individual; it will merely provide the fingerprint examiner with a number of candidates, all of whom have an indistinguishable set of prints in the system's file. The identification must always be made by a final visual comparison of the questioned and file print's ridge characteristics; only these features can impart individuality to a fingerprint. Although ridge patterns impart class characteristics to the print, it is the type and position of ridge characteristics that give it its individual character.

The Henry and FBI classification systems are ten-finger classification schemes useful only for processing a full set of fingerprints. Unfortunately, it is a rarity when the crime scene yields anything more than a single partial print of a suspect. Under such circumstances, a ten-finger file will be of value only when the investigator has the names of known suspects in hand. In this case, by going through a name index, fingerprint cards of suspects on file can be removed and compared to the recovered crime-scene print. However, some police departments also have established a single-fingerprint collection to aid them in their search for suspects. Here, each fingerprint is filed on a separate card and is independently classified. Unfortunately, this approach becomes much too cumbersome when too many individuals are included in the file. Experience shows that single-print collections are useful only for agencies that restrict their members to active criminals who are most likely to engage in crimes that provide the best chance for recovery of fingerprints—for example, house burglaries and car thefts.

AUTOMATED FINGERPRINT IDENTIFICATION SYSTEMS

The Henry system and its subclassifications have proven to be a cumbersome system for storing, retrieving, and searching for fingerprints, particularly as fingerprint collections enlarge. Nevertheless, until the emergence of fingerprint computer technology, this manual approach was the only viable method for the maintenance of fingerprint collections. Since 1970, technological advances have made possible the classification and retrieval of fingerprints by computers. Cautious at first, the law enforcement community was slow to adopt this new technology. Today, caution and skepticism have given way to enthusiasm as state and local agencies are rapidly procuring automated fingerprint identification systems (AFIS) from a number of commercial sources.

The heart of AFIS technology is the ability of a computer to scan and digitally encode fingerprints so that they can be subject to high-speed computer processing. **The AFIS uses automatic scanning devices that convert the image of a fingerprint into digital minutiae that contain data showing ridges at their points of termination (ridge endings) and the branching of ridges into two ridges (bifurcations).** The relative position and orientation of the minutiae are also determined, allowing the computer to store each fingerprint in the form of a digitally recorded geometric pattern. The computer's search algorithm determines the degree of correlation between the location and relationship of the minutiae for both the search and file prints. In this manner, a computer can make thousands of fingerprint comparisons in a second; for example, a set of ten fingerprints can be searched against a file of 500,000 ten-finger prints in about eight-tenths of a second. During the search for a match, the computer uses a scoring system that assigns prints to each of the criteria set by an operator. When the search is complete, the computer then produces a list of file prints that have the closest correlation to the search prints. All of the selected prints are then examined by a trained fingerprint expert, who will make the final verification on the print's identity. Thus, the AFIS makes no final decisions on the identity of a fingerprint, leaving this function to the eyes of a trained examiner.

The speed and accuracy of ten-finger print processing by AFIS have made possible the search of single latent crime-scene fingerprints against an entire file's print collection. Prior to the AFIS, police were usually restricted to searching crime-scene fingerprints against those of known suspects. The impact of the AFIS on no-suspect cases has been dramatic. Minutes after California's AFIS network received its first assignment, the computer scored a direct hit by identifying an individual who had been terrorizing the city of Los Angeles by committing 15 murders. Police estimate that it would have taken a single technician, manually searching the city's 1.7 million print cards, 67 years to come up with the perpetrator's prints. With the AFIS, the search took approximately 20 minutes. In its first year of operation, San Francisco's AFIS computer conducted 5514 latent fingerprint searches and achieved 1001 identifications—a hit rate of 18 percent. This compares to the previous year's average of 8 percent for manual latent print searches. Considering that the national average for manual latent print search hits is only 1 to 5 percent, AFIS technology is destined to become an essential tool of crime-scene investigators.

As an example of how an AFIS computer operates, one system has been designed to automatically filter out imperfections in a latent print, enhance its image, and create a graphic representation of the fingerprint's ridge endings and bifurcations and their direction. The print will then be computer searched against file prints. The image of the latent print and a matching file print will then be displayed side by side on a high-resolution video monitor. The matching latent and file print are then verified and charted by a fingerprint examiner at a video workstation.

AFIS has brought a fundamental change in the way criminal investigators operate, allowing them to spend less time developing suspect lists and more time investigating the suspects generated by the computer. However, investigators must be cautioned against over-reliance on a computer. Sometimes a latent will not make a hit because of the poor quality of the file print. To avoid these potential problems, investigators must still follow the practice of printing all known suspects in a case and manually searching these prints against the crime-scene prints.

AFIS computers are available from several different suppliers. Each system scans fingerprint images and detects and records information about minutiae (ridge endings and bifurcations); however, they do not all incorporate exactly the same features, coordinate systems, or units of measure to record fingerprint information. These incompatibilities have created problems for law enforcement agencies interested in sharing fingerprint information. To resolve this problem, a new American standard has been created, through the sponsorship of the National Bureau of Standards, to provide a means for exchanging data between different makes of AFIS. This data standard defines four types of records that may be used in the exchange of fingerprint information. By selecting the appropriate method, any AFIS user can effectively exchange data with any other AFIS user.

METHODS OF DETECTING FINGERPRINTS

Through common usage, the term *latent fingerprint* has come to be associated with any fingerprint discovered at a crime scene. Sometimes, however, prints found at the scene of a crime are quite visible to the eye, and the word *latent* is a misnomer. Actually, there are three kinds of crime-scene prints: **Visible prints** are made by fingers touching a surface after the ridges have been in contact with a colored material such as blood, paint, grease, or ink; **plastic prints** are ridge impressions left on a soft material such as putty, wax, soap, or dust; and **true latent** or **invisible prints** are impressions caused by the transfer of body perspiration or oils present on finger ridges to the surface of an object.

Locating visible or plastic prints at the crime scene normally presents little problem to the investigator, because these prints are usually distinct and visible to the eye. Locating latent or invisible prints is obviously a much more difficult task and does require the utilization of techniques that will visualize the print. Although the investigator is presented with a number of alternate methods for visualizing a latent print, the method of choice will depend on the type of surface that is being examined.

Hard and nonabsorbent surfaces (e.g., glass, mirror, tile, and painted wood) require different development procedures from surfaces that are soft and porous (e.g., papers, cardboard, and cloth). Prints on the former are preferably developed by the application of a powder, whereas prints on the latter generally require treatment with a chemical.

Fingerprint powders are commercially available in a variety of compositions and colors. These powders, when applied lightly to a nonabsorbent surface with a camel's-hair or fiberglass brush, will readily adhere to perspiration residues and/or deposits of body oils left on the surface. Experienced examiners find that gray and black powders are adequate for most latent print work; the examiner will select the powder that affords the best color contrast with the surface being dusted. Hence, the gray powder, composed of an aluminum dust, is used on dark-colored surfaces. It is also applied to mirrors and metal surfaces that are polished to a mirrorlike finish, because these surfaces will photograph black. The black powder, composed basically of black carbon or charcoal, is applied to white or light-colored surfaces.

Other types of powders are available for developing latent prints. A magnetic-sensitive powder can be spread over a surface with a magnet in the form of a Magna Brush. Since the Magna Brush hasn't any bristles to come in contact with the surface, there is less chance that the print will be destroyed or damaged. The magnetic-sensitive powder comes in black and gray colors and is especially useful on such items as finished leather and rough plastics, where the minute texture of the surface has a tendency to hold particles of ordinary powder. Fluorescent powders are also used to develop latent fingerprints. These powders will fluoresce under ultraviolet light. By photographing the fluorescence pattern of the developing print under UV light, it's possible to avoid having the color of the surface obscure the print.

Of the several chemical methods used for visualizing latent prints, **iodine fuming** is the oldest. Iodine is a solid crystal that, upon being heated, is transformed into a vapor without passing through a liquid phase; such a transformation is called **sublimation.** Most often, the suspect material is placed in an enclosed cabinet along with iodine crystals (see Figure 14–8). As the crystals are heated, the resultant vapors will fill the chamber and combine with constituents of the latent print to make it visible. The reasons why latent prints are visualized by iodine vapors are not yet fully understood. Many believe that the iodine fumes combine with fatty oils; however, there is also convincing evidence to show that the iodine may actually interact with residual water left on a print from perspiration.[2] Unfortunately, iodine prints are not permanent and begin to fade once the fuming process is stopped. It is necessary, therefore, for the examiner to photograph the prints immediately upon development in order to retain a permanent record. Also, iodine-developed prints can be fixed with a 1 percent solution of starch in water, applied by spraying. The print will turn blue and can be expected to last for several weeks to several months.

Another chemical used for visualizing latent prints is **ninhydrin.** The development of latent prints with ninhydrin is dependent on its chemical reaction to form a purple-blue color with amino acids present in trace amounts in perspiration. Ninhydrin (triketohydrindene

[2]J. Almag, Y. Sasson, and A. Anati, "Chemical Reagents for the Development of Latent Fingerprints II: Controlled Addition of Water Vapor to Iodine Fumes—A Solution to the Aging Problem," *Journal of Forensic Sciences,* 24 (1979), 431.

Figure 14–8.
A heated fuming cabinet. *Courtesy* Sirchie Laboratories, Inc., Raleigh, N.C.

hydrate) is commonly sprayed onto the porous surface from an aerosol can. A solution is prepared by mixing the ninhydrin powder with a suitable solvent, such as acetone or ethyl alcohol; a 0.6 percent solution appears to be effective for most applications. Generally, prints begin to appear within an hour or two after ninhydrin application; however, weaker prints may be visualized after 24 to 48 hours. The development can be hastened if the treated specimen is heated in an oven or on a hotplate at a temperature of 80° to 100°C. The ninhydrin method has developed latent prints on paper as old as 15 years.

Silver nitrate is a third chemical used for visualizing latent prints. After the moisture from perspiration has evaporated, a substantial portion of the latent print residue will consist of common salt (sodium chloride). In the presence of the chemical silver nitrate, the chloride ion of the salt will react to form silver chloride. Although silver chloride is colorless, it can be transformed by ultraviolet light into silver. Silver shows up the latent print as black or reddish-brown in color. Commonly, a 3 percent solution of silver nitrate in water is brushed onto a paper or cardboard object suspected of containing a print. The prints are then developed by being exposed to the light.

For most fingerprint examiners, the chemical method of choice is ninhydrin. Its extreme sensitivity and ease of application have all but eliminated the use of iodine for latent print visualization. However, in those instances in which ninhydrin fails, development with silver nitrate may provide identifiable results. Application of silver nitrate will wash away any traces of fatty oils and proteins from an object's surface; **hence, if one wishes to utilize all of the previously mentioned chemical development methods on the same surface, it is necessary to first fume with iodine, follow this treatment with ninhydrin, and then apply silver nitrate to the object.**

In the past, chemical treatment for fingerprint development was reserved for porous surfaces such as paper and cardboard. However, since 1982, a chemical technique known as **Super Glue® fuming** has gained wide popularity for developing latent prints on nonporous surfaces such as metals, electrical tape, leather, and plastic bags.[3] Super Glue is approximately 98 to 99 percent cyanoacrylate ester, and it's this chemical that actually interacts with and visualizes a latent fingerprint. Cyanoacrylate ester fumes can be created when Super Glue is placed on absorbent cotton treated with sodium hydroxide. The fumes can also be created by heating the glue. The fumes and the evidential object are contained within an enclosed chamber for up to 6 hours. Development occurs when fumes from the glue adhere to the latent print, usually producing a white-appearing latent print. Interestingly, small enclosed areas, such as the interior of an automobile, have been successfully processed for latent prints with fumes from Super Glue. Through the use of a small, handheld wand, cyanoacrylate fuming can now easily be accomplished at a crime scene or in a laboratory setting. The wand is designed to heat a small cartridge containing a mix of cyanoacrylate and a fluorescent dye. Once heated the cyanoacrylate and dye mix will vaporize allowing the operator to direct the fumes onto the suspect area (see Figure 14–9).

One of the most exciting and dynamic areas of research in forensic science today is the application of chemical techniques to the

---

[3]F. G. Kendall and B. W. Rehn, "Rapid Method of Super Glue Fuming Application for the Development of Latent Fingerprints," *Journal of Forensic Sciences,* 28 (1983), 777.

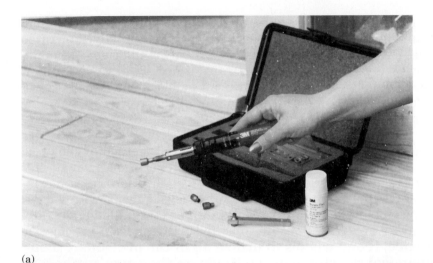

(a)

(b)

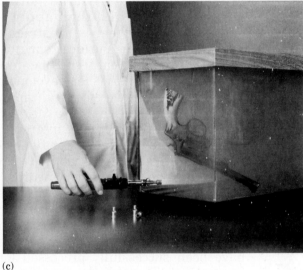

(c)

Figure 14–9.   (a) A handheld fuming wand uses disposable cartridges containing cyanoacrylate and a fluorescent dye. The wand is used to develop prints (b) at the crime scene and (c) within a laboratory. *Courtesy* Lightning Powder Co., Inc., Salem, Oreg.

visualization of latent fingerprints. Changes are occurring very rapidly as researchers are uncovering a variety of processes applicable to the visualization of latent fingerprints. Interestingly, for many years progress in this field was minimal, and fingerprint specialists traditionally relied on the three chemical techniques described earlier— iodine, ninhydrin, and silver nitrate—to reveal the presence of a hidden fingerprint. Then, the finding of Super Glue fuming extended chemical development to prints deposited on nonporous surfaces. The first hint of things to come came with the discovery that latent fingerprints could be visualized by exposure to laser light. This laser method took advantage of the fact that perspiration contains a variety of components that *fluoresce* when illuminated by laser light. Fluorescence is a phenomenon that occurs when a substance absorbs light and re-emits the light in wavelengths longer than the illuminating source. Importantly, substances that emit light or fluoresce are more readily seen with either the naked eye or through photography as compared to non–light-emitting materials. The high sensitivity of fluorescence serves as the underlying principle of many of the new chemical techniques used to visualize latent fingerprints.

The earliest utilization of fluorescence to visualize fingerprints came with the direct illumination of a fingerprint with argon-ion lasers. This laser type was chosen because its blue-green light output induced some of the perspiration components of a fingerprint to fluoresce (see Figure 14–10). The major drawback of this approach was that the perspiration components of a fingerprint are often present in quantities too minute to observe even with the aid of fluorescence. The fingerprint examiner, wearing safety goggles containing optical filters, visually examines the specimen being exposed to the laser light. The filters absorb the laser light and permit the wavelengths at which latent print residues fluoresce to pass through to the eyes of the wearer (see Figure 14–10). The filter also protects the operator against eye damage from scattered or reflected laser light. Likewise, latent print residue producing sufficient fluorescence can be photographed by placing this same filter across the lens of the camera. Examination of

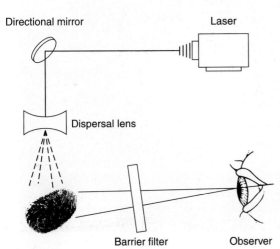

Directional mirror   Laser

Dispersal lens

Barrier filter   Observer

Figure 14–10.
Schematic depicting latent print detection with the aid of a laser. A fingerprint examiner, wearing safety goggles containing optical filters, examines the specimen being exposed to the laser light. The filter absorbs the laser light and permits the wavelengths at which latent print residues fluoresce to pass through to the eyes of the wearer. *Courtesy* Federal Bureau of Investigation, Washington, D.C.

specimens and photography of the fluorescing latent prints are carried out in a darkened room.

The next advancement in latent fingerprint development occurred with the discovery that fingerprints could actually be treated with chemicals that would induce fluorescence when exposed to laser illumination. For example, the application of zinc chloride after ninhydrin treatment or the application of the dye rhodamine 6G after Super Glue fuming caused fluorescence and increased the sensitivity of detection upon exposure to laser illumination (see Figure 14–11). What quickly followed was the discovery of numerous chemical developers for visualizing fingerprints through fluorescence. This knowledge set the stage for the next advance in latent fingerprint development—*the alternate light source.*

With the advent of chemically induced fluorescence, it was no longer necessary to rely on lasers to induce fingerprints to fluoresce through their perspiration residues. High-intensity light sources or "alternate light sources" have proliferated and have all but replaced

Figure 14–11. Evidence can be almost anything. Even a penny found at a crime scene may turn out to be a valuable piece of evidence. A latent print was developed on a penny under laser illumination following Super Glue fuming and the application of rhodamine 6G. *Courtesy* Det. Jeff Thompson, Ocean County, N.J., Sheriff's Dept.

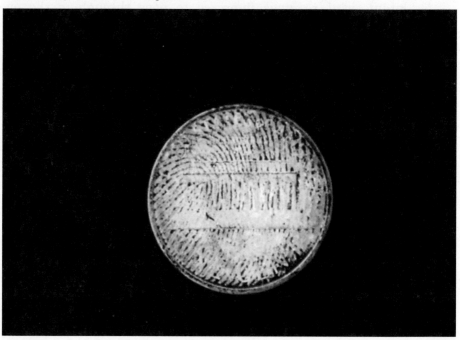

laser lights. High-intensity quartz arc, xenon arc, or indium arc light sources can be focused on a suspect area through a fiber optic cable. This light can be passed through any one of a number of filters giving the user more flexibility in selecting the wavelength of light to be aimed at the latent print. In most cases, these light sources have proven to be as effective as laser light in developing latent prints, and they are commercially available at costs significantly below those of laser illuminators. Furthermore, these light sources are portable and can readily be taken to any crime scene. An alternative light source system is shown in Figure 14–12.

Figure 14–12. An alternate light source system incorporating a high-intensity light source. *Courtesy* Omnichrome, Chino, Calif.

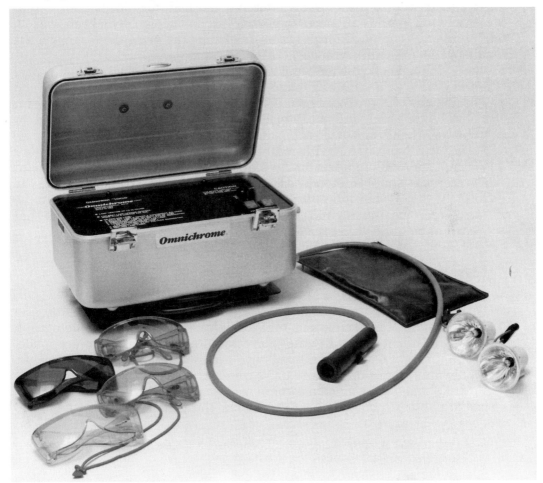

Currently, there are a large number of chemical treatment processes available to the fingerprint examiner (see Color Plate 5 and 6) and the field is still in a constant state of flux. Selection of an appropriate procedure is best left to technicians who have developed their skills through casework experience. Newer chemical processes include a substitute for ninhydrin called DFO (1,8-diaza-fluoren-9-one). This chemical visualizes latent prints on porous materials when exposed to an alternate light source. DFO has been shown to develop 2.5 times more latent prints on paper as compared to ninhydrin. Dye combinations known as RAM, RAY, and MRM 10 when used in conjunction with Super Glue fuming have been shown to be very effective in visualizing latent fingerprints by fluorescence. A silver-based solution known as "physical developer" is now often used in lieu of the conventional silver nitrate method and has also been shown to be a very effective method for developing latent prints on porous articles that may at one time have been wet. A number of chemical formulas useful for latent print development are listed in Appendix V.

The use of powders and chemicals *may* interfere with physical and chemical analysis, particularly in the case of blood, fabrics, and documents. One study has demonstrated that common fingerprint developing agents did not interfere with DNA testing methods used for characterizing bloodstains.[4] Nonetheless, it is recommended that in cases involving items with material adhering to their surfaces and/or items that will require further laboratory examinations, fingerprint processing should not be performed at the crime scene. Rather, the items should be submitted to the laboratory, where they can be processed for fingerprints in conjunction with other examinations that have to be undertaken.

PRESERVATION OF DEVELOPED PRINTS

Once the latent print has been visualized, it must be permanently preserved for future comparison and possible court evidence. A photograph must be taken before any further attempts at preservation are made. Actually, any camera equipped with a close-up lens will do; however, many investigators prefer to use a camera specially designed for fingerprint photography. Such a camera comes equipped with a fixed focus to take photographs on a 1:1 scale when the camera's open eye is held

---

[4]C. Stein et al., "DNA Typing of Fingerprint Reagent Treated Biological Stains," *Journal of Forensic Science,* 41 (1996), 1012.

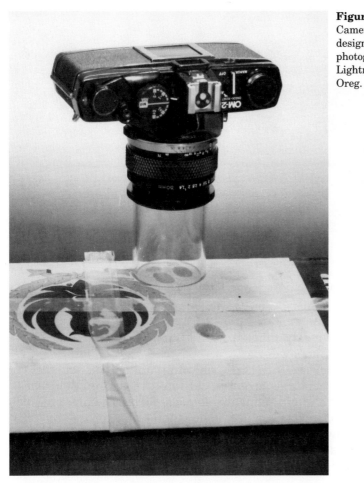

Figure 14–13.
Camera fitted with an adapter
designed to give an approximate 1:1
photograph of a fingerprint. *Courtesy*
Lightning Powder Co., Inc., Salem,
Oreg.

exactly flush against the print's surface (see Figure 14–13). In addition, photographs must be taken to provide an overall view of the print's location with respect to other evidential items at the crime scene.

Once photographs have been secured, one of two procedures is to be followed. If the object is small enough to be transported without destroying the print, it should be preserved in its entirety; the print should be covered with cellophane so it will be protected from damage. On the other hand, prints on large immovable objects that have been developed with a powder can best be preserved by "lifting." The most popular type of lifter is a broad adhesive tape similar to Scotch tape. If the powdered surface is covered with the adhesive side of the tape and pulled up, the powder will be transferred to the tape. Then the

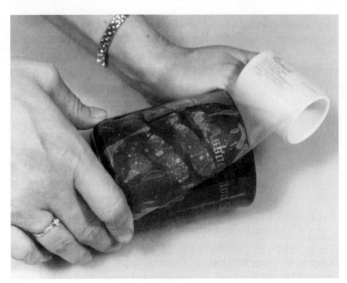

Figure 14–14. "Lifting" a fingerprint. *Courtesy* Lightning Powder
Co., Inc., Salem, Oreg.

tape is placed on a properly labeled card that provides a good background contrast with the powder.

A variation of this procedure is the use of an adhesive-backed clear
plastic sheet that is attached to a colored cardboard backing. Before it is
applied to the print, a celluloid separator is peeled from the plastic sheet
to expose the adhesive lifting surface. The tape is then pressed evenly
and firmly over the powdered print and pulled up (see Figure 14–14). The
sheet containing the adhering powder is now pressed against the cardboard backing to provide a permanent record of the fingerprint.

DIGITAL IMAGING FOR FINGERPRINT ENHANCEMENT

When fingerprints are lifted from a crime scene, they are not usually in
perfect condition, making the analysis that much more difficult. Computers have advanced technology in most fields, and fingerprint identification has not been left behind. With the help of digital-imaging software, fingerprints can now be enhanced for the most accurate and
comprehensive analysis.

Digital imaging is the process in which a picture is converted
into a digital file. The image produced from this digital file is composed of numerous square electronic dots called **pixels.** Images composed of only black and white elements are referred to as gray-scale

images. Each pixel is assigned a number according to its intensity. The gray-scale image is made from the set of numbers to which a pixel may be assigned, ranging from 0 (black) to 255 (white). Once an image is digitally stored, manipulation of the picture is done through computer software that changes the numerical value of each pixel, thus altering the image as directed by the user. **Resolution** reveals the degree of detail that can be seen in an image. It is defined in terms of dimensions, such as 256×256 pixels. The larger the numbers are for these parameters, the closer the digital image resembles the real-world image.

The input of pictures into a digital-imaging system is usually done through the use of scanners, digital cameras, and video cameras. After the picture is changed to its digital image, several methods may be employed to enhance the image. The overall brightness of an image, as well as the contrast between the image and the background, can be adjusted through contrast-enhancement methods. One approach used to enhance an image is spatial filtering. There are several types of filters that produce various effects. A low-pass filter is used to eliminate harsh edges by reducing the intensity difference between pixels (see Figure 14–15). A second filter, the hi-pass filter, operates by modifying a pixel's numerical value to exaggerate its intensity difference from that of its neighbor's. The resulting effect increases the contrast of the edges, thus giving elements high contrast to the background. Frequency analysis, also referred to as Frequency Fourier Transform (FFT), is used to identify periodic or repetitive patterns such as lines or dots that are interfering with the interpretation of the image. These patterns are diminished or eliminated to enhance the appearance of the image. Interestingly, the spacings between fingerprint ridges are themselves periodic. Therefore, the contribution of the fingerprint can be identified in the FFT mode and then enhanced. Likewise, if ridges from overlapping prints are positioned in different directions, their corresponding frequency information will be at different locations in the FFT mode. The ridges of one latent can then be enhanced while the ridges of the other are suppressed.

Color interferences also pose a problem when analyzing an image. For example, a latent fingerprint found on a dollar bill may be difficult to analyze because of the distracting green background. With the imaging software, the green can simply be removed to make the image stand out. If the image itself is of a particular color, such as a ninhydrin-developed print, the purple color can be isolated and enhanced to distinguish it from the background.

Digital-imaging software also provide functions in which portions of the image may be examined individually. Through the use of a scaling and resizing tool, the user can select a part of an image and resize

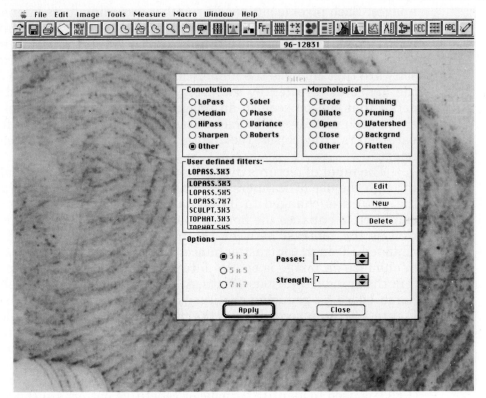

Figure 14–15. A computer screen with a low pass filter image analysis application program running. *Courtesy* Free Radical Enterprises, Fountain Valley, CA 92708, http://www.free-radical.com.

it for a closer look. This function operates much like a magnifying glass, helping the examiner to view fine details of an image.

An important and useful tool, especially for fingerprint identification, is the compare function. This specialized feature places two images side-by-side and allows the examiner to chart the common features on both images simultaneously (see Figure 14–16). In conjunction with the compare tool is the zoom function. The examiner can zoom into a portion of one image, while the second image will automatically zoom into the same portion for a comparison.

Although digital imaging is undoubtedly an effective tool for the enhancement and analysis of images, it can only be as useful as the images it has to work with. If the details do not exist on the original images, the enhancement procedures are not going to work. The benefits of using digital-enhancement methods are apparent when weak images are made more distinguishable.

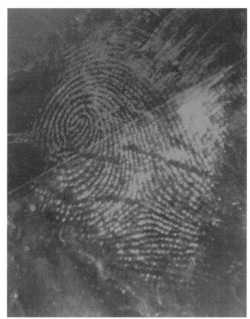

(a) Latent fingerprint visualized by cyanoacrylate fuming.

(b) Fingerprint treated with cyanoacrylate and a blue/green fluorescent dye.

(c) Fingerprint treated with cyanoacrylate and rhodamine 6G fluorescent dye.

(d) Fingerprint treated with cyanoacrylate and the fluorescent dye combination RAM.

Color Plate 5

Source: Photograph B courtesy of 3M Corp., Austin, Tex. Photograph F courtesy of Omnichrome, Chino, Calif. All other photographs courtesy of North Carolina State Bureau of Investigation, Raleigh, N.C.

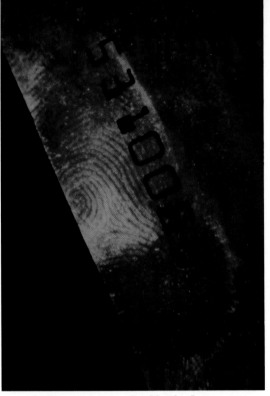

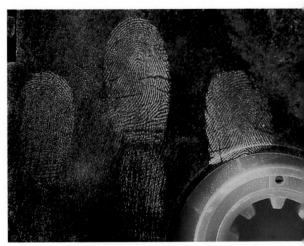

(f) Fingerprint visualized by redwop fluorescent fingerprint powder.

(e) Fingerprint visualized by the fluorescent chemical DFO.

(g) A bloody fingerprint detected by laser light without any chemical treatment.

Color Plate 6

(h) A bloody fingerprint detected by laser light after spraying with merbromin and hydrogen peroxide.

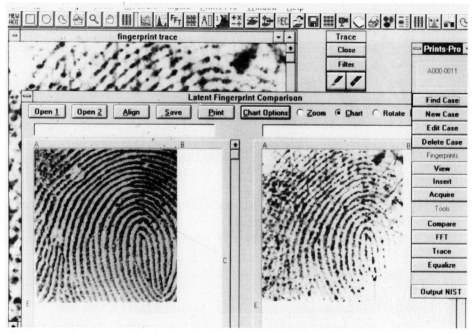

Figure 14–16. Currently available imaging software allows fingerprint analysts to use a dual screen image display with full charting capabilities. The fingerprint examiner can readily compare prints side by side and display important features that are consistent between the fingerprints. *Courtesy* Media Cybernetics, Silver Springs, Md. 20910.

REVIEW QUESTIONS

1. The first systematic attempt at personal identification was devised and introduced by _____.

2. A system of identification relying on precise body measurements is known as _____.

3. The fingerprint classification system used in most English-speaking countries was devised by _____.

4. The first systematic and official use of fingerprints for personal identification in the United States was adopted by the New York City Civil Service Commission. (True, False)

5. The individuality of a fingerprint (is, is not) determined by its pattern.

6. A point-by-point comparison of a fingerprint's _____ must be demonstrated in order to prove identity.

7. _____ are a reproduction of friction skin ridges.

8. The form and pattern of skin ridges are determined by the (epidermis, dermal papillae).

9. A permanent scar will form in the skin only when an injury damages the _____.

10. Fingerprints (can, cannot) be changed during a person's lifetime.

11. The three general patterns into which fingerprints are divided are _____, _____, and _____.

12. The most common fingerprint pattern is the _____.

13. Approximately 5 percent of the population has the _____ fingerprint pattern.

14. A loop pattern that opens toward the thumb is known as a(n) (radial, ulnar) loop.

15. The pattern area of the loop is enclosed by two diverging ridges known as _____.

16. The ridge point nearest the type-line divergence is known as the _____.

17. All loops must have (one, two) delta(s).

18. The approximate center of a loop pattern is called the _____.

19. If an imaginary line drawn between the two deltas of a whorl pattern touches any of the spiral ridges, the pattern is classified as a (plain whorl, central pocket loop).

20. The simplest of all fingerprint patterns is the _____.

21. Arches (have, have no) type lines, deltas, or cores.

22. The presence or absence of the _____ pattern is used as a basis for determining the primary classification in the Henry system.

23. The largest category (25 percent) in the primary classification system is (1/1, 1/2).

24. A fingerprint classification system (can, cannot) unequivocally identify an individual.

25. Computerized fingerprint search systems match prints by comparing the position of bifurcations and ridge endings. (True, False)

26. A fingerprint left by a person with soiled or stained fingertips is called a _____.

27. _____ fingerprints are impressions left on a soft material.

28. Fingerprint impressions that are not readily visible are called _____.

29. Fingerprints on hard and nonabsorbent surfaces are best developed by the application of a _____.

30. Fingerprints on porous surfaces are best developed with _____ treatment.
31. _____ vapors will chemically combine with fatty oils or residual water to visualize a fingerprint.
32. The chemical _____ visualizes fingerprints by its reaction with amino acids.
33. Chemical treatment with _____ visualizes fingerprints by combining with the salt residues of perspiration.
34. A latent fingerprint is first treated with silver nitrate followed by ninhydrin. (True, False)
35. A chemical technique known as _____ is used for developing latent prints on nonporous surfaces such as metal and plastic.
36. _____ is a phenomenon that occurs when a substance absorbs light and re-emits the light in wavelengths longer than the illuminating source.
37. High-intensity light sources known as _____ have proven to be effective in developing latent fingerprints.
38. Once a fingerprint has been visualized, it must be preserved by _____.
39. The image produced from a digital file is composed of numerous square electronic dots called _____.
40. A (hi-pass filter, Frequency Fourier Transform analysis) is used to identify repetitive patterns such as lines or dots that interfere with the interpretation of a digitized fingerprint image.

FURTHER REFERENCES

Cowger, James E., *Friction Ridge Skin*. Boca Raton, Fla.: CRC Press, Inc., 1983.

Hazen, Robert J., "Significant Advances in the Science of Fingerprints," in *Forensic Science,* 2nd ed., G. Davies, ed. Washington, D.C.: American Chemical Society, 1986.

Lee, H. C., and R. E. Gaensleen, eds., *Advances in Fingerprint Technology*. Boca Raton, Fla.: CRC Press, Inc., 1991.

Neudorfer, Charles D., "Fingerprint Automation—Progress in the FBI's Identification Division," *FBI Law Enforcement Bulletin,* 55, no. 3 (1986), 3.

Proceedings of the International Forensic Symposium on Latent Prints. Washington, D.C.: U.S. Government Printing Office, 1987.

The Science of Fingerprints. Washington, D.C.: U.S. Government Printing Office, 1990.

FIREARMS, TOOL MARKS, AND OTHER IMPRESSIONS

Just as natural variations in skin ridge patterns and characteristics provide a key to human identification, minute random markings on surfaces can impart individuality to inanimate objects. Structural variations and irregularities caused by scratches, nicks, breaks, and wear permit the criminalist to relate a bullet to a gun, a scratch or abrasion mark to a single tool, or a tire track to a particular automobile. Individualization, a goal so vigorously pursued in all other areas of criminalistics, frequently becomes an attainable reality in firearm and tool mark examination.

Although a portion of this chapter will be devoted to the comparison of surface features for the purposes of bullet identification, a complete description of the services and capabilities of the modern forensic firearms laboratory cannot be restricted to just this one subject, important as it may be. The high frequency of shooting cases has necessitated that the science of firearms identification extend beyond the mere comparison of bullets to include knowledge of the operation of all types of weapons, the restoration of obliterated serial numbers on weapons, the detection and characterization of gunpowder residues on garments and around wounds, the estimation of muzzle-to-target distances, and the detection of powder residues on hands. Each of these functions will be covered in this chapter.

BULLET COMPARISONS

It is the inner surface of the barrel of a gun that leaves its markings on a bullet passing through it. These markings are peculiar to each gun. Hence, if one bullet found at the scene of a crime and another test-fired from a suspect's gun show the same markings, the suspect is linked to the crime. Because it is these inner surface striations that are so important for bullet comparison, it is important to know why and how they originate.

The gun barrel is produced from a solid bar of steel that has been hollowed out by drilling. The microscopic drill marks left on the barrel's inner surface are randomly irregular and would in themselves serve to impart a uniqueness to each barrel. However, the manufacture of a barrel requires the additional step of impressing its inner surface with spiral **grooves,** a step known as **rifling.** The surfaces of the original bore remaining between the grooves are called **lands** (see Figure 15–1). As a fired bullet travels through a barrel, it engages the rifling grooves; these grooves will then guide the bullet through the barrel, giving it a rapid spin. This is done because a spinning bullet will not tumble end over end on leaving the barrel but will remain instead on a true and accurate course.

The diameter of the gun barrel, sketched in Figure 15–2, measured between opposite lands, is known as the **caliber** of the weapon. Caliber is normally recorded in hundredths of an inch or in millimeters—for example, .22, .38, and 9 mm. Actually, the term *caliber,* as it is commonly applied, is not an exact measurement of the barrel's diameter; for example, a 38 (.38 inches) caliber weapon might actually have a bore diameter that ranges from 0.345 to 0.365 inches.

Before 1940, barrels were rifled by having one or two grooves at a time cut into the surface with steel hook cutters. The cutting tool was rotated as it passed down the barrel, so that the final results were grooves spiraling either to the right or left. However, as the need for

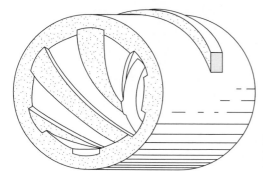

Figure 15–1.
Interior view of a gun barrel, showing the presence of lands and grooves.

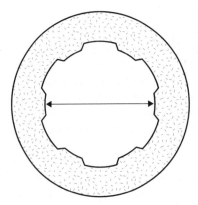

Figure 15–2.
Cross section of a barrel with six grooves. The diameter of the bore is the caliber.

increased speed in the manufacture of weapons became apparent, newer techniques were developed that were far more suitable for the mass production of weapons. The broach cutter, shown in Figure 15–3, consists of a series of concentric steel rings, with each ring slightly larger than the preceding one. As the broach passes through the barrel, it simultaneously cuts all the grooves into the barrel at the required depth. The broach is rotated as it passes through the barrel, giving the grooves their desired direction and rate of twist.

Figure 15–3.   A segment of a broach cutter. *Courtesy* New Jersey State Police.

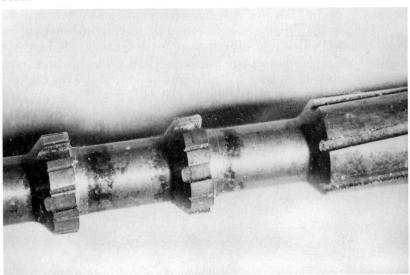

In contrast to the broach, the button process involves no cuttings. Here, a steel plug or "button" impressed with the desired number of grooves is forced under extremely high pressures through the barrel. A single pass of the button down the barrel compresses the metal to create lands and grooves on the barrel walls that are negative forms of those on the button. The button is rotated to produce the desired direction and rate of twist (see Figure 15–4).

Like the button process, the mandrel rifling process involves no cutting of metal. A mandrel is a rod of hardened steel machined so its form is the reverse impression of the rifling it is intended to produce. The mandrel is inserted into a slightly oversized bore, and the barrel is compressed with hammering or heavy rollers into the mandrel's form.

Every firearms manufacturer chooses a rifling process that is best suited to meet the production standards and requirements of its product. Once the choice is made, however, the class characteristics of the weapon's barrel will remain consistent; each will have the same number of lands and grooves, with the same approximate width and direction of twist. For example, .32 caliber Smith & Wesson revolvers have five lands and grooves twisting to the right. On the other hand, Colt

Figure 15–4. (Top) Cross section of a .22 caliber rifled barrel. (Bottom) A button used to produce the lands and grooves in the barrel. *Courtesy* New Jersey State Police.

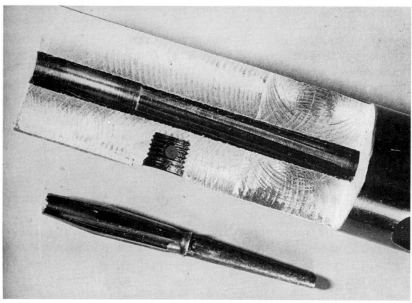

.32 caliber revolvers exhibit six lands and grooves twisting to the left. Although these class characteristics may prove to be of some value in permitting the examiner to distinguish one type or brand-name weapon from another, they will certainly not impart individuality to any one barrel; no class characteristic can do this.

If one could cut a barrel open lengthwise, a careful examination of the interior would reveal the existence of fine lines or striations, many running the length of the barrel's lands and grooves. These striations are impressed into the metal as the negatives of minute imperfections found on the rifling cutter's surface, or they are produced by minute chips of steel pushed against the barrel's inner surface by a moving broach cutter. The fact is that the random distribution and irregularities of these markings are impossible to duplicate exactly in any two barrels. **No two rifled barrels, even those manufactured in succession, will have identical striation markings.** These striations form the individual characteristics of the barrel.

As the bullet passes through the barrel, its surface is impressed with the rifled markings of the barrel. The bullet emerges from the barrel carrying the impressions of the bore's interior surface; these impressions reflect both the class and individual characteristics of the barrel (see Figure 15–5). Because there is no practical way of making a direct comparison between the markings on the fired bullet and those found within a barrel, the examiner must obtain test bullets fired through the suspect barrel for comparison. In order to prevent damage to the test bullet's markings and to facilitate the bullet's recovery, test firings are normally made into a recovery box filled with cotton or into a water tank.

The number of lands and grooves, and their direction of twist, are obvious points of comparison during the initial stages of the examination. Any differences in these class characteristics will immediately serve to eliminate the possibility that both bullets traveled through the same barrel. A bullet having five lands and grooves could not possibly have been fired from a weapon of like caliber having six lands and grooves, nor could one having a right twist have come through a barrel impressed with a left twist. Once it has been ascertained that both bullets carry the same class characteristics, the effort must begin to match the striated markings on both bullets. It is an effort that can be made only with the assistance of the comparison microscope (see Chapter 7).

It is no coincidence that modern firearms identification began with the development and utilization of the comparison microscope. This instrument is the single most important tool at the disposal of the firearms examiner. The test and evidence bullets are mounted on cylindrical adjustable holders beneath the objective lenses of the

Figure 15–5.
A bullet is impressed with the rifling markings of the barrel when it emerges from the weapon. *Courtesy* New Jersey State Police.

microscope, each pointing in the same direction (see Figure 15–6). Both bullets are observed simultaneously within the same field of view, and the examiner rotates one bullet until a well-defined land or groove comes into view. Once the striation markings are located, the other bullet is rotated until a matching region is found. Not only must the lands and grooves of the test and evidence bullet have identical widths, but the longitudinal striations on each must coincide. When a matching area is located, the two bullets are simultaneously rotated to obtain additional matching areas around the periphery of the bullets. Figure 15–7 shows a typical photomicrograph of a bullet match as viewed under a comparison microscope.

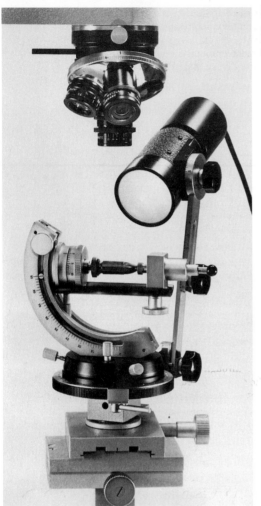

Figure 15–6.
A bullet holder beneath the objective lens of a comparison microscope. *Courtesy* Ernst Leitz.

Unfortunately, the firearms examiner rarely encounters a situation in which a perfect match exists all around the bullet's periphery. The presence of grit and rust can to some degree alter the markings on bullets fired through the same barrel. More commonly, recovered evidence bullets may become so mutilated and distorted on impact as to yield only a small area with intact markings. Furthermore, striation markings on a barrel are not permanent structures; they are subject to continuing change and alteration through wear as succeeding bullets traverse the length of the barrel. Fortunately, in most cases, these changes are not dramatic ones and will not prevent the matching of two bullets fired by the same weapon. As with fingerprint comparison,

Figure 15–7. Photomicrograph of two bullets through a comparison microscope. The test bullet is on the right; the questioned bullet is on the left. *Courtesy* Philadelphia Police Dept. Laboratory.

there are no hard and fast rules governing the minimum number of points required for a bullet comparison. The final opinion must be based upon the judgment, experience, and knowledge of the expert.

Frequently, the firearms examiner is presented with a spent bullet without any accompanying suspect weapon and is requested to provide information with regard to the caliber and possible make of the weapon. If a bullet appears not to have lost its metal, its weight may be one factor in determining its caliber. In some instances, the number of lands and grooves, the direction of twist, and the widths of lands and grooves are useful class characteristics for eliminating certain makes of weapons from consideration. For example, a bullet that has five lands and grooves and twists to the right could not come from a weapon manufactured by Colt, because Colts are not manufactured with these class characteristics. Sometimes a bullet will have rifling marks that set it apart from most other manufactured weapons, as in the case of Marlin rifles. These weapons are rifled by a technique known as "microgrooving" and may have 8 to 24 grooves impressed into their barrels; few other weapons are manufactured in this fashion. In this respect, the FBI maintains a record known as the General Rifling Characteristics File. This file contains listings of class characteristics, such as land and groove width dimensions, for known weapons. It is periodically updated and distributed to the law enforcement community to aid in the identification of rifled weapons from retrieved bullets.

Unlike rifled firearms, a shotgun has a smooth barrel. It therefore follows that projectiles passing through a shotgun barrel will not be impressed with any characteristic markings that can later be related back to the weapon. Shotguns generally fire small lead balls or pellets contained within a shotgun shell (see Figure 15–8). A paper or plastic wad pushes the pellets through the barrel upon ignition of the cartridge's powder charge. By weighing and measuring the diameter of the shot recovered at a crime scene, the examiner can usually determine the size of shot used in the shotshell. The size and shape of the recovered wad may also reveal the gauge of the shotgun used and, in some instances, may indicate the manufacturer of the fired shotshell.

The diameter of the shotgun barrel is expressed by the term **gauge.**[1] The higher the gauge number, the smaller the barrel's diameter. For example, a 12-gauge shotgun has a bore diameter of 0.730 inches as contrasted to 0.670 inches for a 16-gauge shotgun. The exception to this rule is the .410-gauge shotgun, which refers to a barrel 0.410 inches in diameter.

Figure 15–8.   Cross section of a loaded shotgun shell.

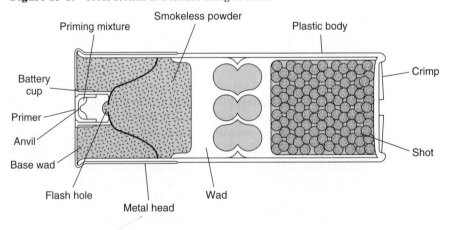

---

[1]Originally, the number of lead balls with the same diameter as the barrel would make a pound. For example, a 20-gauge shotgun is one having an inside diameter equal to the diameter of a lead ball that weighs 1/20 of a pound.

CARTRIDGE CASES

The act of pulling a trigger serves to release the weapon's firing pin, causing it to strike the primer, which in turn ignites the powder. The expanding gases generated by the burning gunpowder propel the bullet forward through the barrel, simultaneously pushing the spent cartridge case or shell back with equal force against the breechblock. As the bullet is marked by its passage through the barrel, the shell is also impressed with markings by its contact with the metal surfaces of the weapon's firing and loading mechanisms. As with bullets, these markings can be reproduced in test-fired cartridges to provide distinctive points of comparison for individualizing a spent shell to a rifled weapon or shotgun.

The shape of the firing pin will be impressed into the relatively soft metal of the primer on the cartridge case, revealing the minute distortions of the firing pin. These imperfections may be sufficiently random to individualize the pin impression to a single weapon. Similarly, the cartridge case, in its rearward thrust, is impressed with the surface markings of the breechblock. The breechblock, like any machined surface, is populated with random striation markings that become a highly distinctive signature for individualizing its surface. Other distinctive markings that may appear on the shell as a result of metal-to-metal contact are caused by the ejector and extractor mechanism and the magazine or clip, as well as by imperfections on the fire chamber walls. Photomicrographs in Figure 15–9 reveal a comparison of the firing pin and breechblock impressions on evidence and test-fired shells.

Firing pin, breechblock, extractor, and ejector marks may also be impressed onto the surface of the brass portion of shells fired by a shotgun. These impressions provide just as valuable points for individualizing the shell to a weapon as do cartridge cases discharged from a rifled firearm. Furthermore, in the absence of a suspect weapon, the size and shape of a firing pin impression and/or the position of ejector marks in relationship to extractor and other markings may provide some clue to the type or make of the weapon that may have fired the questioned shell, or at least may eliminate a large number of possibilities.

AUTOMATED FIREARM SEARCH SYSTEMS

The use of firearms, especially semiautomatic weapons, during the commission of a crime has significantly increased throughout the United States. Because of the expense involved with such firearms,

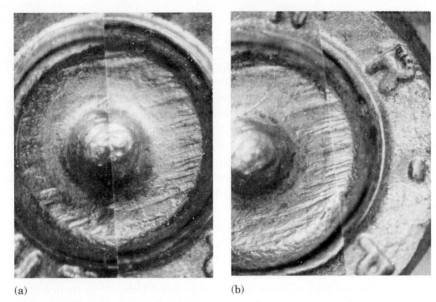

(a)   (b)

Figure 15–9. Comparison microscope photomicrograph showing a match between (a) firing pin impressions and (b) the breechblock markings on two shells. *Courtesy* New Jersey State Police.

the likelihood that a specific weapon will be used in multiple crimes has risen. The advent of computerized imaging technology has made possible the storage of bullet and cartridge surface characteristics in a manner analogous to automated fingerprint files (see pp. 448–450). Using this concept, crime laboratories can be networked, allowing them to share information on bullets and cartridges retrieved at several jurisdictions. The automated search system developed for the FBI is known as DRUGFIRE. This system emphasizes the examination of unique markings on the cartridge casings expended by the weapon. The specimen is analyzed through a microscope attached to a video camera. The magnification allows for a close-up view to identify individual characteristics. The image is captured by the video camera, digitized, and stored in a database. Although DRUGFIRE emphasizes cartridge-case imagery, the images of highly characteristic bullet striations can also be stored in a like manner for comparisons.

The Integrated Ballistic Identification System (IBIS), developed for the Bureau of Alcohol, Tobacco and Firearms, processes digital microscopic images of identifying features found on both expended bullets and cartridge casings. IBIS incorporates two software programs: *Bulletproof,* a bullet-analyzing module, and *Brasscatcher,* a cartridge-case analyzing module. A schematic diagram of *Bulletproof*'s operation is depicted in Figure 15–10.

The DRUGFIRE system currently networks a number of crime laboratories with the FBI. The success of the system has been proven by linking over 1000 cases. For example, in a recent case, two individuals were wounded by gunshots as they were standing near a telephone booth on a Baltimore street corner. Three weeks later, another

Figure 15–10. Bulletproof configuration. The sample is mounted on the specimen manipulator and illuminated by the light source from a microscope. The image is captured by a video camera and digitized. This digital image is then stored in a database, available for retrieval and comparison. The search for a match includes analyzing the width of land and groove impressions along with both rifling and individual characteristics. The *Brasscatcher* software uses the same system configuration but emphasizes the analysis of expended cartridge casings rather than the expended bullets. *Courtesy* Forensic Technology, Montréal, Canada.

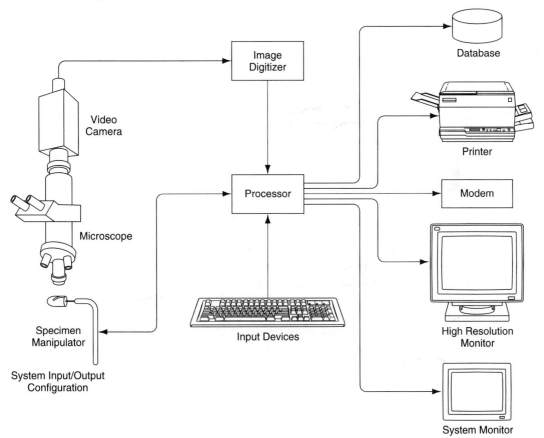

Baltimore citizen was killed by gunshots as he sat on the steps of a house in another area of the city. Five days later, another individual was walking with his wife and a friend down a street in another section of the city when he was fatally wounded by gunshots. All of the shots that struck these four victims were fired by an unknown assailant(s). These three incidents appeared to be unrelated, but the Baltimore Police Department Crime Laboratory was able, with the help of DRUGFIRE, to link the shootings to the same 9 mm firearm. One month after the first shooting incident, police made an arrest and recovered a 9 mm Glock semiautomatic pistol from the suspect's residence. Test-fired specimens from this firearm were entered into the DRUGFIRE system and matched to each of the specimens collected from the three shooting incidents. The associations were verified by traditional firearm examination comparisons performed by the firearm examiner. Before this computerized technology was developed, it would have taken years, or may have been impossible, to link all of these shootings to one single firearm. In another example, the IBIS link between two northern California laboratories produced a hit with a cartridge casing recovered in a double homicide case that was matched with a cartridge casing with test fires from a weapon that was recovered months later.

Both systems, DRUGFIRE and IBIS, serve as screening tools of firearm evidence. It is important to remember that any computerized system does not replace the skills of the firearm examiner. DRUGFIRE and IBIS will be able to screen hundreds of unsolved firearm cases and narrow the possibilities to several firearms. However, the ultimate comparison for making a final conclusion will be determined by the forensic examiner through traditional microscopic methods.

GUNPOWDER RESIDUES

In incidents involving gunshot wounds, it is often necessary to determine the distance from which the weapon was fired. Frequently, in incidents involving a shooting death, the individual apprehended and accused will plead self-defense as the motive for the attack. Such claims are fertile grounds for firing-distance determinations, because finding the proximity of the parties involved in the incident is necessary to establish the true facts of the incident. Similarly, a careful examination of the wounds of suicide victims usually reveals characteristics associated with a very close-range gunshot wound. The absence of such characteristics is a strong indication that the wound was not self-inflicted and signals the possibility of foul play.

Modern ammunition is propelled toward a target by the expanding gases created by the ignition of smokeless powder or nitrocellulose in a cartridge. Under ideal circumstances, it would be expected that all of the powder would be consumed in the process and would be converted into the rapidly expanding gases. However, in practice this is not the case, because the powder is never totally burned. When a firearm is discharged, unburned and partially burned particles of gunpowder in addition to smoke are propelled out of the barrel along with the bullet toward the target. If the muzzle of the weapon is sufficiently close, these products will be deposited onto the target. It is the distribution of gunpowder particles and other discharge residues around the bullet hole that permits an assessment of the distance from which a handgun or rifle was fired.

The accuracy of a distance determination varies according to the circumstances of the case. In instances in which the investigator is unable to recover a suspect weapon, the best that the examiner can do is to state whether or not a shot could have been fired within some distance interval from the target. More exact opinions are possible only when the examiner has the suspect weapon in hand and has knowledge of the type of ammunition used in the shooting.

The precise distance from which a handgun or rifle has been fired must be determined by means of a careful comparison of the powder-residue pattern located on the victim's clothing or skin against test patterns made when the suspect weapon is fired at varying distances from a target. A white cloth or a fabric comparable to the victim's clothing may be used as a test target (see Figure 15–11). Because the spread and density of the residue pattern will vary widely between weapons and ammunition, such a comparison is significant only when it is made with the suspect weapon and ammunition or ammunition of the same type and make. By comparing the test and evidence patterns, the examiner may find enough similarity in shape and density upon which to base an opinion as to the distance from which the shot was fired.

Without the benefit of a weapon, the examiner is restricted to looking for recognizable characteristics around the bullet hole. Such findings are at best approximations made as a result of general observations and knowledge that the examiner has accumulated over an extended period of time spent in firearms examination. However, there are some noticeable characteristics to be looked for. For instance, in the case in which the weapon is held in contact with or less than 1 inch from the target, a heavy concentration of smokelike vaporous lead usually surrounds the bullet entrance hole. Often, loose fibers surrounding a contact hole will show scorch marks from the flame discharge of the weapon, and some synthetic fibers may

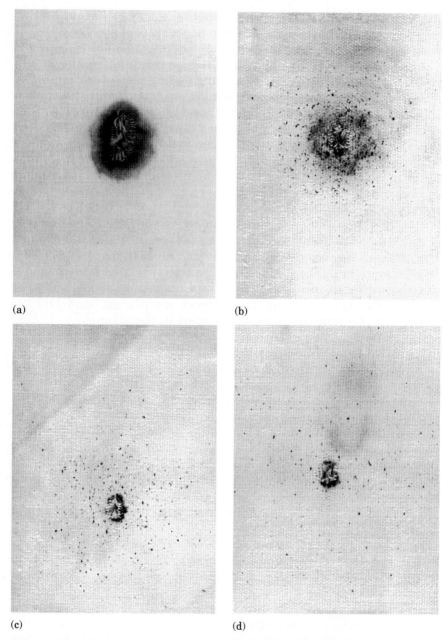

(a)

(b)

(c)

(d)

Figure 15–11.   Test powder patterns made with a .38 Special Smith &
Wesson revolver fired at the following distances from the target: (a) contact,
(b) 6 inches, (c) 12 inches, (d) 18 inches. *Courtesy* New Jersey State Police.

show signs of being melted as a result of the heat from the discharge. Furthermore, the blowback of muzzle gases may produce a stellate (star-shape) tear pattern around the hole. Such a hole will invariably be surrounded by a rim of a smokelike deposit of vaporous lead (see Figure 15–12).

A halo of vaporous lead (smoke) deposited around a bullet hole is normally indicative of a discharge 12 to 18 inches or less from the target. The presence of scattered specks of unburned and partially burned powder grains without any accompanying soot can often be observed at distances up to approximately 25 inches. However, occasionally, scattered gunpowder particles will be noted at a firing distance as far out as 36 inches. With ball powder ammunition, this distance may be extended to 6 to 8 feet. Finally, a weapon that has been fired more than 3 feet from a target will usually not deposit any powder residues onto the target's surface. In these cases, the only visual indication to characterize the hole as being made by a bullet is a dark ring, known as **bullet wipe,** around the perimeter of the entrance hole. Bullet wipe consists of a mixture of carbon, dirt, lubricant, primer residue, and lead wiped off the bullet's surface as it passes through the target. Again, it must be emphasized that in the absence of a suspect weapon, these observations are general guidelines for

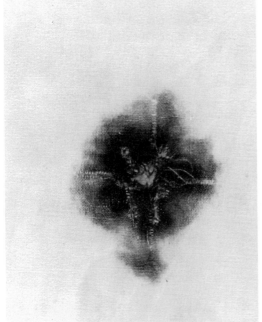

Figure 15–12.
A contact shot. *Courtesy* New Jersey
State Police.

estimating target distances. It must be kept in mind that numerous factors—that is, barrel length, caliber, type of ammunition, and type and condition of the weapon fired—all influence the amount of gunpowder residue deposited on a target.

When garments or other evidence relevant to a shooting are received in the crime laboratory, the surfaces of all items are first examined microscopically for the presence of gunpowder residue. These particles may be identifiable by their characteristic color, sizes, and shapes. However, the absence of visual indications does not preclude the possibility that gunpowder residue is present. Sometimes the lack of color contrast between the powder and garment or the presence of heavily encrusted deposits of blood can obscure the visual detection of gunpowder. Often, an infrared photograph of the suspect area will overcome the problem. Such a photograph may enhance the contrast, thus revealing vaporous lead and powder particles deposited around the hole (see Figure 15–13). In other situations, this may not help, and the analyst will need to use chemical tests to detect gunpowder residues.

Nitrites are one type of chemical product that results from the incomplete combustion of smokeless (nitrocellulose) powder. One test

Figure 5–13.   (a) A shirt bearing a powder stain, photographed under normal light. (b) Infrared photograph of the same shirt. *Courtesy* New Jersey State Police.

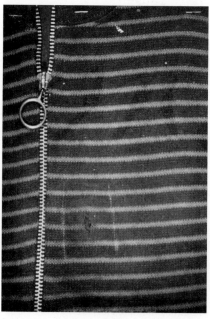
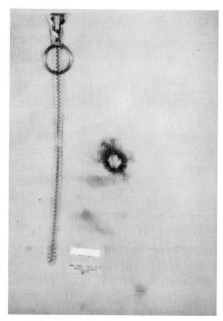

(a)   (b)

method for locating powder residues involves transferring particles embedded on the target surface to chemically treated gelatin-coated photographic paper. This procedure is known as the *Greiss test*. The examiner presses the photographic paper onto the target with a hot iron; once the nitrite particles are on the paper, they are made easily visible by chemical treatment.[2] In addition, comparing the developed nitrite pattern to nitrite patterns obtained from test firings at known distances can be a useful technique for determining the shooting distance from the target. A second chemical test is then performed for the detection of any trace of lead residue that might be around the bullet hole. The procedure is accomplished by spraying the questioned surface with a solution of sodium rhodizonate, followed by a series of oversprays with acid solutions. This treatment will cause lead particles to exhibit a pink color, followed by a blue-violet color.

The determination of firing distances involving shotguns must again be related to test firings performed with the suspect weapon, using the same type of ammunition known to be used in the crime. In the absence of a weapon, the muzzle-to-target distance can be estimated by measuring the spread of the discharged shot. With close-range shots varying in distance up to 4 to 5 feet, the shot charge enters the target as a concentrated mass, producing a hole somewhat larger than the bore of the barrel. As the distance increases, the pellets progressively separate and spread out. Generally speaking, the spread in the pattern made by a 12-gauge shotgun is increased 1 inch for each yard of distance. Thus, a 10-inch pattern would be produced at approximately 10 yards. Of course, this is only a rule of thumb; normally, there are a great number of variables that can affect the shot pattern. Other factors to be taken into consideration include the barrel length, the size and quantity of the pellets fired, the quantity of powder charge used to propel the pellets, and the choke of the gun under examination. **Choke** is the degree of constriction placed at the muzzle end of the barrel. The greater the choke, the narrower will be the shotgun pattern and the faster and farther the pellets will travel.

PRIMER RESIDUES ON THE HANDS

The firing of a weapon not only propels residues toward the target; gunpowder and primer residues are also blown back toward the shooter. As a result, traces of these residues are often deposited on the

---

[2]P. C. Maiti, "Powder Patterns Around Bullet Holes in Bloodstained Articles," *Journal of the Forensic Science Society,* 13 (1973), 197.

firing hand of the shooter, and their detection can provide valuable information as to whether or not an individual has recently fired a weapon.

Early efforts at demonstrating powder residues on the hands centered on chemical tests that could detect the presence of unburned gunpowder or nitrates. For many years, the "dermal nitrate test" enjoyed popularity as such a test. It required the application of hot paraffin or wax to the suspect's hand with a paintbrush. After drying into a solid crust, the paraffin was removed and tested with the chemical diphenylamine. The presence of a blue color was taken as an indication of a positive reaction for nitrates (see Table 11–3). However, during recent years the dermal nitrate test has fallen into disfavor with law enforcement agencies, owing mainly to its lack of specificity. Common materials such as fertilizers, cosmetics, urine, and tobacco are all known to give positive reactions that are indistinguishable from that obtained for gunpowder by this test.

Current efforts to identify a shooter are now centered on the detection of primer residues deposited on the hand of a shooter at the time of firing. With the exception of most .22 caliber ammunition, primers presently manufactured contain a blend of lead styphnate, barium nitrate, and antimony sulfide. Residues from these materials are most likely to be deposited on the thumb web and the back of the firing hand of a shooter, because these areas are in closest proximity to gases escaping along the side or back of the gun during discharge. In addition, individuals who handle a gun without firing it may have primer residues deposited on the palm of the hand coming in contact with the weapon. However, it has been established that with the handling of a used firearm, the passage of time, and the resumption of normal activities following a shooting, gunshot residues from the back of the hand are frequently redistributed to other areas, including the palms. Therefore, it is not unusual to find higher levels of barium and antimony on the palms rather than on the backs of the hands of known shooters in actual case situations. Another possibility is the deposition of significant levels of barium and antimony on the hands of an individual who is near a firearm when it is discharged.

Determination of whether or not a person has fired, handled a weapon, or was near a discharged firearm is normally made by measuring the amount of barium and antimony on the relevant portions of the suspect's hands. A variety of materials and techniques are now utilized for removing these residues. The most popular approach, and certainly the most convenient from the field investigator's point of view, is to remove any residues present by swabbing both the firing and nonfiring hands with cotton that has been moistened with 5 percent nitric acid. The front and back of each hand are separately swabbed. All four swabs, along with a moistened control, are then forwarded to the crime laboratory for analysis (see Appendix II for a detailed description of residue collection procedures).

In any case, once the hands are treated for the collection of barium and antimony, the collection medium must be analyzed for the presence of these elements. The demonstration of high barium and antimony levels on the suspect's hand(s) is a strong indication that that person fired or handled a weapon, or was near a firearm when it was discharged. Because these elements are normally present after a firing in small quantities (less than 10 micrograms), only the most sensitive analytical techniques can be used for their detection.

Unfortunately, even though most specimens submitted for this type of analysis have been from individuals strongly suspected of having fired a gun, there has been a low rate of positive findings. The major difficulty appears to be the short time that primer residues remain on the hands. These residues are readily removed by intentional or unintentional washing, rubbing, or wiping of hands. In fact, one study convincingly demonstrated that it is very difficult to detect primer residues on cotton hand swabs that were taken as soon as two hours after firing a weapon.[3] Hence, as a matter of policy, some laboratories will not accept cotton hand swabs taken from living subjects six or more hours after a firing has occurred. In cases that involve suicide victims, it has been demonstrated that a higher rate of positives for the presence of gunshot residue is obtained when the hand swabbing is conducted before the person's body is moved or when the hands are protected by paper bags.[4] It should be noted, however, that hand swabbing cannot be used to detect firings with most .22 rim-fire ammunition. Such ammunition may contain only barium or neither barium nor antimony in its primer composition.

Neutron activation analysis and flameless atomic absorption spectrophotometry (see Chapter 6) are analytical methods that have demonstrated a sensitivity high enough to be suitable for detecting barium and antimony in gunshot residues in hand swabs. However, the necessity for having access to a neutron source and expensive counting equipment limits neutron activation analysis technology to a small number of crime laboratories. On the other hand, flameless atomic absorption spectrophotometry (see pages 171–173) can be purchased at a cost well within the budgets of most crime laboratories. As a result, the immediate future promises to see more crime laboratories expanding their capabilities to perform primer-residue determinations on hands utilizing the atomic absorption technique.

---

[3]J. W. Kilty, "Activity After Shooting and Its Effect on the Retention of Primer Residues," *Journal of the Forensic Sciences,* 29 (1975), 219.

[4]G. E. Reed et al., "Analysis of Gunshot Residue Test Results in 112 Suicides," *Journal of Forensic Sciences,* 35 (1990), 62.

Another approach to primer-residue detection requires the application of adhesive tape to the hand's surface in order to remove any adhering residue particles.[5] Microscopic primer and gunpowder particles on the tape are then located with the aid of a scanning electron microscope (SEM). These particles have a characteristic size and shape that readily distinguish them from other contaminants present on the hands (see Figure 7–12). When the SEM is linked to an X-ray analyzer (see pp. 197–198), an elemental analysis of the particles can be conducted. A finding of a select combination of elements (e.g., lead, barium, and antimony) confirms that the particles were indeed primer residue (see Appendix II for a detailed description of the SEM residue collection procedure).

The major advantage of the SEM approach for primer-residue detection is its enhanced specificity over hand swabbing. The SEM characterizes primer particles by their size and shape as well as by their chemical composition. Unfortunately, the excessive operator time required to search out and characterize gunshot residue has deterred this technique's use. The availability of automated particle search and identification systems for use with scanning electron microscopes may overcome this problem. Results of work performed with automated systems show it to be significantly faster than a manual approach for searching out gunshot residue particles.[6]

SERIAL NUMBER RESTORATION

Today, many manufactured items, including automobile engine blocks and firearms, are impressed with a serial number for identification. Increasingly, the criminalist is requested to restore such a number when it has been removed or obliterated by grinding, rifling, or punching.

Serial numbers are usually stamped on a metal body or frame, or on a plate, with hard steel dies. These dies strike the metal surface with a force that allows each digit to sink into the metal at a prescribed depth. Restoration of serial numbers can be accomplished because the metal crystals in the stamped zone are placed under a permanent strain that extends a short distance beneath the original numbers. When a suitable etching agent is applied, the strained area will

---

[5]G. M. Woiten et al., "Particle Analysis for the Detection of Gunshot Residue, I: Scanning Electron Microscopy/Energy Dispersive X-Ray Characterization of Hand Deposits from Firing," *Journal of Forensic Sciences,* 24 (1979), 409.

[6]R. S. White and A. D. Owens, "Automation of Gunshot Residue Detection and Analysis by Scanning Electron Microscopy/Energy Dispersive X-Ray Analysis (SEM/EDX)," *Journal of Forensic Sciences,* 32 (1987), 1595. Also, W. L. Tillman, "Automated Gunshot Residue Particle Search and Characterization," *Journal of Forensic Sciences,* 32 (1987), 62.

dissolve at a faster rate as compared to the unaltered metal, thus permitting the etched pattern to appear in the form of the original numbers. However, if the zone of strain has been removed, or if the area has been impressed with a different strain pattern, it is usually not possible to restore the number.

Before any treatment with the etching reagent, the obliterated surface must be thoroughly cleaned of dirt and oil and polished to a mirrorlike finish. The reagent is best applied when the polished metal is swabbed with a moistened cotton ball. The choice of etching reagent will depend on the type of metal surface being worked on. A solution consisting of hydrochloric acid (120 ml), copper chloride (90 g), and water (100 ml) generally works well for steel surfaces.

COLLECTION AND PRESERVATION
OF FIREARM EVIDENCE

FIREARMS

The Hollywood image of an investigator picking up a weapon by its barrel with a pencil or stick in order to protect fingerprints is one that must be avoided. This practice will only serve to disturb powder deposits, rust, or dirt lodged in the barrel, and consequently may alter the striation markings on test-fired bullets. If the recovery of latent fingerprints is a primary concern, it is best to hold the weapon by the edge of the trigger guard or by the checkered portion of the grip, which usually does not retain identifiable fingerprints.

The most important consideration in handling a weapon is safety. Before any weapon is sent to the laboratory, all precautions must be taken to prevent an accidental discharge of a loaded weapon in transit. In most cases, it will be necessary to unload the weapon. If this is done, a record should first be made of the weapon's hammer and safety position; likewise, the location of all fired and unfired ammunition in the weapon must be recorded. When a revolver is recovered, the chamber position in line with the barrel should be indicated by a scratch mark on the cylinder. Each chamber is designated with a number on a diagram, and as each cartridge or casing is removed, it should be marked to correspond to the numbered chambers in the diagram. Knowledge of the cylinder position of a cartridge casing may be useful for later determination of the sequence of events, particularly in shooting cases, when more than one shot was fired. Place each round in a separate box or envelope. If the weapon is an automatic, the magazine must be removed and checked for prints and the chamber then emptied.

Just like any other type of physical evidence recovered at a crime scene, firearm evidence must be marked for identification and a chain of custody must be established. Therefore, when a firearm is recovered, an identification tag should be attached to the trigger guard. The tag should be marked to show appropriate identifying data, including the weapon's serial number, make, model, and the investigator's initials. The firearm itself may be further identified by being marked directly with a sharp-pointed scriber in an inconspicuous area of the weapon—for example, the inside of the trigger guard. This practice will avoid any permanent defacement of the weapon.

When a weapon is recovered from an underwater location, no effort must be made to dry or clean it. Instead, the firearm should be transported to the laboratory in a receptacle containing enough of the same water necessary to keep it submerged. This procedure will prevent rust from developing during transport.

AMMUNITION

The protection of class and individual markings on bullets and cartridge cases must be the primary concern of the field investigator who is handling such evidence. Thus, extreme caution is to be exercised when a lodged bullet must be removed from a wall or other object. If the bullet's surface were accidentally scratched during this operation, valuable striation markings could be obliterated. It is best to free bullets from their target by carefully breaking away the surrounding support material while avoiding direct contact with the projectile.

Bullets recovered at the crime scene are scribed with the investigator's initials, either on the base or on the nose of the bullet (see Figure 15–14). Again, the obliteration of striation markings that may be present on the bullet must be scrupulously avoided. If the bullet is badly deformed and there is no apparent place for identification, it should just be placed in a container that is appropriately marked for identification. In any case, the investigator must protect the bullet by wrapping it in tissue paper before placing it in a pillbox or an envelope for shipment to the crime laboratory. In handling the bullet, the investigator should be conscious of the possibility that minute traces of evidence, such as paint and fibers, may be adhering to the bullet. Care must be taken to leave these trace materials intact. Similarly, a fired casing must be identified in a manner that will avoid the destruction of marks impressed on it from the weapon. The investigator's initials should be placed near the outside or inside mouth of the shell (see Figure 15–15). Discharged shells from shotguns are initialed with ink or indelible pencil on the paper or plastic tube remaining on the shell, or

Figure 15–14.
Discharged evidence bullets should be marked on the base or nose. When there is more than one bullet, a number should accompany the initials. NEVER mark bullets on the side.

on the metal nearest the mouth of the shell. In addition, in situations where semiautomatic or automatic weapons have been fired, the ejection pattern of the casings can help establish the relationship of the suspect to his or her victim. For this reason, the exact location of the place a shell casing was recovered is important information that must be noted by the investigator.

In incidents involving shotguns, any wads recovered are to be packaged and sent to the laboratory. An examination of the size and composition of the wad may reveal information about the type of ammunition used and the gauge of the shotgun.

GUNPOWDER DEPOSITS

The clothing of a firearm victim must be carefully preserved so as to prevent damage or disruption to powder residues deposited around a bullet or shotshell hole. The cutting or tearing of clothing in the area of the holes must be avoided as the clothing is being removed. As a

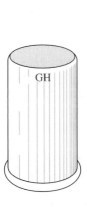

Figure 15–15.
Discharged evidence shells should be marked on the outside or inside, as close as possible to the mouth of the shell. Discharged shotgun shells should be marked on the brass, close to the paper or plastic. NEVER mark the shells where the firing pin strikes the primer.

matter of routine, all wet clothing should be air-dried out of direct sunlight and then folded carefully so as not to disrupt the area around the
bullet hole. Each item should be placed in a separate paper bag.

TOOL MARKS

A tool mark is considered to be any impression, cut, gouge, or abrasion
caused by a tool coming into contact with another object. Most often,
tool marks are encountered at burglary scenes that involve forcible
entry into a building or safe. Generally, these marks occur in the form
of indented impressions into a softer surface or as abrasion marks
caused by the tool cutting or sliding against another object.

Typically, an indented impression is left on the frame of a door or
window as a result of the prying action of a screwdriver or crowbar. A
careful examination of these impressions can reveal important class
characteristics—that is, the size and shape of the tool. However, they
rarely reveal any significant individual characteristics that could permit the examiner to individualize the mark to a single tool. Such characteristics, when they do exist, usually take the form of discernible
random nicks and breaks that the tool has acquired through wear and
use (Figure 15–16).

Just as the machined surfaces of a firearm are impressed with
random striations during its manufacture, the edges of a pry bar,
chisel, screwdriver, knife, and cutting tool will likewise display a
series of microscopic irregularities having the appearance of ridges
and valleys. Such markings are left as a result of the machining
processes used to cut and finish tools. The shape and pattern of such
minute imperfections are further modified by damage and wear during
the life of the tool. Considering the unending variety of patterns that
the hills and valleys can assume, it is highly unlikely that any two
tools will be identical. Hence, it is the presence of these minute imperfections that imparts individuality to each tool.

If the edge of a tool is scraped against a softer surface, it may cut
a series of striated lines that reflect that pattern of the tool's edge.
Markings left in this manner are compared in the laboratory through
a comparison microscope with test tool marks made from the suspect
tool. The result can be a positive comparison, and hence a definitive
association of the tool with the evidence mark, when a sufficient quantity of striations match between the evidence and test markings.

One of the major problems associated with tool mark comparisons
is the difficulty in duplicating in the laboratory the tool mark left at
the crime scene. A thorough comparison requires the preparation of a
series of test marks obtained by applying the suspect tool at various

Figure 15–16.
A comparison of a tool mark with a suspect screwdriver. Note how the presence of nicks and breaks on the tool's edge helps individualize the tool to the mark. *Courtesy* New Jersey State Police.

angles and pressures to a soft metal surface (lead is commonly used). This approach gives the examiner ample opportunity to duplicate many of the details of the original evidence marking. A photomicrograph of a typical tool mark comparison is illustrated in Figure 15–17.

Whenever it is practical, the entire object or the part of the object bearing a tool mark should be submitted to the crime laboratory for examination. When removal of the tool mark is impractical, the only recourse left to the field investigator is to photograph the marked area to scale and make a cast of the mark. Under these circumstances, liquid silicone casting material or dental plaster has been found to be the most satisfactory for reproducing most of the fine details of the mark. However, even under the most optimum conditions, the clarity of many of the tool mark's minute details will be lost or obscured in a photograph or cast. Of course, this will reduce the possibility that the criminalist could individualize the mark to a single tool.

Under no circumstances must the crime-scene investigator attempt to fit the suspect tool into the tool mark. Any contact between

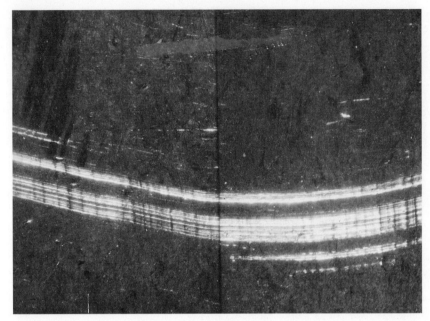

Figure 15–17. A photograph of a tool mark comparison seen under a comparison microscope. *Courtesy* Ernst Leitz.

the tool and the marked surface may alter the mark and will, at the least, raise serious questions about the integrity of the evidence. The suspect tool and mark must be packaged in separate containers, with every precaution taken to avoid contact between the tool or mark with another hard surface. Failure to properly protect the tool or mark from damage could result in the destruction of its individual characteristics. Furthermore, the investigator must bear in mind that the tool or its impression may contain valuable trace evidence. Chips of paint adhering to the mark or tool provide perhaps the best example of how the transfer of trace physical evidence can occur as a result of using a tool to gain forcible entry into a building. Obviously, the presence of trace evidence greatly enhances the evidential value of the tool or its mark and requires that special care be taken in the handling and packaging of the evidence to avoid the loss or destruction of these items.

OTHER IMPRESSIONS

From time to time, impressions of another kind are left at a crime scene. This evidence may take the form of a shoe, tire, or fabric impression and may be as varied as a shoe impression left on a piece of paper at the scene of a burglary (Figure 15–18), a hit-and-run victim's garment that has come into violent contact with an automobile (Figure 15–19), or the impression of a bloody shoe print left on a floor or carpet at a homicide scene (Figure 15–20).

The primary consideration in collecting impressions at the crime scene is the preservation of the impression or its reproduction for later examination in the crime laboratory. Before any impression is moved or otherwise handled, it must be photographed (a scale should be included in the picture) to show all the observable details of the impression. Several shots should be taken directly over the impression as well as at various angles around the impression. The skillful use of side lighting for illumination will help highlight many ridge details that might otherwise remain obscured. Photographs should also be taken to show the position of the questioned impression in relation to the overall crime scene.

Although photography is an important first step in preserving an impression, it still must be considered only as a backup procedure that

Figure 15–18. (a) Impression of shoe found at a crime scene. (b) Test impression made with suspect shoe. A sufficient number of points of comparison exist to support the conclusion that the suspect shoe left the impression at the crime scene. Both photos *courtesy* New Jersey State Police.

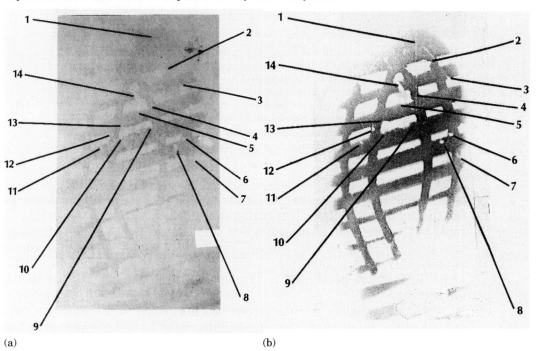

(a)   (b)

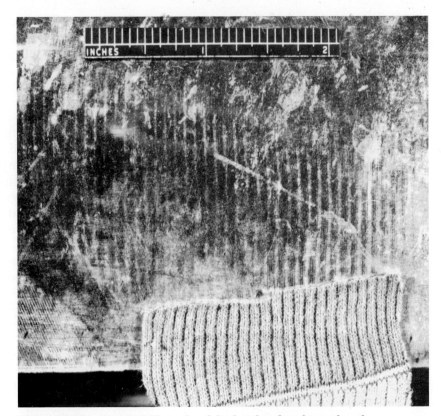

Figure 15–19. A small child was found dead at the edge of a rural road near a railroad crossing, the victim of a hit-and-run driver. A local resident was suspected, but he denied any knowledge of the incident. The investigating officer noted what appeared to be a fabric imprint on the bumper of the suspect's automobile. The weave pattern of the clothing of the deceased was compared with the imprint on the bumper and was found to match. When the suspect was confronted with this information, he admitted his guilt. *Courtesy* Centre of Forensic Sciences, Toronto, Canada.

is available to the examiner if the impression is damaged before reaching the crime laboratory. Naturally, it is preferable for the examiner to receive the original impression for comparison to the suspect shoe, tire, garment, and so forth. In most instances where the impression is on a readily recoverable item, such as glass, paper, or floor tile, little or no difficulty is presented in transporting the evidence intact to the laboratory.

If an impression is encountered on a surface that cannot be submitted to the laboratory, the investigator may be able to preserve the print in a manner that is analogous to lifting a fingerprint. This is

(a) Bloody footprint on cardboard treated with amido black.

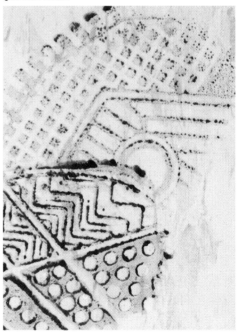

(b) Bloody footprint treated with Hungarian Red dye.

(c) Bloody footprint visualized with leucocrystal violet.

(d) Bloody footprint enhanced with patent blue.

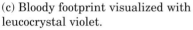

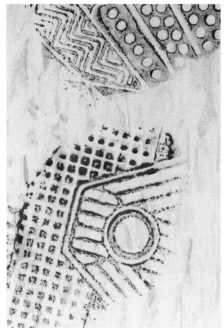

Source: (a) Courtesy Dwane S. Hilderbrand and David P. Coy, Scottsdale Police Crime Laboratory, Scottsdale, AZ. (b) Courtesy ODV, Inc., S. Paris, ME. (c to h) Courtesy William Bodziak, FBI Laboratory.

Color Plate 7

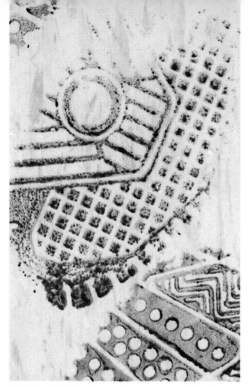

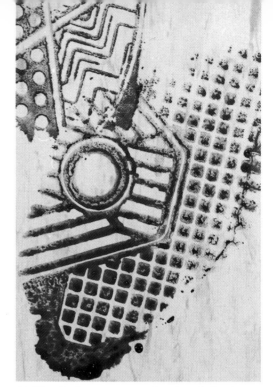

(e) Bloody foot impression treated with amido black.

(f) Bloody footprint visualized with fuschin acid dye.

(g) Bloody foot impression visualized with tartrazine.

(h) Bloody footprint treated with diamino-benzidine.

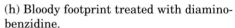

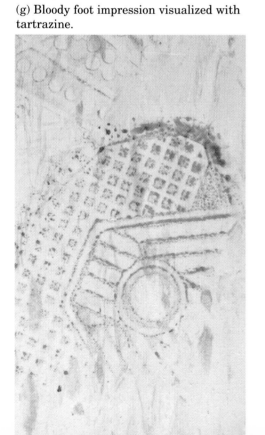

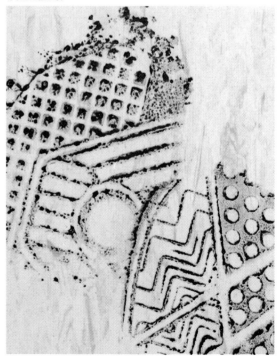

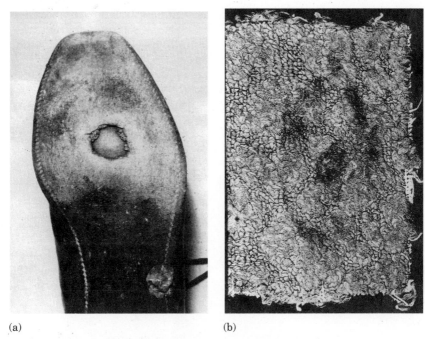

(a)   (b)

Figure 15–20.   A bloody imprint of a shoe was found on the carpet in the home of a homicide victim (b). The suspect's shoe shown in (a) made the impression. Note the distinctive impression of the hole present in the shoe's sole. *Courtesy* Dade County Crime Laboratory, Miami, Fla.

especially true of impressions made in light deposits of dust or dirt. Here, it is desirable that a lifting material large enough to lift the entire impression be used. One product that is excellent for lifting impressions, called "handprint," is available from the Kinderprint Co., Martinez, California. Carefully place the lifting material over the entire impression. Use a fingerprint roller to eliminate any air pockets before lifting the impression off the surface.

Another and more exotic approach to lifting and preserving dust impressions involves the use of a portable electrostatic lifting device known as Pathfinder.[7] The principle employed is similar to creating an electrostatic charge on a comb and using the comb to lift small pieces of tissue paper. A mylar sheet of film is placed on top of the dust mark, and the film is pressed against the impression with the aid of a roller. The high-voltage electrode of the Pathfinder is then placed in contact with the film while the Pathfinder's earth electrodes are placed against a metal plate (earth plate) (see Figure 15–21). A

---

[7]Available from Kinderprint Co., P.O. Box 16, Martinez, Calif. 94553.

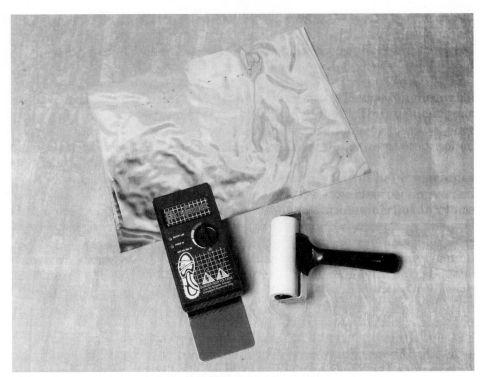

Figure 15–21.   Electrostatic lifting of a dust impression off a floor using a pocket-size powder supply known as Pathfinder. *Courtesy* Ivy Scene of Crime Equipment Ltd., Northampton, U.K.

charge difference develops between the mylar film and the surface below the dust mark so that the dust is attached to the lifting film. In this manner, dust prints off chairs, walls, floors, and the like can be transferred to the mylar film. It has been demonstrated that floor surfaces up to 40 feet in length can be covered with a mylar sheet and searched for dust impressions with the Pathfinder. The electrostatic lifting technique is particularly helpful in recovering barely visible dust prints off colored surfaces. Dust impressions may also be enhanced through chemical development (see Figure 15–22).[8]

When shoe and tire marks are impressed into soft earth at a crime scene, their preservation is best accomplished by photography and casting.[9] Class I dental stone, a form of gypsum, is widely recommended for making casts of shoe and tire impressions. The cast should

---

[8]Source: B. Glattstein, Y. Shor, N. Levin, A. Zeichner, "pH Indicators As Chemical Reagents for the Enhancement of Footwear Marks," *Journal of Forensic Sciences,* 41 (1996), 23.

[9]D. S. Hilderbrand and M. Miller, "Casting Materials—Which One to Use!" *Journal of Forensic Identification,* 45 (1995), 618.

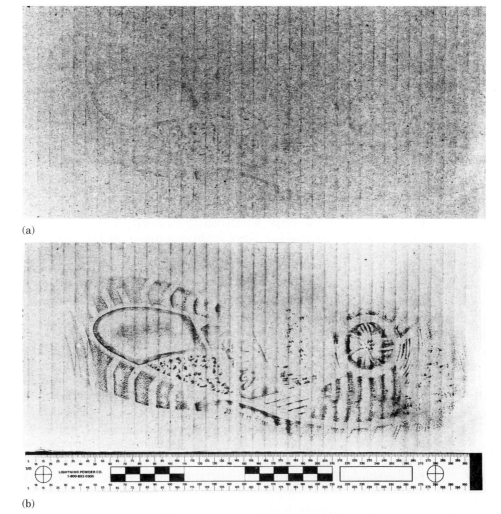

(a)

(b)

Figure 15–22. (a) A dust impression of a shoeprint on cardboard before enhancement. (b) Shoeprint after chemical enhancement with Bromophenol Blue and exposure to water vapor. *Courtesy* Division of Identification and Forensic Science, Israel Police Headquarters, Jerusalem, Israel.

be allowed to air-dry for 24 to 48 hours before it is shipped to the forensic science laboratory for examination. If soil or debris from the impression area is adhering to the cast, no attempt should be made at the crime scene to clean it. An aerosol product known as Snow-Print-Wax is available for casting snow impressions.[10] The recommended procedure is to spray three light coats of the wax at an interval of 1 to

---

[10]Available from Kinderprint Co., P.O. Box 16, Martinez, Calif. 94553.

2 minutes between layers and then let it dry for 10 minutes. A viscous mixture of Class I dental stone is then poured onto the wax-coated impression. After the casting material has hardened, the cast can be removed.

There are a number of chemicals that can be used to develop and enhance footwear impressions made with blood. In areas where a bloody footwear impression is very faint or where the subject has tracked through blood leaving a trail of bloody impressions, chemical enhancement can visualize latent or nearly invisible blood impressions (see Color Plates 7 and 8). A number of chemical formulas useful for bloody footwear impression development are listed in Appendix VI.

Whatever the circumstances, the laboratory procedures used for examining any type of impression remain the same. Of course, a comparison is possible only when an item suspected of having made the impression is recovered. Test impressions may be necessary to compare the characteristics of the suspect item with the evidence impression. The evidential value of the impression will be determined by the number of class and individual characteristics that the examiner finds. Agreement with respect to size, shape, or design may permit the conclusion that the impression *could* have been made by a particular shoe, tire, or garment; however, one cannot entirely exclude other possible sources from having the same class characteristics. More significant is the existence of individual characteristics arising out of wear, cuts, gouges, or other damage. A sufficient number or the uniqueness of such points of comparison will support a finding that both the evidence and test impressions originated from one and only one source.

In situations where tire tread impressions are left at a crime scene, the laboratory can examine the design of the impression and possibly determine the style and/or manufacturer of the tire. This may be particularly helpful to investigators in situations where a suspect tire has not yet been located.

New computer software may be able to assist the forensic scientist in making shoeprint comparisons. For example, an automated shoeprint identification system developed in England, called Shoeprint Image Capture and Retrieval (SICAR), incorporates multiple databases to search known and unknown footwear files for comparison against footwear specimens. Using the system, an impression from a crime scene can be compared to a reference database to find out what type of shoe caused the imprint. That same impression can also be searched in the suspect and crime databases to reveal if that shoeprint matches the shoes of a person who has been in custody or the shoeprints left behind at another crime scene. When matches are made during the searching process, the images are displayed side by side on the computer screen.

Human bite mark impressions on skin and foodstuffs have proven to be important items of evidence for convicting defendants in a number of homicide and rape cases in recent years. If a sufficient number of points of similarity between test and suspect marks are present, a forensic odontologist may conclude that a bite mark was made by one particular individual (see Figure 1–4).

In one case illustrative of the value of bite marks, a wad of used chewing gum was found at a murder site.[11] Examination of the gum revealed the presence of teeth marks. Dental impressions of the victim and two suspects arrested in connection with the murder were then taken. From these, a forensic odontologist was able to make test impressions in silicone for comparison to the chewing gum. Sufficient points of similarity existed to allow the examiner to eliminate the victim and one suspect and to conclude that the gum had been imprinted by the second suspect's teeth.

Tests were also undertaken to determine the blood type of the individual who had chewed the gum. Laboratory tests on the saliva residues on the gum showed that it had been chewed by a secretor with the blood type AB. This type appears in approximately 4 percent of the population and coincided with the blood type of the same suspect selected based on the dental impression.

There was no trial in this case because shortly after these findings were established, a guilty plea of murder was entered by the suspect.

REVIEW QUESTIONS

1. The _____ is the original part of the bore left after rifling grooves are formed.
2. The diameter of the gun barrel is known as its _____.
3. The number of lands and grooves is a(n) (class, individual) characteristic of a barrel.
4. The (individual, class) characteristics of a rifled barrel are formed by striations impressed into the barrel's surface.
5. The single most important instrument for comparing bullets is the _____.
6. If bullets were fired in succession from the same weapon, all the individual characteristics would always be identical. (True, False)
7. It is (always, sometimes) possible to determine the make of a weapon by examining a bullet it fired.

---

[11]H. D. Sperber, "Chewing Gum—An Unusual Clue in a Recent Homicide Investigation," *Journal of Forensic Sciences,* 23 (1978), 792.

8. A shotgun has a (rifled, smooth) barrel.

9. The diameter of a shotgun barrel is expressed by the term _____.

10. Shotgun pellets can be individualized to a single weapon. (True, False)

11. A cartridge case (can, cannot) be individualized to a single weapon.

12. The shape of the indentation caused by the firing pin may be a characteristic peculiar to a firearm. (True, False)

13. The distribution of gunpowder particles and other discharge residues around a bullet hole permits an approximate determination of the distance from which the gun was fired. (True, False)

14. Without the benefit of a weapon, an examiner can make an exact determination of firing distance. (True, False)

15. A halo of vaporous lead (smoke) deposited around a bullet hole is normally indicative of a discharge _____ to _____ inches from the target.

16. An _____ photograph may help visualize gunpowder deposits around a target.

17. One test method for locating powder residues involves transferring particles embedded on the target surface to chemically treated photographic paper. (True, False)

18. As a rule of thumb, the spread in the pattern made by a 12-gauge shotgun is increased 1 inch for every _____ of distance from the target.

19. Current methods for identifying a shooter rely on the detection of (primer, gunpowder) residues on the hands.

20. Determining whether or not an individual has fired a weapon is done by measuring the elements _____ and _____ present on the hands.

21. Firings with all types of ammunition can be detected by hand swabbings with nitric acid. (True, False)

22. Restoration of serial numbers is possible because in the stamped zone the metal is placed under a permanent strain that extends beneath the original numbers. (True, False)

23. It (is, is not) proper to insert a pencil into the barrel in picking up the weapon.

24. Recovered bullets are initialed either on the _____ or _____ of the bullet.

25. Cartridge cases are best marked at the base of the shell. (True, False)

26. The clothing of the victim of a shooting must be handled so as to prevent disruption of _____ around bullet holes.

27. A _____ is any impression caused by a tool coming into contact with another object.
28. Tool marks compare only when a sufficient number of _____ match between the evidence and test markings.
29. A wear pattern can impart (class, individual) characteristics to a shoe.
30. When shoe and tire marks are impressed into soft earth at a crime scene, their preservation is best accomplished by _____ and _____.

FURTHER REFERENCES

Abbott, J. R., and A. C. Germann, *Footwear Evidence.* Springfield, Ill.: Charles C Thomas, Publisher, 1964.

Barnes, F. C., and R. A. Helson, "An Empirical Study of Gunpowder Residue Patterns," *Journal of the Forensic Sciences,* 19 (1974), 448.

Bodziak, William J., *Footwear Impression Evidence.* Boca Raton, Fla.: CRC Press, Inc., 1990.

Cassidy, Michael J., *Footwear Identification.* Ottawa, Canada: Royal Canadian Mounted Police, 1980.

Davis, J., *Tool Marks, Firearms and the Striagraph.* Springfield, Ill.: Charles C Thomas, Publisher, 1958.

Di Maio, V. J. M., *Gunshot Wounds: Practical Aspects of Firearms, Ballistics, and Forensic Techniques.* Boca Raton, Fla.: CRC Press, Inc., 1985.

Heard, Brian J., *Handbook of Firearms and Ballistics,* Chichester, England: Wiley & Sons, 1997.

Kinard, W. D., and C. R. Midkiff, Jr., "Developments in Firearms Residue Detection," in *Forensic Science,* 2nd ed., G. Davies, ed. Washington, D.C.: American Chemical Society, 1986.

McDonald, Peter, *Tire Imprint Evidence.* Boca Raton, Fla.: CRC Press, Inc., 1989.

Moenssens, A. A., J. E. Starrs, C. E. Henderson, and F. E. Inbau, *Scientific Evidence in Civil and Criminal Cases,* 4th ed. Mineola, N.Y.: Foundation Press, 1995.

Rowe, Walter F., "Firearms Identification," in *Forensic Science Handbook,* Vol. 2, R. Saferstein, ed. Englewood Cliffs, N.J.: Prentice Hall, 1988.

Treptow, Richard S., *Handbook of Methods for the Restoration of Obliterated Serial Numbers,* National Aeronautics and Space Administration Contract Report CR-135322. Washington, D.C.: NASA, 1978.

DOCUMENT
AND VOICE
EXAMINATION

Ordinarily, the work of the document examiner involves the examination of handwriting and typewriting to ascertain the source or authenticity of a questioned document. However, document examination is not restricted to a mere visual comparison of words and letters. The document examiner must know how to utilize the techniques of microscopy, photography, and even such analytical methods as chromatography to uncover successfully all efforts, both brazen and subtle, designed to change the content or meaning of a document. Alterations of documents through overwriting, erasures, or the more obvious crossing out of words must be recognized and must be characterized by the examiner as efforts intended to alter or obscure the original meaning of a document. It is the special skills of the document examiner that are relied upon to reconstruct the written contents of charred or burned paper, or to uncover the meaning of indented writings found on a paper pad after the top sheet has been removed.

Any object that contains handwritten or typewritten markings whose source or authenticity is in doubt may be referred to as a "questioned document." Such a broad definition certainly covers all of the written and printed materials that are normally encountered in our daily, social, and business activities. Letters, checks, drivers' licenses, contracts, wills, voter registrations, passports, petitions, and even lottery tickets are the more common specimens received in crime laboratories to be examined. However, we need not restrict our examples to paper documents. Questioned documents may include writings or other markings found on walls, windows, doors, or any other objects.

It must be emphasized that document examiners possess no mystical powers or scientific formulas for identifying the authors of writings. Their success is predicated on applying knowledge gathered through years of training and experience to recognizing and comparing the individual characteristics of questioned and known authentic writings. For this purpose, the gathering of documents of known authorship or origin is critical to the outcome of the examination. Collecting known writings may entail considerable time and effort, and their collection may be further hampered by uncooperative or missing witnesses. However, the uniqueness of handwriting makes this type of physical evidence, like fingerprints, one of few definitive individual characteristics available to the investigator, a fact that certainly justifies an extensive investigative effort.

HANDWRITING COMPARISONS

Document experts continually testify to the fact that no two individuals write exactly alike. This is not to say that there cannot be marked resemblances between two individuals' handwritings, for there are many factors that comprise the total character of a person's writing. Perhaps the most obvious feature of handwriting to the layperson is its general style. As children we all learn to write by attempting to copy letters that match a standard form or style shown to us by our teachers. The style of writing acquired by the learner is that which is fashionable for the particular time and locale. In the United States, for example, the two most widely used systems are the Palmer, first introduced in 1880, and the Zaner-Blosser, introduced in about 1895. To some extent, both of these systems are taught in nearly all of the 50 states.

The early stages that accompany the learning and practicing of handwriting are characterized by a conscious effort on the part of the student to copy standard letter forms. It is not surprising that many pupils in a handwriting class tend at first to have writing styles that are similar to each other, with minor differences attributable to skill in copying. However, as initial writing skills improve, a child normally reaches the stage where the nerve and motor responses associated with the act of writing become subconscious efforts. The individual's writing now begins to take on innumerable habitual shapes and patterns that distinguish it from all others. It is precisely these unique writing traits that the document examiner looks for.

The unconscious handwriting of two different individuals can never be identical. Individual variations associated with mechanical, physical, and mental functions make it extremely unlikely that all these factors can be exactly reproduced by any two people. Thus, variations are expected in angularity, slope, speed, pressure, letter and word spacings, relative dimensions of letters, connections, pen movement, writing skill, and finger dexterity. Furthermore, many other factors besides pure handwriting characteristics are to be considered. The arrangement of the writing on the paper may be as distinctive as the writing itself. Margins, spacings, crowding, insertions, and alignment are all results of personal habits. Spelling, punctuation, phraseology, and grammar can be personal and, if so, combine to individualize the writer.

In a problem involving the authorship of handwriting, all characteristics of both the known and questioned documents must be considered and compared. Dissimilarities between the two writings are a strong indication of two writers, unless these differences can logically be accounted for by the facts surrounding the preparation of the documents. Because any single characteristic, even the most unique one, may be found in the handwriting of other individuals, no single handwriting characteristic can by itself be taken as the basis for a positive comparison. The final conclusion must be based on a sufficient number of common characteristics between the known and questioned writings to effectively preclude the chance of their having originated from two different sources.

What constitutes a sufficient number of personal characteristics? Here again, there are no hard and fast rules for making such a determination. This is a judgment that can be made by the expert examiner only in the context of each particular case.

When the examiner is presented with a reasonable amount of known handwriting for comparison, there is usually little difficulty in finding sufficient evidence to determine the source of a questioned document. Frequently, however, circumstances may prevent a positive conclusion or may permit only the expression of a qualified opinion. Such situations usually develop when an insufficient number of known writings are made available for comparison. Although nothing may be found that definitely points to the questioned and known handwriting being of a different origin, there may not be enough personal characteristics present in the known writings that are consistent with the questioned materials.

Difficulties may also arise when the examiner is presented with questioned writings containing only a few words, all deliberately written in a crude, unnatural form or all very carefully written and thought out so as to disguise the writer's natural style—a situation usually encountered with threatening or obscene letters. It is extremely difficult to compare handwriting that has been very carefully prepared to a document written with such little thought for structural details that it contains only the subconscious writing habits of the writer. However, although it may be relatively easy to change one's writing habits for a few words or sentences, the task of maintaining such an effort grows more difficult with each additional word. When there is an adequate amount of writing available to the examiner, the attempt at total disguise may fail. This was illustrated in the attempt by Clifford Irving to forge letters in the name of the late industrialist Howard Hughes in order to obtain lucrative publishing contracts for Hughes's life story. Figure 16–1 shows the forged signatures of Howard Hughes along with Clifford Irving's known writings. By comparing these signatures, document examiner R. A. Cabbane of the U.S. Postal Inspection Service detected many examples of Irving's personal characteristics in the forged signatures. For example, note the formation of the letter *r* in the word *Howard* on lines 1 and 3, as compared

Figure 16–1. Forged signatures of Howard Hughes and examples of Clifford Irving's writing. Reprinted by permission of the American Society for Testing and Materials from the *Journal of Forensic Sciences,* copyright 1975.

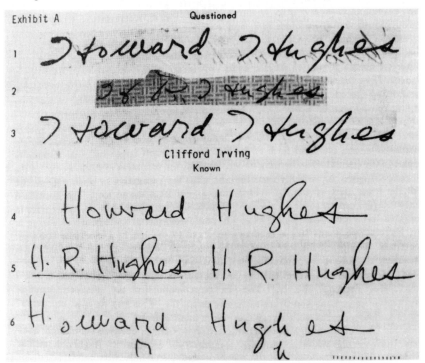

with the composite on line 6. Observe the manner in which the terminal stroke of the letter *r* has a tendency to terminate with a little curve at the baseline of writing on Irving's writing and the forgery. Notice the way the bridge of the *w* drops in line 1 and also in line 6. Also, observe the similarity in the formation of the letter *g* as it appears on line 1 as compared with the second signature on line 5.

The document examiner must also be aware of the fact that writing habits may be altered beyond recognition by the influence of drugs or alcohol. Under these circumstances, it may be impossible to obtain known writings of a suspect written under conditions comparable to those in existence at the time the questioned document was prepared.

COLLECTION OF HANDWRITING EXEMPLARS

It should be fairly obvious by now that the collection of an adequate number of known writings is most critical for determining the outcome of a comparison. Generally, known writings of the suspect furnished to the examiner should be as alike as possible to the questioned document. This is especially true with respect to the writing implement and paper. Styles and habits may be somewhat altered if a person switches from a pencil to a ballpoint pen or to a fountain pen. The way the paper is ruled, or the fact that it is unruled, may also affect the handwriting of a person who has become particularly accustomed to one type or the other. Known writings should also contain some of the words and combinations of letters present in the questioned document.

The known writings must be adequate in number to show the examiner the range of natural variations in a suspect's writing characteristics. No two specimens of writing prepared by one person are ever identical in every detail. Variation is an inherent part of natural writing. In fact, a signature forged by the tracing of an authentic signature can often be detected even if the original and tracing are shown to coincide exactly, because no one ever signs two signatures exactly alike.

There are a great many sources that the investigator can use in establishing the authenticity of the writings of a suspect. An important consideration in selecting sample writings is the age of the genuine document relative to the questioned one. It is important to try to find standards that date closely in time to the questioned document. For most typical adults, basic writing changes are comparatively slow. Therefore, material written within two or three years of the disputed writing is usually found satisfactory for comparison; but as the age difference between the genuine and unknown specimens becomes greater, the standard has a tendency to become less representative.

Despite the many potential sources of handwriting exemplars, it may be difficult or impossible to obtain an adequate set of collected standards. In these situations, handwriting may have to be obtained voluntarily or under court order from the suspect. There is ample case law to support the constitutionality of taking handwriting specimens. In the case of *Gilbert* v. *California*,[1] the Supreme Court upheld the taking of handwriting exemplars before the appointment of counsel. The Court also reasoned that handwriting samples are identifying physical characteristics that lie outside the protection privileges of the Fifth Amendment. Furthermore, in the case of *United States* v. *Mara*,[2] the Supreme Court ruled that the taking of a handwriting sample did not constitute an unreasonable search and seizure of a person and hence was not in violation of Fourth Amendment rights.

As opposed to nonrequested specimens (written without the thought that they may someday be used in a police investigation), requested writing samples may be consciously altered by the writer. However, the investigator can take certain steps to minimize attempts at deception. The requirement of several pages of writing will normally provide the examiner with enough material that is free of attempts at deliberate disguise or nervousness to permit a valid comparison to be made. In addition, the writing of dictation yields exemplars best representative of the suspect's subconscious style and characteristics.

Other steps that can be taken to minimize a conscious writing effort, as well as to ensure conditions approximating those of the questioned writing, can be summarized as follows:

1. The writer should be allowed to write sitting comfortably at a desk or table and without distraction.
2. The suspect should not under any conditions be shown the questioned document or be provided with instructions on how to spell certain words or what punctuation to use.
3. The suspect should be furnished a pen and paper similar to those used in the questioned document.
4. The dictated text should be the same as the contents of the questioned document, or at least should contain many of the same words, phrases, and letter combinations found in the document. In hand-printing cases, the suspect must not be given any instruction on whether to use uppercase (capital) or lowercase (small) lettering. If after writing several pages the writer fails to use the desired type of lettering, he or she can

---

[1]388 U.S. 263 (1967).
[2]410 U.S. 19 (1973).

then be instructed to include it. Altogether, the text must be no shorter than a page.

5. Dictation of the text should take place at least three times. If the writer is making a deliberate effort to disguise the writing, noticeable variations should appear among the three repetitions. Discovering this, the investigator must insist upon continued repetitive dictation of the text.

6. Signature exemplars can best be obtained when the suspect is required to combine other writings with a signature. For example, instead of compiling a set of signatures alone, the writer might be asked to fill out completely 20 to 30 separate checks or receipts, each of which includes a signature.

7. Before requested exemplars are taken from the suspect, a document examiner should be consulted and shown the questioned specimens.

TYPEWRITING COMPARISONS

One mechanical writing device the document examiner encounters is the typewriter. The two requests most often made of the examiner in connection with the examination of these machines are (1) Can the make and model of the typewriter used to type the questioned document be identified? and (2) Can a particular suspect typewriter be identified as having prepared the questioned document?

To answer the first request, the examiner must have access to a complete reference collection of past and present typefaces used by typewriter manufacturers. The two most popular typeface sizes are **pica** (10 letters to the inch) and **elite** (12 letters to the inch). Although there may be a dozen manufacturers utilizing a pica or an elite typeface, many of these are readily distinguishable when a comparison is made of the individual type character's style, shape, and size.

As is true for any mechanical device, use of a typewriter will result in wear and damage to the machine's moving parts. These changes will occur in a fashion that is both random and irregular, thereby imparting individual characteristics to the typewriter. Variations in vertical and horizontal alignment (characters are too high or low or too far left or right of their correct position) and perpendicular misalignment of characters (characters leaning to the left or to the right), as well as defects in each typeface, are most valuable for proving the identity of a typewriter (see Figure 16–2).

The widespread use of business and personal computers is creating a series of new problems to challenge the skills of the document examiner. Personal computers use daisy wheel, dot matrix, and laser printers. More and more, the document examiner will be confronted

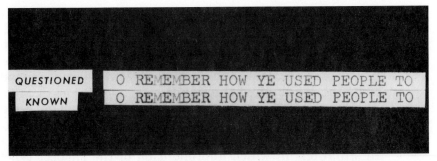

Figure 16–2. A portion of a typewriting comparison points to the conclusion that the same machine typed both specimens. Besides the similarity in the design and size of type, note the light impression consistently made by *M*. Also, *E* slants to the right, almost touching *D* in the word *USED* in both specimens. *Courtesy* New Jersey State Police.

with problems involving these machines, which often produce typed copies that have only inconspicuous defects.

The method of associating a particular typewriter with a typewritten document requires the comparison of the questioned document to exemplars prepared from the suspect typewriter. As with handwriting, the collection of proper standards is the foundation of such comparisons. In this respect, it is preferable if the investigator can directly supply the document examiner with the questioned typewriter. This arrangement gives the examiner the opportunity to prepare an adequate number of exemplars as well as allowing for a direct examination of the machine's typefaces. In the case of IBM Selectric typewriters, the problem of securing the entire typing mechanism is made more difficult because of the interchangeability of type-head spheres. Here, the typewriter as well as the suspect sphere must be secured for examination.

If the investigator has to prepare standards from the questioned machine, a minimum of one copy in full word-for-word order of the questioned typewriting must be obtained. In preparing standards from a machine with an adjustable touch control, partial copies of the questioned text should be typed in light, medium, and heavy touches, respectively. One point that should not be overlooked by either the investigator or the document examiner is the condition of the ribbon. Replacing a worn ribbon with a fresh one makes a significant difference in the typewritten copy. A lightly inked ribbon tends to emphasize slight defects; a well-inked ribbon is likely to obscure them. If exemplars prepared with the ribbon in use differ substantially from the questioned document with respect to inkings, additional standards that more nearly duplicate the questioned document may have to be prepared after consultation with a document examiner. In addition, samples of each character on the keyboard should be typed without the ribbon. To do this, the investigator should set the typewriter in the stencil position and type directly on carbon paper placed over bond paper. This step eliminates any apparent type deformities that may be caused by the condition of the ribbon.

Another area of investigation relates to the ribbon. An examination of the type impressions left on a ribbon may make it possible to find the portion of the ribbon on which a particular text was typed.

In situations in which apprehension of the suspect typewriter is not possible, the investigator must set about gathering known writings that have been typed on the suspect machine. Ideally, material should be selected that contains many of the same combinations of letters and words found on the questioned document. The individual defects that may characterize a typewriter develop and change as the machine is used; some may have altered during the period of time between the preparation of the questioned and standard material. Hence, if a large quantity of specimens is available, those prepared near the time of the disputed document should be collected.

ALTERATIONS, ERASURES, AND OBLITERATIONS

On many occasions, documents are altered or are changed after preparation so that their original intent may be hidden, or so that a forgery may be perpetrated. Documents can be changed in several ways, and for each, the application of a special discovery technique is necessary.

One of the most common ways to alter a document is to try to erase parts of it, using an India rubber eraser, sandpaper, razor blade, or knife to remove writing or type, by abrading or scratching the paper's surface. All such attempts at erasure disturb the upper fibers of the paper. These changes are readily apparent when the suspect area is examined under a microscope using direct light or by allowing the light to strike the paper obliquely from one side (side lighting). Although microscopy may reveal whether or not an erasure has been made, it will not necessarily indicate the original letters or words present. Sometimes so much of the paper has been removed that it is impossible to identify the original contents.

In addition to abrading the paper, the perpetrator may also choose to obliterate words with a chemical erasure. In this case, strong oxidizing agents are placed over the ink, and a reaction occurs that produces a colorless reaction product. Although such an attempt may not be noticeable to the naked eye, examination under the microscope will reveal a discoloration on the treated area of the paper. Sometimes examination of the document under ultraviolet or infrared lighting will reveal the chemically treated portion of the paper.

Some inks, when exposed to blue-green light, will absorb the radiation and will reradiate infrared light. This phenomenon has become known as "infrared luminescence." Thus, if an alteration is made to a document with ink differing from the original, it can sometimes be detected by illuminating the document with blue-green light and using infrared-sensitive film to record the light emanating from the document's surface. In this fashion, any differences in the luminescent properties of the inks will be observed (see Figure 16–3). Infrared luminescence has also been

Figure 16–3. A number of checks were stolen from a government agency and altered by an employee. Part of one check as it appears to the naked eye is shown in (a). An infrared luminescence photograph was prepared of the amount figures at a magnification of 10× in (b). This clearly shows that the number 2 was added with a different ink. The accused pleaded guilty. *Courtesy* Centre of Forensic Sciences, Toronto, Canada.

(a)

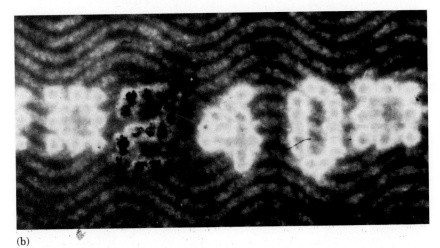

(b)

used successfully to reveal writing that has been erased. Such writings may be recorded by virtue of the fact that invisible residues of the original ink remain embedded in the paper even after an erasure.

    Another important application of infrared photography arises from the observation that inks may differ in their ability to absorb infrared light. Thus, by illuminating a document with infrared light and recording the light reflected off the document's surface with infrared-sensitive film, one may be able to differentiate inks of a dissimilar chemical composition (see Figure 16–4).

(a)

(b)

Figure 16–4.
(a) This photograph, taken under normal illumination, shows the owner of an American Express check to be "Freda C. Brightly Jones." Actually, this signature was altered. The check initially bore the signature "Fred C. Brightly Jr." (b) This photograph taken under infrared illumination, using infrared-sensitive film, clearly shows that the alteration was accomplished by the addition of *a* to *Fred* and *ones* to *Jr.* The ink used to commit these changes is distinguishable because it absorbs infrared light while the original ink does not. *Courtesy* New Jersey State Police.

The intentional obliteration of writing by overwriting or crossing out is seldom used for fraudulent purposes because of its obviousness. Nevertheless, such cases may be encountered in all types of documents. Success at permanently hiding the original writing will depend on the material that is used to cover the writing. If it is done with the same ink as was used to write the original material, recovery will be difficult if not impossible. However, if the two inks are of a different chemical composition, photography with infrared-sensitive film may reveal the original writing. Infrared radiation may pass through the upper layer of writing while being absorbed by the underlying area (see Figure 16–5).

Close examination of a questioned document sometimes reveals crossing strokes or strokes across folds of perforations in the paper that are not in a sequence that is consistent with the natural preparation of the document. Again, these differences can be shown by microscopic and/or photographic scrutiny.

Infrared photography is sometimes successfully used to reveal the contents of a document that has been accidentally or purposely charred in a fire. Another way to decipher charred documents involves reflecting light off the paper's surface at different angles in order to contrast the writing against the charred background (see Figure 16–6).

Digital image processing is the method by which the visual quality of digital pictures is improved or enhanced. Digitizing is the process by which the image is stored into memory. This is done by scanning a continuous image commonly with a TV camera and converting the image by computer into an array of digital intensity values called pixels, or picture elements (see p. 460). An image may be enhanced through lightening, darkening, and contrast control. An example of how the technology is applied to forensic document examination is shown in Figure 16–7.

OTHER DOCUMENT PROBLEMS

Indented writings are the partially visible depressions appearing on a sheet of paper underneath the one on which the visible writing was done. Such depressions are due to the application of pressure on the writing instrument and would appear as a carbon copy of a sheet if carbon paper had been inserted between the pages.

In certain situations, indented writings have proved to be valuable evidence. For example, the top sheet of a bookmaker's records may have been removed and destroyed, but it still may be possible to determine the writing by the impressions left on the pad. These impressions may contain incriminating evidence supporting the

(a)

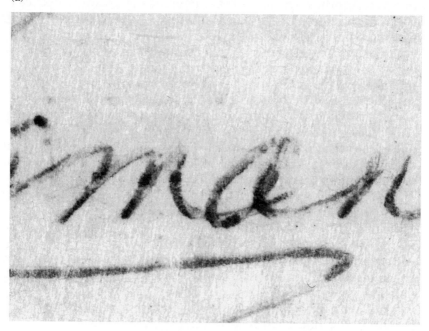

(b)

Figure 16–5. (a) A photograph showing an area of a document that has been blacked out with a heavy layer of ink overwriting. (b) In this photograph, the covering ink has been penetrated by infrared photography to reveal the original writing. *Courtesy* Centre of Forensic Sciences, Toronto, Canada.

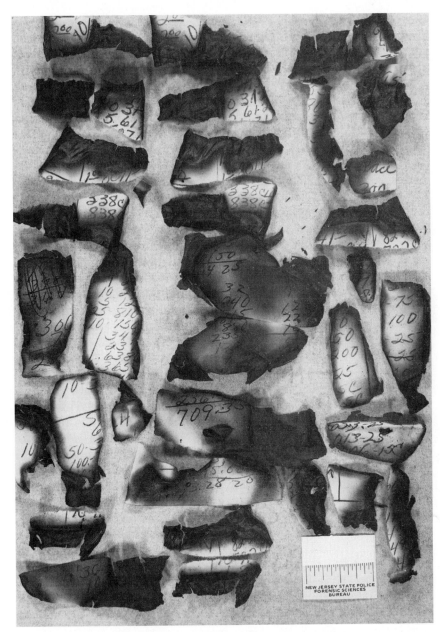

Figure 16–6. Decipherment of charred papers seized in the raid of a suspected bookmaking establishment. The charred documents were photographed with reflected light. *Courtesy* New Jersey State Police.

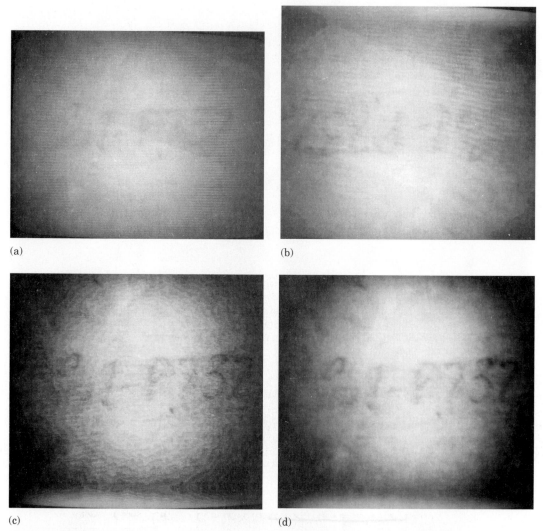

(a)

(b)

(c)

(d)

Figure 16–7. This example of enhancement by digital image processing involves a faint pencil impression found on yellow paper. (a) A live video image of the marking from which a digitized display is constructed. (b) A contrast function was applied to the digitized image. This function increases the contrast of an image by redistributing the range of gray levels. (c) The black intensity of the image is changed as a means of further enhancing the markings. (d) The Hi-Pass function was next applied. This function selectively filters out low-intensity gray levels by emphasizing high-frequency components in the image. This function sharpens the edge detail in the image. *Courtesy* Mary Wenderoth, Cleveland Police Laboratory, Cleveland, Ohio.

charge of illegal gambling activities. When paper is studied under oblique or side lighting, its indented impressions are often readable (see Figure 16–8). An innovative approach to visualizing indented writings has been developed at the London College of Printing in close consultation with the Metropolitan Police Forensic Science Laboratory.[3] The method involves applying an electrostatic charge to the surface of a polymer film that has been placed in close contact with a questioned document. Indented impressions on the document are revealed by applying a toner powder to the charged film. For many cases examined by this process, clearly readable images have been produced from impressions that could not be seen or were barely visible under normal illumination.

An instrument that develops indented writings by electrostatic detection is commercially available and is routinely used by document examiners.

Figure 16–8. A suspected forger was arrested. In his car were found written lists of the victims he intended to defraud. Some of these writings are shown in (a). A writing pad found in his house had indentations on the top page of the pad (b). These indentations corresponded to the writings found in the car, further linking the suspect to the writings. *Courtesy* Centre of Forensic Sciences, Toronto, Canada.

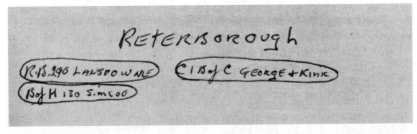

(a)

(b)

---

[3]D. M. Ellen, D. J. Foster, and D. J. Morantz, "The Use of Electrostatic Imaging in the Detection of Indented Impressions," *Forensic Science International*, 15 (1980), 53.

A study of the chemical composition of writing ink present on documents may verify whether or not known and questioned documents were prepared by the same pen. A nondestructive approach to comparing ink lines is accomplished with a visible microspectrophotometer (see pp. 193–195).[4] A case example illustrating the application of this approach to ink analysis appears in Figure 7–9. Thin-layer chromatography is also suitable for ink comparisons. Most commercial inks, especially ballpoint inks, are actually mixtures of several organic dyes. These dyes can readily be separated on a properly developed thin-layer chromatographic plate. The separation pattern of the component dyes is distinctly different for inks having different dye compositions and thus provides many points of comparison between a known and a questioned ink.

Ink can be removed from paper with a hypodermic needle with a blunted point to punch out a small sample from a written line. About 10 plugs or microdots of ink are sufficient for chromatographic analysis. Since 1968, the U.S. Treasury Department has been actively engaged in gathering a complete library of all commercial pen inks. These inks have been systematically cataloged according to dye patterns developed by thin-layer chromatography (see Figure 16–9). On several occasions, this approach has been used to prove that a document has been fraudulently backdated. For example, in one instance, it was possible to establish that a document dated 1958 was backdated because a dye identified in the questioned ink had not been synthesized until 1959.

To further aid forensic chemists in ink-dating matters, several ink manufacturers, at the request of the U.S. Treasury Department, have voluntarily been tagging their inks during the manufacturing process. The tagging program allows inks to be dated to the exact year of manufacture by changing the tags annually.

VOICE EXAMINATION

THE SOUND SPECTROGRAPH

In this era of telephone, radio, and tape-recorder communications, the human voice may often prove to be valuable evidence for associating an individual with a criminal act. The telephoned bomb threat, obscene phone call, or tape-recorded kidnap ransom message have all become frequent enough occurrences to warrant the interest of law

---

[4]P. W. Pfefferli, "Application of Microspectrophotometry in Document Examination," *Forensic Science International*, 23 (1983), 129.

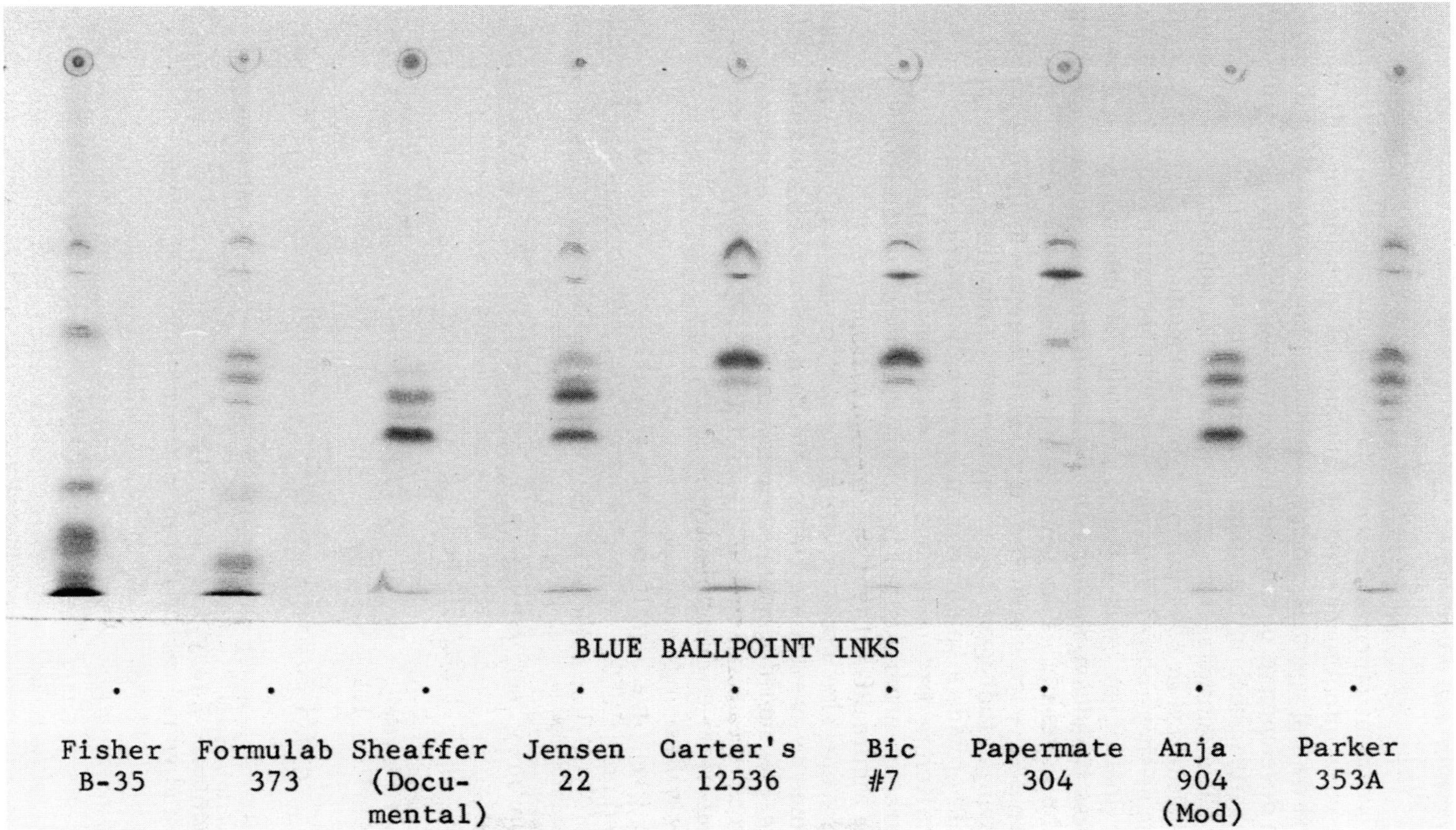

Figure 16-9. Chart demonstrating different TLC patterns of blue ballpoint inks. *Courtesy* Alcohol, Tobacco, and Firearms Laboratory, U.S. Treasury Dept., Washington, D.C.

enforcement officials in scientific techniques capable of transforming the voice into a form suitable for personal identification. To this end, a good deal of research and casework has been generated as a result of the development of the sound spectrograph; this is an instrument that converts speech into a visual graphic display.

The sound spectrograph was first developed at Bell Telephone Laboratories in 1941 during research devoted to studying speech signals as they related to communication services. During World War II, the instrument was used to identify for intelligence purposes the voices broadcast by German military communications. Following the war and during his employment with the company, a Bell System engineer, Lawrence Kersta, worked with this new technique and became convinced that voice spectrograms, or "voiceprints," as he called them, could provide a valuable means of personal identification.

Kersta contended that each voice has its own unique quality and character, arising out of individual variations in the vocal mechanism (see Figure 16–10). The probability that any two individuals will have the same size vocal cavities (throat, nasal, and two oral cavities formed by positioning the tongue) and will coordinate their articulators (lips, teeth, tongue, soft palate, and jaw muscles) in a like manner

Figure 16–10.   Schematic of the vocal mechanism. *Courtesy* Base Ten Systems, Inc.

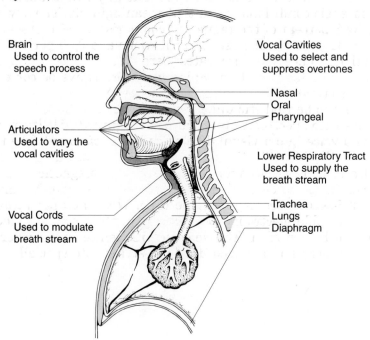

is so small as to make the human voice a unique personal trait. According to Kersta, the voiceprint is simply a graphic display of the unique characteristics of the voice.

As a result of Kersta's claim, the sound spectrograph has attracted great interest among criminal investigators. Many law enforcement laboratories have purchased the instrument, and various courts have been asked to accept its results as evidence of an individual's participation in a crime. However, at this time, there are still conflicting opinions in the courts as to whether the voiceprint has gained a sufficient degree of "general acceptance" within the scientific community to satisfy its admissibility as scientific evidence. A detailed report on voiceprints by the National Academy of Science concluded that "the degree of accuracy and the corresponding error rates of aural-visual voice identification vary widely from case to case, depending upon several conditions including the properties of the voices involved, the conditions under which the voice samples were made, the characteristics of the equipment used, the skill of the examiner making the judgments, and the examiner's knowledge about the case."[5]

The National Academy's concern that there is no adequate scientific basis for legal authorities to judge the reliability of voice spectrographic comparisons was addressed by a 1986 FBI study.[6] A survey of 2000 voice identification comparisons made by FBI examiners under actual forensic conditions found that meaningful decisions were made in only 34.8 percent of the requested comparisons, with observed error rates of 0.31 percent for false identifications and 0.53 percent for false eliminations. Since the error rates were determined from direct feedback from field investigators, which may not always be correct, these percentages represent minimum error rates. An error rate of 1 percent would seem to be realistic under typical case conditions.

The sound spectrograph is shown in Figure 16–11. It converts the sound of a voice into a visual display called a *voiceprint*. The first step in making the identification is to obtain tape recordings of both the suspect and known voices for comparison. The magnetic tape containing the message to be analyzed is fastened to a scanning drum that holds a 2.5-second segment of tape time. With each revolution of the drum, a variable electronic filter permits only a certain band of frequencies to be recorded. The selected frequencies are converted into electrical energy and are recorded by a stylus onto specially prepared

---

[5]*On the Theory and Practice of Voice Identification* (Washington, D.C.: National Academy of Sciences, 1979).

[6]B. E. Koenig, "Spectrographic Voice Identification: A Forensic Survey," *Journal of the Acoustical Society of America,* 79 (1986), 2088.

Figure 16–11.
A sound spectrograph.
Courtesy New Jersey State
Police.

chart paper. As the drum revolves, the variable filter moves to higher and higher frequencies while the stylus simultaneously records the intensity of each selected frequency range. Upon completion of the analysis, a print is produced that represents 2.5 seconds of tape time and contains a pattern of closely spaced lines showing all the audible frequencies in the tape segment.

Figure 16–12 demonstrates a typical voiceprint. The spectrum portrays three parameters of speech: time (horizontal axis), frequency (vertical axis), and the relative intensity or volume of the different frequencies. Intensity is proportional to the degree of darkness within

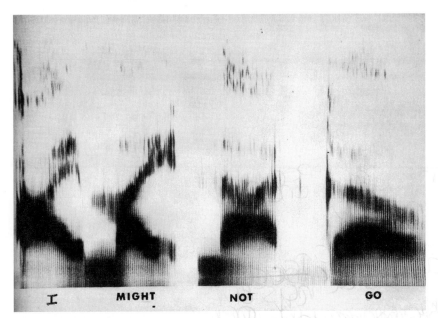

I   MIGHT   NOT   GO

Figure 16–12. A voiceprint. *Courtesy* New Jersey State Police.

each spectrographic region. Hence, in this manner, frequency patterns of identical or like-sounding words are obtained from both the questioned and the known voice for visual comparison. When sufficient similarity exists between the two, a positive conclusion is justified that both voices may have emanated from the same person.

Voiceprints depicting the word *you* are shown in Figure 16–13. As an exercise in voiceprint comparison, the reader can attempt to match the questioned voiceprint on the upper left to the voice of one of the five suspects.

Recent notable applications of voiceprint technology have served to increase the public awareness of this technique. For example, voiceprints played a part in Howard Hughes's refutation of Clifford Irving's purported autobiography of Hughes. A few days after McGraw-Hill and *Life* magazine announced their intent to publish Irving's work, Hughes Tool Company officials arranged for a telephone interview between the reclusive Howard Hughes in the Bahamas and a group of newspaper, radio, and TV reporters assembled in Los Angeles. At the request of one of the major TV networks, spectrographic comparisons of the voice from the Bahamas were made against a known sample of Hughes's voice recorded in 1947. The results proved beyond a doubt that the reporters had been conversing with Howard Hughes and not with an impostor. Irving was eventually found guilty of forging the "Hughes autobiography."

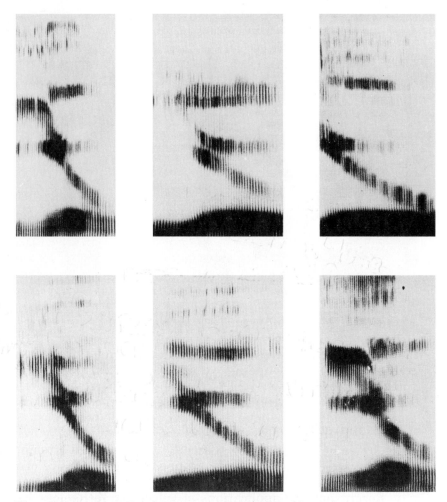

Figure 16–13. A questioned voiceprint and voiceprints of five male speakers uttering *you*. Match the questioned voiceprint on the upper left to the voiceprint of one of the five suspects. (The upper left and lower right voiceprints are of the same person.) *Courtesy* Base Ten Systems, Inc.

In another case, a perpetrator called the police to report that he had killed a woman and to reveal the location of the body. He gave his name as that of an acquaintance. During the course of the investigation, the man whose name was used was eliminated as the caller and the perpetrator was identified through voiceprint comparisons. Based on that identification, the impostor was found guilty and was sentenced to prison.

Present use of forensic voiceprint technology is limited to a relatively small number of active examiners. Legal barriers to the admission of this evidence exist in many jurisdictions. This situation will likely remain unchanged until a consensus develops among the practitioners of this technology with regard to minimum education and experience for spectrographic examiners and a minimum set of uniform criteria for defining and evaluating voiceprint comparisons.

REVIEW QUESTIONS

1. Any object that contains handwriting or typewriting and whose source or authenticity is in doubt is referred to as a _____.
2. Variations in mechanical, physical, and mental functions make it (likely, unlikely) that the writing of two different individuals can be distinguished.
3. In a problem involving the authorship of handwriting, all characteristics of both the _____ and _____ documents must be considered and compared.
4. A single handwriting characteristic can by itself be taken as a basis for a positive comparison. (True, False)
5. Normally, known writings need not contain words and combinations of letters present in the questioned document. (True, False)
6. As the age difference between genuine and unknown specimens becomes greater, the standard has a tendency to become (more, less) representative of the unknown.
7. In the case of _____, the Supreme Court held handwriting to be nontestimonial evidence not protected by Fifth Amendment privileges.
8. When requested writing is being given by a suspect, care must be taken to minimize a _____ writing effort.
9. Random wear and damage to a typewriter will impart it with _____ characteristics.
10. Examination of a document under _____ or _____ lighting may reveal chemical erasures of words or numbers.
11. Some inks, when exposed to blue-green light, will absorb this radiation and emit _____ light.
12. Handwriting containing inks of different chemical compositions may be distinguished by photography with _____ film.
13. _____ writings are partially visible impressions appearing on a sheet of paper underneath the one on which the visible writing was done.
14. Many ink dyes can be separated by the technique of _____ chromatography.

15. The _____ was first developed at Bell Telephone Laboratories in 1941.

16. The sound spectrograph converts sound into a visual display called a _____.

17. Presently, voices analyzed by the sound spectrograph have been widely accepted as evidence in U.S. courts. (True, False)

FURTHER REFERENCES

Brunelle, Richard L., "Questioned Document Examination," in *Forensic Science Handbook,* R. Saferstein, ed. Englewood Cliffs, N.J.: Prentice Hall, 1982.

Brunelle, Richard L., and Robert W. Reed, *Forensic Examination of Ink and Paper.* Springfield, Ill.: Charles C Thomas, Publisher, 1984.

Cantu, Antonio A., "Analytical Methods for Detecting Fraudulent Documents," *Analytical Chemistry,* 63 (1991), 847A.

Ellen, David, *The Scientific Examination of Documents—Methods and Techniques,* 2nd ed. Basingstoke, Hants, England: Taylor & Francis, 1997.

Hilton, Ordway, "The Evolution of Questioned Document Examination in the Last 50 Years," *Journal of Forensic Sciences,* 33 (1987), 1310.

————, *Scientific Examination of Questioned Documents,* rev. ed. Boca Raton, Fla.: CRC Press, Inc., 1982.

Moenssens, André A., J. Starrs, C. E. Henderson, and F. E. Inbau, *Scientific Evidence in Civil and Criminal Cases,* 4th ed. Mineola, N.Y.: Foundation Press, 1995.

On the Theory and Practice of Voice Identification. Washington, D.C.: National Academy of Sciences, 1979.

Proceedings of the International Symposium on Questioned Documents. Washington, D.C.: U.S. Government Printing Office, 1987.

FORENSIC SCIENCE ON THE INTERNET

Today, one cannot read a newspaper or turn on the television without seeing some reference to the Internet. The Internet, often referred to as the "information superhighway," has opened a medium for people to communicate with others and to access millions of pieces of information on computers located anywhere on the globe. No subject or profession remains untouched by the Internet, and this is so for forensic science. Every week many new pages of information are being added to the Internet on the subject of forensic science, providing instant access to updated forensic science news and information. The major impact of the Internet will be to bring together forensic scientists from all parts of the world, linking them into one common electronic community.

The Internet was developed in 1969 by the U.S. Department of Defense with the purpose of providing a connection between computers in different locations. The project, called ARPANET, originated from a group of scientists and engineers funded by the Pentagon's Advanced Research Projects Agency (ARPA). Their idea was based on the premise that the network would still operate even if part of the connection failed. The first successful link was established between computers housed at UCLA and Stanford Research Institute. Shortly thereafter, the sites of USC–Santa Barbara and the University of Utah computers were added to the system. In 1972, there were more than 20 sites connected on the system when the first electronic mail (e-mail) message was sent. In the

1980s, this network of interconnected computers grew with the establishment of the National Science Foundation Network (NSFNet), which encompassed five supercomputing centers across the United States. At about the same time, regional networks were formed around the United States for the purpose of accessing NSFNet. By 1989, ARPANET had closed down and NSFNet, along with its regional networks, began to mushroom into a worldwide network known as the "Internet."[1]

WHAT IS THE INTERNET?

The Internet can be defined as a "network of networks." A single network consists of two or more computers that are connected to share information; the Internet connects thousands of these networks so all of the information can be exchanged worldwide. Connections are made through **modems,** a device that allows computers to exchange and transmit information through telephone lines. Modems transfer the information at a rate of bits per second (bps). Obviously, a modem with high-speed capabilities will assure a faster connection on the Internet. One shouldn't consider connecting to the Internet with a modem that has a transmission speed rate of less than 14.4 bps. Currently, the 28.8 bps modem is recommended for optimum connection speed. Each computer that is linked to the Internet is called a **site.** When you are connected on the Internet, the computer you are using is a local site, and the computers you are communicating with are called the remote sites. The types of organizations that host a site are called **domains.** The most common domains are

> gov . . . government
> mil . . . military
> edu . . . educational institution
> com . . . commercial providers
> org . . . nonprofit organizations

There are several routes that can be taken to connect to the Internet. First, there are commercial online services such as America Online (AOL). These services are the easiest way to get online and are available at a modest cost. For example, most of them, such as America Online and AT&T World Net Service offer their program with unlimited hours for $20 per month. Advantages of commercial online

---

[1]An excellent history of the Internet is to be found in Katie Hefner and Matthew Lyon, *Where Wizards Stay Up Late, The Origins of the Internet* (New York: Simon & Schuster, 1996).

services include offering hourly news stories, electronic mail, and information access in a user-friendly package. A second way to get online is through an Internet service provider. These services typically charge a monthly fee for you to dial into the Internet via their telephone line and also provide an electronic mail account. The access to the Net is usually unlimited and is the most cost-effective way to get online if you plan to spend a lot of time there.

WHERE TO GO ON THE INTERNET

The World Wide Web.   The most popular area of the Internet is the World Wide Web. Also known as WWW, W3, or the Web, it is a collection of documents, called Web pages, that are stored in the computers connected to the Internet throughout the world. Web browsers, such as Netscape Navigator or Microsoft Internet Explorer, are programs that allow the user to explore information stored on the Web and to retrieve Web pages the viewer wishes to read. Most browsers, like the popular Netscape Navigator, perform within a toolbar interface. Various functions such as reload, back, forward, stop, open, and print appear on the toolbar so that with one click on an icon, the user can easily navigate the Internet. Web browsers permit the downloading and capture of documents, as well as printing out selected portions of Web sites. When the program such as Netscape Navigator is accessed, the click of a mouse allows the user to explore all dimensions of the Internet such as the World Wide Web and newsgroups.

Each Web page is stored in a specific Web site that has a unique electronic address that indicates where the document is actually located. The electronic address is called the Uniform Resource Locator (URL). The URL designates the site in which information is stored on the Internet. You can access a page by directly entering the URL into your Internet program. For example, the FBI has a Web site that can be accessed by typing in its URL address:

http://www.fbi.gov

The URL address for the FBI consists of the following components:

http://—hypertext transfer protocol is the programming language the browser uses to locate and read Web pages

www.—denotes the World Wide Web, the place on the Internet where the information is located

fbi.—designates the site; in this case, the Federal Bureau of Investigation

gov—designates the domain

Upon entering the FBI Web site, you are confronted with a multitude of services and information provided by the FBI, such as an overview of the bureau's operation, information regarding ongoing investigations, reports concerning crime statistics, and even a list of the 10 most wanted fugitives. The Internet has made browsing or exploring the Web easy through the existence of **hypertext.** Hypertext is not hard to find since it is highlighted with a different color within the Web page. When selected, the hypertext will allow the user to jump to another Web page related to the subject at hand. For example, if a user is interested in examining the FBI's Law Enforcement Bulletin Web page, one would merely look on the FBI's home page for the highlighted words, *Law Enforcement Bulletin,* and click once with the mouse on the hypertext. The user is immediately transferred to that specific Web site. This Web site has the URL designation *http://www.fbi.gov/leb.htm,* where *leb.htm* designates a document confined within the FBI Web site. The advantage of using hypertext is that the user can quickly switch back and forth between related Web pages without having to type the URL address or to start over at the beginning of the search. It is the existence of hypertext that makes the Internet so user-friendly. With the click of the mouse, the user can navigate from one Web site of the Internet to another, browsing at one's leisure through a succession of documents. Another quick way to reach a site is to designate it as a bookmark or favorite place. Most Internet services provide programs that allow you to customize a list of your favorite Web sites for easy access. This provision allows the user to enter a Web site by merely clicking on an entry contained within the list of favorite sites.

Hundreds of new sites are being added everyday, thus providing the Internet user with a staggering amount of information. One may wish to explore popular Web site locations by using the list of the Top 100 Web Sites compiled by *PC Magazine [http://www.pcmag.com]* (see Table 17-1). Each of the 100 sites is hypertexted so that you can visit a particular site just by clicking on the title. For example, you can easily visit the Library of Congress site and gain access to over 70 million documents. This library offers access to the U.S. Copyright Office, digitized documents of American cultural and historical significance, descriptions of federal events, and indexes. You also can examine the library's current exhibitions or familiarize yourself with its paintings and sculptures. Another Web page listed in the top 100 Web sites is the Four11 Web site. This site is devoted to helping you to locate a long-lost friend or contact relatives who are spread out across the country. A database of names, phone numbers, addresses, and e-mail addresses can easily be searched with a variety of options. The

TABLE 17–1.

A Man's Life
www.manslife.com
Amazon.com
www.amazon.com
American Greetings
www.americangreetings.com
American Medical Association
www.ama-assn.org
AutoWeb
www.autoweb.com
Big Book
www.bigbook.com
Biography Online
www.biography.com
Buzznet
www.buzznet.com
CDNow
www.cdnow.com
City.Net
www.city.net
CitySearch
www.citysearch.com
CNet
www.cnet.com
CNN Interactive
www.cnn.com
Columbia House
www.columbiahouse.com
CyberAtlas
www.cyberatlas.com
Dell
www.dell.com
DineNet Menus Online
www.menusonline.com
Discovery Channel Online
www.discovery.com
E! Online
www.eonline.com
Egghead Software
www.egghead.com
Electric Library
www.elibrary.com
Electric Minds
www.minds.com
Entertainment Drive
www.edrive.com
Epicurious
www.epicurious.com
ESPNet SportsZone
espnet.sportszone.com

Excite Live!
live.excite.com
Family Tree Maker
www.familytreemaker.com
FAO Schwarz
www.faoschwarz.com
Firefly
www.firefly.com
Four11
www.four11.com
Gamelan
www.gamelan.com
Gateway 2000
www.gw2k.com
Happy Puppy Game Site
happypuppy.com
HomeScout
www.homescout.com
HotWired
www.hotwired.com
IBM
www.ibm.com
Industry.Net
www.industry.net
inquiry.com
www.inquiry.com
Internet Movie Database
www.imdb.com
JC Penney
www.jcpenney.com
Joe Boxer
www.joeboxer.com
Kids' World
www.kidsworld.com
Levi's
www.levi.com
Library of Congress
www.loc.gov
LookSmart
www.looksmart.com
Los Angeles Times
www.latimes.com
MapQuest
www.mapquest.com
Match.com
www.match.com
Mercury Center (San Jose Mercury News)
www.sjmercury.com
Microsoft Expedia
www.expedia.msn.com

TABLE 17–1. *continued*

Microsoft Investor
www.investor.msn.com
Microsoft
www.microsoft.com
MIT Media Lab
www.media.mit.edu
MovieLink
www.777film.com
Mr. Showbiz
www.mrshowbiz.com
Museum of Modern Art
www.moma.org
NASA
www.nasa.gov
National Geographic
www.nationalgeographic.com
Nerd World
www.nerdworld.com
Netscape
www.netscape.com
New York Times
www.nytimes.com
NewsPage
www.newspage.com
NPR on the Web
www.npr.org
The Old Farmer's Almanac
www.almanac.com
The Onion
www.theonion.com
Outside Online
outside.starwave.com
Parent Soup
www.parentsoup.com
Pathfinder
www.pathfinder.com
Playbill On-line
piano.symgrp.com/playbill/
PoliticsNow
www.politicsnow.com
PopSci.com
www.popsci.com
Quote.Com
www.quote.com
Rocktropolis
www.rocktropolis.com
Salon
www.salonmagazine.com
Sandy Bay Software's PC Webopaedia
www.sandybay.com/pc-web/index.html
Scholastic Network
www.scholastic.com

Scientific American
www.sciam.com
Stroud's CWS Apps List
www.stroud.com
Suck
www.suck.com
Sun Microsystems
www.sun.com
SupportHelp.com
www.supporthelp.com
Swoon
www.swoon.com
t@p online
www.taponline.com
Thomas: Legislative Information on the Internet
thomas.loc.gov
TUCOWS
www.tucows.com
Tunes.com
www.tunes.com
Tuneup.com
www.tuneup.com
USA Today
www.usatoday.com
w3C Reference Library
www.w3.org/pub/WWW/Library/
Wall Street Journal Interactive Edition
www.wsi.com
Walter Miller's Home Page
pages.prodigy.com/hell/walter/
The Weather Channel
www.weather.com
WebPagesThatSuck
www.webpagesthatsuck.com
webreference.com
www.webreference.com
The Why Files
whyfiles.news.wisc.edu/
Word
www.word.com/
You Don't Know Jack
www.bezerk.com
Your Personal Net
(www.ypn.com)
ZD Net
(www.zdnet.com)
Zoloft
(www.spectacle.com)

Amazon.com Web site provides one of the largest bookstores on the Internet. Here the user can search by keyword, author, subject, or title to locate or purchase books on any topic imaginable. You can even request Amazon.com to e-mail you when books of your personal interests arrive in stock. An interesting Web site that can be helpful to the user is the MapQuest Web site. The user types in the street address, city, and state of his or her point of origin and destination, and MapQuest will generate a map accompanied by directions explaining which roads to follow.

The *PC Magazine* Web site also includes hypertexed sites related to business and commerce; computing; news and sports; entertainment; and reference sources. This Web site opens a gateway to exploring the diversity of the World Wide Web.

Search Engines. Sifting through the enormous amount of information on the World Wide Web can often resemble looking for a needle in a haystack. As the Internet grows, so does the need for automated search tools. Several directories and indexes known as **search engines** are available to assist the user in searching the Internet for a particular topic. Typically, a user will enter a keyword or phrase into a search engine in order to locate sites on the Internet that are relevant to a particular subject. The number of search engines continues to change with new technology, as faster, newer tools are adopted and slower, older ones are phased out. Some of the more popular search engines, along with their URLs, are listed here:

Search engines	URL
Yahoo	http://www.yahoo.com
Excite	http://www.excite.com
Infoseek Guide	http://www.infoseek.com
Alta Vista	http://www.altavista.digital.com
Lycos	http://www.lycos.com
Hot Bot	http://www.hotbot.com

The reader can also find a multitude of search engines on Web site *http://www.search.com*

Search engines contain tools called spiders or robots, which crawl the Web seeking out titles, subjects, and keywords. Through search engines, the user can locate relevant Web pages containing a particular piece of information on the Net. By typing in keywords and phrases related to the needed information, the search engines send their "spiders" out to scan the Web and list all the pages involving the keyword selection. Because each search engine has different capabilities, it is recommended that multiple search engines be used when researching a subject. For example, in compiling this edition, the author had the occasion to search out the subject DRUGFIRE and found a different number of matches for the term *drugfire:*

Engine	*No. of matches*
Hot Bot	94
Excite	46
Alta Vista	51
Lycos	23
Infoseek Guide	50

There are automated search tools called meta-engines that will load a query into several of the Net's leading search engines to compile a single list of results. One example of a meta-engine is MetaCrawler *[http://www.metacrawler.com].* Once a keyword is entered, a typical MetaCrawler search will display the relevant Web pages and indicate which specific search engine found a particular page.

File Transfer Protocol (FTP). Although the most popular feature of the Internet is searching the World Wide Web for information, there are several other services that will allow you to access interesting material. A program called File Transfer Protocol (FTP) enables you to look through files stored on other computers and download those files that interest you. However, as the World Wide Web has expanded in content, the necessity for using FTP has significantly diminished and will be of little interest to the casual user of the Internet. There are many different types of files that may be obtained through FTP. These include government documents, books, computer manuals, games, and word-processing programs. You may also acquire graphics of museum paintings and art, sound programs such as clips of famous speeches, and videos such as movies and cartoons. The subject of forensic science may also be reached via FTP. For example, the National Criminal Justice Reference Service offers a file containing street terms for drugs and drug trade. Once the site ftp.ncjrs.aspensys.com is reached, you can scan the directories, in this case [/pub/ncjrs/] to find the file [street.txt]. After clicking on a file with the mouse, your Internet program provides the option to download the information to either a disk or the hard drive. Once the file is saved, you can open the document and view it through a word-processing program.

Electronic mail and mailing lists. The service that is most commonly used in conjunction with the Internet is electronic mail. Also called **e-mail,** this communication system can transport messages across the world in a matter of seconds. The convenience of e-mail allows persons to communicate on an individual-to-individual basis. In order to utilize e-mail, one has to acquire an e-mail address. This will normally be done through an Internet service provider. Like regular postal mail, you will need an address to receive mail, and you will need to know a recipient's address to send messages. E-mail messages can be sent instantaneously to anywhere on the globe. These messages are stored in an individualized mailbox that can be opened electronically at your convenience. Also, having an e-mail account opens up the opportunity to receive information through mailing lists. A **mailing list** is a discussion group for a selected topic in which related messages are sent directly to your mailbox through e-mail. For example, Forens-L is a mailing list that is dedicated to the discussion of forensic medicine and forensic science and is found to be a quick, useful way to exchange ideas or share information about forensics with people of similar interests around the world. To subscribe to the Forens-L mailing list, access the e-mail address [mailserv@acc.fau.edu] and enter the following message, "SUBSCRIBE FORENS-L *Your real name.*"

Newsgroups.   Another service much like mailing lists involves **newsgroups.** Like a mailing list, a newsgroup is devoted to a particular topic. While a mailing list is usually managed by a single site, a newsgroup networks many sites that are set up by local Internet providers. The result is that a newsgroup joins together a significantly larger audience when compared to a mailing list. A newsgroup is analogous to a bulletin board where articles (messages) are posted by subscribers. When you connect to a newsgroup, you have the ability to quickly scan through a list of article titles, selecting only those that interest you. To find a newsgroup of interest, you can explore USENET, an index for the available newsgroups. The index can be located through search engines such as Alta Vista. USENET can be searched through keywords in the same manner in which the World Wide Web is explored. For example, entering the keyword *law enforcement* into USENET produces a list of articles from any of the newsgroups containing that keyword. The articles are hypertexted so that with a click of the mouse, you can read the article instantaneously. There are also two useful Web sites, http://www.efn.org/~httpnews/UsenetNewsgroups.html and http://www.ttu.edu/newslist/alt.html, that list the available newsgroups in hypertext so that the newsgroup can be accessed directly from the World Wide Web. Commercial services such as AOL allow the user to subscribe to a newsgroup and provide the program that will keep track of how many articles are available, which ones you have read, and which ones you have not read.

EXPLORING FORENSIC SCIENCE ON THE WWW

There are no limits to the amount or type of information that can be found on the Internet. The fields of law enforcement and forensic science have not been left behind by the advancing computerized technology. Extensive information relating to forensic science is available on the Internet. The types of Web pages range from simple explanations of the different fields of forensics to intricate details of crime-scene reconstruction. You can also find information on what colleges offer programs for degrees in forensics or those pages posted by law enforcement agencies that detail the ongoings of their organization, as well as possible employment opportunities. Table 17–2 illustrates a number of Web sites available in the forensic science field [http://tolecs.lab.r1.fws.gov/refs/refs.htm].

Zeno's Forensic Web Page [http://www.simplenet.com/forensic.html] is a valuable starting point and a must for those having any interest in forensic science on the Internet. This site is a collection of hypertexted forensic Web pages that are listed under categories such as new developments in forensics; general forensic information sources, associations, colleges, and societies; literature and journals; forensic laboratories; general Web pages; forensic-related mailing lists and newsgroups; universities; conferences; and various forensic fields of expertise. Another Web site offering a multitude of information related to forensic science is Reddy's Forensic Page [http://haven.ios.com/~nyrc/homepage.html]. Here you can find links to forensic education and expert consultation, as well as information concerning the specific fields of forensic science. An interesting and useful link pertaining to criminal justice resources on the Internet is Mitretek Systems: Criminal Justice Links [http://www.mitretek.org/justice/cjlinks/index.html]. This Web site lists hundreds of hypertexted links to subjects such as law enforcement agencies, law databases, and discussion groups.

An additional Web site for those interested in law enforcement is the Police Officer's Internet Directory [http://www.officer.com]. This comprehensive collection of criminal justice resources is organized into easy-to-read subdirectories that relate to topics such as law enforcement agencies, police association and organization sites, law research pages, and police mailing-list directories.

WEB SITES YOU MAY WISH TO EXPLORE

The Internet contains hundreds of Web pages for the reader who is interested in introductory information on forensic science and criminal investigation. The list on pages 539-540 contains Web sites that serve such a purpose.

TABLE 17–2.
FORENSIC SCIENCE WEB SITES*

American Academy of Forensic Sciences—The American Academy of Forensic Sciences is a professional society dedicated to the application of science to the law. Its membership includes physicians, criminalists, toxicologists, attorneys, dentists, physical anthropologists, document examiners, engineers, psychiatrists, educators, and others who practice and perform research in the many diverse fields relating to forensic science.

American Board of Criminalists—This site contains general information about the ABC, certification requirements, study guides, and bibliographies to aid in preparation for the tests and contact info.

American College of Forensic Examiners—This is a private, not-for-profit scientific and professional society. The mission of the ACFE is to advance the profession of forensic examination and consultation across the many professional fields of its membership, for example, forensic medicine, forensic psychiatry, forensic psychology, forensic accounting, forensic document examination, law, law enforcement, and other fields relating to forensic science.

American Society of Crime Laboratory Directors—This is the home page of the American Society of Crime Lab Directors (ASCLD), a nonprofit professional society organized in 1974 and devoted to the improvement of crime laboratory operations through sound management practices.

Analysis of Volatiles—Headspace/GC/ion-trap MS methods for screening, identification, and quantitation of volatile organic compounds in solid, liquid, or postmortem material are reported. The forensic use of the techniques in the survey of suspected arson death, intoxication, and illicit drug copy is also addressed.

ARBIDAR—Arbidar furnish large kits of natural fibers, furs, and hairs, as well as an information guide on these materials to research, forensic laboratories, and educational institutions.

California Association of Criminalists—From this page on the World Wide Web, you can get information about the CAC, find out who is on the board of directors on various CAC Committees, find out dates of upcoming seminars, and so on.

The Canadian Society of Forensic Science—This page contains information about the Canadian Society of Forensic Sciences (La societe canadienne des sciences judiciares).

California Criminalistics Institute (CCI)—The California Criminalistics Institute is a unit of the California Department of Justice and provides specialized forensic science training to personnel who are practitioners in the field of forensic science. This site contains a list of all current courses, class schedules, and applications.

Barend A. J. Cohen Home Page—The web site of Dr. Barend A. J. Cohen (forensic physician) in Holland emphasizes the importance of international cooperation and highlights the application of forensic medicine in national and international human rights protection.

CRC Press, Forensics—The page provides forensic journal information from CRC Press.

Criminal & Law—This site has links to other sites that have information about criminal law and may provide a good index.

Crime Scene Investigation—This site provides crime-scene investigation information, including documenting crime scenes (with photography, video, and diagrams) and the collection and preservation of evidence.

Crime Scene Training Update—This web page features downloadable clip art for crime-scene illustrations.

Data Discovery—This site searches computer storage media for data that represent evidence and investigative leads.

Dr. Joe Davis' Web Page—Available information includes forensic science education, training, seminars, workshops, expert testimony and case consultation, criminalistics, photography,

TABLE 17–2. *continued*

questioned documents, trace evidence, entomology, investigation, anthropology, criminal profiling, criminology, odontology, pathology, and anatomy for investigators.

Dean's Home Page—This site contains pointers to other law enforcement and forensic information on the Web.

Dr. Robert B. J. Dorion's Homepage—Use this site for information on forensic dentistry or forensic odontology, which is the application of dental and paradental knowledge to the solution of legal issues in civil and in criminal matters.

Forensic Entomology—Want to know how to solve crimes with the help of BUGS? Take a look at this page and get an introduction to the fascinating field of forensic entomology.

ForensicIMAGING Group—This site gives a brief description of a research and development project on craniofacial identification—the reconstruction of faces from decomposed human remains.

Forensic Odontology—This site is located at the University of Queensland and provides a wide variety of links to sites that have information about forensic odontology.

Forensic Psychology Science and Fiction Page—This page contains information about forensic psychology and profiling, in science and in fiction. It contains complete articles, a book list, and links to other forensic psychology pages.

Forensic Science Education Resource—This site contains a compilation of university programs throughout the world that offer degrees or courses with forensic emphases. There are links to the home page of each school, address and phone number information, as well as comments from current and former students of each program.

Forensic Science Resource Guide in a Criminal Fact Investigation—This is a new web site containing a bibliography and resource guide for investigation and litigation of cases involving forensic science evidence.

Forensic Science Society—This site contains digests of *Science & Justice Journal* plus links to other forensic sites.

Hank's Forensic Page—This is the first forensic home page in Taiwan. Both Chinese and English versions are made. You can also enjoy the Chinese music played by the author through ancient Chinese musical instrument "HSIAU."

Hong Kong Government Laboratory—This home page includes details about forensic science in Hong Kong.

Institute of Science and Forensic Medicine—This is a national body responsible for providing forensic science and forensic pathology services in Singapore.

International Association of Bloodstain Pattern Analysts—The IABPA is a professional association dedicated to advancing the forensic discipline of bloodstain pattern analysis.

The International Institute of Forensic Science—This is an independent nonprofit organization that has been established to provide uncompromising investigation into the determination of cause of death and injury.

The McCrone Research Institute—McRI is an Illinois not-for-profit corporation dedicated to teaching and research in applied microscopy.

Michigan State University—This is the School of Criminal Justice web server. The MSU school of Police Administration and Public Safety was established in 1935 as an academic program for those seeking careers in law enforcement. In 1970, the school's name was changed to the School of Criminal Justice.

National Forensic Science Technology Center—The center's vision is to become the premier organization, integrating cross-disciplinary knowledge and technologies; disseminating this information through electronic communications, education and training, and standards implementation; and using the center's resources and influence to promote and create new tools for forensic science practitioners.

Novum Israel, Ltd.—This is the first forensic-related page from Israel. The page includes forensic links and information about new forensic products for identification.

TABLE 17–2. *continued*

Police Forensic Science Laboratory, Dundee, Scotland—The laboratory was set up in 1989 to provide comprehensive service to Tayside Police and Fire Constabulary.

Question Documents Page—By Emily J. Will, this site contains information about question document examinations.

Reddy's Forensic Web Page—This home page has many hot links to forensic organizations, labs, journals, home pages, sites of general forensic science, narcotics/forensic chemistry, questioned documents, digital imaging, image enhancing, and so on.

United Kingdom Police and Forensic Web—For the UK, this site describes emergency services, including law enforcement, investigative agencies, scientific, forensic, fire, rescue and medical response.

USFWS Forensics Laboratory, Ashland, OR—This U.S. Fish and Wildlife Service laboratory provides wildlife forensic support to federal, state, and international wildlife law enforcement agencies.

The Victorian Institute of Forensic Pathology—The institute is a statutory body responsible for forensic pathology and associated forensic services in the State of Victoria. Admin: rik@vifp.monash.edu.au

Zeno's Forensic Page—A great reference page that points to other forensic science, forensic medicine, and forensic psychiatry pages.

Web sites are hypertexted in http://tolecs.lab.r1.fws.gov/refs/refs.htm.

An Introduction to Forensic Firearms Identification [http://www.geocities.com/~jsdoyle/A_Welcome.htm]. This Web site is an extensive collection of information relating to the identification of firearms. An individual can explore in detail how to examine bullets, cartridge cases, clothing for gunshot residues, and suspect shooters' hands for primer residues. Information on the latest technology involving automated firearm search systems Drugfire and IBIS can also be found within this site.

Forensic Science Resources in a Criminal Fact Investigation Index [http://www.tncrimlaw.com/forensic/]. This site provides a bibliography with hypertexted references pertaining to different aspects of criminal investigations involving forensic evidence. For example, the user can find references about DNA, fingerprints, hairs, fibers, and questioned documents as they relate to crime scenes and assist investigations. This Web site is an excellent place to start a research project in forensic science.

Crime-Scene Investigation [http://police2.ucr.edu/csi.html]. For those who are interested in learning the process of a crime-scene investigation, this site provides detailed guidelines and information regarding crime-scene response and the collection and preservation of evidence. For example, information concerning the packaging and analysis of bloodstains, seminal fluids, hairs, fibers, paint, glass, firearms, documents, and fingerprints can be found through this Web site. This Web site explains the importance of inspecting the crime scene and the impact forensic evidence has on the investigation.

Simulation Crime Scene [http://www.crimescene.com/]. This is an interesting Web site that reveals a picture of a crime scene and lists the case specifics such as the type of evidence found, location of evidence in relation to the victim, and circumstances surrounding the crime. The case conclusions are hypertexted so that the user can make the first analysis of the scene and check the results against the case conclusions.

Simulation DQ-Alpha [http://cgi-server.shadow.net/~mchinsee /scripts/simscrpt.pl]. This Web site generates a random DQ-Alpha (DQA1) (see p. 419) strip from a fictitious DNA analysis. The user chooses which alleles he or she thinks are correct and can check the answer against the hypertexted result. This interactive Web site allows the user to learn how to read DQ-Alpha strips and to test his or her interpretive abilities against the computer.

The Science of Crime [http://whyfiles.news.wisc.edu/014/forensic /index.html]. This Web site offers definitions of forensic terms and descriptions of forensic analysis. Topics such as DNA identification, document examiners, and forensic entomology are discussed in layperson's terms. This Web site explains in detail some of the more unusual sides to forensic science.

Questioned Document Examination [http://www.webmasters. net/qde/]. This is a basic, informative Web page that answers frequently asked questions concerning document examination, explains the application of typical document examinations, and details the basic facts and theory of handwriting and signatures. There are also noted document examination cases hypertexted to this Web site for the user to read and recognize the real-life application of forensic document examination.

REVIEW QUESTIONS

1. A _____ consists of two or more computers that are connected to share information.
2. The device that allows computers to exchange and transmit information through telephone lines is a _____.

3. The most popular area of the Internet from which information can be searched and retrieved is known as _____.

4. The (URL, domain) is a unique electronic address that indicates where a document is actually located.

5. The advantage of using hypertext is to be able to quickly switch back and forth between related Web pages without having to type the URL address or to start over at the beginning of the search. (True, False)

6. Typically, a user will enter a keyword or phrase into a _____ in order to locate sites on the Internet that are relevant to a particular subject.

7. (E-mail, USENET) is a communication system that transports messages across the world on an individual-to-individual basis in a matter of seconds.

FURTHER REFERENCES _____

Leshin, C. B., *Internet Investigations in Criminal Justice.* Upper Saddle River, N.J.: Prentice Hall, 1997.

Mario, J., and L. Rourke, "Evaluation of the Internet as a Resource for and About the Forensic Sciences," http://www.li.net/~erin2/forsci.htm.

Tessarolo, A. A., and A. Marignani, "Forensic Science and the Internet," *The Canadian Society of Forensic Science Journal,* 29 (1996), 87.

THE FUTURE

In 1949, Charles O'Hara and James Osterburg, noted criminalistics authors, wrote: "The present position of criminalistics among the sciences may properly be compared with that of chemistry in the nineteenth century." Certainly, the changes that have taken place since this observation was made are nothing short of revolutionary. Forensic science may still have many shortcomings, but it has successfully shed the distinction of being a nineteenth-century science.

Crime laboratories have now become the major benefactors of enormous advancements in scientific technology. Chromatography and spectrophotometry have already had a tremendous impact on forensic methodology. In a very short span of time, DNA typing has developed into a routine forensic science technique. The future promises even more progress. Mass spectrometry, atomic absorption, and high-performance liquid chromatography, among other developments, are rapidly gaining recognition as essential forensic tools. The scanning electron microscope is already enhancing the application of microscopy to the examination of trace physical evidence. An even more impressive tool is the scanning electron microscope linked to an X-ray microanalyzer. This combination gives forensic scientists the ability to examine very small samples nondestructively while plotting the elemental composition of the specimen in view.

Not only will the practitioners of forensic science continue to see the development of new instruments and techniques suitable for solving their unique problems, but the old workhorses of the crime laboratory—that is, the gas chromatograph and the spectrophotometer—have undergone a major facelift thanks to a revolutionary development in electronics called the microprocessor. The microprocessor contains thousands of microscopic transistors, diodes, capacitors, and the like—all hooked together on a quarter-inch chip. The electronic components of a computer that once filled a room are now reduced to the size of a few microprocessor chips. Instrument manufacturers are taking advantage of this development to link personal computers to many types of analytical instrumentation. This will help to further automate and speed the collection of data in the crime laboratory.

However, the unabated progress of analytical technology must not obscure the fact that the profession of forensic science has reached a critical junction in its history. The preoccupation with equipping a crime laboratory with elaborate and sophisticated hardware has left a wide gap between the skill of the scientist and the ability of the criminal investigator to recognize and preserve physical evidence at the crime scene. The crime scene is the critical first step in the process of utilizing scientific services in a criminal investigation. All the expertise and instrumentation that any crime laboratory can muster will be rendered totally impotent if evidence has been left lying unrecognized or ignored on the ground, or if the evidence has been inadvertently destroyed by careless investigators or curiosity seekers. Yet studies confirm that this is precisely what is happening to evidence at many crime scenes (see the references at the end of this chapter).

The theme that there is a need for trained and knowledgeable evidence collectors at crime scenes has been a recurring one throughout this text. Once again, this requirement must be reiterated. How is the evidence collector or investigator to gain the skill and appreciation for recognizing the value of physical evidence? The trend of events seems to be one of conceding past failings and acknowledging the need for creating specialists to perform evidence-collection functions. In growing numbers, police agencies are training and equipping "evidence-collection technicians" to assist criminal investigators in retrieving evidence at the crime scene.

If this program is to have any significant impact on investigative procedures, immediate steps will have to be taken that go beyond the mere designation of an evidence-collection unit within a police agency's table of organization. The effectiveness of such a program should not be measured by the number of oversized and overequipped mobile vans at the unit's disposal; instead, a staff of dedicated operators and administrators trained and experienced in evidence collection has to be assembled. This unit must be recognized as the essential first step in forensic analysis and must become an integral part, both administratively and functionally, of the total forensic service offered by a law enforcement agency.

The education of evidence collectors and investigators is a very critical factor in improving the quality of crime-scene investigation. Although continued in-depth training of the investigators by forensic scientists is an essential ingredient for the success of such a program, many agencies, for lack of space, time, or desire, have not implemented this training. It is therefore gratifying that colleges and universities are emerging as centers of education for law enforcement personnel. Criminal justice or law enforcement programs provide viable forums for teaching the philosophy and theory of criminal investigation and forensic science. However, academia must strive to supplement, not supplant, police in-service training. Police administrators now have the responsibility for selecting the personnel to perform investigative functions. These administrators cannot abdicate their responsibility to create and foster training programs that will assure the competent performance of the investigator's mission.

Whether a college degree will someday be required by all police is still a subject of debate, but the trend is certainly in that direction. Already, nearly 750 higher-education institutions in the United States offer some kind of law enforcement program. It is from the ranks of these students that future generations of criminal investigators and police administrators will be recruited. For the forensic scientist, participation in these programs offers a unique opportunity to teach, develop, and put into practice the philosophy that science is an integral part of criminal investigation.

Of course, education alone will not guarantee the success of the criminal investigator or evidence collector. Experience, perceptive skill, persistence, and precise judgment are all ingredients essential to the makeup of the successful investigator and evidence collector. Combine all these with a careful selection process designed for choosing only those who qualify for this role, and the end result will be a substantial enhancement of the quality of criminal investigative services.

I don't want to leave the reader with the impression that crime laboratories are not being used, or that forensic scientists have difficulty justifying a full day's work. On the contrary, these facilities are overworked and understaffed. Just the demand imposed on them to complete the examination of drug and blood-alcohol evidence is enough to inundate and preoccupy all but the larger crime laboratories. Most facilities can barely keep their heads above water and are drowning in a "sea" of drugs. Furthermore, the disproportionate burden placed on the skills, time, and equipment of the laboratory by drug and blood-alcohol evidence has had a detrimental effect on the capacity of the law enforcement system to process physical evidence generated by more serious crimes.

The solution to the problem may seem obvious: more people, larger facilities, and, of course, more money. In this respect, the crime laboratories must stand in line with other components of the criminal justice system, for the simple truth of the matter is that skyrocketing crime rates have overburdened our police, courts, and correctional institutions. In light of public and political outcries, criminal justice administrators have sought programs geared to producing quick and dramatic reductions in crime rates. In this kind of atmosphere, hiring more scientists or buying a mass spectrometer or a gas chromatograph may hardly seem to many to be the best solution to the problem of crime reduction.

I am not advocating a crash program for building crime laboratories or, for that matter, a crash program aimed at improving the lot of any one segment of the criminal justice community at the expense of the others. The reduction of crime will come about only with a balanced approach to criminal justice, as well as the alleviation of social injustices. In this respect, we must keep the future role of the crime laboratory in its proper perspective while examining the goals and performance that we expect from all components of our criminal justice system.

It must be emphasized to criminal justice planners and administrators that the size and effectiveness of a crime laboratory directly mirror the capability of the investigative agencies that it services. If all or even most of the burglaries, homicides, assaults, rapes, and other types of major offenses were investigated with the thoroughness expected of a proper criminal investigation, the quantity of physical evidence collected would require the existence of better staffed and better equipped crime laboratories.

I can illustrate this point merely by observing that the single most important impetus behind the expansion of crime laboratory services in the United States has been the large influx of drug specimens. A required chemical analysis of these confiscated materials has made the laboratory's participation in prosecution proceedings mandatory. The criminal justice system, faced with the prospect of unreasonable delays due to understaffed laboratories, quickly moved to expand these facilities in order to keep pace with the ever-increasing number of drug seizures. Unfortunately, this same kind of pressure has not yet developed in relation to the collection and analysis of other types of physical evidence related to crimes just as serious as drug offenses, if not more so.

Although the commitment of police to improve the quality of crime-scene investigation is essential, it must be accompanied by a simultaneous effort to improve the caliber of crime laboratory services. Certainly, the thorough collection of crime-scene evidence will necessitate the employment of more forensic scientists to handle the increasing caseloads. However, it would be a mistake for forensic scientists to be lulled into a false sense of security by believing that the tremendous strides made in the development of analytical instruments and techniques are alone sufficient to meet the needs and goals of their profession. In truth, progress can be expected in the future only if crime laboratories are assured of staffs composed of trained and knowledgeable scientists. Unfortunately, because the rapid expansion of criminalistic services has created unprecedented demands for more forensic scientists, it has become exceedingly difficult to locate, train, and assimilate competent individuals into existing crime laboratory operations.

At present, few colleges and universities offer courses or degree programs in criminalistics. For the most part, crime laboratories have to recruit new employees from the ranks of college graduates who have received their formal education in chemistry, biology, geology, or physics. Although some of these individuals may have textbook knowledge of the techniques utilized in forensic analysis, few arrive at the crime laboratory possessing an understanding of the practical aspects of criminal investigation. This deficiency necessitates a prolonged and time-consuming period of intensive training under the direction of trained criminalists. Not only must the new criminalist learn to apply specialized skills to the responsibilities and objectives of a working crime laboratory, he or she must also acquire a familiarity with all phases of crime laboratory operation.

The extent and depth of versatility expected of the forensic scientist are usually determined by the size of the crime laboratory's staff. Scientists in smaller laboratories are often expected to be generalists, performing a wide variety of tasks in order to fulfill the varied objectives of the laboratory. Their counterparts in larger facilities enjoy the luxury of working in specialized areas, relying on a teamwork approach to provide the spectrum of scientific skills needed for the comparison or identification of physical evidence.

In addition to his or her technical responsibilities, the newly trained criminalist must discover and master the role of the expert witness. A good courtroom demeanor and the ability to communicate thoughts and ideas in clear, concise terms are absolutely essential if the scientist's examination and conclusions are to be properly and effectively presented at a hearing or in court.

The present momentum of forensic research could very well falter unless individuals who possess relevant knowledge and skills are attracted to careers in forensic science. The recognition by a sufficient number of colleges and universities of the need for fostering undergraduate and graduate programs in this field is essential for assuring an ample supply of scientists to meet the anticipated personnel needs of the profession. Furthermore, the establishment of forensic education programs, especially at the graduate level, should be accompanied by the formulation of new academic research programs dedicated to investigating fertile areas of research that are pertinent to the expanding role of forensic science in criminal justice. In a university environment, these research programs can be pursued in an atmosphere unaffected by the pressures of everyday casework, a burden that presently weighs heavily on the shoulders of the working forensic scientist.

The prospects for significant technological advances in forensic science in the very near future are great. In fact, the computer-aided fingerprint search of single latent fingerprints is already a reality in most jurisdictions. The ability to search, in a matter of minutes, files composed of millions of prints in order to ascertain a probable match to a latent fingerprint represents the most significant contribution that forensic science has made to criminal investigation since the introduction of the fingerprint itself. Jurisdictions utilizing this approach have reported startling increases in arrests.

Computerized technology is also helping investigators link multiple unrelated shooting cases to a single firearm. The automated search systems DRUGFIRE and IBIS (see pp. 475–478) allow the surface characteristics of a bullet or cartridge case to be scanned and stored in a computerized database. This database is networked throughout various regions of the United States. This technology allows an investigator to search the database for entries bearing similar characteristics to the evidential bullet or cartridge case. If a match is made, multiple crimes may be linked and associated with a single firearm.

Practically every week we read in our newspapers that researchers are developing new products with their ability to manipulate genes. The ability of scientists to penetrate DNA, the basic building block of genes, provides investigators with a powerful forensic tool to individualize blood, semen, and hair. The FBI has initiated an aggressive forensic research program to develop this technology along with an ambitious technical training program to instruct personnel of state and local crime laboratories throughout the United States in the use of this technology. DNA typing has already progressed to the stage where a number of states are developing plans to routinely type offenders involved in sex-related crimes. It's to be expected that within the near future, the reality will be that blood and semen stains recovered from crime scenes will be as revealing of human identity as a fingerprint is today.

Unfortunately, in spite of the fact that crime laboratories are equipped with expensive and sophisticated instruments, seldom can a forensic scientist report to a police officer or a jury that a scientific examination of the evidence has in itself solved a case. More often than not, a conclusive comparison of evidential and control material will not be able to exclude other possible sources. To further complicate matters, the statistical data available to support such conclusions are usually sketchy or nonexistent. In such situations, heavy reliance must necessarily be placed on the experience and opinion of the expert in interpreting the significance of the forensic examination.

Even though class physical evidence for corroborating investigative findings is an important contribution to any criminal case, its nonexclusive character will not always motivate investigators to go all out in their search for class physical evidence. It is no coincidence that the items most sought at the crime site are those that possess potential individual characteristics—that is, fingerprints, firearms, bullets, tool marks, and track impressions—for these are more likely to have the greatest impact on an investigation. Once these avenues have been exhausted, there seems to be little desire to progress any further. Clearly, future research will have to concentrate on defining the value of the much larger category of class evidence so that these items can become statistically more meaningful and attractive to scientist and investigator alike. Forensic science will thrive as a scientific discipline only by supplementing the personal experiences and views of experts, no matter how impartial they may be, with vigorous proof supported by sound experimental data.

A major thrust of forensic research must concentrate on defining the most distinctive properties of evidence and relating these properties to statistics that measure their frequency of occurrence. The creation of data banks to collect, store, and disseminate this kind of information will facilitate the task. Because the responsibility for providing forensic services is spread among more than 350 independent government laboratories in the United States, the task of accumulating meaningful statistical data applicable to the entire country or to large regions is exceedingly difficult. Future progress will depend on the willingness of all crime laboratories to enter into cooperative programs that will ensure uniform standards of analysis as well as providing for the collection and dissemination of analytical and statistical data.

The FBI's Forensic Science Research and Training Center is a key ingredient in the development of criminalistics in the United States. The FBI has made a substantial commitment to the center in terms of personnel and equipment. This facility has established a research program concentrated in the areas of biochemistry, immunology, chemistry, and physics. This program is directed toward the development of new methods for forensic science. The research staff interacts with researchers from academia, industry, and other government and forensic science laboratories. Furthermore, the staff also participates in specialized scientific courses offered by the FBI to state and local crime laboratory personnel. These courses not only have improved the quality of forensic science practices in the United States but have encouraged the standardization of many of the scientific procedures utilized by forensic laboratories throughout the United States.

A foundation of cooperation has been laid; much now remains to be accomplished. How successful our profession will be in fulfilling its present and future obligations to justice will be dependent on the skill, dedication, and ingenuity of its practitioners.

FURTHER REFERENCES _____

Kind, S. S., "Forensic Science in the United Kingdom," *Journal of the Forensic Science Society,* 19 (1979), 117.

Kingston, C. R., and J. L. Peterson, "Forensic Science and the Reduction of Crime," *Journal of Forensic Sciences,* 19 (1974), 417.

Peterson, Joseph L., Steven Mihajlovic, and Michael Gilliand, *Forensic Evidence and the Police: The Effects of Scientific Evidence on Criminal Investigations.* Washington, D.C.: U.S. Government Printing Office, 1984.

Walls, H. J., "What Is 'Reasonable Doubt'? A Forensic Scientist Looks at the Law," in *Forensic Science,* Joseph L. Peterson, ed. New York: AMS Press, Inc., 1975.

◆ CASE READINGS

THE "BOBBY JOE" LONG SERIAL MURDER CASE: A STUDY IN COOPERATION

Capt. Gary Terry
Hillsborough County Sheriff's Office, Tampa, FL

SA Michael P. Malone, M.S.
Hairs and Fiber Unit, Laboratory Division, Federal Bureau of Investigation, Washington, DC

On May 13, 1984, the Hillsborough County Sheriff's Office (HCSO) responded to the scene of a homicide in southern Hillsborough County, where the body of a nude female had been discovered. This was the beginning of an intensive, 8-month investigation into the abduction, rape, and murder of at least 10 women in 3 jurisdictions in the Tampa Bay area. This investigation would ultimately involve personnel from the HCSO, the Federal Bureau of Investigation (FBI), the Tampa Police Department (TPD), the Pasco County Sheriff's Office (PCSO), and the Florida Department of Law Enforcement (FDLE).

Reprinted in part from *FBI Law Enforcement Bulletin,* November and December, 1987.

Never before had the HCSO been involved in a serial murder case of this magnitude. During one period of time in the 8 months, the killer was averaging a murder every other week. This series of grisly killings would eventually end due to the efforts of the homicide detectives who pored over each crime scene striving to find any and all physical evidence, the expertise and skill of the examiners in the FBI Laboratory who analyzed this evidence, the close cooperation and continuous exchange of information between the law enforcement agencies involved, and the fact that the killer released one of his victims alive, yielding physical evidence that would ultimately tie all of the cases together.

The first body, nude and bound, of a young Oriental female was discovered by young boys late in the afternoon, in a remote area of southern Hillsborough County. This victim was identified as Ngeun Thi Long, a 20-year-old Laotian female. She was employed as an exotic dancer at a lounge located on Nebraska Avenue in the City of Tampa. She normally worked the evening shift and was known to use alcohol and drugs. Long was last seen in the apartment complex where she lived. This was in an area near the University of South Florida, where many of the residents were transient. She had been missing for approximately 3 days.

Long had been dead for approximately 48 to 72 hours. She was lying face down with her hands tied behind her back with rope and fabric. A rope was also observed around her neck which had a "leash-like" extension approximately 14 inches in length. It was noted that the ropes around the wrists and neck were different in nature.[1] Under the victim's face was a piece of fabric which may have been used as a gag. The victim's feet were spread apart to a distance of over 5 feet, and it appeared as if the body had been deliberately "displayed" in this manner. The victim's clothing and personal belongings were never found. During the autopsy a large open wound was discovered on the victim's face. Decomposition was extensive in this area, but the cause of death was determined to be strangulation. Tire impressions were found on the roadway leading to the body. It appeared that three of the tires were of different brands and all were worn.

Hillsborough County had been averaging about 30 to 35 homicides per year, and while some prior victims had been bound, none had been bound in this manner. Prior to the death of Long, the HCSO had

---

[1]Ropes and cordages were found in 7 of the 10 homicide cases. All of these were compared with one another. Even though cordages found in one case were sometimes found to be of the same type, there were no instances in which cordages from two or more different cases were found to be similar. However, these cordages and knots did provide a "link" in the patterns which would associate these cases together.

completed a difficult homicide investigation in which the forensic work had been done by the FBI Laboratory. The close cooperation between the HCSO and the FBI Laboratory resulted in the successful conclusion of the case and the conviction of the individual who had committed the murder. Thus, the decision was made to fly the evidence in the Long murder to the FBI Laboratory in Washington, DC, accompanied by a HCSO homicide detective.

The hairs that were removed from the evidence were examined and found to be either the victim's hairs or unsuitable for comparison. The serology examinations were also negative due to the decomposition of the body. The knots in the ropes were examined and were identified; however, these knots were extremely common and not unique to any particular profession or occupation. The tire casts of the tire tread impressions were examined and photographs of these impressions were kept for future reference.

The fibers which were removed from the items in this case were also examined, and this evidence would provide the first important lead in the case. Eventually, it would prove to be the most critical evidence of the entire case. The equipment used for the fiber examinations consisted of a stereoscopic microscope, a comparison microscope, a polarized light microscope, a microspectrophotometer, a melting point apparatus, and eventually, an infrared spectrophotometer. A single lustrous red trilobal nylon fiber was found on a piece of fabric found near the victim. Because of the size, type, and cross-sectional shape of this fiber, it was determined that this fiber was probably a carpet fiber. Because the body had been exposed to the elements for a substantial period of time, and fibers which have been transferred are very transient in nature,[2] it was surmised that most of the carpet fibers which had originally been transferred to the victim's body had been lost. Since the victim's body was found in a remote area, she had probably been transported in a vehicle, and the carpeting of this vehicle is probably the last item she had been in contact with. Furthermore, since there is normally a transference of trace materials (i.e., fibers) when two objects come into close contact, it was also surmised that the killer was probably driving a vehicle with a red carpet. Vehicular carpets readily shed their fibers, and these types of fibers are commonly found on the bodies of victims at crime scenes. These fibers could then provide a critical "link" in determining whether a serial murderer was operating in the Tampa Bay area.

---

[2]C. A. Pounds and K. W. Smalldon, "The Transfer of Fibers between Clothing Materials during Simulated Contacts and Their Persistence during Wear," *Journal of the Forensic Science Society,* 15 (1975), 29.

The above information was provided to the HCSO, with the caution that the fiber information should be kept confidential. Experience has shown that if the existence of fiber evidence is publicized, serial killers might change their pattern and start disposing of the bodies in such a manner that this fiber evidence is either lost or destroyed. The most famous example of this is the Wayne Williams case. [See pp. 81–96.] The possibility also existed that if the killer knew of the existence of the red carpet fibers, he would probably get rid of the vehicle that was the source of this evidence.

Two weeks later, on May 27, 1984, at approximately 11:30 A.M., the body of a young white female was discovered in an isolated area of eastern Hillsborough County. The victim was found nude, with clothing near the body. The victim was on her back, with her hands bound at the waist and a ligature around the neck. Her throat had been cut, and she had sustained multiple blunt trauma injuries to the head. The victim had been at the scene for approximately 8 to 10 hours. The victim's hands were bound to her sides with a clothesline type of rope. The ligature at the neck was made of the same type of rope and was tied in a type of hangman's noose. There was a 3- to 4-foot length of rope extending from the noose. The victim also had what appeared to be a man's green T-shirt binding her upper arms. Hair and fiber evidence were collected from the victim's body.

Several tire tread impressions were located in a dirt roadway that passed approximately 8 feet from the victim's body. These impressions appeared to have been caused by a vehicle turning around in the area next to the victim's location.

The responding homicide detectives believed this homicide was related to the Long case. Since the victim was unidentified, a composite drawing of the victim was made and released to the media. It was through this effort that the victim was identified as Michelle Denise Simms, 22 years old and a native of California. She was last seen the previous night talking with two white males near Kennedy Boulevard in an area that is popular for working prostitutes. Simms had previously worked as a prostitute.

The evidence collected from where Simms was found was immediately flown to the FBI Laboratory. Since this had been a "fresh" site, the chances of recovering significant evidence would be tremendously improved. The tire casts were examined and one of the impressions from the right rear area was identified as being from a Goodyear Viva tire, with the white wall facing inward. The tire impression from the left rear area could not be immediately identified, as it was not in the FBI Laboratory reference files. However, the HCSO was provided with the name of an individual in Akron, Ohio, who was a tire expert, and the tire casts were flown to Akron, where the tire impression was identified as being made by a Vogue tire, an expensive tire that comes only on Cadillacs. A Vogue tire was obtained and photographed in detail.

The fibers removed from the evidence revealed red lustrous trilobal nylon fibers, which matched the Long fiber. In addition, a second type of fiber, a red trilobal delustered fiber, was found, indicating that the killer was driving a vehicle containing two different types of carpet fibers.

Grouping tests conducted on semen stains identified on the clothing of Michelle Simms disclosed the presence of the "B" and "H" blood group substances.

The hairs from the body and clothing of Michelle Simms were examined. Brown, medium-length Caucasian head hairs were found that could have originated from the killer. Human hair is valuable evidence, and in addition to providing information on race, body area, artificial treatment, or other unusual characteristics, it can be strongly associated with a particular individual when matched with a known hair sample from the individual. With this information, the HCSO was able to build a "physical evidence" profile of the killer, which was distributed to other law enforcement agencies; however, the information on the carpet fibers and cordage was kept confidential.

On June 24, 1984, the body of another young white female was found, the third victim in this series of homicides, although this would not be known for a few months. The victim was found in an orange grove in southeastern Hillsborough County. The victim was found fully clothed, and the body was in an advanced stage of decomposition. The total body weight of the victim, including her clothes, was only 25 pounds. There were no ligatures present, and the victim was not found near an interstate as the first two victims had been. During the initial stages of the investigation, the victim's boyfriend failed a polygraph examination and appeared to be an excellent suspect. Evidence from the case was sent to the FBI Laboratory; however, no request was made for this evidence to be compared to the evidence from the previous two homicides until much later.

The victim was identified as Elizabeth B. Loudenback, 22, of Tampa. Loudenback was employed as an assembly line worker and was last seen at approximately 7:00 P.M. on June 8, 1984. She was known to frequent the area of Nebraska Avenue and Skipper Road in northern Hillsborough County, but had no criminal history.

The hairs from the Loudenback case were examined with negative results. Serology examinations were also negative due to the extensive decomposition of the body. The fibers, examined later, were determined to be both types of the red carpet fibers evidenced in the two previous cases. If this examination had been done initially, it would have been immediately known that Loudenback was, in fact, the third victim. When the evidence arrived at the FBI Laboratory, it was not assigned to the examiner who had worked the first two homicides. One of the most important aspects of handling a serial murder investigation is to have the same crime scene technician at all crime scenes and the same forensic examiners at the laboratory, so that one individual can become totally familiar with the forensic portion of the investigation, in order to recognize patterns and associations which might be present.

On October 7, 1984, the nude body of a young black female was discovered near the Pasco/Hillsborough County line, lying next to the dirt entrance road of a cattle ranch. The victim's clothing, except for her bra, was found next to the body. The bra had been tied in a knot and was found hanging from the entrance gate. The head area was in an advanced state of decomposition, much more so than the remainder of the body. The autopsy revealed a puncture wound to the back of the neck, but a gunshot wound to the neck was the cause of death.

The victim was identified as Chanel Devon Williams, an 18-year-old black female. The victim had been previously arrested for prostitution. She was known to frequent a gay bar on Kennedy Boulevard in Tampa. She had been last seen on the night of September 30, 1984, by another prostitute with whom she had been working. The pair were working the area of Nebraska Avenue when Williams' companion was solicited by a "john." They were approximately two-tenths of a mile from the motel where they were conducting their "business." Williams' companion rode back to the motel in the "john's" car, and Williams was instructed to slowly walk back to the motel in order to check on her companion. Williams never made it back to the motel.

The homicide detectives who responded to the place Williams was found began looking for similarities to the previous homicides. Other than the fact that the victim was found nude in a rural area and that Williams was a prostitute, there were no other apparent similarities.

At this point in the investigation, the HCSO requested a criminal personality profile be done by the FBI on the Long, Simms, and Williams cases, and one other homicide in which another female had been shot. A profile was returned (see Figure I–1) indicating strong similarities between the Long case and the Simms case. However, due to various differences (race, lack of ligatures, and cause of death), it was believed that the Williams case and the other above mentioned case were not related.

The evidence from the Williams case was sent to the FBI Laboratory a second time, and both types of the red nylon carpet fibers were found on various articles of her clothing. A brown Caucasian pubic hair, which would ultimately be associated with Robert Long, was also discovered on the victim's sweater. Grouping tests conducted on semen

Race	Caucasian
Age	Mid 20's
Personality	"Macho" Image Assaultive
Employment	Difficulty in Holding Job
Marriage	Probably Divorced
Vehicle	"Flashy Car"
Weapons	Likely to Carry Weapons
Personality	Inclined to Mentally and Physically Taunt and Torture
Victims	Randomly Selected Susceptible to Approach
Geographics	Confine Activity to Given Geographic Region

Figure I–1.
FBI Criminal Personality Profile.

stains identified on Williams' clothing disclosed the presence of the "A" and "H" blood group substances. This was inconsistent with the grouping results found in the Simms case; however, this could be due to their working as prostitutes.

On the morning of October 14, 1984, the body of a white female, nude from the waist down, was discovered in an unpopulated area of northeastern Hillsborough County. The body was found in an orange grove approximately 30 feet from a dirt road, apparently dragged from the roadway. The body had been placed on a gold-colored bedspread, and a blue jogging suit was tied outside the blanket. The bedspread had been tied at both ends with common white string. The victim's hands were bound in front with a red and white handkerchief. Her right wrist and legs were bound with another white string. The victim's feet were bound with a draw string, and there were ligature marks on the victim's throat. She had been struck on the forehead and strangled.

The victim was identified as Karen Beth Dinsfriend, a 28-year-old cocaine user and prostitute. Dinsfriend had been working the area of Nebraska and Hillsborough Avenues and was last seen during the early morning hours of October 14, 1984.

Upon arriving at the scene, the detectives strongly suspected that Dinsfriend's death was related to the previous homicides. The ligatures were almost a "signature" of the offender. Red fibers were found when the body was examined at the medical examiner's office.

By this time, all homicide detectives of the HCSO were assigned to the case. Other assaults, suicides, and unrelated homicides were assigned to property detectives. Six tactical deputies were assigned to do night surveillance in the suspect's "hunting grounds," the area of Nebraska Avenue and West Kennedy Boulevard in North Tampa. The patrol divisions were again given alerts and were continually sending in field interrogation reports (FIR), which were checked. A personal computer was purchased specifically for this investigation and was used to record information on vehicles, vehicular tags, information gathered from talking to prostitutes, and information derived from the FIRs. At this point, the HCSO again went "public" to warn the community about these related homicides. However, the fiber information was kept confidential.

The evidence from the Dinsfriend disposal site was sent directly to the FBI Laboratory, and it yielded valuable evidence. The knots in the ligatures were similar to the knots from the previous cases; a brown Caucasian pubic hair, eventually associated with Robert Long, was found on the bedspread; and semen was found on the bedspread and sweatshirt and tests again disclosed the "A" and "H" blood group substances. The bedspread was tested and found to be composed of gold delustered acrylic fibers. These fibers would also provide a link to Long's vehicle.

Both types of red nylon carpet fibers were again found on most of the items and were microscopically compared to the previous carpet fibers. The color produced by the dyes from the red carpet fibers was also compared using the microspectrophotometer. The microspectrophotometer is one of the most discriminating techniques which can be used in the comparison of fibers. Since these carpet fibers both microscopically and optically matched the red carpet fibers from the previous five cases, it was strongly believed that all of these fibers were consistent with having originated from the same source, and therefore, all of the cases were related.

On October 30, 1984, the nude mummified remains of a white female were discovered near Highway 301 in northern Hillsborough County just south of the Pasco County line. No clothing, ligatures, or any other type of physical evidence were found at the scene. Due to the amount of time the body was exposed to the elements and the fact that the victim was nude, no foreign hairs, fibers, semen, or any other type of evidence were discovered. This victim would not be identified until after the arrest of the suspect, Robert Long, who referred to the victim by her street name, "Sugar." Using this information, the HCSO was able to identify the victim as Kimberly Kyle Hopps, a 22-year-old white female, last seen by her boyfriend getting into a 1977–78 maroon Chrysler Cordoba. Hopps would eventually be associated with

Long's vehicle through a comparison of her head hairs with hairs found in his vehicle.

On November 6, 1984, the remains of a female were discovered near Morris Bridge Road in Pasco County just north of the Hillsborough County Line. The bones of the victim were scattered about a large area; however, a ligature was found. Another ligature was discovered on an arm bone. A shirt, a pair of panties, and some jewelry were also found. Human head hairs, presumed to be from the victim, were also recovered.

On learning of the discovery of this body, the Hillsborough homicide detectives met with the Pasco County detectives, and because of the ligatures, believed that this case was related to their homicides. The two agencies worked together to identify the victim, Virginia Lee Johnson, an 18-year-old white female originally from Connecticut. It was learned that she split her time between Connecticut and the North Tampa area, working as a prostitute in the North Nebraska Avenue area in Hillsborough County.

The evidence from the Johnson site was sent by the PCSO to the FBI Laboratory. Again, due to the extensive decomposition, the body yielded very little physical evidence; however, in the victim's head hair from the crime scene a single red lustrous carpet fiber was found, relating this case to the others. Eventually, Virginia Johnson would also be associated with Robert Long's vehicle through a transfer of her head hairs.

On November 24, 1984, the nude body of a young white female was found on an incline off of North Orient Road in the City of Tampa, involving yet a third jurisdiction in the homicides. The victim had been at the scene less than 24 hours. A wadded pair of blue jeans and a blue flowered top were near the body. The victim was wearing knee high nylons; the body was face down with the head at the lower portion of the incline. Faint tire impressions were observed in the grass next to the roadway, and a piece of wood with possible tire impressions was found. It appeared that the killer had pulled off the road and had thrown the body over the edge and onto the incline. Examination of the body revealed that fecal matter was present on the inside of the victim's legs and on the exterior of the clothing. The body had a pronounced ligature mark on the front portion of the neck. There were also ligature marks on both wrists and on both arms; however, no ligatures were found.

This victim was identified as Kim Marie Swann, a 21-year-old female narcotics user, who worked as a nude dancer. She was last seen walking out of a convenience store near her parent's home at approximately 3:00 P.M. on November 11, 1984.

When the Tampa Police Department responded and noted the ligature marks on the victim, they immediately called the HCSO and requested that they also respond. This homicide was also believed to be related to the previous seven homicides.

The evidence from the Swann disposal site was sent to the FBI Laboratory. The tire tread impressions on the board bore limited design similarities to the tire impressions from the Lana Long and Michelle Simms homicides. Again, red nylon carpet fibers were found on the victim's clothing. The head hair of the victim was examined and would eventually be associated with the suspect's vehicle.

Even though the three jurisdictions now directly involved in the eight homicides continued to work separately on their own cases, there was continual exchange of information among these agencies, which enabled the HCSO to learn that the Tampa Police Department sex crimes detectives were working an abduction and rape of a 17-year-old white female. This exchange of information would ultimately lead to the big "break" in the case, a case which had completely captivated the attention of the Tampa Bay area and one which was beginning to attract national attention as well.

On November 3, 1984, a young girl, Lisa McVey, was leaving a doughnut shop in northern Tampa when she was abducted. The offender took her to an unknown apartment and sexually assaulted her for 26 hours before releasing her. The HCSO urged the Tampa Police Department to send their rape evidence to the FBI Laboratory, and on November 13, 1984, the FBI Laboratory called with the biggest break yet in the serial murder case; they found the same red fibers on McVey's clothes as had been found on the homicide victims.

After the rape case had been linked to the murders, a task force was formed the next day, consisting of the Hillsborough County Sheriff's Office, the Tampa Police Department, the Florida Department of Law Enforcement, the Pasco County Sheriff's Office, and the Federal Bureau of Investigation. The rape victim, McVey, was extensively interviewed and recalled that after leaving the apartment where she was held, the suspect stopped at a "24-hour teller machine" to withdraw some money at approximately 3:00 A.M. She described the suspect's vehicle as being red with a red interior and red carpet, with the word "Magnum" on the dash. Enroute to the release site, the victim recalled peeking out from under the blindfold and seeing a Howard Johnson's motel as they drove up on the interstate.

At this time, there were approximately 30 officers assigned to the task force. They immediately flooded the North Tampa area searching for the apartment and vehicle (only a 1978 Dodge Magnum has the word "Magnum" on the dash). A task force member was flown to the

State capital and returned with a list of every Dodge Magnum registered in Hillsborough County. An examination of the computer printout of these registrations revealed Robert Joe Long's name as a listed owner of a Dodge Magnum.

Each team of detectives was assigned certain areas to search, and as one team drove to their area, they noticed a red Dodge Magnum driving down Nebraska Avenue in North Tampa. The vehicle was stopped, and the driver was told that they were looking for a robbery suspect. The driver, identified as Robert Joe Long, was photographed and a field interrogation report was written.

During the same time period, bank records for all bank machines in North Tampa were being subpoenaed. These bank records revealed that Robert Long had used the 24-hour teller machine close to his apartment at approximately 3:00 A.M. on the morning the rape victim was released. The rape victim identified Long as her assailant from a photo selection. Based on McVey's statements, both an arrest warrant and a search warrant were drawn up and approved by a circuit court judge.

Robert Long was located at his apartment approximately 2 hours after being stopped by the task force members. They began a 24-hour surveillance of Long, also using aircraft to minimize the chances that Long would spot the surveillance teams.

The task force then consulted the Behavioral Science Unit at the FBI Academy for guidelines to use when interviewing the suspect. A Special Agent from the FBI Laboratory in Washington was flown to Tampa for an immediate comparison of fibers from the suspect's apartment and vehicle and to assist in the crime scene searches. An aircraft was standing by so that after the arrest this Agent could be flown immediately to the closest FDLE laboratory which had the special microscope required for comparison of the fiber samples.

The following teams were organized from the task force:

1. Arrest team selected to physically arrest Long. Two of these officers were selected to interview Long at the office after the arrest.
2. Search and seizure team for the vehicle,
3. Search team for the residence, and
4. Neighborhood survey team to interview Long's neighbors in his apartment complex after the arrest and before any information was released to the media.

After all task force teams were at their assigned locations, the signal to effect the arrest was given. By this time, Long was in a movie theater; as Long walked out of the theater, he was arrested. This arrest occurred only 36 hours after the task force was formed.

Long was returned to his apartment where approximately 10 to 15 detectives were waiting. In this jurisdiction (Hillsborough County), it is preferred to serve a search warrant while the owner of the property is there to witness the search. In this case, an embarrassed Long refused to exit the police vehicle and witness the search. Long was then taken to the HCSO operations center for interrogation. The interview was begun after the interviewing officers had consulted with the FBI Agent present who had prepared the criminal personality profile. The Agent advised that this suspect would most likely cooperate if the officers displayed both their authority and a thorough knowledge of the case.

The officers opened the interview by carefully talking only about the McVey rape and abduction until the suspect confessed to the McVey case. Then, the detectives began going into the other homicide cases. Long denied any involvement in the homicides initially.

Meanwhile, the suspect's vehicle had been brought to the Sheriff's office where it was being searched. The vehicle was found to have the Vogue tire and the Goodyear Viva tire, all with the white wall inverted and in the exact location on the vehicle as had been suspected. A sample of the carpet was removed from the vehicle, and the FBI fiber expert was immediately flown with this sample and previous fiber samples to the FDLE lab in Sanford, Florida, which had a comparison microscope. A short time later, the Agent telephoned the HCSO confirming that the fibers from Long's vehicle matched the red carpet fibers found previously on the victims. Long continued to deny committing the murders until the fibers were matched. The interviewing detectives then explained the physical evidence to the suspect. They also explained the significance of the matched fibers and what other comparisons would be done, i.e., hair, blood, etc. At this time, the suspect confessed.

The suspect gave a brief description of each homicide. He admitted killing Loudenback (victim #3) and using her money card. In each case, Long had talked the victims into his vehicle, immediately gaining control of them with a knife and gun. He then bound them and took them to various areas where he sexually assaulted and then murdered them. The suspect also drew a map showing where he had placed victim number nine. This victim had been abducted from the City of Tampa during an earlier part of the investigation, and the Tampa Police Department had informed the HCSO of this fact. They believed she fit the "victim profile" but she remained missing until Long told them where to find the body.

Eventually, a total of 10 homicides which had occurred in and around the Tampa Bay area over a period of approximately 8 months were attributed to Long (see Table I–1). The victims ranged from 18 to

28 years in age, and the majority of the victims were prostitutes. Most victims were strangled and/or asphyxiated; however, one was shot and one died of a cut throat. . . .

As a result of laboratory examinations, numerous associations were made between the various crime scenes, the suspect, the victims, and the suspect's vehicle. (See Table I–2.) The probative value of these

TABLE I–1.

Victim's Name	Date Victim Found	Date Victim Missing	Body Recovery Area	Cause of Death	Age	Occupation
Lana Long	5/13/84	5/10/84	Isolated Area Southern Hillsborough Co.	Asphyxiation	20	Exotic Dancer
Michelle Simms	5/27/84	5/25/84	Isolated Area Eastern Hillsborough Co.	Blunt Force, Cut Throat	22	Prostitute
Elizabeth Loudenback	6/24/84	6/8/84	Orange Grove Southeast Hillsborough Co.	Unknown	22	Factory Worker
Chanel Williams	10/7/84	10/1/84	Isolated Area Northern Hillsborough Co.	Gunshot Wound to Head	18	Prostitute
Karen Dinsfriend	10/14/84	10/13/84	Isolated Area Northeast Hillsborough Co.	Asphyxiation	28	Prostitute
Kimberly Hopps	10/30/84	9/31/84	Isolated Area Northern Hillsborough Co.	Unknown	20's	Prostitute
Juvenile Female	11/4/84	11/3/84	—	—	17	Doughnut Shop Worker
Virginia Johnson	11/6/84	10/15/84	Isolated Area Pasco Co. Near County Line	Strangulation	18	Waitress (Prostitute)
Kim Swann	11/24/84	11/11/84	Tampa Near Rt. 60	Strangulation	21	Student (Part-Time Exotic Dancer)
Vicky Elliot	11/16/84	9/7/84	Isolated Area Northern Hillsborough Co.	Strangulation	21	Waitress
Artis Wick	11/22/84	3/28/84	Isolated Area Southern Hillsborough Co.	Unknown	18	

TABLE I-2.

Name of Victim	Red Delustered Trilobal Nylon Fibers	Red Lustrous Trilobal Nylon Fibers	Yellow Delustered Acrylic Fibers	Hair Transfer Long→Victim	Hair Transfer Victim→Long's Car	Semen	Tire Tread	Cordage/Knots	Misc.
Lana Long	Neg.	Yes	—	Neg.	Head Hair	Neg.	Similar Design and Size	Yes	Partially Decomposed—3 Days
Michelle Simms	Yes	Yes	—	Neg.	Head Hair	"B" & "H"	Similar Design and Size	Yes	Intact Body—2 Days
Elizabeth Loudenback	Yes	Yes	—	Neg.	Neg.	—	—	No	Badly Decomposed—16 Days
Chanel Williams	Yes	Yes	—	Pubic Hair—Sweater	Neg.	"A" & "H"	—	Yes	Badly Decomposed—6 Days
Karen Dinsfriend	Yes	Yes	Blanket to Trunk	Pubic Hair—Blanket	Head Hair	"A" & "H"	Neg.	Yes	Intact Body—1 Day
Kimberly Hopps	Neg.	Neg.	—	Neg.	Head Hair	Neg.	—	No	Skeletonized—1 mo.
Juvenile Female	Yes	Yes	—	Head Hair—Shirt	Neg.	Neg.	—	Yes	Head Hairs Like Victim in Long's Apartment
Virginia Johnson	Neg.	Yes	—	Neg.	Head Hair	—	—	Yes	Skeletonized—3 wks.
Kim Swann	Yes	Yes	—	Neg.	Head Hair	Neg.	Limited Design	No	Intact Body—3 Days
Vicky Elliot	Yes	Yes	—	Neg.	Neg.	Neg.	—	Yes	Skeletonized—60 Days
Artis Wick	Neg.	Neg.	—	Neg.	Neg.	Neg.	—	Yes	Skeletonized—6 mos.

associations was explained to the prosecutors from the Hillsborough County State Attorney's Office and the Pasco County State Attorney's Office. The importance of the fiber evidence was apparent from the beginning, as 8 of the 10 victims were associated with Long's vehicle through fiber comparisons. The importance of the hair evidence also began to emerge as all of the forensic examinations were completed. Six of the victims were associated to Long's vehicle through hair transfers, even though Long had thoroughly vacuumed his Dodge Magnum the day before he was arrested. Two of the 10 victims were associated directly to Long by transfer of his hairs to these victims. The significance of the ligatures and knots should not be overlooked as these provided a valuable link between cases. The tire tread evidence provided many leads and would associate Long's vehicle directly to the crime scene in two of the cases. The importance of the criminal personality profile should also be noted (see Figure I–2). In addition to providing

Figure I–2.   FBI criminal personality profile compared against Robert Long.

Race	Caucasian	Caucasian
Age	Mid 20's	31
Personality	"Macho" Image Assaultive with Weaker Individuals	On Probation for Assault/Lifted Weights/Transferred from S.O. to State Penn.
Employment	Difficulty in Holding Job	Fired from Prev. Job Currently Unemployed
Marriage	Probably Divorced	Divorced
Vehicle	"Flashy Car"	Red Dodge Magnum
Weapons	Likely to Carry Weapons	Carried Gun and Knife
Personality	Inclined to Mentally and Physically Taunt and Torture	Tied "Leash" to some Victims
Victims	Randomly Selected Susceptible to Approach	
Geographics	Confine Activity to Given Geographic Region	Tampa Bay Area

valuable leads, it can also "guide" a case. It cannot, however, take the place of a thorough and competent investigation.

The first trial of Robert Long was held in Dade City, Florida (Pasco County) on April 22, 1985. This was the trial for the murder of Virginia Johnson. The strongest evidence presented at this trial was the hair and fiber associations, as well as the confession of Long. The trial lasted a week and received a great deal of media coverage. Long was found guilty of the murder of Virginia Johnson and was sentenced to die in the electric chair.

It was decided that the first case that would be tried in Hillsborough County would be the Michelle Simms case. This case was picked due to the brutal nature in which she had been killed and the fact that it contained the strongest forensic evidence. The second case to be tried would be the Karen Dinsfriend case. As a result of discussions between the Hillsborough County State Attorney's Office and the Public Defender's Office of Hillsborough County, a plea bargain was agreed upon for eight of the homicides and the abduction and rape of Lisa McVey. Long pled guilty on September 24, 1985, to all of these crimes, receiving 26 life sentences (24 concurrent and 2 to run consecutively to the first 24) and 7 life sentences (no parole for 25 years). In addition, the State retained the option to seek the death penalty for the murder of Michelle Simms. In July of 1986, the penalty phase of the Michelle Simms trial was held in Tampa. It lasted 1 week and again received great media attention. Long was found guilty and was again sentenced to die in Florida's electric chair.

THE ATTEMPTED ASSASSINATION OF ARCHBISHOP MAKARIOS: A FORENSIC SCIENCE CASE STUDY

Julius Grant, MSc, PhD, FRIC

At about 7:05 A.M. on the morning of Sunday, March 8, 1970, the President of the Republic of Cyprus, Archbishop Makarios, boarded his personal helicopter in the courtyard of the archbishop's palace in Nicosia, in order to fly to Macheras Monastery to officiate at a memorial service. He sat on the left of the pilot, Major Zacharias Papadoyiannis. The helicopter took off, and when it had attained the height of the Archbishopric, it made a turn of 150 degrees, still climbing. At a point about 10 metres above the roof of the Archbishopric (Fig. II–1), a shot was heard from the left and rear, and a burst of machine-gun fire came

Reprinted by permission from the *Medico-Legal Journal*, Vol. 40, Part 2, 1972.

Figure II–1.

from the same direction. The Archbishop was not hit, but his pilot sustained a severe wound in the abdomen. With great difficulty in view of his wound, the damage caused to the helicopter and the proximity of buildings and electric cables, the pilot managed to land on an open space on the corner of two neighbouring streets, out of range of the firing (Fig. II–2). The Archbishop and pilot dismounted from the helicopter and ran away from it, having in mind the possibility of an explosion. However, the pilot collapsed and was taken to a hospital where, after a critical illness, he eventually recovered.

The Presidential Guard at the Archbishopric was conscious that the firing came from the roof of the Pancyprian Gymnasium opposite the Archbishop's palace, and they fired in that direction (Fig. II–1). Shortly after the firing occurred, early risers in Thysseos and Othellos Streets, which adjoin the high side wall of the Pancyprian Gymnasium, saw four men climbing over the wall of the school into Thysseos Street. One spectator asked what was happening, but received no reply; he called out to the men to stop or he would shoot them. One then held his hands to his face, and turned back and said to one of the others who was coming up behind him and was holding a pistol, "They are shooting at us." All four then turned into Othellos Street. The spectator and other onlookers then saw the four men board a car waiting

Figure II–2.

nearby and drive off. The first spectator telephoned the police and sub-sequently identified the car by appearance, although he was unable to note the number. Other spectators were able to provide confirmatory evidence regarding the car, although the evidence of identification of the four persons was weak. However, eventually it seems to have been established that the car was of a light blue colour with a white line and was a Fiat, Model 850, registration number ZDR 320. In the meantime the police had been informed of the incident. They entered the Pancyprian Gymnasium, and took possession of the firearms and other exhibits found on the roof.

In another part of Nicosia, at a distance of about a mile from the scene of the attempt, a merchant opening his shop at about 8:30 in the morning noticed a self-drive car having the above description. As this had not been moved by 11:30 A.M. he telephoned the police. On Sunday, March 8, the day of the attempt, at 8:30 in the morning, one G. A. Tal-iadoros went to the Larnaca Road police station and reported that the car which he had hired on February 12 had been stolen from a park-ing place. His agitated condition and confused replies to questions aroused suspicion, and he was questioned about the circumstances of the theft of his car as well as about his own movements. In due course two associates of Taliadoros were also detained. They were questioned as to their whereabouts at the relevant time, and as their answers were deemed to be unsatisfactory, they were held in custody. Further arrests were made subsequently, and six persons, as follows, were ulti-mately detained, namely (Fig. II–3):

Figure II–3.

Adamos Haritonos, 23, student; and associate of Taliadoros
Georghios Alexandrou Taliadoros, 33, estate agent
Antonakis Prokopi Solomonodos, 32, former inspector of police
Antonakis Petrou Yenagritis, 28, police constable
Costas Polykarpou Ioannides, 32, newspaper editor
Polikarpos Antoni Polykarpou, 32, police constable

Monday, March 9, was a holiday and when on Tuesday, the 10th, Maria Constantinou, a cleaner of the Pancyprian school unlocked the toilets, she found below an aperture in the wall two dirty blankets in a heap. One was light grey in colour and the other a darker colour, rather brownish. These also were taken by the police for examination.

The police force acted with great promptitude and efficiency under the direction of Chief Supt. G. Hadjiloizou of the C.I.D. They took possession of the weapons found on the roof of the Pancyprian school and a number of other articles from the school roof, and also the blankets referred to above. At about the same time a shepherd found a cache of arms, also wrapped in two blankets, hidden in a ditch near Nicosia; and these were taken by the Police. They were similar to the arms found on the roof of the Gymnasium and fingerprints were obtainable from them.

Shortly after the above events, I received a telephone call from the High Commissioner for Cyprus in London asking me if I could fly to Cyprus at once; he hinted at the reason. A few days later I attended a Cabinet meeting at the Presidential Palace, where I met the President, and I was formally invited to be responsible for the forensic investigation of the assassination attempt. The resources of the police force and Government Analyst were placed at my disposal, and I take pleasure in paying tribute to the assistance and hospitality I received.

The activities of the police had resulted in the following list of articles of potential importance to be investigated:

> From the school: weapons; two blankets; cigarette ends; button; faecal matter.
>
> From the arms cache: weapons; two blankets.
>
> From the car: dust from the floor; dust from boot; fingerprints; cigarette ends.
>
> From the persons detained: all outer clothing; also some 50 articles of other miscellaneous clothing; dust from a car and blankets from the homes of the persons detained.
>
> Miscellaneous: revolver holster; newspapers; car cover; etc.

The forensic examination of the above is now dealt with in order of importance. The jacket worn by Taliadoros, when he was arrested, bore a smear of white dust on the right shoulder approximately 3×2 cm. in dimensions, and similar in colour to that of the whitewashed walls of the school. Taliadoros said that he picked it up while sitting on a bench and leaning against the wall of the police station where he was originally detained. The police had assiduously taken samples of plaster from the walls of the school along the escape route of the gunmen from the roof to the wall of Thysseos Street, but it was apparent that the mark on the jacket was a surface rubbing, and was a top coat of whitewash and not plaster. In view of the importance of this smear and the lack of wholly positive other forensic evidence concerning Taliadoros, I thought it advisable to make a fresh examination of the scene. Surface rubbings were, therefore, first taken from the areas from which the plaster had been removed. An attempt was then made to reconstruct the early stages of the escape after the shots had been fired.

It will be seen from Fig. II–1 that the gunmen must have climbed down from the flat roof where they had fired at the President on to an open air passage flanked on the right by the high whitewashed wall shown in Fig. II–4. Free passage down the area was prevented on the

Figure II–4.

left by the pitched skylights (four in number) which serve the class-room below and which are apparent in the photograph. It was found that the most convenient way of travelling along this passage in a hurry was to pass between the wall and the skylight, a distance of only 40 cm. This is too small to accommodate a man facing the direction in which he was running. Indeed there was a natural instinct, I found, to half-turn to the left, i.e., away from the wall, on passing between the narrow gaps. If this was done, the right shoulder did not necessarily touch the wall but, as a runner emerged from the gap, there was a distinct probability that his right shoulder would rub against the square-section vertical drainpipes from the roof, which project from the wall to the extent of about 10 cm. When this happened, a smear could be produced on the shoulder of the same size and type and in the same location as that found on Taliadoros's jacket.

A surface rubbing was, therefore, taken from one of the drain-pipes at shoulder level, and it was found that the superficial coating was apparently unlike ordinary whitewash but was consistent with a mixture of whitewash and a white emulsion paint. A likely explanation of this is that it had been found that the whitewash would not cover the metal drainpipe, as well as on the actual wall, and a topcoating of emulsion paint had, therefore, been applied over it. The claim that the smear had come from the police station was easily disposed of, because the bench on which Taliadoros had sat had a wooden back separating the sitter from the wall; and moreover, the whitewash on the wall was not pure white but a pale yellow colour. Below are shown in tabular form the spectroscopic analysis of all the powders collected, from which it will be seen that the powder from the coat and that from the drainpipe matched perfectly; moreover they have no counterpart in any of the other samples, which are characteristic of an ordinary lime wash. The presence of both calcium and titanium is consistent with the use of a paint of good covering power, with the limewash on the pipe; and this occurs also on the coat.

In the course of the hearing the defense pointed out that in Nicosia all the drainpipes of the houses are of this rectangular type, so that the rubbing could have come from one of hundreds in the town. Having foreseen this argument I had spent nearly two hours roaming the streets of the town and rubbing my jacket against drainpipes—often to the mystification of passers-by! Out of many in various parts of the town I found that about 60% were whitewashed, with the white-wash often partly rubbed off, and the remainder were painted with a gloss paint which could not be rubbed off. I did not find one which had the appearance or effect of the drainpipes in the roof corridor at the school. The Court regarded this as significant, according to the Presiding Judge in his summing-up.

Coming now to the two blankets found by the lavatories, these consisted of a grey blanket, torn, with bloodstains and dark stains resembling grease. There was also a brown blanket with several holes, also with dark stains resembling grease. The majority of the fibres comprising it were of wool, and were of a rather unusual shade of

Sample	J	1	2	3	4	5
Aluminum	Minor	Absent	Trace	Minor	Trace	Minor
Barium	Minor	Major	Trace	Minor	Trace	Major
Calcium	Major	Major	Major	Major	Major	Major
Chromium	Trace	Trace	Trace	Trace	Trace	Trace
Iron	Trace	Minor	Trace	Trace	Trace	Trace
Magnesium	Minor	Major	Major	Minor	Major	Major
Silicon	Major	Minor	Trace	Major	Trace	Minor
Titanium	Major	Absent	Absent	Major	Absent	Absent
Zinc	Absent	Minor	Absent	Absent	Trace	Trace

Key
J—Taliadoros's jacket.
1—Landing outside classroom door.
2—Lavatory outside wall.
3—Drainpipe on roof.
4—Lavatory wall where blankets were found.
5—Column at foot of staircase near classroom.

brown. The grease stains were extracted, and it was possible to show that the substance present was similar to a type of greasy lubricant in the stores of the Police Department; and that both were similar to the grease on the weapons, which doubtless was used to prevent them from rusting. Infrared spectroscopy was used for this purpose. There was nothing characteristic about this grease, and this evidence, though contributory, was not in itself conclusive. However, an interesting fact noted was that the grease stains on the blanket and the grease on the weapons, while alike, were completely dissimilar from four other types of oil or grease also kept in the police store. Thus, although the weapons were not police weapons, the grease on them could have come from the police store.

It has been mentioned that bloodstains were found on the grey blanket. These were of human blood. It was thought at first that they were associated with the observation that one of the fugitives seen climbing over the wall had his hand against his face. However, none of the men arrested had any wounds, and examination of the bloodstains showed that they were of the drop rather than of the smear type to be expected from a wound. Medical examination showed no evidence of recent nose-bleeding from any of the men detained. As the stains were old, it was not possible to carry out a grouping test. It was felt that they could have been produced before the relevant date, and this aspect of the evidence was not pursued further.

So far as the weapons found on the scene were concerned, these are shown in Fig. II–1. They comprised a Bren gun, a Lee Enfield rifle, and an M6 rifle; 39 spent cartridges were found, and there were about the same number unused. The only features of importance were the grease referred to above, and fingerprints in the grease. On the weapons were found two prints each having 13 points of diagnostic identity with the right forefinger of Haritonos; one was on the magazine of the Bren gun. On some ammunition was found a print which had 16 points of diagnostic identity with the print from the right forefinger of Yenagritis. On other ammunition was found a print which had 16 points of identity with a print from the left thumb of Solomonodos. On further items of ammunition was found a print which had 16 points of diagnostic identity with a print from the left thumb of Yenagritis. Other prints were found, but were not produced in evidence. On the loaded Bren gun magazine and ammunition found on the roof of the Gymnasium were two prints having 16 points of diagnostic identity with a print from the right thumb of Solomonodos. Other fingerprint evidence attributable to Taliadoros, Haritonos, and Yenagritis was found on the car. Some of these were found near the top edge and on the outside of one of the windows, indicating that the door had been pulled shut, using the partly opened window, by the owner of the print who was sitting inside.

In England 16 points of identity are taken as conclusive evidence of the identity of origin of two fingerprints. In Cyprus, in general the courts accept the same standards as in this country. It will be seen that except in one case the requisite 16 points were obtained. In the case of Haritonos only 13 such points per print were obtained, but points from different parts of more than one print from the same finger can be added together to make the necessary 16. It could be claimed that the lack of further points of identity was due to the poor character of the prints found on the scene in this instance and that there were no dissimilarities between the two prints which could not be accounted for in the same way. Solomonodos, who had been a police officer, accepted that the prints found could have been his. Both he and Yenagritis were in the National Guard in 1963–67, and they stated that they had been in the habit of handling arms and ammunition. In mid-1969 the police authorized the collection of arms surrounded by civilians. Yenagritis and Solomonodos claimed to have been involved in this operation; no Bren guns were among the arms then collected. Haritonos was in the National Guard in 1968 and said that he had handled Bren guns within nine months of the assassination attempt.

This gave rise to a lively controversy as to the age of the fingerprints, which is always difficult to determine with certainty. Supt. Dekatris, the capable fingerprint expert of the Cyprus C.I.D., held the view that the sharpness of the prints indicated recent origin. This was contested by the defence, but I felt that I could support the prosecution's argument because the prints were made in grease, which in the hot climate of Cyprus tends to run; and under these conditions fingerprints become blurred rapidly. An experiment in which prints made in grease on metal were kept at 20°C and 30°C (the summer temperature in Cyprus) for a few days showed a distinct difference in sharpness when developed.

The defense called an expert, formerly of the Greek police force, but he was unable to convince the Court that the fingerprints were old or that the blurring on aging theory was untenable, especially bearing in mind that at least nine months had elapsed since the alleged handling of the weapons and the discovery of the arms. In any case this referred only to the presence of the fingerprints of Solomonodos and Yenagritis, and not to those of their associates.

Fingerprint evidence was also sought from the cigarette ends. These were found on the scene, in the car, and in the police station after detention. Practically all were of the same make and had been smoked in the same way, i.e., to the extent of two-thirds of their length. They were then stubbed out in a similar way by being bent almost at right-angles. It was hoped that the stubbing-out operation would have left a fingerprint on the cigarette paper, but unfortunately nothing that could be satisfactorily used as evidence was found when we used the ninhydrin test. On the other hand, experiments in which we produced similar stubs did leave fingerprints. The reason for this difference may have been the greater heat of burning in the case of the cigarette ends believed to have been associated with the accused; or because the smoker was one of the few people whose fingerprints do not respond to the ninhydrin test. It would have been interesting to have tested the fingerprints of the six men on paper to check this. A saliva grouping test on the cigarette ends might also have been helpful, but facilities were not available.

Much of the forensic work concerned fibres. The objective was to link the fibres from one or more blankets with one or more of the accused. This applied both to the fibres of which the blankets were made and to adventitious fibres found on the blankets. To this end a large collection from the wardrobes of the six men was seized and thoroughly examined, including the pocket linings—since the latest style in trousers can apparently contain as many as seven pockets! In all some 60 outer garments, including shoes, were tested; also included were contents of cars and blankets from the homes of the accused, which the defence alleged were the source of certain of the fibres found. This was extremely laborious work but was fully justified. The connecting links in the evidence were small in number but important. In my evidence on this aspect I thought it advisable to make clear the significance and limitation of evidence based on fibres. This disarmed some anticipated cross-examination.

In making a comparison between fibres found on a suspect and fibres found at the scene of a crime or on an article associated with it, there are three principal criteria to be taken into account, namely:

(a) the material of which the fibre is made;

(b) the colour of the fibre;

(c) its dimensions, i.e., shape and size.

1. Now, if one has two single fibres, one from the scene and one from the suspect, and they are alike in all the three above respects, then one can say that the fibres could have come from the same source, but that there is no certainty that they did so.

2. On the other hand if the fibres being compared are unusual in some respect as well as being alike, then the chance that they come from the same source is greater.

3. Finally, if one is examining groups of fibres, i.e., tufts of fibres of different kinds and different colours, then if the two groups contain the same fibres in the same proportions, then the possibility that they come from the same source is very high indeed; but one still cannot say with absolute certainty that they did so.

On the jacket belonging to Taliadoros, which had the white smear referred to above, I found a number of fibres which were not part of the composition of the jacket, i.e., extraneous fibers. On the left shoulder of the jacket was such a brown fibre, which matched closely the principal fibres of the brown blanket found at the scene of the assassination attempt. Since this was an unusual fibre, I placed it in category 2 above. This could not be regarded as conclusive evidence because the brown fibre could have come from some other source. However, as stated, the shade of the colour was unusual and it is interesting to note that although some hundreds of fibres from various items of clothing, car dust, etc. were examined, in no case did a brown fibre similar to that from the blanket occur except on the left shoulder of Taliadoros's jacket. It should be added that the police took a multi-coloured blanket from the home of Taliadoros. It contained brown fibres, which were said to have accounted for the fibre on his jacket; there was a superficial resemblance, but microscopical methods showed the fibres to be quite different.

In the right-hand pocket of the trousers of Taliadoros I found a tuft of fibres which was similar to the fibres comprising one of the blankets used to wrap the weapons. Since this consisted of no less than four fibres of different colours and types in each case, I placed this in the third category, representing the strongest possibility of identity.

On a pullover belonging to Yenagritis I found a human hair which was similar to a human hair which I found on one of the blankets from the school lavatory. It is impossible to say with complete certainty that two human hairs are or are not identical. However, these were alike in colour; they were both relatively long, too long for a male hair, even in these days; and I felt that the possibility that they came from the same source was strong. This was another link between Yenagritis and the blanket.

On the left arm of the jacket of Polykarpou I also found a tuft of fibres similar to those of one of the blankets, and the nature of these was such as to put them in the third category, of the strongest possibility. I also examined debris I collected from the body and boot of the car of Solomonodos and here I found a tuft of fibres similar to those of one of the blankets presumably used to wrap the guns. Here again the nature and the proportions of the fibres placed them in the category of maximum possibility.

The forensic evidence established links as follows:

Linking:

> Arms to blankets—grease.
> Arms to accused—fingerprints.
> Blanket to accused—fibres.
> Scene to accused—white smears (Taliadoros).
> Car to accused—fingerprints and fibres.

The preliminary enquiry was heard in Nicosia starting April 15, 1970, with Mr. A. Frangos, Senior Counsel of the Republic, for the prosecution. Ninety-five witnesses were called by the prosecution; cross-examination was reserved.

The subsequent trial was held in the assize court room of Nicosia in October 1970. The prosecution was conducted by Mr. Talarides, Senior Counsel, and Mr. Frangos. In Cyprus legal procedure resembles that of England except that there is no jury, the verdict resting with the three presiding Judges. In a small country such as Cyprus this is regarded as a more desirable procedure. Apart from the prosecution's forensic evidence, testimony was largely concerned with the actions, behaviour, and alleged alibis of the accused. The Defence sought to establish alibis and to prove reasonable doubt as to the forensic evidence, but the combined effect of the latter apparently convinced the Judges. The charge against Polykarpou was withdrawn at the first hearing due to lack of evidence; only that from the fibres being available. Ioannides was acquitted owing to insufficient evidence; he was expelled from Cyprus. The remaining four were sentenced to 14 years imprisonment in Nicosia and, according to the press, they subsequently confessed that theirs was one of several plots which were due to take place at the time of the attempted assassination and which undoubtedly would have done so had it not been for the prompt action of the authorities. The accused instructed their respective Counsel not to place any factors in mitigation before the Court; Haritonos stated that he did not pray for leniency.

The author is indebted to the Government of Cyprus for permission to reproduce the illustrations; and to Chief Supt. Hadjiloizou for his cooperation in the preparation of this paper.

TEAMWORK IN THE FORENSIC SCIENCES: REPORT OF A CASE

L. W. Bradford and A. A. Biasotti

Director and Supervising Criminalist, respectively, Laboratory of Criminalistics, San José, California

The scene in which the following events occurred is a single story dwelling in a quiet residential neighborhood where the victim lived. The victim was a 45-year-old woman who lived in the second house on a particular cul-de-sac street next to a red house on the corner (which is of later significance). A street light is situated here.

The investigative events began with the discovery of the victim lying face up over the foot of her bed with the top of her head completely blown off. Tissue debris covered both walls and the ceiling surrounding the victim. The gruesome discovery was made and reported immediately at 2:30 A.M. by an elderly male boarder who rented one bedroom in the victim's house. The boarder had entered the house, using his key, at about 1:15 A.M. after working as a bartender since 4 P.M. the previous day. He went directly to his bedroom and read for about an hour. When ready to retire, he noticed lights in the victim's bedroom and kitchen. Investigating, he discovered the victim. The first patrol unit arrived at the scene within minutes. The patrol officer found no weapon and, after a quick search for a possible intruder on the premises, called for assistance.

The detective team arrived at the scene within ten minutes and was followed within the hour by a team of four investigators who were immediately deployed to interview neighbors for possible leads. A more detailed search of the scene revealed that:

1. All doors were locked and there were no signs of forced entry.
2. The victim's clothing was neatly arranged on a chair next to her bed.
3. There was no indication of a struggle prior to the fatal shot.
4. Valuables appear to be intact and undisturbed.

After photographing the victim and the scene, the body was removed; and a search was made for the projectile which caused the extensive trauma to the victim. A high-velocity weapon was assumed to be the cause of death.

Reprinted by permission of the American Society for Testing and Materials from *Journal of Forensic Sciences.*

The major portion of a 150 grain, military type, jacketed bullet was recovered in the wall space back of the headboard of the victim's bed. A projection of the bullet path through the mattress, headboard, and wall, in conjunction with the position of the body, an apparent "defense" type wound on the lower right wrist of the victim, and the lack of powder residues indicated that the victim was shot while sitting on the end of the bed, leaning back at about a 30-degree angle, and holding her right arm in defensive fashion over her face. Class characteristics of the rifle impressed on the .30 caliber bullet indicated the possibility of Remington Rifles, Model numbers 721 to 760.

This fatal bullet was destined to be the vital link in connecting the suspect with the victim, but in a very unusual manner. The second vital link, discovered later in the investigation, was a cancelled check, which will be discussed separately.

Canvassing of the immediate neighbors developed several witnesses who on the evening before:

1. Heard a loud "bang" or "back fire" between 10:15 P.M. and 10:30 P.M.
2. Saw a red station wagon with white top, round tail lights, and loud muffler start up and drive out of cul-de-sac within a few minutes after hearing the "loud bang." The license number was not obtained.
3. Described the driver of the vehicle as a male—without further details.

It was also learned from persons in the neighborhood that a vehicle similar to the described station wagon had been parked near the scene on several occasions.

Careful and methodical interrogation of all the neighbors, known friends, and former husband (amicably separated) of the victim continued until such time that a conference was called by the detective-in-charge to summarize and evaluate the information assembled. Logical suspects, including the boarder, the former husband, and several known acquaintances, were quickly eliminated because alibis were confirmed by investigation. One lead, however, needed to be followed. It was learned from friends that the victim frequented a local commercial dance studio. Questioning of persons present during Wednesday afternoon at the dance studio indicated that most of the victim's dancing lessons had been with a part-time instructor who would be in a position to give more information about the victim's acquaintances and habits than anyone else.

Through further leads and contacts, the address of this man was found to be an apartment in an adjacent city. The instructor was 23 years old and married with two children. Two detectives, upon arriving at the suspect's apartment, noted a red and white 1955 Ford station wagon parked in the stall of the apartment. Upon knocking and identifying themselves they were invited into the living room by the instructor. While questioning him about the victim, her acquaintances, and his actions the night of the murder, the detectives noted a marble-topped coffee table, end table, and lamp which fitted the description of furniture taken in a burglary of the victim's residence several months prior. When asked about this furniture, the instructor said that he had purchased it somewhere at a department store. He later changed his story indicating that it was given to him by a friend. The suspect further stated that he had visited the victim the previous week to borrow $50; but instead he sold her a painting for $140. He denied any knowledge of the murder or of owning a .30 caliber rifle.

He had a good alibi for the night of the murder. He had taken his wife (a waitress) to work early Wednesday evening, taking their children (girl, age 5; boy, age 3) with them and returned home to baby-sit, clean house, and watch TV until about 12:30 A.M. when he departed, leaving the children at home alone, to pick up his wife at work.

As the result of this initial questioning, during which the suspect had changed some of his story, and considering the presence of the stolen furniture, the investigators asked the suspect to go to police headquarters for further questioning, which he did willingly. Further interrogation of the suspect at headquarters, and interrogation of his wife, separately, strengthened the investigators' suspicions that the suspect was not telling the truth and knew more about the murder than he had admitted. At the conclusion of these interviews, the man and wife accepted the police opinion that the furniture was stolen property and allowed it to be taken from their apartment. The man was released at this time after agreeing to a polygraph examination the following day.

Shortly after midnight when the investigators arrived at the suspect's apartment to recover the furniture, they learned from a neighbor adjacent to the suspect's apartment that their apartment had been burglarized about three weeks earlier while she and her husband were away for that weekend. This burglary had been investigated and revealed a forced entry by cutting a screen over the bathroom window and entry through an unlocked window. Reported stolen were a Remington .30-'06 Model 760 Gamemaster rifle and $10 in cash. With this information in hand, a warrant to search the suspect's apartment and station wagon was obtained and executed on Friday afternoon, the second day following the murder.

The search of the suspect's apartment brought forth the following:

1. A paper target with bullet holes which appeared to be about .30 caliber.
2. One fired caliber .30-'06 cartridge case (established by laboratory examination to be not connected with the stolen rifle).

3. A caliber .22 rifle, a .410 gauge shotgun, and a caliber .25 pistol.

4. An electric shaver identified as belonging to the boarder living in the victim's house and reported stolen in a burglary.

5. A pair of stained trousers (lab examination revealed no blood or human tissue on these trousers).

The search of the suspect's station wagon developed the following:

1. Cuff links identified as taken with the electric shaver found in the apartment.

2. A large "gunshot" penetration from interior to exterior at about a 45 degree angle in the right side with the entry in line with the top of the rear-seat cushion.

The "gunshot" hole in the suspect's vehicle was an unexplained event which later developed into yet another interesting speculative aspect of this case. From an examination of the penetration, powder, pattern, and lead pellets found in the vehicle, it was determined that this hole was consistent with the firing of a .410 gauge shotgun. It was found that this single shot, bolt action Mossberg, Model 173 A, .410 gauge shotgun found in the suspect's apartment would fire when dropped on its butt with the thumb safety in the "fire" position. This information at the time did little more than add mystery to the investigation. About 19 days after the murder, however, this event assumed new significance when one of the investigators in checking out the neighborhood near the scene observed what appeared to be a pellet pattern on the sidewalk next to the curb in front of the house on the corner next to the victim's residence. This was the area in which the red and white station wagon had been observed parked on previous occasions. Examination of the pattern in conjunction with the hole in the vehicle indicated that the pattern, size, shape, shot imprints, and angle were all consistent with the hypothesis that the suspect's .410 shotgun discharged through the right side while parked at the curb. No statements had been given by the suspect to the point of this evidence.

When again questioned about the items recovered in the search and his alibis, the suspect refused to answer most questions without his attorney. He did, however, attempt to explain the target with the caliber .30 bullet holes by saying that he had recently been to a local outdoor shooting ranch where he was shooting a "large caliber rifle" which he described as "more than a .22 and smaller than a cannon." This statement, which must have been an inadvertent "slip" by the suspect, provided a useful clue.

All information thus far obtained pointed to a connection between the suspect and the victim, the burglaries, and possibly the murder; but a direct link with the crime was not a matter of established fact. Based upon these tenuous developments and on the advice of the District Attorney of Santa Clara County, the suspect was arrested and charged with Burglary, Receiving Stolen Property, and Murder. After the arrest the chief detective found a key in the personal property taken from the suspect at the time of booking which appeared to be identical with the house key to the victim's residence. The suspect when questioned about the key said that it was for a prior residence in the area and gave an address. A check of this alibi address revealed that the suspect and his wife had lived at that address. The locks had not been changed after they had moved, and the key taken from the suspect and matching the victim's key did not open any of the locks at the alibi address; but it did open the entrance door to the victim's house. How or when the suspect obtained this key has never been determined, but it was known that the victim stored her wraps and purse in the cloak room at dancing periods when the suspect was present. Consequently, he had an opportunity to make a duplicate.

At this point, a service station attendant was located who tentatively identified the suspect as one who had stopped at his gas station in the vicinity of the death scene on the night of the murder.

The suspect, when faced with all of the apparent contradictions to his alibis, accused the police of lying and attempting to falsely implicate him and refused to answer further questions. When the time for an agreed polygraph examination arrived, he refused to undergo the examination. From this point on no further information was obtained directly from the suspect which would aid in the solution of the case.

Two days after the murder, the police were faced with an array of alibis, contradictions, and facts which appeared to be pieces of a puzzle, but which defied fitting together in any logical way. It was again time for reflection and contemplation before planning the next move. A review of the progress to date indicated that the next two main lines of investigation should be:

1. To contact the neighbors of the suspect who resided in the apartment adjacent to the suspect to determine whether any fired components from the caliber .30-'06 Remington Model 760 rifle were available from the period prior to the time of the burglary in which the rifle was taken.

2. To investigate the shooting range for spent bullets where the suspect indicated that he may have fired a rifle.

The neighbors were contacted first, and three fired .30-'06 cartridge cases were obtained which had been fired from the rifle before it was stolen. When asked when and where the rifle had last been fired, the neighbor replied that it had been at a pine tree during the recent fall deer hunting season in the Sierra Nevada mountains located about 150 miles from his apartment. This occurred while he was hunting with a friend and a nephew. The neighbor had his .30-'06 Remington Model 760 rifle; the friend had a .30–'06 Springfield Model 1903 rifle; and his nephew had a .30-30 Winchester Model 94 rifle. He said that he and his nephew had sighted in their rifles with targets placed against a large pine tree at a distance of about 150 feet from a clearing near a road. Several shots were fired. He thought that he could locate the tree. Four days after the murder, the neighbor guided investigators to a pine tree approximately 100 feet tall and about 30-in. in diameter. A small section surrounding one apparent bullet hole was cut out, and a jacketed bullet was recovered and returned to the laboratory in San Jose for examination. This bullet was found to be from a caliber .30 weapon of six right-hand riflings with a land width consistent with the Model 94 Winchester used by the neighbor's nephew. A second trip to the pine tree was made; and with permission and assistance of the U.S. Forest Service, the tree was felled. A five-foot section of the trunk was returned to Santa Clara County where it was split and dissected. With the aid of X-ray equipment, a second bullet was recovered. The bullet was fully mushroomed, leading to a cover over the rifling marks which had preserved the class and individual characteristics on the base portion of the metal jacket. The bullet proved to be a soft point fired from a caliber .30 weapon with class characteristics consistent with a Remington Model 760 rifle. These class characteristics were the same as those of the fatal bullet. Further study revealed a significant similarity of individual characteristics between the fatal bullet and the bullet from the tree indicating that both had been fired by the neighbor's stolen rifle (Figs. III–1 and III–2).

The next phase of the investigation proceeded to the shooting range where it was believed that the suspect may have fired a rifle prior to the murder. Nine days after the murder the range master of the Sunnyvale Rod and Gun Club was contacted, and it was determined that the range had opened about a month prior to the murder after renovating the sandstone-shale embankment which served as a backstop at 100 yards from the firing point. The range had been closed for about three months while the embankment was scraped and cleared. When shown a photo of the suspect and asked if he recognized the person, the range master stated that the photo resembled a person using the range during the past month who was shooting a .30-'06 Remington Model Gamemaster "pump-action" rifle. Entries on the sign-in register required for all persons using the range were hastily

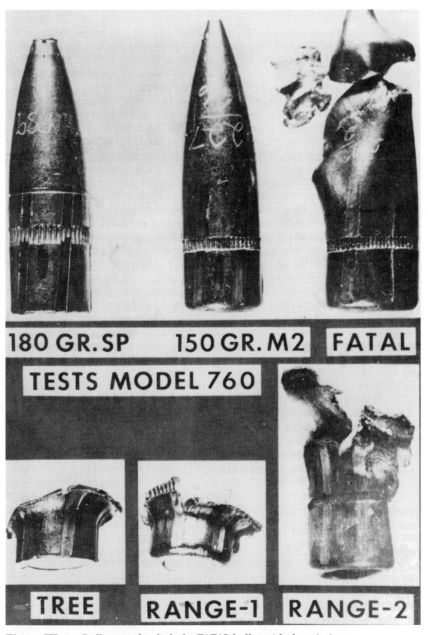

Figure III–1. Bullets used to link the FATAL bullet with the missing murder rifle. The FATAL bullet and the two RANGE bullets are metal-jacketed, spitzer, 150 grain M2 ball (U.S. Army) military type. The bullet from the TREE is a 180 grain soft point corresponding to ammunition possessed by the owner of the stolen rifle. The two tests were *not* fired by the murder weapon and are included solely for the purpose of illustrating bullet type and class characteristics of rifling marks.

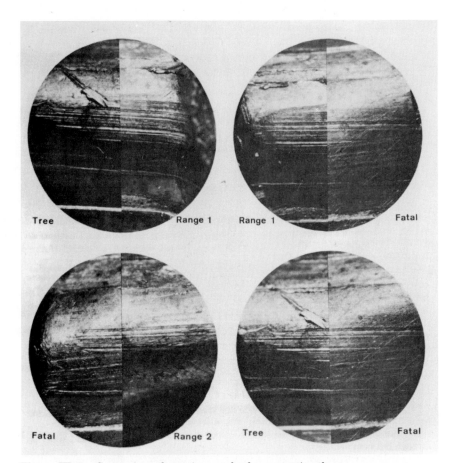

Figure III-2.   Comparison photomicrographs demonstrating the
identification between the bullets shown in Figure III-1.

searched for the name and address of the suspect. None being found,
the list was submitted to the Laboratory of Criminalistics for a handwriting examination to determine whether or not the suspect could
have signed the register using an assumed name.

When the register was examined at the Laboratory, the only immediately available authentic specimen of handwriting of the suspect was
his endorsement of a $140 check which he had earlier mentioned in con-
nection with the purported sale of a painting to the victim. An examination of the complete range record revealed the name of the suspect
one week later than the date first indicated by the range master. This
name was identified with the writing on the check endorsement. There
was further examination of the check which will be discussed separately. The signature on the range record was dated three days prior to

the murder. The register indicated that he was assigned to firing Point #29. Point #30 was the last firing position. A man and his son assigned lanes 27 and 28 and another person assigned lane 30 were immediately contacted and questioned. Lanes 29 and 30 were customarily the only targets used for high velocity weapons.

The man and his son from shooting lanes 27 and 28 identified the suspect from a photograph and said he was firing a .30-'06 Remington Model 742 or 760 in lane 29. Also that he was firing military type ammunition and when asked if they could have his brass, the suspect replied that he was saving it for a friend. They further noted that a girl, about 5, and a boy, about 3, accompanied the suspect at the range. Based upon this information the embankment covering targets #28, 29, and 30 was searched with the aid of a screen. Several buckets of metal jacket fragments were recovered. The buckets of projectiles were taken to the laboratory where rapid sorting based on gross class characteristics eliminated all but a few jackets and jacket fragments with class characteristics similar to the fatal bullet (Fig. III–1).

A detailed comparison microscope examination was now begun which revealed that two bullet jackets from the range had class and individual characteristics that established an identity between the .30 caliber bullet from the tree and the fatal bullet (Figs. III–1 and III–2). Thus, about three weeks after the murder, the two bullets from the range provided the needed missing link between the stolen rifle and the fatal bullet. Without this evidence a connection between the stolen rifle and the fatal bullet would never have been established because the rifle had not been found. The physical evidence had now provided a link between the murder weapon and the suspect and the fatal bullet. To strengthen this link further, a third trip was made to the area from which the neighbor had fired at the pine tree. With the aid of a metal detector, three fired .30-'06 cartridge cases were found. Microscopic comparisons of breech bolt marks on these cases led to an identification with the three fired cases previously obtained from the neighbor (Fig. III–3).

Returning to the subject of the $140 check, the endorsement was of interest as an exemplar of the defendant's signature for the purpose of comparison with the range record. Much to the surprise of the investigators during the preliminary examination of this document at the laboratory, it was discovered that the entire face of the check was traced. It was further determined that the payer signature was traced from an authentic victim's signature and the remainder of the check was traced from authentic writing of the suspect, including his own name as payee.

The document examiner, upon this finding, asked the detectives to obtain the victim's check stubs for the period involved with the $140 check.

Figure III–3.   Comparison photomicrographs demonstrating the identification between cartridge cases recovered near tree to cases from the owner of stolen rifle.

It was found that the traced check was numbered in a sequence different from those covering the period of her stubs. The traced check was number 330. A new group of five personalized checkbooks had recently been received from the bank by mail. Four of these were found by the detectives in an opened bank envelope on the victim's desk. The fifth book containing checks No. 325 through 349 was missing. Speculate now as to the reason that check No. 330 was cashed by the defendant rather than Nos. 325, 326, 327, 328, and 329.

The prosecutor charged first degree murder. The defendant was found guilty and was sentenced to life. The prosecutor used the following lines of argument following the presentation of all the evidence:

1. The victim was a lonely woman who had spent several thousand dollars for dancing lessons over a period of years as a form of recreation.
2. The defendant gained a knowledge of the victim's habits, address, and situation through frequent association as a dance instructor.
3. Through access to the defendant's wraps and purse while at dancing sessions, the defendant gained possession of a key by either replication or theft.
4. Using this illicit key, the defendant had made visits to the victim's home while she was attending dance sessions in other areas. He had taken

property from this home on several occasions. This included the furniture, boarder's cuff links, and checkbook.

5. The defendant had burglarized his neighbor's apartment and had taken the .30-'06 rifle. When entering the victim's home, he was armed, first with the .410 gauge shotgun, later with the .30-'06 rifle. The long-barreled weapons were concealed by placing them on the floor behind the driver's seat of the vehicle. On one of these occasions, while the vehicle was parked near the victim's home, the shotgun was accidentally discharged while in the act of placing or removing it from this position.

6. The defendant traced the victim's signature on check No. 325, using the technique of carbon paper; however, when he covered the tracing with ink, it was a different color than his freehand writing on the remainder of the check face. He continued practicing the forgery until he learned that tracing the entire check face was the only method of avoiding a difference in appearance of the ink color between the payer line and remaining entries. In this way he used up checks Nos. 325, 326, 327, 328, and 329, and finally perfected the forgery on check No. 330.

7. After cashing the check, the defendant waited until the day that he thought cancelled checks through the mail would arrive at the victim's house, at which time he again entered the home armed with the rifle intending to remove the cancelled check No. 330 and destroy it in order to conceal the forgery; he unexpectedly encountered the victim and killed her.

The case is bizarre for several reasons:

1. The connection of the fatal bullet with the suspect without the rifle is exceptionally uncommon.
2. The fact of a defendant tracing his own name is very peculiar.
3. The good fortune of finding exemplar bullets in examinable condition from the tree and range under the circumstances described is unlikely.

It is to the credit of the investigators, examiners, and prosecutors that they recognized the value and significance of all the facets of the evidence and were able to communicate with each other in a manner which made the most effective use of all of it.

GLOSSARY

Acid A compound capable of donating a hydrogen ion (H^+) to another compound.

Agglutination The clumping together of red blood cells by the action of an antibody.

Allele Any of several alternative forms of a gene located at the same point on a particular pair of chromosomes. For example, the genes determining the blood types A and B are alleles.

Alpha Ray A type of radiation emitted by a radioactive element. The radiation is composed of helium atoms minus their orbiting electrons.

Alveolus A small sac in the lungs through whose walls air and other vapors are exchanged between the breath and the blood.

Amino Acids The building blocks of proteins. There are 20 common amino acids. Amino acids are linked together to form a protein. The types of amino acid and the order in which they're linked determines the character of each protein.

Amorphous Solid A solid in which the constituent atoms or molecules are arranged in random or disordered positions. There is no regular order in amorphous solids.

Analgesic A drug or substance that lessens or eliminates pain.

Anthropometry A system of identification of individuals by measurements of parts of the body, developed by Alphonse Bertillon.

Antibody A protein that destroys or inactivates a specific antigen. Antibodies are found in the blood serum.

Anticoagulant A substance that prevents coagulation or clotting of the blood.

Antigen A substance, usually a protein, that stimulates the body to produce antibodies against it.

Antiserum Blood serum in which there are specific antibodies.

Artery A blood vessel that carries blood away from the heart.

Aspermia The absence of sperm; sterility in males.

Atom The smallest unit of an element; not divisible by ordinary chemical means. Atoms are made up of electrons, protons, and neutrons plus other subatomic particles.

Atomic Mass The sum of the number of protons and neutrons in the nucleus of an atom.

Atomic Number The number of protons in the nucleus of the atom. Each element has its own unique atomic number.

Base A compound capable of accepting a hydrogen ion (H^+).

Becke Line A bright halo that is observed near the border of a particle immersed in a liquid of a different refractive index.

Beta Ray A type of radiation emitted by a radioactive element. The radiation consists of electrons.

Birefringence A difference in the two indices of refraction exhibited by some crystalline materials.

Black Powder Normally, a mixture of potassium nitrate, carbon, and sulfur in the ratio 75/15/10.

Caliber The diameter of the bore of a rifled firearm. The caliber is usually expressed in hundredths of an inch, or millimeters, e.g., .22 caliber and 9 mm.

Capillary A tiny blood vessel across whose walls exchange of materials between the blood and the tissues takes place; receives blood from arteries and carries it to veins.

Catalyst A substance that accelerates the rates of chemical reactions but is not itself permanently changed by the reaction.

Cell The smallest component of life capable of independent reproduction and from which DNA is isolated.

Celsius Scale The temperature scale using the melting point of ice as 0 and the boiling point of water as 100, with 100 equal divisions or degrees between.

Chemical Property Describes the behavior of a substance when it reacts or combines with another substance.

Chromosome A rodlike structure in the cell nucleus, along which the genes are located. It is composed of DNA surrounded by other material, mainly proteins.

Class Characteristics Properties of evidence that can only be associated with a group and never with a single source.

Combustion The rapid combination of oxygen with another substance accompanied by the production of noticeable heat and light.

Compound A pure substance composed of two or more elements.

Continuous Spectrum A type of emission spectrum showing a continuous band of colors all blending into one another.

Crystalline Solid A solid in which the constituent atoms have a regular arrangement.

Deflagration A very rapid oxidation reaction accompanied by the generation of a low-intensity pressure wave that can have a disruptive effect on the surroundings.

Density A physical property of matter that is equivalent to the mass per unit volume of a substance.

Depressant A substance used to depress the functions of the central nervous system. Depressants calm irritability and anxiety and may induce sleep.

Depth of Focus The thickness of a specimen entirely in focus under a microscope.

Detonating Cord A cordlike explosive containing a core of high-explosive material, usually PETN. Also called *primacord*.

Detonation An extremely rapid oxidation reaction accompanied by a violent disruptive effect and an intense, high-speed shock wave.

Digital Imaging A process through which a picture is converted into a series of square electronic dots known as pixels. Manipulation of the picture is accomplished through computer software that changes the numerical value of each pixel.

Dispersion The separation of light into its component wavelengths.

DNA Abbreviation for deoxyribonucleic acid—the molecules carrying the body's genetic information. DNA is double-stranded in the shape of a double helix.

Egg The female reproductive cell.

Ejector The mechanism in a firearm that throws the cartridge or fired case from the firearm.

Electron   A very light, negatively charged particle that is one of the fundamental structural units of the atom.

Electron Orbitals   The pathway of electrons as they move around the nuclei of atoms. Each orbital is associated with a particular electronic energy level.

Electrophoresis   A technique for the separation of molecules through their migration on a support medium while under the influence of an electrical potential.

Element   A collection of atoms all having the same atomic number. An element cannot be broken down into simpler substances by chemical means.

Emission Spectrum   Light emitted from a source and separated into its component colors or frequencies.

Endothermic Reaction   A chemical transformation in which heat energy is absorbed from the surroundings.

Energy   The combined ability or potential of a system or material to do work. Some forms of energy are heat energy, chemical energy, and electrical energy.

Enzyme   A type of protein that acts as a catalyst for certain specific reactions.

Erythrocyte   A red blood cell.

Exothermic Reaction   A chemical transformation in which heat energy is liberated.

Explosion   A chemical or mechanical action resulting in the rapid expansion of gases.

Extractor   The mechanism in a firearm by which a cartridge of a fired case is withdrawn from the chamber.

Fahrenheit Scale   The temperature scale using the melting point of ice as 32° and the boiling point of water as 212°, with 180 equal divisions or degrees between.

Flash Point   The minimum temperature at which a liquid fuel will produce enough vapor to burn.

Fluoresce   To emit visible light when exposed to light of a shorter wavelength—i.e., ultraviolet light.

Frequency   The number of waves that pass a given point per second.

Gamma Ray   A high-energy form of electromagnetic radiation emitted by a radioactive element.

Gas   A state of matter in which the attractive forces between molecules are small enough to permit them to move with complete freedom.

Gauge   Size designation of a shotgun, originally the number of lead balls with the same diameter as the barrel that would make a pound. For example, a 12-gauge shotgun would have a bore diameter of a lead ball 1/12 pound in weight. The only exception is the .410 shotgun, in which bore size is 0.41 inch.

Gene   A unit of inheritance consisting of a DNA segment located on a chromosome.

Genetic Code   A series of three DNA bases coding for a specific amino acid.

Genotype   The particular combination of genes present in the cells of an individual.

Glowing Combustion   Burning at the fuel air interface. Examples are a red-hot charcoal or a burning cigarette.

Hallucinogen   A substance that induces changes in mood, attitude, thought, or perception.

Heat of Combustion   The heat evolved when a substance is burned in oxygen.

Hemoglobin   A red blood cell protein responsible for transporting oxygen in the bloodstream and the red coloring of blood.

Heterozygous   Having two different allelic genes on two corresponding positions of a pair of chromosomes.

High Explosive   Explosive with a velocity of detonation greater than 1000 meters per second. For example, dynamite and RDX.

Homozygous   Having two identical allelic genes on two corresponding positions of a pair of chromosomes.

Hybridization   The process of joining two complementary strands of DNA together to form a double-stranded molecule.

Hydrocarbon   Any compound consisting only of carbon and hydrogen.

Ignition Temperature   The minimum temperature at which a fuel will spontaneously ignite.

Individual Characteristics   Properties of evidence that can be attributed to a common source with an extremely high degree of certainty.

Inorganic Compound   A chemical compound not based on carbon.

Ion   An atom or molecule bearing a positive or negative charge.

Iso-enzymes   Multiple molecular forms of an enzyme, each having the same or very similar enzyme activities.

Isotope   An atom differing from another atom of the same element in the number of neutrons it has in its nucleus.

Laser   Light Amplification by the Simulated Emission of Radiation. Light that has all its waves pulsating in unison.

Latent Fingerprint	A fingerprint made by the deposit of oils and/or perspiration. It is invisible to the naked eye.
Line Spectrum	A type of emission spectrum showing a series of lines separated by black areas. Each line represents a definite wavelength or frequency.
Liquid	A state of matter in which molecules are in contact with one another but are not rigidly held in place.
Livor Mortis	The medical condition that occurs after death and results in the settling of blood in areas of the body closest to the ground.
Low Explosive	Explosive with a velocity of detonation less than 1000 meters per second. For example, black powder and smokeless powder.
Mass	A constant property of matter that reflects the amount of material present.
Matter	All things of substance. Matter is composed of atoms or molecules.
Microcrystalline Tests	Tests to identify specific substances by the color and morphology of the crystals formed when the substance is mixed with specific reagents.
Mineral	A naturally occurring crystalline solid.
Molecule	Two or more atoms held together by chemical bonds.
Monochromatic Light	Light having a single wavelength or frequency.
Monomer	The basic unit of structure from which a polymer is constructed.
Narcotic	Analgesic or pain-killing substance that depresses vital body functions such as blood pressure, pulse rate, and breathing rate. The regular administration of narcotics will produce physical dependence.
Neutron	A particle having no electrical charge, which along with the proton is a basic unit in the structure of the nucleus of an atom.
Nucleotide	The unit of DNA consisting of one of four bases—adenine, guanine cytosine, or thymine—attached to a phosphate-sugar group.
Nucleus	The core of an atom in which the protons and neutrons exist.
Oligospermia	A condition describing an abnormally low sperm count.
Organic Compound	Substance composed of carbon and hydrogen, and, often, smaller amounts of oxygen, nitrogen, chlorine, phosphorus, or other elements.

Oxidation   The combination of oxygen with other substances to produce new products.

Oxidizing Agent   A substance that supplies oxygen to a chemical reaction.

Parfocal   Construction of a microscope such that when an image is focused with one objective in position, the other objective can be rotated into place and the field will remain in focus.

Periodic Table   Chart of elements arranged according to their atomic numbers. Vertical rows are called *groups* or *families,* horizontal rows are called *series.*

pH   A symbol used to express the basicity or acidity of a substance. A pH of 7 is neutral; lower values are acidic, higher values basic.

Phase   A uniform piece of matter. Different phases are separated by definite visible boundaries.

Phenotype   The physical manifestation of a genetic trait such as shape, color, and blood type.

Photon   A small packet of electromagnetic radiation energy. Each photon contains a unit of energy equal to the product of Plank's constant and the frequency of radiation: $E = hf.$

Physical Dependence   Physiological need for a drug that has been brought about by its regular use. Dependence is characterized by withdrawal sickness when administration of the drug is abruptly stopped.

Physical Evidence   Any object that can establish that a crime has been committed or can provide a link between a crime and its victim or between a crime and its perpetrator.

Physical Property   Describes the behavior of a substance without having to alter the substance's composition through a chemical reaction.

Pixel   An electronic square dot that is used to compose a digital image.

Plane-Polarized Light   Light confined to a single plane of vibration.

Plasma   The fluid portion of unclotted blood.

Plastic Fingerprint   A fingerprint impressed in a soft surface.

Polymer   A substance composed of a large number of atoms. These atoms are usually arranged in repeating units or monomers.

Polymerase Chain Reaction (PCR)   A technique for replicating or copying a portion of a DNA strand outside a living cell. This technique leads to millions of copies of the DNA strand.

Polymorphism	The existence of more than one form of a genetic trait.
Precipitin	An antibody that reacts with its corresponding antigen to form a precipitate.
Preservative	A substance added to blood in order to inhibit the growth of microorganisms. Sodium fluoride is a common preservative.
Proteins	Polymers of amino acids that play basic roles in the structures and functions of living things.
Proton	A positively charged particle that is one of the basic structures in the nucleus of an atom.
Psychological Dependence	The conditioned use of a drug caused by underlying emotional needs.
Pyrolysis	The decomposition of organic matter by heat.
Radioactivity	The particle and/or gamma ray radiation emitted by the unstable nucleus of some isotopes.
Real Image	An image formed by the actual convergence of light rays upon a screen.
Reconstruction	The method used to support a likely sequence of events by the observation and evaluation of physical evidence, as well as statements made by those involved with the incident.
Refraction	The bending of a light wave as it passes from one medium to another.
Refractive Index	The ratio of the speed of light in a vacuum to its speed in a given substance.
Replication	The synthesis of new DNA from existing DNA.
Restriction Enzymes	Chemicals that act as scissors to cut DNA molecules at specific locations.
Restriction Fragment Length Polymorphisms (RFLP)	Different fragment lengths of base pairs that result from cutting a DNA molecule with restriction enzymes.
Ridge Characteristics	Ridge endings, bifurcations, enclosures, and other ridge details, which must match in two fingerprints in order for their common origin to be established. Also called *minutiae*.
Rigor Mortis	The medical condition that occurs after death and results in the shortening of muscle tissue and the stiffening of body parts in the position they are in when death occurs.
Safety Fuse	A cord containing a core of black powder. It is used to carry a flame at a uniform rate to an explosive charge.

Secretor	An individual who secretes his or her blood-type antigen(s) in body fluids. Approximately 80 percent of the population are secretors.
Serology	The study of antigen–antibody reactions.
Serum	The liquid that separates from the blood when a clot is formed.
Short Tandem Repeats (STR)	Regions of a DNA molecule that contain short, segments consisting of three to seven repeating base pairs.
Smokeless Powder (double-base)	An explosive consisting of a mixture of nitrocellulose and nitroglycerin.
Smokeless Powder (single-base)	An explosive consisting of nitrocellulose.
Solid	A state of matter in which the molecules are held closely together in a rigid state.
Sperm	The male reproductive cell.
Spontaneous Combustion	A fire caused by a natural heat-producing process in the presence of sufficient air and fuel.
Stimulant	A substance taken to increase alertness or activity.
Sublimation	A physical change from the solid directly into the gaseous state.
Titration	The analytical operation of adding a reagent until a reaction is complete, and then measuring the volume so added.
Vein	A blood vessel that transports blood toward the heart.
Virtual Image	An image that cannot be seen directly. It can only be seen by a viewer looking through a lens.
Wavelength	The distance between crests of adjacent waves.
Weight	A property of matter that depends both on the mass of a substance and the effects of gravity on that mass.
X Chromosome	The female sex chromosome.
X-ray	A high-energy, short-wavelength form of electromagnetic radiation.
Y Chromosome	The male sex chromosome.

APPENDICES

APPENDIX I
GUIDES TO THE COLLECTION OF PHYSICAL EVIDENCE—FBI*

| Specimen | Amount Desired | | Send By |
	Standard	Evidence	
Abrasives	Not less than one ounce.	All	Registered mail or equivalent
Acids	10 ml.	All to 100 ml.	Call Chemistry-Toxicology Unit at (202) 324-4318 for instructions.
Alkalies: Caustic Soda, Potash, Ammonia, etc.	10 ml. of liquids. 10 g. of solids.	All to 100 ml. All to 100 g.	Call Chemistry-Toxicology Unit at (202) 324-4318 for instructions.
Ammunition (Live Cartridges)			Call Firearms-Toolmarks Unit at (202) 324-4378 for instructions.
Anonymous Letters, Extortion Letters, and Bank Robbery Notes		All **original** documents.	Registered mail or equivalent
Blood: 1. Liquid Known Samples	One tube each (sterile) 5cc–10cc blood only. No preservatives.	All	Registered mail or equivalent

Courtesy of the Federal Bureau of Investigation, Quantico, Va.

Identification	Wrapping and Packing	Remarks
Outside container: type of material, date obtained, investigator's name or initials.	Use film canister or plastic vial. Seal to prevent any loss.	Avoid use of envelopes.
Same as above.	Use plastic/glass bottle. Pack in sawdust, glass, or rock wool. Use bakelite or paraffin-lined bottle for hydrofluoric acid.	Label acid, corrosive, etc.
Same as above.	Use plastic or glass bottle with rubber stopper held with adhesive tape.	Label alkali, corrosive, etc.
Same as above.	Call Firearms-Toolmarks Unit at (202) 324-4378 for instructions.	Unless specific examination of the cartridge is essential, do not submit.
Initial and date each document, if advisable.	Use proper enclosure. Place in envelope and seal with "Evidence" tape or transparent cellophane tape. Flap side of envelope should show: (1) wording "Enclosure(s) to FBIHQ from (name of submitting office)," (2) title of case, (3) brief description of contents, (4) file number, if known. Staple to original letter of transmittal.	Do not handle with bare hands. Advise if evidence should be treated for latent fingerprints.
Outside test tube: use adhesive tape. Name of donor, date taken, doctor's name, investigator's name or initials.	Wrap in cotton/soft paper. Place in mailing tube or suitable strong mailing carton.	Submit immediately. Don't hold awaiting additional items for comparison. Do not freeze, keep refrigerated until mailing. Do not add refrigerants and/or dry ice to sample during transit. Label "Fragile."

Specimen	Amount Desired		Send By
	Standard	*Evidence*	
2. Small quantities:			
a. Liquid Questioned Samples		All	Registered mail or equivalent
b. Dry stains Not on fabrics		As much as possible.	Registered mail or equivalent
c. For toxicological use		20 cc of blood and preservative mixture.	Registered mail or equivalent
3. Stained clothing, fabric, etc.		As found.	Registered mail or equivalent
Bullets (projector without cartridge)		All found.	Registered mail or equivalent
Cartridges (live ammunition)		All found.	Call Firearms-Toolmarks Unit at (202) 324-4378 for instructions.
Cartridge Cases (shells only)		All	Registered mail or equivalent
Casts (Dental or Die Stone Casts of Tire Treads and Shoe Prints)	Send in suspect's shoes and tires. Photographs and sample impressions are usually not suitable for comparison.	All shoe prints and entire circumference of tires.	Registered mail or equivalent

Identification	*Wrapping and Packing*	*Remarks*
Same as above.	Same as above.	*If unable to expeditiously furnish sample:* Dry on nonporous surface, scrape off or collect (use eye droppers or clean spoon), transfer to nonporous surface or absorb in sterile gauze and let it dry.
Outside pillbox or plastic vial: label with type of specimen, date secured, investigator's name or initials.	Seal to prevent leakage.	Keep it dry. Do not use envelopes.
Same as liquid samples.	Medical examiner should use a standard blood collection kit.	Preservative desired (identify preservation used). Refrigerate. Can freeze.
Use tag or mark directly on clothes: type of specimens, date secured, investigator's name or initials.	Wrap each article separately. Label outside package as to contents. Place in strong box to prevent shifting of contents.	If wet when found, dry by hanging. DO NOT USE HEAT TO DRY. Avoid direct sunlight while drying. Do not use preservatives.
Initials on base, nose or mutilated area.	Pack tightly in cotton or soft paper in pill, match, or powder box. Place in box. Label outside of box as to contents.	Unnecessary handling obliterates marks.
Initials on outside of case near bullet end.	Same as above.	Live ammunition is dangerous. Handle with care.
Initials preferably on inside near open end and/or on outside near open end.	Same as above.	Spent cartridge cases.
On back of cast before it hardens, write location and date taken, and investigator's name or initials.	Wrap in paper and cover with suitable packing material to prevent breakage.	Label "Fragile." Plaster of Paris is no longer recommended.

| | Amount Desired | | |
Specimen	Standard	Evidence	Send By
Checks (fraudulent)		All	Registered mail or equivalent
Check Protector, Rubber Stamp, and/or Date Stamp Known Standards (if possible, send actual device)	Obtain several copies in full word-for-word order of each questioned check-writer impression. If unable to forward rubber stamps, prepare numerous samples with different degrees of pressure.		Registered mail or equivalent
Clothing		All	Registered mail or equivalent
Codes and Ciphers (found on items of racketeering cases)		All	Registered mail or equivalent
Documents (charred or burned)		All	Registered mail or equivalent
Drugs: 1. Liquids		All	Registered mail or equivalent
2. Powders, Pills, and Solids		All to 30 g.	Registered mail or equivalent

EXPLOSIVES: Detonators, Blasting Caps, Detonating Cord, Black Powder, Smokeless Laboratory, (202) 324-2696, for shipping instructions. (For an emergency after regular

Fibers	Entire garment or other cloth item.	All	Registered mail or equivalent

Identification	*Wrapping and Packing*	*Remarks*
See Anonymous Letters on pages 598–599.	See Anonymous Letters on pages 598–599.	Advise what parts are questioned or known. Furnish physical description of subject.
Place name or initials, date, name of make and model, etc., on sample impressions.	See Anonymous Letters on pages 598–599.	Do not disturb inking mechanisms on printing devices.
Mark directly on garment or use string tag indicating type of evidence, date obtained, investigator's name or initials.	Wrap each article individually. Place in strong container with identification written on outside of package.	Do not cut out stains, leave clothing whole. If wet, hang in room to dry before packing.
See Anonymous Letters on pages 598–599.	See Anonymous Letters on pages 598–599.	Furnish to Racketeering Records Analysis Unit.
Outside container: indicate if fragile, date obtained, investigator's name or initials.	Pack in rigid container between layers of cotton.	If moisture is added use atomizer, otherwise, not recommended.
Affix label to bottle in which found, including date it was found and investigator's name or initials.	Make sure container does not leak. Seal with tape to prevent any loss.	Mark "Fragile." If possible, use heat-seal plastic bags.
Outside of pillbox: affix label with date found and investigator's name or initials.	Seal with tape to prevent any loss.	If powder, pills, or solids are found in paper bags, place them in plastic bags to prevent any loss.

Power, High Explosives and Explosive Accessories, call the Explosives Unit, FBI hours, call (202) 324-3000.)

Outside container or on the object fibers are adhering, include date and investigator's name or initials.	Use folder paper or pillbox. Seal edges and openings with tape.	Do not place loose in an envelope.

| | Amount Desired | | |
Specimen	Standard	Evidence	Send By
Firearms (unloaded weapons)		All	Registered mail or equivalent
Flash Paper	One sheet	All to 5 sheets.	Call Racketeering Records Analysis Unit (RRAU) at (202) 324-2500 for instructions.
Gasoline	10 ml.	All to 10 ml.	Call Chemistry-Toxicology Unit at (202) 324-4318 for instructions.
Gems		All	Insured, registered mail or equivalent
General Unknown: **1.** Solids (non-hazardous)	10 gms.	All to 10 gms.	Registered mail or equivalent
2. Liquids (non-hazardous)	10 ml.	All to 10 ml.	Registered mail or equivalent
Glass Fractures		All	Registered mail or equivalent
Glass Particles	All of bottle or headlight. Small piece of each broken pane.	All	Registered mail or equivalent

Identification	*Wrapping and Packing*	*Remarks*
Identify gun with a string tag bearing complete description. Mark inconspicuously and have investigative notes reflecting how and where gun is marked.	Wrap in paper and identify contents of packages. Place in cardboard box or wooden box.	Unload all weapons before shipping. Keep from rusting. See Ammunition on pages 598–599, if applicable.
Outside container: label indicating date and investigator's name or initials.	Place in individual polyethylene envelopes, double-wrap in manila envelopes, and seal with paper tape the inner wrapper.	Fireproof, place in vented location away from any other combustible materials and, if feasible, place in watertight container immersed in water. Mark inner wrapper "Flash Paper," "Flammable."
Outside container: label indicating type of material, date, and investigator's name or initials.	Use an all-metal container packed in wooden box.	An all-metal container should be used for its fireproof qualities.
Outside container: label indicating date and investigator's name or initials.	Use jeweler's box or place in cotton in pillbox.	
Outside container: label indicating date and investigator's name or initials.	Same as Drugs, see pages 602–603.	Call Chemistry-Toxicology Unit at (202) 324-4318 for instructions.
Same as Liquid Drugs, see pages 602–603.	Same as Liquid Drugs, see pages 602–603.	Same as above.
Separate questioned from known. Mark which is the interior or exterior of glass removed from frame.	Wrap each piece separately in cotton. Pack in sturdy container to prevent shifting and breakage. Identify contents.	Avoid chipping. Mark "Fragile."
Outside container: Label indicating date and investigator's name or initials.	Place in film cannister or plastic vial. Seal and protect against breakage.	Do not use envelopes, paper, or plastic bags.

Specimen	Amount Desired		Send By
	Standard	*Evidence*	*Send By*
Gunshot Residues			
1. Cotton applicator swabs with plastic shafts. **(Do not use wood shafts.)**		All	Registered mail or equivalent
2. On cloth Only to determine weapon to target distance.		All	Registered mail or equivalent
Hair	Twenty-five full-length hairs from different parts of head and/or pubic region.	All	Registered mail or equivalent
Handwriting and Hand Printing Known Standards			Registered mail or equivalent
Insulation			
1. Glass Wool	1″ mass from each suspect area.	All	Registered mail or equivalent
2. Safe	Sample all damaged areas.	All	Registered mail or equivalent
Matches	One to two books of paper. One full box of wood.	All	Federal Express, UPS, or equivalent
Metal	1 lb.	All to 1 lb.	Registered mail or equivalent
Oil	10 ml. together with specifications.	All to 10 ml.	Federal Express, UPS, or equivalent

Identification	*Wrapping and Packing*	*Remarks*
Outside container: Date and name or initial. Label as to name of person and which hand (left/right).	Place swabs in plastic containers.	Do not use glass containers.
Outside container: Indicate date, obtained from whom, description, name or initials.	Dry and package individually in **unused** brown wrapping paper or brown grocery bag.	Do not mix items. Use more than one bag, or wrap different items separately.
Outside container: Type of material, date, and investigator's name or initials.	Folded paper or pillbox. Seal edges and openings with tape.	Do not place loose in envelope.
Indicate from whom obtained, voluntary statement included in appropriate place, date obtained, and investigator's name or initials.	Same as Anonymous Letters, see pages 598–599.	Same as Anonymous Letters, see pages 598–599.
Outside container: type of material, date, name or initials.	Use pillbox or plastic vial. Seal to prevent any loss.	Avoid use of glass containers and envelopes.
Same as above.	Same as above.	Same as above.
Outside container: label indicating type of material, date, and investigator's name or initials.	Pack in metal container and in larger package to prevent shifting. Pack matches in box or metal container to prevent friction between matches.	Keep and label: "Keep away from fire."
Outside container: label indicating type of material, date, and investigator's name or initials.	Use paper boxes or containers. Seal and use strong paper or wooden box.	Melt number, heat treatment, and other specifications of foundry if available. Keep from rusting.
Same as above.	Use metal container with tight screw top. Seal to prevent leakage.	DO NOT USE DIRT OR SAND FOR PACKING MATERIAL. Keep away from fire.

| Specimen | Amount Desired | | Send By |
	Standard	Evidence	
Obliterated, Eradicated, or Indented Writing		All	Registered mail or equivalent
Organs of the Body		200 g. of each organ.	Call Chemistry-Toxicology Unit at (202) 324-4318 for instructions.
Paint:			
1. Liquid	Original unopened container up to 1/4 pint, if possible.	All to 1/4 pint.	Registered mail or equivalent
2. Solid (paint chips or scrapings)	At least 1/2 sq. in. of solid, with all layers represented.	All. If on small object, send object.	Registered mail or equivalent
Rope, Twine, and Cordage	One yard or amount available.	All	Registered mail or equivalent
Saliva Samples	1.5″ diameter stain in center of filter paper.	All	Registered mail or equivalent
Shoe Print Lifts (impressions on hard surfaces)	Photograph before making of dust impression.	All	Registered mail or equivalent
Soils and Minerals	Samples from areas near pertinent spot.	All	Registered mail

Identification	*Wrapping and Packing*	*Remarks*
Same as Anonymous Letters, see pages 598–599.	Same as Anonymous Letters, see pages 598–599.	Advise whether bleaching or staining methods may be used. Avoid folding.
Outside container: Victim's name, date of death, date of autopsy, name of doctor, investigator's name or initials.	Plastic or glass containers. Metal lids must have liners.	Call Chemistry-Toxicology Unit at (202) 324-4318 for instructions.
Outside container: Type of material, origin if known, date, investigator's name or initials.	Use friction-top paint can or large-mouth, screw-top jar. If glass, pack to prevent breakage. Use heavy corrugated paper or wooden box.	Protect spray can nozzles to keep them from going off. Avoid contact w/adhesive materials. Wrap to protect paint smears. Do not use envelopes, paper/plastic bags, or glass vials.
Same as above.	If small amount, use round pillbox or small glass vial with screw top. Seal to prevent leakage. Do not use envelopes. Do not pack in cotton.	Avoid contact with adhesive materials. Wrap so as to protect smear. *If small amount:* seal round pillbox, film cannister, or plastic vial to protect against leakage/breakage.
On tag or container: Type of material, date, investigator's name or initials.	Wrap securely.	
Outside envelope and on filter paper: Type of sample, name of donor, date of collection, and collector's initials or name.	Seal in envelope.	Stain should be circled in pencil for identification. Filter paper available from hospitals and drugstores. Allow to dry.
On lifting tape or paper attached to tape: date, investigator's name or initials.	Prints in dust are easily damaged. Fasten print or lift to bottom of box so that nothing will rub against it.	Always secure crime scene area until shoe prints or tire treads are located and preserved.
Outside container: type of material, date, investigator's name or initials.	Use pillbox or plastic vial.	Avoid glass containers and envelopes.

Specimen	Amount Desired		Send By
	Standard	*Evidence*	
Tape (Adhesive Tape)	Recovered roll.	All	Registered mail or equivalent
Tools/Toolmarks	Send in the tool. If impractical, make several impressions on similar materials as evidence using entire marking area of tool.	All	Registered mail or equivalent
Typewriting, known standards	For instructions on known standards: see Documents on pages 602–603.		Registered mail or equivalent
Urine	Preferably all urine voided over a period of 24 hours.	All	Registered mail or equivalent
Vaginal Samples 1. Slides (microscope)	Minimum of two slides.	Minimum of two swabs.	Registered mail or equivalent
2. Swabs	Two unstained swabs from same package as stained.		Registered mail or equivalent
Water	100 ml.	100 ml.	Registered mail or equivalent
Wire	3 ft. (Do not kink).	All (Do not kink).	Registered mail or equivalent
Wood	One foot or amount available.	All	Registered mail or equivalent

Identification	*Wrapping and Packing*	*Remarks*
Same as above.	Place on waxed paper, cellophane, or plastic.	Do not cut, wad, distort, or separate tapes that are stuck together.
On object or on tag attached to an opposite end from where toolmarks appear: date recovered and investigator's name or initials.	After marks have been protected with soft paper, wrap in strong wrapping paper, place in strong box, and pack to prevent shifting.	If necessary to remove item from its source by cutting, indicate where item was cut.
On specimens: serial number, brand, model, etc., date recovered, and investigator's name or initials.	Same as Anonymous Letters on pages 598–599.	Examine ribbon for evidence of questioned message.
Outside container: name of liquid, date taken, investigator's name or initials.	Use plastic specimen container. Seal tight with lid.	Make sure that package does not leak.
Outside envelope and on filter paper: type of sample, name of donor, date of collection, and collector's name or initials.	Use commercial slide box.	Slide box available at hospitals. Doctors should not fix slides. No cover slips. Air-dry.
Same as above.	Seal in envelope.	Allow swabs to dry before packaging.
Same as Urine.	Same as Urine.	Same as Urine.
On label or tab: describe type of material, date, investigator's name or initials.	Wrap securely.	Do not kink wire.
Same as above.	Wrap securely.	

APPENDIX II

INSTRUCTIONS FOR COLLECTING GUNSHOT RESIDUE (GSR)
for Scanning Electron Microscopy and Atomic Absorption Analysis

─────────── NOTE ───────────

In control test firings, it has been shown that the concentration of gunshot residue significantly declines on living subjects after approximately 4 hours. In view of these findings, if more than 4 hours have passed since the shooting, it is recommended that you check with your crime laboratory before submitting samples for analysis.

─────────── S.E.M. COLLECTION PROCEDURE ───────────

(A) When the covering is removed from the metal stubs, the adhesive collecting surface is exposed and care must be used to not drop the stub or contaminate the collecting surface by allowing this exposed surface to come in contact with an object other than the area that is to be sampled. (See Figure 1.)

(B) *Do not* return paper stub cover to stubs after collection. (*Discard stub covers.*)

(C) Heavily soiled or bloody areas should be avoided if possible.

(D) When pressing the stubs on the questioned areas, use enough pressure to cause a mild indentation on the surface of the subject's hand.

STEP 1 Fill out all information requested on the enclosed Gunshot Residue Analysis Information Form.

STEP 2 Put on the disposable plastic gloves provided in this kit. *Do not substitute with other gloves!*

> NOTE: If there is blood on the subject's hands or clothing, the investigating officer should put on latex or other approved barrier gloves to protect him/her from bloodborne pathogens, then put on the plastic gloves provided in this kit.

STEP 3 <u>RIGHT BACK:</u>

(A) Carefully remove the cap from the vial labeled RIGHT BACK, then remove the paper covering from the metal sample stub.

(B) While holding the vial cap, press the collecting surface of the stub onto the back of the subject's right hand until the area shown below in Figure 2 has been covered.

(C) After sampling the back of the subject's right hand, return the cap, with metal stub, to the RIGHT BACK vial. *Do not return paper covering to metal stub!*

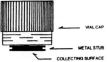

Fig. 1

STEP 4 <u>RIGHT PALM:</u>

Repeat the procedure described in Step 3, using the metal stub in the vial marked RIGHT PALM. Make sure to sample the area shown below in Figure 3.

STEP 5 <u>LEFT BACK and LEFT PALM:</u>

For collection from the left hand, repeat Steps 3 and 4 using the vials labeled LEFT BACK and LEFT PALM.

STEP 6 After sampling all four areas, return capped vials to kit envelope.

Fig. 2 (BACK)

Fig. 3 (PALM)

Source: Tri-Tech, Inc., Southport, N.C.

A.A. COLLECTION PROCEDURE

NOTE: (A) This second part of the GSR collection is *ONLY* to be performed *AFTER* sampling with the SEM stubs.

(B) If you feel that during the SEM collection procedure you have contaminated the gloves, discard contaminated gloves, then thoroughly wash your hands with soap and water and dry with a clean towel. At no time during the collection process should your hands (with or without gloves) come into contact with the cotton tip of the swab.

(C) When dispensing nitric acid, use 2 - 3 drops of 5% nitric acid solution to moisten each swab (do not over-moisten). In order to dispense an appropriate amount of the nitric acid solution, hold the acid dispenser in a horizontal position above and *almost* touching the top of the swab, and squeeze gently.

(D) To swab the subject's hands, the investigator should grasp the subject's arm above the wrist with one hand and swab with the other. The subject's hand should be in a "spread" position. Thorough swabbing of the hands is carried out by using moderate pressure while swabbing. The swab should be rotated during this procedure to insure that all of the surface of the cotton tip is utilized. At least 30 seconds per swab is required.

(E) When placing swabs in tubes, always place cotton tips *FACE DOWN*.

STEP 7 CONTROL SWABS: Remove *two* of the swabs from the unmarked ziplock bag. Moisten both swabs with 2 - 3 drops of the 5% nitric acid solution supplied in kit (do not substitute). Place both swabs in the tube labeled CONTROL. Then recap tube and set it aside.

STEP 8 RIGHT BACK:

(A) Moisten the tip of *ONE* swab with 2 - 3 drops of nitric acid solution, then thoroughly swab the back of the subject's right hand including the back of the fingers and all of the web area which would be exposed while holding a weapon. Fig. 4 illustrates the area of hand for swabbing. Place swab used in the tube labeled RIGHT BACK.

Fig. 4 (BACK)

(B) Repeat the above procedure using a *SECOND* swab. Place the second swab used in the RIGHT BACK tube, then recap tube and set it aside.

STEP 9 RIGHT PALM:

(A) Moisten the tip of *ONE* swab with 2 - 3 drops of nitric acid solution, then thoroughly swab the palm of the subject's right hand as shown in Fig. 5. Place swab used in the tube labeled RIGHT PALM.

(B) Repeat the above procedure using a *SECOND* swab. Place the second swab used in the RIGHT PALM tube, then recap tube and set it aside.

Fig. 5 (PALM)

STEP 10 LEFT BACK/LEFT PALM: Follow the same procedures described in Steps 8 and 9, but swabbing the subject's left hand.

STEP 11 CARTRIDGE CASE:

NOTE: For .22 cal and foreign manufactured ammunition, it is necessary that either Steps A and B described below be completed *OR* the casings be submitted to the laboratory. If latent prints are required on the expended casing(s), Steps A and B should be omitted and the casings should be submitted for latent print processing. If for any reason the CARTRIDGE CASE swabs are not used, mark the tube "*NOT USED*".

(A) Moisten the tip of *ONE* swab with 2 - 3 drops of nitric acid solution, then thoroughly swab the inside of the cartridge case. Place swab used in the tube labeled CARTRIDGE CASE.

(B) Repeat the above procedure using a *SECOND* swab. Place second swab used in the CARTRIDGE CASE tube, and then recap tube and set it aside.

FINAL INSTRUCTIONS

(A) Fill out all information requested on the front of the kit envelope.

(B) With the exception of the 5% nitric acid dispenser and the disposable gloves, return all other kit components, used or unused, to kit envelope.

(C) Moisten kit envelope flap, then seal envelope. Affix Police Evidence Seal where indicated, then initial seal.

(D) Mail or hand deliver sealed kit to the crime laboratory for analysis. (If mailed, package kit in a cardboard box to prevent damage in transit.)

APPENDIX III
FBI POLICY FOR SUBMITTING
DNA EVIDENCE

The FBI Laboratory will accept evidence for DNA analysis from current, violent personal crimes where appropriate standards for comparison are available. Specifically, DNA analysis on state and local cases will be limited to homicide, sexual assault, and serious aggravated assault cases in which a suspect has been identified. In certain cases, evidence will be accepted by the FBI Laboratory for DNA analysis even though a suspect has not been identified. These exceptions include serial homicide/rape cases and sexual assaults on young children. A known blood sample from the victim and suspect is required for comparison purposes.

Requests for DNA Analysis

Requests for DNA analysis on previously adjudicated cases should not be submitted to the FBI Laboratory but should be referred by the investigating agency to one of the private DNA testing laboratories. Names and addresses of these laboratories can be provided upon request.

It is the policy of the FBI Laboratory that no examinations will be conducted on evidence which has been previously examined by another expert. However, the Laboratory will accept evidence samples for DNA analysis, even though another crime laboratory may have conducted traditional serological tests on the evidence items if that crime laboratory does not have the capability to perform the DNA tests and if the submitted samples are determined to be of a quality and condition conducive to DNA analysis. The local crime laboratory should contact the DNA Analysis Unit of the FBI Laboratory prior to submitting this type of evidence.

Law enforcement agencies requesting DNA analysis are encouraged to submit evidence to their local crime laboratory for traditional serological testing prior to submitting samples to the FBI Laboratory for DNA testing.

Packaging and Shipment of DNA Evidence

Body fluid-stained evidence, submitted to the FBI Laboratory for serological and/or DNA analysis, should be completely air-dried before packaging and submitted promptly. Blood samples from the suspect and victim should be collected by medical personnel in two vacutainer tubes, one containing EDTA for DNA analysis and the other containing no preservative for serological analysis. These blood samples should be submitted to the Laboratory without delay. In the event there will be a delay in submission of the dried stain evidence to the Laboratory, it should be kept frozen. Questions regarding the collection, preservation, and submission of evidence to the FBI Laboratory for DNA analysis should be directed to the Laboratory's DNA Analysis Unit, telephone (202) 324-5436.

FBI Laboratory Mitochondrial DNA Case Acceptance Policy

The FBI Laboratory has recently initiated mitochondrial DNA (mtDNA) analysis on appropriate forensic specimens examined within the FBI Laboratory. Mitochondrial DNA analysis may be applied in forensic cases where the amount of extracted DNA is very small or degraded, as in tissues such as telogen hairs, old bone, and teeth.

The maternal mode of inheritance of mtDNA also makes mtDNA analysis helpful in forensic cases involving missing persons or unidentified bodies. It is helpful in cases where known maternal relatives can provide reference samples for direct comparison to a mtDNA type from a questioned tissue.

Due to the limited number of qualified personnel, characterization of mtDNA from forensic specimens is currently limited to FBI cases only. The FBI Laboratory case acceptance policy for mtDNA analysis extracted from various tissues is outlined as follows:

Hairs

Analysis will be performed on human head hairs and pubic hairs that are associated through comparison microscopy and confirmed according to FBI Laboratory Hairs and Fibers Unit (HFU) protocols. Hairs that have been microscopically compared prior to submission to the FBI Laboratory will be compared and confirmed according to HFU protocols before being subjected to mtDNA analysis.

Other human hairs will be subjected to mtDNA analysis as deemed appropriate by the FBI Laboratory examiner.

Bones and Teeth

All contributors must telephone the FBI Laboratory prior to submitting a case requiring the mtDNA analysis of bones or teeth. A letter accompanying the incoming evidence must reference the telephone conversation in which approval was granted by FBI Laboratory personnel for the acceptance of a case consisting of bone or teeth evidence for requested mtDNA analysis.

Bodily Fluids

Bodily fluids will be subjected to mtDNA analysis at the discretion of a qualified FBI Laboratory examiner.

All questions regarding mtDNA analysis should be directed to the FBI Laboratory Hairs and Fibers Unit (telephone: 202-324-4344 or fax: 202-324-8080). All questions regarding nuclear DNA testing should continue to be directed to the FBI DNA Analysis Unit (telephone: 202-324-5436 or fax: 202-324-8090).

APPENDIX IV
CHROMATOGRAPHIC AND
SPECTROPHOTOMETRIC PARAMETERS
FOR FIGURES CONTAINED WITHIN THE TEXT

---

1. *Figures 5–6 (a) and (b)*
   $3' \times 1/4''$ glass column; 3% OV-17 on Varaport 30, 80/100 mesh.
   T(injection port) = 280°C, T(defector) = 280°C, T(column) = 200°C
   Carrier Gas: Nitrogen at 50 ml/min
2. *Figure 5–7*
   $8' \times 1/8''$ stainless steel, 15% carbowax 20M, AW-DMCS treated 80/100 mesh chromosorb W plus $3' \times 1/8''$ stainless steel, 10% silicone D.C. 200 in series.
   Temperature unknown
   Carrier Gas: Nitrogen

3. *Figure 5–9*
   Absorbent: Silica Gel G
   Development Solvent: Benzene
   Visualizer: Fast Blue B Salt
4. *Figure 5–10*
   Absorbent: Silica Gel G
   Developing Solvent: Chloroform-Diethylamine (9:1)
   Visualizer: Iodoplatinate
5. *Figure 5–16*
   Solvent: 0.1N HCL
6. *Figure 5–17(a)*
   Heroin hydrochloride in KBr
7. *Figure 5–17 (b)*
   Secobarbital (free acid) in KBr
8. *Figure 8–18 (a) and (b)*
   Same as Figure 5–7.
9. *Figure 9–8*
   Solvent: 0.1N HCL
10. *Figure 10–9*
    Ethanol in whole blood analyzed by "head space" technique.
    A porous polymer column was used.
    T(injection port) = 132°C, T(detector) = 132°C, T(column) = 132°C
    Carrier Gas: Helium (thermal conductivity detector was used).
11. *Figure 11–5*
    30 m × 0.75 mm I.D. glass capillary column, SPB-1, bonded phase with a 1.0 μm
    film thickness. Column oven temperature program: 40°C for 3 min., 12°C/min.
    up to 250°C. FID temperature 280°C. Injection port temperature 250°C. Helium
    carrier and make-up gas.
12. *Figure 11–7*
    60 m × 0.25 mm I.D. glass capillary column, DB-1, bonded phase with a 1.0 μm
    film thickness. Hydrogen was used as carrier gas at a linear velocity of
    approximately 45 cm/s. The oven was temperature programmed from 35°C (2
    min.) to 260°C at 8°C/min. Column operated at 50:1 or 250:1 split ratios.
13. *Figure 11–10*
    RDX in KBr
14. *Figure 16–9*
    Absorbent: Silica Gel
    Developing Solvent: Ethyl acetate, absolute ethanol, water (70:35:30)

APPENDIX V
CHEMICAL FORMULAS FOR LATENT
FINGERPRINT DEVELOPMENT*

Iodine Spray Reagent

1. Prepare the following stock solutions:

Solution A	Solution B
Dissolve 1 gram of Iodine in 1 liter of Cyclohexane	Dissolve 5 grams of a-Naphthoflavone in 40 ml of Methylene Chloride (Dichloramethane)

Source: FBI Latent Fingerprint Section Research Team

2. Add 2 ml of Solution B to 100 ml of Solution A. Using a magnetic stirrer, mix thoroughly for 5 minutes.
3. Filter the solution through a facial tissue, paper towel, filter paper, etc., into a beaker. The solution should be *lightly* sprayed on the specimen using an aerosol spray unit or a mini-spray gun powered with compressed air.
4. Lightly spray the suspect area with several applications until latent prints sufficiently develop.

Remarks

- Solution A may be stored at room temperature. Shelf life is in excess of 30 days.
- Solution B must be refrigerated. Shelf life is in excess of 30 days.
- The combined working solution (A and B) should be used within 24 hours after mixing.
- The Iodine Spray solution is effective on most surfaces (porous and nonporous).
- A fine spray mist is the most effective form of application.
- The Cyanoacrylate (super glue) process *cannot* be used prior to the Iodine Spray Reagent Process. Cyanoacrylate may be used, however, after the Iodine Spray Reagent.
- On porous surfaces, DFO and/or Ninhydrin may be used after the Iodine Spray.
- Propanol may be used to remove the staining of the Iodine Spray Reagent.
- 1,1,2 Trichlorotrifluoroethane may be substituted for Cyclohexane.

1,8-Diazafluoren-9-one (DFO)

Step 1: Stock solution: Dissolve 1 gram DFO in 200 ml Methanol, 200 ml Ethyl Acetate, and 40 ml Acetic Acid.

Step 2: Working solution (make as needed): Start with stock solution and dilute to 2 liters with Petroleum Ether (40° to 60° boiling point fraction). Pentane can also be used. Solution should be clear.

Dip the paper document into the working solution and allow to dry. Dip again and allow to dry.

When completely dry, apply heat (200° for 10 to 20 minutes). An oven, hair dryer, or dry iron can be used.

Visualize with an alternate light source at 450, 485, 525, and 530 nm and observe through orange goggles. If the surface paper is yellow, such as legal paper, it may be necessary to visualize the paper at 570 nm and view it through red goggles.

Ninhydrin

20 grams Ninhydrin
3,300 ml Acetone
Shelf life is approximately one month
or

5 grams Ninhydrin
30 ml Methanol
40 ml 2-Propanol
930 ml Petroleum Ether
Shelf life is approximately one year

Dip the paper document in the working solution and allow to dry. Dip again and allow to dry. When completely dry, heat may be applied. A steam iron should be used on the steam setting. Do not touch the iron directly to the paper. Rather, hold the iron above the paper and allow the steam to heat it.

Zinc Chloride Solution (Post-Ninhydrin Treatment)

5 grams of Zinc Chloride crystals
2 ml of Glacial Acetic Acid
100 ml of Methyl Alcohol
Add 400 ml of 1,1,2 Trichlorotrifluoroethane to the mixture and stir.
Add 2 ml of 5 percent Sodium Hypochlorite solution (commercially available liquid bleach such as Clorox, Purex, and others).

Lightly spray the paper with the Zinc solution. Repeat the spraying as needed. Do not overdo the spraying.

The ninhydrin-developed prints treated with this solution may fluoresce at room temperature with an alternate light source. For maximum fluorescence, place the paper in a bath of liquid nitrogen and examine again with an alternate light source.

Physical Developer

When mixing and using these solutions, make sure the glassware, processing trays, stirring rods, and stirring magnets are absolutely clean. Do not use metal trays or tweezer.

Stock Detergent Solution: 3 grams of N-Dodecylamine Acetate are combined with 4 grams of Synperonic-N mixed in 1 liter of distilled water.

Silver Nitrate Solution: 20 grams of Silver Nitrate crystals are mixed in 100 milliliters of distilled water.

Redox Solution: 60 grams of Ferric Nitrate are mixed in 1,800 milliliters of distilled water. After this solution is thoroughly mixed, add 160 grams of Ferrous Ammonium Sulfate, mix thoroughly and add 40 grams of Citric Acid, mix thoroughly.

Maleic Acid Solution: Put 50 grams of Maleic Acid into 2 liters of distilled water.

Physical Developer Working Solution: Begin with 2,125 milliliters of the Redox Solution and add 80 milliliters of the Stock Detergent Solution, mix well, then add 100 milliliters of the Silver Nitrate Solution and mix well. Appropriate divisions can be used if smaller amounts of the working solution are desired.

Immerse specimen in maleic acid solution for 10 minutes
Incubate item in PD working solution for 15–20 minutes
Thoroughly rinse specimen in tap water for 20 minutes
Air-dry and photograph

Cyanoacrylate Fluorescent Enhancement Reagents

Rhodamine 6G

Stock Solution

Working Solution

100 mg Rhodamine 6G
100 ml Methanol
(Stir until thoroughly dissolved.)

3 ml Rhodamine 6G Stock Solution
15 ml Acetone
10 ml Acetonitrile
15 ml Methanol
32 ml 2-Propanol
925 ml Petroleum Ether
(Combine in order listed.)

Ardrox

2 ml Ardrox P-133D
10 ml Acetone
25 ml Methanol
10 ml 2-Propanol
8 ml Acetonitrile
945 ml Petroleum Ether

MBD
7-(p-methoxybenzylaminol)-4-nitrobenz-2-oxa-1,3-diazole

Stock Solution

100 mg MBD
100 ml Acetone

Working Solution

10 ml MBD Stock Solution
30 ml Methanol
10 ml 2-Propanol
950 ml Petroleum Ether
(Combine in order listed.)

Yellow 40 (Maxilon Flavine 10 GFF)

2 grams Yellow 40
1 liter Methanol

RAM Combination Enhancer

3 ml Rhodamine 6G Stock Solution
2 ml Ardrox P-133D

7 ml MBD Stock Solution
20 ml Methanol
10 ml 2-Propanol
8 ml Acetonitrile
950 ml Petroleum Ether
(Combine in order listed.)

Modified RAM

.03 g MBD
25 ml Acetone
40 ml Ethanol
15 ml 2-Propanol
950 ml Petroleum Ether
1 ml Ardrox P-133D
5 ml Rhodamine 6G Stock (1 gram Rhodamine in 1,000 ml Ethanol)
20 ml Acetonitrile
(Combine in order listed.)

RAY Combination Enhancer*

To 940 ml of either isopropyl alcohol or denatured ethyl alcohol add:

1.0 gram of Yellow 40
0.1 gram of Rhodamine 6G
8 ml of Ardrox P-133D
50 ml of acetonitrile (optional, but dye stain of prints will appear more brilliant)

MRM 10 Combination Enhancer

3 ml Rhodamine 6G Stock Solution
3 ml Yellow 40 Stock Solution
7 ml MBD Stock Solution
20 ml Methanol
10 ml 2-Propanol
8 ml Acetonitrile
950 ml Petroleum Ether
(Combine in order listed.)

The above solutions are used on evidence which has been treated with cyanoacrylate (Super Glue) fumes. These solutions dye the cyanoacrylate residue adhering to the latent print residue. Wash the dye over the evidence. It may be necessary to rinse the surface with a solvent, such as Petroleum Ether, to remove the excess stain.

CAUTION: These solutions contain solvents which may be respiratory irritants so they should be mixed and used in a fume hood or while wearing a full-face breathing

Source: John H. Olenik, Fremont, Ohio.

apparatus. Also, these solvents may damage some plastics, cloth, wood, and painted surfaces.

Because of the respiratory irritation possible and the general inefficiency of spraying, it is *not* recommended to spray these solutions. To obtain the maximum benefit and coverage, it is recommended that evidence be soaked, submerged, or washed with these types of solutions.

Source of Chemicals

Ardrox P-133D may be obtained from:

Radiatronics NDT, Inc.
P. O. Box 12308
Overland Park, KS 66212
Telephone Number: (913) 432-7080

Lightning Powder Company, Inc.
Salem, OR 97302-2121
Telephone Number: 1-800-852-0300

MBD may be obtained from:

Sigma Chemical Company
P. O. Box 14508
St. Louis, MO 63178
Telephone Number: 1-800-325-3010

Maxilon Flavine 10 GFF may be obtained from:

CIBA-GIEGY Corporation
410 Swing Road
Greensboro, NC 27409
Telephone Number: 1-800-334-9481

APPENDIX VI

CHEMICAL FORMULAS FOR DEVELOPMENT OF FOOTWEAR IMPRESSIONS IN BLOOD

Amido Black

Staining Solution:
0.2 g Napthalene 12B or Napthol Blue Black
10 ml Glacial Acetic Acid
90 ml Methanol

Rinsing Solution:
90 ml Methanol
10 ml Glacial Acetic Acid

Stain the impression by spraying or immersing the item in the staining solution for approximately one minute. Next, treat with the rinsing solution to remove stain from nonimpression area. Then rinse well with distilled water.

Coomassie Blue

Staining Solution: (Add in this order)
0.44 g Coomassie Brilliant Blue
200 ml Methanol
40 ml Glacial Acetic Acid
200 ml Distilled Water

Rinsing Solution:
40 ml Glacial Acetic Acid
200 ml Methanol
200 ml Distilled Water

Spray object with the staining solution, completely covering the area of interest. Then spray the object with rinsing solution, clearing the background. Allow object to air-dry.

Diaminobenzidine (DAB)

Solution A (Fixer solution):
20 g 5-sulphosalicylic acid
Dissolved in 1L distilled water

Solution B:
100 ml 1M Phosphate Buffer (pH 7.4)
800 ml distilled water

Solution C:
1 g diaminobenzidine
Dissolved in 100 ml distilled water

Working Solution (Mix just prior to use):
900 ml solution B
100 ml solution C
5 ml 30% Hydrogen peroxide

Immerse impression area in fixer solution A for approximately 4 minutes. Remove and rinse in distilled water. Immerse impression area for approximately 4 minutes in the working solution or until print is fully developed. Remove and rinse in distilled water.

Fuchsin Acid

20 g sulfosalicylic acid
2 g fuchsin acid
Dissolved in 1L distilled water

Stain the impression by spraying or immersing the item in the dye solution for approximately one minute. Rinse well with distilled water.

Hungarian Red

This product is available from:
ODV, Inc.
P.O. Box 180
S.Paris, ME 04281
1-800-422-3784

Leucocrystal Violet

10 g 5-Sulfosalicylic Acid
500 ml 3% Hydrogen Peroxide
3.7 g Sodium Acetate
1 g Leucocrystal Violet

If Leucocrystal violet crystals are yellow instead of white; do not use. This indicates crystals are old and solution will not work.

Spray the object until completely covered. Then allow object to air dry. Development of impressions will occur within 30 seconds. Store the solution in amber glassware and refrigerate.

Leucomalachite Green

1 g Leucomalachite Green
70 ml Ethyl Ether
10 drops Glacial Acetic Acid
5 drops Hydrogen Peroxide

Spray the object until completely covered. Then allow object to air dry.

Patent Blue

20 g sulfosalicylic acid
2 g Patent Blue V (VF)
Dissolved in 1L distilled water

Stain object by spraying or immersing the item in the dye solution for approximately one minute. Rinse well with distilled water.

Tartrazine

20 g sulfosalicylic acid
2 g tartrazine
Dissolved in 1L distilled water

Stain object by spraying or immersing the item in the dye solution for approximately one minute. Rinse well with distilled water.

◆ ANSWERS

CHAPTER 1

1. forensic science
3. Alphonse Bertillon
5. Leone Lattes
7. Albert Osborn
9. Edmond Locard
11. California
13. drug
15. federal, state, county, and municipal
17. biology
19. toxicology
21. *Frye* v. *United States*
23. *Coppolino* v. *State*
25. True
27. training
29. True

CHAPTER 2

1. physical evidence
3. False
5. photography, sketching, notes
7. close-ups
9. systematic
11. clothing; fingernail scrapings; head and pubic hairs; blood; vaginal, anal, and oral swabs; bullets; and hand swabs.
13. separate
15. is not
17. False
19. control
21. arson or fire

CHAPTER 3

1. identification
3. comparative
5. individual
7. True
9. weight
11. False
13. False

CHAPTER 4

1. physical
3. metric
5. 1/100
7. 200
9. True
11. True
13. 180
15. mass
17. density
19. refraction

21. True
23. birefringence
25. glass
27. density, refractive index
29. Becke line
31. radial
33. False
35. will
37. minerals
39. True

CHAPTER 5

1. matter
3. 109
5. atom
7. molecule
9. has no
11. less
13. organic
15. qualitative, quantitative
17. chromatography
19. higher
21. gas chromatography
23. pyrolyzed

25. thin-layer chromatography
27. R_f
29. electrophoresis
31. wavelength
33. electromagnetic
35. laser
37. True
39. can
41. spectrophotometer
43. infrared
45. True

CHAPTER 6

1. oxygen, silicon
3. trace
5. emission spectrum
7. line
9. False
11. carbon
13. does
15. proton, neutron, electron
17. positive

19. protons
21. True
23. light
25. isotopes
27. alpha rays, beta rays, gamma rays
29. gamma rays
31. neutron activation analysis
33. crystalline

CHAPTER 7

1. lenses
3. compound
5. eyepiece or ocular lens
7. True
9. vertical or reflected
11. parfocal
13. magnifying power
15. numerical aperture

17. decreases
19. decreases
21. True
23. False
25. plane-polarized
27. polarizing
29. microspectrophotometer
31. X-rays

CHAPTER 8

1. hair follicle
3. True
5. medulla
7. 1/3, 1/2
9. animal
11. comparison
13. is
15. often
17. 50
19. Natural

21. True
23. False
25. monomer
27. True
29. thin-layer
31. infrared
33. color and layer structure
35. layer structure
37. colorcoat or basecoat
39. inorganic

CHAPTER 9

1. True
3. physical
5. False
7. analgesics, depressive
9. morphine
11. True
13. Hashish
15. True
17. lysergic acid
19. depresses
21. long-
23. Tranquilizers
25. Amphetamines
27. clandestine
29. sniffed
31. Anabolic
33. five
35. IV
37. Marquis
39. marijuana
41. Microcrystalline
43. infrared
45. cystolitic

CHAPTER 10

1. ethyl alcohol
3. is
5. faster
7. watery
9. oxidized
11. breath
13. stomach, small intestine
15. pulmonary
17. 2100
19. potassium dichromate
21. catalyst
23. infrared
25. 45
27. decline
29. *Schmerber* v. *California*
31. blood, urine
33. greater
35. pH
37. screening, confirmation
39. percent saturation
41. synergistic
43. corroborate

CHAPTER 11

1. False
3. False
5. chemical, mechanical
7. absorb, liberate
9. exothermic
11. endothermic
13. ignition
15. flash point
17. Glowing combustion or smouldering
19. Spontaneous combustion
21. potassium nitrate, charcoal, sulfur
23. origin
25. porous
27. gas chromatograph
29. True
31. cannot
33. low
35. black powder, smokeless powder
37. False
39. is not
41. RDX
43. initiating
45. collection
47. acetone
49. infrared spectroscopy

CHAPTER 12

1. type
3. Plasma
5. Red blood cells
7. A
9. A,B
11. antibodies
13. True
15. neither
17. serology
19. A
21. radioimmunoassay (RIA) or enzyme-multiplied immuno-assay technique
23. 3
25. benzidine
27. precipitin
29. absorption-elution
31. Enzymes
33. electrophoresis
35. dry
37. gene
39. 23
41. alleles
43. phenotype
45. will
47. AA, BB, AB

49. acid phosphatase
51. oligospermia

53. can
55. True

CHAPTER 13

1. gene
3. polymer
5. nucleotides
7. double helix
9. A-C-G-T
11. Proteins
13. True

15. restriction enzymes
17. repeating
19. electrophoresis
21. True
23. two
25. twenty-eight
27. multiplexing

CHAPTER 14

1. Alphonse Bertillon
3. Sir Edward Richard Henry
5. is not
7. Fingerprints
9. dermal papillae
11. loop, whorls, arches
13. arch
15. type lines
17. one
19. plain whorl

21. have no
23. 1/1
25. True
27. Plastic
29. powder
31. Iodine
33. silver nitrate
35. Super Glue® fuming
37. alternate light sources
39. pixels

CHAPTER 15

1. land
3. class
5. comparison microscope
7. sometimes
9. gauge
11. can
13. True
15. 12, 18

17. True
19. primer
21. False
23. is not
25. False
27. tool mark
29. individual

CHAPTER 16

1. questioned document
3. known, questioned
5. False
7. *Gilbert* v. *California*
9. individual

11. infrared
13. Indented
15. sound spectrograph
17. False

CHAPTER 17

1. network
3. World Wide Web
5. True
7. E-mail

INDEX

Internet site for, 540
laboratory services for examination of, 11
primer residues from, 45, 483–86
rifling of, 467–70
serial number restoration on, 486–87
Fires:
　analysis of evidence recovered from,
　　339–43
　chemistry of, 327–34
　collection of physical evidence from, 47,
　　337–39
　fuel-air mixture and, 332, 347
　initiation of, 330
Flash point, 331
Florence test, 390
Flotation, 111
Fluorescence, 455–56, 458
Forensic laboratories (*see* Crime laboratories)
Forensic science:
　definition and scope of, 1–3
　future of, 542–49
　history and development of, 3–7
Forensic scientist:
　functions of, 14–20
Frequency of light:
　definition, 149
　energy of photon and, 149–50, 175
Freud, Sigmund, 271
Frye v. U.S., 14–16

Galton, Francis, 4, 438
Gamma rays, 177
Gas, definition of, 133
Gas chromatography:
　applications of, 139–41, 241–42, 282,
　　283–84, 306, 315, 339–43
　description of, 137–41
　use with mass spectroscopy, 155–59,
　　283–84, 315–16
　(*See also* Pyrolysis gas chromatography)
Gasoline, analysis of, 339–43
Gauge, 474
Gel diffusion, 372
Genes, 386–88, 403
Genetic code, 408
Genotype, 387–88
Geology, forensic aspects of, 11, 122–23
Gilbert v. California, 507
Glass:
　collection of, 46, 119–20
　comparison of, 109–15
　composition of, 109
　density, 111
　fractures of, 117–19
　headlight, 109
　holes in, 117–19
　laminated, 109
　refractive index of, 114–15
　significance of, 114–15
　tempered, 109
　trace elements in, 111, 167

Glowing combustion, 332
"Glue Sniffing," 269
Goddard, Calvin, 5
Greiss test, 483
Gross, Hans, 5
Gun Control Act of 1968, 9
Gunpowder residues, 178, 478–83, 489–90

Hair:
　age of, 219
　collection of, 46, 221, 394
　cross-section of, 218–19
　DNA in, 220, 416, 419
　examination of, 215–21
　forcible removal of, 219–20
　forensic significance of, 49, 217
　medullary index, 213
　morphology of, 211–15
　pigments of, 213, 217
　race of, 218–19
　scale patterns, 213
　sexing of, 219
　species of, 213
Hair follicle, 212, 219–20
Hallucinogens:
　definition of, 261
　types of, 261–67
Handbuch fur Untersuchungsrichter
　(Gross), 5
Handwriting:
　collection of exemplars of, 506–508
　comparison of, 503–506
　individual characteristics of, 503–506
　styles of, 503
H-antigen, 392
Hashish, 261, 284
Hashish oil, 263, 284
Headlight filaments, 120
Heat of combustion, 329
　table, 329
Heavy metals, 316
Hemoglobin, 317, 370, 406–408
Henry, Edward Richard, 439
Henry, William, 136
Henry's Law, 136, 296–97
Henry's system of fingerprint classification,
　439, 446–47
Hepatitis B, 51
Heredity, 385–88
Heroin:
　administration of, 259
　analysis of, 97–98, 145, 154–55, 159,
　　279–80, 283
　diluents of, 260
　effect of, 259
　legal control of, 262, 275
　metabolism of, 312
　physical dependence on, 256
　psychological dependence on, 255
　synthesis of, 258–59
Herschel, William, 438